READINGS IN
POLITICAL IDEOLOGIES
SINCE THE RISE OF MODERN SCIENCE

H.B. McCullough · Wolfgang Depner

OXFORD
UNIVERSITY PRESS

OXFORD
UNIVERSITY PRESS

Oxford University Press is a department of the University of Oxford.
It furthers the University's objective of excellence in research, scholarship,
and education by publishing worldwide. Oxford is a registered trade mark of
Oxford University Press in the UK and in certain other countries.

Published in Canada by
Oxford University Press
8 Sampson Mews, Suite 204,
Don Mills, Ontario M3C 0H5 Canada

www.oupcanada.com

Library and Archives Canada Cataloguing in Publication

Readings in political ideologies since the rise of modern
science / H.B. McCullough & Wolfgang Depner.

Includes bibliographical references.

ISBN 978-0-19-544547-3

1. Political science—Textbooks. I. McCullough, H.B., 1944–
II. Depner, Wolfgang

JA66.R42 2013   320   C2012-906228-6

Oxford University Press is committed to our environment.
This book is printed on Forest Stewardship Council® certified paper
and comes from responsible sources.

Cover image: Yagi Studio/Digital vision/Getty Images

Printed and bound in Canada

3 4 — 16 15

Contents

Part X   Environmentalism

Part XI   Religious Fundamentalism

Acknowledgements

The editors wish to thank Shelby Wolfe and Barbara Wilke for their unceasing efforts in seeing this book to its conclusion, Courtney Wallsmith for her creative endeavours in tracking down suitable photographs, and Keith Thompson for his ongoing support in this field over many years. The editors are deeply appreciative of the meticulous work of copy editing and proofreading undertaken by Wendy Yano and Jennie Worden. In addition, the editors wish to thank Allan McCullough and Maria and Peter Depner for their guidance both before and throughout this project.

The editors, along with Oxford University Press, would like to acknowledge the reviewers whose thoughtful comments and suggestions have helped to shape this text:

Graham Dodds, Concordia University
Chris Erickson, University of British Columbia
James Ingram, McMaster University
Edward King, Concordia University
Peter Prontzos, Langara College
Christopher Wood, Lakehead University
Jason Zorbas, University of Saskatchewan

Introduction

We know little about the life of Mohammed Bouazizi, the young Muslim Arab who set himself on fire 17 December 2010 after he had suffered yet another round of humiliation by the harassing officials serving the corrupt government of then–Tunisian dictator Ben Ali. We know that he hailed from a humble background, which eventually forced him to abandon his ambitions to acquire a higher education. We know that he managed to make ends meet by selling produce on the dusty streets of Sidi Bouzid, an uncertain existence since it depended on his ever-changing ability to bribe government officials. And finally, we know that he could no longer endure their arbitrary whims after they had seized his cart for his failure to give them what was never theirs to take in the first place.

To express his frustration, Bouazizi chose one of the most drastic and dramatic forms of protest—self-immolation, a gruesome practice whose history stretches back centuries, across religious and cultural traditions. News of this solitary, desperate act of defiance soon spread throughout the Arab world and turned Bouazizi into a martyr for the cause of greater economic, social, and political liberties, at least in the minds of millions chafing under authoritarian potentates such as Ben Ali or Egypt's Hosni Mubarak. As such, Bouazizi became the inspirational face of the Arab Spring, a historic period of political turmoil across the Middle East, which witnessed the demise of several regional regimes that had clung to power for decades, often with the help of Western nations that had coddled them for economic and strategic reasons.

Whether Bouazizi actually triggered this transformation and its subsequent tangents—as this idealized narrative suggests—remains an open question, at best. Some other incident elsewhere in the Arab world might have had the same effect of unleashing this deep human reservoir of frustrated ambitions and unsatisfied yearnings, which had been stifled for decades behind a protective but ultimately porous dam made out of foreign military aid, corruption, and state-sponsored terrorism. But it would be difficult to deny the conclusion that Bouazizi acted on a collection of beliefs that constitute a political ideology—here, tentatively defined as a pattern of social, political, economic, technological, and philosophical beliefs that help us organize the world around us. We will see in a moment why our definition claims to be neither complete nor comprehensive, for it coexists with countless others, some of which have invited considerable controversy.

If our definition of political ideology strikes readers as rather abstract, they may also think of political ideologies as metaphorical nets, with which they can capture reality, or at least a measure of it. In this sense, political ideologies comment on human nature, the role of government, economics arrangements, and so on. Yet political ideologies are capable of much more than just describing the world as it might appear. They also have the power to change reality in profound, previously unimaginable ways, because they also make normative statements about its future shape. They aim to infuse values and inspire actions, a prescriptive process that frequently features the transformation of beliefs into sanctified dogma, deemed to be irrefutable and unfalsifiable.

This transformation can have two effects. For one, it can motivate seemingly heroic acts of selfless sacrifice as in the case of Mohammed Bouazizi. Or it can inspire previously unimaginable deeds of collective barbarism so unfathomable that they obliterate all human reserves for rational thought. This second possibility certainly defined much of the twentieth century, as an escalating series of ideological clashes created a global topography of horrors, of which the battlefields of two global world wars and Auschwitz mark only the most infamous coordinates on a dark journey that led all of humanity to the very brink of nuclear self-immolation. It is precisely this history that has cast political ideologies in a pale, unflattering light. It is precisely this history that has many yearning for a post-ideological world, freed from the ferocious conflicts of the past.

Indeed, some, most notably Francis Fukuyama, proclaimed the arrival of this very state at the end of the Cold War, when the Marxist-communist bloc under the leadership of the former Soviet Union disintegrated following four decades of ideological warfare in various guises with the capitalistic bloc under the leadership of the United States. "What we may be witnessing is not just the end of the Cold War, or the passing of a particular period of postwar history, but the end of history as such . . . that is the end point of mankind's ideological evolution and the universalization of Western liberal democracy as the final form of human government," he wrote.[1]

But this premature pronouncement—which its author has since modified—has turned out to be presumptuous in light of events since 1989. Genocides in Africa (notably Rwanda) and the former Yugoslavia, the emergence of the Internet, the events of 9/11, the subsequent invasions of Afghanistan and Iraq by Western forces under the leadership of the United States, the emergence of new global powers that reject Western notions of democracy even as they embrace capitalism (China, Russia), the Great Recession of 2008, and the Arab Spring have only underscored the robust place of political ideologies in the lives of humans around the globe. While the age of political ideologies might have started with the rise of modern science, the Enlightenment, and the

French Revolution in 1789, it certainly did not end with the fall of the Berlin Wall 200 years later. Nor did it resume, as some have argued, after 9/11, after some kind of sleeping beauty slumber. Political ideologies will continue to shape our lives. This is precisely the reason that makes the study of political ideologies so relevant, even urgent.

As shocking as it may sound, we are all political ideologues at heart. At one stage or another in our lives, all of us will have developed, digested, and disseminated some morsels of political ideology, whether or not we are conscious of it. Some of us will actively participate in this process by acquiring reams of material through various mediums (like this book) on the subject. Others may receive their ideological education more subtly by either mimicking or questioning the prevailing ideological beliefs of their social environment and peers. Others, meanwhile, may openly confess that they possess no interest in the subject of political ideologies whatsoever. Such individuals might sometimes classify themselves as subscribers to a set of ideas they might call pragmatic in raising doubts about the validity of the various –isms (conservatism, liberalism, and so on) that float through the intellectual ether. But this commitment to pragmatism might be perfunctory, for it does not prevent these individuals from expressing their respective ideological commitments through their day-to-day actions (or non-actions). Not every single decision (be it of a private or a public nature) has a political dimension that reveals some ideological position, but it does not take much to arrive at such a point. It is therefore imperative to possess a scheme that grants us the power to perceive this moment, even if our "net" to capture this reality has holes in it. But where does one begin?

The literature on the subject of political ideology is immense and occasionally intimidating. This book offers to clear away some of this debris by presenting readers with a taste of this diversity. Readers may therefore think of this book as a sampler, designed to whet intellectual appetites and curiosities. Some of the selections find their way into this book because of their status as so-called classics. This selection criterion played a particularly prominent role in the early chapters, where readers will find selections from writers whose very names might be synonymous with the Western tradition. They include John Locke, Edmund Burke, Adam Smith, and Immanuel Kant. We tried to balance our obligation toward honouring the standards by recognizing the contributions of perhaps lesser-known historical figures, such as Italian artist Filippo Tommaso Marinetti, an intellectual forefather of Fascism, and Frédéric Bastiat, a classical French economist from the nineteenth century, whose sometimes-forgotten works have become increasingly popular among neo-liberals of the early twenty-first century. We have also sought to highlight the modern relevance of various ideologies by finding a contemporary representative, when and where possible, as it was the case with Dutch populist Geert Wilders, whose views about Muslims and the European Union might be despicable, but are unavoidable in light of their contemporary relevance. Finally, we have given our book a distinct Canadian flavour, alerting readers to the valuable but often unrecognized contributions of past and present Canadian thinkers, such as the authors of the Regina Manifesto, Pierre Elliott Trudeau, Will Kymlicka, Ursula Franklin, and Lorraine Code, among others.

This book will not attempt to place the described political ideologies within some longitudinal and latitudinal system that measures their various commitments to economic and social liberties. We would rather let these ideologies speak for themselves, unfiltered and unvarnished, for we trust the intelligence of our readers to draw their own conclusions in finding their own path. Nor will this book attempt to assemble an all-encompassing theory about the nature of ideology per se, for such an ambitious agenda lies outside its mandate. But it is our firm belief that students would nonetheless benefit from a brief survey of the treacherous terrain that confronts contemporary scholars. The contours of this field come into sharp relief the very moment one dares to define the term *ideology* itself. Recognizing the vast diversity of possible definitions that even a cursory review of the literature will reveal, let us consider six perspectives, as discussed by Terry Eagleton.[2]

- Ideology as the totality of lived social practices. This view proposed by French philosopher Louis Althusser connects humans to the dominant economic system and sidesteps questions about the truthfulness of ideological claims and grounds ideology in personal behaviour rather than empirical observations.
- Ideology as a collection of ideas and belief (whether they might be true or false) that characterize a socially significant class.
- Ideology as a tool with which various competing social groups (regardless of their status) promote and legitimize their respective interests as they compete against each other for societal dominance.
- Ideology as the self-serving tool of the ruling class, whose members in turn rely on it to acquire the acquiescence of their societal subordinates. Such an application of ideology often features the heavy use of myths and symbols to naturalize and legitimize pervasive power structures. Phrased differently, this view images ideology as a retardant rather than as a propellant of political conflict.
- Ideology as a falsifying device with which ruling elites mislead and manipulate the unwashed masses into actions that serve the narrow interests of their masters without being aware of it. This view perceives ideology as a form of false consciousness,

as a camera obscura that turns the material world on its head.

- Ideology as a tool to legitimize the material structure of society at large. This decidedly Marxist view proposes that ideology promotes and perpetuates more than just the narrow interests of the ruling class.

Note that some of these definitions harmonize with others, whereas others sound practically incompatible. Note also that these various definitions differ in their cognitive treatment of ideology as a term. Some paint it in with neutral, even positive colours. Others coat it with dark cynicism to give the term a pejorative connotation. We hope readers will pick up on these distinctions as they read our selections. Above all, we hope that our chosen selections will enrich the intellectual life of students, be it by expanding their horizons or deepening their previous knowledge about the subject. We certainly do not expect students to agree with every word we have written for this book. We certainly do not expect them to develop an affinity for any one particular ideology presented here. But we do hope that our book will give students an appreciation for the scale of political thought, whatever its tone might be.

Notes

1. For more, see Francis Fukuyama, (1989) "The End of History?" *The National Interest 16* (Summer): 3–18.
2. Terry Eagleton, (1991) *Ideology: An Introduction.* London: Verso, pp. 28–31.

Part I

Classical Liberalism

Classical Liberalism

Classical liberalism stands for an undiluted affirmation of individual liberty, the rule of law, constitutionalism, and representative government. From the perspective of classical liberalism, the rule of law is of particular importance inasmuch as it works to protect possession of property and the faith of contracts. As an ideology, it emerged with the rise of the bourgeoisie at the time of the Glorious Revolution in 1688 in England. Protectionism that accompanied the economic philosophy of its earliest proponents gave way to laissez-faireism around the time of the American Revolution in 1776. By the middle of the nineteenth century—in other words, by the time of the full blast of the Industrial Revolution—classical liberalism began to experience problems in the arena of monopoly control and exploitation, thereby undercutting some of its democratic values—values espoused by Montesquieu, Kant, and Madison. This development set the stage for the development of reform liberalism, Marxism, and democratic socialism.

Major Figures

John Locke (1632–1704), Charles de Montesquieu (1689–1755), Adam Smith (1723–1790), Immanuel Kant (1724–1804), and James Madison (1751–1836)

Period of Greatest Influence

1690 to 1830s

Introduction

The birth of the modern nation-state in 1648, the revolt of Protestantism beginning in the early sixteenth century and continuing into the seventeenth century, and the rise of modern science in 1660 set the stage for the development of classical liberalism. Here is a political ideology that stands apart from Greek, Roman, and medieval worldviews. Indeed, it is a political ideology that is quite new. There is no better starting point for understanding this ideology than John Locke (1632–1704), for it is he who gives a coherent account of its main ideas, including an affirmation of the rights of life, liberty, and property; the rule of law; the social contract; representative democracy; and the night watchman approach to the role of government in the economy. The staying power of Locke's ideas is evident in the role that his ideas have played in contemporary neoliberalism and public choice theory as these are understood in both domestic and international politics.

While it is John Locke who sets the stage for classical liberalism, it is Charles de Montesquieu (1689–1755) and Adam Smith (1723–1790) who develop some of the ideas laid down by Locke. Montesquieu develops Locke's notion of the rule of law in a liberal direction in his justly famous *L'Esprit des Lois* (1748), a work that touches on law and politics. The arguments of the book consist of three issues: first, the classification of governments into republics based on virtue, monarchies based on honour, and despotism based on fear; second, the separation of powers among the legislature, executive, and judiciary; and third, the influence of climate on politics. In exploring each of these arguments, Montesquieu touches upon a multitude of topics including laws in general, laws derived from the nature of government, laws in relation to force, laws that establish liberty, laws and slavery, laws and commerce, and laws and religion. For anyone well-versed in Locke's writings, the thematic connection between Locke and Montesquieu is obvious. Montesquieu stands tall as a political philosopher advocating liberty and rejecting intolerance.

As for Adam Smith (1723–1790), he explores in considerable detail Locke's notion of liberty in an economic direction. He does this by examining such notions as the division of labour, the restless desire of humans to better their conditions, the institution of money, the theory of the invisible hand, mercantilism, physiocracy, comparative advantage, and laissez-faireism. These are notions that Smith discusses against the background of human nature that he explores, not in his famous *Wealth of Nations* (1776) but in his *Theory of Moral Sentiments* (1759). This latter work shows Smith's versatility in addressing not only economic ideas but also the psychological profile that is assumed in exploring these economic ideas. Too often it is forgotten that Smith was the Professor of Logic and Moral Philosophy when he lectured at Glasgow University, but his versatility makes clear that this is a fact to be remembered.

Following Smith, the next great classical liberal is Immanuel Kant (1724–1804). Kant's contribution is philosophical and is found in some of his famous works, including his *Critique of Pure Reason* and his *Critique of Practical Reason*. While he is known primarily as a metaphysician and epistemologist, Kant does make a contribution of some significance on the topic of freedom, especially in his famous essay "What is

Enlightenment?" In this essay, he offers a passionate defence of freedom by attacking self-incurred tutelage, a tutelage that is rooted in a lack of resolution and courage. Kant sees this self-incurred tutelage resulting in a form of deferential living: the book understands for me, the pastor becomes my conscience, and the physician decides my diet. Kant recoils from this deferential living and maintains instead that enlightenment surely follows the granting of freedom. What Kant affirms as a classical liberal is liberty in the same spirit as Locke.

The last of the classical liberals considered here is James Madison (1751–1836). Madison was the fourth president of the United States of America and one of the contributors to the famous *Federalist Papers* (1787–1788), along with Alexander Hamilton and John Jay. Standing in the contractarian tradition of John Locke, Madison develops, at the time of the American Revolution, federalist theory as well as fundamental ideas of constitutionalism. In "Federalist Paper No. 10," he aims to combat factionalism—the fatal social disease that Plato addresses in the *Republic*—by calling attention to the virtues of a republic: first, its representative nature; and second, the greater number of its citizens and greater sphere of a republican country. Whilst being sensitive to the Kantian ideal of enlightenment, Madison does not think the enlightened statesman will be able to adjust the clashing interests that give rise to factionalism; rather, Madison proposes protecting the liberty of all and containing the evils of factionalism by the adoption of republicanism and its concomitant virtues. Madison certainly carries one beyond Locke, but, at the same time, he makes use of Locke's ideas, including the idea of representation and the need for the rule of law such that no man is allowed to be the judge in his own case. This is nothing but vintage classical liberalism as understood by Locke.

Common to those who stand in the school of classical liberalism are an endorsement of the right to liberty of the individual, an affirmation of the rule of law and constitutionalism, and an endorsement of laissez-faireism. Both Locke and Kant are notable advocates of the autonomy of the individual, including the right to liberty. Smith focuses this right to liberty in an economic direction and, in the process, effectively attacks protectionism and monopoly control while supporting laissez-faireism. Both Montesquieu and Madison, however, argue for constitutionalism as the undergirding structure of the rule of law. The resulting school of thought amounts to a formidable bastion.

CHAPTER 1

Of Property

John Locke

§ 27. Though the earth, and all inferior creatures, be common to all men, yet every man has a property in his own person: this nobody has any right to but himself. The labour of his body, and the work of his hands, we may say, are properly his. Whatsoever then he removes out of the state that nature hath provided, and left it in, he hath mixed his labour with, and joined to it something that is his own, and thereby makes it his property. It being by him removed from the common state nature hath placed it in, it hath by this labour something annexed to it that excludes the common right of other men. For this labour being the unquestionable property of the labourer, no man but he can have a right to what that is once joined to, at least where there is enough, and as good, left in common for others.

§ 28. He that is nourished by the acorns he picked up under an oak, or the apples he gathered from the trees in the wood, has certainly appropriated them to himself. Nobody can deny but the nourishment is his. I ask then, when did they begin to be his? when he digested? or when he ate? or when he boiled? or when he brought them home? or when he picked them up? and it is plain, if the first gathering made them not his, nothing else could. That labour put a distinction between them and common: that added something to them more than nature, the common mother of all, had done; and so they became his private right. And will any one say, he had no right to those acorns or apples he thus appropriated, because he had not the consent of all mankind to make them his? Was it a robbery thus to assume to himself what belonged to all in common? If such a consent as that was necessary, man had starved, notwithstanding the plenty God had given him. We see in commons, which remain so by compact, that it is the taking any part of what is common, and removing it out of the state nature leaves it in, which begins the property; without which the common is of no use. And the taking of this or that part does not depend on the express consent of all the commoners. Thus the grass my horse has bit; the turfs my servant has cut; and the ore I have digged in any place, where I have a right to them in common with others; become my property, without the assignation or consent of any body. The labour that was mine, removing them out of that common state they were in, hath fixed my property in them.

§ 29. By making an explicit consent of every commoner necessary to any one's appropriating to himself any part of what is given in common, children or servants could not cut the meat, which their father or master had provided for them in common, without assigning to every one his peculiar part. Though the water running in the fountain be every one's, yet who can doubt but that in the pitcher is his only who drew it out? His labour hath taken it out of the hands of nature, where it was common, and belonged equally to all her children, and hath thereby appropriated it to himself.

§ 30. Thus this law of reason makes the deer that Indian's who hath killed it; it is allowed to be his goods who hath bestowed his labour upon it, though before it was the common right of every one. And amongst those who are counted the civilized part of mankind, who have made and multiplied positive laws to determine property, this original law of nature, for the beginning of property, in what was before common, still takes place; and by virtue thereof, what fish any one catches in the ocean, that great and still remaining common of mankind; or what ambergris any one takes up here, is by the labour that removes it out of that common state nature left it in made his property who takes that pains about it. And even amongst us, the hare that any one is hunting is thought his who pursues her during the chase: for being a beast that is still looked upon as common, and no man's private possession; whoever has employed so much labour about any of that kind, as to find and pursue her, has thereby removed her from the state of nature, wherein she was common, and hath begun a property.

§ 31. It will perhaps be objected to this, that "if gathering the acorns, or other fruits of the earth, &c. makes a right to them, then any one may engross as much as he will." To which I answer, Not so. The same law of nature, that does by this means give us property, does also bound that property too. "God has given us all things richly," 1 Tim. vi. 17, is the voice of reason confirmed by inspiration. But how far has he given it us? To enjoy. As much as any one can make use of to any advantage of life before it spoils, so much he may by his labour fix a property in: whatever is beyond this, is more than his share, and belongs to others. Nothing was made by God for man to spoil or destroy. And thus, considering the plenty of natural provisions there was a long time in the world,

and the few spenders; and to how small a part of that provision the industry of one man could extend itself, and engross it to the prejudice of others; especially keeping within the bounds, set by reason, of what might serve for his use; there could be then little room for quarrels or contentions about property so established.

§ 32. But the chief matter of property being now not the fruits of the earth, and the beasts that subsist on it, but the earth itself; as that which takes in, and carries with it all the rest; I think it is plain, that property in that too is acquired as the former. As much land as a man tills, plants, improves, cultivates, and can use the product of, so much is his property. He by his labour does, as it were, enclose it from the common. Nor will it invalidate his right, to say every body else has an equal title to it, and therefore he cannot appropriate, he cannot enclose, without the consent of all his fellow-commoners, all mankind. God, when he gave the world in common to all mankind, commanded man also to labour, and the penury of his condition required it of him. God and his reason commanded him to subdue the earth, i.e., improve it for the benefit of life, and therein lay out something upon it that was his own, his labour. He that, in obedience to this command of God, subdued, tilled, and sowed any part of it, thereby annexed to it something that was his property, which another had no title to, nor could without injury take from him.

§ 33. Nor was this appropriation of any parcel of land, by improving it, any prejudice to any other man, since there was still enough, and as good left; and more than the yet unprovided could use. So that, in effect, there was never the less left for others because of his enclosure for himself: for he that leaves as much as another can make use of, does as good as take nothing at all. Nobody could think himself injured by the drinking of another man, though he took a good draught, who had a whole river of the same water left him to quench his thirst;

and the case of land and water, where there is enough of both, is perfectly the same.

§ 34. God gave the world to men in common; but since he gave it them for their benefit, and the greatest conveniencies of life they were capable to draw from it, it cannot be supposed he meant it should always remain common and uncultivated. He gave it to the use of the industrious and rational (and labour was to be his title to it), not to the fancy or covetousness of the quarrelsome and contentious. He that had as good left for his improvement as was already taken up, needed not complain, ought not to meddle with what was already improved by another's labour: if he did, it is plain he desired the benefit of another's pains, which he had no right to, and not the ground which God had given him in common with others to labour on, and whereof there was as good left as that already possessed, and more than he knew what to do with, or his industry could reach to.

§ 35. It is true, in land that is common in England, or any other country, where there is plenty of people under government, who have money and commerce, no one can enclose or appropriate any part without the consent of all his fellow-commoners; because this is left common by compact, i.e., by the law of the land, which is not to be violated. And though it be common, in respect of some men, it is not so to all mankind, but is the joint property of this county, or this parish. Besides, the remainder, after such enclosure, would not be as good to the rest of the commoners as the whole was when they could all make use of the whole; whereas in the beginning and first peopling of the great common of the world it was quite otherwise. The law man was under was rather for appropriating. God commanded, and his wants forced him to labour. That was his property which could not be taken from him wherever he had fixed it. And hence subduing or cultivating the earth, and having dominion, we see are joined together. The one gave title to the other.

So that God, by commanding to subdue, gave authority so far to appropriate: and the condition of human life, which requires labour and materials to work on, necessarily introduces private possessions.

§ 36. The measure of property nature has well set by the extent of men's labour and the conveniencies of life: no man's labour could subdue, or appropriate all; nor could his enjoyment consume more than a small part; so that it was impossible for any man, this way, to intrench upon the right of another, or acquire to himself a property, to the prejudice of his neighbour, who would still have room for as good and as large a possession (after the other had taken out his) as before it was appropriated. This measure did confine every man's possession to a very moderate proportion, and such as he might appropriate to himself, without injury to any body, in the first ages of the world, when men were more in danger to be lost, by wandering from their company, in the then vast wilderness of the earth, than to be straitened for want of room to plant in. And the same measure may be allowed still without prejudice to any body, as full as the world seems: for supposing a man, or family, in the state they were at first peopling of the world by the children of Adam, or Noah; let him plant in some inland, vacant places of America, we shall find that the possessions he could make himself, upon the measures we have given, would not be very large, nor, even to this day, prejudice the rest of mankind, or give them reason to complain, or think themselves injured by this man's encroachment; though the race of men have now spread themselves to all the corners of the world, and do infinitely exceed the small number was at the beginning. Nay, the extent of ground is of so little value, without labour, that I have heard it affirmed, that in Spain itself a man may be permitted to plough, sow, and reap, without being disturbed, upon land he has no other title to, but only his making use of it. But, on the contrary, the inhabitants think themselves beholden to him, who, by his industry on neglected, and consequently waste land, has increased the stock of corn, which they wanted. But be this as it will, which I lay no stress on; this I dare boldly affirm, that the same rule of propriety, viz, that every man should have as much as he could make use of, would hold still in the world, without straitening any body; since there is land enough in the world to suffice double the inhabitants, had not the invention of money, and the tacit agreement of men to put a value on it, introduced (by consent) larger possessions, and a right to them; which, how it has done, I shall by and by show more at large.

§ 37. This is certain, that in the beginning, before the desire of having more than man needed had altered the intrinsic value of things, which depends only on their usefulness to the life of man; or had agreed, that a little piece of yellow metal, which would keep without wasting or decay, should be worth a great piece of flesh, or a whole heap of corn; though men had a right to appropriate, by their labour, each one to himself, as much of the things of nature as he could use: yet this could not be much, nor to the prejudice of others, where the same plenty was still left to those who would use the same industry. To which let me add, that he who appropriates land to himself by his labour, does not lessen, but increase the common stock of mankind: for the provisions serving to the support of human life, produced by one acre of enclosed and cultivated land, are (to speak much within compass) ten times more than those which are yielded by an acre of land of an equal richness lying waste in common. And therefore he that encloses land, and has a greater plenty of the conveniencies of life from ten acres, than he could have from an hundred left to nature, may truly be said to give ninety acres to mankind: for his labour now supplies him with provisions out of ten acres, which were by the product of an hundred lying in common. I have here rated the improved land very low, in making its product but as ten to one, when it is much nearer an hundred to one: for I ask, whether in the wild woods and uncultivated waste of America, left to nature, without any improvement, tillage, or husbandry, a thousand acres yield the needy and wretched inhabitants as many conveniencies of life as ten acres equally fertile land do in Devonshire, where they are well cultivated?

Before the appropriation of land, he who gathered as much of the wild fruit, killed, caught, or tamed, as many of the beasts, as he could; he that so employed his pains about any of the spontaneous products of nature, as any way to alter them from the state which nature put them in, by placing any of his labour on them, did thereby acquire a propriety in them: but if they perished, in his possession, without their due use; if the fruits rotted, or the venison putrefied, before he could spend it; he offended against the common law of nature, and was liable to be punished; he invaded his neighbour's share, for he had no right, farther than his use called for any of them, and they might serve to afford him conveniencies of life.

§ 38. The same measures governed the possession of land too: whatsoever he tilled and reaped, laid up and made use of, before it spoiled, that was his peculiar right; whatsoever he enclosed, and could feed, and make use of, the cattle and product was also his. But if either the grass of his enclosure rotted on the ground, or the fruit of his planting perished without gathering and laying up; this part of the earth, notwithstanding his enclosure, was still to be looked on as waste, and might be the possession of any other. Thus, at the beginning, Cain might take as much ground as he could till, and make it his own land, and yet leave enough to Abel's sheep to feed on; a few acres would serve for both their possessions. But as families increased, and industry enlarged their stocks, their possessions enlarged with the need of them; but yet it was commonly without any fixed property in the ground they made use of, till they incorporated, settled themselves together, and built cities; and then, by consent, they came in time to set out the bounds of their distinct territories, and agree on limits between them and their neighbours; and by laws within themselves settled the properties of those of the same society: for we see that in that part of the world which was first inhabited, and therefore like to be best peopled, even as low down as Abraham's time, they wandered with their flocks, and their herds, which was their substance, freely up and down; and this Abraham did, in a country where he was a stranger. Whence it is plain, that at least a great part of the land lay in common; that the inhabitants valued it not, nor claimed property in any more than they made use of. But when there was not room enough in the same place for their herds to feed together, they by consent, as Abraham and Lot did, Gen. xiii. 5, separated and enlarged their pasture, where it best liked them. And for the same reason Esau went from his father, and his brother, and planted in mount Seir, Gen. xxxvi. 6.

§ 39. And thus, without supposing any private dominion and property in Adam, over all the world, exclusive of all other men, which can no way be proved, nor any one's property be made out from it; but supposing the world given, as it was, to the children of men in common, we see how labour could make men distinct titles to several parcels of it, for their private uses; wherein there could be no doubt of right, no room for quarrel.

§ 40. Nor is it so strange, as perhaps before consideration it may appear, that the property of labour should be able to overbalance the community of land: for it is labour indeed that put the difference of value on every thing; and let any one consider what the difference is between an acre of land planted with tobacco or sugar, sown with wheat or barley, and an acre

of the same land lying in common, without any husbandry upon it, and he will find, that the improvement of labour makes the far greater part of the value. I think it will be but a very modest computation to say, that of the products of the earth useful to the life of man, nine-tenths are the effects of labour: nay, if we will rightly estimate things as they come to our use, and cast up the several expenses about them, what in them is purely owing to nature, and what to labour, we shall find, that in most of them ninety-nine hundredths are wholly to be put on the account of labour.

§ 41. There cannot be a clearer demonstration of any thing, than several nations of the Americans are of this, who are rich in land, and poor in all the comforts of life; whom nature having furnished as liberally as any other people with the materials of plenty, i.e., a fruitful soil, apt to produce in abundance what might serve for food, raiment, and delight; yet, for want of improving it by labour, have not one-hundredth part of the conveniencies we enjoy: and a king of a large and fruitful territory there feeds, lodges, and is clad worse than a day-labourer in England.

§ 42. To make this a little clear, let us but trace some of the ordinary provisions of life, through their several progresses, before they come to our use, and see how much of their value they receive from human industry. Bread, wine, and cloth, are things of daily use, and great plenty; yet notwithstanding, acorns, water, and leaves, or skins, must be our bread, drink, and clothing, did not labour furnish us with these more useful commodities: for whatever bread is more worth than acorns, wine than water, and cloth or silk than leaves, skins, or moss, that is wholly owing to labour and industry; the one of these being the food and raiment which unassisted nature furnishes us with; the other, provisions which our industry and pains prepare for us; which, how much they exceed the other in value, when any one hath computed, he will then see how much labour makes the far greatest part of the value of things we enjoy in this world: and the ground which produces the materials is scarce to be reckoned in as any, or, at most, but a very small part of it; so little, that even amongst us, land that is left wholly to nature, that hath no improvement of pasturage, tillage, or planting, is called, as indeed it is, waste; and we shall find the benefit of it amount to little more than nothing.

This shows how much numbers of men are to be preferred to largeness of dominions; and that the increase of lands, and the right of employing of them, is the great art of government: and that prince, who shall be so wise and god-like, as by established laws of liberty to secure protection and encouragement to the honest industry of mankind, against the oppression of power and narrowness of party, will quickly be too hard for his neighbours: but this by the by. To return to the argument in hand.

§ 43. An acre of land, that bears here twenty bushels of wheat, and another in America, which, with the same husbandry, would do the like, are, without doubt, of the same natural intrinsic value: but yet the benefit mankind receives from the one in a year is worth 5*l.* and from the other possibly not worth a penny, if all the profit an Indian received from it were to be valued, and sold here; at least, I may truly say, not one thousandth. It is labour, then, which puts the greatest part of the value upon land, without which it would scarcely be worth any thing: it is to that we owe the greatest part of all its useful products; for all that the straw, bran, bread, of that acre of wheat, is more worth than the product of an acre of as good land, which lies waste, is all the effect of labour: for it is not barely the ploughman's pains, the reaper's and thresher's toil, and the baker's sweat, is to be counted into the bread we eat; the labour of those who broke the oxen, who digged and wrought the iron and stones, who felled and framed the timber employed about the plough,

mill, oven, or any other utensils, which are a vast number, requisite to this corn, from its being seed to be sown to its being made bread, must all be charged on the account of labour, and received as an effect of that: nature and the earth furnished only the almost worthless materials, as in themselves. It would be a strange "catalogue of things, that industry provided and made use of, about every loaf of bread," before it came to our use, if we could trace them; iron, wood, leather, bark, timber, stone, bricks, coals, lime, cloth, dyeing, drugs, pitch, tar, masts, ropes, and all the materials made use of in the ship, that brought any of the commodities used by any of the workmen, to any part of the work: all which it would be almost impossible, at least too long, to reckon up.

§ 44. From all which it is evident, that though the things of nature are given in common, yet man, by being master of himself, and "proprietor of his own person, and the actions or labour of it, had still in himself the great foundation of property"; and that which made up the greater part of what he applied to the support or comfort of his being, when invention and arts had improved the conveniencies of life, was perfectly his own, and did not belong in common to others.

§ 45. Thus labour, in the beginning, gave a right of property wherever any one was pleased to employ it upon what was common, which remained a long while the far greater part, and is yet more than mankind makes use of. Men, at first, for the most part, contented themselves with what unassisted nature offered to their necessities: and though afterwards, in some parts of the world, (where the increase of people and stock, with the use of money, had made land scarce, and so of some value) the several communities settled the bounds of their distinct territories, and by laws within themselves regulated the properties of the private men of their society, and so, by compact and agreement, settled the property which labour and industry began: and the leagues that have been made between several states and kingdoms, either expressly or tacitly disowning all claim and right to the land in the others' possession, have, by common consent, given up their pretences to their natural common right, which originally they had to those countries, and so have, by positive agreement, settled a property amongst themselves, in distinct parts and parcels of the earth; yet there are still great tracts of ground to be found, which (the inhabitants thereof not having joined with the rest of mankind in the consent of the use of their common money) lie waste, and are more than the people who dwell on it do or can make use of, and so still lie in common; though this can scarce happen amongst that part of mankind that have consented to the use of money.

§ 46. The greatest part of things really useful to the life of man, and such as the necessity of subsisting made the first commoners of the world look after, as it doth the Americans now, are generally things of short duration; such as, if they are not consumed by use, will decay and perish of themselves: gold, silver, and diamonds, are things that fancy or agreement hath put the value on, more than real use, and the necessary support of life. Now of those good things which nature hath provided in common, every one had a right (as hath been said) to as much as he could use, and property in all that he could effect with his labour; all that his industry could extend to, to alter from the state nature had put it in, was his. He that gathered a hundred bushels of acorns or apples, had thereby a property in them; they were his goods as soon as gathered. He was only to look that he used them before they spoiled, else he took more than his share, and robbed others. And indeed it was a foolish thing, as well as dishonest, to hoard up more than he could make use of. If he gave away a part to any body else, so that it perished not uselessly in his possession, these he also made use of. And if

he also bartered away plums, that would have rotted in a week, for nuts that would last good for his eating a whole year, he did no injury; he wasted not the common stock; destroyed no part of the portion of the goods that belonged to others, so long as nothing perished uselessly in his hands. Again, if he would give his nuts for a piece of metal, pleased with its colour; or exchange his sheep for shells, or wool for a sparkling pebble or a diamond, and keep those by him all his life, he invaded not the right of others; he might heap as much of these durable things as he pleased; the exceeding of the bounds of his just property not lying in the largeness of his possession, but the perishing of any thing uselessly in it.

§ 47. And thus came in the use of money, some lasting thing that men might keep without spoiling, and that by mutual consent men would take in exchange for the truly useful, but perishable supports of life.

§ 48. And as different degrees of industry were apt to give men possessions in different proportions, so this invention of money gave them the opportunity to continue and enlarge them: for supposing an island, separate from all possible commerce with the rest of the world, wherein there were but an hundred families, but there were sheep, horses, and cows, with other useful animals, wholesome fruits, and land enough for corn for a hundred thousand times as many, but nothing in the island, either because of its commonness, or perishableness, fit to supply the place of money; what reason could any one have there to enlarge his possessions beyond the use of his family and a plentiful supply to its consumption, either in what their own industry produced, or they could barter for like perishable, useful commodities with others? Where there is not something, both lasting and scarce, and so valuable, to be hoarded up, there men will not be apt to enlarge their possessions of land, were it ever so rich, ever so free for them to take: for I ask, what would a man value ten thousand, or an hundred thousand acres of excellent land, ready culti-vated, and well stocked too with cattle, in the middle of the inland parts of America, where he had no hopes of commerce with other parts of the world, to draw money to him by the sale of the product? It would not be worth the en-closing, and we should see him give up again to the wild common of nature, whatever was more than would supply the conveniencies of life to be had there for him and his family.

§ 49. Thus in the beginning all the world was America, and more so than that is now; for no such thing as money was any where known. Find out something that hath the use and value of money amongst his neighbours, you shall see the same man will begin presently to enlarge his possessions.

§ 50. But since gold and silver, being little useful to the life of man in proportion to food, raiment, and carriage, has its value only from the consent of men, whereof labour yet makes, in great part, the measure; it is plain, that men have agreed to a disproportionate and unequal possession of the earth; they having, by a tacit and voluntary consent, found out a way how a man may fairly possess more land than he himself can use the product of, by receiving, in exchange for the overplus, gold and silver, which may be hoarded up without injury to any one; these metals not spoiling or decaying in the hands of the possessor. This partage of things in an inequality of private possessions, men have made practicable out of the bounds of society, and without compact; only by put-ting a value on gold and silver, and tacitly agreeing in the use of money: for in govern-ments, the laws regulate the right of property, and the possession of land is determined by positive constitutions.

CHAPTER 2

Of the Principles of the Three Kinds of Government

Charles de Secondat, Baron de Montesquieu

1. *Difference between the Nature and Principle of Government.* Having examined the laws in rela-tion to the nature of each government, we must investigate those which relate to its principle.

There is this difference between the nature and principle[1] of government, that the former is that by which it is constituted, the latter that by which it is made to act. One is its particular structure, and the other the human passions which set it in motion.

Now, laws ought no less to relate to the prin-ciple than to the nature of each government. We must, therefore, inquire into this principle, which shall be the subject of this third book.

2. *Of the Principle of different Governments.* I have already observed that it is the nature of a republican government that either the collec-tive body of the people, or particular families, should be possessed of the supreme power;

of a monarchy, that the prince should have this power, but in the execution of it should be directed by established laws; of a despotic government, that a single person should rule according to his own will and caprice. This enables me to discover their three principles; which are thence naturally derived. I shall begin with a republican government, and in particular with that of democracy.

3. *Of the Principle of Democracy.* There is no great share of probity necessary to support a monarchical or despotic government. The force of laws in one, and the prince's arm in the other, are sufficient to direct and maintain the whole. But in a popular state, one spring more is necessary, namely, virtue.

What I have here advanced is confirmed by the unanimous testimony of historians, and is extremely agreeable to the nature of things. For it is clear that in a monarchy, where he who commands the execution of the laws generally thinks himself above them, there is less need of virtue than in a popular government, where the person entrusted with the execution of the laws is sensible of his being subject to their direction.

Clear is it also that a monarch who, through bad advice or indolence, ceases to enforce the execution of the laws, may easily repair the evil; he has only to follow other advice; or to shake off this indolence. But when, in a popular government, there is a suspension of the laws, as this can proceed only from the corruption of the republic, the state is certainly undone.

A very droll spectacle it was in the last century to behold the impotent efforts of the English towards the establishment of democracy. As they who had a share in the direction of public affairs were void of virtue; as their ambition was inflamed by the success of the most daring of their members;[2] as the prevailing parties were successively animated by the spirit of faction, the government was continually changing: the people, amazed at so many revolutions, in vain attempted to erect a commonwealth. At length, when the country had undergone the most violent shocks, they were obliged to have recourse to the very government which they had so wantonly proscribed.

When Sylla thought of restoring Rome to her liberty, this unhappy city was incapable of receiving that blessing. She had only the feeble remains of virtue, which were continually diminishing. Instead of being roused from her lethargy by Caesar, Tiberius, Caius Claudius, Nero, and Domitian, she riveted every day her chains: if she struck some blows, her aim was at the tyrant, not at the tyranny.

The politic Greeks, who lived under a popular government, knew no other support than virtue. The modern inhabitants of that country are entirely taken up with manufacture, commerce, finances, opulence, and luxury.

When virtue is banished, ambition invades the minds of those who are disposed to receive it, and avarice possesses the whole community. The objects of their desires are changed; what they were fond of before has become indifferent; they were free while under the restraint of laws, but they would fain now be free to act against law; and as each citizen is like a slave who has run away from his master, that which was a maxim of equity he calls rigour; that which was a rule of action he styles constraint; and to precaution he gives the name of fear. Frugality, and not the thirst of gain, now passes for avarice. Formerly the wealth of individuals constituted the public treasure; but now this has become the patrimony of private persons. The members of the commonwealth riot on the public spoils, and its strength is only the power of a few, and the licence of many.

Athens was possessed of the same number of forces when she triumphed so gloriously as when with such infamy she was enslaved. She had twenty thousand citizens,[3] when she defended the Greeks against the Persians, when she contended for empire with Sparta, and invaded Sicily. She had twenty thousand when Demetrius Phalereus numbered them,[4] as slaves are told by the head in a marketplace. When Philip attempted to lord it over Greece, and appeared at the gates of Athens,[5] she had even then lost nothing but time. We may see in Demosthenes how difficult it was to awaken her; she dreaded Philip, not as the enemy of her liberty, but of her pleasures.[6] This famous city, which had withstood so many defeats, and having been so often destroyed had as often risen out of her ashes, was overthrown at Chaeronea, and at one blow deprived of all hopes of resource. What does it avail her that Philip sends back her prisoners, if he does not return her men? It was ever after as easy to triumph over the forces of Athens as it had been difficult to subdue her virtue.

How was it possible for Carthage to maintain her ground? When Hannibal, upon his being made praetor, endeavoured to hinder the magistrates from plundering the republic, did not they complain of him to the Romans? Wretches, who would fain be citizens without a city, and be beholden for their riches to their very destroyers! Rome soon insisted upon having three hundred of their principal citizens as hostages; she obliged them next to surrender their arms and ships; and then she declared war.[7] From the desperate efforts of this defenceless city, one may judge of what she might have performed in her full vigour, and assisted by virtue.

4. *Of the Principle of Aristocracy.* As virtue is necessary in a popular government, it is requisite also in an aristocracy. True it is that in the latter it is not so absolutely requisite.

The people, who in respect to the nobility are the same as the subjects with regard to a monarch, are restrained by their laws. They have, therefore, less occasion for virtue than the people in a democracy. But how are the nobility to be restrained? They who are to execute the laws against their colleagues will immediately perceive that they are acting against themselves. Virtue is therefore necessary in this body, from the very nature of the constitution.

An aristocratic government has an inherent vigour, unknown to democracy. The nobles form a body, who by their prerogative, and for their own particular interest, restrain the people; it is sufficient that there are laws in being to see them executed.

But easy as it may be for the body of the nobles to restrain the people, it is difficult to restrain themselves.[8] Such is the nature of this constitution, that it seems to subject the very same persons to the power of the laws, and at the same time to exempt them.

Now such a body as this can restrain itself only in two ways; either by a very eminent virtue, which puts the nobility in some measure on a level with the people, and may be the means of forming a great republic; or by an inferior virtue, which puts them at least upon a level with one another, and upon this their preservation depends.

Moderation is therefore the very soul of this government; a moderation, I mean, founded on virtue, not that which proceeds from indolence and pusillanimity.

5. *That Virtue is not the Principle of a Monarchical Government.* In monarchies, policy effects great things with as little virtue as possible. Thus in the nicest machines, art has reduced the number of movements, springs, and wheels.

The state subsists independently of the love of our country, of the thirst of true glory, of self-denial, of the sacrifice of our dearest interests, and of all those heroic virtues which we admire in the ancients, and to us are known only by tradition.

The laws supply here the place of those virtues; they are by no means wanted, and the state dispenses with them: an action performed here in secret is in some measure of no consequence.

Though all crimes be in their own nature public, yet there is a distinction between crimes really public and those that are private, which are so called because they are more injurious to individuals than to the community.

Now in republics private crimes are more public, that is, they attack the constitution more than they do individuals; and in monarchies, public crimes are more private, that is, they are more prejudicial to private people than to the constitution.

I beg that no one will be offended with what I have been saying; my observations are founded on the unanimous testimony of historians. I am not ignorant that virtuous princes are so very rare; but I venture to affirm that in a monarchy it is extremely difficult for the people to be virtuous.[9]

Let us compare what the historians of all ages have asserted concerning the courts of monarchs; let us recollect the conversations and sentiments of people of all countries, in respect to the wretched character of courtiers, and we shall find that these are not airy speculations, but truths confirmed by a sad and melancholy experience.

Ambition in idleness; meanness mixed with pride; a desire of riches without industry; aversion to truth; flattery, perfidy, violation of engagements, contempt of civil duties, fear of the prince's virtue, hope from his weakness, but, above all, a perpetual ridicule cast upon virtue, are, I think, the characteristics by which most courtiers in all ages and countries have been constantly distinguished. Now, it is exceedingly difficult for the leading men of the nation to be knaves, and the inferior sort to be honest; for the former to be cheats, and the latter to rest satisfied with being only dupes.

But if there should chance to be some unlucky honest man[10] among the people, Cardinal Richelieu, in his political testament, seems to hint that a prince should take care not to employ him.[11] So true is it that virtue is not the spring of this government! It is not indeed excluded, but it is not the spring of government.

6. *In what Manner Virtue is supplied in a Monarchical Government.* But it is high time for me to have done with this subject, lest I should be suspected of writing a satire against monarchical government. Far be it from me; if monarchy wants one spring, it is provided with another. Honour, that is, the prejudice of every person and rank, supplies the place of the political virtue of which I have been speaking, and is everywhere her representative: here it is capable of inspiring the most glorious actions, and, joined with the force of laws, may lead us to the end of government as well as virtue itself.

Hence, in well-regulated monarchies, they are almost all good subjects, and very few good men; for to be a good man,[12] a good intention is necessary, and we should love our country, not so much on our own account, as out of regard to the community.

7. *Of the Principle of Monarchy.* A monarchical government supposes, as we have already observed, pre-eminences and ranks, as likewise a noble descent. Now since it is the nature of honour to aspire to preferments and titles, it is properly placed in this government.

Ambition is pernicious in a republic. But in a monarchy it has some good effects; it gives life to the government, and is attended with this advantage, that it is in no way dangerous, because it may be continually checked.

It is with this kind of government as with the system of the universe, in which there is a power that constantly repels all bodies from the centre, and a power of gravitation that attracts them to it. Honour sets all the parts of the body politic in motion, and by its very action connects them; thus each individual advances the public good, while he only thinks of promoting his own interest.

True it is that, philosophically speaking, it is a false honour which moves all the parts of the government; but even this false honour is as useful to the public as true honour could possibly be to private persons.

Is it not very exacting to oblige men to perform the most difficult actions, such as require an extraordinary exertion of fortitude and resolution, without other recompense than that of glory and applause?

Notes

1. This is a very important distinction, whence I shall draw many consequences; for it is the key of an infinite number of laws.
2. Cromwell.
3. Plutarch, *Pericles;* Plato, in *Critias.*
4. She had at that time twenty-one thousand citizens, ten thousand strangers, and four hundred thousand slaves. See Athenaeus, vi.
5. She had then twenty thousand citizens. See Demosthenes in *Aristog.*
6. They had passed a law, which rendered it a capital crime for any one to propose applying the money designed for the theatres to military service.
7. This lasted three years.
8. Public crimes may be punished, because it is here a common concern; but private crimes will go unpunished, because it is the common interest not to punish them.
9. I speak here of political virtue, which is also moral virtue as it is directed to the public good; very little of private moral virtue, and not at all of hat virtue which relates to revealed truths. This will appear better in v. 2.
10. This is to be understood in the sense of the preceding note.
11. We must not, says he, employ people of mean extraction; they are too rigid and morose.— *Testament Polit.*, 4.
12. This word *good man* is understood here in a political sense only.

CHAPTER 3

Of Restraints upon the Importation from Foreign Countries of Such Goods as Can Be Produced at Home

Adam Smith

Book IV.

By restraining, either by high duties, or by absolute prohibitions, the importation of such goods from foreign countries as can be produced at home, the monopoly of the home-market is more or less secured to the domestic industry employed in producing them. Thus the prohibition of importing either live cattle or salt provisions from foreign countries secures to the graziers of Great Britain the monopoly of the home-market for butchers'-meat. The high duties upon the importation of corn, which in times of moderate plenty amount to a prohibition, give a like advantage to the growers of that commodity. The prohibition of the importation of foreign woollens is equally favourable to the woollen manufactures. The silk manufacture, though altogether employed upon foreign materials, has lately obtained the same advantage. The linen manufacture has not yet obtained it, but is making great strides towards it. Many other sorts of manufactures have, in the same manner, obtained in Great Britain, either altogether, or very nearly a monopoly against their countrymen. The variety of goods of which the importation into Great Britain is prohibited, either absolutely, or under certain circumstances, greatly exceeds what can easily be suspected by those who are not well acquainted with the laws of the customs.

That this monopoly of the home-market frequently gives great encouragement to that particular species of industry which enjoys it, and frequently turns towards that employment a greater share of both the labour and stock of the society than would otherwise have gone to it, cannot be doubted. But whether it tends either to increase the general industry of the society, or to give it the most advantageous direction, is not, perhaps, altogether so evident.

The general industry of the society never can exceed what the capital of the society can employ. As the number of workmen that can be kept in employment by any particular person must bear a certain proportion to his capital, so the number of those that can be continually employed by all the members of a great society, must bear a certain proportion to the whole capital of that society, and never can exceed that proportion. No regulation of commerce can increase the quantity of industry in any society beyond what its capital can maintain. It can only divert a part of it into a direction into which it might not otherwise have gone; and it is by no means certain that this artificial direction is likely to be more advantageous to the society than that into which it would have gone of its own accord.

Every individual is continually exerting himself to find out the most advantageous employment for whatever capital he can command. It is his own advantage, indeed, and not that of the society, which he has in view. But the study of his own advantage naturally, or rather necessarily, leads him to prefer that employment which is most advantageous to the society.

First, every individual endeavours to employ his capital as near home as he can, and consequently as much as he can in the support of domestic industry; provided always that he can thereby obtain the ordinary, or not a great deal less than the ordinary profits of stock.

Thus upon equal or nearly equal profits, every wholesale merchant naturally prefers the home-trade to the foreign trade of consumption, and the foreign trade of consumption to the carrying trade. In the home-trade his capital is never so long out of his sight as it frequently is in the foreign trade of consumption. He can know better the character and situation of the persons whom he trusts, and if he should happen to be deceived, he knows better the laws of the country from which he must seek redress. In the carrying trade, the capital of the merchant is, as it were, divided between two foreign countries, and no part of it is ever necessarily brought home, or placed under his own immediate view and command. The capital which an Amsterdam merchant employs in carrying corn from Konnigsberg to Lisbon, and fruit and wine from Lisbon to Konnigsberg, must generally be the one-half of it at Konnigsberg and the other half at Lisbon. No part of it need ever come to Amsterdam. The natural residence of such a merchant should either be at Konnigsberg or Lisbon, and it can only be some very particular circumstances which can make him prefer the residence of Amsterdam. The uneasiness, however, which he feels at being separated so far from his capital, generally determines him to bring part both of the Konnigsberg goods which he destines for the market of Lisbon, and of the Lisbon goods which he destines for that of Konnigsberg, to Amsterdam: and though this necessarily subjects him to a double charge of loading and unloading, as well as to the payment of some duties and customs, yet for the sake of having some part of his capital always under his own view and command, he willingly submits to this extraordinary charge; and it is in this manner that every country which has any considerable share of the carrying trade, becomes always the emporium, or general market, for the goods of all the different countries whose trade it carries on. The merchant, in order to save a second loading and unloading, endeavours always to sell in the home-market as much of the goods of all those different countries as he can, and thus, so far as he can, to convert his carrying trade into a foreign trade of consumption. A merchant, in the same manner, who is engaged in the foreign trade of consumption, when he collects goods for foreign markets, will always be glad, upon equal or nearly equal profits, to sell as great a part of them at home as he can. He saves himself the risk and trouble of exportation, when, so far as he can, he thus converts his foreign trade of consumption into a home trade. Home is in this manner the centre, if I may say so, round which the capitals of the inhabitants of every country are continually circulating, and towards which they are always tending, though by particular causes they may sometimes be driven off and repelled from it towards more distant employments. But a capital employed in the home-trade, it has already been shown, necessarily puts into motion a greater quantity of domestic industry, and gives revenue and employment to a greater number of the inhabitants of the country, than an equal capital employed in the foreign trade of consumption: and one employed in the foreign trade of consumption has the same advantage over an equal capital employed in the carrying trade. Upon equal, or only nearly equal profits, therefore, every individual naturally inclines to employ his capital in the manner in which it is likely to afford the greatest support to domestic industry, and to

give revenue and employment to the greatest number of people of his own country.

Secondly, every individual who employs his capital in the support of domestic industry, necessarily endeavours so to direct that industry, that its produce may be of the greatest possible value.

The produce of industry is what it adds to the subject or materials upon which it is employed. In proportion as the value of this produce is great or small, so will likewise be the profits of the employer. But it is only for the sake of profit that any man employs a capital in the support of industry; and he will always, therefore, endeavour to employ it in the support of that industry of which the produce is likely to be of the greatest value, or to exchange for the greatest quantity either of money or of other goods.

But the annual revenue of every society is always precisely equal to the exchangeable value of the whole annual produce of its industry, or rather is precisely the same thing with that exchangeable value. As every individual, therefore, endeavours as much as he can both to employ his capital in the support of domestic industry, and so to direct that industry that its produce may be of the greatest value; every individual necessarily labours to render the annual revenue of the society as great as he can. He generally, indeed, neither intends to promote the public interest, nor knows how much he is promoting it. By preferring the support of domestic to that of foreign industry, he intends only his own security; and by directing that industry in such a manner as its produce may be of the greatest value, he intends only his own gain, and he is in this, as in many other cases, led by an invisible hand to promote an end which was no part of his intention. Nor is it always the worse for the society that it was no part of it. By pursuing his own interest he frequently promotes that of the society more effectually than when he really intends to promote it. I have never known much good done by those who affected to trade for the public good. It is an affectation, indeed, not very common among merchants, and very few words need be employed in dissuading them from it.

What is the species of domestic industry which his capital can employ, and of which the produce is likely to be of the greatest value, every individual, it is evident, can, in his local situation, judge much better than any statesman or lawgiver can do for him. The statesman, who should attempt to direct private people in what manner they ought to employ their capitals, would not only load himself with a most unnecessary attention, but assume an authority which could safely be trusted, not only to no single person, but to no council or senate whatever, and which would nowhere be so dangerous as in the hands of a man who had folly and presumption enough to fancy himself fit to exercise it.

To give the monopoly of the home-market to the produce of domestic industry, in any particular art or manufacture, is in some measure to direct private people in what manner they ought to employ their capitals, and must, in almost all cases, be either a useless or a hurtful regulation. If the produce of domestic can be brought there as cheap as that of foreign industry, the regulation is evidently useless. If it cannot, it must generally be hurtful. It is the maxim of every prudent master of a family, never to attempt to make at home what it will cost him more to make than to buy. The tailor does not attempt to make his own shoes, but buys them of the shoemaker. The shoemaker does not attempt to make his own clothes, but employs a tailor. The farmer attempts to make neither the one nor the other, but employs those different artificers. All of them find it for their interest to employ their whole industry in a way in which they have some advantage over their neighbours, and to purchase with a part of its produce, or what is the same thing, with

the price of a part of it, whatever else they have occasion for.

What is prudence in the conduct of every private family, can scarce be folly in that of a great kingdom. If a foreign country can supply us with a commodity cheaper than we ourselves can make it, better buy it of them with some part of the produce of our own industry, employed in a way in which we have some advantage. The general industry of the country, being always in proportion to the capital which employs it, will not thereby be diminished, no more than that of the above-mentioned artificers; but only left to find out the way in which it can be employed with the greatest advantage. It is certainly not employed to the greatest advantage, when it is thus directed towards an object which it can buy cheaper than it can make. The value of its annual produce is certainly more or less diminished, when it is thus turned away from producing commodities evidently of more value than the commodity which it is directed to produce. According to the supposition, that commodity could be purchased from foreign countries cheaper than it can be made at home. It could, therefore, have been purchased with a part only of the commodities, or, what is the same thing, with a part only of the price of the commodities, which the industry employed by an equal capital would have produced at home, had it been left to follow its natural course. The industry of the country, therefore, is thus turned away from a more to a less advantageous employment, and the exchangeable value of its annual produce, instead of being increased, according to the intention of the lawgiver, must necessarily be diminished by every such regulation.

By means of such regulations, indeed, a particular manufacture may sometimes be acquired sooner than it could have been otherwise, and after a certain time may be made at home as cheap or cheaper than in the foreign country. But though the industry of the society may be thus carried with advantage into a particular channel sooner than it could have been otherwise, it will by no means follow that the sum total, either of its industry, or of its revenue, can ever be augmented by any such regulation. The industry of the society can augment only in proportion as its capital augments, and its capital can augment only in proportion to what can be gradually saved out of its revenue. But the immediate effect of every such regulation is to diminish its revenue, and what diminishes its revenue is certainly not very likely to augment its capital faster than it would have augmented of its own accord, had both capital and industry been left to find out their natural employments.

Though for want of such regulations the society should never acquire the proposed manufacture, it would not, upon that account, necessarily be the poorer in any one period of its duration. In every period of its duration its whole capital and industry might still have been employed, though upon different objects, in the manner that was most advantageous at the time. In every period its revenue might have been the greatest which its capital could afford, and both capital and revenue might have been augmented with the greatest possible rapidity.

The natural advantages which one country has over another in producing particular commodities are sometimes so great, that it is acknowledged by all the world to be in vain to struggle with them. By means of glasses, hotbeds, and hotwalls, very good grapes can be raised in Scotland, and very good wine too can be made of them at about thirty times the expense for which at least equally good can be brought from foreign countries. Would it be a reasonable law to prohibit the importation of all foreign wines, merely to encourage the making of claret and burgundy in Scotland? But if there would be a manifest absurdity in turning towards any employment, thirty times more of the capital and industry of the country than would be necessary to purchase from foreign countries an equal quantity of the commodities wanted, there must be an absurdity, though not altogether so glaring, yet exactly of the same kind, in turning towards any such employment a thirtieth, or even a three hundredth part more of either. Whether the advantages which one country has over another, be natural or acquired, is in this respect of no consequence. As long as the one country has those advantages, and the other wants them, it will always be more advantageous for the latter, rather to buy of the former than to make. It is an acquired advantage only, which one artificer has over his neighbour, who exercises another trade; and yet they both find it more advantageous to buy of one another, than to make what does not belong to their particular trades.

CHAPTER 4

What Is Enlightenment?

Immanuel Kant

Enlightenment is man's release from his self-incurred tutelage. Tutelage is man's inability to make use of his understanding without direction from another. Self-incurred is this tutelage when its cause lies not in lack of reason but in lack of resolution and courage to use it without direction from another. *Sapere aude!* "Have courage to use your own reason!"—that is the motto of enlightenment.

Laziness and cowardice are the reasons why so great a portion of mankind, after nature has long since discharged them from external direction (*naturaliter maiorennes*), nevertheless remains under lifelong tutelage, and why it is so easy for others to set themselves up as their guardians. It is so easy not to be of age. If I have a book which understands for me, a pastor who has a conscience for me, a physician who decides my diet, and so forth, I need not trouble myself. I need not think, if I can only pay—others will readily undertake the irksome work for me.

That the step to competence is held to be very dangerous by the far greater portion of mankind (and by the entire fair sex)—quite apart from its being arduous—is seen to by those guardians who have so kindly assumed superintendence over them. After the guardians have first made their domestic cattle dumb and have made sure that these placid creatures will not dare take a single step without the harness of the cart to which they are tethered, the guardians then show them the danger which threatens if they try to go alone. Actually, however, this danger is not so great, for by falling a few times they would finally learn to walk alone. But an example of this failure makes them timid and ordinarily frightens them away from all further trials.

For any single individual to work himself out of the life under tutelage which has become almost his nature is very difficult. He has come to be fond of this state, and he is for the present really incapable of making use of his reason, for no one has ever let him try it out. Statutes and formulas, those mechanical tools of the rational employment or rather misemployment of his natural gifts, are the fetters of an everlasting tutelage. Whoever throws them off makes only an uncertain leap over the narrowest ditch because he is not accustomed to that kind of free motion. Therefore, there are few who have succeeded by their own exercise of mind both in freeing themselves from incompetence and in achieving a steady pace.

But that the public should enlighten itself is more possible; indeed, if only freedom is granted, enlightenment is almost sure to follow. For there will always be some independent thinkers, even among the established guardians of the great masses, who, after throwing off the yoke of tutelage from their own shoulders, will disseminate the spirit of the rational appreciation of both their own worth and every man's vocation for thinking for himself. But be it noted that the public, which has first been brought under this yoke by their guardians, forces the guardians themselves to remain bound when it is incited to do so by some of the guardians who are themselves capable of some enlightenment—so harmful is it to implant prejudices, for they later take vengeance on their cultivators or on their descendants. Thus the public can only slowly attain enlightenment. Perhaps a fall of personal despotism or of avaricious or tyrannical oppression may be accomplished by revolution, but never a true reform in ways of thinking. Rather, new prejudices will serve as well as old ones to harness the great unthinking masses.

For this enlightenment, however, nothing is required but freedom, and indeed the most harmless among all the things to which this term can properly be applied. It is the freedom to make public use of one's reason at every point. But I hear on all sides, "Do not argue!" The officer says: "Do not argue but drill!" The tax collector: "Do not argue but pay!" The cleric: "Do not argue but believe!" Only one prince in the world says, "Argue as much as you will, and about what you will, but obey!" Everywhere there is restriction on freedom.

Which restriction is an obstacle to enlightenment, and which is not an obstacle but a promoter of it? I answer: The public use of one's reason must always be free, and it alone can bring about enlightenment among men. The private use of reason, on the other hand, may often be very narrowly restricted without particularly hindering the progress of enlightenment. By the public use of one's reason I understand the use which a person makes of it as a scholar before the reading public. Private use I call that which one may make of it in a particular civil post or office which is entrusted to him. Many affairs which are conducted in the interest of the community require a certain mechanism through which some members of the community must passively conduct themselves with an artificial unanimity, so that the government may direct them to public ends, or at least prevent them from destroying those ends. Here argument is certainly not allowed—one must obey. But so far as a part of the mechanism regards himself at the same time as a member of the whole community or of a society of world citizens, and thus in the role of a scholar who addresses the public (in the proper sense of the word) through his writings, he certainly can argue without hurting the affairs for which he is in part responsible as a passive member. Thus it would be ruinous for an officer in service to debate about the suitability or utility of a command given to him by his superior; he must obey. But the right to make remarks on errors in the military service and to lay them before the public for judgment cannot equitably be refused him as a scholar. The citizen cannot refuse to pay the taxes imposed on him; indeed, an impudent complaint at those levied on him can be punished as a scandal (as it could occasion general refractoriness). But the same person nevertheless does not act contrary to his duty as a citizen when, as a scholar, he publicly expresses his thoughts on the inappropriateness or even the injustice of these levies. Similarly a clergyman is obligated to make his sermon to his pupils in catechism and his congregation conform to the symbol of the church which he serves, for he has been accepted on his condition. But as a scholar he has complete freedom, even the calling, to communicate to the public all his carefully tested and well-meaning thoughts on that which is erroneous in the symbol and to make suggestions for the better organization of the religious body and church. In doing this there is nothing that could be laid as a burden on his conscience. For what he teaches as a consequence of his office as a representative of the church, this he considers something about which he has no freedom to teach according to his own lights; it is something which he is appointed to propound at the dictation of and in the name of another. He will say, "Our church teaches this or that; those are the proofs which it adduces." He thus extracts all practical uses for his congregation from statutes to which he himself would not subscribe with full conviction but to the enunciation of which he can very well pledge himself because it is not impossible that truth lies hidden in them, and, in any case, there is at least nothing in them contradictory to inner religion. For if he believed he had found such in them, he could not conscientiously discharge the duties of his office; he would have to give it up. The use, therefore, which an appointed teacher makes of his reason before his congregation is merely private, because this congregation is only a domestic one (even if it be a large gathering); with respect to it, as a priest, he is not free, nor can he be free, because he carries out the orders of another. But as a scholar, whose writings speak to his public, the world, the clergyman in the public use of his reason enjoys an unlimited freedom to use his own reason and to speak in his own person. That the guardians of the people (in spiritual things) should themselves be incompetent is an absurdity which amounts to the eternalization of absurdities.

But would not a society of clergymen, perhaps a church conference or a venerable classis (as they call themselves among the Dutch), be justified in obligating itself by oath to a certain unchangeable symbol in order to enjoy an unceasing guardianship over each of its members and thereby over the people as a whole, and even to make it eternal? I answer that this is altogether impossible. Such a contract, made to shut off all further enlightenment from the human race, is absolutely null and void even if confirmed by the supreme power, by parliaments, and by the most ceremonious of peace treaties. An age cannot bind itself and ordain to put the succeeding one into such a condition that it cannot extend its (at best very occasional) knowledge, purify itself of errors, and progress in general enlightenment. That would be a crime against human nature, the proper destination of which lies precisely in this progress; and the descendants would be fully justified in rejecting those decrees as having been made in an unwarranted and malicious manner.

The touchstone of everything that can be concluded as a law for a people lies in the question whether the people could have imposed such a law on itself. Now such a religious compact might be possible for a short and definitely limited time, as it were, in expectation of a better. One might let every citizen, and especially the clergyman, in the role of scholar, make his comments freely and publicly, i.e., through writing, on the erroneous aspects of the present institution. The newly introduced order might last until insight into the nature of these things had become so general and widely approved that through uniting their voices (even if not unanimously) they could bring a proposal to the throne to take those congregations under protection which had united into a changed religious organization according to their better ideas, without, however, hindering others who wish to remain in the order. But to unite in a permanent religious institution which is not to

be subject to doubt before the public even in the lifetime of one man, and thereby to make a period of time fruitless in the progress of mankind toward improvement, thus working to the disadvantage of posterity—that is absolutely forbidden. For himself (and only for a short time) a man may postpone enlightenment in what he ought to know, but to renounce it for himself and even more to renounce it for posterity is to injure and trample on the rights of mankind.

And what a people may not decree for itself can even less be decreed for them by a monarch, for his law-giving authority rests on his uniting the general public will in his own. If he only sees to it that all true or alleged improvement stands together with civil order, he can leave it to his subjects to do what they find necessary for their spiritual welfare. This is not his concern, though it is incumbent on him to prevent one of them from violently hindering another in determining and promoting this welfare to the best of his ability. To meddle in these matters lowers his own majesty, since by the writings in which his subjects seek to present their views he may evaluate his own governance. He can do this when, with deepest understanding, he lays upon himself the reproach, "Caesar non est supra grammaticos." Far more does he injure his own majesty when he degrades his supreme power by supporting the ecclesiastical despotism of some tyrants in his state over his other subjects.

If we are asked, "Do we now live in an *enlightened age?*" the answer is, "No," but we do live in an *age of enlightenment*. As things now stand, much is lacking which prevents men from being, or easily becoming, capable of correctly using their own reason in religious matters with assurance and free from outside direction. But, on the other hand, we have clear indications that the field has now been opened wherein men may freely deal with these things and that the obstacles to general enlightenment or the release from self-imposed tutelage are gradually being reduced. In this respect, this is the age of enlightenment, or the century of Frederick.

A prince who does not find it unworthy of himself to say that he holds it to be his duty to prescribe nothing to men in religious matters but to give them complete freedom while renouncing the haughty name of *tolerance*, is himself enlightened and deserves to be esteemed by the grateful world and posterity as the first, at least from the side of government, who divested the human race of its tutelage and left each man free to make use of his reason in matters of conscience. Under him venerable ecclesiastics are allowed, in the role of scholars, and without infringing on their official duties, freely to submit for public testing their judgments and views which here and there diverge from the established symbol. And an even greater freedom is enjoyed by those who are restricted by no official duties. This spirit of freedom spreads beyond this land, even to those in which it must struggle with external obstacles erected by a government which misunderstands its own interest. For an example gives evidence to such a government that in freedom there is not the least cause for concern about public peace and the stability of the community. Men work themselves gradually out of barbarity if only intentional artifices are not made to hold them in it.

I have placed the main point of enlightenment—the escape of men from their self-incurred tutelage—chiefly in matters of religion because our rulers have no interest in playing the guardian with respect to the arts and sciences and also because religious incompetence is not only the most harmful but also the most degrading of all. But the manner of thinking of the head of a state who favours religious enlightenment goes further, and he sees that there is no danger to his law-giving in allowing his subjects to make public use of their reason and to publish their thoughts on a better formulation of his legislation and even their open-minded criticisms of the laws already made. Of this we have a shining example wherein no monarch is superior to him whom we honour.

But only one who is himself enlightened is not afraid of shadows, and who has a numerous and well-disciplined army to assure public peace, can say: "Argue as much as you will, and about what you will, only obey!" A republic could not dare say such a thing. Here is shown a strange and unexpected trend in human affairs in which almost everything, looked at in the large, is paradoxical. A greater degree of civil freedom appears advantageous to the freedom of mind of the people, and yet it places inescapable limitations upon it; a lower degree of civil freedom, on the contrary, provides the mind with room for each man to extend himself to his full capacity. As nature has uncovered from under this hard shell the seed for which she most tenderly cares—the propensity and vocation to free thinking—this gradually works back upon the character of the people, who thereby gradually become capable of managing freedom; finally, it affects the principles of government, which finds it to its advantage to treat men, who are now more than machines, in accordance with their dignity.[1]

Note

1. Today I read in the *Büschingsche Wöchentliche Nachrichten* for September 13 an announcement of the *Berlinische Monatsschrift* for this month, which cites the answer to the same question by Mr Mendelssohn. But this issue has not yet come to me; if it had, I would have held back the present essay, which is now put forth only in order to see how much agreement in thought can be brought about by chance.

CHAPTER 5

No. 10

James Madison

Among the numerous advantages promised by a well-constructed Union, none deserves to be more accurately developed than its tendency to break and control the violence of faction. The friend of popular governments never finds himself so much alarmed for their character and fate as when he contemplates their propensity to this dangerous vice. He will not fail, therefore, to set a due value on any plan which, without violating the principles to which he is attached, provides a proper cure for it. The instability, injustice, and confusion introduced into the public councils have, in truth, been the mortal diseases under which popular governments have everywhere perished, as they continue to be the favourite and fruitful topics from which the adversaries to liberty derive their most specious declamations. The valuable improvements made by the American constitutions on the popular models, both ancient and modern, cannot certainly be too much admired; but it would be an unwarrantable partiality to contend that they have as effectually obviated the danger on this side, as was wished and expected. Complaints are everywhere heard from our most considerate and virtuous citizens, equally the friends of public and private faith and of public and personal liberty, that our governments are too unstable, that the public good is disregarded in the conflicts of rival parties, and that measures are too often decided, not according to the rules of justice and the rights of the minor party, but by the superior force of an interested and overbearing majority. However anxiously we may wish that these complaints had no foundation, the evidence of known facts will not permit us to deny that they are in some degree true. It will be found, indeed, on a candid review of our situation, that some of the distresses under which we labour have been erroneously charged on the operation of our governments; but it will be found, at the same time, that other causes will not alone account for many of our heaviest misfortunes; and, particularly, for that prevailing and increasing distrust of public engagements and alarm for private rights which are echoed from one end of the continent to the other. These must be chiefly, if not wholly, effects of the unsteadiness and injustice with which a factious spirit has tainted our public administration.

By a faction I understand a number of citizens, whether amounting to a majority or minority of the whole, who are united and actuated by some common impulse of passion, or of interest, adverse to the rights of other citizens, or to the permanent and aggregate interests of the community.

There are two methods of curing the mischiefs of faction: the one, by removing its causes; the other, by controlling its effects.

There are again two methods of removing the causes of faction: the one, by destroying the liberty which is essential to its existence; the other, by giving to every citizen the same opinions, the same passions, and the same interests.

It could never be more truly said than of the first remedy that it was worse than the disease. Liberty is to faction what air is to fire, an ailment without which it instantly expires. But it could not be a less folly to abolish liberty, which is essential to political life, because it nourishes faction than it would be to wish the annihilation of air, which is essential to animal life, because it imparts to fire its destructive agency.

The second expedient is as impracticable as the first would be unwise. As long as the reason of man continues fallible, and he is at liberty to exercise it, different opinions will be formed. As long as the connection subsists between his reason and his self-love, his opinions and his passions will have a reciprocal influence on each other; and the former will be objects to which the latter will attach themselves. The diversity in the faculties of men, from which the rights of property originate, is not less an insuperable obstacle to a uniformity of interests. The protection of these faculties is the first object of government. From the protection of different and unequal faculties of acquiring property, the possession of different degrees and kinds of property immediately results; and from the influence of these on the sentiments and views of the respective proprietors ensues a division of the society into different interests and parties.

The latent causes of faction are thus sown in the nature of man; and we see them everywhere brought into different degrees of activity, according to the different circumstances of civil society. A zeal for different opinions concerning religion, concerning government, and many other points, as well of speculation as of practice; an attachment to different leaders ambitiously contending for pre-eminence and power; or to persons of other descriptions whose fortunes have been interesting to the human passions, have, in turn, divided mankind into parties, inflamed them with mutual animosity, and rendered them much more disposed to vex and oppress each other than to co-operate for their common good. So strong is this propensity of mankind to fall into mutual animosities that where no substantial occasion presents itself the most frivolous and fanciful

distinctions have been sufficient to kindle their unfriendly passions and excite their most violent conflicts. But the most common and durable source of factions has been the verious and unequal distribution of property. Those who hold and those who are without property have ever formed distinct interests in society. Those who are creditors, and those who are debtors, fall under a like discrimination. A landed interest, a manufacturing interest, a mercantile interest, a moneyed interest, with many lesser interests, grow up of necessity in civilized nations, and divide them into different classes, actuated by different sentiments and views. The regulation of these various and interfering interests forms the principal task of modern legislation and involves the spirit of party and faction in the necessary and ordinary operations of government.

No man is allowed to be a judge in his own cause, because his interest would certainly bias his judgment, and, not improbably, corrupt his integrity. With equal, nay with greater reason, a body of men are unfit to be both judges and parties at the same time; yet what are many of the most important acts of legislation but so many judicial determinations, not indeed concerning the rights of single persons, but concerning the rights of large bodies of citizens? And what are the different classes of legislators but advocates and parties to the causes which they determine? Is a law proposed concerning private debts? It is a question to which the creditors are parties on one side and the debtors on the other. Justice ought to hold the balance between them. Yet the parties are, and must be, themselves the judges; and the most numerous party, or in other words, the most powerful faction must be expected to prevail. Shall domestic manufacturers be encouraged, and in what degree, by restrictions on foreign manufacturers? are questions which would be differently decided by the landed and the manufacturing classes, and probably by neither with a sole regard to justice and the public good. The apportionment of taxes on the various descriptions of property is an act which seems to require the most exact impartiality; yet there is, perhaps, no legislative act in which greater opportunity and temptation are given to a predominant party to trample on the rules of justice. Every shilling with which they overburden the inferior number is a shilling saved to their own pockets.

It is in vain to say that enlightened statesmen will be able to adjust these clashing interests and render them all subservient to the public good. Enlightened statesmen will not always be at the helm. Nor, in many cases, can such an adjustment be made at all without taking into view indirect and remote considerations, which will rarely prevail over the immediate interest which one party may find in disregarding the rights of another or the good of the whole.

The inference to which we are brought is that the *causes* of faction cannot be removed and that relief is only to be sought in the means of controlling its *effects.*

If a faction consists of less than a majority, relief is supplied by the republican principle, which enables the majority to defeat its sinister views by regular vote. It may clog the administration, it may convulse the society; but it will be unable to execute and mask its violence under the forms of the Constitution. When a majority is included in a faction, the form of popular government, on the other hand, enables it to sacrifice to its ruling passion or interest both the public good and the rights of other citizens. To secure the public good and private rights against the danger of such a faction, and at the same time to preserve the spirit and the form of popular government, is then the great object to which our inquiries are directed. Let me add that it is the great desideratum by which alone this form of government can be rescued from the opprobrium under which it has so long laboured and be recommended to the esteem and adoption of mankind.

By what means is this object attainable? Evidently by one of two only. Either the existence of the same passion or interest in a majority at the same time must be prevented, or the majority, having such coexistent passion or interest, must be rendered, by their number and local situation, unable to concert and carry into effect schemes of oppression. If the impulse and the opportunity be suffered to coincide, we well know that neither moral nor religious motives can be relied on as an adequate control. They are not found to be such on the injustice and violence of individuals, and lose their efficacy in proportion to the number combined together, that is, in proportion as their efficacy becomes needful.

From this view of the subject it may be concluded that a pure democracy, by which I mean a society consisting of a small number of citizens, who assemble and administer the government in person, can admit of no cure for the mischiefs of faction. A common passion or interest will, in almost every case, be felt by a majority of the whole; a communication and concert results from the form of government itself; and there is nothing to check the inducements to sacrifice the weaker party or an obnoxious individual. Hence it is that such democracies have ever been spectacles of turbulence and contention; have ever been found incompatible with personal security or the rights of property; and have in general been as short in their lives as they have been violent in their deaths. Theoretic politicians, who have patronized this species of government, have erroneously supposed that by reducing mankind to a perfect equality in their political rights, they would at the same time be perfectly equalized and assimilated in their possessions, their opinions, and their passions.

A republic, by which I mean a government in which the scheme of representation takes place, opens a different prospect and promises the cure for which we are seeking. Let us examine the points in which it varies from pure democracy, and we shall comprehend both the nature of the cure and the efficacy which it must derive from the Union.

The two great points of difference between a democracy and a republic are: first, the delegation of the government, in the latter, to a small number of citizens elected by the rest; secondly, the greater number of citizens and greater sphere of country over which the latter may be extended.

The effect of the first difference is, on the one hand, to refine and enlarge the public views by passing them through the medium of a chosen body of citizens, whose wisdom may best discern the true interest of their country and whose patriotism and love of justice will be least likely to sacrifice it to temporary or partial considerations. Under such a regulation it may well happen that the public voice, pronounced by the representatives of the people, will be more consonant to the public good than if pronounced by the people themselves, convened for the purpose. On the other hand, the effect may be inverted. Men of factious tempers, of local prejudices, or of sinister designs, may, by intrigue, by corruption, or by other means, first obtain the suffrages, and then betray the interests of the people. The question resulting is, whether small or extensive republics are most favourable to the election of proper guardians of the public weal; and it is clearly decided in favour of the latter by two obvious considerations.

In the first place it is to be remarked that however small the republic may be the representatives must be raised to a certain number in order to guard against the cabals of a few; and that however large it may be they must be limited to a certain number in order to guard against the confusion of a multitude. Hence, the number of representatives in the two cases not being in proportion to that of the constituents, and being proportionally greatest in the small

republic, it follows that if the proportion of fit characters be not less in the large than in the small republic, the former will present a greater option, and consequently a greater probability of a fit choice.

In the next place, as each representative will be chosen by a greater number of citizens in the large than in the small republic, it will be more difficult for unworthy candidates to practise with success the vicious arts by which elections are too often carried; and the suffrages of the people being more free, will be more likely to centre on men who possess the most attractive merit and the most diffusive and established characters.

It must be confessed that in this, as in most other cases, there is a mean, on both sides of which inconveniencies will be found to lie. By enlarging too much the number of electors, you render the representative too little acquainted with all their local circumstances and lesser interests; as by reducing it too much, you render him unduly attached to these, and too little fit to comprehend and pursue great and national objects. The federal Constitution forms a happy combination in this respect; the great and aggregate interests being referred to the national, the local and particular to the State legislatures.

The other point of difference is the greater number of citizens and extent of territory which may be brought within the compass of republican than of democratic government; and it is this circumstance principally which renders factious combinations less to be dreaded in the former than in the latter. The smaller the society, the fewer probably will be the distinct parties and interests composing it; the fewer the distinct parties and interests, the more frequently will a majority be found of the same party; and the smaller the number of individuals composing a majority, and the smaller the compass within which they are placed, the more easily will they concert and execute their plans of oppression. Extend the sphere and you take in a greater variety of parties and interests; you make it less probable that a majority of the whole will have a common motive to invade the rights of other citizens; or if such a common motive exists, it will be more difficult for all who feel it to discover their own strength and to act in unison with each other. Besides other impediments, it may be remarked that, where there is a consciousness of unjust or dishonourable purposes, communication is always checked by distrust in proportion to the number whose concurrence is necessary.

Hence, it clearly appears that the same advantage which a republic has over a democracy in controlling the effects of faction is enjoyed by a large over a small republic—is enjoyed by the Union over the States composing it. Does this advantage consist in the substitution of representatives whose enlightened views and virtuous sentiments render them superior to local prejudices and to schemes of injustice? It will not be denied that the representation of the Union will be most likely to possess these requisite endowments. Does it consist in the greater security afforded by a greater variety of parties, against the event of any one party being able to outnumber and oppress the rest? In an equal degree does the increased variety of parties comprised within the Union increase

this security. Does it, in fine, consist in the greater obstacles opposed to the concert and accomplishment of the secret wishes of an unjust and interested majority? Here again the extent of the Union gives it the most palpable advantage.

The influence of factious leaders may kindle a flame within their particular States but will be unable to spread a general conflagration through the other States. A religious sect may degenerate into a political faction in a part of the Confederacy; but the variety of sects dispersed over the entire face of it must secure the national councils against any danger from that source. A rage for paper money, for an abolition of debts, for an equal division of property, or for any other improper or wicked project, will be less apt to pervade the whole body of the Union than a particular member of it, in the same proportion as such a malady is more likely to taint a particular county or district than an entire State.

In the extent and proper structure of the Union, therefore, we behold a republican remedy for the diseases most incident to republican government. And according to the degree of pleasure and pride we feel in being republicans ought to be our zeal in cherishing the spirit and supporting the character of federalists.

Critical Thinking Questions

1. What three limitations does John Locke think exist on one's right to property prior to the introduction of money?

2. According to Montesquieu, virtue is necessary in a popular (democratic) government. Is he correct in saying of such governments "when virtue is banished, ambition invades the minds of those disposed to receive it, and avarice possesses the whole community"? Do we have any contemporary evidence of this today? Do the contrasts that Montesquieu makes among democracies, aristocracies, and monarchies have any relevance today?

3. What is Adam Smith's Theory of the Invisible Hand? What is his Theory of Comparative Advantage? Do either of these theories have any application today?

4. What is enlightenment, according to Kant? What condition is needed in order to have enlightenment, in his opinion?

5. How does Madison address the problem of factionalism in a civil society? Do you find his argument convincing?

Biographies

John Locke (1632–1704)

 Besides being a physician, John Locke was a philosopher who wrote extensively on the subject of epistemology and politics. He was one of the three great British empiricists, along with George Berkeley and David Hume. His two most famous works are *An Essay Concerning Human Understanding* and *Two Treatises on Government*.

Charles de Montesquieu (1689–1755)

Known as an aristocrat, satirist, stylist, and intellectual in and about France, Montesquieu, after a lengthy study of law, history, economics, geography, and politics, wrote *The Spirit of Laws*, a work that was influenced by the political views of John Locke. While Locke had spoken of the executive and legislative branches of government, he did not see the judiciary as something separate from the latter. Montesquieu, for his part, saw the judiciary as something separate from both the executive and legislative branches of government. This idea of Montesquieu's was picked up by the founding fathers of the United States' constitution.

Adam Smith (1723–1790)

Smith was a Scottish moral philosopher, logician, and economist. Having already published *The Theory of Moral Stentiments*, Smith became famous for his publication of *The Nature and Causes of the Wealth of Nations*. He was for some time a tutor at Balliol College, Oxford, before becoming a professor at Glasgow University in 1751. In 1764, he resigned his position in Glasgow to become the tutor of the Duke of Buccleuch.

Immanuel Kant (1724–1804)

The most acclaimed German epistemologist and metaphysician, Kant attempted to come to terms with the skepticism unleashed by David Hume, a friend of Adam Smith. Kant's most famous works include *The Critique of Pure Reason*, *The Critique of Practical*

Reason, and *Prolegomena to Any Future Metaphysics*. In addition to these writings, Kant also wrote, more sparingly, essays on perpetual peace, the conjectural beginning of history, the end of all things, and enlightenment.

James Madison (1751–1836)

First a member of the US Congress, Secretary of State from 1801 to 1809, and then the fourth president of the United States of America (1809–1817), Madison contributed extensively to the writing of *The Federalist Papers*. His contribution to the defence of federalism in the emerging republic guaranteed a place for him in the halls of political and constitutional theory. Madison placed in new dress many of the social contractarian ideas of Locke, and in this way moved away from talk of custom and convention found in the writings of Edmund Burke. A strong critic of slavery, Madison used his pen to persuade his readers to accept republican principles as a means of defeating factionalism. He thereby endorsed representative government together with control over a large territory. In addition to being influenced by John Locke, Madison was affected in his political thinking by David Hume and Voltaire.

Part II

Conservatism

Conservatism

"Better to stick with that which has worked than subscribe to utopian dreams" could well be considered the rallying cry for all conservatives. That which has worked, according to the likes of Edmund Burke and Russell Kirk, is what has stood the test of time as found in the institutions of our societies. These institutions represent the wisdom of the species and should not be tampered with—at most, only reformed but not changed. Though conservatism has ancient roots in Aristotle (384–322 BCE) and then Richard Hooker (1554–1600), more recent conservatism began with Edmund Burke in response to the challenge to the establishment resulting from the French Revolution in 1789. The prevailing views of Burkean conservatism had social ideals taking priority over the economic ideals of capitalism, reflecting aristocratic values over bourgeois values. But with the passage of time and the rise of neo-conservatism in the 1970s and early 1980s, this priority was reversed. The effect of this was to produce an underlying tension at the heart of contemporary conservatism, a fact somewhat reflected in the underlying tension in the present-day Republican Party in the United States.

Major Figures

David Hume (1711–1776), Edmund Burke (1729–1797), Thomas Carlyle (1795–1881), Aldous Huxley (1894–1963), Michael Oakeshott (1901–1990), Ronald Reagan (1911–2004), Russell Kirk (1918–1994), William F. Buckley Jr (1925–2008), Margaret Thatcher (1925–), and Roger Scruton (1944–)

Period of Greatest Influence

1789 to the middle of the nineteenth century and then again from 1979 to the present

Introduction

The revolution that abruptly ended the self-serving French absolutism of King Louis XVI in eighteenth-century France, the Reign of Terror that subsequently dragged an "enlightened" society into a blood-drenched nightmare of state-sponsored violence, and the Napoleonic era that eventually carried the "contagion" of republicanism throughout continental Europe serve as the historical context and cause of conservatism as a modern political philosophy.

The foregoing comments do not mean to diminish the historical contributions that English philosopher Thomas Hobbes (1588–1679) and Greek thinkers before him have made to our contemporary understanding of conservatism. But they remind readers that conservatism emerged primarily as a response—critics might say reaction—to the events and legacy of 1789, when liberal ideas about inalienable human rights codified through social contracts mobilized an increasingly literate, confident, and prosperous citizenry—only to serve as thin justifications for rationalized barbarism and collective totalitarianism.

The French Revolution certainly looms large in the writings of Edmund Burke (1729–1797), an Irish-born writer whose publishing career eventually propelled him into the House of Commons. The excesses of the French Revolution, whose sympathizers included many leading lights of English society, stunned Burke, who favoured slow, organic change over revolutionary turmoil in preserving the best elements of society. He responded to the shock of the French Revolution by penning his perhaps most famous piece, *Reflections on the Revolution in France*, the source of the first selection found in this part. The piece enunciates crucial elements of conservatism, such as the importance of customs and conventions as the true sources of political life and institutions. This conservative reverence for tradition also finds expression in Burke's contempt for intrusive governments that act in the abstract without the benefit of experience. Burke's warning against "plausible schemes" that "have often shameful and lamentable conclusions" rings eerily true when we hold it up against the horrors of the twentieth century.

In our second selection, Aldous Huxley (1894–1963), who witnessed many of these horrors, echoes this concern about the effects of human hubris. The pursuit of some "utopian destination" through the "religion" of technological progress is "the hope and faith (in the teeth of all human experience) that one gets something for nothing." As Huxley says, the "technological imperialism" of scientific progress exacts a moral price, which few are willing to consider in the first place. This cost–benefit analysis of scientific progress remains as relevant in the early twenty-first century as it did during the middle of the twentieth century, whether we are talking about aerial warfare (as Huxley did in 1945) or stem-cell research today. Huxley's critique of progress also exemplifies the tense, hostile relations between conservatism and modern science. No one would deny that conservatism's critical attitude toward science can be beneficial. But opponents of conservatism often use this criticism to paint conservatives as rubes who believe the world is flat after God created it in six days.

The role of religion in shaping conservative thought appears as one of the major themes in the writings of Russell Kirk (1918–1994). As Kirk writes in our third selection, conservatives believe in the existence of an "enduring moral order." While Kirk fails to disclose the source of this order, he leaves enough verbal clues behind to make a case for Judeo-Christian principles. But Kirk (who became increasingly religious toward the end of his life as he embraced Catholicism) does not see faith and reason as antagonistic forces. Nor do conservatives oppose progress, per se, he argues. The "thinking conservative" reconciles permanence and change to maintaining a "vigorous" and "diverse" society that consists out of "many sorts of inequality." The opposite of this condition—forced equality through "narrowing uniformity and deadening egalitarianism"—leads at best to "social stagnation," Kirk concludes.

William F. Buckley Jr (1925–2008) meanwhile makes us aware of another central conundrum facing contemporary conservatism: if conservatives have been historically skeptical of government schemes that serve some abstract purpose, how far will they go in sacrificing said principle in the face of a presumptive threat that deserves a collective response? Buckley's answer, in short: whatever it takes. Buckley justifies this position as a response to the "messianic" threat of Islamic terrorism following the end of the Cold War (during which the United States expanded the role of government, a fact obliquely acknowledged) and the events of 9/11. Guantanamo Bay and Abu Ghraib are the direct consequences of this position. Naturally, not all conservatives, such as Andrew Sullivan, have agreed with this apparent sacrifice of principle in rejecting the politics of torture, a position that has earned them the status of a minority, at least within conservative circles.

The last of the conservatives considered here, Roger Scruton (1944–), reminds readers that conservatives can easily appear as radicals who attack rather than defend accepted conventions. Whereas Buckley challenges the generally accepted prohibition against torture, Scruton takes dead aim at the dominance of popular culture and the secularization of society, which he links in the chosen selection. One might even surrender to the temptation of accusing Scruton of committing iconoclasm when he attacks television, once a forum of Buckley and of Ronald Reagan, the most revered US president among conservatives. But Scruton's behaviour is not inconsistent if we return to our starting point. Few listened to Burke in 1790. Yet few of us living today would dare to quibble with his prophesy. This foresight confirms the enduring power of conservatism and its message, whose core is a commandment for thoughtful continuity in the face of humanity's compulsive instinct for change and self-improvement. Sometimes, conservatives argue, it might be better to err on the side of caution, a thought as relevant today as it was during the days of Burke.

CHAPTER 6

Reflections on the Revolution in France

Edmund Burke

Far am I from denying in theory; full as far is my heart from withholding in practice (if I were of power to give or to withhold) the *real* rights of men. In denying their false claims of right, I do not mean to injure those which are real, and are such as their pretended rights would totally destroy. If civil society be made for the advantage of man, all the advantages for which it is made become his right. It is an institution of beneficence; and law itself is only beneficence acting by a rule. Men have a right to live by that rule; they have a right to justice; as between their fellows, whether their fellows are in politic function or in ordinary occupation. They have a right to the fruits of their industry and to the means of making their industry fruitful. They have a right to the acquisitions of their parents; to the nourishment and improvement of their offspring; to instruction in life, and to consolation in death. Whatever each man can separately do, without trespassing upon others, he has a right to do for himself; and he has a right to a fair portion of all which society, with all its combinations of skill and force, can do in his favour. In this partnership all men have equal rights; but not to equal things. He that has but five shillings in the partnership, has as good a right to it, as he that has five hundred pound has to his larger proportion. But he has not a right to an equal dividend in the product of the joint stock; as to the share of power, authority, and direction which each individual ought to have in the management of the state, that I must deny to be amongst the direct original rights of man in civil society; for I have in my contemplation the civil social man, and no other. It is a thing to be settled by convention.

If civil society be the offspring of convention, that convention must be its law. That convention must limit and modify all the descriptions of constitution which are formed under it. Every sort of legislative, judicial, or executory power are its creatures. They can have no being in any other state of things; and how can any man claim, under the conventions of civil society, rights which do not so much as suppose its existence? Rights which are absolutely repugnant to it? One of the first motives to civil society, and which becomes one of its fundamental rules, is *that no man should be judge in his own cause*. By this each person has at once divested himself of the first fundamental right of uncovenanted man, that is, to judge for himself, and to assert his own cause. He abdicates all right to be his own governor. He inclusively, in a great measure, abandons the right of self-defence, the first law of nature. Men cannot enjoy the rights of an uncivil and of a civil state together. That he may obtain justice he gives up his right of determining what it is in points the most essential to him. That he may secure some liberty, he makes a surrender in trust of the whole of it.

Government is not made in virtue of natural rights, which may and do exist in total independence of it; and exist in much greater clearness, and in a much greater degree of abstract perfection: but their abstract perfection is their practical defect. By having a right to every thing they want every thing. Government is a contrivance of human wisdom to provide for human *wants*. Men have a right that these wants should be provided for by this wisdom. Among these wants is to be reckoned the want, out of civil society, of a sufficient restraint upon their passions. Society requires not only that the passions of individuals should be subjected, but that even in the mass and body as well as in the individuals, the inclinations of men should frequently be thwarted, their will controlled, and their passions brought into subjection. This can only be done *by a power out of themselves*; and not, in the exercise of its function, subject to that will and to those passions which it is its office to bridle and subdue. In this sense the restraints on men, as well as their liberties, are to be reckoned among their rights. But as the liberties and the restrictions vary with times and circumstances, and admit of infinite modifications, they cannot be settled upon any abstract rule; and nothing is so foolish as to discuss them upon that principle.

The moment you abate any thing from the full rights of men, each to govern himself, and suffer any artificial positive limitation upon those rights, from that moment the whole organization of government becomes a consideration of convenience. This it is which makes the constitution of a state, and the due distribution of its powers, a matter of the most delicate and complicated skill. It requires a deep knowledge of human nature and human necessities, and of the things which facilitate or obstruct the various ends which are to be pursued by the mechanism of civil institutions. The state is to

have recruits to its strength, and remedies to its distempers. What is the use of discussing a man's abstract right to food or to medicine? The question is upon the method of procuring and administering them. In that deliberation I shall always advise to call in the aid of the farmer and the physician, rather than the professor of metaphysics.

The science of constructing a commonwealth, or renovating it, or reforming it, is, like every other experimental science, not to be taught *a priori*. Nor is it a short experience that can instruct us in that practical science; because the real effects of moral causes are not always immediate; but that which in the first instance is prejudicial may be excellent in its remoter operation; and its excellence may arise even from the ill effects it produces in the beginning. The reverse also happens; and very plausible schemes, with very pleasing commencements, have often shameful and lamentable conclusions. In states there are often some obscure and almost latent causes, things which appear at first view of little moment, on which a very great part of its prosperity or adversity may most essentially depend. The science of government being therefore so practical in itself, and intended for such practical purposes, a matter which requires experience, and even more experience than any person can gain in his whole life, however sagacious and observing he may be, it is with infinite caution that any man ought to venture upon pulling down an edifice which has answered in any tolerable degree for ages the common purposes of society, or on building it up again, without having models and patterns of approved utility before his eyes.

These metaphysic rights entering into common life, like rays of light which pierce into a dense medium, are, by the laws of nature, refracted from their straight line. Indeed in the gross and complicated mass of human passions and concerns, the primitive rights of men undergo such a variety of refractions and reflections, that it becomes absurd to talk of them as if they continued in the simplicity of their original direction. The nature of man is intricate; the objects of society are of the greatest possible complexity and therefore no simple disposition or direction of power can be suitable either to man's nature, or to the quality of his affairs. When I hear the simplicity of contrivance aimed at the boasted of in any new political constitutions, I am at no loss to decide that the artificers are grossly ignorant of their trade, or totally negligent of their duty. The simple governments are fundamentally defective, to say no worse of them. If you were to contemplate society in but one point of view, all these simple modes of polity are infinitely captivating. In effect each would answer its single end much more perfectly than the more complex is able to attain all its complex purposes. But it is better that the whole should be imperfectly and anomalously answered, than that, while some parts are provided for with great exactness, others might be totally neglected, or perhaps materially injured, by the over-care of a favourite member.

The pretended rights of these theorists are all extremes; and in proportion as they are metaphysically true, they are morally and politically false. The rights of men are in a sort of *middle*, incapable of definition, but not impossible to be discerned. The rights of men in governments are their advantages; and these are often in balances between differences of good; in compromises sometimes between good and evil, and sometimes, between evil and evil. Political reason is a computing principle; adding, subtracting, multiplying, and dividing, morally and not metaphysically or mathematically, true moral denominations.

CHAPTER 7

The Perennial Philosophy

Aldous Huxley

The Greeks believed that *hubris* was always followed by *nemesis*, that if you went too far you would get a knock on the head to remind you that the gods will not tolerate insolence on the part of mortal men. In the sphere of human relations, the modern mind understands the doctrine of *hubris* and regards it as mainly true. We wish pride to have a fall, and we see that very often it does fall.

To have too much power over one's fellows, to be too rich, too violent, too ambitious—all this invites punishment, and in the long run, we notice, punishment of one sort or another duly comes. But the Greeks did not stop there. Because they regarded Nature as in some way divine, they felt that it had to be respected and they were convinced that a hubristic lack of respect for Nature would be punished by avenging *nemesis*. In "The Persians," Aeschylus gives the reasons—the ultimate, metaphysical reasons—for the barbarians' defeat. Xerxes was punished for two offences—overweening imperialism directed against the Athenians, and overweening imperialism directed against

Nature. He tried to enslave his fellow men, and he tried to enslave the sea, by building a bridge across the Hellespont.

Atossa
From shore to shore he bridged the Hellespont.

Ghost of Darius
What, could he chain the mighty Bosphorous?

Atossa
Even so, some god assisting his design.

Ghost of Darius
Some god of power to cloud his better sense.

Today we recognize and condemn the first kind of imperialism; but most of us ignore the existence and even the very possibility of the second. And yet the author of *Erewhon* was certainly not a fool, and now that we are paying the appalling price for our much touted "conquest of Nature" his book seems more than ever topical. And Butler was not the only nineteenth century skeptic in regard to Inevitable Progress. A generation or more before him, Alfred de Vigny was writing about the new technological marvel of his days, the steam engine—writing in a tone very different from the enthusiastic roarings and trumpetings of his great contemporary, Victor Hugo.

Sur le taureau de fer, qui fume, souffle et beugle,
L'homme est monté trop tôt. Nul ne connaît encor
Quels orages en lui porte ce rude aveugle,
Et le gai voyageur lui livre son trésor.

And a little later in the same poem he adds,

Tous se sont dit: "Allons," mais aucun n'est le maître

D'un dragon mugissant qu'un savant a fait naître.
Nous nous sommes joués à plus fort que nous tous.

Looking backwards across the carnage and the devastation, we can see that Vigny was perfectly right. None of those gay travellers, of whom Victor Hugo was the most vociferously eloquent, had the faintest notion where that first, funny little Puffing Billy was taking them. Or rather they had a very clear notion, but it happened to be entirely false. For they were convinced that Puffing Billy was hauling them at full speed toward universal peace and the brotherhood of man; while the newspapers which they were so proud of being able to read, as the train rumbled along toward its Utopian destination not more than 50 years or so away, were the guarantee that liberty and reason would soon be everywhere triumphant. Puffing Billy has now turned into a four-motored bomber loaded with white phosphorus and high explosives, and the free press is everywhere the servant of its advertisers, of a pressure group, or of the government. And yet, for some inexplicable reason, the travellers (now far from gay) still hold fast to the religion of Inevitable Progress—which is, in the last analysis, the hope and faith (in the teeth of all human experience) that one can get something for nothing. How much saner and more realistic is the Greek view that every victory has to be paid for, and that, for some victories, the price exacted is so high that it outweighs any advantage that may be obtained! Modern man no longer regards Nature as being in any sense divine and feels perfectly free to behave toward her as an overweening conqueror and tyrant. The spoils of recent technological imperialism have been enormous; but meanwhile *nemesis* has seen to it that we get our kicks as well as halfpence. For example, has the ability to travel in 12 hours from New York to Los Angeles given more pleasure to the human race than the dropping of bombs and fire has given pain? There is no known method of computing the amount of felicity or goodness in the world at large. What is obvious, however, is that the advantages accruing from recent technological advances—or, in Greek phraseology, from recent acts of *hubris* directed against Nature—are generally accompanied by corresponding disadvantages, that gains in one direction entail losses in other directions, and that we never get something except for something. Whether the net result of these elaborate credit and debit operations is a genuine Progress in virtue, happiness, charity, and intelligence is something we can never definitely determine. It is because the reality of Progress can never be determined that the nineteenth and twentieth centuries have had to treat it as an article of religious faith. To the exponents of the Perennial Philosophy, the question whether Progress is inevitable or even real is not a matter of primary importance. For them, the important thing is that individual men and women should come to the unitive knowledge of the divine Ground, and what interests them in regard to the social environment is not its progressiveness or non-progressiveness (whatever those terms may mean), but the degree to which it helps or hinders individuals in their advance toward man's final end.

CHAPTER 8

Ten Conservative Principles

Russell Kirk

Being neither a religion nor an ideology, the body of opinion termed *conservatism* possesses no Holy Writ and no *Das Kapital* to provide dogmata. So far as it is possible to determine what conservatives believe, the first principles of the conservative persuasion are derived from what leading conservative writers and public men have professed during the past two centuries. After some introductory remarks on this general theme, I will proceed to list ten such conservative principles.

[...]

Perhaps it would be well, most of the time, to use this word "conservative" as an adjective chiefly. For there exists no Model Conservative, and conservatism is the negation of ideology: it is a state of mind, a type of character, a way of looking at the civil social order.

The attitude we call conservatism is sustained by a body of sentiments, rather than by a system of ideological dogmata. It is almost true that a conservative may be defined as a person who thinks himself such. The conservative movement or body of opinion can accommodate a considerable diversity of views on a good many subjects, there being no Test Act or Thirty-Nine Articles of the conservative creed.

In essence, the conservative person is simply one who finds the permanent things more pleasing than Chaos and Old Night. (Yet conservatives know, with Burke, that healthy "change is the means of our preservation.") A people's historic continuity of experience, says the conservative, offers a guide to policy far better than the abstract designs of coffee-house philosophers. But of course there is more to the conservative persuasion than this general attitude.

It is not possible to draw up a neat catalogue of conservatives' convictions; nevertheless, I offer you, summarily, ten general principles; it seems safe to say that most conservatives would subscribe to most of these maxims. In various editions of my book *The Conservative Mind* I have listed certain canons of conservative thought—the list differing somewhat from edition to edition; in my anthology *The Portable Conservative Reader* I offer variations upon this theme. Now I present to you a summary of conservative assumptions differing somewhat from my canons in those two books of mine. In fine, the diversity of ways in which conservative views may find expression is itself proof that conservatism is no fixed ideology. What particular principles conservatives emphasize during any given time will vary with the circumstances and necessities of that era. The following ten articles of belief reflect the emphases of conservatives in America nowadays.

First, the conservative believes that there exists an enduring moral order. That order is made for man, and man is made for it: human nature is a constant, and moral truths are permanent.

This word *order* signifies harmony. There are two aspects or types of order: the inner order of the soul, and the outer order of the commonwealth. Twenty-five centuries ago, Plato taught this doctrine, but even the educated nowadays find it difficult to understand. The problem of order has been a principal concern of conservatives ever since *conservative* became a term of politics.

Our twentieth-century world has experienced the hideous consequences of the collapse of belief in a moral order. Like the atrocities and disasters of Greece in the fifth century before Christ, the ruin of great nations in our century shows us the pit into which fall societies that mistake clever self-interest, or ingenious

social controls, for pleasing alternatives to an old-fangled moral order.

It has been said by liberal intellectuals that the conservative believes all social questions, at heart, to be questions of private morality. Properly understood, this statement is quite true. A society in which men and women are governed by belief in an enduring moral order, by a strong sense of right and wrong, by personal convictions about justice and honour, will be a good society—whatever political machinery it may utilize; while a society in which men and women are morally adrift, ignorant of norms, and intent chiefly upon gratification of appetites, will be a bad society—no matter how many people vote and no matter how liberal its formal constitution may be. [. . .]

Second, the conservative adheres to custom, convention, and continuity. It is old custom that enables people to live together peaceably: the destroyers of custom demolish more than they know or desire. It is through convention—a word much abused in our time—that we contrive to avoid perpetual disputes about rights and duties: law at base is a body of conventions. Continuity is the means of linking generation to generation; it matters as much for society as it does for the individual; without it, life is meaningless. When successful revolutionaries have effaced old customs, derided old conventions, and broken the continuity of social institutions—why, presently they discover the necessity of establishing fresh customs, conventions, and continuity; but that process is painful and slow; and the new social order that eventually emerges may be much inferior to the old order that radicals overthrew in their zeal for the Earthly Paradise.

Conservatives are champions of custom, convention, and continuity because they prefer the devil they know to the devil they don't know. Order and justice and freedom, they believe, are the artificial products of a long social experience, the result of centuries of trial and reflection and sacrifice. Thus the body social is a kind of spiritual corporation, comparable to the church; it may even be called a community of souls. Human society is no machine, to be treated mechanically. The continuity, the life-blood, of a society must not be interrupted. Burke's reminder of the necessity for prudent change is in the mind of the conservative. But necessary change, conservatives argue, ought to be gradual and discriminatory, never unfixing old interests at once.

Third, conservatives believe in what may be called the principle of prescription. Conservatives sense that modern people are dwarfs on the shoulders of giants, able to see farther than their ancestors only because of the great stature of those who have preceded us in time. Therefore conservatives very often emphasize the importance of *prescription*—that is, of things established by immemorial usage, so that the mind of man runneth not to the contrary. There exist rights of which the chief sanction is their antiquity—including rights to property, often. Similarly, our morals are prescriptive in great part. Conservatives argue that we are unlikely, we moderns, to make any brave new discoveries in morals or politics or taste. It is perilous to weigh every passing issue on the basis of private judgment and private rationality. The individual is foolish, but the species is wise, Burke declared. In politics we do well to abide by precedent and precept and even prejudice, for the great mysterious incorporation of the human race has acquired a prescriptive wisdom far greater than any man's petty private rationality.

Fourth, conservatives are guided by their principle of prudence. Burke agrees with Plato that in the statesman, prudence is chief among virtues. Any public measure ought to be judged by its probable long-run consequences, not merely by temporary advantage or popularity. Liberals and radicals, the conservative says, are imprudent: for they dash at their objectives without giving much heed to the risk of new abuses worse than the evils they hope to sweep away. As John Randolph of Roanoke put it, Providence moves slowly, but the devil always hurries. Human society being complex, remedies cannot be simple if they are to be efficacious. The conservative declares that he acts only after sufficient reflection, having weighed the consequences. Sudden and slashing reforms are as perilous as sudden and slashing surgery.

Fifth, conservatives pay attention to the principle of variety. They feel affection for the proliferating intricacy of long-established social institutions and modes of life, as distinguished from the narrowing uniformity and deadening egalitarianism of radical systems. For the preservation of a healthy diversity in any civilization, there must survive orders and classes, differences in material condition, and many sorts of inequality. The only true forms of equality are equality at the Last Judgment and equality before a just court of law; all other attempts at levelling must lead, at best, to social stagnation. Society requires honest and able leadership; and if natural and institutional differences are destroyed, presently some tyrant or host of squalid oligarchs will create new forms of inequality.

Sixth, conservatives are chastened by their principle of imperfectability. Human nature suffers irremediably from certain grave faults, the conservatives know. Man being imperfect, no perfect social order ever can be created. Because of human restlessness, mankind would grow rebellious under any utopian domination, and would break out once more in violent discontent—or else expire of boredom. To seek for utopia is to end in disaster, the conservative says: we are not made for perfect things. All that we reasonably can expect is a tolerably ordered, just, and free society, in which some evils, maladjustments, and suffering will continue to lurk. By proper attention to prudent reform, we may preserve and improve this tolerable order. But if the old institutional and moral safeguards of a nation are neglected, then the anarchic impulse in humankind breaks loose: "the ceremony of innocence is drowned." The ideologues who promise the perfection of man and society have converted a great part of the twentieth-century world into a terrestrial hell.

Seventh, conservatives are persuaded that freedom and property are closely linked. Separate property from private possession, and Leviathan becomes master of all. Upon the foundation of private property, great civilizations are built. The more widespread is the possession of private property, the more stable and productive is a commonwealth. Economic levelling, conservatives maintain, is not economic progress. Getting and spending are not the chief aims of human existence; but a sound economic basis for the person, the family, and the commonwealth is much to be desired.

Sir Henry Maine, in his *Village Communities,* puts strongly the case for private property, as distinguished from communal property: "Nobody is at liberty to attack several property and to say at the same time that he values civilization. The history of the two cannot be disentangled." For the institution of several property—that is, private property—has been a powerful instrument for teaching men and women responsibility, for providing motives to integrity, for supporting general culture, for raising mankind above the level of mere drudgery, for affording leisure to think and freedom to act. To be able to retain the fruits of one's labour; to be able to see one's work made permanent; to be able to bequeath one's property to one's posterity; to be able to rise from the natural condition of grinding poverty to the security of enduring accomplishment; to have something that is really one's own—these are advantages difficult to deny. The conservative acknowledges that the possession of property fixes certain duties upon the possessor; he accepts those moral and legal obligations cheerfully.

Eighth, conservatives uphold voluntary community, quite as they oppose involuntary collectivism. Although Americans have been attached strongly to privacy and private rights, they also have been a people conspicuous for a successful spirit of community. In a genuine community, the decisions most directly affecting the lives of citizens are made locally and voluntarily. Some of these functions are carried out by local political bodies, others by private associations: so long as they are kept local, and are marked by the general agreement of those affected, they constitute healthy community. But when these functions pass by default or usurpation to centralized authority, then community is in serious danger. Whatever is beneficent and prudent in modern democracy is made possible through co-operative volition. If, then, in the name of an abstract Democracy, the functions of community are transferred to distant political direction—why, real government by the consent of the governed gives way to a standardizing process hostile to freedom and human dignity.

For a nation is no stronger than the numerous little communities of which it is composed. A central administration, or a corps of select managers and civil servants, however well intentioned and well trained, cannot confer justice and prosperity and tranquility upon a mass of men and women deprived of their old responsibilities. That experiment has been made before; and it has been disastrous. It is the performance of our duties in community that teaches us prudence and efficiency and charity.

Ninth, the conservative perceives the need for prudent restraints upon power and upon human passions. Politically speaking, power is the ability to do as one likes, regardless of the wills of one's fellows. A state in which an individual or a small group are able to dominate the wills of their fellows without check is a despotism, whether it is called monarchical or aristocratic or democratic. When every person claims to be a power unto himself, then society falls into anarchy. Anarchy never lasts long, being intolerable for everyone, and contrary to the ineluctable fact that some persons are more strong and more clever than their neighbours. To anarchy there succeeds tyranny or oligarchy, in which power is monopolized by a very few.

The conservative endeavours to so limit and balance political power that anarchy or tyranny may not arise. In every age, nevertheless, men and women are tempted to overthrow the limitations upon power, for the sake of some fancied temporary advantage. It is characteristic of the radical that he thinks of power as a force for good—so long as the power falls into his hands. In the name of liberty, the French and Russian revolutionaries abolished the old restraints upon power; but power cannot be abolished; it always finds its way into someone's hands. That power which the revolutionaries had thought oppressive in the hands of the old regime became many times as tyrannical in the hands of the radical new masters of the state.

Knowing human nature for a mixture of good and evil, the conservative does not put his trust in mere benevolence. Constitutional restrictions, political checks and balances, adequate enforcement of the laws, the old intricate web of restraints upon will and appetite—these the conservative approves as instruments of freedom and order. A just government maintains a healthy tension between the claims of authority and the claims of liberty.

Tenth, the thinking conservative understands that permanence and change must be recognized and reconciled in a vigorous society. The conservative is not opposed to social improvement, although he doubts whether there is any such force as a mystical Progress, with a Roman P, at work in the world. When a society is progressing in some respects, usually it is declining in other respects. The conservative knows that any healthy society is influenced by two forces, which Samuel Taylor Coleridge called its Permanence and its Progression. The Permanence of a society

is formed by those enduring interests and convictions that give us stability and continuity; without that Permanence, the fountains of the great deep are broken up, society slipping into anarchy. The Progression in a society is that spirit and that body of talents which urge us on to prudent reform and improvement; without that Progression, a people stagnate.

Therefore the intelligent conservative endeavours to reconcile the claims of Permanence and the claims of Progression. He thinks that the liberal and the radical, blind to the just claims of Permanence, would endanger the heritage bequeathed to us, in an endeavour to hurry us into some dubious Terrestrial Paradise. The conservative, in short, favours reasoned and temperate progress; he is opposed to the cult of Progress, whose votaries believe that everything new necessarily is superior to everything old.

Change is essential to the body social, the conservative reasons, just as it is essential to the human body. A body that has ceased to renew itself has begun to die. But if that body is to be vigorous, the change must occur in a regular manner, harmonizing with the form and nature of that body; otherwise change produces a monstrous growth, a cancer, which devours its host. The conservative takes care that nothing in a society should ever be wholly old, and that nothing should ever be wholly new. This is the means of the conservation of a nation, quite as it is the means of conservation of a living organism. Just how much change a society requires, and what sort of change, depend upon the circumstances of an age and a nation.

Such, then, are ten principles that have loomed large during the two centuries of modern conservative thought. Other principles of equal importance might have been discussed here: the conservative understanding of justice, for one, or the conservative view of education. But such subjects, time running on, I must leave to your private investigation.

Chapter 9

To Preserve What We Have

William F. Buckley Jr

When in 1955 I set out to publish a journal devoted to the interests of US conservatism, I stressed in a preliminary circular pretty much what one would have expected on the subject. It was necessary then, and would be necessary for most of the balance of the millennium, to confront directly the challenge of Soviet-based communism; to explain, and to plead, that whatever the pains and dangers of resisting it, these were worth undergoing. In retrospect, it appears obvious that the effort was worthwhile, but it was less than obvious at crisis points, among them Hungary, Berlin, Cuba, and Vietnam. History will document that the high cost of nuclear-stakes resistance dismayed more merely than US Catholic bishops. Resistance à outrance engendered flesh and blood perspectives. It came down to: *Is it really worth it?* What do we end up having in hand, by developing and redeveloping and updating a nuclear inventory and the hardware to deliver nuclear strikes, whether pre-emptively or punitively?

American conservatism needed to say and to think through the philosophical vocabulary for saying: It is worth any cost to preserve what we have.

And what was it that we *did* have? [. . .]

Conservatives could list, bit by bit, those things that distinguished American life from life in the Soviet Union. A large inventory springs readily to mind. There were the different levels of self-sovereignty. The individual—conservatives argued—has certain rights over his own direction in life. These rights are subject to biological constraints: You can't, without consequence, ignore diet and exercise. And there are social restraints: You can't defy American orthodoxy without bumping into civil blockades. You can't marry three people simultaneously or refuse to send your child to school.

Then there was sovereignty at the next level, the freedom to choose, politically and economically. There the American, unlike the Soviet citizen, was substantially freer, though here there was a domestic struggle, still going on after 50 years. Acquisitive members of society are always seeking to enhance their jurisdiction. What we had in America, and continue to have, is an inchoate sense of proportion in the matter. The conservative instinctively rejects collectivization. Fifty years ago (and contention goes on today) it was thought by many an improvement in social management to pool those concerns that aren't irrevocably personal (whom shall I marry?), by letting collective authority decide how much steel should be produced or property permitted to an individual or his heir. Grander perspectives were thought to be served by socializing education and health care. In 1954, the US hovered between the New Deal and the Great Society. Conservatives fought on, winning some, losing some. With the increase in regulations and extension of custody, the public throne sprouted more and more emeralds and baubles. The sovereignty of the public sector reached to over 40 per cent of the gross national income.

Even so, the Utopians were slowed down, and that was mostly the doing of American conservatives. To hinder, let alone to check rampant collectivization, conservatives needed to do two things. The first was to take empirical note of the failures of those societies that sought collective answers to every problem. Such failures needed to be publicized, and the correlative consequences of yielding authority to the state thought through. The challenge has been to decoct from empirical history relevant lessons. John Adams taught that the state tends to turn every contingency into an excuse for enhancing itself. That is 200-year-old wisdom, but in 1955, and today, it has become a faintly remembered, quaint aphorism of a founding father learned, but grouchy. The lesson required reiteration in modern times, in hard-boiled, contemporaneous philosophical jousting.

American conservatives, in order to enliven the principles they stood by, needed to observe life under communism in the Soviet Union and China, to learn from their failures but simultaneously to reinforce philosophical prejudices, liberal in origin. If human freedom is the fountainhead of American conservative thought, then its preservation becomes its principal concern. That means that the knights-errant of conservatism have to find fresh and communicable ways of burnishing the goals of individual authority and of free choice. Everybody is prepared to stipulate that all men should be free to choose between Coca-Cola and Pepsi-Cola. It is something else to document the advantages, real and ideal, of private health care over public health care.

Conservatives do not vest in the free market ontological authority. But we believe that the marketplace is the operative mechanism by which individual choice is transcribed. It is true that the free market produces wealth beyond the resources of socialism, but what conservatives are engaged in defending isn't the proposition that Coca-Cola is better than Pepsi. On such matters conservatives are nescient, never knowing which of the two is "better," capable

only of knowing which is in greater demand—while discerning, in the course of submitting to the free market, that what is important isn't the relative merit of the goods, but the inherent meaning of the individual's expression of choice. That freedom magnifies to the high level espied by G.K. Chesterton when he said simply that we should be free to be our own potty little selves.

[. . .]

Conservatives (unlike anarchists, or Objectivists) know that sacrifices are necessary, even as diet is necessary for organic health. Exactly what it is necessary to forgo is always debatable. Some good men thought it wrong to go to war to end slavery, or to go to Congress to end Jim Crow. Conservatives correctly assumed, in 1955, that to resist the Soviet aggression meant such things as taxes and even a draft. Today the enemy has another face, and we need to remind ourselves that designs on our freedoms don't disappear; they express themselves variously, in entirely different ballistic design. Al Qaeda is messianic, not Utopian, but the ugly genius of science creates weapons of mass destruction, and the market facilitates their assembly and distribution. Put your mind to it, compel the state's treasury to cooperate, and you have an atom bomb. Can we imagine what is needed to thwart explosions in Bali nightclubs? Conservatives know only that whatever is needed, we must come up with it.

Above all, conservatives tend to intuit that materialism terminology is insufficient to express the depth of American attachments to their ideals. It remains, for some reason, arresting that one speaks of the "sanctity" of life, of our "devotion" to our ideals, of the "holy" causes in which we engage. American conservatives never exclude those who discountenance transcendent perspectives, but we tend to live by them.

Chapter 10

Leisure, Cult, and Culture

Roger Scruton

Culture is the product of leisure: it is created and enjoyed in those moments, or those states of mind, when the immediate urgencies of practical life are in abeyance. Our culture was, historically, the product of a leisured class—a class with a virtual monopoly on leisure. But today we live in a society in which leisure is universally available, even to those who lack a use for it. This is one cause of the deep uncertainty about "Western culture." There seems a radical disjunction between our aristocratic and high-bourgeois inheritance, the product of an educated class of priests, prophets, and noblemen, and the works of our newly emancipated "common man"—whose fanfare, however, was composed by Aaron Copland, a most uncommon member of the educated elite. In order to clarify our predicament, it is worth reflecting on leisure, and its connection with religion on the one hand, and culture on the other.

Leisure, Play, and the Aesthetic

The Greeks took leisure seriously, a fact recorded in the subsequent history of their word for it—*schole*—which became *scola* in Latin, and school in English. Leisure, for Aristotle, was the purpose of work—not work in the sense of any specific activity but in the general sense of *ascholia* (leisurelessness).[1] *Ascholia* was Aristotle's term for business, and it has its equivalent in Latin (*neg-otium*), and survives, too, in French. The *negociant* is the one who is always busy, and who therefore has the question before him: why? What purpose is served by business, and

when is that purpose fulfilled? For Aristotle the answer was clear: you work in order to free yourself for leisure, and in leisure you are truly free: free to pursue the contemplative life which, for Aristotle, was the highest good.

In that account you see a radically different set of priorities from those that animate a modern economy. Work, for Aristotle, is mere "leisurelessness," a condition of lack, which we strive to overcome so as to enjoy our true human fulfillment, which is the life of contemplation. This emphasis on contemplation may seem like so much philosophical snobbery. What Aristotle had in mind, however, was an activity which is its own reward, and which therefore illustrates the condition of contentment. For the philosopher, the question "Why contemplate?" neither has nor deserves an answer. Contemplation is not a means to an end, but an end in itself. And this, Aristotle implies, is what all true *schole* involves.

For a great many people today leisure is not a state of contemplation but one of physical activity—although activity which, like Aristotle's contemplation, is *its own reward*. Recreation, sport, and games are all to be understood in the spirit of Aristotle's *schole*—as activities which are not means to an end but ends in themselves. That is why these activities, however strenuous, are activities in which we are *at rest*: for our plans and projects *come to rest* in them. This, we are apt to say, is the point of it all, what we worked for, the goal to which our labour was a means.

What I am saying about leisure was said, in another tone of voice but for a connected purpose, by Schiller, not about leisure but about play, which is its prototype in the world of the child. In his *Letters on the Aesthetic Education of Man*,[2] Schiller described play as the higher condition to which we aspire whenever we relinquish our practical concerns. The contrast he had in mind was not that between play and work, but that between playing and being in earnest. And he used that distinction to make an interesting remark about aesthetics. "With the good and the useful," he wrote, "man is merely in earnest; but with the beautiful he plays." That phrase "merely in earnest" is of course heavily ironic, but it expresses a systematic rejection of the workaday world. Fulfillment does not come through purpose, Schiller is implying, but only when purpose is set aside. And for Schiller, the paradigm of fulfillment is the aesthetic experience—not contemplation as Aristotle understood it, but the disinterested contemplation of *appearances*, the self-conscious alertness to *the presented meaning* of things.

Schiller believed that we can understand aesthetic judgment if we refer it back to the world of play—a world in which nothing really has a purpose, and where every action is engaged in for its own sake, as something intrinsically delightful. Art returns us to that world of primal innocence, by enabling us to set our purposes aside. It is not merely that the work of art is valued for its own sake, and without reference to a purpose. It is also that we, in the act of appreciation, reassume the mantle of a child, allowing our emotions and impressions to follow imaginative paths, constraining them to no purpose, no goal, no earnest endeavour. And just as a child learns through play, so do we learn through the aesthetic experience, by exercising our feelings in imaginary realms, enlarging our vision of humanity, and coming to see the world as imbued with intrinsic values, meaningful in itself and without reference to our own self-centred interests.

Leisure and Distraction

Schiller saw culture as the sphere of "aesthetic education," and play as its archetype. And through uniting the two ideas he hoped to show that the decline of religion had not bereft mankind of intrinsic values. Through "aesthetic education"—in other words, culture—we could reconnect to those primordial experiences of wonder and awe which show us the lasting meaning of our life on earth. That is why culture matters: it is a vessel in which intrinsic values are captured and handed on.

Aristotle and Schiller both emphasize the active nature of leisure and its connection to contemplative forms of mental life. But we can switch off from work without switching on to any higher purpose. We can pass from activity to passivity, in which our mind does not engage the world but is rather engaged by it, distracted by external things rather than interested in them. And someone might suggest that distraction is more and more the normal position of people when their work is set aside. Television techniques are increasingly designed to capture attention, rather than to provide a point of interest, and recent research[3] has demonstrated the extent to which the normal channels of information gathering have been short-circuited by TV, producing widespread attention disorders and an addiction to visual stimulation. If this is leisure, many people say, let's have less of it.

The distinction between distraction and interest is hard to draw exactly. After all, you cannot be distracted by something without also being interested in it. But the interest stops with the next distraction. The mind does not *keep hold* of the first object of attention, since it is incapable of pursuing its interest if the stimulus is not renewed. Art lovers standing before a painting look and look, and even when they look away, their thoughts are of the picture. Each detail interests them; each shape and colour has a meaning, and they search the picture for a human significance that they may try to put into words, if they are critically inclined, or which they may store silently in their hearts. Here all the attention comes from the viewers: they are actively engaged in interpreting what they see, and their viewing is in a certain measure a creative act. They are creating the object of their own awareness, but also receiving from it a vision of repose.

By contrast the couch potato in front of the television screen, his eyes led from image to image by the five-second cut, is barely able to attend to one thing before his mind is captured by another. Here there is still scope for mental activity—for example, a judgment of the aesthetic, moral, or philosophical worth of the scene on the screen. But the object of attention is not the product of this mental activity, and stays in view only because it is able constantly to distract the mind of the viewer from its previous focus.

The TV is a paradigm of the distracting process, but it is not the only instance. Many forms of popular entertainment have a similar character, of diverting attention while neutralizing thought. And when sociologists speak of the "recreational" use of drugs, alcohol, and other things (sex included), they are really talking of distraction. Recreation, in this sense, means maintaining mental vacancy, even in the midst of activities like sex, which require the full engagement of the person if they are to deliver what they mean. If popular entertainment is mere distraction, then we might reasonably suggest that leisure, in the sense intended by Aristotle, has vanished from the world of popular entertainment, that the final emancipation of the workers from their work has led to the loss of the one thing that they were really working for.

[…]

Culture and Cult

What I have just described is another use of leisure: one in which leisure means not activity but the involvement in a spectacle, valued for its meaning as an end in itself. This involvement was once imbued with far-reaching mythical and religious meanings, and even today awakens some of the passions associated with the cults of gods and heroes. And it points to another connection—not that between leisure and culture, but that between leisure and cult.

In the Book of Genesis is told the story of God's creation of the world, expressed with admirable succinctness and simplicity, and through imagery which recreates some of that primordial wonder which we witness also in the Lascaux caves. And on the seventh day, the story tells us, God rested, thereby setting an example to his creatures who, in honour of all those things that are ends in themselves, of which their Creator is the supreme example, devote one day a week to worshipping Him. This, their day of recreation, is also a day of re-creation, in which the spirit is renewed, and the meaning of life unfolded.

This story points to an important feature of human communities, though one that is not easily observed in the modern world. In the spirit of Genesis, we might indulge in our own fanciful genealogy of the human condition, and one more in keeping, perhaps, with modern science. Imagine, then, a hunter-gatherer community, which tracks its large quarry for several days and finally triumphs. The community can rest at last, can gather round together for a feast, but it will experience also a flow of gratitude, perhaps offering the first burnt morsel to a god. All kinds of explanations have been offered for the ancient practice of ritual sacrifice.[4] But perhaps the simplest and most plausible is that it is the survival of that primitive feast, in which the gods were summoned down among their worshippers, so as to taste the gifts that they themselves provided. Later—agricultural—communities did not need to hunt for their meals, but the need for ceremonial killing, for gratitude and feasting, was by then immovable. And something of this survives in the feast of 'Eid, in the Christian Communion, in the Jewish Passover, and in the Chinese festival of the New Year.

In time, we might suppose, the gods detached themselves from the feasts in which they were revealed, to become objects of theological study. But their festivals remained, as the principal way in which communities rehearsed their membership, through recreational activities that restored the shared meaning of their world. One such festival was that devoted to Dionysus in Athens, when poets competed for the approval of the crowd with their tragic tales of gods and heroes. And some of these tragedies survive, examples of the highest art and testimony to a long tradition of speculation and insight.

That genealogy is, of course, a fiction. But it is, I believe, an illuminating fiction, one that spells out in time the timeless connections between contiguous things. It takes us from the species-needs of the hunter-gatherer to the birth of revealed religion, thence to organized worship and the communal festival and finally to culture as a genial by-product of our festive celebrations. The connection between cult and culture can be made in other ways,[5] but its intrinsic plausibility is displayed in the story that I told, and that story prompts the following thought:

Culture grows from religion, and religion from a species-need. But the culture engendered by a religion may also turn upon its parent with a skeptical eye. This has often happened, and indeed was already happening in the Greek theatre. Not only were the gods and heroes lampooned by Aristophanes; their solemn stories were told by Aeschylus and Euripides with an air of detachment, as allegories of the human condition rather than literal descriptions of immortal goings-on.

Not that the tragedians disbelieved in the gods. Judging from their surviving works, they neither believed nor disbelieved, regarding belief as in some way irrelevant to their task, which was to capture and illustrate the *meaning of the world*. Like Plato and Socrates, they saw the stories of the gods as myths, and treated myth as another mode of knowledge, distinct from both rational science and storytelling. They believed in God rather than the gods, and their God was, like that of Plato, Socrates, and Aristotle, infinite, eternal, inscrutable, standing in judgment over a world that does not really contain Him.

Growing away from Religion

The tendency of high culture to detach itself from its religious origin can be witnessed in many places and at many times. The Augustan poets of Rome are already standing back from their religious inheritance, with Lucretius expressly pouring scorn on it. The Sufi poets of Persia (Hafiz, Rumi, and Omar Khayyam), profoundly religious though their sentiments are, have only an awkward and tangential relation to the Islamic orthodoxies of their surrounding society. Shakespeare's plays neither endorse nor condemn the Christian vision, but stand at such a distance from it as to prompt the views that he was an atheist, a pagan, a Protestant, and even a Catholic recusant, each interpretation compellingly illustrated from the texts.[6] And since the Enlightenment it has been clear that poetry, music, and art—while they may often express profound religious faith—are equally able to continue in a spirit of skepticism, invoking the values of community and endowing all that they touch with a spiritual nimbus, while at the same time refraining from any commitment to theological doctrine or even pouring scorn on that doctrine, in the manner of Diderot, Shelley, and Nietzsche.

This process of "growing away" from religion creates the great divide between the leisure interests of ordinary people and the culture of the critical elite. In the conditions of scarcity from which civilizations begin, the religious festival and the weekly worship are the only times in which the spirit of leisure can possess the ordinary person—and they are times dedicated to religion, and to the affirmation of the community through ritual, song, and prayer. But, as the mastery over the environment advances, so does leisure increase. And while the elite devotes this newly abundant leisure to contemplation and high culture, ordinary people use it to engage in forms of recreation and distraction remote from the contemplative ideal espoused by Aristotle. The extreme point has been reached today, in which neither the elite culture nor popular entertainment belong to the practice of religion, but where both, in secret or not-so-secret ways, bear the impress of religion, and carry into the world of enlightened common sense that now surrounds us, precious canisters of the intriguing darkness from which humanity began and for which some part of us still yearns.

Notes

1. *Nicomachean Ethics* 1177b4-6, which remarks that we are busy for the sake of leisure, just as we make war for the sake of peace.
2. Friedrich von Schiller, *Letters on the Aesthetic Education of Man*, tr. E. Wilkinson and L.A. Willoughby, Oxford (1967).
3. By Mihaly Csikszentmihalyi and Robert Kubey (summarized in *Scientific American*, 23 February 2002).
4. See Walter Burkert, *Homo Necans: The Anthropology of Ancient Greek Ritual and Myth*, tr. Peter Bing, Berkeley, CA, Univ. of California Press (1983); René Girard, *La Violence et le sacré*, Paris, Grasset (1972).
5. See Josef Pieper, *Leisure: the Basis of Culture* (Musse und Kult, 1948), tr. G. Malsbary, South Bend, Indiana, St. Augustine's Press (1997).
6. The Catholic recusant theory had had a striking boost recently from Patrick H. Martin and John Finnis: "The Identity of 'Anthony Rivers,'" *Recusant History* 26 (2002), pp. 39–74.

Critical Thinking Questions

1. Describe Burke's position on abstract rights. Where does Burke locate the source of all legislative, judicial, and executive powers? Which form of knowledge should not guide the "science of constructing a commonwealth," according to Burke?

2. What does Huxley mean when he speaks of "hubris"? Can you think of recent or current examples that confirm Huxley's negative view of technology?

3. William F. Buckley Jr suggests in his essay that conservatives should not restrain themselves in their response to the threat of al Qaeda (here serving as a shorthand for "Islamic" terrorism). How consistent is this position with the broader principles of conservatism? You may evaluate Buckley's appeal against his earlier claim that "if human freedom is the fountainhead of American conservatism, then its preservation becomes its principal concern."

4. Among the ten articles of conservative belief cited by Kirk, which do you believe is most important to most conservatives? Do any other ideologies adhere to any of these ten articles? Do Burke and Kirk share the same attitude toward change in social practices and institutions?

5. What does Scruton blame for the gap between the leisure interests of ordinary people (such as television, recreational drugs) and the critical elite? How convincing is this argument? What do you make of Scruton's broader suggestion that we can differentiate between forms of entertainment, some of which are worthy of conserving, while others are not?

Biographies

Edmund Burke (1729–1797)

This Irish-born critic of social contract theory began his public career as a writer of pieces that defended social customs and traditions. He then translated his literary successes into a political career, during which he served in the House of Commons. Burke, whose oratory skills never matched his written rhetoric, combined his opposition to the French Revolution with support for various emancipatory causes inside and outside of England during his time in office.

Aldous Huxley (1894–1963)

 A member of a prominent English family, whose accomplishments and ambitions stretch across multiple fields, Huxley gained literary acclaim with writings that challenged scientific progress. *Brave New World* ranks as the most famous manifestation of the cultural pessimism that pervaded the philosophy of Huxley. Some see Huxley, who promoted Indian mysticism and English romanticism, as an intellectual godfather of the LSD-fuelled counterculture movement of the 1960s, an ironic twist by any measure.

Russell Kirk (1918–1994)

This American philosopher formally codified the canons of conservatism, first through interpretation, then through synthesis. Kirk—who received considerable credit for reviving the legacy of Burke in North America during his early career—viewed the relationship between Christianity and Western civilization as symbiotic toward the end of his life. But Kirk, whose central work, *The Conservative Mind*, remains a staple of readings lists, was not above challenging conventional positions when he criticized American policy in the Middle East.

William F. Buckley Jr (1925–2008)

A public intellectual, journalist, diplomat, and bon vivant, Buckley combined graceful manners with a razor-shaped mind. This blend, which has completely disappeared from modern-day American conservatism, often allowed Buckley to charm and defeat his opponents at the same time as he made a very public case for a cocktail of laissez-faire capitalism and strident anti-communism served with a heavy pinch of cultural sophistication that rejected the fringe elements of American conservatism. First Barry Goldwater, then later Ronald Reagan, drank from this mix.

Roger Scruton (1944–)

Combative, if not iconoclastic, toward modern society, Scruton has rarely shied away from controversial positions on topics such as homosexuality, popular culture, and environmentalism. This apparent absence of moderation in the attempted defeat of what Scruton considers vice has earned him considerable attention in his native England, where he frequently appears as a public defender of classical art, music, and literature.

Part III

Reform Liberalism

Reform Liberalism

Reform liberalism promotes a robust kind of freedom, namely positive liberty, together with procedural and substantive justice. It also affirms the importance of the individual and the community. Originating in Britain with the writings of John Stuart Mill and T.H. Green, and then later John Maynard Keynes, reform liberalism had its own North American proponents including John Dewey, Pierre Elliott Trudeau, and John Rawls in the twentieth century. Both the Industrial Revolution of the nineteenth century and, much later, the Great Depression of 1929 fuelled the fires of reform liberalism and provided an ideological platform for progressive policy initiatives in the social, economic, and civil spheres. Since 1979 with the rise of neo-liberalism and the forces of globalization, reform liberalism has faced steady opposition. The near eclipse of the Liberal Party of Canada, the marginalization of the Liberal part of the Cameron/Clegg coalition in the United Kingdom, and the intolerance of American media for liberal ideas are evidence of this opposition.

Major Figures

John Stuart Mill (1806–1873), T.H. Green (1836–1882), J.A. Hobson (1858–1940), John Dewey (1859–1952), L.T. Hobhouse (1864–1929), John Maynard Keynes (1883–1946), John Kenneth Galbraith (1908–2006), Pierre Elliott Trudeau (1919–2000), John Rawls (1921–2002), Ronald Dworkin (1931–), and Will Kymlicka (1962–)

Period of Greatest Influence

1859 to 1918, and then again from 1929 to 1979

Introduction

The Industrial Revolution of the eighteenth and nineteenth centuries ushered in social and economic problems that began to challenge the integrity of classical liberalism. Two of these problems were the exploitation of workers and the monopolistic control of industries. It was Charles Dickens who described the wretchedness of the workers in his fictional novels and thereby etched permanently in our minds what it might have been like to live during those times, but it would be social critics and reformers of different stripes who would share the conviction that classical liberalism had outlived its usefulness as an economic and political philosophy. What resulted was the shattering of classical liberalism and the birth of three new schools of thinking: reform liberalism, Marxism, and democratic socialism. It is with the first of these that we are presently concerned.

Reform liberalism begins with John Stuart Mill (1806–1873) and is robustly defended in *On Liberty* (1859) in undoubtedly the most spirited defence of freedom offered in the English language. Grounding his political philosophy in the moral code of utilitarianism, Mill affirms the following principle: the only purpose for which power can be rightfully exercised over any member of a civilized community, against one's will, is to prevent harm to others. Mill then proceeds in analytical fashion to examine this principle in light of freedom of thought, freedom of action, and freedom of association. But Mill does not stop here, for he is eager to give an even more nuanced treatment of his principle of liberty by considering practical cases. These practical cases include specific examples of state control over drugs, religious practices, alcoholic consumption, polygamy, and other practices. But perhaps what stands out in Mill as a reform liberal is his linking happiness to human development and individuality, and linking these in turn to freedom. What Mill offers, in the end, is a sufficiently large enough understanding of "harm" that leaves room for positive state action in creating favourable conditions for the individual.

While John Stuart Mill offers a philosophical perspective of reform liberalism, John Dewey (1859–1952) offers a social scientific perspective as he alerts us to the need for thoroughgoing changes in the set-up of institutions that surround the individual. Here, Dewey thinks of schools, hospitals, churches, courts, political parties, families, and others that perform essential functions in nourishing the growth and development of the whole person. Whereas Marx might endorse a similar view of the importance of institutions to the well-being of the individual, Dewey differs from Marx in his unwillingness to endorse the use of violence in effecting the changes necessary to have supportive institutions. Dewey is a democrat and believes in the value of education in changing people's minds, in educating people, to achieve reform. Finally, it should be noted that Dewey denies that freedom is something ready-made but instead sees it as needing to be continually reconstructed, especially as this relates to supporting social structures.

The economic face of reform liberalism is unquestionably provided by John Maynard Keynes (1883–1946). He creates the initiative for a new school of economics, Keynesianism, which Roosevelt makes use of during the era of the New Deal in the United States and which has resurfaced in light of the serious downturn in the world economy beginning in 2008. A Cambridge scholar at the time of Bertrand Russell, Keynes unleashes his mathematical mind and economic skills upon a variety of topics, including an explanation of the success of laissez-faireism and an economic and philosophical refutation of this same brand of Adam Smith's economic thinking. Keynes is not timid about "venturing into the den of the lions" to attack the flagging economic theory behind classical liberalism.

Years after Keynes, Pierre Elliott Trudeau (1919–2000) became Minister of Justice in Lester B. Pearson's Liberal government in Ottawa. Within short order, he would go on to become the next prime minister of Canada in resounding fashion and was viewed by Canadians outside of Quebec as the answer to the problem of Quebec and its search for independence. In the present extract, Trudeau makes clear his commitment to liberal principles as he tries to define his political philosophy. What he seeks to do is to spell out a position that stands equal distance from authority on the one hand and freedom on the other. Shunning ideological commitment on the grounds of ideology being the true enemy of freedom, Trudeau goes on to support checks and balances in the political arena—checks and balances that translate into a practical equilibrium. It is the unworkability of "special status" for Quebec that he criticizes in this context. Its unworkability is grounded in the ideological thinking of French Canadians—a form of thought, he believes, that remains unresponsive to changing historical and political circumstances.

Five years after Trudeau's book, John Rawls (1921–2002) in his magnum opus, *A Theory of Justice* (1972), establishes philosophical space for reform liberalism by developing a set of principles that those living behind a veil of ignorance will choose to live by. His principles have become known as the principle of liberty and the principle of difference. In a later work, *The Law of Peoples* (1999), Rawls applies his earlier findings to the international community and tries to tease out traditional principles of justice among free and democratic peoples. He confronts in due course the problem of all liberals: the problem of the toleration of non-liberal peoples. By confronting the issue of the liberal's toleration of non-liberals, Rawls ends up extending Mill's principle to its logical limit by allowing ample room for a people's self-determination.

And so to the last of the political thinkers studied in this chapter, Will Kymlicka (1962–)—Kymlicka picks up where Trudeau leaves off. Whereas Trudeau addresses cultural dualism in the context of Canadian liberalism, Kymlicka examines cultural pluralism in the context of liberal theory. He does this by examining, among other things, the effort by the Trudeau government to dismantle the Canadian *Indian Act* that created, in effect, two kinds of Canadian citizenship: Indian and non-Indian. According to those who think like Trudeau, the granting of permanent rights to a special class of citizens seems impossible in an ideology such as liberalism, an ideology which maintains the principle of equal consideration. Kymlicka traces effectively the worries that liberals have of deviating from the principle of equal individual rights, and at the same time points out clearly the resistance that minority groups, such as Canadian aboriginals, have to making the Canadian Constitution colourblind and insensitive to their special place in the body politic.

Reform liberals share a commitment to a robust sense of political liberty and freedom, shorn of any metaphysical commitment to a theory of the invisible hand. What is condemned by reform liberals, as Mill would say, is harm to individuals; what is applauded, as Dewey would say, is opportunity for development of the individual. The liberty of reform liberals is a liberty that is supported by institutional structures such as schools, families, governmental agencies, and religious entities. To the reform liberals such as Keynes, Trudeau, and Kymlicka, the liberty of the classical liberals looks economical naive and morally defective, especially when the principle of equality is introduced. Finally, reform liberals such as Rawls, Trudeau, and Kymlicka wrestle unevenly with the principle of equality, with Rawls allowing room for a principle of difference, Kymlicka attempting to accommodate special treatment for minorities inside the liberal state, and Trudeau distancing himself from special status for French Canadians and Canadian aboriginals.

CHAPTER 11

Introductory

John Stuart Mill

The object of this Essay is to assert one very simple principle, as entitled to govern absolutely the dealings of society with the individual in the way of compulsion and control, whether the means used be physical force in the form of legal penalties, or the moral coercion of public opinion. That principle is, that the sole end for which mankind are warranted, individually or collectively, in interfering with the liberty of action of any of their number, is self-protection. That the only purpose for which power can be rightfully exercised over any member of a civilized community, against his will, is to prevent harm to others. His own good, either physical or moral, is not a sufficient warrant. He cannot rightfully be compelled to do or forbear because it will be better for him to do so, because it will make him happier, because, in the opinions of others, to do so would be wise, or even right. These are good reasons for remonstrating with him, or reasoning with him, or persuading him, or entreating him, but not for compelling him, or visiting him with any evil in case he do otherwise. To justify that, the conduct from which it is desired to deter him, must be calculated to produce evil to some one else. The only part of the conduct of any one, for which he is amenable to society, is that which concerns others. In the part which merely concerns himself, his independence is, of right, absolute. Over himself, over his own body and mind, the individual is sovereign.

It is, perhaps, hardly necessary to say that this doctrine is meant to apply only to human beings in the maturity of their faculties. We are not speaking of children, or of young persons below the age which the law may fix as manhood or womanhood. Those who are still in a state to require being taken care of by others, must be protected against their own actions as well as against external injury. For the same reason, we may leave out of consideration those backward states of society in which the race itself may be considered as in its nonage. The early difficulties in the way of spontaneous progress are so great, that there is seldom any choice of means for overcoming them; and a ruler full of the spirit of improvement is warranted in the use of any expedients that will attain an end, perhaps otherwise unattainable. Despotism is a legitimate mode of government in dealing with barbarians, provided the end be their improvement, and the means justified by actually effecting that end. Liberty, as a principle, has no application to any state of things anterior to the time when mankind have become capable of being improved by free and equal discussion. Until then, there is nothing for them but implicit obedience to an Akbar or a Charlemagne, if they are so fortunate as to find one. But as soon as mankind have attained the capacity of being guided to their own improvement by conviction or persuasion (a period long since reached in all nations with whom we need here concern ourselves), compulsion, either in the direct form or in that of pains and penalties for non-compliance, is no longer admissible as to their own good, and justifiable only for the security of others.

[. . .]

But there is a sphere of action in which society, as distinguished from the individual, has, if any, only an indirect interest; comprehending all that portion of a person's life and conduct which affects only himself, or if it also affects others, only with their free, voluntary, and undeceived consent and participation. When I say only himself, I mean directly, and in the first instance: for whatever affects himself, may affect others through himself; and the objection which may be grounded on this contingency, will receive consideration in the sequel. This, then, is the appropriate region of human liberty. It comprises, first, the inward domain of consciousness; demanding liberty of conscience, in the most comprehensive sense; liberty of thought and feeling; absolute freedom of opinion and sentiment on all subjects, practical or speculative, scientific, moral, or theological. The liberty of expressing and publishing opinions may seem to fall under a different principle, since it belongs to that part of the conduct of an individual which concerns other people; but, being almost of as much importance as the liberty of thought itself, and resting in great part on the same reasons, is practically inseparable from it. Secondly, the principle requires liberty of tastes and pursuits; of framing the plan of our life to suit our own character; of doing as we like, subject to such consequences as may follow: without impediment from our fellow-creatures, so long as what we do does not harm them, even though they should think our conduct foolish, perverse, or wrong. Thirdly, from this liberty of each individual, follows the liberty, within the same limits, of combination among individuals; freedom to unite, for any purpose not involving harm to others: the persons combining being supposed to be of full age, and not forced or deceived.

CHAPTER 12

Renascent Liberalism

John Dewey

When, then, I say that the first object of a renascent liberalism is education, I mean that its task is to aid in producing the habits of mind and character, the intellectual and moral patterns, that are somewhere near even with the actual movements of events. It is, I repeat, the split between the latter as they have externally occurred and the ways of desiring, thinking, and of putting emotion and purpose into execution that is the basic cause of present confusion in mind and paralysis in action. The educational task cannot be accomplished merely by working upon men's minds, without action that effects actual change in institutions. The idea that dispositions and attitudes can be altered by merely "moral" means conceived of as something that goes on wholly inside of persons is itself one of the old patterns that has to be changed. Thought, desire, and purpose exist in a constant give and take of interaction with environing conditions. But resolute thought is the first step in that change of action that will itself carry further the needed change in patterns of mind and character.

In short, liberalism must now become radical, meaning by "radical" perception of the necessity of thoroughgoing changes in the set-up of institutions and corresponding activity to bring the changes to pass. For the gulf between what the actual situation makes possible and the actual state itself is so great that it cannot be bridged by piecemeal policies undertaken *ad hoc*. The process of producing the changes will be, in any case, a gradual one. But "reforms" that deal now with this abuse and now with that without having a social goal based upon an inclusive plan, differ entirely from effort at re-forming, in its literal sense, the institutional scheme of things. The liberals of more than a century ago were denounced in their time as subversive radicals, and only when the new economic order was established did they become apologists for the *status quo* or else content with social patchwork. If radicalism be defined as perception of need for radical change, then today any liberalism which is not also radicalism is irrelevant and doomed.

But radicalism also means, in the minds of many, both supporters and opponents, dependence upon use of violence as the main method of effecting drastic changes. Here the liberal parts company. For he is committed to the organization of intelligent action as the chief method. Any frank discussion of the issue must recognize the extent to which those who decry the use of any violence are themselves willing to resort to violence and are ready to put their will into operation. Their fundamental objection is to change in the economic institution that now exists, and for its maintenance they resort to the use of the force that is placed in their hands by this very institution. They do not need to advocate the use of force; their only need is to employ it. Force, rather than intelligence, is built into the procedures of the existing social system, regularly as coercion, in times of crisis as overt violence. The legal system, conspicuously in its penal aspect, more subtly in civil practice, rests upon coercion. Wars are the methods recurrently used in settlement of disputes between nations. One school of radicals dwells upon the fact that in the past the transfer of power in one society has either been accomplished by or attended with violence. But what we need to realize is that physical force is used, at least in the form of coercion, in the very set-up of our society. That the competitive system, which was thought of by early liberals as the means by which the latent abilities of individuals were to be evoked and directed into socially useful channels, is now in fact a state of scarcely disguised battle hardly needs to be dwelt upon. That the control of the means of production by the few in legal possession operates as a standing agency of coercion of the many, may need emphasis in statement, but is surely evident to one who is willing to observe and honestly report the existing scene. It is foolish to regard the political state as the only agency now endowed with coercive power. Its exercise of this power is pale in contrast with that exercised by concentrated and organized property interests.

It is not surprising in view of our standing dependence upon the use of coercive force that at every time of crisis coercion breaks out into open violence. In this country, with its tradition of violence fostered by frontier conditions and by the conditions under which immigration went on during the greater part of our history, resort to violence is especially recurrent on the part of those who are in power. In times of imminent change, our verbal and sentimental worship of the Constitution, with its guarantees of civil liberties of expression, publication, and assemblage, readily goes overboard. Often the officials of the law are the worst offenders, acting as agents of some power that rules the economic life of a community. What is said about the value of free speech as a safety valve is then forgotten with the utmost of ease: a comment, perhaps, upon the weakness of the defence of freedom of expression that values it simply as a means of blowing-off steam.

It is not pleasant to face the extent to which, as matter of fact, coercive and violent force is relied upon in the present social system as a means of social control. It is much more agreeable to evade the fact. But unless the fact is acknowledged as a fact in its full depth and breadth, the meaning of dependence upon intelligence as the alternative method of social direction will not be grasped. Failure in acknowledgment signifies, among other things, failure to realize that those who propagate the dogma of dependence upon force have the sanction of much that is already entrenched in the existing system. They would but turn the use of it to opposite ends. The assumption that the method of intelligence already rules and that those who urge the use of violence are introducing a new element into the social picture may not be hypocritical but it is unintelligently unaware of what is actually involved in intelligence as an alternative method of social action.

I begin with an example of what is really involved in the issue. Why is it, apart from our tradition of violence, that liberty of expression is tolerated and even lauded when social affairs seem to be going in a quiet fashion, and yet is so readily destroyed whenever matters grow critical? The general answer, of course, is that at bottom social institutions have habituated us to the use of force in some veiled form. But a part of the answer is found in our ingrained habit of regarding intelligence as an individual possession and its exercise as an individual right. It is false that freedom of inquiry and of expression are not modes of action. They are exceedingly potent modes of action. The reactionary grasps this fact, in practice if not in express idea, more quickly than the liberal, who is too much given to holding that this freedom is innocent of consequences, as well as being a merely individual right. The result is that this liberty is tolerated as long as it does not seem to menace in any way the *status quo* of society. When it does, every effort is put forth to identify the established order with the public good. When this identification is established, it follows that any merely individual right must yield to the general welfare. As long as freedom of thought and speech is claimed as a merely individual right, it will give way, as do other merely personal claims, when it is, or is successfully represented to be, in opposition to the general welfare.

I would not in the least disparage the noble fight waged by early liberals in behalf of individual freedom of thought and expression. We owe more to them than it is possible to record in words. No more eloquent words have ever come from any one than those of Justice Brandeis in the case of a legislative act that in fact restrained freedom of political expression. He said: "Those who won our independence believed that the final end of the State was to make men free to develop their faculties, and that in its government the deliberative faculties should prevail over the arbitrary. They valued liberty both as an end and as a means. They believed liberty to be the secret of happiness and courage to be the secret of liberty. They believed that freedom to think as you will and to speak as you think are means indispensable to the discovery and spread of political truth; that without free speech and assembly discussion would be futile; that with them, discussion affords ordinarily adequate protection against the dissemination of noxious doctrines; that the greatest menace to freedom is an inert people; that public discussion is a political duty; and that this should be a fundamental principle of the American government." This is the creed of a fighting liberalism. But the issue I am raising is connected with the fact that these words are found in a dissenting, a minority opinion of the Supreme Court of the United States. The public function of free individual thought and speech is clearly recognized in the words quoted. But the reception of the truth of the words is met by an obstacle: the old habit of defending liberty of thought and expression as something inhering in individuals apart from and even in opposition to social claims.

CHAPTER 13

The End of Laissez-Faire

John Maynard Keynes

The disposition toward public affairs, which we conveniently sum up as individualism and *laissez-faire*, drew its sustenance from many different rivulets of thought and springs of feeling. For more than a hundred years our philosophers ruled us because, by a miracle, they nearly all agreed or seemed to agree on this one thing. We do not dance even yet to a new tune. But a change is in the air. We hear but indistinctly what were once the clearest and most distinguishable voices which have ever instructed political mankind. The orchestra of diverse instruments, the chorus of articulate sound, is receding at last into the distance.

[...]

The parallelism between economic *laissez-faire* and Darwinianism, already briefly noted, is now seen, as Herbert Spencer was foremost to recognize, to be very close indeed. Just as Darwin invoked sexual love, acting through sexual selection, as an adjutant to natural selection by competition, to direct evolution along lines which should be desirable as well as effective, so the individualist invokes the love of money, acting through the pursuit of profit, as an adjutant to natural selection, to bring about the production on the greatest possible scale of what is most strongly desired as measured by exchange value.

The beauty and the simplicity of such a theory are so great that it is easy to forget that it follows not from the actual facts, but from an incomplete hypothesis introduced for the sake of simplicity. Apart from other objections to be mentioned later, the conclusion that individuals acting independently for their own advantage will produce the greatest aggregate of wealth, depends on a variety of unreal assumptions to the effect that the processes of production and consumption are in no way organic, that there exists a sufficient foreknowledge of conditions and requirements, and that there are adequate opportunities of obtaining this foreknowledge. For economists generally reserve for a later stage of their argument the complications which arise—(1) when the efficient units of production are large relatively to the units of consumption, (2) when overhead costs or joint costs are present, (3) when internal economies tend to the aggregation of production, (4) when the time required for adjustments is long, (5) when ignorance prevails over knowledge, and (6) when monopolies and combinations interfere with equality in bargaining—they reserve, that is to say, for a later stage their analysis of the actual facts. Moreover, many of those who recognize that the simplified hypothesis does not accurately correspond to fact conclude nevertheless that it does represent what is "natural" and therefore ideal. They regard the simplified hypothesis as health, and the further complications as disease.

Yet besides this question of fact there are other considerations, familiar enough, which rightly bring into the calculation the cost and character of the competitive struggle itself, and the tendency for wealth to be distributed where it is not appreciated most. If we have the welfare of the giraffes at heart, we must not overlook the sufferings of the shorter necks who are starved out, or the sweet leaves which fall to the ground and are trampled underfoot in the struggle, or the overfeeding of the long-necked ones, or the evil look of anxiety or struggling greediness which overcasts the mild faces of the herd.

But the principles of *laissez-faire* have had other allies besides economic textbooks. It must be admitted that they have been confirmed in the minds of sound thinkers and the reasonable public by the poor quality of the opponent proposals—protectionism on one hand, and Marxian socialism on the other. Yet these doctrines are both characterized, not only or chiefly by their infringing the general presumption in favour of *laissez-faire*, but by mere logical fallacy. Both are examples of poor thinking, of inability to analyze a process and follow it out to its conclusion. The arguments against them, though reinforced by the principle of *laissez-faire*, do not strictly require it. Of the two, protectionism is at least plausible, and the forces making for its popularity are nothing to wonder at. But Marxian socialism must always remain a portent to the historians of opinion—how a doctrine so illogical and so dull can have exercised so powerful and enduring an influence over the minds of men and, through them, the events of history. At any rate, the obvious scientific deficiencies of these two schools greatly contributed to the prestige and authority of nineteenth-century *laissez-faire*.

Nor has the most notable divergence into centralized social action on a great scale—the conduct of the late war—encouraged reformers or dispelled old-fashioned prejudices. There is much to be said, it is true, on both sides. War experience in the organization of socialized production has left some near observers optimistically anxious to repeat it in peace conditions. War socialism unquestionably achieved a production of wealth on a scale far greater than we ever knew in peace, for though the goods and services delivered were destined for

immediate and fruitless extinction, nonetheless they were wealth. Nevertheless, the dissipation of effort was also prodigious, and the atmosphere of waste and not counting the cost was disgusting to any thrifty or provident spirit.

Finally, individualism and *laissez-faire* could not, in spite of their deep roots in the political and moral philosophies of the late eighteenth and early nineteenth centuries, have secured their lasting hold over the conduct of public affairs, if it had not been for their conformity with the needs and wishes of the business world of the day. They gave full scope to our erstwhile heroes, the great business men. "At least one half of the best ability in the Western world," Marshall used to say, "is engaged in business." A great part of "the higher imagination" of the age was thus employed. It was on the activities of these men that our hopes of progress were centred.

Men of this class [Marshall wrote][1] live in constantly shifting visions, fashioned in their own brains, of various routes to their desired end; of the difficulties which Nature will oppose to them on each route, and of the contrivances by which they hope to get the better of her opposition. This imagination gains little credit with the people, because it is not allowed to run riot; its strength is disciplined by a stronger will; and its highest glory is to have attained great ends by means so simple that no one will know, and none but experts will even guess, how a dozen other expedients, each suggesting as much brilliancy to the hasty observer, were set aside in favour of it. The imagination of such a man is employed, like that of the master chess-player, in forecasting the obstacles which may be opposed to the successful issue of his far-reaching projects, and constantly rejecting brilliant suggestions because he has pictured to himself the counter-strokes to them. His strong nervous force is at the opposite extreme of human nature from that nervous irresponsibility which conceives hasty Utopian schemes, and which is rather to be compared to the bold facility of a weak player, who will speedily solve the most difficult chess problem by taking on himself to move the black men as well as the white.

This is a fine picture of the great captain of industry, the master-individualist, who serves us in serving himself, just as any other artist does. Yet this one, in his turn, is becoming a tarnished idol. We grow more doubtful whether it is he who will lead us into paradise by the hand.

These many elements have contributed to the current intellectual bias, the mental makeup, the orthodoxy of the day. The compelling force of many of the original reasons has disappeared but, as usual, the vitality of the conclusions outlasts them. To suggest social action for the public good to the City of London is like discussing the *Origin of Species* with a bishop 60 years ago. The first reaction is not intellectual, but moral. An orthodoxy is in question, and the more persuasive the arguments the graver the offence. Nevertheless, venturing into the den of the lethargic monster, at any rate I have traced his claims and pedigree so as to show that he has ruled over us rather by hereditary right than by personal merit.

IV§

Let us clear from the ground the metaphysical or general principles upon which, from time to time, *laissez-faire* has been founded. It is *not* true that individuals possess a prescriptive "natural liberty" in their economic activities. There is *no* "compact" conferring perpetual rights on those who Have or on those who Acquire. The world is *not* so governed from above that private and social interest always coincide. It is *not* so managed here below that in practice they coincide.

It is *not* a correct deduction from the principles of economics that enlightened self-interest always operates in the public interest. Nor is it true that self-interest generally *is* enlightened; more often individuals acting separately to promote their own ends are too ignorant or too weak to attain even these. Experience does *not* show that individuals, when they make up a social unit, are always less clear-sighted than when they act separately.

We cannot therefore settle on abstract grounds, but must handle on its merits in detail what Burke termed "one of the finest problems in legislation, namely, to determine what the State ought to take upon itself to direct by the public wisdom, and what it ought to leave, with as little interference as possible, to individual exertion."[2] We have to discriminate between what Bentham, in his forgotten but useful nomenclature, used to term *Agenda* and *Non-Agenda*, and to do this without Bentham's prior presumption that interference is, at the same time, "generally needless" and "generally pernicious."[3] Perhaps the chief task of economists at this hour is to distinguish afresh the *Agenda* of government from the *Non-Agenda*; and the companion task of politics is to devise forms of government within a democracy which shall be capable of accomplishing the *Agenda*. I will illustrate what I have in mind by two examples.

(1) I believe that in many cases the ideal size for the unit of control and organization lies somewhere between the individual and the modern State. I suggest, therefore, that progress lies in the growth and the recognition of semi-autonomous bodies within the State—bodies whose criterion of action within their own field is solely the public good as they understand it, and from whose deliberations motives of private advantage are excluded, though some place it may still be necessary to leave, until the ambit of men's altruism grows wider, to the separate advantage of particular groups, classes, or

faculties—bodies which in the ordinary course of affairs are mainly autonomous within their prescribed limitations, but are subject in the last resort to the sovereignty of the democracy expressed through Parliament.

I propose a return, it may be said, toward medieval conceptions of separate autonomies. But, in England at any rate, corporations are a mode of government which has never ceased to be important and is sympathetic to our institutions. It is easy to give examples, from what already exists, of separate autonomies which have attained or are approaching the mode I designate—the universities, the Bank of England, the Port of London Authority, even perhaps the railway companies. In Germany there are doubtless analogous instances.

But more interesting than these is the trend of joint stock institutions, when they have reached a certain age and size, to approximate to the status of public corporations rather than that of individualistic private enterprise. One of the most interesting and unnoticed developments of recent decades has been the tendency of big enterprise to socialize itself. A point arrives in the growth of a big institution—particularly a big railway or big public utility enterprise, but also a big bank or a big insurance company—at which the owners of the capital, i.e., the shareholders, are almost entirely dissociated from the management, with the result that the direct personal interest of the latter in the making of great profit becomes quite secondary. When this stage is reached, the general stability and reputation of the institution are the more considered by the management than the maximum of profit for the shareholders. The shareholders must be satisfied by conventionally adequate dividends; but once this is secured, the direct interest of the management often consists in avoiding criticism from the public and from the customers of the concern. This is particularly the case if their great size or semi-monopolistic position renders them conspicuous in the public eye and vulnerable to public attack. The extreme instance, perhaps, of this tendency in the case of an institution, theoretically the unrestricted property of private persons, is the Bank of England. It is almost true to say that there is no class of persons in the kingdom of whom the Governor of the Bank of England thinks less when he decides on his policy than of his shareholders. Their rights, in excess of their conventional dividend, have already sunk to the neighbourhood of zero. But the same thing is partly true of many other big institutions. They are, as time goes on, socializing themselves.

Not that this is unmixed gain. The same causes promote conservatism and a waning of enterprise. In fact, we already have in these cases many of the faults as well as the advantages of State Socialism. Nevertheless, we see here, I think, a natural line of evolution. The battle of Socialism against unlimited private profit is being won in detail hour by hour. In these particular fields—it remains acute elsewhere—this is no longer the pressing problem. There is, for instance, no so-called important political question so really unimportant, so irrelevant to the reorganization of the economic life of Great Britain, as the nationalization of the railways.

It is true that many big undertakings, particularly public utility enterprises and other business requiring a large fixed capital, still need to be semi-socialized. But we must keep our minds flexible regarding the forms of this semi-socialism. We must take full advantage of the natural tendencies of the day, and we must probably prefer semi-autonomous corporations to organs of the central government for which ministers of State are directly responsible.

I criticize doctrinaire State Socialism, not because it seeks to engage men's altruistic impulses in the service of society, or because it departs from *laissez-faire*, or because it takes away from man's natural liberty to make a million, or because it has courage for bold experiments. All these things I applaud. I criticize it because it misses the significance of what is actually happening; because it is, in fact, little better than a dusty survival of a plan to meet the problems of 50 years ago, based on a misunderstanding of what someone said a hundred years ago. Nineteenth-century State Socialism sprang from Bentham, free competition, etc., and is in some respects a clearer, in some respects a more muddled version of just the same philosophy as underlies nineteenth-century individualism. Both equally laid all their stress on freedom, the one negatively to avoid limitations on existing freedom, the other positively to destroy natural or acquired monopolies. They are different reactions to the same intellectual atmosphere.

(2) I come next to a criterion of *Agenda* which is particularly relevant to what it is urgent and desirable to do in the near future. We must aim at separating those services which are *technically social* from those which are *technically individual*. The most important *Agenda* of the State relate not to those activities which private individuals are already fulfilling, but to those functions which fall outside the sphere of the individual, to those decisions which are made by *no one* if the State does not make them. The important thing for government is not to do things which individuals are doing already, and to do them a little better or a little worse; but to do those things which at present are not done at all.

It is not within the scope of my purpose on this occasion to develop practical policies. I limit myself therefore, to naming some instances of what I mean from amongst those problems about which I happen to have thought most.

Many of the greatest economic evils of our time are the fruits of risk, uncertainty, and ignorance. It is because particular individuals, fortunate in situation or in abilities, are able to take advantage of uncertainty and ignorance, and also because for the same reason big business is often a lottery, that great inequalities of wealth come about; and these same factors are also the cause of the unemployment of labour, or the disappointment of reasonable business expectations, and of the impairment of efficiency and production. Yet the cure lies outside the operations of individuals; it may even be to the interest of individuals to aggravate the disease. I believe that the cure for these things is partly to be sought in the deliberate control of the currency and of credit by a central institution, and partly in the collection and dissemination on a great scale of data relating to the business situation, including the full publicity, by law if necessary, of all business facts which it is useful to know. These measures would involve society in exercising directive intelligence through some appropriate organ of action over many of the inner intricacies of private business, yet it would leave private initiative and enterprise unhindered. Even if these measures prove insufficient, nevertheless, they will furnish us with better knowledge than we have now for taking the next step.

My second example relates to savings and investment. I believe that some coordinated act of intelligent judgement is required as to the scale on which it is desirable that the community as a whole should save, the scale on which these savings should go abroad in the form of foreign investments, and whether the present organization of the investment market distributes savings along the most nationally productive channels. I do not think that these matters should be left entirely to the chances of private judgement and private profits, as they are at present.

My third example concerns population. The time has already come when each country needs a considered national policy about what size of population, whether larger or smaller than at present or the same, is most expedient.

And having settled this policy, we must take steps to carry it into operation. The time may arrive a little later when the community as a whole must pay attention to the innate quality as well as to the mere numbers of its future members.

Notes

1. "The Social Possibilities of Economic Chivalry," *Economic Journal*, XVII (1907), 9.
2. Quoted by McCulloch in his *Principles of Political Economy*.
3. Bentham's *Manual of Political Economy*, published posthumously, in Bowring's edition (1843).

CHAPTER 14

Federalism and the French Canadians

Pierre Elliott Trudeau

Foreword

In joining the Liberals, I turned my back on the socialist party for which I had campaigned at a time when Quebec considered socialism to be treason and heresy; but I had no regrets because by then—in 1965—most of its Quebec followers were in fact exchanging socialism for nationalism. They did this in the hope of finding a foothold in Quebec, but as a result they merely drew closer to the rising *bourgeoisie*. The latter was beginning to use Marxist terminology to justify its preaching of *national socialism*.

[. . .]

In Canada, and this includes Quebec, we have never known tyranny except in its figurative forms, for example the tyranny of public opinion. I am, however, far from considering that particular form the least terrible. For public opinion seeks to impose its domination over everything. Its aim is to reduce all action, all thought, and all feeling to a common denominator. It forbids independence and kills inventiveness; condemns those who ignore it and banishes those who oppose it. (Anyone who thinks I am exaggerating may count the number of times I have been called a "traitor" in recent years by the nationalist pundits of Quebec.)

I early realized that ideological systems are the true enemies of freedom. On the political front, accepted opinions are not only inhibiting to the mind, they contain the very source of error. When a political ideology is universally accepted by the elite, when the people who "define situations" embrace and venerate it, this means that it is high time free men were fighting it. For political freedom finds its essential strength in a sense of balance and proportion. As soon as any one tendency becomes too strong, it constitutes a menace.

The oldest problem of political philosophy, although it is not the only one, is to justify authority without destroying the independence of human beings in the process. How can an individual be reconciled with a society? The need for privacy with the need to live in groups? Love for freedom with need for order? . . . The most useful conclusion philosophy has come to is that one must keep an equal distance from both alternatives. Too much authority, or too little, and that is the end of freedom. For oppression also arises from lack of order, from the tyranny of the masses: it is then called the Reign of Terror.

In this sense it is possible to say that there are no absolute truths in politics. The best ideologies, having arisen at specific times to combat given abuses, become the worst if they survive the needs which gave them birth. Throughout history all great reformers were sooner or later betrayed by the excessive fidelity of their disciples. When a reform starts to be universally popular, it is more than likely that it has already become reactionary, and free men must then oppose it.

There is thus the danger that mass media—to the extent that they claim to reflect public opinion—constitute a vehicle for error, if not indeed an instrument of oppression. For my part, I have never been able to read newspapers without a sense of uneasiness, especially newspapers of opinion. They follow their customers and are therefore always lagging behind reality.

Since the function of political science is to seek and define the conditions of progress in advanced societies, this discipline naturally favours institutions that guarantee freedom without destroying order. This is the reason for their great interest in parliamentary and federal systems. The former, because they make the various organs of power independent of each other and give a prominent role to the opposition. The latter, because they divide the exercise of sovereignty between the various levels of government, and give none of them full powers over the citizen. Strangely enough, the classic analyses of these two systems are found in French thinkers: Montesquieu observing the British parliamentary system, and de Tocqueville describing American democracy. (In view of the fact that it was the Canadian Constitution that united the qualities of these two systems for the first time in history, it is rather paradoxical that French-Canadian "thinkers" should have such difficulty in perceiving its merits.)

The theory of checks and balances, so acutely analyzed by these two writers, has always had my full support. It translates into practical terms the concept of equilibrium that is inseparable from freedom in the realm of ideas. It incorporates a corrective for abuses and excesses into the very functioning of political institutions.

My political action, or my theory—insomuch as I can be said to have one—can be expressed very simply: create counterweights. As I have explained, it was because of the federal government's weakness that I allowed myself to be catapulted into it.

With these principles, and being a citizen of this country, I would have become a French Canadian by adoption had I not been one by birth. And had French Canadians needed someone to preach collective pride to them, no doubt I would have been first on the soap-box. But good God! that is all we've had, sermons on pride and divine missions! We possessed a wealth of immense syntheses and elaborate superstructures; we went overboard on constitutional or judicial reforms, the most obvious merit of which was their lack of contact with reality. Lenin said that such superstructures were *bourgeois* fads, and I can well understand why: they allow the middle class to play around with a great many concepts, to give the impression that nearly everything is to be reformed, and yet never be forced to change the slightest thing in actual fact.

In the introduction to *La Grève de l'amiante* (Editions Cité Libre, 1956), I demonstrated that our history has been riddled with these elaborate constructions, each one designed to make a great nation of us. During the thirties, it was the theory of corporatism. I do not think I am far wrong in saying that during this period nearly all French-Canadian thinkers, politicians, journalists, and editors advocated corporatism as a kind of extraordinary panacea; in any case, no one was far-sighted or courageous enough to say that it was all nonsense. The consequence was that we had to wait 20 years for the only reform that really counts: education. Net result? Of all Canada's ethnic groups, French Canadians have the second lowest standard in education, barely above that of the poor immigrants just arrived from Sicily.

Well, times have not changed much. Or if they have, it is for the worse. The fads are not the same, but official French-Canadian thinking has become even more monolithic and sterile, its supporters more intolerant: I do not think that using dynamite in a country that enjoys freedom of speech can be considered a sign of rational progress.

"Special status" (a completely illogical concept) has now taken the place that corporatism occupied a generation ago and is showing approximately the same characteristics. In the past, people neither wanted, nor were able, to abolish capitalism; but the dominating theories required them to pretend they did: hence all the talk about corporatism. Today, people neither want, nor are able, to *really* make Quebec independent, so they speak of "special status." We must have the expression, if nothing else. It is a way of assuring ourselves that the Constitution will be fundamentally transformed, while telling the rest of the country that it will not.

A woollier concept would be hard to imagine: and it is unanimously supported simply because anyone can give it whatever meaning he wishes. In fact, there are as many interpretations of "special status" as there are persons discussing it. The most striking example of this is the New Democratic Party which interprets it in two diametrically opposed ways, according to whether it is speaking to English or French Canadians. (On this point, Professor Ramsay Cook has done an essential job of clarifying the issues, in the *Globe and Mail*, 5 August 1967.)

We French Canadians are terribly lacking in tenacity. Rather than devote all our efforts to the real improvement of our intellectual, social, and economic condition, we let ourselves be carried away by legal superstructures without even inquiring whether they will work.

All the various kinds of "special status" which have been discussed until now, whatever their content, lead to the following logical problem: how can a constitution be devised to give Quebec greater powers than other provinces, without reducing Quebec's power in Ottawa? How can citizens of other provinces be made to accept the fact that they would have less power over Quebec at the federal level than Quebec would have over them? How, for example, can Quebec assume powers in foreign affairs, which other provinces do not have, without accepting a reduction of its influence in the field of foreign affairs through the federal government? How can Quebec be made the national state of French Canadians, with really *special* powers, without abandoning at the same time demands for the parity of French and English in Ottawa and throughout the rest of the country?

These questions remain unanswered, because they are unanswerable. For to think about them is to realize that we must have the courage and lucidity to make a choice.

Either the federal government exercises approximately the same powers over Quebec as it does over other provinces; Quebeckers will then be entitled to be represented in Ottawa in exactly the same way as other Canadians. This option would obviously not prevent Quebeckers from adopting whatever special policies they wished *within their provincial jurisdiction*, for example through the Civil Code, social legislation, development of resources, or a completely revised *provincial* constitution. This option would also allow parity between the English and French languages in all federal institutions, and the same parity could eventually be negotiated with other provinces.

Or, the central government's power over Quebec is substantially reduced compared to what it is over other provinces. Quebec's constitutional position having thus become really special, its electorate would not be entitled to demand complete representation at the federal level; and, more specifically, it would have to accept that the French fact be limited, legally and politically, to the province of Quebec.

The second alternative is the "special status" one. We can adopt it, or not. But those who think that they can have both options are deceiving themselves.

I have had the same ideas on our Constitution for a long time, as these essays will demonstrate. But as soon as I started expressing them in Parliament—which was after all the purpose of my being elected—*Le Droit* accused me of having become a slave to the Pearson government!

"Progressive" circles in Quebec, on the other hand, had condemned me for joining an "old party," maintaining that it was impossible to exert a significant influence within it. A year later I was accused of exerting too much influence, and the federal Members were warned against my ideas on the grounds that I did not speak "on behalf of French Canadians."

When I think of all the nonsense that has been spoken "on behalf of French Canadians" in the past 50 years, I am not very worried by this accusation. In any case, I never claimed to speak "on behalf" of anyone; if the Party does not agree with my opinions, it can repudiate me; if my constituents do not, they can elect someone else.

To "ready-made" or second-hand ideas, I have always preferred my own. They form the substance of this book, and together constitute what Mr. Pelletier has very kindly called my theory of politics.

CHAPTER 15

Principles of the Law of Peoples

John Rawls

Proceeding in a way analogous to the procedure in *A Theory of Justice*,[1] let's look first at familiar and traditional principles of justice among free and democratic peoples:[2]

1. Peoples are free and independent, and their freedom and independence are to be respected by other peoples.
2. Peoples are to observe treaties and undertakings.
3. Peoples are equal and are parties to the agreements that bind them.
4. Peoples are to observe a duty of non-intervention.
5. Peoples have the right of self-defence but no right to instigate war for reasons other than self-defence.
6. Peoples are to honour human rights.
7. Peoples are to observe certain specified restrictions in the conduct of war.
8. Peoples have a duty to assist other peoples living under unfavourable conditions that prevent their having a just or decent political and social regime.[3]

Notes

1. See *A Theory of Justice* (Harvard University Press, 1971), where chapter 2 discusses the principles of justice and chapter 3 gives the reasoning from the original position concerning the selection of principles.

2. See J.L. Brierly, *The Law of Nations: An Introduc-* *tion to the Law of Peace*, 6th edn (Oxford: Clarendon Press, 1963), and Terry Nardin, *Law, Morality, and the Relations of States* (Princeton: Princeton University Press, 1983). Both Brierly and Nardin give similar lists as principles of international law.

3. This principle is especially controversial. I discuss it in §§15–16.

CHAPTER 16

Liberalism in Culturally Plural Societies

Will Kymlicka

What explains the common liberal opposition to such minority rights? It's not difficult to see why liberals have opposed them. Liberalism, as I've presented it, is characterized both by a certain kind of *individualism*—that is, individuals are viewed as the ultimate units of moral worth, as having moral standing as ends in themselves, as "self-originating sources of valid claims" (Rawls 1980 p. 543); and by a certain kind of *egalitarianism*—that is, every individual has an equal moral status, and hence is to be treated as an equal by the government, with equal concern and respect (Dworkin p. 24; Rawls 1971 p. 511). Since individuals have ultimate moral status, and since each individual is to be respected as an equal by the government, liberals have demanded that each individual have equal rights and entitlements. Liberals have disagreed amongst themselves as to what these rights should be, because they have different views about what it is to treat people with equal concern and respect. But most would accept that these rights should include rights to mobility, to personal property, and to political participation in one's community. The new Canadian Charter of Rights and Freedoms embodies these liberal principles, guaranteeing such rights to every citizen, regardless of race or sex, ethnicity or language, etc. (Asch pp. 86–7; Schwartz ch. 1).

There seems to be no room within the moral ontology of liberalism for the idea of collective rights. The community, unlike the individual, is not a "self-originating source of valid claims." Once individuals have been treated as equals, with the respect and concern owed them as moral beings, there is no further obligation to treat the communities to which they belong as equals. The community has no moral existence or claims of its own. It is not that community is unimportant to the liberal, but simply that it is important for what it contributes to the lives of individuals, and so cannot ultimately conflict with the claims of individuals. Individual and collective rights cannot compete for the same moral space, in liberal theory, since the value of the collective derives from its contribution to the value of individual lives.

The constitutional embodiment of these liberal principles, in Canada and elsewhere, has played an important role in many of liberalism's greatest achievements in fighting against unjust legislation. For example, in the *Brown v. Board of Education* case, ([1954] 347 US 483), the Fourteenth Amendment of the American Constitution, guaranteeing equal protection of the law to all its citizens, was used to strike down legislation that segregated blacks in the American South. The "separate but equal" doctrine which had governed racial segregation in the United States for 60 years denied blacks the equal protection of the law. That case dealt solely with segregated school facilities, but it was a major impetus behind the removal of other segregationist legislation in the 1950s, the passage of the Civil Rights and Voting Rights Acts in the 1960s, and the development of mandatory busing, "head start," and affirmative action programs in the 1970s; which in turn were the catalyst for similar programs to benefit other groups—Hispanics, women, the handicapped, etc. Indeed, "its educative and moral impact in areas other than public education and, in fact, its whole thrust toward equality and opportunity for all men has been of immeasurable importance" (Kaplan p. 228). The "thrust" of this movement was sufficiently powerful to shape non-discrimination and equal protection legislation in countries around the world, and it provided the model for various international covenants on human rights (especially the Convention on the Elimination of All Forms of Racial Discrimination, adopted by the UN General Assembly in 1965). It also underlies the prominent philosophical accounts of liberal equality.

The history of these developments is one of the high points of Western liberalism in the twentieth century, for there is a powerful ideal of equality at work here in the political morality of the community—the idea that every citizen has a right to full and equal participation in the political, economic, and cultural life of the country, without regard to race, sex, religion, physical handicap—without regard to any of the classifications which have traditionally kept people separate and behind.

The logical conclusion of these liberal principles seems to be a "colour-blind" constitution—the removal of all legislation differentiating people in terms of their race or ethnicity (except for temporary measures, like affirmative action, which are believed necessary to reach a colour-blind society). Liberal equality requires the "universal" mode of incorporating citizens into the state. And this indeed has often been the conclusion drawn by courts in Canada and the United States.

This movement exercised an enormous influence on Canadian Indian policy as well (Berger p. 94). The desirability of a colour blind constitution was the explicit motivation behind the 1969 proposals for reforming the Indian Act in Canada. In 1968 Pierre Trudeau was elected Prime Minister of Canada on a platform of social justice that was clearly influenced by the American political movements. Canada didn't have a policy of segregating blacks, but it did have something which looked very similar. As in the United States, the native Indian population was predominantly living on segregated reserves, and was subject to a complex array of legislation which treated Indians and non-Indians differentially. While every Indian had the right to live on the land of her band, there were restrictions on her ability to use the land, or dispose of her estate as she saw fit, and there was a total prohibition on any alienation of the land. The reservation system also placed restrictions on the mobility, residence, and voting rights of non-Indians in the Indian territory; and in the case of voting rights, the restriction remained even when the non-Indian married into the Indian community. There were, in other words, two kinds of Canadian citizenship, Indian and non-Indian, with different rights and duties, differential access to public services, and different opportunities for participating in the various institutions of Canadian government.

Dismantling this system was one of the top priorities of Trudeau's "Just Society" policy, and early in 1969 the government released a White Paper on Indian Policy which recommended an end to the special constitutional status of Indians (DIAND). The government proposed that the reservation system, which had protected Indian communities from assimilation, be dismantled. Indians would not, of course, be compelled to disperse and assimilate. They would be free to choose to associate with one another, and co-ordinate the way they used their resources in the market, so as to preserve their way of life. Freedom of association is one of the individual rights to be universally guaranteed in a colour-blind constitution. But they would receive no legal or constitutional help in their efforts. Legislation discriminating against non-Indians in terms of property rights, mobility rights, or political rights would not be allowed.

From its very conception to the choice of language in the final draft, the policy reflected the powerful influence of the ideal of racial equality which was developing in the United States and the United Nations. Paraphrasing UN human rights instruments, the authors said that the policy rested "upon the fundamental right of Indian people to full and equal participation in the cultural, social, economic and political life of Canada," and this required that the legislative and constitutional bases of discrimination be removed (DIAND pp. 201–2). Echoing the *Brown* decision, the policy proposed that Indians no longer receive separate services from separate agencies, because "separate but equal services do not provide truly equal treatment" (DIAND p. 204). Echoing Justice Harlan's famous dictum that the American Constitution should be colour-blind, the Canadian proposal said that "The ultimate aim of removing the specific references to Indians from the constitution may take some time, but it is a goal to

be kept constantly in view" (DIAND p. 202). Perhaps it was the weight of all this normative authority that gave the authors such a sense of righteousness. It is, they said, "self-evident" that the constitution should be colour-blind, an "undeniable part of equality" that Indians should have equal access to common services; "There can be no argument . . . It is right" (DIAND pp. 202–3).

It is worth emphasizing that the issue was not about temporary measures to help Indians overcome their disadvantaged position in the broader society. While not all liberals are prepared to allow even temporary measures which differentiate on the basis of race or ethnicity, the government proposal followed the more common view that measures such as affirmative action are acceptable. But they are acceptable precisely because they are viewed as appropriate or necessary means to the pursuit of the ideal of a colour-blind constitution. Affirmative action of this sort appeals to the values embodied in that ideal, not to competing values. The issue posed by the special status of Canada's Indians, therefore, was not that of affirmative action, but "whether the granting of permanent political rights to a special class of citizens (rather than special rights on a temporary basis) is possible within an ideology that maintains the principle of equality of consideration" (Asch p. 76). And for the liberal architects of the 1969 proposal, the answer was that liberal equality was incompatible with the permanent assigning of collective rights to a minority culture.

The proposal was immediately applauded by the media, even by opposition parties, as a triumph for liberal justice. Indians, on the other hand, were furious, and after six months of bitter and occasionally violent Indian protest, the policy was withdrawn. In the words of one commentator, the policy was a response "to white liberal demands from the public, not to Indian demands" (Weaver 1981 p. 196). But liberals have only reluctantly retreated from that policy, despite the almost unanimous opposition it received from the Indians themselves. Liberals fear that any deviation from the strict principle of equal individual rights would be the first step down the road to apartheid, to a system where some individuals are viewed as first-class citizens and others only second-class, in virtue of their race or ethnic affiliation. These fears are strengthened when liberals see white South African leaders invoke minority rights in defence of their system of apartheid, and compare their system of tribal homelands to our system of Indian reservations and homelands (*International Herald Tribune* p. 2; *Toronto Star* p. B3). If we allow Indians to discriminate against non-Indians in the name of their collective rights, how can we criticize white South Africans for

discriminating against blacks in the name of their collective rights?

So liberals have viewed the idea of collective rights for minority cultures as both theoretically incoherent and practically dangerous. Many commentators have argued that this liberal antipathy is the biggest stumbling block to a satisfactory settlement of aboriginal claims in Canada (Weaver 1981 pp. 55–6, 196; 1985 pp. 141–2; Ponting and Gibbins pp. 327–31; Asch pp. 75–88, 100–4; Dacks pp. 63–79), and in the United States (Svensson pp. 430–3; Van Dyke pp. 28–30; Morgan p. 41; Barsh and Henderson pp. 241–8). And Schwartz's account of the recent constitutional conferences in Canada on aboriginal rights bears out the continued relevance of these liberal principles amongst government and court officials (Schwartz).

Bibliography

Asch, M. (1984). *Home and Native Land: Aboriginal Rights and the Canadian Constitution*. Methuen, Toronto.

Barsh, R., and Henderson, J.Y. (1980). *The Road: Indian Tribes and Political Liberty*. University of Toronto Press, Toronto.

Berger, T. (1984). "Towards the Regime of Tolerance." In *Political Thought in Canada: Contemporary Perspectives*. Ed. S. Brooks. Irwin Publishing, Toronto.

Boldt, M., and Long, J.A. (1985). *The Quest for Justice: Aboriginal Peoples and Aboriginal Rights*. University of Toronto Press, Toronto.

Bowles, R., Hanley, J., Hodgins, B., and Rawlyk, G. (1972). *The Indian: Assimilation, Integration or Separation?* Prentice-Hall, Scarborough, Ont.

Dacks, G. (1981). *A Choice of Futures: Politics in the Canadian North*. Methuen, Toronto.

DIAND (Department of Indian Affairs and Northern Development). (1969). "A Statement of the Government of Canada on Indian Policy." In Bowles et al. (1972).

Dworkin, R. (1983). "In Defense of Equality." *Social Philosophy and Policy*. Vol. I.

International Herald Tribune. (1985). "Botha Rejects Plea From Within Party to End Home School Segregation." 3 Oct.

Kaplan, J. (1964). "Comment on 'The Decade of School Desegregation.'" *Columbia Law Review*. Vol. 64.

Morgan, E. (1984). "Self-Government and the Constitution: A Comparative Look at Native Canadians and American Indians." *American Indian Law Review*. Vol. 12.

Ponting, J., and Gibbins, R. (1980). *Out of Irrelevance: A Socio-political Introduction to Indian Affairs in Canada*. Butterworth, Toronto.

Rawls, J. (1971). *A Theory of Justice*. Oxford University Press, London.

———. 1980). "Kantian Constructivism in Moral Theory." *Journal of Philosophy*. Vol. 77.

Schwartz, B. (1986). *First Principles, Second Thoughts: Aboriginal Peoples, Constitutional Reform and Canadian Statecraft*. The Institute for Research on Public Policy, Montreal.

Svensson, F. (1979). "Liberal Democracy and Group Rights: The legacy of Individualism and its Impact on American Indian Tribes." *Political Studies*. Vol. 27.

Toronto Star. (1986). "Botha's Warning." 28 Sept.

Van Dyke, V. (1982). "Collective Entities and Moral Rights: Problems in Liberal-Democratic Thought." *Journal of Politics.* Vol. 44.

Weaver, S. (1981). *Making Canadian Indian Policy.* University of Toronto Press, Toronto.

——. (1985). "Federal Difficulties with Aboriginal Rights Demands." In Boldt and Long (1985).

Critical Thinking Questions

1. What is the condition that Mill imposes on the state before it can exercise its power of "compulsion and control" over individual members of society? What does this condition reveal about Mill's own view about humanity? Which freedoms exist within the "region of human liberty" as defined by Mill? What is Mill's broader commentary about the link between utility and liberty?

2. What, according to Dewey, is liberalism's primary means of revolutionary change? Dewey accuses corporate interests of coercing individuals and corrupting their political liberties through control of the government. How convincing is this claim in light of historical and contemporary evidence? How would you rate Dewey's confidence in his own cause?

3. When Keynes rejects the view that "enlightened self-interest always operates in the public interest," who (or what) is under attack? What is Keynes' (devastating) definition of state socialism? Keynes defines unfettered capitalism and state socialism as different answers to the same "intellectual atmosphere." What does he mean? Keynes denounces the unmerited idolatry of powerful industrialists as the "orthodoxy" of his era. Which contemporary economic policies and positions might deserve this kind of criticism today? Why?

4. Identify the oldest problem of political philosophy, as Trudeau describes it. Which general solutions does Trudeau propose in resolving this problem? More specifically, Trudeau endorses a specific institution. Which one? Trudeau frames his broader argument against ideological dogma against the backdrop of Quebecois nationalism and its quest for "special status" within Canada. Why does Trudeau oppose this ambition? Can you think of reasons that might justify "special status" for any particular group?

5. Which of the principles of justice identified by Rawls are most easily implementable in that part of the international community which is free and democratic? Can these principles be extended in a modified form to non-democratic peoples? Do Rawls' principles shed light on the principle of self-determination as it applies to aboriginal groups inside existing democratic countries?

6. According to Kymlicka's account, why does the "moral ontology of liberalism" reject the idea of collective rights or special status for minority groups? Explain this apparent default position of liberalism with references to the history of race relations in Canada and elsewhere. Do you find this position to be practical in light of economic and social imbalances between groups in a society? How might globalization impact the long-term viability of this position?

Biographies

John Stuart Mill (1806–1873)

Any list of English-speaking philosophers in the nineteenth century must begin with British philosopher John Stuart Mill, whose views remain as relevant today as they did in the Victorian era when his most famous work, *On Liberty*, first appeared. Mill began his multifaceted career at an early age under the supervision of his father James and British philosopher Jeremy Bentham, then eclipsed both by extending and expanding refining their utilitarian thoughts. While Mill never thoroughly rejected the utilitarian principle of maximizing welfare, he warned against its excesses in enunciating a theory of liberty that identified individual liberties (such as the freedom of expression) as the source of general utility. This view—which stresses the sanctity of the individual—is also a rejection of tyranny in its myriad forms, including the democratic variety.

John Dewey (1859–1952)

Dewey was an American philosopher and educator who argued that the stability of a modern democratic society depends on the intellectual habits and environment of its citizenry. This unshakable belief in the instrumental role of education as a shield and sword against the natural but potentially harmful effects of progress nourished Dewey, who identified "resolute thought" as the inaugural step toward practical change. Dewey developed his pragmatic views about education during a long and productive career at various universities, including the University of Chicago, where he field-tested his theories at his famed Laboratory School. Contemporary liberals continue to recognize and revere Dewey's impressive accomplishments.

John Maynard Keynes (1883–1946)

Keynes was a British economist whose theories founded the modern welfare state. Keynes forged his views after attending the Paris Peace Conference following World War I. Keynes' critical assessment of the Versailles Treaty—which he considered harsh and short-sighted—predicted many of its consequences, including the rise of totalitarianism in a defeated but vengeful Germany. Keynes' reputation rose in the

1930s when western countries such as the United States increased government spending to stimulate demand and lower unemployment in response to the Great Depression. Keynes' star remained high after World War II as western states sought to moderate the swings of capitalism. While the political popularity of Keynesian measures waned during the late twentieth century, the most recent economic turmoil has once revived interest in Keynes' writings such as *A Treatise on Money* and *The General Theory of Employment.*

Pierre Elliott Trudeau (1919–2000)

 Pierre Elliott Trudeau had represented striking asbestos miners as a lawyer in his native Quebec before launching a productive, often provocative career in Canadian politics in the mid-1960s. Blessed with a combination of charm and intelligence that often appeared as arrogance, Trudeau rarely shunned the spotlight as Canada's fifteenth prime minister for nearly 16 years, from 1968 to 1984, minus a brief stint on the opposition benches. The passage of the *Canadian Charter of Rights and Freedoms* as part of a constitutional package that formally established Canadian sovereignty ranks as Trudeau's most significant achievement. The *Charter* acknowledged the emergence of a liberal, cosmopolitan Canada and sought to ameliorate the cleavages of a multi-ethnic state stretching across a continent. The national euphoria that accompanied Trudeau's rise to power has faded, but his intellectual legacy remains.

John Rawls (1921–2002)

This American-born philosopher turned down a career in the army after serving in World War II to pursue an academic career in philosophy on both sides of the Atlantic. He eventually settled at Harvard, where he influenced an entire generation of contemporary liberal thinkers such as Martha Nussbaum. We can also measure Rawls' intellectual wattage by the compliments which he received from his contemporaries, including his chief critic, Robert Nozick, who praised Rawls' sophisticated analysis, even as he challenged its conclusions. Rawls remained productive throughout his career, publishing new material on subjects such as international development and weapons of mass destruction well up to his death. *A Theory of Justice*, however, towers above Rawls' entire body of work, as an incomplete but ultimately inspiring blueprint for what an ideal liberal society might look like.

Will Kymlicka (1962–)

Kymlicka is a Canadian-born philosopher who has developed his liberal defence of group rights over the course of a career that has earned him acclaim in Europe, the United States, and his home country. Kymlicka, who currently teaches at Queen's University in Kingston, ON, has also advised the Canadian government on immigration and multiculturalism. Kymlicka's primary publications, such as *Multicultural Citizenship: A Liberal*

Theory of Minority Rights and *Politics in the Vernacular: Nationalism, Multiculturalism and Citizenship,* continue to generate interest around the world, including in Europe where political elites are trying to reconcile the economic challenges of their aging societies with the frequently xenophobic politics of integrating various minorities. While the optics of this process might cause confusion among Canadian observers used to living in a diverse society, they have no reasons to feel smug or superior thanks to unresolved historical wrongs. Yet they can take comfort in Kymlicka's intellectual guidance.

Part IV

Marxism

Marxism

Marxism affirms the primacy of modes of production and class struggle in explaining institutional structures associated with law, religion, education, family, marriage, to name only a few. As an ideology, it speaks on behalf of the working class, or proletariat, against the capitalists, or bourgeoisie. Unlike reform liberalism, which rejects the use of violence in order to effect social change, Marxism endorses as a necessity the use of force. Equality ranks among its highest ideals. Originating with Karl Marx in the early 1840s in Germany and surrounding countries, the ideology underwent important modification at the hands of Lenin in the early part of the twentieth century and again at the hands of Mao Tse-Tung in the 1930s and 1940s—the former adding new ideas about imperialism, and the latter new ideas of the revolutionary role of the peasantry.

Major Figures

Karl Marx (1818–1883), Friedrich Engels (1820–1895), Rosa Luxemburg (1871–1919), Vladimir Ilyich Ulyanov Lenin (1870–1924), Joseph Stalin (1879–1953), Mao Tse-Tung (1893–1976), and Fidel Castro (1926–)

Period of Greatest Influence

1843 to 1989

Introduction

In addition to the ideological reaction of reform liberalism and democratic social-ism to the Industrial Revolution, there stands Marxism like a giant colossus. Central to Marxism are, of course, Karl Marx and Friedrich Engels, but they are not by any means alone. Others who have to be mentioned include Vladimir Ulyanov, otherwise known as Lenin, as well as Rosa Luxemburg and Mao Tse-Tung. They are all consid-ered individuals who fall well within the list of those who are established Marxists. However, there are two other individuals that deserve consideration in any discussion of Marxism: one because he is a critic of this ideology, and one because he presents in modern dress a Marxist interpretation of international law. Respectively, these indi-viduals are the famous psychoanalyst Sigmund Freud and renowned international legal scholar B.S. Chimni.

Among the more famous of the publications of Karl Marx (1818–1883) and Friedrich Engels (1820–1895) is *The Communist Manifesto,* published in 1848. In communist lit-erature it is perhaps only overshadowed by Marx's *Das Kapital (Capitalism),* published initially in its first volumes in 1867. Attention here focuses upon the *Manifesto* owing to its clarity and influence. In the selected extract, one sees Marx and Engels at their acerbic best as they define history in terms of class struggle and the executive of the state in terms of a committee to manage the common affairs of the bourgeoisie. They care-fully outline their argument of the immiseration of the proletariat as it sinks deeper and deeper below the sustainable level. Then, notwithstanding the revolutionary nature of the bourgeoisie in opening new trade routes like the Cape of Good Hope and discover-ing new markets for goods produced, Marx and Engels put their fingers on the seeds of the destruction of the bourgeoisie: namely the combination or unionization of members of the proletariat class. In Marx and Engels' own terms, the bourgeoisie in effect pro-duces its own gravediggers. This is a theme that Marx echoes over and over in both earlier and later writings, though sometimes he contextualizes the theme in terms of economic determinism as he outlines the impact of changing modes of production on property relations or class ownership.

Once one turns attention to others in the tradition of Marxism, eyes soon set on V.I. Lenin (1870–1924), leader of the Bolshevik Revolution (1917), strategist, and edi-tor of the newspaper *The Spark*. He shares with Marx a background in the study of law but not in the study of philosophy. Hegelian notions that influence Marx are left undeveloped by Lenin as he pushes his analysis of capitalism further and further in the direction of considerations of economics. Of prime importance to Lenin is the monopo-lization of production and capital as well as the merging of bank capital with industrial capital. These developments when coupled with the territorial division of the whole world among the biggest capitalist powers amount to, what Lenin defines as, imperial-ism. Lenin expresses these ideas in one of his two most well-known works, *Imperialism, the Highest Stage of Capitalism* published in 1912. His other equally well-known work is *What is to Be Done?* also published in the same year. This latter work (not discussed here) seeks to drag out of the closet, kicking and screaming, those reformers who call themselves democratic socialists and who direct their bourgeois criticism at Marxism.

Lenin is exceptionally effective in his attack on social democrats, an attack that matches his criticism of imperialism.

Never one to shy away from intellectual confrontation, Sigmund Freud (1856–1939), in his *Civilization and Its Discontents*, challenges the ideas of communists such as Marx and Lenin. His attack is quite different from that of Mikhail Bakunin, and in fact one cannot help but believe he would have, given enough time, subjected Bakunin to an equally effective criticism to that which he unleashes on Marx and the communists. Whatever the truth in this matter, what can be said is that Freud challenges, very plausibly, Marx and other communists' belief that the root of human evil is found in the institution of private property. Once Freud becomes convinced that a monistic theory of human motivation (i.e., a theory based on libidinal instinct alone) is insufficient to account for human behaviour—behaviour such as revealed in World War I and vividly described by Wilfrid Owen in his war poems—he finds himself well placed to take aim at Marx and his "untenable illusion" of believing in the effectiveness of ridding humanity of evil by abolishing private possessions. Freud acknowledges quite openly his inability to comment on the economic viability of such an abolition, but he affirms with force his conviction of the unacceptability of the psychological premises on which this theory is constructed. Freud leans on his new dualism of human motivation—libidinal (life) instinct and thanatos (death) instinct—to dismiss the psychological profile that Marx relies upon.

The next extract in the Marxist readings is that of Mao Tse-Tung (1893–1976). Mao was the leader of the Chinese Communist Revolution (1949) and massaged Marxist ideas to fit the Chinese situation in the interwar years. In this selection, Mao vigorously adopts the Hegelian idea of the dialectic. He defends this by arguing for the existence of two conceptions concerning the development of the universe: one being the metaphysical conception, and the other being the dialectical conception. Once he distinguishes these two conceptions, he moves on to affirm the validity of the second of these at the expense of the first. Happily for Mao, the position he affirms is one also advanced by Lenin. Mao's intent in the extract is to combat dogmatism in the Chinese Communist Party, and he attempts to do this by showing that the dialectic of Marxism overcomes the isolated and static nature of the vulgar metaphysical worldview and replaces it with the interrelated and dynamic nature of the Marxist worldview. This dynamic nature studies things "internally" and "in relation to other things" with the "fundamental cause of development" lying in the opposition or contradictoriness within "the thing." Unsurprisingly for Mao, one easily moves from contradictoriness to opposition and from opposition to antagonism, an antagonism that relates easily to Marx's idea of history being the history of class struggle.

"The Nationalities Question" of Rosa Luxemburg provides the penultimate reading of this part. Rosa Luxemburg (1871–1919) was a strong crusader for Marxist socialism. Born into a Jewish merchant's family, Luxemburg discovered Marxism at an early age in her country of birth, Poland. While in Switzerland some years later, she came to know many of the future well-known figures of the Russian Revolution, including Lenin, Georgi Plekhanov, and Pavel Axelrod. Though familiar with the thinking of these individuals, she by no means copies their thinking and indeed, as shown in

"The Nationalities Question," takes aim specifically at Lenin and his slogan of "the right of self-determination." Recognizing the ideological tendency of Lenin to be obstinate and rigid with respect to this slogan, Luxemburg points out that the principle of self-determination not only runs counter to Lenin's other principle of democratic centralism but, unsurprisingly, supplies the bourgeoisie with the most desirable pretext for counter-revolution. It is to Luxemburg's credit that she recognizes something that Lenin does not, namely the day of reckoning that awaits international socialism at the hands of the nationalist movement and self-determination. Luxemburg obviously understands the rather comical nature of Lenin adhering to the same principle of self-determination as that advanced by the bourgeois idealist Woodrow Wilson.

Attempting to fill the gap left by Marxists' neglect of international law, B.S. Chimni (1952–) argues that contemporary international law is, in an unprecedented way, "congealing inequities in the international system." Chimni sees international law and institutions as putty being shaped by the forces of globalization, where "globalization" is defined as the shift of principal venue of capital accumulation from the nation to the global arena. In Chimni's opinion, the era of globalization has two main objectives: (1) the removal of local impediments to the rule of capital, and (2) the dismantling of international laws of distribution, which are based on the notion of market intervention. In detailed fashion he goes on to discuss each of these in terms of the privatization of the public sector in the third world, the growing network of international laws which free transnational capital, the privatization of the global technology regime, the privatization of the global commons, the extension of the global commons to the environment, and the elimination of national courts in resolving disputes between transnational corporations and the state. These and other observations of Chimni make a case for acknowledging the new role of international law that emerged in the 1980s and that began to displace the international law of the 1970s, which aimed at an equitable international law of distribution. Chimni makes for compelling reading!

From its inception, Marxism did not stand still. While Marx applies his thinking to economic determinism and the class struggle, Lenin sees the delay of the overthrow of capitalism as attributable to a higher stage of capitalism, namely imperialism. And Mao Tse-Tung develops Marx's class struggle and applies it to the peasantry. Mao does this all the while bearing in mind the Hegelian nature of Marx's thinking, at the core of which are found opposition and contradictoriness. Luxemburg for her part looks askance at the approach Lenin takes to the nationalities question and self-determination, realizing the dangers that lurk within. But beyond those who support Marx and his ideology, it is a tribute to the impact Marx and Marxism had upon history and intellectual thought that it attracted critics as significant as Sigmund Freud. However, the resilience of Marxist thought, notwithstanding what Freud says and what Keynes in another context says, is amply demonstrated by the acute observations, in a contemporary setting, proffered by B.S. Chimni. Chimni makes clear that Marxism provides powerful analytical tools for subjecting the idealism of international law to a very materialistic attack. With this in mind, and as others have suggested, one could well say of Marxism: here is an ideology that has intellectual aspects, revolutionary appeal, and mythical attributes that both attract and repel proponents and critics respectively.

CHAPTER 17

Bourgeois and Proletarians

Karl Marx and Friedrich Engels

A spectre is haunting Europe, the spectre of Communism. All the powers of old Europe have entered into a holy alliance to exorcise this spectre; Pope and Czar, Metternich and Guizot, French Radicals and German police-spies.

Where is the party in opposition that has not been decried as communistic by its opponents in power? Where is the Opposition that has not hurled back the branding reproach of Communism, against the more advanced opposition parties, as well as against its reactionary adversaries?

Two things result from this fact:

1. Communism is already acknowledged by all European powers to be itself a power.
2. It is high time that Communists should openly, in the face of the whole world, publish their views, their aims, their tendencies, and meet this nursery tale of the spectre of Communism with a manifesto of the party itself.

To this end, Communists of various nationalities have assembled in London, and sketched the following manifesto, to be published in the English, French, German, Italian, Flemish, and Danish languages.

I Bourgeois and Proletarians

The history of all hitherto existing society is the history of class struggles.

Freeman and slave, patrician and plebeian, lord and serf, guild-master and journeyman, in a word, oppressor and oppressed, stood in constant opposition to one another, carried on an uninterrupted, now hidden, now open fight, a fight that each time ended either in a revolutionary reconstitution of society at large, or in the common ruin of the contending classes.

In the earlier epochs of history, we find almost every where a complicated arrangement of society into various orders, a manifold gradation of social rank. In ancient Rome we have patricians, knights, plebeians, slaves; in the Middle Ages, feudal lords, vassals, guild-masters, journeymen, apprentices, serfs; in almost all of these classes, again, subordinate gradations.

The modern bourgeois society that has sprouted from the ruins of feudal society has not done away with class antagonisms. It has but established new classes, new conditions of oppression, new forms of struggle in place of the old ones.

Our epoch, the epoch of the bourgeoisie, possesses, however, this distinctive feature; it has simplified the class antagonisms. Society as a whole is more and more splitting up into two great hostile camps, into two great classes directly facing each other: Bourgeoisie and Proletariat.

From the serfs of the Middle Ages sprang the chartered burghers of the earliest towns. From these burgesses the first elements of the bourgeoisie were developed.

The discovery of America, the rounding of the Cape, opened up fresh ground for the rising bourgeoisie. The East-Indian and Chinese markets, the colonization of America, trade with the colonies, the increase in the means of exchange and in commodities generally, gave to commerce to navigation, to industry, an impulse never before known, and thereby, to the revolutionary element in the tottering feudal society, a rapid development.

The feudal system of industry, in which industrial production was monopolized by closed guilds, now no longer sufficed for the growing wants of the new markets. The manufacturing system took its place. The guild-masters were pushed on one side by the manufacturing middle-class; division of labour between the different corporate guilds vanished in the face of division of labour in each single workshop. Meantime the markets kept ever growing, the demand, ever rising. Even manufacture no longer sufficed. Thereupon steam and machinery revolutionized industrial production. The place of manufacture was now taken by the giant, modern industry, the place of the industrial middle-class, by industrial millionaires, the leaders of whole industrial armies, the modern bourgeois.

Modern industry has established the world-market, for which the discovery of America paved the way. This market has given an immense development to commerce, to navigation, to communication by land. This development has, in its turn, reacted on the extension of industry; and in proportion as industry, commerce, navigation, railways extended, in the same proportion the bourgeoisie developed, increased its capital, and pushed into the background every class handed down from the Middle Ages.

We see, therefore, how the modern bourgeoisie is itself the product of a long course of development, of a series of revolutions in the modes of production and of exchange.

Each step in the development of the bourgeoisie was accompanied by a corresponding political advance of that class. An oppressed class under the sway of the feudal nobility, it became an armed and self-governing association in the medieval commune; here independent urban republic (as in Italy and Germany), there taxable "third estate" of the monarchy (as in France); afterwards, in the period of manufacture proper, serving either the semi-feudal or the absolute monarchy as a counterpoise against the nobility, and, in fact, cornerstone of the great monarchies in general, the bourgeoisie has at last, since the establishment of Modern Industry and of the world-market, conquered for itself, in the modern representative State, exclusive political sway. The executive of the modern State is but a committee for managing the common affairs of the whole bourgeoisie.

The bourgeoisie has played a most revolutionary role in history.

The bourgeoisie, wherever it has got the upper hand, has put an end to all feudal, patriarchal, idyllic relations. It has pitilessly torn asunder the motley feudal ties that bound man to his "natural superiors," and has left remaining no other bond between man and man than naked self-interest, than callous "cash payment." It has drowned the most heavenly ecstasies of religious fervour, of chivalrous enthusiasm, of philistine sentimentalism, in the icy water of egotistical calculation. It has resolved personal worth into exchange value, and in place of the numberless indefeasible chartered freedoms, has set up that single, unconscionable freedom, Free Trade. In one word, for exploitation, veiled by religious and political illusions, it has substituted naked, shameless, direct, brutal exploitation.

The bourgeoisie has stripped of its halo every occupation hitherto honoured and looked up to with reverent awe. It has converted the physician, the lawyer, the priest, the poet, the man of science, into its paid wage-labourers.

The bourgeoisie has torn away from the family its sentimental veil, and has reduced the family relation to a mere money relation.

The bourgeoisie has disclosed how it came to pass that the brutal display of vigour in the

Middle Ages, which Reactionists so much admire, found its fitting complement in the most slothful indolence. It has been the first to show what man's activity can bring about. It has accomplished wonders far surpassing Egyptian pyramids, Roman aqueducts, and Gothic cathedrals; it has conducted expeditions that put in the shade all former migrations of nations and crusades.

The bourgeoisie cannot exist without constantly revolutionizing the instruments of production, and thereby the relations of production, and with them the whole relations of society. Conservation of the old modes of production in unaltered form was, on the contrary, the first condition of existence for all earlier industrial classes. Constant revolutionizing of production, uninterrupted disturbance of all social conditions, everlasting uncertainty and agitation distinguish the bourgeois epoch from all earlier ones. All fixed, fast-frozen relations, with their train of ancient and venerable prejudices and opinions, are swept away, all new-formed ones become antiquated before they can ossify. All that is solid melts into air, all that is holy is profaned, and man is at last compelled to face with sober senses his real conditions of life, and his relations with his kind.

The need of a constantly expanding market for its products chases the bourgeoisie over the whole surface of the globe. It must nestle everywhere, settle everywhere, establish connections everywhere.

The bourgeoisie has through its exploitation of the world-market given a cosmopolitan character to production and consumption in every country. To the great chagrin of Reactionists, it has drawn from under the feet of industry the national ground on which it stood. All old-established national industries have been destroyed or are daily being destroyed. They are dislodged by new industries, whose introduction becomes a life and death question for all civilized nations, by industries that no longer work up indigenous raw material, but raw material drawn from the remotest zones; industries whose products are consumed, not only at home, but in every quarter of the globe. In place of the old wants, satisfied by the production of the country, we find new wants, requiring for their satisfaction the products of distant lands and climes. In place of the old local and national seclusion and self-sufficiency, we have intercourse in every direction, universal interdependence of nations. And as in material, so also in intellectual production. The intellectual creations of individual nations become common property. National one-sidedness and narrow-mindedness become more and more impossible, and from the numerous national and local literatures there arises a world literature.

The bourgeoisie, by the rapid improvement of all instruments of production, by the immensely facilitated means of communication, draws all, even the most barbarian, nations into civilization. The cheap prices of its commodities are the heavy artillery with which it batters down all Chinese walls, with which it forces the barbarians' intensely obstinate hatred of foreigners to capitulate. It compels all nations, on pain of extinction, to adopt the bourgeois mode of production; it compels them to introduce what it calls civilization into their midst, i.e., to become bourgeois themselves. In a word, it creates a world after its own image.

The bourgeoisie has subjected the country to the rule of the towns. It has created enormous cities, has greatly increased the urban population as compared with the rural, and has thus rescued a considerable part of the population from the idiocy of rural life. Just as it has made the country dependent on the towns, so it has made barbarian and semi-barbarian countries dependent on the civilized ones, nations of peasants on nations of bourgeois, the East on the West.

The bourgeoisie keeps more and more doing away with the scattered state of the population, of the means of production, and of property. It has agglomerated population, centralized means of production, and has concentrated property in a few hands. The necessary consequence of this was political centralization. Independent, or but loosely connected provinces, with separate interests, laws, systems of taxation, and governments, became lumped together in one nation, with one government, one code of laws, one national class-interest, one frontier, and one customs tariff.

The bourgeoisie, during its rule of scarce one hundred years, has created more massive and more colossal productive forces than have all preceding generations together. Subjection of Nature's forces to man, machinery, application of chemistry to industry and agriculture, steam-navigation, railways, electric telegraphs, clearing of whole continents for cultivation, canalization of rivers, whole populations conjured out of the ground. What earlier century had even a presentiment that such productive forces slumbered in the lap of social labour?

We see then: the means of production and of exchange on whose foundation the bourgeoisie built itself up were generated in feudal society. At a certain stage in the development of these means of production and of exchange, the conditions under which feudal society produced and exchanged the feudal organization of agriculture and manufacturing industry, in one word, the feudal relations of property became no longer compatible with the already developed productive forces; they became so many fetters. They had to burst asunder; they were burst asunder.

Into their places stepped free competition, accompanied by a social and political constitution adapted to it, and by the economical and political sway of the bourgeois class.

A similar movement is going on before our own eyes. Modern bourgeois society with its relations of production, of exchange and of property, a society that has conjured up

such gigantic means of production and of exchange, is like the sorcerer, who is no longer able to control the powers of the nether world whom he has called up by his spells. For many a decade past the history of industry and commerce is but the history of the revolt of modern productive forces against modern conditions of production, against the property relations that are the conditions for the existence of the bourgeoisie and of its rule. It is enough to mention the commercial crises that by their periodical return put on its trial, each time more threateningly, the existence of the entire bourgeois society. In these crises a great part not only of the existing products but also of the previously created productive forces are periodically destroyed. In these crises there breaks out an epidemic that, in all earlier epochs, would have seemed an absurdity, the epidemic of overproduction. Society suddenly finds itself put back into a state of momentary barbarism; it appears as if a famine, a universal war of devastation had cut off the supply of every means of subsistence; industry and commerce seem to be destroyed; and why? Because there is too much civilization, too much means of subsistence, too much industry, too much commerce. The productive forces at the disposal of society no longer tend to further the development of the conditions of bourgeois property; on the contrary, they have become too powerful for these conditions, by which they are fettered, and so soon as they overcome these fetters, they bring disorder into the whole of bourgeois society, endanger the existence of bourgeois property. The conditions of bourgeois society are too narrow to comprise the wealth created by them. And how does the bourgeoisie get over these crises? On the one hand by enforced destruction of a mass of productive forces; on the other, by the conquest of new markets, and by the more thorough exploitation of the old ones. That is to say, by paving the way for more extensive and more destructive crises, and by diminishing the means whereby crises are prevented.

The weapons with which the bourgeoisie felled feudalism to the ground are now turned against the bourgeoisie itself.

But not only has the bourgeoisie forged the weapons that bring death to itself; it has also called into existence the men who are to wield those weapons, the modern working-class, the proletarians.

In proportion as the bourgeoisie, i.e., capital, is developed, in the same proportion is the proletariat, the modern working-class, developed, a class of labourers, who live only so long as they find work, and who find work only so long as their labour increases capital. These labourers, who must sell themselves piecemeal, are a commodity, like every other article of commerce, and are consequently exposed to all the vicissitudes of competition, to all the fluctuations of the market.

Owing to the extensive use of machinery and to division of labour, the work of the proletarians has lost all individual character, and, consequently, all charm for the workman. He becomes an appendage of the machine, and it is only the most simple, most monotonous, and most easily acquired knack that is required of him. Hence, the cost of production of a workman is restricted, almost entirely, to the means of subsistence that he requires for his maintenance, and for the propagation of his race. But the price of a commodity, and also of labour, is equal to its cost of production. In proportion, therefore, as the repulsiveness of the work increases, the wage decreases. Nay more, in proportion as the use of machinery and division of labour increases, in the same proportion the burden of toil also increases, whether by prolongation of the working hours, by increase of the work enacted in a given time, or by increased speed of the machinery, etc.

Modern industry has converted the little workshop of the patriarchal master into the great factory of the industrial capitalist. Masses of labourers, crowded into the factory, are organized like soldiers. As privates of the industrial army they are placed under the command of a perfect hierarchy of officers and sergeants. Not only are they the slaves of the bourgeois class, and of the bourgeois State, they are daily and hourly enslaved by the machine, by the overlooker, and, above all, by the individual bourgeois manufacturer himself. The more openly this despotism proclaims gain to be its end and aim, the more petty, the more hateful and the more embittering it is.

The less the skill and exertion or strength implied in manual labour, in other words, the more modern industry becomes developed, the more is the labour of men superseded by that of women. Differences of age and sex have no longer any distinctive social validity for the working class. All are instruments of labour, more or less expensive to use, according to their age and sex.

No sooner is the exploitation of the labourer by the manufacturer, so far at an end, that he receives his wages in cash, than he is set upon by the other portions of the bourgeoisie, the landlord, the shopkeeper, the pawnbroker, etc.

The lower strata of the middle-class, the small tradespeople, shopkeepers, and retired tradesmen generally, the handicraftsmen and peasants, all these sink gradually into the proletariat, partly because their diminutive capital does not suffice for the scale on which Modern Industry is carried on, and is swamped in the competition with the large capitalists, partly because their specialized skill is rendered worthless by new methods of production. Thus the proletariat is recruited from all classes of the population.

The proletariat goes through various stages of development. With its birth begins its struggle with the bourgeoisie. At first the contest is carried on by individual labourers, then by the workpeople of a factory, then by the operatives of one trade, in one locality, against the individual bourgeois who directly exploits them. They direct their attacks not against the bourgeois conditions of production, but against the instruments of production themselves; they destroy imported wares that compete with their labour, they smash to pieces machinery, they set factories ablaze, they seek to restore by force the vanished status of the workman of the Middle Ages.

At this stage the labourers still form an incoherent mass scattered over the whole country, and broken up by their mutual competition. If anywhere they unite to form more compact bodies, this is not yet the consequence of their own active union, but of the union of the bourgeoisie, which class, in order to attain its own political ends, is compelled to set the whole proletariat in motion, and is moreover yet, for a time, able to do so. At this stage, therefore, the proletarians do not fight their enemies, but the enemies of their enemies, the remnants of absolute monarchy, the landowners, the non-industrial bourgeois, the petty bourgeoisie. Thus the whole historical movement is concentrated in the hands of the bourgeoisie; every victory so obtained is a victory for the bourgeoisie.

But with the development of industry the proletariat not only increases in number, it becomes concentrated in greater masses, its strength grows, and it feels that strength more. The various interests and conditions of life within the ranks of the proletariat are more and more equalized, in proportion as machinery obliterates all distinctions of labour, and nearly everywhere reduces wages to the same low level. The growing competition among the bourgeois, and the resulting commercial crises, make the wages of the workers ever more fluctuating. The unceasing improvement of machinery, ever more rapidly developing, makes their livelihood more and more precarious; the collisions between individual workmen and individual bourgeois take more and more the character of collisions between two classes.

Thereupon the workers begin to form combinations (Trades' Unions) against the bourgeois; they club together in order to keep up the rate of wages; they found permanent associations in order to make provision beforehand for these occasional revolts. Here and there the contest breaks out into riots.

Now and then the workers are victorious, but only for a time. The real fruit of their battles lies, not in the immediate result, but in the ever expanding union of the workers. This union is helped on by the improved means of communication that are created by modern industry, and that place the workers of different localities in contact with one another. It was just this contact that was needed to centralize the numerous local struggles, all of the same character, into one national struggle between classes. But every class struggle is a political struggle. And that union, to attain which the burghers of the Middle Ages, with their miserable highways, required centuries, the modern proletarians, thanks to railways, achieve in a few years.

This organization of the proletarians into a class, and consequently into a political party, is continually being upset again by the competition between the workers themselves. But it ever rises up again, stronger, firmer, mightier. It compels legislative recognition of particular interests of the workers by taking advantage of the divisions among the bourgeoisie itself. Thus the ten-hour bill in England was carried.

Altogether collisions between the classes of the old society further, in many ways, the course of development of the proletariat. The bourgeoisie finds itself involved in a constant battle. At first with the aristocracy; later on with those portions of the bourgeoisie itself, whose interests have become antagonistic to the progress of industry; at all times, with the bourgeoisie of foreign countries. In all these battles it sees itself compelled to appeal to the proletariat, to ask for its help, and thus to drag it into the political arena. The bourgeoisie itself, therefore, supplies the proletariat with its own elements of political and general education, in other words, it furnishes the proletariat with weapons for fighting the bourgeoisie.

Further, as we have already seen, entire sections of the ruling classes are, by the advance of industry, precipitated into the proletariat, or are at least threatened in their conditions of existence. These also supply the proletariat with fresh elements of enlightenment and progress.

Finally, in times when the class-struggle nears the decisive hour, the process of dissolution going on within the ruling class, in fact, within the whole range of old society, assumes such a violent, glaring character, that a small section of the ruling class cuts itself adrift, and joins the revolutionary class, the class that holds the future in its hands. Just as, therefore, at an earlier period, a section of the nobility went over to the bourgeoisie, so now a portion of the bourgeoisie goes over to the proletariat, and in particular, a portion of the bourgeois ideologists, who have raised themselves to the level of comprehending theoretically the historical movements as a whole.

Of all the classes that stand face to face with the bourgeoisie today, the proletariat alone is a really revolutionary class. The other classes decay and finally disappear in the face of modern industry, the proletariat is its special and essential product.

The lower middle-class, the small manufacturer, the shopkeeper, the artisan, the peasant, all these fight against the bourgeoisie, to save from extinction their existence as fractions of the middle-class. They are, therefore, not revolutionary, but conservative. Nay more, they are reactionary, for they try to roll back the wheel of history. If by chance they are revolutionary, they are so, only in view of their impending transfer into the proletariat, they thus defend not their present, but their future interests, they desert their own standpoint to place themselves at that of the proletariat.

The "dangerous class," the social scum, that passively rotting mass thrown off by the lowest layers of old society, may, here and there, be swept into the movement by a proletarian revolution; its conditions of life, however, prepare it far more for the part of a bribed tool of reactionary intrigue.

In the conditions of the proletariat, those of old society at large are already virtually swamped. The proletarian is without property; his relation to his wife and children has no longer anything in common with the bourgeois family relations, modern industrial labour, modern subjection to capital, the same in England as in France, in America as in Germany, has stripped him of every trace of national character. Law, morality, religion, are to him so many bourgeois prejudices, behind which lurk in ambush just as many bourgeois interests. All the preceding classes that got the upper hand sought to fortify their already acquired status by subjecting society at large to their conditions of appropriation. The proletarians cannot become masters of the productive forces of society, except by abolishing their own previous mode of appropriation, and thereby also every other previous mode of appropriation. They have nothing of their own to secure and to fortify; their mission is to destroy all previous securities for, and insurances of, individual property.

All previous historical movements were movements of minorities, or in the interest of minorities. The proletarian movement is the self-conscious, independent movement of the immense majority, in the interest of the immense majority. The proletariat, the lowest stratum of our present society, cannot stir, cannot raise itself up, without the whole superincumbent strata of official society being sprung into the air.

Though not in substance, yet in form, the struggle of the proletariat with the bourgeoisie is at first a national struggle. The proletariat of each country must first of all settle matters with its bourgeoisie. In depicting the most general phases of the development of the proletariat, we traced the more or less veiled civil war, raging within existing society, up to the point where that war breaks out into open revolution, and where the violent overthrow of the bourgeoisie, lays the foundation for the sway of the proletariat.

Hitherto, every form of society has been based, as we have already seen, on the antagonism of oppressing and oppressed classes. But in order to oppress a class, certain conditions must be assured to it under which it can, at least, continue its slavish existence. The serf, in the period of serfdom, raised himself to membership in the commune, just as the petty bourgeois, under the yoke of feudal absolutism, managed to develop into a bourgeois. The modern labourer, on the contrary, instead of rising with the progress of industry, sinks deeper and deeper below the conditions of existence of his own class. He becomes a pauper, and pauperism develops more rapidly than population and wealth. And here it becomes evident that the bourgeoisie is unfit

any longer to be the ruling class in society, and to impose its conditions of existence upon society, as an overriding law. It is unfit to rule, because it is incompetent to assure an existence to its slave within his slavery, because it cannot help letting him sink into such a state that it has to feed him. Society can no longer live under this bourgeoisie, in other words, its existence is no longer compatible with society.

The essential condition for the existence, and for the sway of the bourgeois class, is the formation and augmentation of capital; the condition for capital is wage-labour. Wage-labour rests exclusively on competition between the labourers. The advance of industry, whose involuntary promoter is the bourgeoisie, replaces the isolation of the labourers, due to competition, by their involuntary combination, due to association. The development of Modern Industry therefore cuts from under its feet the very foundation on which the bourgeoisie produces and appropriates products. What the bourgeoisie therefore produces, above all, are its own gravediggers. Its fall and the victory of the proletariat are equally inevitable.

CHAPTER 18

Imperialism, as a Special Stage of Capitalism

Vladimir I. Lenin

We must now try to sum up, put together, what has been said above on the subject of imperialism. Imperialism emerged as the development and direct continuation of the fundamental characteristics of capitalism

in general. But capitalism only became capitalist imperialism at a definite and very high stage of its development, when certain of its fundamental characteristics began to change into their opposites, when the features of the epoch of transition from capitalism to a higher social and economic system had taken shape and revealed themselves all along the line. Economically, the main thing in this process is the displacement of capitalist free competition by capitalist monopoly. Free competition is the fundamental characteristic of capitalism, and of commodity production generally; monopoly is the exact opposite of free competition, but we have seen the latter being transformed into monopoly before our eyes, creating large-scale industry and forcing out small industry, replacing large-scale by still larger-scale industry, and carrying concentration of production and capital to the point where out of it has grown and is growing monopoly: cartels, syndicates, and trusts, and merging with them, the capital of a dozen or so banks, which manipulate thousands of millions. At the same time the monopolies, which have grown out of free competition, do not eliminate the latter, but exist over it and alongside of it, and thereby give rise to a number of very acute, intense antagonisms, frictions, and conflicts. Monopoly is the transition from capitalism to a higher system.

If it were necessary to give the briefest possible definition of imperialism we should have to say that imperialism is the monopoly stage of capitalism. Such a definition would include what is most important, for, on the one hand, finance capital is the bank capital of a few very big monopolist banks, merged with the capital of the monopolist combines of industrialists; and, on the other hand, the division of the world is the transition from a colonial policy which has extended without hindrance to territories unseized by any capitalist power, to a colonial policy of monopolistic possession of the territory of the world which has been completely divided up.

But very brief definitions, although convenient, for they sum up the main points, are nevertheless inadequate, since very important features of the phenomenon that has to be defined have to be especially deduced. And so, without forgetting the conditional and relative value of all definitions in general, which can never embrace all the concatenations of a phenomenon in its complete development, we must give a definition of imperialism that will include the following five of its basic features: 1) the concentration of production and capital has developed to such a high stage that it has created monopolies which play a decisive role in economic life; 2) the merging of bank capital with industrial capital, and the creation, on the basis of this "finance capital," of a financial oligarchy; 3) the export of capital as distinguished from the export of commodities acquires exceptional importance; 4) the formation of international monopolist capitalist combines which share the world among themselves, and 5) the territorial division of the whole world among the biggest capitalist powers is completed. Imperialism is capitalism in that stage of development in which the dominance of monopolies and finance capital has established itself; in which the export of capital has acquired pronounced importance; in which the division of the world among the international trusts has begun; in which the division of all territories of the globe among the biggest capitalist powers has been completed.

We shall see later that imperialism can and must be defined differently if we bear in mind, not only the basic, purely economic concepts—to which the above definition is limited—but also the historical place of this stage of capitalism in relation to capitalism in general, or the relation between imperialism and the two main trends in the working-class movement. The point to be noted just now is that imperialism, as interpreted above, undoubtedly represents a special stage in the development of capitalism. To enable the reader to obtain the most well-grounded idea of imperialism possible, we deliberately tried to quote as largely as possible *bourgeois* economists who are obliged to admit the particularly incontrovertible facts concerning the latest stage of capitalist economy. With the same object in view, we have quoted detailed statistics which enable one to see to what degree bank capital, etc., has grown, in what precisely the transformation of quantity into quality, of developed capitalism into imperialism, was expressed. Needless to say, of course, all boundaries in nature and in society are conditional and changeable, that it would be absurd to argue, for example, about the particular year or decade in which imperialism "definitely" became established.

In the matter of defining imperialism, however, we have to enter into controversy, primarily, with K. Kautsky, the principal Marxian theoretician of the epoch of the so-called Second International—that is, of the 25 years between 1889 and 1914. The fundamental ideas expressed in our definition of imperialism were very resolutely attacked by Kautsky in 1915, and even in November 1914, when he said that imperialism must not be regarded as a "phase" or stage of economy, but as a policy, a definite policy "preferred" by finance capital; that imperialism must not be "identified" with "present-day capitalism"; that if imperialism is to be understood to mean "all the phenomena of present-day capitalism"—cartels, protection, the domination of the financiers, and colonial policy—then the question as to whether imperialism is necessary to capitalism becomes reduced to the "flattest tautology," because, in that case, "imperialism is naturally a vital necessity for capitalism," and so on. The best way to present Kautsky's idea is to quote his own definition of imperialism, which is diametrically opposed to the substance of the ideas which we have set forth (for the objections coming from the camp of the German Marxists, who have been advocating similar ideas for many years already, have been long known to Kautsky as the objections of a definite trend in Marxism).

Kautsky's definition is as follows:

> Imperialism is a product of highly developed industrial capitalism. It consists in the striving of every industrial capitalist nation to bring under its control or to annex larger and larger areas of *agrarian* (Kautsky's italics) territory, irrespective of what nations inhabit those regions.[1]

This definition is utterly worthless because it one-sidedly, i.e., arbitrarily, singles out only the national question (although the latter is extremely important in itself as well as in its relation to imperialism), it arbitrarily and *inaccurately* connects this question *only* with industrial capital in the countries which annex other nations, and in an equally arbitrary and inaccurate manner pushes into the forefront the annexation of agrarian regions.

Imperialism is a striving for annexations—this is what the *political* part of Kautsky's definition amounts to. It is correct, but very incomplete, for politically, imperialism is, in general, a striving toward violence and reaction. For the moment, however, we are interested in the *economic* aspect of the question, which Kautsky *himself* introduced into *his* definition. The inaccuracies in Kautsky's definition are glaring. The characteristic feature of imperialism is *not* industrial *but* finance capital. It is not an accident that in France it was precisely the extraordinarily rapid development of *finance* capital, and the weakening of industrial capital, that, from the 'eighties onwards, gave rise to the extreme intensification of annexationist (colonial) policy. The characteristic feature of imperialism is precisely that it strives to annex *not only* agrarian territories, but even most highly industrialized regions (German appetite for Belgium; French appetite for Lorraine), because 1) the fact that the world is already divided up obliges those contemplating a *redivision* to reach out for *every kind* of territory, and 2) an essential feature of imperialism is the rivalry between several Great Powers in the striving for hegemony, i.e., for the conquest of territory, not so much directly for themselves as to weaken the adversary and undermine *his* hegemony. (Belgium is particularly important for Germany as a base for operations against England; England needs Bagdad as a base for operations against Germany, etc.)

Kautsky refers especially—and repeatedly—to Englishmen who, he alleges, have given a purely political meaning to the word "imperialism" in the sense that he, Kautsky, understands it. We take up the work by the Englishman Hobson, *Imperialism*, which appeared in 1902, and there we read:

> The new imperialism differs from the older, first, in substituting for the ambition of a single growing empire the theory and the practice of competing empires, each motivated by similar lusts of political aggrandizement and commercial gain; secondly, in the dominance of financial or investing over mercantile interests.[2]

We see that Kautsky is absolutely wrong in referring to Englishmen generally (unless he meant the vulgar English imperialists, or the avowed apologists for imperialism). We see that Kautsky, while claiming that he continues to advocate Marxism, as a matter of fact takes a step backward compared with the *social-liberal* Hobson, who *more correctly* takes into account two "historically concrete" (Kautsky's definition is a mockery of historical concreteness!) features of modern imperialism: 1) the competition between *several* imperialisms, and 2) the predominance of the financier over the merchant. If it is chiefly a question of the annexation of agrarian countries by industrial countries, then the role of the merchant is put in the forefront.

Kautsky's definition is not only wrong and un-Marxian. It serves as a basis for a whole system of views which signify a rupture with Marxian theory and Marxian practice all along the line. We shall refer to this later. The argument about words which Kautsky raises as to whether the latest stage of capitalism should be called "imperialism" or "the stage of finance capital" is absolutely frivolous. Call it what you will, it makes no difference. The essence of the matter is that Kautsky detaches the politics of imperialism from its economics, speaks of annexations as being a policy "preferred" by finance capital, and opposes to it another bourgeois policy which, he alleges, is possible on this very same basis of finance capital. It follows, then, that monopolies in economics are compatible with non-monopolistic, non-violent, non-annexationist methods in politics. It follows, then, that the territorial division of the world, which was completed precisely during the epoch of finance capital, and which constitutes the basis of the present peculiar forms of rivalry between the biggest capitalist states, is compatible with a non-imperialist policy. The result is a slurring-over and a blunting of the most profound contradictions of the latest stage of capitalism, instead of an exposure of their depth; the result is bourgeois reformism instead of Marxism.

Kautsky enters into controversy with the German apologist of imperialism and annexations, Cunow, who clumsily and cynically argues that imperialism is present-day capitalism; the development of capitalism is inevitable and progressive; therefore imperialism is progressive; therefore, we should grovel before it and glorify it! This is something like the caricature of the Russian Marxists which the Narodniks drew in 1894–95. They argued: if the Marxists believe that capitalism is inevitable in Russia, that it is progressive, then they ought to open a tavern and begin to implant capitalism!

Kautsky's reply to Cunow is as follows: imperialism is not present-day capitalism; it is only one of the forms of the policy of present-day capitalism. This policy we can and should fight, fight imperialism, annexations, etc.

Notes

1. *Die Neue Zeit*, 1914, 2 (Vol. 32), p. 909, Sept. 11, 1914; cf. 1915, 2, p. 107 et seq.
2. Hobson, *Imperialism*, London, 1902, p. 324.

CHAPTER 19

Civilization and Its Discontents

Sigmund Freud

The existence of this inclination to aggression, which we can detect in ourselves and justly assume to be present in others, is the factor which disturbs our relations with our neighbour and which forces civilization into such a high expenditure [of energy]. In consequence of this primary mutual hostility of human beings, civilized society is perpetually threatened with disintegration. The interest of work in common would not hold it together; instinctual passions are stronger than reasonable interests. Civilization has to use its utmost efforts in order to set limits to man's aggressive instincts and to hold the manifestations of them in check by psychical reaction-formations. Hence, therefore, the use of methods intended to incite people into identifications and aim-inhibited relationships of love, hence the restriction upon sexual life, and hence too the ideal's commandment to love one's neighbour as oneself—a commandment which is really justified by the fact that nothing else runs so strongly counter to the original nature of man. In spite of every effort, these endeavours of civilization have not so far achieved very much. It hopes to prevent the crudest excesses of brutal violence by itself assuming the right to use violence against criminals, but the law is not able to lay hold of the more cautious and refined manifestations of human aggressiveness. The time comes when each one of us has to give up as illusions the expectations which, in his youth, he pinned upon his fellow-men, and when he may learn how much difficulty and pain has been added to his life by their ill-will. At the same time, it would be unfair to reproach civilization with trying to eliminate strife and competition from human activity. These things are undoubtedly indispensable. But opposition is not necessarily enmity; it is merely misused and made an *occasion* for enmity.

The communists believe that they have found the path to deliverance from our evils. According to them, man is wholly good and is well-disposed to his neighbour; but the institution of private property has corrupted his nature. The ownership of private wealth gives the individual power, and with it the temptation to ill-treat his neighbour; while the man who is excluded from possession is bound to rebel in hostility against his oppressor. If private property were abolished, all wealth held in common, and everyone allowed to share in the enjoyment of it, ill-will and hostility would disappear among men. Since everyone's needs would be satisfied, no one would have any reason to regard another as his enemy; all would willingly undertake the work that was necessary. I have no concern with any economic criticisms of the communist system; I cannot enquire into whether the abolition of private property is expedient or advantageous.[1] But I am able to recognize that the psychological premises on which the system is based are an untenable illusion. In abolishing private property we deprive the human love of aggression of one of its instruments, certainly a strong one, though certainly not the strongest; but we have in no way altered the differences in power and influence which are misused by aggressiveness, nor have we altered anything in its nature. Aggressiveness was not created by property. It reigned almost without limit in primitive times, when property was still very scanty, and it already shows itself in the nursery almost before property has given up its primal, anal form; it forms the basis of every relation of affection and love among people (with the single exception, perhaps, of the mother's relation to her male child). If we do away with personal rights over material wealth, there still remains prerogative in the field of sexual relationships, which is bound to become the source of the strongest dislike and the most violent hostility among men who in other respects are on an equal footing. If we were to remove this factor, too, by allowing complete freedom of sexual life and thus abolishing the family, the germ-cell of civilization, we cannot, it is true, easily foresee what new paths the development of civilization could take; but one thing we can expect, and that is that this indestructible feature of human nature will follow it there.

Note

1. Anyone who has tasted the miseries of poverty in his own youth and has experienced the indifference and arrogance of the well-to-do, should be safe from the suspicion of having no understanding or good will toward endeavours to fight against the inequality of wealth among men and all that it leads to. To be sure, if an attempt is made to base this fight upon an abstract demand, in the name of justice, for equality for all men, there is a very obvious objection to be made—that nature, by endowing individuals with extremely unequal physical attributes and mental capacities, has introduced injustices against which there is no remedy.

CHAPTER 20

On Contradiction

Mao Tse-Tung

August 1937

The law of contradiction in things, that is, the law of the unity of opposites, is the basic law of materialist dialectics. Lenin said, "Dialectics in the proper sense is the study of contradiction *in the very essence of objects*."[1] Lenin often called this law the essence of dialectics; he also called it the kernel of dialectics.[2] In studying this law, therefore, we cannot but touch upon a variety of questions, upon a number of philosophical problems. If we can become clear on all these problems, we shall arrive at a fundamental understanding of materialist dialectics. The problems are: the two world outlooks, the universality of contradiction, the particularity of contradiction, the principal contradiction and the principal aspect of a contradiction, the identity and struggle of the aspects of a contradiction, and the place of antagonism in contradiction.

The criticism to which the idealism of the Deborin school has been subjected in Soviet philosophical circles in recent years has aroused great interest among us. Deborin's idealism has exerted a very bad influence in the Chinese Communist Party, and it cannot be said that the dogmatist thinking in our Party is unrelated to the approach of that school. Our present study of philosophy should therefore have the eradication of dogmatist thinking as its main objective.

I. The Two World Outlooks

Throughout the history of human knowledge, there have been two conceptions concerning the law of development of the universe, the metaphysical conception and the dialectical conception, which form two opposing world outlooks. Lenin said:

> The two basic (or two possible? or two historically observable?) conceptions of development (evolution) are: development as decrease and increase, as repetition, *and* development as a unity of opposites (the division of a unity into mutually exclusive opposites and their reciprocal relation).[3]

Here Lenin was referring to these two different world outlooks.

In China another name for metaphysics is *hsuan-hsueh*. For a long period in history whether in China or in Europe, this way of thinking, which is part and parcel of the idealist world outlook, occupied a dominant position in human thought. In Europe, the materialism of the bourgeoisie in its early days was also metaphysical. As the social economy of many European countries advanced to the stage of highly developed capitalism, as the forces of production, the class struggle, and the sciences developed to a level unprecedented in history, and as the industrial proletariat became the greatest motive force in historical development, there arose the Marxist world outlook of materialist dialectics. Then, in addition to open and barefaced reactionary idealism, vulgar evolutionism emerged among the bourgeoisie to oppose materialist dialectics.

The metaphysical or vulgar evolutionist world outlook sees things as isolated, static, and one-sided. It regards all things in the universe, their forms and their species, as eternally isolated from one another and immutable. Such change as there is can only be an increase or decrease in quantity or a change of place. Moreover, the cause of such an increase or decrease or change of place is not inside things but outside them, that is, the motive force is external. Metaphysicians hold that all the different kinds of things in the universe and all their characteristics have been the same ever since they first came into being. All subsequent changes have simply been increases or decreases in quantity. They contend that a thing can only keep on repeating itself as the same kind of thing and cannot change into anything different. In their opinion, capitalist exploitation, capitalist competition, the individualist ideology of capitalist society, and so on, can all be found in ancient slave society, or even in primitive society, and will exist forever unchanged. They ascribe the causes of social development to factors external to society, such as geography and climate. They search in an over-simplified way outside a thing for the causes of its development, and they deny the theory of materialist dialectics which holds that development arises from the contradictions inside a thing. Consequently they can explain neither the qualitative diversity of things, nor the phenomenon of one quality changing into another. In Europe, this mode of thinking existed as mechanical materialism in the seventeenth and eighteenth centuries and as vulgar evolutionism at the end of the nineteenth and the beginning of the twentieth centuries. In China, there was the metaphysical thinking exemplified in the saying "Heaven changeth not, likewise the Tao changeth not,"[4] and it was supported by the decadent feudal ruling classes for a long time. Mechanical materialism and vulgar evolutionism, which were imported from Europe in the last hundred years, are supported by the bourgeoisie.

As opposed to the metaphysical world outlook, the world outlook of materialist dialectics holds that in order to understand the development of a thing we should study it internally and in its relations with other things; in other words, the development of things should be seen as their internal and necessary self-movement, while each thing in its movement is interrelated with and interacts on the things around it. The fundamental cause of the development of a thing is not external but internal; it lies in the contradictoriness within the thing. There is internal contradiction in every single thing, hence its motion and development. Contradictoriness within a thing is the fundamental cause of its development, while its interrelations and interactions with other things are secondary causes. Thus materialist dialectics effectively combats the theory of external causes, or of an external motive force, advanced by metaphysical mechanical materialism and vulgar evolutionism. It is evident that purely external causes can only give rise to mechanical motion, that is, to changes in scale or quantity, but cannot explain why things differ qualitatively in thousands of ways and why one thing changes into another. As a matter of fact, even mechanical motion under external force occurs through the internal contradictoriness of things. Simple growth in plants and animals, their quantitative development,

is likewise chiefly the result of their internal contradictions. Similarly, social development is due chiefly not to external but to internal causes. Countries with almost the same geographical and climatic conditions display great diversity and unevenness in their development. Moreover, great social changes may take place in one and the same country although its geography and climate remain unchanged. Imperialist Russia changed into the socialist Soviet Union, and feudal Japan, which had locked its doors against the world, changed into imperialist Japan, although no change occurred in the geography and climate of either country. Long dominated by feudalism, China has undergone great changes in the last hundred years and is now changing in the direction of a new China, liberated and free, and yet no change has occurred in her geography and climate. Changes do take place in the geography and climate of the earth as a whole and in every part of it, but they are insignificant when compared with changes in society; geographical and climatic changes manifest themselves in terms of tens of thousands of years, while social changes manifest themselves in thousands, hundreds, or tens of years, and even in a few years or months in times of revolution. According to materialist dialectics, changes in nature are due chiefly to the development of the internal contradictions in nature. Changes in society are due chiefly to the development of the internal contradictions in society, that is, the contradiction between the productive forces and the relations of production, the contradiction between classes and the contradiction between the old and the new; it is the development of these contradictions that pushes society forward and gives the impetus for the supersession of the old society by the new. Does materialist dialectics exclude external causes? Not at all. It holds that external causes are the condition of change and internal causes are the basis of change, and that external causes become operative through internal causes. In a suitable temperature an egg changes into a chicken, but no temperature can change a stone into a chicken, because each has a different basis. There is constant interaction between the peoples of different countries. In the era of capitalism, and especially in the era of imperialism and proletarian revolution, the interaction and mutual impact of different countries in the political, economic, and cultural spheres are extremely great. The October Socialist Revolution ushered in a new epoch in world history as well as in Russian history. It exerted influence on internal changes in the other countries in the world and, similarly and in a particularly profound way, on internal changes in China. These changes, however, were effected through the inner laws of development of these countries, China included. In battle, one army is victorious and the other is defeated; both the victory and the defeat are determined by internal causes. The one is victorious either because it is strong or because of its competent generalship, the other is vanquished either because it is weak or because of its incompetent generalship; it is through internal causes that external causes become operative. In China in 1927, the defeat of the proletariat by the big bourgeoisie came about through the opportunism then to be found within the Chinese proletariat itself (inside the Chinese Communist Party). When we liquidated this opportunism, the Chinese revolution resumed its advance. Later, the Chinese revolution again suffered severe setbacks at the hands of the enemy, because adventurism had risen within our Party. When we liquidated this adventurism, our cause advanced once again. Thus it can be seen that to lead the revolution to victory, a political party must depend on the correctness of its own political line and the solidity of its own organization.

The dialectical world outlook emerged in ancient times both in China and in Europe. Ancient dialectics, however, had a somewhat spontaneous and naive character; in the social and historical conditions then prevailing, it was not yet able to form a theoretical system, hence it could not fully explain the world and was supplanted by metaphysics. The famous German philosopher Hegel, who lived in the late eighteenth and early nineteenth centuries, made most important contributions to dialectics, but his dialectics was idealist. It was not until Marx and Engels, the great protagonists of the proletarian movement, had synthesized the positive achievements in the history of human knowledge and, in particular, critically absorbed the rational elements of Hegelian dialectics and created the great theory of dialectical and historical materialism that an unprecedented revolution occurred in the history of human knowledge. This theory was further developed by Lenin and Stalin. As soon as it spread to China, it wrought tremendous changes in the world of Chinese thought.

This dialectical world outlook teaches us primarily how to observe and analyze the movement of opposites in different things and, on the basis of such analysis, to indicate the methods for resolving contradictions. It is therefore most important for us to understand the law of contradiction in things in a concrete way.

[. . .]

VI. The Place of Antagonism in Contradiction

The question of the struggle of opposites includes the question of what is antagonism. Our answer is that antagonism is one form, but not the only form, of the struggle of opposites.

In human history, antagonism between classes exists as a particular manifestation of the struggle of opposites. Consider the contradiction between the exploiting and the exploited classes. Such contradictory classes co-exist for a long time in the same society, be it slave society, feudal society, or capitalist society, and they struggle with each other; but it is not until the contradiction between the two classes develops to a certain stage that it assumes the form of open antagonism and develops into revolution. The same holds for the transformation of peace into war in class society.

Before it explodes, a bomb is a single entity in which opposites co-exist in given conditions. The explosion takes place only when a new condition, ignition, is present. An analogous situation arises in all those natural phenomena which finally assume the form of open conflict to resolve old contradictions and produce new things.

It is highly important to grasp this fact. It enables us to understand that revolutions and revolutionary wars are inevitable in class society and that without them, it is impossible to accomplish any leap in social development and to overthrow the reactionary ruling classes and therefore impossible for the people to win political power. Communists must expose the deceitful propaganda of the reactionaries, such as the assertion that social revolution is unnecessary and impossible. They must firmly uphold the Marxist–Leninist theory of social revolution and enable the people to understand that social revolution is not only entirely necessary but also entirely practicable, and that the whole history of mankind and the triumph of the Soviet Union have confirmed this scientific truth.

However, we must make a concrete study of the circumstances of each specific struggle of opposites and should not arbitrarily apply the formula discussed above to everything. Contradiction and struggle are universal and absolute, but the methods of resolving contradictions, that is, the forms of struggle, differ according to the differences in the nature of the contradictions. Some contradictions are characterized by open antagonism, others are not. In accordance with the concrete development of things, some contradictions which were originally non-antagonistic develop into antagonistic ones, while others which were originally antagonistic develop into non-antagonistic ones.

As already mentioned, so long as classes exist, contradictions between correct and incorrect ideas in the Communist Party are reflections within the Party of class contradictions. At first, with regard to certain issues, such contradictions may not manifest themselves as antagonistic. But with the development of the class struggle, they may grow and become antagonistic. The history of the Communist Party of the Soviet Union shows us that the contradictions between the correct thinking of Lenin and Stalin and the fallacious thinking of Trotsky, Bukharin, and others did not at first manifest themselves in an antagonistic form, but that later they did develop into antagonism. There are similar cases in the history of the Chinese Communist Party. At first the contradictions between the correct thinking of many of our Party comrades and the fallacious thinking of Chen Tu-hsiu, Chang Kuo-tao, and others also did not manifest themselves in an antagonistic form, but later they did develop into antagonism. At present the contradiction between correct and incorrect thinking in our Party does not manifest itself in an antagonistic form, and if comrades who have committed mistakes can correct them, it will not develop into antagonism. Therefore, the Party must on the one hand wage a serious struggle against erroneous thinking, and on the other give the comrades who have committed errors ample opportunity to wake up. This being the case, excessive struggle is obviously inappropriate. But if the people who have committed errors persist in them and aggravate them, there is the possibility that this contradiction will develop into antagonism.

Economically, the contradiction between town and country is an extremely antagonistic one both in capitalist society, where under the rule of the bourgeoisie the towns ruthlessly plunder the countryside, and in the Kuomintang areas in China, where under the rule of foreign imperialism and the Chinese big comprador bourgeoisie the towns most rapaciously plunder the countryside. But in a socialist country and in our revolutionary base areas, this antagonistic contradiction has changed into one that is non-antagonistic; and when communist society is reached it will be abolished.

Lenin said, "Antagonism and contradiction are not at all one and the same. Under socialism, the first will disappear, the second will remain."[5] That is to say, antagonism is one form, but not the only form, of the struggle of opposites; the formula of antagonism cannot be arbitrarily applied everywhere.

Notes

1. V.I. Lenin, "Conspectus of Hegel's *Lectures on the History of Philosophy*," *Collected Works*, Russ. ed., Moscow, 1958, Vol. 38, p. 249.

2. In his essay "On the Question of Dialectics," Lenin said, "The splitting in two of a single whole and the cognition of its contradictory parts (see the quotation from Philo on Heraclitus at the beginning of Section 3 'On Cognition' in Lassalle's book on Heraclitus) is the *essence* (one of the 'essentials,' one of the principal, if not the principal, characteristics or features) of dialectics." (*Collected Works*, Russ. ed., Moscow, 1958, Vol. 38, p. 357.) In his "Conspectus of Hegel's *The Science of Logic*," he said, "In brief, dialectics can be defined as the doctrine of the unity of opposites. This grasps the kernel of dialectics, but it requires explanations and development." (Ibid., p. 215.)

3. V.I. Lenin, "On the Question of Dialectics," *Collected Works*, Russ. ed., Moscow, 1958, Vol. 38, p. 358.

4. A saying of Tung Chung-shu (179–104 BCE), a well-known exponent of Confucianism in the Han Dynasty.

5. V.I. Lenin, "Remarks on N.I. Bukharin's *Economics of the Transitional Period*," *Selected Works*, Russ. ed., Moscow-Leningrad, 1931, Vol. 11, p. 357.

CHAPTER 21

The Nationalities Question

Rosa Luxemburg

The Bolsheviks are in part responsible for the fact that the military defeat was transformed into the collapse and breakdown of Russia. Moreover, the Bolsheviks themselves have, to a great extent, sharpened the objective difficulties of this situation by a slogan which they placed in the foreground of their policies: the so-called right of self-determination of peoples, or—something which was really implicit in this slogan—the disintegration of Russia.

The formula of the right of the various nationalities of the Russian Empire to determine their fate independently "even to the point of the right of governmental separation from Russia," was proclaimed again with doctrinaire obstinacy as a special battle cry of Lenin and his comrades during their opposition against Miliukovist, and then Kerenskyan imperialism. It constituted the axis of their inner policy after the October Revolution also. And it constituted the entire platform of the Bolsheviks at Brest-Litovsk, all they had to oppose to the display of force by German imperialism.

One is immediately struck with the obstinacy and rigid consistency with which Lenin and his comrades stuck to this slogan, a slogan which is in sharp contradiction to their otherwise outspoken centralism in politics as well as to the attitude they have assumed toward other democratic principles. While they showed a quite cool contempt for the Constituent Assembly, universal suffrage, freedom of press and assemblage, in short, for the whole apparatus of the basic democratic liberties of the people which, taken all together, constituted the "right of self-determination" inside Russia, they treated the right of self-determination of peoples as a jewel of democratic policy for the sake of which all practical considerations of real criticism had to be stilled. While they did not permit themselves to be imposed upon in the slightest by the plebiscite for the Constituent Assembly in Russia, a plebiscite on the basis of the most democratic suffrage in the world, carried out in the full freedom of a popular republic, and while they simply declared this plebiscite null and void on the basis of a very sober evaluation of its results, still they championed the "popular vote" of the foreign nationalities of Russia on the question of which land they wanted to belong to, as the true palladium of all freedom and democracy, the unadulterated quintessence of the will of the peoples and as the court of last resort in questions of the political fate of nations.

The contradiction that is so obvious here is all the harder to understand since the democratic forms of political life in each land, as we shall see, actually involve the most valuable and even indispensable foundations of socialist policy, whereas the famous "right of self-determination of nations" is nothing but hollow, petty-bourgeois phraseology and humbug.

Indeed, what is this right supposed to signify? It belongs to the ABC of socialist policy that socialism opposes every form of oppression, including also that of one nation by another.

If, despite all this, such generally sober and critical politicians as Lenin and Trotsky and their friends, who have nothing but an ironical shrug for every sort of utopian phrase such as disarmament, league of nations, etc., have in this case made a hollow phrase of exactly the same kind into their special hobby, this arose, it seems to us, as a result of some kind of policy made to order for the occasion. Lenin and his comrades clearly calculated that there was no surer method of binding the many foreign peoples within the Russian Empire to the cause of the revolution, to the cause of the socialist proletariat, than that of offering them, in the name of the revolution and of socialism, the most extreme and most unlimited freedom to determine their own fate. This was analogous to the policy of the Bolsheviks toward the Russian peasants, whose land-hunger was satisfied by the slogan of direct seizure of the noble estates and who were supposed to be bound thereby to the banner of the revolution and the proletarian government. In both cases, unfortunately, the calculation was entirely wrong.

While Lenin and his comrades clearly expected that, as champions of national freedom even to the extent of "separation," they would turn Finland, the Ukraine, Poland, Lithuania, the Baltic countries, the Caucasus, etc., into so many faithful allies of the Russian Revolution, we have witnessed the opposite spectacle. One after another, these "nations" used the freshly granted freedom to ally themselves with German imperialism against the Russian Revolution as its mortal enemy, and, under German protection, to carry the banner of counter-revolution into Russia itself. The little game with the Ukraine at Brest, which caused a decisive turn of affairs in those negotiations and brought about the entire inner and outer political situation at present prevailing for the Bolsheviks, is a perfect case in point. The conduct of Finland, Poland, Lithuania, the Baltic lands, the peoples of the Caucasus, shows most convincingly that we are not dealing here with an exceptional case, but with a typical phenomenon.

To be sure, in all these cases, it was really not the "people" who engaged in these reactionary policies, but only the bourgeois and petty-bourgeois classes, who—in sharpest opposition to their own proletarian masses—perverted the "national right of self-determination" into an instrument of their counter-revolutionary class policies. But—and here we come to the very heart of the question—it is in this that the utopian, petty-bourgeois character of this nationalistic slogan resides: that in the midst of the crude realities of class society and when class antagonisms are sharpened to the uttermost, it is simply converted into a means of bourgeois class rule. The Bolsheviks were to be taught to their own great hurt and that of the revolution, that under the rule of capitalism there is no self-determination of peoples, that in a class society each class of the nation strives to "determine itself" in a different fashion, and that, for the bourgeois classes, the standpoint of national freedom is fully subordinated to that of class rule. The Finnish bourgeoisie, like the Ukrainian bourgeoisie, were unanimous in preferring the violent rule of Germany to national freedom, if the latter should be bound up with Bolshevism.

The hope of transforming these actual class relationships somehow into their opposite and of getting a majority vote for union with the Russian Revolution by depending on the revolutionary masses—if it was seriously meant by Lenin and Trotsky—represented an incomprehensible degree of optimism. And if it was only meant as a tactical flourish in the duel with the German politics of force, then it represented dangerous playing with fire. Even without German military occupation, the famous "popular plebiscite," supposing that it had come to

that in the border states, would have yielded a result, in all probability, which would have given the Bolsheviks little cause for rejoicing; for we must take into consideration the psychology of the peasant masses and of great sections of the petty bourgeoisie, and the thousand ways in which the bourgeoisie could have influenced the vote. Indeed, it can be taken as an unbreakable rule in these matters of plebiscites on the national question that the ruling class will either know how to prevent them where it doesn't suit their purpose, or where they somehow occur, will know how to influence their results by all sorts of means, big and little, the same means which make it impossible to introduce socialism by a popular vote.

The mere fact that the question of national aspirations and tendencies toward separation were injected at all into the midst of the revolutionary struggle, and were even pushed into the foreground and made into the shibboleth of socialist and revolutionary policy as a result of the Brest peace, has served to bring the greatest confusion into socialist ranks and has actually destroyed the position of the proletariat in the border countries.

In Finland, so long as the socialist proletariat fought as a part of the closed Russian revolutionary phalanx, it possessed a position of dominant power: it had the majority in the Finnish parliament, in the army; it had reduced its own bourgeoisie to complete impotence, and was master of the situation within its borders.

Or take the Ukraine. At the beginning of the century, before the tomfoolery of "Ukrainian nationalism" with its silver rubles and its "Universals" and Lenin's hobby of an "independent Ukraine" had been invented, the Ukraine was the stronghold of the Russian revolutionary movement. From there, from Rostov, from Odessa, from the Donetz region, flowed out the first lava-streams of the revolution (as early as 1902–04) which kindled all South Russia into a sea of flame, thereby preparing the uprising of 1905. The same thing was repeated in the present revolution, in which the South Russian proletariat supplied the picked troops of the proletarian phalanx. Poland and the Baltic lands have been since 1905 the mightiest and most dependable hearths of revolution, and in them the socialist proletariat has played an outstanding role.

How does it happen then that in all these lands the counter-revolution suddenly triumphs? The nationalist movement, just because it tore the proletariat loose from Russia, crippled it thereby, and delivered it into the hands of the bourgeoisie of the border countries.

Instead of acting in the same spirit of genuine international class policy which they represented in other matters, instead of working for the most compact union of the revolutionary forces throughout the area of the Empire, instead of defending tooth and nail the integrity of the Russian Empire as an area of revolution and opposing to all forms of separatism the solidarity and inseparability of the proletarians in all lands within the sphere of the Russian Revolution as the highest command of politics, the Bolsheviks, by their hollow nationalistic phraseology concerning the "right of self-determination to the point of separation," have accomplished quite the contrary and supplied the bourgeoisie in all border states with the finest, the most desirable pretext, the very banner of the counter-revolutionary efforts. Instead of warning the proletariat in the border countries against all forms of separatism as mere bourgeois traps, they did nothing but confuse the masses in all the border countries by their slogan and delivered them up to the demagogy of the bourgeois classes. By this nationalistic demand they brought on the disintegration of Russia itself, pressed into the enemy's hand the knife which it was to thrust into the heart of the Russian Revolution.

To be sure, without the help of German imperialism, without "the German rifle butts in German fists," as Kautsky's *Neue Zeit* put it, the Lubinskys and other little scoundrels of the Ukraine, the Erichs and Mannerheims of Finland, and the Baltic barons, would never have gotten the better of the socialist masses of the workers in their respective lands. But national separatism was the Trojan horse inside which the German "comrades," bayonet in hand, made their entrance into all those lands. The real class antagonisms and relations of military force brought about German intervention. But the Bolsheviks provided the ideology which masked this campaign of counter-revolution; they strengthened the position of the bourgeoisie and weakened that of the proletariat.

The best proof is the Ukraine, which was to play so frightful a role in the fate of the Russian Revolution. Ukrainian nationalism in Russia was something quite different from, let us say, Czechish, Polish, or Finnish nationalism in that the former was a mere whim, a folly of a few dozen petty-bourgeois intellectuals without the slightest roots in the economic, political, or psychological relationships of the country; it was without any historical tradition, since the Ukraine never formed a nation or government, was without any national culture, except for the reactionary-romantic poems of Shevschenko. It is exactly as if, one fine day, the people living in the *Wasserkante*[1] should want to found a new Low-German (*Plattdeutsche*) nation and government! And this ridiculous pose of a few university professors and students was inflated into a political force by Lenin and his comrades through their doctrinaire agitation concerning the "right of self-determination including etc." To what was at first a mere farce they lent such importance that the farce became a matter of the most deadly seriousness—not as a serious national movement for which, afterward as before, there are no roots at all, but as a shingle and rallying flag of counter-revolution! At Brest, out of this addled egg crept the German bayonets.

There are times when such phrases have a very real meaning in the history of class struggles. It is the unhappy lot of socialism that in this World War it was given to it to supply the ideological screens for counter-revolutionary policy. At the outbreak of the war, German Social-Democracy hastened to deck the predatory expedition of German imperialism with an ideological shield from the lumber-room of Marxism by declaring it to be a liberating expedition against Russian Czarism, such as our old teachers (Marx and Engels) had longed for. And to the lot of the Bolsheviks, who were the very antipodes of our government socialists, did it fall to supply grist for the mill of counter-revolution with their phrases about self-determination of peoples; and thereby to supply not alone the ideology for the strangling of the Russian Revolution itself, but even for the plans for settling the entire crisis arising out of the World War.

We have good reason to examine very carefully the policies of the Bolsheviks in this regard. The "right of self-determination of peoples," coupled with the league of nations and disarmament by the grace of President Wilson, constitute the battle-cry under which the coming reckoning of international socialism with the bourgeoisie is to be settled. It is obvious that the phrases concerning self-determination and the entire nationalist movement, which at present constitute the greatest danger for international socialism, have experienced an extraordinary strengthening from the Russian Revolution and the Brest negotiations. We shall yet have to go into this platform thoroughly. The tragic fate of these phrases in the Russian Revolution, on the thorns of which the Bolsheviks were themselves destined to be caught and bloodily scratched, must serve the international proletariat as a warning and lesson.

And from all this there followed the dictatorship of Germany from the time of the Brest treaty to the time of the "supplementary treaty." The two hundred expiatory sacrifices in Moscow. From this situation arose the terror and the suppression of democracy.

Note

1. A region in Germany where the German dialect known as *Plattdeutsch* is spoken.

CHAPTER 22

Marxism and International Law

B.S. Chimni

I. Introduction

International law is today playing an unprecedented role in creating and congealing inequities in the international system. The period after the Second World War has witnessed the exponential growth of international law.[1] No longer confined to questions of war and peace or diplomacy, international law has, on the one hand, come to govern the use of oceans and outer space, and on the other, regulate core aspects of national economic, social, and cultural life. Recent years in particular have seen the adoption of a network of laws which seek to establish the legal and institutional framework favourable to the accumulation of capital in the era of globalization.

Generally speaking, three overlapping features can be said to mark the growth of international law in the last two decades. First, it is the principle instrument through which the rule of private property is being extended in the world economy. Second, it is the means through which the rights of transnational capital are being safeguarded, among other things, by prescribing uniform global standards—ignoring the phenomenon of uneven development—in key areas such as technology and foreign investment. Third, it guarantees the observance of these standards through endowing international institutions with the means to enforce them.

But despite the critical role international law has come to play in building and sustaining the contemporary international system Marxists have entirely neglected its study.[2] While an attempt was made in the former Soviet Union to articulate a Marxist approach to international law, its content was dictated less by Marxism-Leninism than by the need to rationalize Soviet foreign policy.[3] The principle task of Soviet international lawyers was seen as providing post facto justifications for the acts of omission and commission of the state in its external relations. No serious effort was undertaken to engage with bourgeois international legal scholarship in order to highlight the distinctive nature of the Marxist approach. Consequently, the field of international law still represents a wasteland insofar as Marxism is concerned. In this essay we make a preliminary attempt to fill the gap in the literature by reflecting on the condition of international law and institutions at the end of the twentieth century.

[. . .]

III. Globalization and International Law-I

International law and institutions are today being transformed to facilitate the process of globalisation. Globalization may be said to refer "to the shift of the principal venue of capital accumulation from the nation-state to the global arena" [Teeple 1997:15].[4] There is, as Teeple points out, "an historical parallel to the present shift":

> The development of national forms of capital in the 18th and 19th centuries required the destruction of local and regional jurisdictions. Numerous differences in laws, standards, currencies, weights and measures, taxes, customs duties, political and religious rights and privileges made trade and commerce over a large geographic area extremely difficult. Just as these barriers to the expansion of capital had to be overcome to make the modern nation-state, so today the systems of governance in the nation-state have to be dismantled in order to remove the barriers to accumulation for global corporations. It follows that laws, regulations, standards, and governing agencies since World War II have been and continue to be reconstituted at the global level. [Teeple 1997:16]

Since the early 1980s, the advanced capitalist world has, under the guidance of the hegemonic transnationalized fractions of its national bourgeoisies, and with the assistance of the transnationalized fractions of national capital in the third world, pushed through a series of changes in international economic law which lay the legal foundation for capital accumulation in the era of globalization [Robinson 1996:13–31]. These changes appear to have two principal objectives: (i) to extend and deepen worldwide the rule of capital through the removal of "local" impediments; and (ii) to dismantle international laws of distribution which are based on the principle of market intervention. We identify below the different measures which have been taken in the world of international law to translate these objectives into reality.

(A) Extending and Deepening
the Reign of Capital

A series of developments in the past two decades have sought to deepen and extend the reign of capital.

First, reference may be made to the privatization of the public sector in the third world. This objective is being achieved through the instrument of international monetary law which legitimizes and enforces conditionalities imposed by international financial institutions.[5] As has been pointed out, "forced privatization was the standard feature of all structural adjustment programmes" [Hoogvelt 1997:138, 172]. By 1992 more than 80 countries around the world had privatized some 6,800 previously state-owned enterprises, mostly monopoly suppliers of essential public services like water, electricity, or telephones [Hoogvelt 1997:138].[6]

Second, a growing network of international laws seeks to free transnational capital of all spatial and temporal constraints. The trend towards strengthening the rights of foreign capital, initiated in the mid-1970s (the move from nationalism to pragmatism), continues unabated [. . .].

Third, the global technology regime has been privatized.[7] The adoption of Agreement on Trade related Intellectual Property Rights (hereafter the TRIPs Text) as a part of the GATT Final Act has been a crucial step in this regard with its preamble baldly stating that "intellectual property rights are private rights". There is little justification for such a pronouncement. Indeed, a review of the literature on intellectual property rights (IPRs) reveals that such a view is difficult to sustain [Chimni 1994:315–33].

[. . .]

Fourth, the global commons have been subjected to the process of privatization. Consider the developments in the Law of the Sea which regulates the use of the oceans. In 1982, after a decade of negotiations, the Third United Nations Conference adopted the Law of the Sea Convention. It was widely welcomed by the international community—despite the skepticism of some of us—as a legal regime which was fair to all the participants. Under the convention the principle of common heritage of (hu)mankind applies to the non-living resources of the ocean floor and its subsoil beyond the limits of the Exclusive Economic Zone (extending to 200 miles) and the Continental Shelf. It is to be operationalized through a parallel regime which requires (vide Article 153) every exploitable site to be divided into two parts, one for the mining company that has made a claim, and the other for UN's Enterprise, the operational arm of the International Sea-Bed Authority established by the convention. Writing in 1982 we had contended that the revolutionary concept of common heritage of mankind harboured reactionary content as it essentially envisaged the private exploitation of the resources of the seabed beyond national jurisdiction [Chimni 1982:407–12]. [. . .]

Fifth, the idea of the global commons is sought to be extended by the industrialized world to the environment, including resources (e.g., forests) which are located within the territory of third world countries [Imber 1994:58ff]. In addressing the issue intertemporal considerations are not given due weight implying a change in the distribution of property rights to the detriment of the third world countries. For "as industrial countries developed, global private rights were granted to polluters; now, developing countries are asked to agree to a redistribution of those property rights without compensation for already depleted resources" [Uimonen and Whalley 1997:66]. This "redistribution" of course goes hand in hand with an

IPR regime which makes environment friendly technology costly to access. On the other hand, there is a push to universalize northern regulatory norms since they promote the interests of transnational capital: the leading 50 environmental corporations in the world are located in the advanced capitalist countries [for details see Pratt and Montgomery 1997:75–96].

Sixth, there have been established alternative dispute settlement mechanisms which seek to eliminate the role of national courts in resolving disputes between TNCs and the state. Today, international commercial arbitration is the preferred mode of settling disputes for TNCs. Since the late 1970s there has been a tremendous growth in the number of arbitration centres, arbitrators, and arbitrations [Dezelay and Garth 1996]. "By the mid-1980s," according to a close observer, "it had become recognized that arbitration was the normal way of settlement of international commercial disputes" [Lalive 1995:2]. International commercial arbitration, it needs to be underlined, is essentially a private interests regime in which parties have "autonomy" in terms of the selection of the arbitrators, the substantial law to be applied, and the place of arbitration. Support for it rests on a certain assumption of the proper sphere of state activities. In fact it reproduces the public/private divide in international law. Community policy comes into play only at the time of enforcement of an award and that too in the exceptional circumstance that the "public policy" of a state has been violated, a concept increasingly narrowly interpreted. While, without doubt, international commercial arbitration has a significant role to play in routine cases involving international business transactions, it is not a suitable method for resolving disputes in core areas of national economic life like, for example, the exploration and exploitation of natural resources [Sornarajah 1991:79].

[. . .]

(B) Remaking the International Laws of Distribution

Accompanying the network of laws which extend and deepen the reign of capital have been attacks on principles and agreements which attempted to inject, as a part of the effort to usher in a NIEO, the traditional international law of distribution with elements of equity and justice. Two examples would suffice. First, is the rejection of the special and differential treatment (SDT) principle which calls for preferential treatment to be given to third world countries.

[. . .]

Second, dating from the arrival of the Reagan and Thatcher administrations in the US and UK respectively, an all-out attack was launched on international commodity agreements (ICAs) whose primary aim is to stabilize the prices of primary commodities by intervening in the world market through the use of export quotas and/or buffer stock mechanisms [Chimni 1987:ch 3]. It may be recalled that the NIEO program of action had recommended the "expeditious formulation of commodity agreements" and CERDS had stated that "it is the duty of states to contribute to the development of international trade in goods" through concluding ICAs [ibid:3–4]. These instruments were however represented by the Reagan and Thatcher administrations as distorting free markets. The timing of the offensive was impeccable. It came at a point when primary commodity prices were at the lowest since the great depression.[8] The unfortunate collapse of the Fifth International Tin Agreement in 1985 was used to completely discredit the instrument of ICAs disregarding their role in ensuring a more equal distribution of gains from the sale of raw materials, as also the fact that the idea of free market was a myth [ibid:197–212]. What the industrialized world wanted to ensure was that prices of primary commodities remained low through staving off intervention in markets through ICAs.

[. . .]

VII. Conclusion

The aim of this paper was to draw attention to the crucial role international law and institutions have come to play in the contemporary international system. With capitalism entering the phase of globalization international law is playing a role akin to the one which internal law performed in the early stages of capitalism in removing local impediments to the process of accumulation. The international legal process is being used to control the content of national laws in crucial areas of economic, political, and social life, as also to relocate powers from sovereign states to international institutions in order to facilitate their surveillance and enforcement. These developments have considerably eroded the capacity of third world states to carry out independent and self-reliant development.

For a period of time in the 1970s there was optimism that international laws could be transformed by a global coalition of third world countries to meet their particular concerns. An equitable international law of distribution was sought to be shaped through the adoption of the SDT principle and by promoting ICAs to realize just prices. Negotiations were also initiated to draft codes of conduct to regulate TNCs and the transfer of technology, and to revise the Paris convention on industrial property. Radical concepts such as the "common heritage of mankind" were advanced in the process of arriving at rules to govern the use of the oceans. Attempts were made to democratize the decision-making process in the IMF and the World Bank. But these initiatives floundered on the rock of neo-colonialism. Form the beginning of the 1980s, an increasingly hostile international economic environment saw the third world countries abandon the strategy of global coalition, hoping to separately encash their dependent status.

Meanwhile, capitalism entered the phase of globalization. It was now the turn of the advanced capitalist countries to seek changes in the body of international law. These changes involved, first, the rejection of the proposals which had emerged in the 1970s in the form of a program and declaration of action on NIEO and CERDS. Second, it called for the adoption of legal instruments to free transnational capital of spatial and temporal constraints. Third, an international law of distribution based on market ethics was given shape, eliminating all chances of injecting equity into international economic relations. Fourth, changes were initiated in the relevant international legal regime to enable the strict control of voluntary and forced migration. Fifth, international state apparatuses were sought to be established to ensure the effective implementation of the rules which facilitate and promote accumulation in the era of globalization.

These changes in the body of international law reflect the domination of the transnationalized fractions of the bourgeoisie in the advanced capitalist countries. They have in this regard the active consent of their counterparts in the third world. The latter not only faithfully act as transmission belts for the ideas emerging from the advanced capitalist world but vigorously support it in a bid to profit from becoming junior partners in the global domination project. At the receiving end are the working classes and disadvantaged groups in the first and the third worlds. Their condition has seriously worsened in the last two decades.[9] On the other hand, as a result of the relocation of powers from nation-states to international institutions, the capacity of the left and democratic movements to resist developments which adversely affect their interests has declined [Robinson 1996:27]. If the global progressive forces hope to interrupt and thwart the reproduction of the relations of transnational domination then they must, among other things, think of ways and means to enhance their own role in the international law-making and law enforcement process. This calls for much greater attention to be paid to international legal developments than is being done at present. The international legal strategy must in turn form an integral part of a transnational counter-hegemonic project which, even as it continues to have its principal base in national struggles, comes to form transnational alliances in order to resist the vision of globalized capitalism.

Notes

1. "Perhaps the most important of the revolutions in the dimension of modern international law lies in its expanding scope, in the addition of new subjects to the field of international law" [Friedmann 1968].

2. Seven decades ago, in his preface to the second Russian edition of his book on law and Marxism, Pashukanis [1978:38] wrote that " . . . the Marxist critique has not even touched on such fields as that of international law yet." The situation is no different today.

3. For a critique of the Soviet International Law approach as articulated by its chief spokesman G.I. Tunkin in the period after the Second World War see Chimni [1993:chapter V].

4. We recognize that "globalization" is an essentially contested concept [Hirst and Thompson 1995; Hoogvelt 1997]. What we adopt here is a working definition which highlights its general feature.

5. It is often forgotten that the IMF/WB combine achieve their goals through imposing legal obligations on states. International Monetary Law has evolved through, among other things, the interpretation of the Articles of Agreement of the IMF. According to Dam [1982:117], "the history of interpretation of the Fund's Articles of Agreement is nothing more, and nothing less, than the record of the rules of the Fund." He then goes on to point out that "perhaps the most interesting evolution has occurred with respect to those rules dealing with access to Fund resources and, in particular, what has come to be known in Fund parlance as 'conditionality.' That term refers to the conditions that the Fund may impose on access to its resources and on their subsequent use by member countries." See also Gold [1984]. At a later point in this article we discuss the anti-democratic nature of the decision-making process in the IMF.

6. Hoogvelt [1997:172] cites one senior World Bank manager who resigned after 12 years as stating: "Everything we did from 1983 onwards was based on our new sense of mission to have the south 'privatized' or die: toward this end we ignominiously created economic bedlam in Latin America and Africa."

7. This is in contrast to the view that "technology is the archetypal common heritage of mankind since it is the expression of man's spirit, his boldness and his conquests, of the advance of science and human knowledge over the centuries and beyond state boundaries" [Bedjaoui 1979:231].

8. " . . . the general level of real commodity prices had fallen by 1986 to below the nadir reached in 1932 during the Great Depression of the interwar era" [Maizels 1994:53].

9. See the annual Human Development Reports in this regard.

References

Bedjaoui, Mohammed (1979): *Towards a New International Economic Order*, Holmes and Meir Publishers, New York.

Chimni, B.S. (1982): "Law of the Sea: Imperialism All the Way," *Economic and Political Weekly*, Vol. 17, No. 11, March 13.

——(1987): *International Commodity Agreements: A Legal Study*, Croom Helm, London.

——(1993): *International Law and World Order: A Critique of Contemporary Approaches*, Sage, New Delhi.

——(1994): "Hard Patent Regime Completely Unjustifiable" in S.R. Chowdhury, E.M.G. Denters, and Paul J.I.M. de Waart (eds). *The Right to Development in International Law*, Martinus Nijhoff Publishers, Dordrecht, pp. 315–33.

Dam, W. Kenneth (1982): *The Rules of the Game: Reform and Evolution of the International*

Monetary System, The University of Chicago Press, Chicago.

Dezelay, Y., and B. Garth (1996): *Dealing in Virtue: International Commercial Arbitration and the Construction of a Transnational Legal Order*. The University of Chicago Press, Chicago.

Friedmann, Wolfgang (1968): *The Changing Structure of International Law*, Columbia University Press, Columbia.

Gold, Joseph (1984): *Legal and Institutional Aspects of the International Monetary System*, IMF, Washington, DC.

Hirst, Paul, and Grahame Thompson (1995): *Globalisation in Question*. Polity Press, Cambridge.

Hoogvelt, Ankie (1997): *Globalisation and the Postcolonial World: The New Political Economy of Development*, Macmillan Press, London.

Imber, Mark F. (1994): *Environment, Security and UN Reform*, St Martin's Press, New York.

Lalive, Pierre, cited in W.L. Craig (1995): "Some Trends and Developments in the Laws and Practice of International Commercial Arbitration," *Texas International Law Journal*, Vol. 30, No. 1, winter, pp. 1–59.

Maizels, Alfred (1994): "Commodity Market Trends and Instabilities: Policy Options for Developing Countries" in *UNCTAD Review*, UN, New Delhi.

Pashukanis, B. Evgeny (1978): *Law and Marxism: A General Theory*, Ink Links, London.

Pratt, Larry, and Wendy Montgomery (1997): "Green Imperialism: Pollution, Penitence, Profits," *Socialist Register*, 1997.

Robinson, I. William (1996): "Gloablisation: Nine These[s] on Our Epoch." *Race and Class*, Vol. 38: pp. 13–31.

Sornarajah, M. (1991): "The Climate of International Arbitration," *Journal of International Arbitration*, Vol. 8, No. 2, pp. 47–86.

Teeple, Gary (1997): "Globalisation as the Triumph of Capitalism: Private Property, Economic Justice and the New World Order" in Ted Schrecker (ed.), *Surviving Globalism: The Social and Environmental Challenges*, Macmillan Press, Wiltshire, pp. 15–38.

Uimonen, P., and J. Whalley (1997): *Environmental Issues in the New Trading Systems*, Macmillan Press, London.

Critical Thinking Questions

1. What is the universal source of historical change as Marx and Engels describe it? Marx and Engels identify the bourgeoisie and the proletariat as the central antagonists of their "epoch." How relevant does this assessment remain today? What is the role of the modern state, as Marx and Engels describe it? Do you agree?

2. What is Lenin's shorthand definition of imperialism? Lenin offers his definition as he attacks Karl Kautsky's alternative definition as inaccurate and incomplete. What are the differences between the competing definitions? Which do you find more convincing? Review the basic elements of imperialism as the highest (and final) stage of capitalism as explained by Lenin. Based on your reading, what is the likelihood that capitalism would ever reach this threshold, if it has not already?

3. How does Freud assess the proposed abolishment of private property as advocated by Marxism? Do you agree with his diagnosis? What is Freud's view about

Marxism's larger ambition to forge a society free of material conflict and competition? How might he have reached this view? What is your assessment of this view?

4. Mao's description of dialectic materialism identifies "internal contradictions" as the primary instigators of social progress. Identify two indispensable elements of this progress. Mao encourages his readers to study the "law of contradiction" at the heart of his dialectical world outlook. Why?

5. According to Luxemburg, how did leaders of the Bolshevik Revolution such as Lenin and Trotsky among others end up handing their various enemies the very "knife" aimed at the heart of the same revolution? Why does Luxemburg accuse Lenin and Trotsky of naivety and, worse, hypocrisy on matters of national self-determination? What is Luxemburg's view of nationalism?

6. According to Chimni, how does international law facilitate globalization? Identify some of the institutions that play a prominent role in this process. Which broad characteristics do they share? What does Chimni recommend toward the end of the selection?

Biographies

Karl Marx (1818–1883)

A disciple of German philosopher Hegel (1770–1831), Marx turned into the high priest of the ideology bearing his name after the upheavals of the 1840s radicalized him. The Prussian government forced Marx to flee his native Rhineland for the then-capital of capitalism—London—where he gained liberty in exchange for a crushing poverty that denied him and his family basic comforts. Sustained financially and otherwise by a small but devoted circle of lifetime supporters, including collaborator Friedrich Engels (1820–1895), he overcame these conditions through effort and energy to publish countless manuscripts on political economy and social theory. This collection—which *Das Kapital* crowns—remains as relevant and controversial today. For some, it has the status of divine Scripture; for others, it is nothing less than an evil spectre.

Friedrich Engels (1820–1895)

The son of a wealthy industrialist, Engels became an advocate for the working class after a trip to England in the early 1840s had exposed him to the plight of the proletariat. While Engels had already met Karl Marx before travelling to England, the experience drew Engels ever closer to Marx, with whom he shared a growing antagonism toward authority and an affinity for the dialectic of Hegel (1770–1831). This relationship with Marx reached an early climax in 1848 when the two men co-published *The Communist Manifesto*, with Engels clearly the junior partner in terms of his contributions. But Marxism might not have had the intellectual reach, had it not been for Engels, a tireless publisher whose engaging writing style reflects his early literary ambitions. Not only did Engels sharpen the theories of Marx, he also extended them into subjects beyond economics, while remaining Marx's most faithful disciple.

Vladimir Ilyich Ulyanov Lenin (1870–1924)

As Winston Churchill suggested, Lenin might well have been the best and worst thing that ever happened to millions of people inside and outside of Russia, where he was born into the ruling aristocracy. Nobody would deny that he soaked his hands in blood, first as leader of the Bolshevik Revolution (1917) that ended centuries of Romanov rule, then as principal defender of the new tyranny as it struggled for survival during the ensuing civil war (1917–1922). Nor would anyone question the analytical skills and practical abilities that allowed Lenin to succeed in situations where others would have failed. He nearly always knew what was to be done. This penchant for perseverance transformed Lenin into an icon for revolutionaries around the world. Ultimately, Lenin proved Marx wrong. He turned a feudal-agrarian country into the inaugural testing site for proletarian rule, an improvement by some measure, but far, far removed from the utopian idealism informing Marxism, in light of the horrors that befell the newly formed Soviet Union after his death.

Sigmund Freud (1856–1939)

The now clichéd image of Freud (but not necessarily his work) has become an unquestioned part of modern Western thought. While few would deny the influence Freud exerted on the twentieth century through his groundbreaking work in the field of psychoanalysis, many would reject the soundness and empirical rigour of his "discoveries" about the role of sexuality in shaping human behaviour. Notwithstanding this contemporary and not undeserving criticism, classic titles such as *The Interpretation of Dreams* remain much read. Freud also achieved a sterling reputation as a critic of his times, particularly on religious matters, during his life. It began in the illusionary splendour of the declining Habsburg Empire in what is now the Czech Republic only to end in the cold comfort of his British exile after Nazi Germany had annexed Austria (1938). A heavy smoker, Freud committed assisted suicide that spared him the pain of learning that much of his extended family fell victim to the madness of the Holocaust.

Mao Tse-Tung (1893–1976)

Mao, like Lenin, often strayed from the theoretical precepts of Marxism to serve his often-disastrous agenda of transforming an agrarian state into a global power. Born as the son of a peasant, Mao participated as a soldier in the republican revolution that ended imperial rule in China, then discovered Marxism during university. Rising through the ranks of China's communist party during the Warlord Era (1916–1928), Mao's star ironically rose during a military defeat, the Long March (1934–1935), as communist forces retreated into northern China in the face of the superior Nationalist army under Mao's principal adversary, General Chiang Kai-shek (1887–1975). While the two sides forged a temporary alliance during the Second Sino-Japanese War (1937–1945), Mao's leadership ensured communist control of Mainland China in the aftermath of the war. The Great Leap Forward (1958–1961), the Cultural Revolution (1966–1976), and the visit of US President Richard Nixon (1972) stand among the defining events of the Mao era, which set the stage for China's rise at the cost of millions of lives lost through famine and political violence.

Rosa Luxemburg (1871–1919)

Conflicts and contradictions defined the life of Luxemburg who often stood between places, geographically and politically. Born to Polish parents in what was at the time Czarist Russia, Luxemburg showed early promise as an organizer, as she sought Polish independence through the global overthrow of capitalism. This position put her at odds with Lenin (1870–1924), who viewed nationalism as a necessary precursor to the decline of capitalism. Luxemburg, who eventually moved to Germany, also broke with the militarism of the German Social Democratic Party, which had embraced the nationalist agenda of the Prussian aristocracy leading to World War I. This position turned Luxemburg and follow communist Wilhelm Liebknecht (1871–1919) into targets for *Freikorps* members, who murdered the pair during the early, violent days of the Weimar Republic. Luxemburg's legacy has primarily lived on in Germany, where opponents of the former East German state once used one of her quotations to embarrass the communist regime. The quotation might well be a *leitmotif* for Luxemburg: "Freedom is always and exclusively freedom for the one who thinks differently."

B.S. Chimni (1952–)

"The threat of recolonization is haunting the third world." So opens the manifesto, which B.S. Chimni penned in 2006 on behalf of scholars who survey international law from the varied perspectives of the developing world. While this multi-dimensional prism owes an obvious intellectual debt to Karl Marx, Chimni is much more than just a mere recycler of well-worn Marxian rhetoric. His prominent guest lectures and prestigious appointments to world-leading universities (Harvard Law) as well as institutions (United Nations) identify Chimni as one of the most important scholars of international law, whether or not one agrees with his ideological positions. Indeed, it might not be a stretch to suggest that Chimni might be on par with Marx himself, at least in one way. Whereas Marx had the ability to admire and admonish capitalism in the same context, Chimni has reached the conclusion that international law might well offer the worst and best hope for the third world to break its social, political, and economic chains.

Part V

Democratic Socialism

Democratic Socialism

Democratic socialism places considerable weight upon not just political and civil equality but also social and economic equality, especially when thought of in terms of parity of opportunities people have to fulfill themselves. Typically, democratic socialists attempt to combine freedom and equality in one world; absent this, as R.H. Tawney maintains, "freedom for the pike is death for the minnow." Originating in continental Europe and Britain in the mid-nineteenth century, this ideology in a very significant way helped bring about the establishment of the welfare state with all its safety nets for unemployment, health, and retirement. Democratic socialism played an active role in Europe and elsewhere in tempering the effects of the Great Depression from 1929 onward. More recently, it has been under attack from the unrelenting pressures of neo-liberalism.

Major Figures

Henri de Saint-Simon (1760–1825), Robert Owen (1771–1858), Charles Fourier (1772–1837), Eduard Bernstein (1850–1932), R.H. Tawney (1880–1962), Tommy Douglas (1904–1986), Stuart Hampshire (1914–2004), Alec Nove (1915–1994), C.A.R. Crosland (1918–1977), Peter Self (1919–1999), Anthony Giddens (1938–), and Linda McQuaig (1951–)

Period of Greatest Influence

1830 to 1995

Introduction

By the middle of the nineteenth century, democratic socialism in Europe had become an ideology with which to be reckoned. It, along with reform liberalism and Marxism, exploded on the scene. What differentiates democratic socialism from reform liberalism is the role that social and economic inequalities play. Democratic socialists tend to emphasize economic and social rights, while reform liberals—though giving a nodding endorsement to these rights—tend to emphasize political and civil rights. As for what differentiates democratic socialism from Marxism, one can say that the former decries the use of violence to bring about equality, while the latter openly endorses it in the form of the proletarian revolution.

While there is some advantage to starting any discussion of democratic socialism with Robert Owen (1771–1858) because of his efforts to blunt the hard edge of capitalism in his cotton factory at New Lanark, Scotland, and even further advantage to starting the discussion with Eduard Bernstein (1850–1932) because of his analytical and critical thinking, there is more to be gained by beginning with R.H. Tawney (1880–1962) and his nuanced treatment of economic equality in the building of a just society. So it is to Tawney that we turn.

The Methodist-educated English economic historian R.H. Tawney is inspired by the watchwords of the French Revolution: liberty, equality, and fraternity—with a strong emphasis on the first two of these. His commitment to socialist principles rooted in his Christian beliefs leads Tawney to classify communities by their economic and social structure—a classification that allows him to distinguish between communities where economic initiative is widely diffused and class differences small and trivial, and those where the majority exercise little influence on the economic enterprise and class differences are great. Tawney believes in light of this inequality that the extension of liberty from the political to the economic sphere is among the most urgent tasks of industrial societies and that this extension makes the traditional opposition between liberty and equality untenable. Noting that "freedom for the pike is death for the minnow," Tawney maintains that equality is not to be contrasted with liberty but only with a particular interpretation of it. Shunning the belief in liberty as consisting exclusively in security against government oppression, Tawney embraces a belief in liberty that places restraint on the strong, on the rich, and the gifted. It is this view of liberty that he sees as compatible with equality.

It was not just in Europe and Britain that social democratic ideas had traction. They also had traction in what was known in 1933 as the Dominion of Canada (since changed officially to simply "Canada"). Under the influence of the League for Social Reconstruction (LSR)—an organization that embraced individuals such as Frank Underhill, Frank Scott, Eugene Forsey, Harry Cassidy, Graham Spry, and Irene Bliss—the Co-Operative Commonwealth Federation (CCF), a democratic socialist political party, issued a manifesto, the *Regina Manifesto* by name. The CCF Party itself could claim membership from the likes of Tommy Douglas, David Lewis, M.J. Coldwell, and J.S. Woodsworth. This was the party of the *Regina Manifesto*, influenced as it was by the LSR. The contents of this document are as clear as they are bold and different from the classical liberalism of Adam Smith and John Locke, and indeed quite distinguishable from the reform liberalism of Dewey and Keynes. The document lays down a social and economic blueprint for Canada that includes among other things: a planned socialized economic order, effective control of banking and currency, a national labour code, socialized health services, and a new taxation policy to lessen glaring inequalities of income and to provide social services. What the *Regina Manifesto* presents are ideas very much in the spirit of Bernstein and Tawney, but decidedly more focused. Here, the *Regina Manifesto* acts like a blueprint for a social democratic ideology.

A more contemporary interpretation of democratic socialism is provided by Peter Self (1919–1999), who was Emeritus Professor at the London School of Economics and Professor at the Australian National University. On the basis of his wide experience in public administration (consultant to the OECD, chair of leading voluntary bodies, and chair of government committees in Britain and Australia), Self rejects neo-liberal and libertarian values and instead advances arguments in favour of particular interpretations of equality and liberty. With respect to the first of these, he supports egalitarianism that embraces "equal moral worth to each individual." With respect to the second of these, he supports a balance "between the pulls of private freedom to lead one's own life, and a social responsibility to contribute to the common good." However, Self does not restrict his democratic socialist thinking to the foregoing socialists values, but advances ideas that would make for a democracy "on the march." These ideas are three-fold: the workings of democracy should be spread more widely throughout society, property and wealth should not exercise "disproportionate political influence," and responsible exercise of democratic rights requires "clear political support." The prescient nature of Self's observations emerges in connection with the last of these three when he expands on his ideas by saying that "clear political support" means, among other things, that there should be limits on media ownership. His remarks are prescient in light of the 2011 British tabloid scandal—a scandal revealing the "unusually close relationship between politicians, newspaper owners, and some senior journalists in Britain"—centred around Australian media mogul Rupert Murdoch. One has the unmistakable sense in reading Self that here is someone with a keen understanding of the workings of modern industrialized democratic societies. There is much to be gained from an attentive reading of his ideas.

British democratic socialism underwent a change in the 1980s and 1990s, a change that became known as the Third Way. At the centre of this metamorphosis was Anthony Giddens (1938–). Giddens was a former director of the London School of Economics and sociologist as well as a person of influence on former British Prime Minister Tony Blair. In his earlier writings, Giddens emphasizes the dilemmas facing democratic socialists, including those of globalization, individualism, political agency, and ecological problems. His approach in addressing these is that of proposing a framework of policy-making that stands apart from old-style social democracy and new-style liberalism—hence, the Third Way. In the present article, Giddens makes clear that the Third Way is not a program linked to the New Democrats in the United States or New Labour in Britain, but rather a form of politics that stands in the tradition of democratic socialism that stretches back to Eduard Bernstein. Moreover, Giddens asserts, the Third Way is not a middle way but instead a way of thinking directed at two aims: electoral recovery and the development of a riposte to neo-liberalism. Linked to these aims is a new citizenship contract of rights and responsibilities and not globalization—internationalism. In brief, Giddens advocates a "breakout" for social democrats, a breakout that he calls "neoprogressivism."

Finally, we come to Linda McQuaig (1951–), Canadian columnist and non-fiction writer. In her selection, she examines the way in which greed and the pursuit of material gain have become the "central organizing principles" of our society. McQuaig argues— echoing the earlier views of Karl Polanyi, historian and anthropologist—that in the past few centuries, greed and the endless pursuit of material gain have displaced other aspects of life such as religion, family, clan, community, and kingdom. In the opening chapter of her 2002 book *All You Can Eat: Greed, Lust, and the Triumph of the New Capitalism*, McQuaig claims that an international legal system has been constructed to ensure not only legal protection for greed and materialism, but also to ensure their supremacy. Taking issue with the preoccupation of those who would defer to the model *Homo Economicus*—a model that stands behind the fascination with greed and materialism— McQuaig maintains with plausibility that this model applies only to human behaviour as "capitalism has attempted to reshape it" and does not apply to human behaviour that addresses the social aspect of our behaviour. At issue here is the one-dimensional nature of *Homo Economicus* and its applicability to everyday persons. It is this to which McQuaig takes exception and inclines instead toward the multi-dimensional view of persons encapsulated in Aristotle's notion of persons as social animals, a notion of persons that fits nicely into the democratic socialist's notion of the welfare state. For McQuaig, government intervention and market regulation are in and laissez-faireism is out.

In a world driven by neo-liberalism with its penchant for globalization, the ideas of democratic socialists such as Tawney, the writers of the *Regina Manifesto*, Self, Giddens, and McQuaig seem out of step with the time. But in a world where poverty is acute, exploitation is rife, environmental decay is present, and economic problems prevail, issues of social justice—issues that cry out for a different solution than that offered by neo-liberalism—demand a reconsideration of the ideas of democratic socialism. Despite the hegemonic power that neo-liberalism enjoys as an ideology and as a practising system of belief, the jury is still out on whether it can deliver the "goods," so to speak, as promised by some of its ardent defenders such as Ayn Rand (1905–1982) and Friedrich Hayek (1899–1992). The foregoing democratic socialists demand an opportunity to present their case to this same jury.

CHAPTER 23

Liberty and Equality

R.H. Tawney

Liberty and equality have usually in England been considered antithetic; and, since fraternity has rarely been considered at all, the famous trilogy has been easily dismissed as a hybrid abortion. Equality implies the deliberate acceptance of social restraints upon individual expansion. It involves the prevention of sensational extremes of wealth and power by public action for the public good. If liberty means, therefore, that every individual shall be free, according to his opportunities, to indulge without limit his appetite for either, it is clearly incompatible, not only with economic and social, but with civil and political, equality, which also prevent the strong exploiting to the full the advantages of their strength, and, indeed, with any habit of life save that of the Cyclops. But freedom for the pike is death for the minnows. It is possible that equality is to be contrasted, not with liberty, but only with a particular interpretation of it.

The test of a principle is that it can be generalized, so that the advantages of applying it are not particular, but universal. Since it is impossible for every individual, as for every nation, simultaneously to be stronger than his neighbours, it is a truism that liberty, as distinct from the liberties of special persons and classes, can exist only in so far as it is limited by rules, which secure that freedom for some is not slavery for others. The spiritual energy of human beings, in all the wealth of their infinite diversities, is the end to which external arrangements, whether political or economic, are merely means. Hence institutions which guarantee to men the opportunity of becoming the best of which they are capable are the supreme political good, and liberty is rightly preferred to equality, when the two are in conflict. The question is whether, in the conditions of modern society, they conflict or not. It is whether the defined and limited freedom, which alone can be generally enjoyed, is most likely to be attained by a community which encourages violent inequalities, or by one which represses them.

Inequality of power is not necessarily inimical to liberty. On the contrary, it is the condition of it. Liberty implies the ability to act, not merely to resist. Neither society as a whole, nor any group within it, can carry out its will except through organs; and, in order that such organs may function with effect, they must be sufficiently differentiated to perform their varying tasks, of which direction is one and execution another. But, while inequality of power is the condition of liberty, since it is the condition of any effective action, it is also a menace to it, for power which is sufficient to use is sufficient to abuse. Hence, in the political sphere, where the danger is familiar, all civilized communities have established safeguards, by which the advantages of differentiation of function, with the varying degrees of power which it involves, may be preserved, and the risk that power may be tyrannical, or perverted to private ends, averted or diminished. They have endeavoured, for example, as in England, to protect civil liberty by requiring that, with certain exceptions, the officers of the State shall be subject to the ordinary tribunals, and political liberty by insisting that those who take decisions on matters affecting the public shall be responsible to an assembly chosen by it. The precautions may be criticized as inadequate, but the need for precautions is not today disputed. It is recognized that political power must rest ultimately on consent, and that its exercise must be limited by rules of law.

The dangers arising from inequalities of economic power have been less commonly recognized. They exist, however, whether recognized or not. For the excess or abuse of power, and its divorce from responsibility, which results in oppression, are not confined to the relations which arise between men as members of a state. They are not a malady which is peculiar to political systems, as was typhus to slums, and from which other departments of life can be regarded as immune. They are a disease, not of political organization, but of organization. They occur, in the absence of preventive measures, in political associations, because they occur in all forms of association in which large numbers of individuals are massed for collective action. The isolated worker may purchase security against exploitation at the cost of poverty, as the hermit may avoid the corruptions of civilization by forgoing its advantages. But, as soon as he is associated with his fellows in a common undertaking, his duties must be specified and his rights defined; and, in so far as they are not, the undertaking is impeded. The problem of securing a livelihood ceases to be merely economic, and becomes social and political. The struggle with nature continues, but on a different plane. Its efficiency is heightened by co-operation. Its character is complicated by the emergence of the question of the terms on which co-operation shall take place.

In an industrial civilization, when its first phase is over, most economic activity is corporate activity. It is carried on, not by individuals, but by groups, which are endowed by the State with a legal status, and the larger of which, in size, complexity, specialization of functions and unity of control, resemble less the private enterprise of the past than a public department.

As far as certain great industries are concerned, employment must be found in the service of these corporations, or not at all. Hence the mass of mankind pass their working lives under the direction of a hierarchy, whose heads define, as they think most profitable, the lines on which the common enterprise is to proceed, and determine, subject to the intervention of the State and voluntary organizations, the economic, and to a considerable, though diminishing, extent, the social environment of their employees. Possessing the reality of power, without the decorative trappings—unless, as in England is often the case, it thinks it worthwhile to buy them—this business oligarchy is the effective aristocracy of industrial nations, and the aristocracy of tradition and prestige, when such still exists, carries out its wishes and courts its favours. In such conditions, authority over human beings is exercised, not only through political, but through economic, organs. The problem of liberty, therefore, is necessarily concerned, not only with political, but also with economic, relations.

It is true, of course, that the problems are different. But to suppose that the abuses of economic power are trivial, or that they are automatically prevented by political democracy, is to be deceived by words. Freedom is always, no doubt, a matter of degree; no man enjoys all the requirements of full personal development, and all men possess some of them. It is not only compatible with conditions in which all men are fellow-servants, but would find in such conditions its most perfect expression. What it excludes is a society where only some are servants, while others are masters.

For, whatever else the idea involves, it implies at least, that no man shall be amenable to an authority which is arbitrary in its proceedings, exorbitant in its demands, or incapable of being called to account when it abuses its office for personal advantage. Insofar as his livelihood is at the mercy of an irresponsible superior, whether political or economic, who can compel his reluctant obedience by *force majeure*, whose actions he is unable to modify or resist, save at the cost of grave personal injury to himself and his dependents, and whose favour he must court, even when he despises it, he may possess a profusion of more tangible blessings, from beer to motor-bicycles, but he cannot be said to be in possession of freedom. Insofar as an economic system grades mankind into groups, of which some can wield, if unconsciously, the force of economic duress for their own profit or convenience, while others must submit to it, its effect is that freedom itself is similarly graded. Society is divided, in its economic and social relations, into classes which are ends, and classes which are instruments. Like property, with which in the past it has been closely connected, liberty becomes the privilege of a class, not the possession of a nation.

Political principles resemble military tactics; they are usually designed for a war which is over. Freedom is commonly interpreted in England in political terms, because it was in the political arena that the most resounding of its recent victories were won. It is regarded as belonging to human beings as citizens, rather than to citizens as human beings; so that it is possible for a nation, the majority of whose members have as little influence on the decisions that determine their economic destinies as on the motions of the planets, to applaud the idea with self-congratulatory gestures of decorous enthusiasm, as though history were of the past, but not of the present. If the attitude of the ages from which it inherits a belief in liberty had been equally ladylike, there would have been, it is probable, little liberty to applaud.

For freedom is always relative to power, and the kind of freedom which at any moment it is most urgent to affirm depends on the nature of the power which is prevalent and established. Since political arrangements may be such as to check excess of power, while economic arrangements permit or encourage them, a society, or a large part of it, may be both politically free and economically the opposite. It may be protected against arbitrary action by the agents of government, and be without the security against economic oppression which corresponds to civil liberty. It may possess the political institutions of an advanced democracy, and lack the will and ability to control the conduct of those powerful in its economic affairs, which is the economic analogy of political freedom.

The extension of liberty from the political to the economic sphere is evidently among the most urgent tasks of industrial societies. It is evident also, however, that, insofar as this extension takes place, the traditional antithesis between liberty and equality will no longer be valid. As long as liberty is interpreted as consisting exclusively in security against oppression by the agents of the State, or as a share in its government, it is plausible, perhaps, to dissociate it from equality; for, though experience suggests that, even in this meagre and restricted sense, it is not easily maintained in the presence of extreme disparities of wealth and influence, it is possible for it to be enjoyed, in form at least, by pauper and millionaire. Such disparities, however, though they do not enable one group to become the political master of another, necessarily cause it to exercise a preponderant influence on the economic life of the rest of society.

Hence, when liberty is construed, realistically, or implying, not merely a minimum of civil and political rights, but securities that the economically weak will not be at the mercy of the economically strong, and that the control of those aspects of economic life by which all are affected will be amenable, in the last resort, to the will of all, a large measure of equality, so far from being inimical to liberty, is essential to it. In conditions which impose co-operative, rather than merely individual, effort, liberty is, in fact, equality in action, in the sense, not that all men perform identical functions or wield the same degree of power, but that all men are equally protected against the abuse of power, and equally entitled to insist that power shall be used, not for personal ends, but for the general advantage. Civil and political liberty obviously imply, not that all men shall be members of parliament, cabinet ministers, or civil servants, but the absence of such civil and political inequalities as enable one class to impose its will on another by legal coercion. It should be not less obvious that economic liberty implies, not that all men shall initiate, plan, direct, manage, or administer, but the absence of such economic inequalities as can be used as a means of economic constraint.

The danger to liberty which is caused by inequality varies with differences of economic organization and public policy. When the mass of the population are independent producers, or when, if they are dependent on great undertakings, the latter are subject to strict public control, it may be absent or remote. It is seen at its height when important departments of economic activity are the province of large organizations, which, if they do not themselves, as sometimes occurs, control the State, are sufficiently powerful to resist control by it. Among the numerous interesting phenomena which impress the foreign observer of American economic life, not the least interesting is the occasional emergence of industrial enterprises which appear to him, and, indeed, to some Americans, to have developed the characteristics, not merely of an economic undertaking, but of a kind of polity. Their rule may be a mild and benevolent paternalism, lavishing rest-rooms, schools, gymnasia, and guarantees for constitutional behaviour on care-free employees; or it may be a harsh and suspicious tyranny. But, whether as amiable as Solon, or as ferocious as Lycurgus, their features are cast in a heroic mould. Their gestures are those of the sovereigns of little commonwealths rather than of mere mundane employers.

American official documents have, on occasion, called attention to the tendency of the bare stem of business to burgeon, in a favourable environment, with almost tropical exuberance, so that it clothes itself with functions that elsewhere are regarded as belonging to political authorities. The corporations controlled by six financial groups, stated the Report of the United States Commission on Industrial Relations some 20 years ago, employ 2,651,684 wage-earners, or 440,000 per group. Some of these companies own, not merely the plant and equipment of industry, but the homes of the workers, and streets through which they pass to work, and the halls in which, if they are allowed to meet, their meetings must be held. They employ private spies and detectives, private police and, sometimes, it appears, private troops, and engage, when they deem it expedient, in private war. While organized themselves, they forbid organization among their employees, and enforce their will by evicting malcontents from their homes, and even, on occasion, by the use of armed force. In such conditions business may continue in its modesty, since its object is money, to describe itself as business; but, in fact, it is a tyranny. "The main objection to the large corporation," remarks Mr Justice Brandeis, who, as a judge of the Supreme Court, should know the facts, "is that it makes possible—and in many cases makes inevitable—the exercise of industrial absolutism." Property in capital, thus inflated and emancipated, acquires attributes analogous to those of property in land in a feudal society. It carries with it the disposal, in fact, if not in law, of an authority which is quasi-governmental. Its owners possess what would have been called in the ages of darkness a private jurisdiction, and their relations to their dependents, though contractual in form, resemble rather those of ruler and subject than of equal parties to a commercial venture. The liberty which they defend against the encroachments of trade unionism and the State is most properly to be regarded, not as freedom, but as a franchise.[1]

The conventional assertion that inequality is inseparable from liberty is obviously, in such circumstances, unreal and unconvincing; for the existence of the former is a menace to the latter, and the latter is most likely to be secured by curtailing the former. It is true that in England, where three generations of trade unionism and state intervention have done something to tame it, the exercise of economic power is, at ordinary times, less tyrannical than it once was. It still remains, nevertheless, a formidable menace to the freedom of common men. The pressure of such power is felt by the consumer, when he purchases necessaries which, directly or indirectly, are controlled by a monopoly. It is felt in the workshop, where, within the limits set by industrial legislation and collective agreements, the comfort and amenity of the wage-earners' surroundings, the discipline and tone of factory life, the security of employment and methods of promotion, the recruitment and dismissal of workers, the degree to which successive relays of cheap juvenile labour are employed, the opportunity to secure consideration for grievances, depend ultimately upon the policy pursued by a board of directors, who may have little love, indeed, for their shareholders, but who represent, in the last resort, their financial interests, and who, insofar as they are shareholders themselves, are necessarily judges in their own cause.

The effects of such autocracy are even graver in the sphere of economic strategy, which settles the ground upon which these tactical issues are fought out, and, in practice, not infrequently determines their decision before they arise. In such matters as the changes in organization most likely to restore prosperity to an embarrassed industry, and, therefore, to secure a tolerable livelihood to the workers engaged in it; methods of averting or meeting a depression; rationalization, the closing of plants and the concentration of production; the sale of a business on which a whole community depends or its amalgamation with a rival—not to mention the critical field of financial policy, with its possibilities, not merely of watered capital and of the squandering in dividends of resources which should be held as reserves, but of a sensational redistribution of wealth and widespread unemployment as a result of decisions taken by bankers—the diplomacy of business, like that of governments before 1914, is still commonly conducted over the heads of those most affected by it. The interests of the public, as workers and consumers, may receive consideration when these matters are determined; but the normal organization of economic life does not offer reliable guarantee that they will be considered. Nor can it plausibly be asserted that, if they are not, those aggrieved can be certain of any redress.

Power over the public is public power. It does not cease to be public merely because private persons are permitted to buy and sell, own and bequeath it, as they deem most profitable. To retort that its masters are themselves little more than half-conscious instruments, whose decisions register and transmit the impact of forces that they can neither anticipate nor control, though not wholly unveracious, is, nevertheless, superficial. The question is not whether there are economic movements which elude human control, for obviously there are. It is whether the public possesses adequate guarantees that those which are controllable are controlled in the general interest, not in that of a minority. Like the gods of Homer, who were subject themselves to a fate behind the fates, but were not thereby precluded from interfering at their pleasure in the affairs of men, the potentates of the economic world exercise discretion, not, indeed, as to the situation which they will meet, but as to the manner in which they will meet it. They hold the initiative, have such freedom to manoeuvre as circumstances allow, can force an issue or postpone it, and, if open conflict seems inevitable or expedient, can choose, as best suits themselves, the ground where it shall take place.

"Even if socialism were practicable without the destruction of freedom," writes Lord Lothian, "would there be any advantage in converting the whole population into wage or salary earners, directed by the relatively few, also salaried, officials, who by ability, or promotion, or 'pull,' could work their way to the top of the political machine or the permanent bureaucracy? . . . Is not that community the best, and, in the widest sense of the word, the most healthy, which has the largest proportion of citizens who have the enterprise, and energy, and initiative, to create new things and new methods for themselves, and not merely to wait to carry out the orders of somebody 'higher up'?"[2] In view of the practice, of some parts, at least, of the business world, the less said about "pull," perhaps, the better. But how true in substance! And how different the liner looks from the saloon-deck and the stokehold! And how striking that the conditions which Lord Lothian deplores as a hypothetical danger should be precisely those which ordinary men experience daily as an ever-present fact!

For, in England at any rate, as a glance at the Registrar-General's reports would have sufficed to show him, not only the majority of the population, but the great majority, are today "wage or salary earners," who, for quite a long time, have been "directed by the relatively few," and who, if they did not "wait to carry out the orders of somebody higher up," would be sent about their business with surprising promptitude. Unless Lord Lothian proposes to abolish, not only a particular political doctrine, but banks, railways, coal-mines and cotton-mills, the question is not whether orders shall be given, but who shall give them; whether there

shall be guarantees that they are given in the general interest; and whether those to whom they are given shall have a reasonable security that, when their welfare is at stake, their views will receive an unbiased consideration.

Freedom may be, as he insists, more important than comfort. But is a miner, who is not subject to a bureaucracy, or at least, to a bureaucracy of the kind which alarms Lord Lothian, conspicuously more free than a teacher, who is? If a man eats bread made of flour produced to the extent of 40 per cent by two milling combines and meat supplied by an international meat trust, and lives in a house built of materials of which 25 per cent are controlled by a ring, and buys his tobacco from one amalgamation, and his matches from another, while his wife's sewing-thread is provided by a third, which has added eight millionaires to the national roll of honour in the last 20 years, is he free as a consumer? Is he free as a worker, if he is liable to have his piece-rates cut at the discretion of his employer, and, on expressing his annoyance, to be dismissed as an agitator, and to be thrown on the scrap-heap without warning because his employer has decided to shut down a plant, or bankers to restrict credit, and to be told, when he points out that the industry on which his livelihood depends is being injured by mismanagement, that his job is to work, and that the management in question will do his thinking for him? And if, in such circumstances, he is but partially free as a consumer and a worker, is not his freedom as a citizen itself also partial, rather than as Lord Lothian would desire, unqualified and complete?

Lord Lothian is misled as to liberty, because he has omitted to consider the bearing upon it of another phenomenon, the phenomenon of inequality. The truth is that, when the economic scales are so unevenly weighted, to interpret liberty as a political principle, which belongs to one world, the world of politics and government, while equality belongs—if, indeed, it belongs anywhere—to another world, the world of economic affairs, is to do violence to realities. Governments, it is true, exercise powers of a great and special kind, and freedom requires that they should be held strictly to account. But the administration of things is not easily distinguished, under modern conditions of mass organization, from the control of persons, and both are in the hands, to some not inconsiderable degree, of the minority who move the levers of the economic mechanism. The truth of the matter is put by Professor Pollard in his admirable study, *The Evolution of Parliament*. "There is only one solution," he writes, "of the problem of liberty, and it lies in equality. . . . Men vary in physical strength; but so far as their social relations go that inequality has been abolished. . . . Yet there must have been a period in social evolution when this refusal to permit the strong man to do what he liked with his own physical strength seemed, at least to the strong, an outrageous interference with personal liberty. . . . There is, in fact, no more reason why a man should be allowed to use his wealth or his brain than his physical

strength as he likes. . . . The liberty of the weak depends upon the restraint of the strong, that of the poor upon the restraint of the rich, and that of the simpler-minded upon the restraint of the sharper. Every man should have this liberty and no more, to do unto others as he would that they should do unto him; upon that common foundation rest liberty, equality, and morality."[3]

Notes

1. For evidence on these points see USA, *Final Report of Commission on Industrial Relations*, 1916; *Report of the Steel Strike of 1919* and *Public Opinion and the Steel Strike* (Reports of the Commission of Inquiry, Interchurch World Movement), New York, 1920 and 1921; H.C. Butler, *Industrial Relations in the United States* (ILO, *Studies and Reports*, Series A, no. 27), 1927. The Quotation from Mr Justice Brandeis occurs in the *Final Report on Industrial Relations*, p. 63.
2. *Manchester Guardian*, 8 January 1930.
3. A.F. Pollard, *The Evolution of Parliament*, 1920, pp. 183–4.

CHAPTER 24

Regina Manifesto

David Lewis and Frank Scott

Adopted at First National Convention Held at Regina, Sask., July, 1933

The CCF is a federation of organizations whose purpose is the establishment in Canada of a Co-operative Commonwealth in which the principle regulating production, distribution, and exchange will be the supplying of human needs and not the making of profits.

We aim to replace the present capitalist system, with its inherent injustice and inhumanity by a social order from which the domination and exploitation of one class by another will be eliminated, in which economic planning will supersede unregulated private enterprise and competition, and in which genuine democratic self-government, based upon economic equality will be possible. The present order is marked by glaring inequalities of wealth and opportunity, by chaotic waste and instability; and in an age of plenty it condemns the great mass of the people to poverty and insecurity. Power has become more and more concentrated into the hands of a small irresponsible minority of financiers and industrialists and to their predatory interests the majority are habitually sacrificed. When private profit is the main stimulus to economic effort, our society oscillates between periods of feverish prosperity in which the main benefits go to speculators and profiteers, and of catastrophic depression, in which the common man's normal state of insecurity and hardship is accentuated. We believe that these evils can be removed only in a planned and socialized economy in which our natural resources and the principal means of production and distribution are owned, controlled, and operated by the people.

The new social order at which we aim is not one in which individuality will be crushed out by a system of regimentation. Nor shall we interfere with cultural rights of racial or religious minorities. What we seek is a proper collective organization of our economic resources such as will make possible a much greater degree of leisure and a much richer individual life for every citizen.

This social and economic transformation can be brought about by political action, through the election of a government inspired by the ideal of a Co-operative Commonwealth and supported by a majority of the people. We do not believe in change by violence. We consider that both the old parties in Canada are the instruments of capitalist interests and cannot serve as agents of social reconstruction, and that whatever the superficial differences between them, they are bound to carry on government

in accordance with the dictates of the big business interests who finance them. The CCF aims at political power in order to put an end to this capitalistic domination of our political life. It is a democratic movement, a federation of farmer, labour, and socialist organizations, financed by its own members and seeking to achieve its ends solely by constitutional methods. It appeals for support to all who believe that the time has come for a far-reaching reconstruction of our economic and political institutions and who are willing to work together for the carrying out of the following policies:

1. Planning

The establishment of a planned, socialized economic order, in order to make possible the most efficient development of the national resources and the most equitable distribution of the national income.

The first step in this direction will be the setting up of a National Planning Commission consisting of a small body of economists, engineers, and statisticians assisted by an appropriate technical staff.

The task of the Commission will be to plan for the production, distribution, and exchange of all goods and services necessary to the efficient functioning of the economy; to coordinate the activities of the socialized industries; to provide for a satisfactory balance between the producing and consuming power; and to carry on continuous research into all branches of the national economy in order to acquire the detailed information necessary to efficient planning.

The Commission will be responsible to the Cabinet and will work in co-operation with the Managing Boards of the Socialized Industries.

It is now certain that in every industrial country some form of planning will replace the disintegrating capitalist system. The CCF will provide that in Canada the planning shall be done, not by a small group of capitalist magnates in their own interest, but by public servants acting in the public interest and responsible to the people as a whole.

2. Socialization of Finance

Socialization of all financial machinery—banking, currency credit, and insurance, to make possible the effective control of currency, credit, and prices, and the supplying of new productive equipment for socially desirable purposes.

Planning by itself will be of little use if the public authority has not the power to carry its plans into effect. Such power will require the control of finance and of all those vital industries and services, which, if they remain in private hands, can be used to thwart or corrupt the will of the public authority. Control of finance is the first step to the control of the whole economy. The chartered banks must be socialized and removed from the control of private profit-seeking interests; and the national banking system thus established must have at its head a Central Bank to control the flow of credit and the general price level, and to regulate foreign exchange operations. A National Investment Board must also be set up, working in cooperation with the socialized banking system to mobilize and direct the unused surpluses of production for socially desired purposes as determined by the Planning Commission.

Insurance Companies, which provide one of the main channels for the investment of individual savings and which, under their present competitive organization, charge needlessly high premiums for the social services that they render, must also be socialized.

3. Social Ownership

Socialization (Dominion, Provincial, or Municipal) of transportation, communications, electric power, and all other industries and services essential to social planning and their operation under the general direction of the Planning Commission by competent managements freed from day-to-day political interference.

Public utilities must be operated for the public benefit and not for the private profit of a small group of owners or financial manipulators. Our natural resources must be developed by the same methods. Such a program means the continuance and extension of the public ownership enterprises in which most governments in Canada have already gone some distance. Only by such public ownership, operated on a planned economy, can our main industries be saved from the wasteful competition or the ruinous over-development and over-capitalization which are the inevitable outcome of capitalism. Only in a regime of public ownership and operation will the full benefits accruing from centralized control and mass production be passed on to the consuming public.

Transportation, communications, and electric power must come first in a list of industries to be socialized. Others, such as mining, pulp and paper, and the distribution of milk, bread, coal, and gasoline, in which exploitation, waste, or financial malpractices are particularly prominent, must next be brought under social ownership and operation.

In restoring to the community its natural resources and in taking over industrial enterprises from private into public control, we do not propose any policy of outright confiscation. What we desire is the most stable and equitable transition to the Co-operative Commonwealth. It is impossible to decide the policies to be followed in particular cases in an uncertain future, but we insist upon certain broad principles. The welfare of the community must take supremacy over the claims of private wealth. In times of war, human life has been conscripted. Should economic circumstances call for it, conscription of wealth would be more justifiable.

We recognize the need for compensation in the case of individuals and institutions which must receive adequate maintenance during the transitional period before the planned economy becomes fully operative. But a CCF government will not play the role of rescuing bankrupt private concerns for the benefit of promoters and of stock and bond holders. It will not pile up a deadweight burden of unremunerative debt which represents claims upon the public treasury of a functionless owner class.

The management of publicly owned enterprises will be vested in boards who will be appointed for their competence in the industry and will conduct each particular enterprise on efficient economic lines. The machinery of management may well vary from industry to industry, but the rigidity of Civil Service rules should be avoided and likewise the evils of the patronage system as exemplified in so many departments of the Government today. Workers in these public industries must be free to organize in trade unions and must be given the right to participate in the management of the industry.

4. Agriculture

Security of tenure for the farmer upon his farm on conditions to be laid down by individual provinces; insurance against unavoidable crop failure; removal of the tariff burden from the operations of agriculture; encouragement of producers' and consumers' co-operatives; the restoration and maintenance of an equitable relationship between prices of agricultural products and those of other commodities and services; and improving the efficiency of export trade in farm products.

The security of tenure for the farmer upon his farm which is imperilled by the present disastrous situation of the whole industry, together with adequate social insurance, ought to be guaranteed under equitable conditions.

The prosperity of agriculture, the greatest Canadian industry, depends upon a rising volume of purchasing power of the masses in Canada for all farm goods consumed at home, and upon the maintenance of large scale exports of the stable commodities at satisfactory prices or equitable commodity exchange.

The intense depression in agriculture today is a consequence of the general world crisis caused by the normal workings of the capitalistic system resulting in: (1) Economic nationalism expressing itself in tariff barriers and other restrictions of world trade; (2) The decreased purchasing power of unemployed and underemployed workers and of the Canadian people in general; (3) The exploitation of both primary producers and consumers by monopolistic corporations who absorb a great proportion of the selling price of farm products. (This last is true, for example, of the distribution of milk and dairy products, the packing industry, and milling.)

The immediate cause of agricultural depression is the catastrophic fall in the world prices of foodstuffs as compared with other prices, this fall being due in large measure to the deflation of currency and credit. To counteract the worst effect of this, the internal price level should be raised so that the farmers' purchasing power may be restored.

We propose therefore:

(1) The improvement of the position of the farmer by the increase of purchasing power made possible by the social control of the financial system. This control must be directed towards the increase of employment as laid down elsewhere and towards raising the prices of farm commodities by appropriate credit and foreign exchange policies.

(2) Whilst the family farm is the accepted basis for agricultural production in Canada the position of the farmer may be much improved by:

(a) The extension of consumers' co-operatives for the purchase of farm supplies and domestic requirements; and

(b) The extension of co-operative institutions for the processing and marketing of farm products.

Both of the foregoing to have suitable encouragement and assistance.

(3) The adoption of a planned system of agricultural development based upon scientific soil surveys directed towards better land utilization, and a scientific policy of agricultural development for the whole of Canada.

(4) The substitution for the present system of foreign trade, of a system of import and export boards to improve the efficiency of overseas marketing, to control prices, and to integrate the foreign trade policy with the requirements of the national economic plan.

5. External Trade

The regulation in accordance with the National plan of external trade through import and export boards.

Canada is dependent on external sources of supply for many of her essential requirements of raw materials and manufactured products. These she can obtain only by large exports of the goods she is best fitted to produce. The strangling of our export trade by insane protectionist policies must be brought to an end. But the old controversies between free traders and protectionists are now largely obsolete. In a world of nationally organized economies Canada must organize the buying and selling of her main imports and exports under public boards; and take steps to regulate the flow of less important commodities by a system of licences. By so doing she will be enabled to make the best trade agreements possible with foreign countries, put a stop to the exploitation of both primary producer and ultimate consumer, make possible the coordination of internal processing, transportation, and marketing of farm products, and facilitate the establishment of stable prices for such export commodities.

6. Co-operative Institutions

The encouragement by the public authority of both producers' and consumers' co-operative institutions.

In agriculture, as already mentioned, the primary producer can receive a larger net revenue through co-operative organization of purchases and marketing. Similarly in retail distribution of staple commodities such as milk, there is room for development both of public municipal operation and of consumers' co-operatives, and such co-operative organization can be extended into wholesale distribution and into manufacturing. Co-operative enterprises should be assisted by the state through appropriate legislation and through the provision of adequate credit facilities.

7. Labour Code

A National Labour Code to secure for the worker maximum income and leisure, insurance covering illness, accident, old age, and unemployment, freedom of association and effective participation in the management of his industry or profession.

The spectre of poverty and insecurity which still haunts every worker, though technological developments have made possible a high standard of living for everyone, is a disgrace which must be removed from our civilization. The community must organize its resources to effect progressive reduction of the hours of work in accordance with technological development and to provide a constantly rising standard of life to everyone who is willing to work. A labour code must be developed which will include state regulation of all wages, equal reward and equal opportunity of advancement for equal services, irrespective of sex; measures to guarantee the right to work or the right to maintenance through stabilization of employment and through unemployment insurance;

social insurance to protect workers and their families against the hazards of sickness, death, industrial accident, and old age; limitation of hours of work and protection of health and safety in industry. Both wages and insurance benefits should be varied in accordance with family needs.

In addition workers must be guaranteed the undisputed right to freedom of association, and should be encouraged and assisted by the state to organize themselves in trade unions. By means of collective agreements and participation in works councils, the workers can achieve fair working rules and share in the control of industry and professions; and their organizations will be indispensable elements in a system of genuine industrial democracy.

The labour code should be uniform throughout the country. But the achievement of this end is difficult so long as jurisdiction over labour legislation under the BNA Act is mainly in the hands of the provinces. It is urgently necessary, therefore, that the BNA Act be amended to make such a national labour code possible.

8. Socialized Health Services

Publicly organized health, hospital, and medical services.

With the advance of medical science the maintenance of a healthy population has become a function for which every civilized community should undertake responsibility. Health services should be made at least as freely available as are educational services today. But under a system which is still mainly one of private enterprise the costs of proper medical care, such as the wealthier members of society can easily afford, are at present prohibitive for great masses of the people. A properly organized system of public health services including medical and dental care, which would stress the prevention rather than the cure of illness, should be

extended to all our people in both rural and urban areas. This is an enterprise in which Dominion, Provincial, and Municipal authorities, as well as the medical and dental professions, can co-operate.

9. BNA Act

The amendment of the Canadian Constitution, without infringing upon racial or religious minority rights or upon legitimate provincial claims to autonomy, so as to give the Dominion Government adequate powers to deal effectively with urgent economic problems which are essentially national in scope; the abolition of the Canadian Senate.

We propose that the necessary amendments to the BNA Act shall be obtained as speedily as required, safeguards being inserted to ensure that the existing rights of racial and religious minorities shall not be changed without their own consent. What is chiefly needed today is the placing in the hands of the national government of more power to control national economic development. In a rapidly changing economic environment our political constitution must be reasonably flexible. The present division of powers between Dominion and Provinces reflects the conditions of a pioneer, mainly agricultural, community in 1867. Our constitution must be brought into line with the increasing industrialization of the country and the consequent centralization of economic and financial power which has taken place in the last two generations. The principle laid down in the Quebec Resolutions of the Fathers of Confederation should be applied to the conditions of 1933, that "there be a general government charged with matters of common interest to the whole country and local governments for each of the provinces charged with the control of local matters in their respective sections."

The Canadian Senate, which was originally

created to protect provincial rights, but has failed even in this function, has developed into a bulwark of capitalist interests, as is illustrated by the large number of company directorships held by its aged members. In its peculiar composition of a fixed number of members appointed for life it is one of the most reactionary assemblies in the civilized world. It is a standing obstacle to all progressive legislation, and the only permanently satisfactory method of dealing with the constitutional difficulties it creates is to abolish it.

10. External Relations

A Foreign Policy designed to obtain international economic co-operation and to promote disarmament and world peace.

Canada has a vital interest in world peace. We propose, therefore, to do everything in our power to advance the idea of international co-operation as represented by the League of Nations and the International Labor Organization. We would extend our diplomatic machinery for keeping in touch with the main centres of world interest. But we believe that genuine international co-operation is incompatible with the capitalist regime which is in force in most countries, and that strenuous efforts are needed to rescue the League from its present condition of being mainly a League of capitalist Great Powers. We stand resolutely against all participation in imperialist wars. Within the British Commonwealth, Canada must maintain her autonomy as a completely self-governing nation. We must resist all attempts to build up a new economic British Empire in place of the old political one, since such attempts readily lend themselves to the purposes of capitalist exploitation and may easily lead to further world wars. Canada must refuse to be entangled in any more wars fought to make the world safe for capitalism.

11. Taxation and Public Finance

A new taxation policy designed not only to raise public revenues but also to lessen the glaring inequalities of income and to provide funds for social services and the socialization of industry; the cessation of the debt creating system of Public Finance.

In the type of economy that we envisage, the need for taxation, as we now understand it, will have largely disappeared. It will nevertheless be essential, during the transition period, to use the taxing powers, along with the other methods proposed elsewhere, as a means for providing for the socialization of industry, and for extending the benefits of increased Social Services.

At the present time capitalist governments in Canada raise a large proportion of their revenues from such levies as customs duties and sales taxes, the main burden of which falls upon the masses. In place of such taxes upon articles of general consumption, we propose a drastic extension of income, corporation, and inheritance taxes, steeply graduated according to ability to pay. Full publicity must be given to income tax payments and our tax collection system must be brought up to the English standard of efficiency.

We also believe in the necessity for an immediate revision of the basis of Dominion and Provincial sources of revenue, so as to produce a coordinated and equitable system of taxation throughout Canada.

An inevitable effect of the capitalist system is the debt creating character of public financing. All public debts have enormously increased, and the fixed interest charges paid thereon now amount to the largest single item of so-called uncontrollable public expenditures. The CCF proposes that in future no public financing shall be permitted which facilitates the perpetuation of the parasitic interest-receiving class; that capital shall be provided through the medium of the National

Investment Board and free from perpetual interest charges.

We propose that all Public Works, as directed by the Planning Commission, shall be financed by the issuance of credit as suggested, based upon the national wealth of Canada.

12. Freedom

Freedom of speech and assembly for all; repeal of Section 98 of the Criminal Code; amendment of the Immigration Act to prevent the present inhuman policy of deportation; equal treatment before the law of all residents of Canada irrespective of race, nationality, or religious or political beliefs.

In recent years, Canada has seen an alarming growth of Fascist tendencies among all governmental authorities. The most elementary rights of freedom of speech and assembly have been arbitrarily denied to workers and to all whose political and social views do not meet with the approval of those in power. The lawless and brutal conduct of the police in certain centres in preventing public meetings and in dealing with political prisoners must cease. Section 98 of the Criminal Code which has been used as a weapon of political oppression by a panic-stricken capitalist government, must be wiped off the statute book and those who have been imprisoned under it must be released. An end must be put to the inhuman practice of deporting immigrants who were brought to this country by immigration propaganda and now,

through no fault of their own, find themselves victims of an executive department against whom there is no appeal to the courts of the land. We stand for full economic, political, and religious liberty for all.

13. Social Justice

The establishment of a commission composed of psychiatrists, psychologists, socially minded jurists, and social workers, to deal with all matters pertaining to crime and punishment and the general administration of law, in order to humanize the law and to bring it into harmony with the needs of the people.

While the removal of economic inequality will do much to overcome the most glaring injustices in the treatment of those who come into conflict with the law, our present archaic system must be changed and brought into accordance with a modern concept of human relationships. This new system must not be based, as is the present one, upon vengeance and fear, but upon an understanding of human behaviour. For this reason its planning and control cannot be left in the hands of those steeped in an outworn legal tradition; and therefore it is proposed that there shall be established a national commission composed of psychiatrists, psychologists, socially minded jurists, and social workers, whose duty it shall be to devise a system of prevention and correction consistent with other features of the new social order.

CHAPTER 25

The Revival of Political Choice

Peter Self

This chapter is concerned with ways of exercising political choice in modern democratic societies. In the future more decisions are likely to be taken internationally or regionally, and, it is hoped, also locally, so as to reduce the historic sovereignty of the nation-state. Both movements of functions—upwards and downwards—correspond with economic and social changes in the world, and are clearly evident in Europe, where the transfer of powers to the European Union has gone hand in hand with other transfers to the elected regional bodies which exist in Germany, France, Spain, and elsewhere. However, for the foreseeable future the nation-state will remain the key player in political life, because international political power is still too weak and fragmented, and localized sources of political power—however valuable—cannot possibly cope with global impacts. The nation-state still has a vital and in some respects expanding role to play in devising a more balanced and equitable framework for the market system and in organizing a comprehensive but partly devolved system of public services.

Accordingly, the chapter will start by drawing together the book's conclusions into a discussion of the future character and role of democratic states, followed by a consideration of how the state might relate more effectively to community opinion and initiatives. The third section seeks a solution to perhaps the state's greatest failure, the missing links between work and welfare. Finally comes consideration of how economic thought needs to be drastically altered to take account of its neglected or overridden social impacts, and how a democratically elected counter-revolution of ideas might be established.

The Regenerated State?

The nation-state has become a beleaguered institution. Some see it as failing to meet its responsibilities. Others see it as too remote and authoritarian for the requirements of an increasingly individualist society. A favourite remedy is to fall back upon the more voluntaristic basis of civil society. This viewpoint has important merits and lessons for both the state and the economy, but also strong limitations. A more vibrant civil society can in practice only flourish within the framework of a supportive and purposeful state, which shares and expresses similar democratic values.

[. . .] The notion of a minimum state with few functions is a chimerical one. The factors which influenced the growth of the state—the impacts of industrialization, urbanization, technology, and rapid economic and social change—are proceeding faster than ever. The withering of the state would not anyhow be possible without a parallel withering of the global economy, and the latter process is harder since economic power is entrenched at the global not the national level.

Neo-liberals and libertarians seem to want to combine an extreme freedom of the individual from any form of state intervention with a simple endorsement of the global capitalist economy. This is an impossible combination, which is met with some fanciful beliefs. Thus writers such as Nozick (1974) make play with a utopia in which any group of people can choose to live in the kind of economic and social system which they prefer. This idea would only work at all if a strong state protected these groups from external pressures, especially the strong ones for global market penetration.

[. . .] [C]apitalism could not work effectively without the support of a wide array of public functions. Capitalist markets depend comprehensively upon a framework of laws and regulations established by the state, and the triumph of capitalism has been dependent upon supportive political measures which could be reversed or modified. Market liberalization and privatization can work tolerably and effectively only with the aid of an increased range of public regulations—over abuses of monopoly, dangerous drugs, consumer protection, environmental impacts, and much else. The state is expected to sacrifice cherished social objectives in order to assist market "efficiency," yet capitalism depends completely upon the social infrastructure provided by the state for producing educated, capable, and fit workers, services which could never be provided for the mass of the population on a profitable basis. The state must also cope with all the casualties of the market system as well as the discontents and frustrations which its erratic course produces.

Many politicians now see the first aim of the state as being to promote the international competitiveness of the national economy. Other goals must be subordinated to this supreme aim. The argument goes that if a nation fails to attract sufficient investment and jobs in the highly competitive international arena, it will sink into economic decline and its social aims will be frustrated. This seems to be the ruling belief even of a centre-left party such as New Labour in Britain, while in one powerful version European unity is desirable, not for the better protection of social and environmental standards, but for forging a powerful competitive bloc in the global arena.

Against this position it can be claimed that the state is essential for protecting social and community values which are being persistently undermined by global capitalism. Also the capitalist "virtues" of competition and consumers' choice are often applied inappropriately or operate perversely on closer examination. Because of the dependence of capitalism upon the state, the state has both a right and a duty to make capitalism more equitable and socially responsive.

Given the remoteness of exercises of economic power, the state should do all it can to assist the decentralization of the economy. Some measures to this effect, such as support for community banks and producer co-operatives, were suggested [earlier]. Reversion to a more localized economy would probably do more than anything else to restore social trust in the market. The state could make capitalism more equitable and acceptable through giving more protection to the weaker parties in the law of contract, and putting limits to the acquisition and inheritance of capital. It could demonstrate the virtues of co-operative working in its own services instead of slavishly and often inappropriately copying market disciplines and incentives. A more balanced relationship between the state and capitalism would itself check the destructively imperialist tendencies of the latter.

A second vital mission for the state is to rehabilitate its role and credentials as a service provider, which has been damaged by exaggerated and indiscriminate attacks upon bureaucracy. The public choice theory that bureaucrats have an inevitable tendency to pervert public policy to their own personal advantage, amounts to guilt by association and has no empirical roots in a sociological analysis of actual bureaucracies whose behaviour varies widely. Yet this impressionistic reasoning buttresses the familiar belief that governments are big, bloated, and "inefficient" compared with business enterprises.

These assertions miss the point that the functional requirements of the state have been expanding for sound reasons. The greater labour intensity of many public services increases their proportionate demand on the economy; demands for education and health are naturally increasing, and developments in medical technology bring a sharp and continuous escalation in costs; the rising number of old people and of children needing care and protection places heavier demands on the personal social services; public environmental responsibilities and many forms of regulation are growing rapidly. It is often pointed out that the stringent controls since the 1970s checked the growth but failed in most Western countries to reduce the size of public expenditure as a proportion of national income. Politicians, armed with market dogmas, continue to argue that cuts can always be covered by increased efficiency, and to blame bureaucrats for any consequent service failures. But given the demonstrable reason for growth in so many spheres of the public domain, this result looks not a failure but a remarkable degree of containment.

It has become politically unfashionable to say so, but there are good reasons for understanding and accepting, not just opposing, the growth of the public sector. Actually, [. . .] the resources devoted to public service consumption are relatively modest—under one-fifth of gross domestic product in OECD countries, the balance of public expenditure consisting of transfer payments which have also needed to increase because of more unemployment and poverty. [Earlier were] reasons for keeping the expanding requirements of social services within a democratic political framework of comprehensive coverage, rather than accepting their gradual erosion by privatization until only a still substantial but inferior public system

remains. There is no need to repeat those arguments. They are central to any reasonable view of equality of opportunity, and they represent a form of collective social insurance which is relatively cheap and a main source of social cohesion. It does not follow that these collective services need to be centrally provided and tightly controlled. The future role of the state is better seen as orchestrating the operations of a variety of service providers. However, the framework still needs to combine the case for diversity with a reasonable degree of equality in access to services. It is not an easy balance to achieve.

The present image of the state is a strongly negative one. Political leaders give the impression of disbelief in the worth of the state's functions and rarely are political voices raised in praise of what the state does or could accomplish. All eyes are fixed upon the supposed wonders and benefits of economic competition and growth. It is no wonder then that there is much ignorance about the actual range, benefits, and problems of public functions. The "public" has become an almost dirty word under the weight of the ruling market dogmas.

A revived democratic state could be expected to pursue more positive purposes. It would seek new means of stimulating and channelling the energies and resources of society so as to meet neglected social goals and aspirations. Its role would be less to order or coerce and more to energize and orchestrate within a new framework of enabling legislation and resource allocation. Resources will always remain too limited in terms of the state's tasks, but the need for a substantial public sector would be accepted and not denigrated. Present political beliefs minimize the value of research and planning for distinctive public purposes and rely upon crude political management. A more purposive stance would enlist intelligent and dedicated public servants to assist in the pursuit of complex goals.

The state's support for capitalist markets carries with it an endorsement of the values of that system as it currently operates. Economic goals are continually allowed to override their own adverse impacts, as when governments respond to mounting evidence of the grim effects of addictive gambling, not by ending their support for casinos but by requiring them to make a small contribution towards alleviating the disease they have first produced. At present, legislators seem quite unable to relate the severe social problems which they encounter in their constituencies to the economic "imperatives" which they continue to pursue. A more purposive state, however, would be prepared to question the values of the market and, with enough community support, actively promote alternative values and goals.

Many may consider that this sketch of a more active state, less beholden to the market and more socially responsive, is an unrealistic reversion to the past. Certainly there would need to be a drastic transformation in the state's present orientations, without which few would be keen to strengthen its capacities. The state is in danger of losing democratic trust. It still remains the creature of a political process and could be regenerated by the emergence of a more active and responsible democracy, and by a reversion to the quest for a common good, which can be described as "a set of shared purposes and standards which are fundamental to the way of life prized together by the participants" (Connolly, 1981, p. 91). Skeptics sneer at the notion of a common good, which Brennan and Buchanan (1985, pp. 37–9) see as a vain quest or "organismic monstrosity." But, if there is no such thing as common good, why should we embrace such purposes as "free market" or economic growth? The common good is a contestable term and the quest will always be open-ended. There is no warranty that a more active democracy would pursue any particular goals and it could have different priorities from those espoused here, but there are also reasons to suppose that a greater stress on social considerations and objectives is congruent with basic democratic values.

These values turn on interpretations of equality and liberty. A genuine democracy is egalitarian in the sense that it accords equal moral worth to each individual. There can never be equal political influence and there will always be wide variations in political participation. Many individuals can quite reasonably opt to leave policy issues to their chosen representatives, but what they need anyhow to judge is the social values of their chosen representative rather than his technical political skills. At the same time more direct political participation is itself a good to be encouraged and fostered. In particular, if participation is to be more of a reality, it is vital to reduce the baleful political influence of wealth and economic power which contribute a lot to the alienation of ordinary citizens.

Liberty when intelligently understood implies always a balance between the pulls of private freedom to lead one's own life, and a social responsibility to contribute to the common good. Liberty then implies a responsible exercise of democratic rights. In human terms the individual's engagement with her immediate social environment may always be greater than with the more formal and often remote political environment; yet the political is a necessary framework for the social. It is because of this situation that efforts to promote a responsible, and discourage a frivolous, treatment of citizenship are so important. A genuinely democratic society would promote all forms of free discussion and debate, and repudiate commercial attempts to subordinate democratic concerns to market criteria.

[. . .]

Democratic Counter-revolution?

This chapter has assumed that a democratic revival is possible. But what does a more active, equal, and responsible democracy entail? It is often assumed that Western societies exhibit the basic requisites of democracy and attention is fixed upon fine-tuning of their procedures and safeguards; but this approach fails to consider the wider social and political conditions within which democracies actually function. If democracy is to become a more meaningful element in the life of society, and hence in the constructive exercise of political choice, three lines of reform need to be pursued, which will be briefly summarized.

First, the workings of democracy should be spread more widely throughout society so as to permeate other institutions besides the state. The development of economic democracy through the promotion of co-operation and consultation in the workplace [. . .] would be one element in this process. The strengthening of elected local government and voluntary bodies is vital both for developing more informed political participation and for delivering public services in an acceptable way. More than this, one must regret the monopolization of office by a narrow political class and look for ways of injecting a broader range of representation into legislatures. One such method is to have the upper house of the legislature elected by a variety of organizations, such as the professions, academia, business, trade unions, local governments, and so on. While an acceptable scheme of this kind is difficult to devise, the principle behind it offers the bridge between the state and civil society which many people want to build.

Second, democracy will continue to be halt and lame so long as the possession of wealth and property exercise such disproportionate political influence, both indirectly and directly. Obvious measures here are to place strong curbs upon political donations and electoral expenses, to limit total electoral expenditure and to provide some assistance to poorer candidates from a public fund. More basically it is hard to see democracy working fairly without a reduction in the extreme economic inequalities of modern societies, especially the concentration of wealth in a tiny class of the very rich. Sooner or later some limit must be placed on the unlimited rights of personal acquisition and the inheritance of vast fortunes.

Third, the responsible exercise of democratic rights, which is surely the ultimate point of citizenship, requires clear political support. Essential measures here are to reduce the permitted limits of media ownership, require more space for informed political discussion as a condition of television licences, promote independent public broadcasting systems, prohibit quick and slick electoral advertising, tax media advertising, and assist the emergence of a wider variety of media outlets. All these measures are within the existing powers of governments and represent little more than elementary conditions of a responsible democracy.

While efforts to strengthen democracy face formidable obstacles, they will be helped by widening perceptions of the need for change. Until recently, political pressures for reform were weak and the personal need to adapt to a rapidly changing economic system seemed dominant. The future was liberally greased with promises about economic growth, and reform efforts were sublimated (as they still are) into the never-ending guests to "increase the competitiveness" of some industry, occupation, city, region, or nation. The world was (and still is) presented as a vast arena of competition which rewarded the worthy and punished the lazy. It was overlooked that this competition did not occur on a level playing field and had many of the attributes of a zero-sum game. However, perspectives are changing rapidly. In the two years since this book's inception, protest against the capitalist market system has grown from a trickle into a stream of critical books, articles, and letters.

Political mobilization is the necessary means for pursuing new goals. It is both helped and hindered by the single-issue politics which is a feature of modern society. These various causes pursue their own agenda and can sometimes be appeased by minor concessions made within the framework of the dominant orthodoxy.

However, the need for integrated action is becoming more apparent. Environmentalists are hardening in their opposition to the principles of the global economy, but effective progress with their aims requires an equally sensitive understanding of social frustrations and aspirations. Feminist efforts to make competitive entry into senior positions as open to women as men needs to be combined with advocacy for the numerous women suffering from new forms of economic exploitation. Ethnic groups are particularly liable to economic disadvantage, but their response needs to be the advocacy of better economic policies not attempts at social segregation and an elusive self-sufficiency or autonomy. These various currents can come together within a framework which reasserts the interests of workers against the dominance of the profit motive, of citizens against the erosion of common resources, and of the disadvantaged against their neglect and marginalization.

The battle of ideas is central to this reform project. It is necessary to challenge the ruling interpretation of liberal individualism. The liberal concept that an individual should be free to choose his own beliefs and lifestyle so long as he does not seriously harm others represented in its day an important advance in freedom and toleration; but its founders never imagined that it could be used to justify a "hands off" approach to the regulation of severely depraved activities which cause grave harm to others as well as their perpetrators. It is time to recognize

that there is a difference between vice and virtue which society needs to blame or condemn, even if not too dogmatically. Governments have a direct responsibility to regulate activities which do serious harm to others and to assist the efforts of schools and communities to instil those virtues which make for social harmony and co-operation as well as tolerance.

Liberal theorists have rediscovered the need for social responsibility as the condition of individual freedom. This welcome discovery has still to be made politically effective in a world where "liberalism" is crudely identified with the assertion of individual rights. In particular, the rights to private property and unlimited acquisition have been pushed to the point of highly destructive effects upon the common life and interests of society. It is important to demonstrate these effects and to show how the possession of common assets is essential to a satisfactory life (especially for the poor) and can be sensibly managed. What sort of "common good" can exist in a world where the affluent isolate themselves in gated communities and where predatory activities become normal?

The revolution in economic ideas ought already to have started with the many intellectual demolitions of the orthodox neo-classical model. That so many people still cling to it may be ascribed to its usefulness (actually a much qualified one) for appearing to justify capitalist markets, in much the same way as the medieval scholastics could argue about how many angels can dance on the top of a needle and still be a useful aid to the power of the medieval church. There is no need to reject the use of formal models as such because, even with unrealistic assumptions, they may offer some insight into reality. The trouble with the neo-classical model lies not only in its degree of unrealism, but with assumptions which are socially and ethically mistaken; labour and land, for example, cannot and should not be treated as simply "commodities," nor is it right to treat individual preferences as "exogenous" and independent of their social formation.

It may be questioned whether it is possible to produce a satisfactory model which combines economic and social elements. But whether this is so or not, economics can offer only limited guidance on such issues as desirable patterns of ownership, the distribution of wealth, and the importance of public services, and cannot say much about largely "non-quantitative" matters such as the quality of life or the conditions of social co-operation. Economic policy works within the possible limits of the system which it is serving, so that a different system will mean a changed spectrum of economic possibilities which cannot be constructed out of theories tied to unconstrained market relationships and interpreted along capitalist lines.

The future is uncertain. It may be that the logic of capitalist markets has become too tight-knit, and the supporting interests too strong, for any piecemeal reform to prove possible. Capitalism might then be eventually superseded by a system whose character can only be guessed at. This book has been written in the hope that piecemeal reform *is* possible, and that the better aspects of competitive markets can be retained within a more balanced and stable system, which will be more socially oriented and less environmentally destructive. From a limited start further progress towards these goals should be possible; but even a limited start entails an awakening of the latent power of what David Lilienthal (1945) once termed (in the context of the Tennessee Valley Authority) "democracy on the march."

Bibliography

Brennan, G. and Buchanan, J.H., *The Reason of Rules: Constitutional Political Economy* (Cambridge University Press, 1985).

Connolly, W.E., *Appearance and Reality in Politics* (Cambridge University Press, 1981).

Lilienthal, D., *TVA: Democracy on the March* (Penguin Books, 1945).

Nozick, R., *Anarchy, State and Utopia* (Blackwell, 1974).

CHAPTER 26

Neoprogressivism: A New Agenda for Social Democracy

Anthony Giddens

It is said that anyone who goes to a restaurant should never make a joke to the waiter about the food or the menu. The waiter's smile will inevitably be forced, because he will have heard the same observation many times before. I feel much the same about the third way. I have been to many countries discussing third way politics. I have lost count of the number of times people have said what we really should be looking for is a fourth way. I have usually answered that we are already on the fifteenth way, meaning that the third way discussion is a continuing and evolving debate, which it is.

But now I have come to see that in a certain sense they are right. At this juncture in political thinking and policy-making, we have to go beyond where third way thinking has got so far. There are two reasons. The main one is simply that the world has moved on since the late 1980s and early 1990s, the time at which third way ideas, in their contemporary guise, were initiated. The second is that there were some weaknesses in these ideas, understandable in the context in which they developed, but that also now need to be remedied.

The Third Way: What It Was and Is

Let me first of all comment upon some misconceptions about the third way debate. The third way, at least in my understanding of it, is *not* a program specifically linked to the New Democrats in the US or to New Labour in Britain. It is not, in other words, a label for a distinctively Anglo-Saxon approach to political analysis and policy-making. The notion stretches much more widely, to the efforts of social democratic parties across the world to rethink their policies in the post-1989 period. Another word for the third way is simply progressivism. Third way politics stands in traditions of social democratic revisionism that stretch back to Eduard Bernstein and Karl Kautsky.

The third way is *not* a "middle way"—specifically, it is not an attempt to find a halfway point between the Old Left and free market fundamentalism. It seeks to transcend both of these. Neither of these earlier two "ways" is adequate to cope with the social and economic problems we face today. The third way is a distinctively left-of-centre project—it is about the modernization of social democracy. When I wrote my book *The Third Way* in 1998,[1] I gave it the subtitle "The Renewal of Social Democracy," and that to me is what the third way means. Finally, the third way is *not* an empty PR exercise. On the contrary, from its beginnings it has been a policy-driven response to change. We live in a world marked by rapid and dramatic transformations—globalization being the most important—and it is the role of third way thinking to seek to show how to cope with them.

Third way thinking has been directed to two main aims. One is *electoral recovery*. By the early 1990s, social democratic parties had been out of power in some of the leading industrial countries, such as the UK, Germany, and France, for a long while. In the US, until Bill Clinton came to office in 1993, there had been no Democratic president for 12 years. Left-of-centre parties had been slow to adjust to a society in which their traditional constituency, the working class, was shrinking away. A generation ago, in the EU countries, over 40 per cent of the labour force worked in manufacture; that proportion has dwindled to 16 per cent, and it is still declining. The old industrial economy has increasingly been replaced by a knowledge-based economy, in a society where the middle class is easily the dominant grouping.

Second, the centre left had to respond to the *crisis of Keynesianism*, the counterpart in Western countries to the dissolution of East European state socialism. Globalization was the prime force behind both of these transitions. It is not possible to have national demand management in a globalized marketplace. At that time, free market fundamentalism—the belief that most of our problems can be resolved through the spread of markets—seemed triumphant, even in those countries that did not directly experience Thatcherite or neo-liberal rule. The third way developed essentially as a critical riposte to neo-liberalism, and it was a highly effective one. The emerging synthesis stressed that active government is an essential prerequisite both for successful economic development and social justice. But it recognized that some established notions and policies of the left had to be rejected or rethought.

Contrary to what some critics say, the policy framework of the third way is coherent and intellectually powerful. It can be sketched out in brief as follows. Government and the state need thoroughgoing reform, to make them faster moving, more effective and responsive, and to reflect the need for greater transparency and diversity in a society where consumer choice has become a prime force. The state should become more of an enabler rather than a direct provider or producer. "Command and control" has visibly failed, not only in the Soviet Union, but also in its milder versions in Western societies, where it took the shape of nationalization of the "commanding heights" of the economy. The emphasis of the state should now be upon helping people to help themselves.

Public investment, however, has to be geared to what a society can afford. "Tax and spend" in the past for the left often meant "tax and overspend." In place of this attitude modernizing social democrats place an emphasis upon fiscal discipline, and upon improving the conditions of economic competitiveness. Economic development and social justice can go hand in hand if we concentrate upon promoting high levels of job creation. A society with a high proportion of people in work is likely to be increasingly prosperous, but is also able to free up resources to pay for public investment. Having a job, above the floor of a decent minimum wage, is the best route out of poverty for anyone able to work.

These ideas presume a new citizenship contract, based upon responsibilities as well as rights. The state helps provide citizens with the resources to make their own lives, but in return they have to recognize their obligations to the community. T.H. Marshall's famous citizenship triad, the classical source for traditional social democratic thought, mentioned only rights—social, political, and economic.[2] Today we should recognize that most rights are conditional. People who claim unemployment benefits, for example, should have the obligation to look for work.

We have to add a further citizenship right to those mentioned by Marshall—the right to live free from the fear of crime. In third way thinking, there should be no policy areas accepted as the inevitable terrain of the right. Voters in the past have tended to trust social democrats on issues such as welfare and education, but not with questions to do with crime, immigration, and defence. The point is not, or should not be, for social democrats to take over rightist policies on these issues, but to offer persuasive left-of-centre approaches and solutions to them.

Finally, the third way framework is internationalist. It is not naively "pro-globalization." It recognizes that globalization produces insecurities, tensions, and conflicts alongside its benefits. Yet many of these benefits, including those generated by free trade, are real. Globalization is also intrinsically related to the spread of democracy. It isn't only in the industrial countries that people are becoming more active citizens, wishing to have more control over what they do, and less inclined than in the past to accept the dictates of authority.

Third way type parties registered a string of successes during the 1990s. At one point, the Democrats held the White House, while 13 out of 15 EU countries were ruled by centre left parties or coalitions. As of 2003, by contrast, the Republicans rule the roost in the US, holding not only the presidency, but both houses of Congress too. Only some six countries in the EU are now governed from the left of centre. The last few years have also seen the rise of far right populism in Europe, with some far right parties polling heavily among erstwhile social democratic voters.

The implications of these changes for the third way have to be put into perspective. In the US election of 2001, the Democratic candidate Al Gore won a higher percentage of the popular vote than George Bush, and but for a few thousand dimpled chads would have been president. Some of the reverses suffered by the centre left in EU countries resulted from tactical errors rather than from swings in public consciousness. Mr Jospin, for instance, lost the chance to get into the presidential run-off in France because the left-of-centre vote in the first stage became too fragmented. In Italy, following the period of government of the Olive Tree Coalition, the left was also divided, allowing Mr Berlusconi to come through for victory. We should also note that centre left coalitions have recently won power in a number of East European countries, including Poland, the Czech Republic, and Hungary.

The electoral setbacks of the centre left came not from the fact that the third way failed, but because it was not embraced actively enough. Governments or parties that did not move sufficiently in a third way direction either fell from power or were not able to attain it. Some governments, for example, were unwilling or unable to push through labour market reforms. As a result, unemployment remained higher than it needed to be. The Lisbon program in the EU was heavily influenced by third way thinking, and is crucial to a resumption of economic growth and to job generation in Europe—yet it has by no means always been endorsed in practice. The Lisbon summit set a target of 70 per cent or more of the labour force in work by 2010. Progress thus far has been slow. The employment ratio of the EU countries in 2002 was 64 per cent—compared to over 75 per cent in the US.

Some parties failed to respond to voter concerns about crime and immigration. They tried to tack on new policies in these areas only after the rise of the far right had shaken them out of their complacency—and too late to register effectively with the voters. Al Gore might very well have emerged a clear winner had he stuck more closely to the policies that helped generate such exceptional economic prosperity in the US during the Clinton years.

I have no doubt at all in my mind that many of the core ideas of the third way are valid and should be sustained. The third way was right to challenge traditional leftist thinking. It was successful wherever it managed to reach out to the new middle class groups and embrace individual aspiration. It was right to reject old-style tax and spend. It was right to relate rights to responsibilities as the basis of a new citizenship contract. It was right about the primacy of work over benefits and the welfare reforms needed to produce such a change of emphasis. It was right about the need to react to the changed economic conditions of the knowledge economy. And, filtered through all of these, it was right to argue that globalization is altering fundamental aspects both of our own societies and the international arena, calling for new policy responses.

Today, nevertheless, we do stand at an important transition point. The challenges and the social context of 2003 are not those of 1993. Moreover, a certain degree of self-criticism is necessary. The third way was developed above all as a critique of the neo-liberal right. It was defined too much in terms of what it was against rather than what it was for. Social democrats need, I shall argue, a greater *ideological breakout* from this situation than has been achieved so far. This ideological breakaway demands new *concepts* and new *policy perspectives*. We must continue to think *radically*, but radicalism means being open to *fresh ideas*, not relapsing back into the traditional leftism of the past. I shan't in fact call this new perspective the fourth way, although the idea is tempting. Instead I shall speak of *neoprogressivism* and the *neoprogressives* (*neoprogs*). The neoprogs need to develop a social democratic agenda as ambitious and comprehensive as the neoconservatives have done in the US and elsewhere.

We need, as I would see it, to create more *deep support* for left-of-centre policies than was generated by the first wave of third way policies. We should not be content with a pragmatic appeal. Deep support means touching an emotional chord among citizens, not just appealing to their pragmatic interests. It means recovering some of that capacity the left had to a much greater degree before 1989, the capacity to inspire. It means having ideals that show what we are for, rather than only what we reject. It means conveying a notion of the type of society, and the type of world, we want to create.

Ideological Breakout

What should neoprogressives stand for? My answer, in brief, would be: a strong public sphere, coupled to a thriving market economy; a pluralistic, but inclusive society; and a cosmopolitan wider world, founded upon principles of international law. Making a renewed case for public interests and public goods (nationally and internationally) seems to me the most crucial, for it is here that the reactive nature of earlier third way thinking is most evident. A healthy economy needs well-functioning markets, but it also needs a well-developed public domain, in which the state retains an essential role.

Strengthening public life does not imply returning to the nanny state. It means rethinking what the state is, and what it is for, in relation to concepts of the public interest and the public good. I call the process *publicization*. The early post-war period was the era of the bureaucratic state. Then we had a time of privatization and deregulation. Now we are potentially entering another phase again—marked not by the return of the bureaucratic state, but by a more inclusive definition of the public purpose. After privatization comes publicization. By publicization I mean defending the core importance of the public sphere to a decent society—one in which citizens can pursue their aspirations, but feel protected and secure. First-wave third way thinking was good at helping with the first, but was less well able to provide for the second.

Notes

1. Anthony Giddens, *The Third Way*, Cambridge: Polity Press, 1998.
2. T.H. Marshall, *Class, Citizenship and Social Development*, Westport: Greenwood Press, 1973.

CHAPTER 27

Nudists and Capitalists

Linda McQuaig

This [chapter] is about greed—not about how bad it is or how guilty we should feel about giving in to it and indulging ourselves. Rather, [it] is about the curious way our society has made greed and material acquisitiveness its central organizing principles. I describe this as "curious" because there is nothing natural or inevitable about our approach. Indeed, our approach is something of an aberration. The pursuit of private profit and the impulse to accumulate material possessions have always been present, in some form, in human societies. But through most of history and in just about every corner of the globe, the pursuit of material gain was not the central activity of society, as it is today. Rather it was relegated to a lower position, considered less important than other aspects of life—like religion, family, clan, community, and kingdom. The attainment of material possessions was considered a less important mark of distinction and status than the display of other forms of human behaviour—like bravery, loyalty, devotion, service, honour, and dedication to duty.

The late economic historian and anthropologist Karl Polanyi—whose ideas are central to this [chapter]—made the provocative point that it is only in the last few centuries, and only in parts of the Western world, that greed and the endless pursuit of material gain have been given almost free rein, that they have been massaged, encouraged, and even considered the very essence of the human personality. This amounts to a massive transformation of society, and this book will explore aspects of this transformation and their impact on the world. Polanyi went on to argue that this transformation was not part of some natural evolution, based on the reality of human nature, but rather was a deliberately imposed redesign of society, carried out by a small but powerful elite in order to enhance its own interests. It could be added that it is only in the last decade or so that things have been pushed an amazing step further—to the point where elaborate international legal systems have been put in place to ensure not only that greed and the pursuit of material gain are given legal protection, but that they are given *supremacy*.

[. . .]

We take it as self-evident that the desire to endlessly accumulate material possessions is basic to the human condition. Some people consider it virtually the only thing basic to the human condition. In the study of economics, for instance, it occupies the very centre of the compass. The central character in economics is *Homo Economicus*, the human prototype, who is pretty much just a walking set of insatiable material desires. He uses his rational abilities to ensure the satisfaction of all his wants, which are the key to his motivation. And he isn't considered some weirdo; the whole point of him is that he represents traits basic to all of us—*Homo Economicus* "R" Us, as it were. This constancy in basic human programming makes it possible, according to economists, to predict human behaviour. Offer enough material incentive, for instance, and we can push corporate executives into a frenzy of hard work; reduce support for welfare recipients, and they'll soon get their financial houses in order and hold down a job. Sure, human beings are intelligent and complex, but their basic motivation is quite simple, the theory goes, and it starts—and usually ends—with a voracious appetite for material gain.

One of the reasons for the success of this theory is that it is so obviously true—or at least partly true. The argument that humans are greedy and have large appetites for material possessions is hardly one that requires supporting evidence. Just state the argument and everyone will nod immediately in agreement—partly because they recognize that sort of inclination in themselves, partly because they've seen it constantly in others. It's pretty clear: *Homo Economicus* rules. After a while, any slight deviation from the *Homo Economicus* model starts to seem implausible or even suspect. Why would anybody do this or that without pay? Must be up to something.

But while the case for *Homo Economicus*—or the centrality if greed and insatiable acquisitiveness in the human personality—appears incontestable, it may hold true mostly for our own society. It may be, in other words, that such strongly acquisitive behaviour isn't really rooted in our nature, but rather is an acquired habit based on the institutions, attitudes, and incentives that shape our society.

Polanyi noted that in primitive and traditional societies, the satisfaction of human material needs was an integral part of the overall life of the community. In other words, the quest for food and material goods was simply part of the overall process and organization of society. The function of meeting material needs was thus "embedded" in one's broader social relations, part of one's role as a member of family, clan, and the larger community. Capitalism changed this, by redesigning society in a way that separated out human material desires, stimulated them and pushed them to the forefront, greatly expanding their importance. The quest for material goods became a world of its own—a world that was given precedence over all other aspects of society. Thus, under capitalism, the material motive was "dis-embedded" from society and from social control, with far-reaching implications for humans and their surroundings.

So the *Homo Economicus* model isn't really a model of human behaviour but rather a model of human behaviour as *capitalism has attempted to reshape it*. The intense focus on material acquisitiveness is something that capitalism has cultivated in us. The point is not to suggest that humans are nicer than the *Homo Economicus* model implies, simply different. By highlighting the individualistic, materialistic motive, capitalism has moved the focus away from what Polanyi insists is the most basic aspect of our nature—that we are social animals.

The essentially social nature of humans was identified centuries ago by Aristotle, and has been observed extensively in the social sciences—particularly psychology, sociology, and anthropology—as well as being the subject of much theory in philosophy and religion. The point is that humans naturally seek to relate to and be accepted by other humans. They want to belong, to feel part of a larger human community. As part of that community—whether family, clan, club, gang, social network, or society at large—they will generally participate and contribute willingly. In addition to a sense of belonging, they want position and status in the social order. They desire approval, recognition, and respect from others; they want to be appreciated and considered worthy by their fellow humans. The more ambitious may dream of being honoured, treated like a "big man on campus" or fawned over by enthusiastic fans.

In emphasizing this social nature, Polanyi is not suggesting that humans are unselfish or uninterested in their own welfare. On the contrary, he is suggesting they are primarily concerned about their own welfare (although not always exclusively so). But this focus on their own welfare doesn't mean that their motivation is primarily materialistic in nature. In fact, their individual welfare hinges, to a large extent, on their social relationships and on the preservation and viability of their communities. To the extent that humans are focused on specifically material goals, their motivation may be largely based on their desire to achieve status and position in the social order. "[Man] does not aim at safeguarding his individual interest in the acquisition of material possessions, but rather at ensuring social good will, social status, social assets," argues Polanyi. "He values possessions primarily as a means to that end."

[. . .]

So here's another way to look at things. *Homo Economicus* is a one-dimensional character who serves a useful purpose in the economics-textbook version of human reality. *Homo's* energetic and cunning pursuit of material gain is necessary for the main plot line of capitalism, and it makes for a compelling cartoon-variety tale. But as a meaningful representation of the human personality and human needs, *Homo*

Economicus seems deficient, even fraudulent. If we look at human societies over time and place—not just restricting our view to the past few centuries in the West—we see that the one consistent thing that can be said about humans is not that they are driven to endlessly acquire material possessions; at times, they seem quite indifferent to this goal. The one thing that is truly consistent, as noted as far back as Aristotle, is that they are social. They travel in packs. They build societies. They may go hunting alone, but they return to the tribe's campfire at night. Tom Hanks illustrated Aristotle's point nicely in the movie *Castaway*: even on the best beach in paradise, by himself he's a miserable guy. One suspects that he would remain so even if he had plenty of steaks and lime daiquiris, an endless supply of Gucci shoes and a wrap-around DVD system.

[. . .]

There is plenty of historical evidence of societies that collectively sought to curb individual acquisitiveness. The medieval world considered greed to be a destructive force that could wreak havoc on the well-being of the community. A merchant was permitted to make a fair return—that is, one that would allow him to live in a manner appropriate for someone of his social position—but those who tried to squeeze an extra profit were considered anti-social and even repulsive. Such people, who would be considered smart businesspeople today, were denounced back in the fourteenth century as "enemies both to God and man, opposite both to Grace and Nature." In case there was any remaining doubt about the merits of such people, the denunciation went on to depict them as "Man-haters, opposite to the Common good, as if the world were made only for them." (To which Mitsubishi would now reply: "Not yet, but we're working on it.")

The transformation of traditional societies into our modern capitalist world is in many ways the story of the repositioning of greed and material acquisitiveness in the overall scheme of society—that is, greed's meteoric rise from the status of the dirty scoundrel of human existence to that of liberator and world-class superstar. But in our celebration of greed as the poster boy of our age, and our rush to conclude that its spirit alone shapes us all, we have blotted out a huge part of our history and risk blinding ourselves to a huge part of our present—the desire for collective action to resist the full force of private greed, to seek what Polanyi called "the protection of society."

This impulse to collectively resist the market is a recurrent theme in the history of the past four of five centuries, according to Polanyi. Indeed, right from the emergence of the market economy, about five centuries ago, there was widespread resistance [. . .] . This resistance has continued in many forms over the centuries. Polanyi argued that true laissez-faire capitalism, in which individual greed is essentially allowed to run loose beyond the reach of social control, only really existed briefly in Britain from the 1840s to the 1870s—and has now been revived, to some extent, in the past two decades in certain parts of the world. Certainly, if we look back at the past five centuries, we are struck by what Polanyi considered a double movement—the implementation of capitalism, but also, each step of the way, the determined attempt of people to come together to protect themselves from the potential damage of newly released market forces. The history of the past five hundred years is the history of the rise of capitalism, but it's also the history of the *resistance* to the harshness of capitalism.

The development of the welfare state in the early post-war period is an important example of this resistance to capitalism's excesses. After the era of fairly free-wheeling capitalism in the early part of the twentieth century, and the disastrous effects of this approach during the Great Depression, there was a clear public sentiment in Western nations in favour of government intervention and market regulation. Although the results varied from country to country, the basic thrust of public policy in the West during the first few decades after the Second World War was towards using the collective power of government to regulate the marketplace and ensure a more equitable distribution of resources among citizens. By imposing higher taxes on the well-to-do, governments were able to redistribute income to those lower down the ladder, and to establish national programs for delivering public services to all. While the post-war system kept capitalism intact, it modified it considerably in the name of protecting the public. There was a widely shared belief that the public interest—as represented by the government—should be given precedence over the powerful private interests that dominated the economic sphere, that ultimately power should rest with the people and their democratically elected representatives. This amounted to what Polanyi described as an attempt to "re-embed" the economy back into society—that is, to make the economy serve the interests of society, not the other way around.

It would be a mistake to overstate the trend towards equality in that early post-war period. There was certainly plenty of inequality, and large corporations were enormously powerful and influential with governments. Popular empowerment had a long way to go. But it would also be a mistake to understate how different the attitudes of policy-makers and the public were in those decades. The trend seemed to be clearly, if slowly, moving in the direction of expanding the democratic rights and sense of economic entitlement of ordinary people—a trend that some in the elite felt angered and threatened by. After all, where would it lead? Would the elite's dominion over the economy and claim to its profits be compromised? When the world economy slowed down in the 1970s, those who disliked the new egalitarian trends saw an opportunity, at last, to move against them.

The attempt to roll back these egalitarian advances is, in a nutshell, the story of the new capitalism. The financial elite has tried to take away the egalitarian gains and the popular sense of entitlement that was achieved during the early post-war decades. To stop this trend towards equality, the elite has sought to strip governments of their power, to return to a laissez-faire approach to the marketplace and to free up corporations—and the rich in general—from the burden of having to transfer what seems to them to be an unduly large part of their wealth to the public purse. Of course, this isn't an entirely "new" capitalism so much as it is an attempt to return to an old capitalism, to create something closer to the unfettered, laissez-faire capitalism that had prevailed in mid-nineteenth-century Britain.

Critical Thinking Questions

1. Tawney distinguishes between economic and political liberty. Based on this distinction, what are the four possible states of any given society? According to Tawney, what ranks as one of the most important goals of modern industrial society? How relevant does this goal remain for contemporary society? Critics of Tawney would argue that his demand for greater equality poses a threat to liberty. How does he respond to this criticism?

2. The *Regina Manifesto* appeared in a specific historic context. How relevant is this context today? How would you rate the success of the *Regina Manifesto* in promoting change?

3. Critics of the *Regina Manifesto* would charge that it undermines economic liberties. How would you judge this criticism?

4. Self concedes that the state suffers from a "strongly negative" image. Which factors have contributed to this condition? He argues "governments have a direct responsibility to regulate activities which do serious harms to others" and "instill those virtues which make for social harmony and cooperation as well as tolerance." If that is that the case, how should government decide which activities are harmful and which virtues promote social harmony? Does the state have a direct responsibility, at all?

5. Giddens argues the policies of the Third Way are "coherent and intellectual powerful." How credible is this claim? How does Giddens attempt to justify the toleration of globalization as a fundamental element of the Third Way? Compare Giddens' *Progressive Manifesto* with the *Regina Manifesto*. Which document has won the day?

6. McQuaig frames the rise of the public welfare state as a response to the excesses of private greed. What other reasons might justify the welfare state? McQuaig's argument rests on the premise of rejecting *Homo Economicus* as an accurate model of human behaviour. Does she advance a suitable alternative?

Biographies

R.H. Tawney (1880–1962)

Born in India, Tawney could have followed his father into the British civil service after graduating from Oxford in 1903. He instead entered the charitable sector. This step had a profound impact on Tawney's personal and professional life. First, it led to his marriage with Jeanette, the sister of his long-time friend William Beveridge (1879–1963), the founder of the modern welfare state in the United Kingdom. More importantly, the experience convinced Tawney of the need for significant societal reforms, a belief that intensified after his front-line service in World War I. Tawney, a devout Protestant who kept his personal faith private, paid particular attention as an economic historian to the immoral and selfish dimensions of capitalism, a topic that would dominate his most important works such as *The Acquisitive Society* (1920) and *Equality* (1931).

Authors of the *Regina Manifesto*

A single person did not write the *Regina Manifesto*. Instead, it qualifies as a collaborative effort under the leadership of League for Social Reconstruction (LSR), an organization that embraced individuals such as Frank Underhill, F.R. Scott, Eugene Forsey, Harry Cassidy, Graham Spry, and Irene Bliss. This circle of intellectuals would go on to hold considerable sway over the Co-operative Commonwealth Federation, the forerunner of the contemporary New Democratic Party, arguably the most successful social democratic party in English-speaking North America. This status rests primarily but not exclusive on its role in creating Canada's public healthcare system dating back to its origins in Saskatchewan, the party's historical and spiritual home. While the political fortunes of the party have waxed and waned throughout the latter decades of the twentieth century, it recently experienced an unprecedented resurgence when it won more than 100 seats during the 2011 federal election to claim the status of Official Opposition, a historic achievement by any measure.

Peter Self (1919–1999)

Gentle despite his striking physical presence, courageous despite the occasional crisis of confidence, Self shaped the public and political life of two countries—his native England and his adopted home of Australia. Born into a middle-class family headed by a leading civil servant of the era, Self spent World War II (1939–1945) as a conscientious objector working various jobs. Before the war ended, Self secured a staff position with *The Economist*, where he wrote about subjects such as local government that would animate his later academic career. Mostly associated with the London School of Economics, Self advanced the scholarship of public administration and planning during his career in the United Kingdom. Disenchanted by the personal politics of academia and disgusted by the public policies of Tory Prime Minister Margaret Thatcher (1925–), Self moved to Australia in the early 1980s, where he once again held senior posts in government and academia. While Self questioned some of his personal decisions, most notably his decision to sit out the war, he never apologized for his vision of a society that fused individual liberty with collective responsibility.

Anthony Giddens (1938–)

Born in London during the declining days of the British Empire, Giddens pursued an academic career in sociology that eventually propelled him to the commanding heights of intellectual and political life at the dawn of the twenty-first century. As the former director of the renowned London School of Economics (1997–2003) and as an advisor to governments around the world, Giddens' ideas have influenced countless students of sociology and politics. Giddens' hold on the intellectual imagination reached its undeniable apex in the 1990s when his ideas about the Third Way greatly influenced then–British Prime Minister Tony Blair (New Labour) and former US President Bill Clinton.

Linda McQuaig (1951–)

A columnist and non-fiction author, McQuaig rose to prominence during the late 1980s when she revealed the criminal doings of a senior Ontario bureaucrat who had funnelled charitable donations into the campaign coffers of the ruling provincial Liberals. This exposure turned McQuaig into a national figure who has since used her prominent perch in the Canadian media environment to crusade against the corrupting influence of corporations on political affairs. This campaign—which has spanned across a series of books and countless columns—has led to unflattering comparisons with American documentary filmmaker Michael Moore. Yes, McQuaig, like Moore, occasionally relies on a piece of pointed humour or polemic to make her point. But McQuaig has succeeded where Moore has failed, as she has earned the grudging respect of her one-time foes, including former newspaper baron Conrad Black. After McQuaig had attacked his business dealings, he publicly lashed out at her. Yet Black respected her work to the point that he hired her.

Part VI

Fascism and Neo-nationalism

Fascism and Neo-nationalism

Fascism stands at the juncture of conservatism and nationalism. It venerates the culture, "race," and values of a single nation and backs up this veneration with totalitarian power. Typically, it sets aside constitutionalism and the rule of law so much so that justice is eviscerated. Though it has variegated roots in the nineteenth century, as an ideology Fascism came to a head with the March on Rome in 1922 in Italy and with the passing of the Enabling Bill in 1933 in Germany. The contemporary challenge to multiculturalism in the European Union, especially in the Netherlands and France, has resulted in the birth of Fascist-like ideas—ideas that are recombining with neo-national ideals. The resulting neo-nationalism competes with neo-liberalism for the hearts and minds of contemporary Europeans.

Major Figures

F.T. Marinetti (1876–1944), Benito Mussolini (1883–1945), Adolf Hitler (1889–1945), Viktor Orban (1963–), and Geert Wilders (1963–)

Period of Greatest Influence

1922 to 1945

Introduction

The birth of Darwinism in 1859 coupled with rising nationalism and the debacle of World War I gave birth to a radical ideology hitherto not confronted. This new ideology was Fascism and was characterized by a marked hostility to ideas and principles that classical liberals, conservatives, reform liberals, and even, at times, Marxists took for granted. These ideas and principles included tolerance, democratic sensibilities, the universal brotherhood and incompletely recognized sisterhood of mankind, free trade, the principle of equality, and procedural justice. The clarion call of Fascism was the Treaty of Versailles of 1919, which failed to reward Italy for its contributions to the outcome of the war, and its war guilt clause, Article 231, which aimed to punish Germany. The ink was hardly dry on the Treaty when, on 24 February 1920, an upstart named Adolf Hitler (1883–1945) delivered his speech of "Twenty Five Points." In retrospect, this virtual manifesto revealed everything about the way Fascists would conduct themselves if ever given power in Germany, but its demands were simply not given much credence until years later. However, before turning to Hitler's speech, we discuss the remarks of a proto-Fascist in the years preceding the Treaty and those of Benito Mussolini (1883–1945) some years later.

Though one can easily cite the motifs of social Darwinism, self-sufficiency (autarky), and nationalism as the nineteenth-century precursors of Fascism, a much neglected cluster of related themes is provided by the Italian Filippo Tommaso Marinetti (1876–1944) in his *Futurist Manifesto* published in 1909 in *Le Figaro*. In the *Manifesto*, Marinetti glorifies courage, rebellion, and aggressive action (which find their way into the visual grammar of Fascism in heroic art); affirms the validity of delirious primordial elements; extols the future and condemns the past; and lacerates museum, libraries, and academies of any sort. There is something nihilistic in Marinetti's ideas, where one thinks of nihilism as the radical rejection of values—certainly the rejection of conventional values. In their place, Marinetti offers radically new values that eventually work their way into the platform of the *Partito Politico Futurista* (Futurist Political Party), which he helped found in 1918 and which one year later was itself folded into Benito Mussolini's Italian Fascist Party. Clearly, there is a line of thought in the history of ideas that leads from Marinetti to Mussolini.

The political ideas of Benito Mussolini are articulated in a bold and uncompromising way in a pamphlet entitled *The Political and Social Doctrine of Fascist* published in 1933. They, more than the ideas found in Hitler's "Twenty-Five Points," encapsulate much of the strident and nihilistic tone of Marinetti. Such is the case when Mussolini—who, along with his Fascist black shirts, had already risen to power—denounces universalism, pacifism, democracy, equality, and liberalism, thereby implicitly rejecting international endeavours such as the League of Nations. There is a self-confidence in the words of Mussolini that reveals his certainty of the vulnerability of liberalism, both classical and reform, as a spent spiritual force quite unable to meet the needs of the Italian people in the 1930s. Drenched in self-assuredness and echoing some of the themes of Nietzsche (1844–1900), a Prussian existentialist, in *Thus Spoke Zarathustra*, Mussolini declares categorically that the temples of liberalism are deserted. Only too ready is Mussolini to provide different temples for new gods and a new doctrine, thereby showing the religious dimensions to the ideology he advocates.

Like those of Mussolini, the demands made by Hitler in his "Twenty-Five Points" are as uncompromising as they are bold and challenging. They take seething aim—white-hot aim—at the provisions of the Treaty of Versailles. Seizing on the suggestions of Lenin and Woodrow Wilson regarding the validity of self-determination, Hitler demands the right of all Germans to form a nation based on this principle. He then moves in rapid succession to a denunciation of the Treaty and of non-German immigration and to an affirmation of racial purity and control of the press. These are by no means all of his demands, but they set the tone for the remainder of his speech and for more strident demands that he makes during the years immediately preceding the outbreak of World War II, including those demands with respect to Austria and Czechoslovakia. A few years later in *Mein Kampf* (1925–1926), Hitler explores broader themes of the "philosophy" standing behind his "Twenty-Five Points." Here, Hitler describes the way in which the ideal image of a folkish state is to be transformed into a practical reality, the key being fanatical intolerance. In other words, the way forward for Hitler lies in a program that amounts to a declaration of war against the existing order and that roots itself in fanatical faith, unquestioned leadership, and a few guiding principles. At the heart of this existing order, according to Hitler, lie the Jews and their communist allies, as well as their Jewish state, a state that must be eliminated to be replaced by the folkish state of the master race, the Aryan nation. One finds in the words of Hitler more than an intimation of things to come in Germany after the Crash of 1929, the Great Depression, the disintegrating Weimar Republic, and the passage of the Enabling Bill in 1933. It is this bill, after all, that finally consolidates in a "legal" way Hitler's hold on dictatorial power as Chancellor of Germany and enables his implementing many of the things aspired after in the "Twenty-Five Points."

The culmination of the extreme ideas of Fascism—at least as articulated in Germany—was unquestionably the Final Solution (*Endlösung*), during which some six million Jews were systematically exterminated either by being gassed or shot. Hannah Arendt (1906–1975) writes persuasively of the banality of evil as personified in the attitude and actions of Adolf Eichmann, Head of Jewish Affairs in the Gestapo in 1941, regarding the Final Solution. Of particular interest to Arendt is the manner in which National Socialists in Germany—acting under direct orders from the Führer and filtered via the chain of command from Hermann Göring to Reinhard Heydrich—subjected all correspondence to a rigid set of "language rules" so as to replace words such as "killing," "extermination," and "liquidation" with more acceptable words such as "final solution," "evacuation," and "special treatment." Arendt speaks of the disembodied voice of Eichmann heard during his trial in Jerusalem, and in so doing Arendt attempts, as Bernard Wasserstein suggests, to flesh out a central concern evident in all her writings: the conflict between civilization and barbarism. In this she stands in the good company of such distinguished historians as Herodotus and Gibbon.

In the extract from his article "International Law and the Third Reich," Detlev Vagts summarily describes the impact of National Socialism, German Fascism, on international law. According to Vagts, National Socialism gave rise to its antithesis: the ratification of the Genocide Convention, the judgement at Nuremberg, the prohibition on the use of force in the United Nations Charter, and the tightening of the Hague and Geneva rules for waging war. Vagts effectively outlines the different responses made by international lawyers in Germany after 1933, responses that range from those who withdrew from international law studies to those who collaborated with the Nazis. Those who collaborated, as Vagts says, had difficulty producing an intellectual structure to serve as a bridge between racist conceptions of the state and international law. In penetrating fashion, Vagts ends by exploring the question of whether the experience of international lawyers under the Third Reich has lessons for international lawyers in other places and times.

Following the War Crimes Tribunals in Nuremberg and Tokyo, the prevailing view in Western liberal democracies was that the odious aspects of Fascism were dead. To the surprise of most people, events after the carnage of the Twin Towers and 9/11, including the economic uncertainty surrounding hedge funds, derivatives, and sub-prime mortgages, as well as demographic changes, have conspired to fan the flames of a new nationalism in European countries, one that took a devastatingly tragic turn in July 2011, when Norwegian right-wing extremist Andres Behring Breivik killed 69 people, mostly teenagers. A self-styled "modern-day crusader," Breivik described his actions "as atrocious but necessary" in the defence of European Christianity against Islam and Marxism. This new form of what Norwegian scholar Thomas Hegghammer has called "macro-nationalism" is explicitly praised by the author of our next selection.

Enter Geert Wilders, a xenophobic Dutch nationalist, who condemned Breivik's actions. In his anthologized speech, Wilders addresses Germans in Berlin for the purpose of encouraging them to form a political movement, like his in Holland, in order to oppose the Islamization of Germany. Drawing on Marx's introduction to *The Communist Manifesto* Wilder warns Germans that a spectre is haunting Europe, to wit, the spectre of Islam. Wilders attempts to distance himself from those who would attack Muslims. Rather, he targets Islam on the grounds that it is an intolerant ideology that allows no room for compromise, thereby threatening the identities of European countries. For Wilders, this inflexible ideology compromises national identity by discouraging assimilation among Muslims. He claims to have no quarrel with Muslims but only with their ideology. While the political stance of Wilders is not Fascism, it is a new breed of nationalism with overtones of racism only slightly veiled.

The twentieth century saw an agitated ideology surface in the form of Fascism. Both Mussolini and Hitler had pretentious claims to their tenure in power and in something less than the "fullness of time," their political and military strength faded away. It was up to democratic liberal regimes to set the house in order—a house that had been so badly disturbed during the period from 1920 to 1945. But though it can be said that Fascism has pretty well faded as an influential force in the international community, aspects of it remain, one aspect being neo-nationalism. The voice of Wilders makes this abundantly clear.

CHAPTER 28

The Futurist Manifesto

F.T. Marinetti

1. We want to sing about the love of danger, about the use of energy and recklessness as common, daily practice.
2. Courage, boldness, and rebellion will be essential elements in our poetry.
3. Up to now, literature has extolled a contemplative stillness, rapture, and reverie. We intend to glorify aggressive action, a restive wakefulness, life at the double, the slap and the punching fist.
4. We believe that this wonderful world has been further enriched by a new beauty, the beauty of speed. A racing car, its bonnet decked out with exhaust pipes like serpents with galvanic breath . . . a roaring motorcar, which seems to race on like machine-gun fire, is more beautiful than the Winged Victory of Samothrace.[1]
5. We wish to sing the praises of the man behind the steering wheel, whose sleek shaft traverses the earth, which itself is hurtling at breakneck speed along the racetrack of its orbit.
6. The poet will have to do all in his power, passionately, flamboyantly, and with generosity of spirit, to increase the delirious fervour of the primordial elements.
7. There is no longer any beauty except the struggle. Any work of art that lacks a sense of aggression can never be a masterpiece. Poetry must be thought of as a violent assault upon the forces of the unknown with the intention of making them prostrate themselves at the feet of mankind.
8. We stand upon the furthest promontory of the ages! . . . Why should we be looking back over our shoulders, if what we desire is to smash down the mysterious doors of the Impossible? Time and Space died yesterday.[2] We are already living in the realms of the Absolute, for we have already created infinite, omnipresent speed.
9. We wish to glorify war—the sole cleanser of the world[3]—militarism, patriotism, the destructive act of the libertarian,[4] beautiful ideas worth dying for, and scorn for women.[5]
10. We wish to destroy museums, libraries, academies of any sort, and fight against moralism, feminism,[6] and every kind of materialistic, self-serving cowardice.
11. We shall sing of the great multitudes[7] who are roused up by work, by pleasure, or by rebellion; of the many-hued, many-voiced tides of revolution in our modern capitals; of the pulsating, nightly ardour of arsenals and shipyards, ablaze with their violent electric moons; of railway stations, voraciously devouring smoke-belching serpents; of workshops hanging from the clouds by their twisted threads of smoke; of bridges which, like giant gymnasts, bestride the rivers, flashing in the sunlight like gleaming knives; of intrepid steamships that sniff out the horizon; of broad-breasted locomotives, champing on their wheels like enormous steel horses, bridled with pipes; and of the lissome flight of the airplane, whose propeller flutters like a flag in the wind, seeming to applaud, like a crowd excited.

It is from Italy that we hurl at the whole world this utterly violent, inflammatory manifesto of ours, with which today we are founding "Futurism," because we wish to free our country from the stinking canker of its professors, archaeologists, tour guides, and antiquarians.

For far too long has Italy been a marketplace for junk dealers. We want to free our country from the endless number of museums that everywhere cover her like countless graveyards. Museums, graveyards! . . . They're the same thing, really, because of their grim profusion of corpses that no one remembers. Museums. They're just public flophouses, where things sleep on forever, alongside other loathsome or nameless things! Museums: ridiculous abattoirs for painters and sculptors, who are furiously stabbing one another to death with colours and lines, all along the walls where they vie for space.

Sure, people may go there on pilgrimage about once a year, just as they do to the cemetery on All Souls Day—I'll grant you that! And yes, once a year a wreath of flowers is laid at the feet of the *Gioconda*[8]—I'll grant you that too! But what I won't allow is that all our miseries, our fragile courage, or our sickly anxieties get marched daily around these museums. Why should we want to poison ourselves? Why should we want to rot?

What on earth is there to be discovered in an old painting other than the laboured contortions of the artist, trying to break down the insuperable barriers which prevent him from giving full expression to his artistic dream? . . . Admiring an old painting is just like pouring our purest feelings into a funerary urn, instead of projecting them far and wide, in violent outbursts of creation and of action.

Do you really want to waste all your best energies in this unending, futile veneration for the past, from which you emerge fatally exhausted, diminished, trampled down?

Make no mistake, I'm convinced that for an artist to go every day to museums and libraries and academies (the cemeteries of wasted effort, calvaries of crucified dreams, records of impulses cut short! . . .) is every bit as harmful as the prolonged overprotectiveness of parents for certain young people who get carried away by their talent and ambition. For those who are dying anyway, for the invalids, for the prisoners—who cares? The admirable past may be a balm to their worries, since for them the future is a closed book . . . but we, the powerful young Futurists, don't want to have anything to do with it, the past!

So let them come, the happy-go-lucky fire raisers with their blackened fingers! Here they come! Here they are! . . . Come on then! Set fire to the library shelves! . . . Divert the canals so they can flood the museums! . . . Oh, what a pleasure it is to see those revered old canvases, washed out and tattered, drifting away in the water! . . . Grab your picks and your axes and your hammers and then demolish, pitilessly demolish, all venerated cities!

Notes

1. A famous marble sculpture commissioned around 190 BCE by the citizens of Rhodes to commemorate their naval victory over the Seleucid king, Antiochus III. It portrays Nike, the Greek goddess of victory, standing on a ship's prow, with her wings spread and her clinging garments rippling in the wind. The sculpture was discovered in 1863 on the Aegean island of Samothrace and given a new home in the Louvre.

2. This is a reference to recent inventions and technologies that allowed human beings to overcome the age-old limitations imposed by time and space, for example, high-speed travel (steam trains, bicycles, automobiles, airplanes) and the use of new means of communication (telegraph, telephone).

3. On Marinetti's concept of health and hygiene see, *War, the Sole Cleanser of the World.*

4. This is a reference to the spectacular assassinations of Tsar Alexander II (1881) and King Umberto I of Savoy (1900) and the anarchist bomb attacks that shook Paris in 1892–94. When Marinetti was studying in Paris, he had plenty of opportunity for acquainting himself with the doctrines of Anarchism. After his return to Italy he became friends with the Revolutionary Syndicalist Walter Mocchi and the anarchist poets Gian Pietro Lucini and Umberto Notari. Together they frequented the anarchist and syndicalist circles in Lombardy and recruited there some of the early supporters of the Futurist movement. The iconoclastic mentality of the artists Marinetti gathered around himself was also reflected in his own writing, which often celebrated the anarchists' *beaux gestes libertaires.* It has even been suggested that Marinetti's early poetry was influenced by the style and tone of anarchist magazines, brochures, and posters. See Fanette Roche-Pézard, "Marinetti et l'anarchie."

In Jean-Claude Marcadé, ed., *Présence de F.T. Marinetti* (Lausanne: L'Âge d'Homme, 1982), pp. 67–85; and Giovanni Lista, "Marinetti et les anarcho-syndicalistes," ibid., pp. 127–33.

5. The phrase "scorn for women" caused considerable discussion and forced Marinetti to clarify the issue in the preface to *Mafarka* and in *Against Sentimentalized Love and Parliamentarianism.*

6. As Marinetti elucidated in his interview with Comoedia, he made a distinction between the feminist movement "as it triumphs in France today, thanks to a magnificent elite of intellectual women," and its variant in Italy, "where it is confined to unbridled and small-minded careerism and oratory ambitions." See also his comments on the English suffragettes in *Against Sentimentalized Love and Parliamentarianism* and in *Lecture to the English on Futurism.*

7. Marinetti was familiar with and influenced by Gustave Le Bon's analysis of the burgeoning mass society.

8. This is a reference to Leonardo da Vinci's *Mona Lisa* painting in the Louvre.

CHAPTER 29

The Political and Social Doctrine of Fascism

Benito Mussolini

Fascism is now a completely individual thing, not only as a regime but as a doctrine. And this means that today Fascism, exercising its critical sense upon itself and upon others, has formed its own distinct and peculiar point of view, to which it can refer and upon which, therefore, it can act in the face of all problems, practical or intellectual, which confront the world.

And above all, Fascism, the more it considers and observes the future and the development of humanity quite apart from political considerations of the moment, believes neither in the possibility nor the utility of perpetual peace. It thus repudiates the doctrine of Pacifism—born of a renunciation of the struggle and an act of cowardice in the face of sacrifice. War alone up to its highest tension all human energy and puts the stamp of nobility upon the peoples who have the courage meet it. All other trials are substitutes, which never really put men into the position where they have to make the great decision—the alternative of life or death. Thus a doctrine which is founded upon this harmful postulate of peace is hostile to Fascism. And thus hostile to the spirit of Fascism, though accepted for what use they can be in dealing with particular political situations, are all the international leagues and societies which, as history will show, can be scattered to the winds when once strong national feeling is aroused by any motive—sentimental, ideal, or practical. This anti-Pacifist spirit is carried by Fascism even into the life of the individual; the proud motto of the *Squadrista*, "Me ne frego," written on the bandage of the wound, is an act of philosophy not only stoic, the summary of a doctrine not only political—it is the education to combat, the acceptation of the risks which combat implies, and a new way of life for Italy. Thus the Fascist accepts life and loves it, knowing nothing of and despising suicide: he rather conceives of life as duty and struggle and conquest, life which should be high and full, lived for oneself, but above all for others—those who are at hand and those who are far distant, contemporaries, and those who will come after.

This "demographic" policy of the regime is the result of the above premise. Thus the Fascist loves in actual fact his neighbour, but this "neighbour" is not merely a vague and undefined concept, this love for one's neighbour puts no obstacle in the way of necessary educational severity, and still less to differentiation of status and to physical distance. Fascism repudiates any universal embrace, and in order to live worthily in the community of civilized peoples watches its contemporaries with vigilant eyes, takes good note of their state of mind and, in the changing trend of their interests, does not allow itself to be deceived by temporary and fallacious appearances.

Such a conception of life makes Fascism the complete opposite of that doctrine, the base of so-called scientific and Marxian Socialism, the materialist conception of history; according to which the history of human civilization can be explained simply through the conflict of interests among the various social groups and by the change and development in the means and instruments of production. That the changes in the economic field—new discoveries of raw materials, new methods of working them, and the inventions of science—have their importance no one can deny; but that these factors are sufficient to explain the history of humanity excluding all others is an absurd delusion. Fascism, now and always, believes in holiness and in heroism; that is to say, in actions influenced by no economic motive, direct or indirect. And if the economic conception of history be denied, according to which theory men are no more than puppets, carried to and fro by the waves of chance, while the real directing forces are quite out of their control, it follows that the existence of an unchangeable and unchanging class-war is also denied—the natural progeny of the economic conception of history. And above all Fascism denies that class-war can be the preponderant force in the transformation of society. These two fundamental concepts of Socialism being this refuted, nothing is left of it but the sentimental aspiration—as old as humanity itself—toward a social convention in which the sorrows and sufferings of the humblest shall be alleviated. But here again Fascism repudiates the conception of "economic" happiness, to be realized by Socialism and, as it were, at a given moment in economic evolution to assure to everyone the maximum of well-being. Fascism denies the materialist conception of happiness as a possibility, and abandons it to its inventors, the economists of the first half of the nineteenth century: that is to say, Fascism denies the validity of the equation, well-being=happiness, which would reduce men to the level of animals, caring for one thing only—to be fat and well-fed—and would thus degrade humanity to a purely physical existence.

After Socialism, Fascism combats the whole complex system of democratic ideology, and repudiates it, whether in its theoretical premises or in its practical application. Fascism denies that the majority, by the simple fact that it is a majority, can direct human society; it denies that numbers alone can govern by means of a periodical consultation, and it affirms the immutable, beneficial, and fruitful inequality of mankind, which can never be permanently levelled through the mere operation of a mechanical process such as universal suffrage. The democratic regime may be defined as from time to time giving the people the illusion of sovereignty, while the real effective sovereignty lies in the hands of other concealed and irresponsible forces. Democracy is a regime nominally without a king, but it is ruled by many kings—more absolute, tyrannical, and ruinous than one sole king, even though a tyrant. This explains why Fascism, having first in 1922 (for reasons of expediency) assumed an attitude tending towards republicanism, renounced this point of view before the march to Rome; being convinced that the question of political form is not today of prime importance, and after having studied the examples of monarchies and republics past and present reached the conclusion that monarchy or republicanism are not to be judged, as it were, by an absolute standard; but that they represent forms in which the evolution—political, historical, traditional, or psychological—of a particular country has expressed itself. Fascism supersedes the antithesis monarchy or republicanism, while democracy still tarries beneath the domination of this idea, forever pointing out the insufficiency of the first and forever the praising of the second as the perfect regime. Today, it can be seen that

there are republics innately reactionary and absolutist, and also monarchies which incorporate the most ardent social and political hopes of the future.

"Reason and science," says Renan (one of the inspired pre-Fascists) in his philosophical meditations, "are products of humanity, but to expect reason as a direct product of the people and a direct result of their action is to deceive oneself by a chimera. It is not necessary for the existence of reason that everybody should understand it. And in any case, if such a decimation of truth were necessary, it could not be achieved in a low-class democracy, which seems as though it must of its very nature extinguish any kind of noble training. The principle that society exists solely through the well-being and the personal liberty of all the individuals of which it is composed does not appear to be conformable to the plans of nature, in whose workings the race alone seems to be taken into consideration, and the individual sacrificed to it. It is greatly to be feared that the last stage of such a conception of democracy (though I must hasten to point out that the term 'democracy' may be interpreted in various ways) would end in a condition of society in which a degenerate herd would have no other preoccupation but the satisfaction of the lowest desires of common men." Thus Renan. Fascism denies, in democracy, the absurd conventional untruth of political equality dressed out in the garb of collective irresponsibility, and the myth of "happiness" and indefinite progress. But, if democracy may be conceived in diverse forms—that is to say, taking democracy to mean a state of society in which the populace are not reduced to impotence in the State—Fascism may write itself down as "an organized, centralized, and authoritative democracy."

Fascism has taken up an attitude of complete opposition to the doctrines of Liberalism, both in the political field and the field of economics. There should be no undue exaggeration (simply with the object of immediate success in controversy) of the importance of Liberalism in the last century, nor should what was but one among many theories which appeared in that period be put forward as a religion for humanity for all time, present and to come. Liberalism only flourished for half a century. It was born in 1830 in reaction against the Holy Alliance, which had been formed with the object of diverting the destinies of Europe back to the period before 1789, and the highest point of its success was the year 1848, when even Pius IX was a Liberal. Immediately after that date it began to decay, for if the year 1848 was a year of light and hope, the following year, 1849, was a year of darkness and tragedy. The Republic of Rome was dealt a mortal blow by a sister-republic—that of France—and in the same year Marx launched the gospel of the Socialist religion, the famous Communist Manifesto. In 1851, Napoleon III carried out his far from Liberal *coup d'etat* and reigned in France until 1870, when he was deposed by a popular movement as the consequence of a military defeat which must be counted as one of the most decisive in history. The victor was Bismarck, who knew nothing of the religion of liberty, or the prophets by which that faith was revealed. And it is symptomatic that such a highly civilized people as the Germans were completely ignorant of the religion of liberty during the whole of the nineteenth century. It was nothing but a parenthesis, represented by that body which has been called "The ridiculous Parliament of Frankfort," which lasted only for a short period. Germany attained her national unity quite outside the doctrines of Liberalism—a doctrine which seems entirely foreign to the German mind, a mind essentially monarchic—while Liberalism is the logical and, indeed, historical forerunner of anarchy. The stages in the achievement of German unity are the three wars of '64, '66, and '70, which were guided by such "Liberals" as Von Moltke and Bismarck. As for Italian unity,

its debt to Liberalism is completely inferior in contrast to that which it owes to the work of Mazzini and Garibaldi, who were not Liberals. Had it not been for the intervention of the anti-Liberal Napoleon, we should not have gained Lombardy; and without the help of the again anti-Liberal Bismarck at Sadowa and Sedan it is very probable that we should never have gained the province of Venice in '66, or been able to enter Rome in '70. From 1870 to 1914 a period began during which even the very high priests of the religion themselves had to recognize the gathering twilight of their faith—defeated as it was by the decadence of literature and atavism in practice—that is to say, Nationalism, Futurism, Fascism. The era of Liberalism, after having accumulated an infinity of Gordian knots, tried to untie them in the slaughter of the World War—and never has any religion demanded of its votaries such a monstrous sacrifice. Perhaps the Liberal Gods were athirst for blood? But now, today, the Liberal faith must shut the doors of its deserted temples, deserted because the peoples of the world realize that its worship—agnostic in the field of economics and indifferent in the field of politics and morals—will lead, as it has already led, to certain ruin. In addition to this, let it be pointed out that all the political hopes of the present day are anti-Liberal, and it is therefore supremely ridiculous to try to classify this sole creed as outside the judgment of history, as though history were a hunting ground reserved for the professors of Liberalism alone—as though Liberalism were the final unalterable verdict of civilization.

But the Fascist negation of Socialism, Democracy, and Liberalism must not be taken to mean that Fascism desires to lead the world back to the state of affairs before 1789, the date which seems to be indicated as the opening years of the succeeding semi-Liberal century: we do not desire to turn back; Fascism has not chosen De Maistre for its high-priest. Absolute monarchy has been and can never return, any more than blind acceptance of ecclesiastical authority.

So, too, the privileges of the feudal system "have been," and the division of society into castes impenetrable from outside, and with no inter-communication among themselves: the Fascist conception of authority has nothing to do with such a polity. A party which entirely governs a nation is a fact entirely new to history, there are no possible references or parallels. Fascism uses in its construction whatever elements in the Liberal, Social, or Democratic doctrines still have a living value; it maintains what may be called the certainties which we owe to history, but it rejects all the rest—that is to say, the conception that there can be any doctrine of unquestioned efficacy for all times and all peoples. Given that the nineteenth century was the century of Socialism, of Liberalism, and of Democracy, it does not necessarily follow that the twentieth century must also be a century of Socialism, Liberalism, and Democracy: political doctrines pass, but humanity remains; and it may rather be expected that this will be a century of authority, a century of the Left, a century of Fascism. For if the nineteenth century was a century of individualism (Liberalism always signifying individualism) it may be expected that this will be the century of collectivism, and hence, the century of the State. It is a perfectly logical deduction that a new doctrine can utilize all the still vital elements of previous doctrines.

No doctrine has ever been born completely new, completely defined and owing nothing to the past; no doctrine can boast a character of complete originality; it must always derive, if only historically, from the doctrines which have preceded it and develop into further doctrines which will follow. Thus the scientific Socialism of Marx is the heir of the Utopian Socialism of Fourier, of the Owens, and of Saint-Simon; thus again the Liberalism of the eighteenth century is linked with all the advanced thought of the seventeenth century, and thus the doctrines of Democracy are the heirs of the Encyclopedists. Every doctrine tends to direct human activity towards a determined objective; but the action of men also reacts upon the doctrine, transforms it, adapts it to new needs, or supersedes it with something else. A doctrine then must be no mere exercise in words, but a living act; and thus the value of Fascism lies in the fact that it is veined with pragmatism, but at the same time has a will to exist and a will to power, a firm front in face of the reality of "violence."

The foundation of Fascism is the conception of the State, its character, its duty, and its aim. Fascism conceives of the State as an absolute, in comparison with which all individuals or groups are relative, only to be conceived of in their relation to the State. The conception of the Liberal State is not that of a directing force, guiding the play and development, both material and spiritual, of a collective body, but merely a force limited to the function of recording results: on the other hand, the Fascist State is itself conscious, and has itself a will and a personality—thus it may be called the "ethic" State. In 1929, at the first five-yearly assembly of the Fascist regime, I said:

> For us Fascists, the State is not merely a guardian, preoccupied solely with the duty of assuring the personal safety of the citizens; nor is it an organization with purely material aims, such as to guarantee a certain level of well-being and peaceful conditions of life; for a mere council of administration would be sufficient to realize such objects. Nor is it a purely political creation, divorced from all contact with the complex material reality which makes up the life of the individual and the life of the people as a whole. The State, as conceived of and as created by Fascism, is a spiritual and moral fact in itself, since its political, juridical, and economic organization of the nation is a concrete thing: and such an

organization must be in its origins and development a manifestation of the spirit. The State is the guarantor of security both internal and external, but it is also the custodian and transmitter of the spirit of the people, as it has grown up through the centuries in language, in customs, and in faith. And the State is not only a living reality of the present, it is also linked with the past and above all with the future, and thus transcending the brief limits of individual life, it represents the immanent spirit of the nation. The forms in which States express themselves may change, but the necessity for such forms is eternal. It is the State which educates its citizens in civic virtue, gives them a consciousness of their mission and welds them into unity; harmonizing their various interests through justice, and transmitting to future generations the mental conquests of science, of art, of law, and the solidarity of humanity. It leads men from primitive tribal life to that highest expression of human power which is Empire: it links up through the centuries the names of those of its members who have died for its existence and in obedience to its laws, it holds up the memory of the leaders who have increased its territory and the geniuses who have illumined it with glory as an example to be followed by future generations. When the conception of the State declines, and disunifying and centrifugal tendencies prevail, whether of individuals or of particular groups, the nations where such phenomena appear are in their decline.

From 1929 until today, evolution, both political and economic, has everywhere gone to prove the validity of these doctrinal premises. Of such gigantic importance is the State. It is the force which alone can provide a solution to the dramatic contradictions of capitalism, and that state of affairs which we call the crisis can only be dealt with by the State, as between other States. Where is the shade of Jules Simon, who in the dawn of Liberalism proclaimed that, "The State must labour to make itself unnecessary, and prepare the way for its own dismissal"? Or of McCulloch, who, in the second half of the last century, affirmed that the State must guard against the danger of governing too much? What would the Englishman, Bentham, say today to the continual and inevitably invoked intervention of the State in the sphere of economics, while according to his theories industry should ask no more of the State than to be left in peace? Or the German Humboldt, according to whom the "lazy" State should be considered the best? It is true that the second wave of Liberal economists were less extreme than the first, and Adam Smith himself opened the door—if only very cautiously—which leads to State intervention in the economic field: but whoever says Liberalism implies individualism, and whoever says Fascism implies the State. Yet the Fascist State is unique, and an original creation. It is not reactionary, but revolutionary, in that it anticipates the solution of the universal political problems which elsewhere have to be settled in the political field by the rivalry of parties, the excessive power of the Parliamentary regime and the irresponsibility of political assemblies; while it meets the problems of the economic field by a system of syndicalism which is continually increasing in importance, as much in the sphere of labour as of industry: and in the moral field enforces order, discipline, and obedience to that which is the determined moral code of the country. Fascism desires the State to be a strong and organic body, at the same time reposing upon broad and popular support. The Fascist State has drawn into itself even the economic activities of the nation, and, through the corporative social and educational institutions created by it, its influence reaches every aspect of the national life and includes, framed in their respective organizations, all the political, economic, and spiritual forces of the nation. A State which reposes upon the support of millions of individuals who recognize its authority, are continually conscious of its power and are ready to serve it, is not the old tyrannical State of the medieval lord nor has it anything in common with the absolute governments either before or after 1789. The individual in the Fascist State is not annulled but rather multiplied, just in the same way that a soldier in a regiment is not diminished but rather increased by the number of his comrades. The Fascist State organizes the nation, but leaves a sufficient margin of liberty to the individual; the latter is deprived of all useless and possibly harmful freedom, but retains what is essential; the deciding power in this question cannot be the individual, but the State alone.

The Fascist State is not indifferent to the fact of religion in general, or to that particular and positive faith which is Italian Catholicism. The State professes no theology, but a morality, and in the Fascist State religion is considered as one of the deepest manifestations of the spirit of man, thus it is not only respected but defended and protected. The Fascist State has never tried to create its own God, as at one moment Robespierre and the wildest extremists of the Convention tried to do; nor does it vainly seek to obliterate religion from the hearts of men as does Bolshevism: Fascism respects the God of the ascetics, the saints, and heroes, and equally, God as He is perceived and worshipped by simple people.

The Fascist State is an embodied will to power and government: the Roman tradition is here an ideal of force in action. According to Fascism, government is not so much a thing to be expressed in territorial or military terms as in terms of morality and the spirit. It must be thought of as an Empire—that is to say, a nation which directly or indirectly rules other nations, without the need for conquering a single square yard of territory. For Fascism, the growth of Empire, that is to say the expansion of the nation, is an essential manifestation of vitality, and its opposite a sign of decadence. Peoples which are rising, or rising again after a period of decadence, are always imperialist; any renunciation is a sign of decay and of death. Fascism is the doctrine best adapted to represent the tendencies and the aspirations of a people, like the people of Italy, who are rising again after many centuries of abasement and foreign servitude. But Empire demands discipline, the coordination of all forces and a deeply felt sense of duty and sacrifice: this fact explains many aspects of the practical working of the regime, the character of many forces in the State, and the necessarily severe measures which must be taken against those who would oppose this spontaneous and inevitable movement of Italy in the twentieth century, and would oppose it by recalling the outworn ideology of the nineteenth century—repudiated wheresoever there has been the courage to undertake great experiments of social and political transformation: for never before has the nation stood more in need of authority, of direction, and of order. If every age has its own characteristic doctrine, there are a thousand signs which point to Fascism as the characteristic doctrine of our time. For if a doctrine must be a living thing, this is proved by the fact that Fascism has created a living faith; and that this faith is very powerful in the minds of men, is demonstrated by those who have suffered and died for it.

Fascism has henceforth in the world the universality of all those doctrines which, in realizing themselves, have represented a stage in the history of the human spirit.

CHAPTER 30

The Twenty-Five Points of the German Workers' Party, 1920*

Adolf Hitler

The program of the German Workers' Party is limited as to period. The leaders have no intention, once the aims announced in it have been achieved, of setting up fresh ones, merely in order to increase the discontent of the masses artificially, and so ensure the continued existence of the party.

1. We demand the union of all Germans to form a Great Germany on the basis of the right of self-determination enjoyed by nations.
2. We demand equality of rights for the German people in its dealings with other nations, and abolition of the peace treaties of Versailles and Saint-Germain.
3. We demand land and territory (colonies) for the nourishment of our people and for settling our excess population.
4. None but members of the nation may be citizens of the state. None but those of German blood, whatever their creed, may be members of the nation. No Jew, therefore, may be a member of the nation.
5. Anyone who is not a citizen of the state may live in Germany only as a guest and must be regarded as being subject to foreign laws.
6. The right of voting on the leadership and legislation is to be enjoyed by the state alone. We demand therefore that all official appointments, of whatever kind, whether in the Reich, in the country, or in the smaller localities, shall be granted to citizens of the state alone. We oppose the corrupting custom of Parliament of filling posts merely with a view to party considerations, and without reference to character or capacity.
7. We demand that the state shall make it its first duty to promote the industry and livelihood of citizens of the state. If it is not possible to nourish the entire population of the state, foreign nationals (non-citizens of the state) must be excluded from the Reich.
8. All non-German immigration must be prevented. . . .
9. All citizens of the state shall be equal as regards rights and duties.
10. It must be the first duty of each citizen of the state to work with his mind or with his body. The activities of the individual may not clash with the interests of the whole, but must proceed within the frame of the community and be for the general good.

We demand therefore:

11. Abolition of incomes unearned by work.
12. In view of the enormous sacrifice of life and property demanded of a nation by every war, personal enrichment due to a war must be regarded as a crime against the nation. We demand therefore ruthless confiscation of all war gains.

13. We demand nationalization of all businesses (trusts). . . .
14. We demand that the profits from wholesale trade shall be shared.
15. We demand extensive development of provision for old age.
16. We demand creation and maintenance of a healthy middle class, immediate communalization of wholesale business premises, and their lease at a cheap rate to small traders, and that extreme consideration shall be shown to all small purveyors to the state, district authorities, and smaller localities.
17. We demand land reform suitable to our national requirements. . . .
18. We demand ruthless prosecution of those whose activities are injurious to the common interest. Sordid criminals against the nation, usurers, profiteers, etc., must be punished with death, whatever their creed or race.
19. We demand that the Roman Law, which serves the materialistic world order, shall be replaced by a legal system for all Germany.
20. With the aim of opening to every capable and industrious German the possibility of higher education and of thus obtaining advancement, the state must consider a thorough reconstruction of our national system of education. . . .
21. The state must see to raising the standard of health in the nation by protecting mothers and infants, prohibiting child labour, increasing bodily efficiency by obligatory gymnastics and sports laid down by law, and by extensive support of clubs engaged in the bodily development of the young.
22. We demand abolition of a paid army and formation of a national army.
23. We demand legal warfare against conscious political lying and its dissemination in the press. In order to facilitate creation of a German national press we demand:
    a) that all editors of newspapers and their assistants, employing the German language, must be members of the nation;
    b) that special permission from the state shall be necessary before non-German newspapers may appear. These are not necessarily printed in the German language;
    c) that non-Germans shall be prohibited by law from participation financially in or influencing German newspapers. . . .

    It must be forbidden to publish papers which do not conduce to the national welfare. We demand legal prosecution of all tendencies in art and literature of a kind likely to disintegrate our life as a nation, and the suppression of institutions which militate against the requirements above-mentioned.
24. We demand liberty for all religious denominations in the state, so far as they are not a danger to it and do not militate against the moral feelings of the German race.

    The party, as such, stands for positive Christianity, but does not bind itself in the matter of creed to any particular confession. It combats the Jewish-materialist spirit within us and without us. . . .
25. That all the foregoing may be realized we demand the creation of a strong central power of the state. Unquestioned authority of the politically centralized Parliament over the entire Reich and its organizations; and formation of chambers for classes and occupations for the purpose of carrying out the general laws promulgated

by the Reich in the various states of the confederation.

The leaders of the party swear to go straight forward—if necessary to sacrifice their lives—in securing fulfillment of the foregoing points.

Note

*   Raymond E. Murphy, ed., *National Socialism*, U.S. Department of State, Publication 1864 (Washington, 1943), pp. 222–225. It was not until August, 1920, that the name of The German Workers' Party was changed to The National Socialist German Workers' Party (National-sozialistische Deutsche Arbeiterpartei—NSDAP, or Nazi party).

CHAPTER 31

An Expert on the Jewish Question

Hannah Arendt

It was the year 1935, when Germany, contrary to the stipulations of the Treaty of Versailles, introduced general conscription and publicly announced plans for rearmament, including the building of an air force and a navy. It was also the year when Germany, having left the League of Nations in 1933, prepared neither quietly nor secretly the occupation of the demilitarized zone of the Rhineland. It was the time of Hitler's peace speeches—"Germany needs peace and desires peace," "We recognize Poland as the home of a great and nationally conscious people," "Germany neither intends nor wishes to interfere in the internal affairs of Austria, to annex Austria, or to conclude an *Anschluss*"—and, above all, it was the year when the Nazi regime won general and, unhappily, genuine recognition in Germany and abroad, when Hitler was admired everywhere as a great national statesman. In Germany itself, it was a time of transition. Because of the enormous rearmament program, unemployment had been liquidated, the initial resistance of the working class was broken, and the hostility of

the regime, which had at first been directed primarily against "anti-Fascists"—Communists, Socialists, left-wing intellectuals, and Jews in prominent positions—had not yet shifted entirely to persecution of the Jews qua Jews.

To be sure, one of the first steps taken by the Nazi government, back in 1933, had been the exclusion of Jews from the Civil Service (which in Germany included all teaching positions, from grammar school to university, and most branches of the entertainment industry, including radio, the theatre, the opera, and concerts) and, in general, their removal from public offices. But private business remained almost untouched until 1938, and even the legal and medical professions were only gradually abolished, although Jewish students were excluded from most universities and were nowhere permitted to graduate. Emigration of Jews in these years proceeded in a not unduly accelerated and generally orderly fashion, and the currency restrictions that made it difficult, but not impossible, for Jews to take their money, or at least the greater part of it, out of the country were the same for non-Jews; they dated back to the days of the Weimar Republic. There were a certain number of *Einzelaktionen,* individual actions putting pressure on Jews to sell their property at often ridiculously low prices, but these usually occurred in small towns and, indeed, could be traced to the spontaneous, "individual" initiative of some enterprising Storm Troopers, the so-called SA men, who, except for their officer corps, were mostly recruited from the lower classes. The police, it is true, never stopped these "excesses," but the Nazi authorities were not too happy about them, because they affected the value of real estate all over the country. The emigrants, unless they were political refugees, were young people who realized that there was no future for them in Germany. And since they soon found out that there was hardly any future for them in other European countries either, some Jewish emigrants actually returned during this period. When Eichmann was asked how he had reconciled his personal feelings about Jews with the outspoken and violent anti-Semitism of the Party he had joined, he replied with the proverb: "Nothing's as hot when you eat it as when it's being cooked"—a proverb that was then on the lips of many Jews as well. They lived in a fool's paradise, in which, for a few years, even Streicher spoke of a "legal solution" of the Jewish problem. It took the organized pogroms of November 1938, the so-called *Kristallnacht* or Night of Broken Glass, when 7500 Jewish shop windows were broken, all synagogues went up in flames, and 20,000 Jewish men were taken off to concentration camps, to expel them from it.

The frequently forgotten point of the matter is that the famous Nuremberg Laws, issued in the fall of 1935, had failed to do the trick. The testimony of three witnesses from Germany, high-ranking former officials of the Zionist organization who left Germany shortly before the outbreak of the war, gave only the barest glimpse into the true state of affairs during the first five years of the Nazi regime. The Nuremberg Laws had deprived the Jews of their political but not of their civil rights; they were no longer citizens *(Reichsbürger)*, but they remained members of the German state *(Staatsangehörige)*. Even if they emigrated, they were not automatically stateless. Sexual intercourse between Jews and Germans, and the contraction of mixed marriages, were forbidden. Also, no German woman under the age of 45 could be employed in a Jewish household. Of these stipulations, only the last was of practical significance; the others merely legalized a *de facto* situation. Hence, the Nuremberg Laws were felt to have stabilized the new situation of Jews in the German Reich. They had been second-class citizens, to put it mildly, since 30 January 1933; their almost complete separation from the rest of the population had been achieved in a matter of weeks or months—through terror but also through the more than ordinary connivance of those around them. "There was a wall between Gentiles and Jews," Dr. Benno Cohn of Berlin testified. "I cannot remember speaking to a Christian during all my journeys over Germany." Now, the Jews felt, they had received laws of their own and would no longer be outlawed. If they kept to themselves, as they had been forced to do anyhow, they would be able to live unmolested. In the words of the *Reichsvertretung* of the Jews in Germany (the national association of all communities and organizations, which had been founded in September 1933, on the initiative of the Berlin community, and was in no way Nazi-appointed), the intention of the Nuremberg Laws was "to establish a level on which a bearable relationship between the German and the Jewish people [became] possible," to which a member of the Berlin community, a radical Zionist, added: "Life is possible under every law. However, in complete ignorance of what is permitted and what is not one cannot live. A useful and respected citizen one can also be as a member of a minority in the midst of a great people" (Hans Lamm, *Über die Entwicklung des deutschen Judentums*, 1951). And since Hitler, in the Röhm purge in 1934, had broken the power of the SA, the Storm Troopers in brown shirts who had been almost exclusively responsible for the early pogroms and atrocities, and since the Jews were blissfully unaware of the growing power of the black-shirted SS, who ordinarily abstained from what Eichmann contemptuously called the *"Stürmer* methods," they generally believed that a *modus vivendi* would be possible; they even offered to co-operate in "the solution of the Jewish question." In short, when Eichmann entered upon his apprenticeship in Jewish affairs, on which, four years later, he was to be the recognized "expert," and when he made his first contacts with Jewish functionaries, both Zionists and Assimilationists talked in terms of a great "Jewish revival," a "great constructive movement of German Jewry," and they still quarreled among themselves in ideological terms about the desirability of Jewish emigration, as though this depended upon their own decisions.

Eichmann's account during the police examination of how he was introduced into the new department—distorted, of course, but not wholly devoid of truth—oddly recalls this fool's paradise. The first thing that happened was that his new boss, a certain von Mildenstein, who shortly thereafter got himself transferred to Albert Speer's *Organisation Todt,* where he was in charge of highway construction (he was what Eichmann pretended to be, an engineer by profession), required him to read Theodor Herzl's *Der Judenstaat,* the famous Zionist classic, which converted Eichmann promptly and forever to Zionism. This seems to have been the first serious book he ever read and it made a lasting impression on him. From then on, as he repeated over and over, he thought of hardly anything but a "political solution" (as opposed to the later "physical solution," the first meaning expulsion and the second extermination) and how to "get some firm ground under the feet of the Jews." (It may be worth mentioning that, as late as 1939, he seems to have protested against desecrators of Herzl's grave in Vienna, and there are reports of his presence in civilian clothes at the commemoration of the 35th anniversary of Herzl's death. Strangely enough, he did not talk about these things in Jerusalem, where he continuously boasted of his good relations with Jewish officials.) In order to help in this enterprise, he began spreading the gospel among his SS comrades, giving lectures and writing pamphlets. He then acquired a smattering of Hebrew, which enabled him to read haltingly a Yiddish newspaper—not a very difficult accomplishment, since Yiddish, basically an old German dialect written in Hebrew letters, can be understood by any German-speaking person who has mastered a few dozen Hebrew words. He even read one more book, Adolf Böhm's *History of Zionism* (during the trial he kept confusing it with Herzl's *Judenstaat),* and this was perhaps a considerable achievement for a man who, by his own account, had always been utterly reluctant to read anything except newspapers, and who, to the distress of his father, had never availed himself of the books in the family library. Following up Böhm, he studied the organizational set-up of the Zionist movement, with all its parties, youth groups, and different programs. This did not yet make him an "authority," but it was enough to earn him an assignment as official spy on the Zionist offices and on their meetings; it is worth noting that his schooling in Jewish affairs was almost entirely concerned with Zionism.

[. . .]

Long before all this happened, Eichmann was given his first opportunity to apply in practice what he had learned during his apprenticeship. After the *Anschluss* (the incorporation of Austria into the Reich), in March 1938, he was sent to Vienna to organize a kind of emigration that had been utterly unknown in Germany, where up to the fall of 1938 the fiction was maintained that Jews if they so desired were permitted, but were not believed in the fiction was the program of the NSDAP, formulated in 1920, which shared with the Weimar Constitution the curious fate of never being officially abolished; its Twenty-Five Points had even been declared "unalterable" by Hitler. Seen in the light of later events, its anti-Semite provisions were harmless indeed: Jews could not be full-fledged citizens, they could not hold Civil Service positions, they were to be excluded from the press, and all those who had acquired German citizenship after 2 August 1914—the date of the outbreak of the First World War—were to be denaturalized, which meant they were subject to expulsion. (Characteristically, the denaturalization was carried out immediately, but the wholesale expulsion of some 15,000 Jews, who from one day to the next were shoved across the Polish border at Zbaszyn, where they were promptly put into camps, took place only five years later, when no one expected it any longer.) The Party program was never taken seriously by Nazi officials; they prided themselves on belonging to a movement, as distinguished from a party, and a movement could not be bound by a program. Even before the Nazis' rise to power, these Twenty-Five Points had been no more than a concession to the party system and to such prospective voters as were old-fashioned enough to ask what was the program of the party they were going to join. Eichmann, as we have seen, was free of such deplorable habits, and when he told the Jerusalem court that he had not known Hitler's program he very likely spoke the truth; "The Party program did not matter, you knew what you were joining." The Jews, on the other hand, were old-fashioned enough to know the Twenty-Five Points by heart and to believe in them; whatever contradicted the legal implementation of the Party

program they tended to ascribe to temporary, "revolutionary excesses" of undisciplined members or groups.

But what happened in Vienna in March 1938, was altogether different. Eichmann's task had been defined as "forced emigration," and the words meant exactly what they said: all Jews, regardless of their desires and regardless of their citizenship, were to be forced to emigrate—an act which in ordinary language is called expulsion. Whenever Eichmann thought back to the 12 years that were his life, he singled out his year in Vienna as head of the Center for Emigration of Austrian Jews as its happiest and most successful period. Shortly before, he had been promoted to officer's rank, becoming an *Untersturmführer,* or lieutenant, and he had been commended for his "comprehensive knowledge of the methods of organization and ideology of the opponent, Jewry." The assignment in Vienna was his first important job, his whole career, which had progressed rather slowly, was in the balance. He must have been frantic to make good, and his success was spectacular: in eight months, 45,000 Jews left Austria, whereas no more than 19,000 left Germany in the same period; in less than 18 months, Austria was "cleansed" of close to 150,000 people, roughly 60 per cent of its Jewish population, all of whom left the country "legally"; even after the outbreak of the war, some 60,000 Jews could escape. How did he do it? The basic idea that made all this possible was of course not his but, almost certainly, a specific directive by Heydrich, who had sent him to Vienna in the first place. (Eichmann was vague on the question of authorship, which he claimed, however, by implication; the Israeli authorities, on the other hand, bound [as Yad Vashem's *Bulletin* put it] to the fantastic "thesis of the all-inclusive responsibility of Adolf Eichmann" and the even more fantastic "supposition that one [i.e., his] mind was behind it all," helped him considerably in his efforts to deck himself in borrowed plumes, for which he had in any case a great inclination.) The idea, as explained by Heydrich in a conference with Göring on the morning of the *Kristallnacht,* was simple and ingenious enough: "Through the Jewish community, we extracted a certain amount of money from the rich Jews who wanted to emigrate. By paying this amount, and an additional sum in foreign currency, they made it possible for poor Jews to leave. The problem was not to make the rich Jews leave, but to get rid of the Jewish mob." And this "problem" was not solved by Eichmann. Not until the trial was over was it learned from the Netherlands State Institute for War Documentation that Erich Rajakowitsch, a "brilliant lawyer" whom Eichmann, according to his own testimony, "employed for the handling of legal questions in the central offices for Jewish emigration in Vienna, Prague, and Berlin," had originated the idea of the "emigration funds." Somewhat later, in April 1941, Rajakowitsch was sent to Holland by Heydrich in order to "establish there a central office which was to serve as a model for the 'solution of the Jewish question' in all occupied countries in Europe."

Still, enough problems remained that could be solved only in the course of the operation, and there is no doubt that here Eichmann, for the first time in his life, discovered in himself some special qualities. There were two things he could do well, better than others: he could organize and he could negotiate. Immediately upon his arrival, he opened negotiations with the representatives of the Jewish community, whom he had first to liberate from prisons and concentration camps, since the "revolutionary zeal" in Austria, greatly exceeding the early "excesses" in Germany, had resulted in the imprisonment of practically all prominent Jews. After this experience, the Jewish functionaries did not need Eichmann to convince them of the desirability of emigration. Rather, they informed him of the enormous difficulties which lay ahead. Apart from the financial problem, already "solved," the chief difficulty lay in the number of papers every emigrant had to assemble before he could leave the country. Each of the papers was valid only for a limited time, so that the validity of the first had usually expired long before the last could be obtained. Once Eichmann understood how the whole thing worked, or, rather, did not work, he "took counsel with himself" and "gave birth to the idea which I thought would do justice to both parties." He imagined "an assembly line, at whose beginnings the first document is put, and then the other papers, and at its end the passport would have to come out as the end product." This could be realized if all the officers concerned—the Ministry of Finance, the income tax people, the police, the Jewish community, etc.—were housed under the same roof and forced to do their work on the spot, in the presence of the applicant, who would no longer have to run from office to office and who, presumably, would also be spared having some humiliating chicaneries practised on him, and certain expenses for bribes. When everything was ready and the assembly line was doing its work smoothly and quickly, Eichmann "invited" the Jewish functionaries from Berlin to inspect it. They were appalled: "This is like an automatic factory, like a flour mill connected with some bakery. At one end you put in a Jew who still has some property, a factory, or a shop, or a bank account, and he goes through the building from counter to counter, from office to office, and comes out at the other end without any money, without any rights, with only a passport on which it says: 'You must leave the country within a fortnight. Otherwise you will go to a concentration camp.'"

This, of course, was essentially the truth about the procedure, but it was not the whole truth. For these Jews could not be left "without any money," for the simple reason that without it no country at this date would have taken them. They needed, and were given, their *Vorzeigegeld,* the amount they had to show in order to obtain their visas and to pass the immigration controls of the recipient country. For this amount, they needed foreign currency, which the Reich had no intention of wasting on its Jews. These needs could not be met by Jewish accounts in foreign countries, which, in any event, were difficult to get at because they had been illegal for many years; Eichmann therefore sent Jewish functionaries abroad to solicit funds from the great Jewish organizations, and these funds were then sold by the Jewish community to the prospective emigrants at a considerable profit—one dollar, for instance, was sold for 10 or 20 marks when its market value was 4.20 marks. It was chiefly in this way that the community acquired not only the money necessary for poor Jews and people without accounts abroad, but also the funds it needed for its own hugely expanded activities. Eichmann did not make possible this deal without encountering considerable opposition from the German financial authorities, the Ministry, and the Treasury, which, after all, could not remain unaware of the fact that these transactions amounted to a devaluation of the mark.

Bibliography

Lamm, Hans, *Über die Entwicklung des deutschen Judentums im Dritten Reich,* mimeographed dissertation, Erlangen, 1951.

CHAPTER 32

International Law in the Third Reich

Detlev F. Vagts

The abiding interest in the encounter of National Socialism with international law lies not in its doctrinal impact on the law of nations but in its role as an episode in intellectual history. In terms of Nazism's influence on the corpus of international law, one can say that it was zero, except in a negative sense. The determination of Hitler to wipe out races he characterized as inferior gave rise to the Genocide Convention. His willingness to wage war against his neighbours set the stage for the Judgment in the Nuremberg war crimes trial and the prohibition on the use of force in Article 2(4) of the United Nations Charter, which reflected the post–World War I efforts of Kellogg and Briand. The Führer's choice of methods in waging those wars caused a tightening of the Hague and Geneva rules. But there is something to be learned from the process used by the Nazi movement to make its international jurists produce the doctrines that it wanted and from the way that the international law community in Germany responded.

The seizure of power in 1933 confronted a small community of international lawyers whose thinking had been shaped by working on a body of law created only in part by Germany itself. They were linked in various ways with colleagues outside Germany whose writings they read and reviewed, whom they met at conferences and with whom they dealt on behalf of their government. They were also part of the special and separate German academic community. The responses of the universities, institutes, and other institutions were at best passive, and sometimes welcoming, to the new order of things. The responses of individuals are distributed over a fairly wide range. One can say that the internationalists behaved marginally better than other German jurists. Of those who did not sympathize with Nazism, some had little manoeuvering ground since their racial heritage or political activities had indelibly stamped them as worthless in the party's eyes. Some of those who survived the first Nazi purge were on the defensive because of their shortcomings from the Nazi perspective. A few internationalists resisted, at great cost to themselves in the end, although most had preserved their position from which they could resist only by rendering services to the state system. A number withdrew from active participation in contemporary international law studies. A few did manage to maintain some contact with foreign literature and institutions.[1]

The collaborators produced the type of writing the Nazis desired. In the first stage, the Nazis wanted the world and Germans to believe that they were committed to peaceful change. It was fairly easy for the establishment to produce this sort of assurance since peaceful revision of the Versailles imposition had been the goal of almost all Germans since 1919. What the publicists had more difficulty with was producing a coherent intellectual structure to serve as a bridge between racist concepts of the state and law and a meaningful international law. There

is something grimly comic about the united effort to suppress Ludwig Schecher and his all-too-clear demonstration that under Nazism there could be no international law but only German foreign relations law.[2]

After 1937, the emphasis came to be on building justifications for a new order in Europe, led by the Reich, that would be unequal and achieved by force. The old guard of internationalists, now rather few in number, seem to have been unable to bring themselves to move in this direction; hence, it was left to the younger generation, composed of men with few international contacts and intense exposure to Nazism, to carry this load. The older lawyers did continue to serve the Reich by arguing, for example, that traditional rules of neutrality outlawed American intervention into what was happening in Europe.

Did international lawyers really succeed in helping the Third Reich? They probably helped in some measure to slow the awakening of observers at home and abroad to the fact that Hitler's reworking of the European state structure was going to be more radical and violent than what had gone before. But those who wrote the critical literature outside Germany were quite hostile to what the Germans produced and it is unlikely that other foreign internationalists were much persuaded. German output after 1940 was largely for internal consumption. The denigration of Russian and other Slavic peoples that appeared in the German international law literature must have contributed somewhat to the utter ruthlessness with which Germans conducted the war in the east and to the lack of meaningful protest against those measures.

On the other hand, German internationalists were further removed from the scenes of true horror than, say, the criminal lawyers, and what they wrote was less vulgarly racist than what purely domestic branches of law generated during those years. It was possible, if one was well established in 1933, to write a fairly neutral and unobjectionable type of work. But it took steady nerves to do that and to resist the temptation to curry favour by saying the "right" things. It was a frightening time in which to live and one's judgments about what people did during that time must take account of those pressures.

Does this experience have implications for international lawyers in other times and places? Any affirmative suggestion must be hedged with many qualifications, for the Nazi experience was, and, one hopes, will remain, unique even for repressive and fascistic states. But some readers of the *Journal* may find themselves in countries where for the present the normal freedoms have been withdrawn by a military or authoritarian regime; others may find themselves in governmental positions where they are asked to do or say things that run against their conscientious views even though the state overall is not undemocratic. One might thus venture a few general observations. First, even in so-called totalitarian regimes there is some room for moral decisions, though opposition actions may have little practical effect. They may at a minimum give comfort to persons in trouble with the regime. Second, politically, failure to resign or protest will in some quarters be taken as approval of government measures as a matter of legality or policy or both. Third, attention must be paid to the dynamics of an authoritarian government, its tendency to demand more and more in the name of loyalty and to discard people of an increasingly centrist position. What is yielded today is not enough tomorrow. Fourth, it must not be assumed that by staying in one's governmental or academic position one can prevent even worse things from happening. The actor must take into account the fact that his or her judgment is apt to be warped by the all-too-human frailties of inertia, financial self-interest, and a sense of irreplaceability. Exit is thus less apt to be the worst solution than our

judgment at the time makes it appear to be.

Finally, a reminder that nothing lasts forever, not even dictatorships. The Thousand Year Reich barely made it to 12. Nowadays most military dictatorships endure about a decade. The 70-year endurance of the Communist regime in Russia and its 40-year survival in Eastern Europe are unique. This knowledge should serve as encouragement to holding out and as a reminder that though the mills of the gods do not grind as finely as they should, they do grind. The situation of those who took indefensible positions during one period of history can be rather unpleasant when times change.

Notes

1. One moving testimony to this connection is the emotional reaction of Viktor Bruns's coworkers at receiving Borchard's 1943 tribute in Borchard, *Death of Dr. Viktor Bruns*, 37 AJIL 658 (1943), which "transcended all the battle lines." On the destruction of both the library and unpublished writings at the Kaiser Wilhelm Institute, see Makarov, *Berthold Schenk Graf von Stauffenberg (1905–1944)*, 47 *Friedenswarte* 360, 364 (1947).

2. L. Schecher, *Deutsches Aussenstaatsrecht* 136 (1933):
   In a complete sense the new principle of the state as the organization of a "national body set aside by its folk qualities, closed to outsiders by its race," is unthinkable without the primacy of state law. The unqualified connection of all members of a *Volk* with their *Volk* as the highest value on earth can, as a matter of law, be established only on *the* basis that the national state is the highest creator of order for its total living relationships, upon which no *legal* limitation of its competence is binding. (emphasis in original)
   A whole mass of critiques of Schecher is listed in E. Bristler, *Die Völkerrechtslehre des Nationalsozialismus* (1938), at 67–68 (written in fact by John Herz, and in Geneva, not, as stated in the book, in Paris). This was done to protect the author's family, then still in Germany. *See* J. Herz, *Vom Überleben: Wie ein Weltbild*

Enstand 111 (1984). Portions of the 1938 book were published as Herz, *The National Socialist Doctrine of International Law and the Problems of International Organization*, 54 Pol. Sci. Q. 536 (1939); and *Bolshevist and National Socialist Doctrines of International Law*, 7 Soc. Res. 1 (1940) (with J. Florin). *See also* H. Mosler, *Die Intervention im Völkerrecht* 77 (1937). In Mosler's case, this assertion of the reality of international law seems to have been part of an effort to keep Nazism from feeling free from the limits of that law. In his speech at the fiftieth anniversary of Mosler's doctorate, Tomuschat noted that Mosler advocated the legitimacy of intervention in cases of extensive religious persecution, etc. B. Knobbe-Keuk, C. Tomuschat & H. Mosler, *Reden Zum 50. Doktorjubiläum 9,* 11 (1988).

CHAPTER 33

Speech

Geert Wilders

Dear Friends,

[. . .]

Despite my busy schedule at home, however, I insisted on coming to Berlin, because Germany, too, needs a political movement to defend German identity and to oppose the Islamization of Germany. Chancellor Angela Merkel says that the Islamization of Germany is inevitable. She conveys the message that citizens have to be prepared for more changes as a result of immigration. She wants the Germans to adapt to this situation. The Christian-Democrat leader said: "More than before mosques will be an integral part of our cities."

[. . .]

Dear friends, tomorrow is the Day of German Unity. Tomorrow exactly 20 years ago, your great nation was reunified after the collapse of the totalitarian Communist ideology. The Day of German Unity is an important day for the whole of Europe. Germany is the largest democracy in Europe. Germany is Europe's economic powerhouse. The well-being and prosperity of Germany is a benefit to all of us, because the well-being and prosperity of Germany is a prerequisite for the well-being and prosperity of Europe.

Today I am here, however, to warn you for looming disunity. Germany's national identity, its democracy and economic prosperity, is being threatened by the political ideology of Islam. In 1848, Karl Marx began his Communist Manifesto with the famous words: "A spectre is haunting Europe—the specter of communism." Today, another spectre is haunting Europe. It is the spectre of Islam. This danger, too, is political. Islam is not merely a religion, as many people seem to think: Islam is mainly a political ideology.

This insight is not new.

I quote from the bestselling book and BBC television series *The Triumph of the West* which the renowned Oxford historian J.M. Roberts wrote in 1985: "Although we carelessly speak of Islam as a 'religion'; that word carries many overtones of the special history of Western Europe. The Muslim is primarily a member of a community, the follower of a certain way, an adherent to a system of law, rather than someone holding particular theological views." The

Flemish Professor Urbain Vermeulen, the former president of the European Union of Arabists and Islamicists, too, points out that "Islam is primarily a legal system, a law," rather than a religion.

The American political scientist Mark Alexander writes that "One of our greatest mistakes is to think of Islam as just another one of the world's great religions. We shouldn't. Islam is politics or it is nothing at all, but, of course, it is politics with a spiritual dimension, . . . which will stop at nothing until the West is no more, until the West has . . . been well and truly Islamized."

These are not just statements by opponents of Islam. Islamic scholars say the same thing. There cannot be any doubt about the nature of Islam to those who have read the Koran, the Sira, and the Hadith. Abul Ala Maududi, the influential twentieth-century Pakistani Islamic thinker, wrote—I quote, emphasizing that these are not my words but those of a leading Islamic scholar—"Islam is not merely a religious creed [but] a revolutionary ideology and jihad refers to that revolutionary struggle . . . to destroy all states and governments anywhere on the face of the earth, which are opposed to the ideology and program of Islam."

[. . .]

A dispassionate study of the beginnings of Islamic history reveals clearly that Muhammad's objective was first to conquer his own people, the Arabs, and to unify them under his rule, and then to conquer and rule the world. That was the original cause; it was obviously political and was backed by military force. "I was ordered to fight all men until they say 'There is no god but Allah,'" Muhammad said in his final address. He did so in accordance with the Koranic command in Sura 8:39: "Fight them until there is no more dissension and the religion is entirely Allah's."

According to the mythology, Muhammad founded Islam in Mecca after the Angel Gabriel visited him for the first time in the year 610. The first 12 years of Islam, when Islam was religious rather than political, were not a success. In 622, Muhammad emigrated to Yathrib, a predominantly Jewish oasis, with his small band of 150 followers. There he established the first mosque in history, took over political power, gave Yathrib the name of Medina, which means the "City of the Prophet," and began his career as a military and a political leader who conquered all of Arabia. Tellingly, the Islamic calendar starts with the hijra, the migration to Medina—the moment when Islam became a political movement.

After Muhammad's death, based upon his words and deeds, Islam developed Sharia, an elaborate legal system which justified the repressive governance of the world by divine right—including rules for jihad and for the absolute control of believers and non-believers. Sharia is the law of Saudi Arabia and Iran, among other Islamic states. It is also central to the Organization of the Islamic Conference, which in article 24 of its Cairo Declaration of Human Rights in Islam, proclaims that "all rights and freedoms are subject to the Islamic Sharia." The OIC is not a religious institution; it is a political body. It constitutes the largest voting block in the United Nations and writes reports on so-called "Islamophobia" in Western countries which accuse us of human rights violations. To speak in biblical terms: They look for a speck in our eye, but deny the beam in their own.

Under Sharia law people in the conquered territories have no legal rights, not even the right to life and to own property, unless they convert to Islam.

Before I continue, and in order to avoid any misunderstandings, I want to emphasize that I am talking about Islam, not about Muslims. I always make a clear distinction between the people and the ideology, between Muslims and Islam. There are many moderate Muslims, but the political ideology of Islam is not moderate and has global ambitions. It aims to impose Islamic law or Sharia upon the whole world. The way to achieve this is through jihad. The good news is that millions of Muslims around the world—including many in Germany and the Netherlands—do not follow the directives of Sharia, let alone engage in jihad. The bad news, however, is that those who do are prepared to use all available means to achieve their ideological, revolutionary goal.

In 1954, in his essay Communism and Islam, Professor Bernard Lewis spoke of "the totalitarianism, of the Islamic political tradition." Professor Lewis said that "The traditional Islamic division of the world into the House of Islam and the House of War, . . . has obvious parallels in the Communist view of world affairs. . . . The aggressive fanaticism of the believer is the same."

The American political scientist Mark Alexander states that the nature of Islam differs very little—and only in detail rather than style—from despicable and totalitarian political ideologies such as National-Socialism and Communism. He lists the following characteristics for these three ideologies.

- They use political purges to "cleanse" society of what they consider undesirable;
- They tolerate only a single political party. Where Islam allows more parties, it insists that all parties be Islamic ones;
- They coerce the people along the road that it must follow;
- They obliterate the liberal distinction between areas of private judgment and of public control;
- They turn the educational system into an apparatus for the purpose of universal indoctrination;
- They lay down rules for art, for literature, for science, and for religion;
- They subdue people who are given second-class status;

- They induce a frame of mind akin to fanaticism. Adjustment takes place by struggle and dominance;
- They are abusive to their opponents and regard any concession on their own part as a temporary expedient and on a rival's part as a sign of weakness;
- They regard politics as an expression of power;
- They are anti-Semitic.

There is one more striking parallel, but this is not a characteristic of the three political ideologies, but one of the West. It is the apparent inability of the West to see the danger. The prerequisite to understanding political danger, is a willingness to see the truth, even if it is unpleasant. Unfortunately, modern Western politicians seem to have lost this capacity. Our inability leads us to reject the logical and historical conclusions to be drawn from the facts, though we could, and should know better. What is wrong with modern Western man that we make the same mistake over and over again?

There is no better place to ponder this question than here in Berlin, the former capital of the evil empire of Nazi Germany and a city which was held captive by the so-called German "Democratic" Republic for over 40 years.

When the citizens of Eastern Europe rejected Communism in 1989, they were inspired by dissidents such as Aleksandr Solzhenitsyn, Václav Havel, Vladimir Bukovsky, and others, who told them that people have a right, but also an obligation, to "live within the truth." Freedom requires eternal vigilance; so it is with truth. Solzhenitsyn added, however, that "truth is seldom sweet; it is almost invariably bitter." Let us face the bitter truth: We have lost our capacity to see the danger and understand the truth because we no longer value freedom.

Politicians from almost all establishment politicians today are facilitating Islamization. They are cheering for every new Islamic school,

Islamic bank, Islamic court. They regard Islam as being equal to our own culture. Islam or freedom? It does not really matter to them. But it does matter to us. The entire establishment elite—universities, churches, trade unions, the media, politicians—are putting our hard-earned liberties at risk. They talk about equality, but amazingly fail to see how in Islam women have fewer rights than men and infidels have fewer rights than adherents of Islam.

Are we about to repeat the fatal mistake of the Weimar Republic? Are we succumbing to Islam because our commitment to freedom is already dead? No, it will not happen. We are not like Frau Merkel. We do not accept Islamization as inevitable. We have to keep freedom alive. And, to the extent that we have already lost it, we must reclaim it in our democratic elections. That is why we need political parties that defend freedom. To support such parties I have established the International Freedom Alliance.

[...]

One of the things we are no longer allowed to say is that our culture is superior to certain other cultures. This is seen as a discriminatory statement—a statement of hatred even. We are indoctrinated on a daily basis, in the schools and through the media, with the message that all cultures are equal and that, if one culture is worse than all the rest, it is our own. We are inundated with feelings of guilt and shame about our own identity and what we stand for. We are exhorted to respect everyone and everything, except ourselves. That is the message of the Left and the politically correct ruling establishment. They want us to feel so ashamed about our own identity that we refuse to fight for it.

The detrimental obsession of our cultural and political elites with Western guilt reinforces the view which Islam has of us. The Koran says that non-Muslims are kuffar (the plural of kafir), which literally means "rejecters" or "ingrates." Hence, infidels are "guilty." Islam teaches that in our natural state we have all

been born as believers. Islam teaches that if we are not believers today this is by our own or by our forefathers' fault. Subsequently, we are always kafir—guilty—because either we or our fathers are apostates. And, hence, according to some, we deserve subjugation.

Our contemporary leftist intellectuals are blind to the dangers of Islam.

Former Soviet dissident Vladimir Bukovsky argues that after the fall of communism, the West failed to expose those who had collaborated with the Communists by advocating policies of détente, improved relations, relaxation of international tension, peaceful coexistence. He points out that the Cold War was "a war we never won. We never even fought it. . . . Most of the time the West engaged in a policy of appeasement toward the Soviet bloc—and appeasers don't win wars."

Islam is the Communism of today. But, because of our failure to come clean with Communism, we are unable to deal with it, trapped as we are in the old Communist habit of deceit and double-speak that used to haunt the countries in the East and that now haunts all of us. Because of this failure, the same leftist people who turned a blind eye to Communism then, turn a blind eye to Islam today. They are using exactly the same arguments in favour of détente, improved relations, and appeasement as before. They argue that our enemy is as peace-loving as we are, that if we meet him half-way he will do the same, that he only asks respect and that if we respect him he will respect us. We even hear a repetition of the old moral equivalence mantra. They used to say that Western "imperialism" was as bad as Soviet imperialism; they are now saying that Western "imperialism" is as bad as Islamic terrorism.

In my speech near Ground Zero in New York on September 11, I emphasized that we must stop the "Blame the West, Blame America"-game which Islamic spokesmen are playing with us. And we must stop playing this game ourselves. I have the same message for you. It is an insult to tell us that we are guilty and deserve what is happening to us. We do not deserve becoming strangers in our own land. We should not accept such insults. First of all, Western civilization is the freest and most prosperous on earth, which is why so many immigrants are moving here, instead of Westerners moving there. And secondly, there is no such thing as collective guilt. Free individuals are free moral agents who are responsible for their own deeds only.

I am very happy to be here in Berlin today to give this message which is extremely important, especially in Germany. Whatever happened in your country in the past, the present generation is not responsible for it. Whatever happened in the past, it is no excuse for punishing the Germans today. But it is also no excuse for you to refuse to fight for your own identity. Your only responsibility is to avoid the mistakes of the past. It is your duty to stand with those threatened by the ideology of Islam, such as the State of Israel and your Jewish compatriots. The Weimar Republic refused to fight for freedom and was overrun by a totalitarian ideology, with catastrophic consequences for Germany, the rest of Europe, and the world. Do not fail to fight for your freedom today.

[. . .]

In these difficult times, where our national identity is under threat, we must stop feeling guilty about who we are. We are not "kafir"; we are not guilty. Like other peoples, Germans have the right to remain who they are. Germans must not become French, nor Dutch, nor Americans, nor Turks. They should remain Germans. When the Turkish Prime Minister Erdogan visited your country in 2008, he told the Turks living here that they had to remain Turks. He literally said that "assimilation is a crime against humanity." Erdogan would have been right if he had been addressing the Turks in Turkey. However, Germany is the land

of the Germans. Hence, the Germans have a right to demand that those who come to live in Germany assimilate; they have the right—no they have a duty to their children—to demand that newcomers respect the German identity of the German nation and Germany's right to preserve its identity.

We must realize that Islam expands in two ways. Since it is not a religion, conversion is only a marginal phenomenon. Historically, Islam expanded either by military conquest or by using the weapon of hijra, immigration. Muhammad conquered Medina through immigration. Hijra is also what we are experiencing today. The Islamization of Europe continues all the time. But the West has no strategy for dealing with the Islamic ideology, because our elites say that we must adapt to them rather than the other way round.

There is a lesson which we can learn in this regard from America, the freest nation on earth. Americans are proud of their nation, its achievements, and its flag. We, too, should be proud of our nation. The United States has always been a nation of immigrants. US President Theodore Roosevelt was very clear about the duty of immigrants. Here is what he said: "We should insist that if the immigrant who comes here in good faith becomes an American and assimilates himself to us, he shall be treated on an exact equality with everyone else . . . But this is predicated upon the man's becoming in very fact an American, and nothing but an American. . . . There can be no divided allegiance here. . . . We have room for but one sole loyalty and that is a loyalty to the American people."

It is not up to me to define what Germany's national identity consists of. That is entirely up to you. I do know, however, that German culture, like that of neighbouring countries, such as my own, is rooted in Judeo-Christian and humanist values. Every responsible politician has a political obligation to preserve these values against ideologies which threaten them. A Germany full of mosques and veiled women is no longer the Germany of Goethe, Schiller and Heine, Bach and Mendelssohn. It will be a loss to us all. It is important that you cherish and preserve your roots as a nation. Otherwise you will not be able to safeguard your identity; you will be abolished as a people, and you will lose your freedom. And the rest of Europe will lose its freedom with you.

Critical Thinking Questions

1. Discuss Marinetti's desire to "glorify war—the sole cleanser of the world" with an eye toward contemporary attitudes and depictions of armed conflict. Marinetti's *Manifesto* (particularly its eleventh point) clothes technology in a veil of romantic danger, which we should embrace. Discuss the possible consequences—whether positive or negative—of such a submission.

2. Mussolini writes that Fascism "denies the materialistic conception of (human) happiness." Which alternative concept(s) does he advance? What does Mussolini imply when he mocks the suggestion that liberalism represents "the final unalterable verdict of civilization"? Discuss Mussolini's claim that the "Fascist state is itself conscious, and has itself a will and a personality." What does he mean by this rhetoric?

3. Describe some of the "language rules" that the Nazis used in committing the Holocaust, as Arendt describes them. What were their effects? Based on Arendt's account, describe Adolf Eichmann's reaction when confronted with direct visual evidence that showed the consequences of his actions. Describe Eichmann's attitude and demeanour (as described by Arendt) during his trial.

4. Describe at least three additions to international law whose origins date back to the Nazi experience, as described by Vagts. How successful have these institutional changes proven themselves? Discuss with reference to recent developments on the international stage post–Cold War and post-9/11. Vagts suggests that repressive regimes lack permanency. What might give him this confidence?

5. Discuss Wilders' attempt to draw a parallel between the rise of Fascism during the 1930s and the rise of Islamism. How appropriate is this comparison? Wilders' argument that newcomers must conform to traditions, cultures, and values of their new homes raises the following question: who bears the burden of accommodation? Wilders stresses the sanctity of national identity, yet also invokes more universal values, when convenient. Assess the reconcilability of this position.

Biographies

Filippo Tommaso Marinetti (1876–1944)

A lawyer by profession and poet by passion, Marinetti founded the Futurist Movement in 1909 and remained its most pre-eminent figure until his death. While Marinetti often disagreed with specific policies of Italian Fascism, his aggressive, even nihilistic views about the role of war, for example, clearly shaped the intellectual evolution of Fascism. Indeed, Marinetti volunteered in World War I, served briefly in the cabinet of Benito Mussolini during the interwar period, and joined the Italian campaign in Russia during World War II in his mid-60s, a move that eventually robbed him of his health and his life. Irony of ironies: the artists who drew inspiration from Futurism soon found themselves in the crosshairs of Fascism, especially in Nazi Germany.

Benito Mussolini (1883–1945)

Il Duce's personal and political journey from petty criminal and socialist agitator before World War I to Europe's first Fascist dictator after it could be symbolic of the opportunism and intellectual confusion that defines Fascism specifically and Europe between the wars generally. Mussolini's improbable but well-choreographed rise to power in 1920s certainly inspired one certain disgruntled army veteran floundering in Weimar Germany, namely Adolf Hitler. Mussolini initially treated Hitler with disdain, only to realize later that his dreams for a new Roman Empire depended increasingly on the army of the Austrian-born dictator, whose fate he eventually shared.

Adolf Hitler (1889–1945)

A mix of favourable conditions such as the economic turmoil of the Great Depression, a divided opposition, genuine political skills, and occasional bouts of luck permitted this former art school dropout and his henchmen to seize control of a modern but anxious society seemingly mired in defeat and decline following World War I. Whether the broader phenomenon of National Socialism represents an aberration of German history or its natural evolution of its "*Sonderweg*" (special path) up to that point is for others to decide. One fact remains though: Hitler's geo-political hubris and racial theories as expressed in *Mein Kampf* and partially actualized between 1933 and 1945 have left an irreparable stain on civilization. Hitler might have escaped personal accountability by suicide during the final days of World War II, but the burden of his legacy will outlast his fiction of a Thousand-Year Reich.

Hannah Arendt (1906–1975)

A scholar of political power and authority, Arendt studied philosophy under Karl Jaspers. Still later, she studied under Martin Heidegger, with whom she had a romantic relationship. The affair earned Arendt—who was born into a family of secular German Jews—much criticism because Heidegger later revealed himself to be a supporter of Adolf Hitler, whose genocidal regime Arendt had barely escaped, first to France, then to the United States. Three works define Arendt: *The Origins of Totalitarianism* (1951), *The Human Condition* (1958), and her reports of the Adolf Eichmann trial, which evolved into *Eichmann in Jerusalem: A Report on the Banality of Evil* (1963), a chilling exposé of the crime of the century.

Detlev Vagts (1929–)

It would be difficult to divorce the research interest of Vagts from his biography—the son of Miriam Beard, the daughter of the influential American historian Charles A. Beard, and Alfred Vagts, a German World War I veteran who wrote widely about military history after leaving Germany in 1932. One is not surprised to read then that Vagts pursued similar academic interests. They included American history, international law, and National Socialism. A graduate of Harvard, Vagts taught at his alma mater for 46 years, retiring in 2005.

Geert Wilders (1963–)

This Dutch politician has become one of the most controversial but equally powerful voices in European affairs. Wilders' platform—which rejects European integration and rails against immigrants particularly if they come from Muslim countries—has generated a strong following in Holland, where his Party for Freedom plays a leading role. This success has also earned Wilders attention outside this home country, where he has managed to impress—seduce, if you wish—an international audience in Europe, Israel, and the United States with harsh anti-Islamist sentiments that appeal to both voters on the right concerned about cultural asphyxiation and voters on the left concerned about shrinking welfare states.

Part VII

Pacifism

Pacifism

The Sermon on the Mount as delivered by Jesus of Nazareth provides the main inspiration for pacifism. As advocated by Jesus, pacifism represents non-violence in the face of forces of darkness. Through the millennia that followed, this ideology, called *satyagraha* by Mohandas Gandhi, developed to embrace civil disobedience and non-co-operation. Gandhi is probably the reformer most frequently associated with this political thought, undoubtedly owing to his effective deployment of it in combating British imperialism in India. However, Gandhi was not the only political reformer to make use of *satyagraha*. During the early 1960s, Martin Luther King Jr also effectively deployed it in his struggle for the civil rights of blacks in the United States, specifically with the Montgomery Bus Boycott of 1955 and the Birmingham Campaign of the early 1960s.

Major Figures

Jesus of Nazareth (6 BCE–c. 30 CE), Tertullian (c. 160–c. 220 CE), Origen (185–254 CE), Petr Chelčický (c. 1390–c. 1460), George Fox (1624–1691), David Thoreau (1817–1862), Leo Tolstoy (1828–1910), Mohandas Gandhi (1869–1948), Bertrand Russell (1872–1970), Aldous Huxley (1894–1963), Ursula Franklin (1921–), and Martin Luther King Jr (1929–1968)

Period of Greatest Influence

1915 to 1968

Introduction

Fascism took aim at not only Marxism and democratic liberalism in its attempt to consolidate its hold on the minds of nationalists during the 1920s and 1930s. It also took aim at pacifism, an ideology reflected in the teachings of Jesus (6 BCE–c. 30 CE), Leo Tolstoy (1828–1910), Mohandas Gandhi (1869–1948), Bertrand Russell (1872–1970), Aldous Huxley (1894–1963), and Ursula Franklin (1921–). But what exactly is this philosophy of pacifism? And is it a philosophy that has intellectual traction? These are questions that all pacifists attempt to answer.

The teachings and beatitudes of Jesus undoubtedly serve as a compelling starting point for any discussion of pacifism, especially the teaching found in the Sermon on the Mount: "Love your enemies, do good to those who hate you, bless those who curse you, and pray for those who treat you badly" (Luke 6: 27–29), and the beatitude: "Blessed are the peacemakers, for they will be called the sons of God" (Matthew 5:9). As others say, Jesus' words are unmistakably words of love, non-retaliation, and non-violence. Yet, when considering even Christian societies, one cannot think of a society that has actually put these words into effect. Indeed, there seems a profound divide between the political principles of moral persons and the political principles of immoral society. This truth notwithstanding, pacifism has captured the imagination of spiritual and political figures who have managed successfully to put it into practice. Notable among such figures are Mohandas Gandhi, champion of India's independence movement in the 1940s, and Martin Luther King Jr (1929–1968), leader of the black civil rights movement in the United States during the 1950s and 1960s.

The discussion below, while acknowledging the profound impact of Jesus' words, will focus on more recent figures, beginning with Leo Tolstoy, a Russian thinker deeply influenced by the ideas of Jesus. From Tolstoy, the discussion will move to other figures already mentioned: Gandhi, Huxley, Russell, and Franklin.

Tolstoy draws a line from the Sermon on the Mount to the principle of non-resistance in response to the violence of others. Tolstoy is deferential to the role of reason in the mutual interaction of human beings. He sees in rational persuasion a mechanism for furthering the welfare of the world. In brief, Tolstoy replaces persuasion for conflict rooted in violence, domination, and coercion. What this reveals is a belief on the part of Tolstoy that non-resistance can be effectively employed not just in taking issue with militarism, but also in taking issue with other social injustices such as slavery, imprisonment in foul-smelling cells, distraining for debt, running the gauntlet, and burning at the stake. What is striking about Tolstoy's position here is that Tolstoy maintains it in spite of his knowledge of the violent, coercive, and unjust measures taken by various Russian czars in their treatment of Poles and Doukhobors. It cannot be said, therefore, of Tolstoy that his pacifism is rooted in his ignorance of the Machiavellian world of politics.

The great spiritual leader Mohandas Gandhi, through his actions in South Africa but particularly in India, gives proof of the political efficacy of the pacifism that he endorses under the name *satyagraha*, a philosophy that embraces *ahimsa* or non-violence, civil disobedience, and non-co-operation. He distinguishes non-violence from passive resistance on the grounds that unlike the latter, non-violence is a weapon of the strong and it rules out the commitment of any violent act. He describes civil disobedience as the deliberate breach of any statutory law that is immoral, where the violator invokes the sanction of the law and willingly suffers imprisonment. Non-co-operation implies withdrawing from the state when the state has been, in the view of the non-co-operator, corrupt. Gandhi develops these ideas further by laying down the pre-requisites of *satyagraha*; they include reasoned and willing obedience to the morally defensible laws of the state, tolerance, and suffering. "Insistence on the truth" is what Gandhi argues *satyagraha* literally means, and it is this which he claims, in memorable words, "arms the votary with matchless power."

For the prolific Aldous Huxley, the doctrine of *ahimsa* stands as the foundational point upon which he builds the philosophy of pacifism and humanitarianism. Pacifism, for Huxley, is simply the application of principles of individual morality to the problems of politics, society, and economics. In short, pacifism, or what he sometimes calls "constructive pacifism," is a complete philosophy of life embracing democratic and non-violent principles. It is not just opposition to war but opposition to inter-tribal conflicts, large-scale conflicts, consumer exploitation, capitalism, imperialism, and organized religion. Huxley's views on humanitarianism are less developed than his views on pacifism, but some of Huxley's comments on the former suggest that he has in mind the actions and deeds of followers of Jainism and Buddhism as practitioners of *ahimsa*. Though not a well-known activist in the spirit of Gandhi, Huxley nonetheless does unhesitatingly openly criticize a sacred cow in Britain by endorsing the War Resisters' International Peace Pledge. It is clear that his idealism is balanced by a heavy dose of realism when he declares that the three causes of war are the pursuit of wealth, the pursuit of glory, and the advocacy of a creed.

About the same time that Huxley published *An Encyclopaedia of Pacifism*, Bertrand Russell published *Which Way to Peace?* Both of these books were written just before the outbreak of World War II and, owing to this, have a sense of urgency about them. Russell's pacifism is not rooted in religious conviction, something impossible given Russell's atheistic convictions. In place of religion, Russell leans upon reason and a comparison of the consequences of war versus the consequences of an unjust peace and in the end concludes that an unjust peace with no war is better than war itself. It is evident that Russell's pacifism is one that focuses upon non-militarism, in the spirit of Tertullian (c. 160–c. 220 CE) and Origen (185–254 CE), and is not the embracing pacifism as defended by Gandhi. Ever mindful of the obstacles to pacifism—that is, ever mindful of fear, pride, and greed—Russell in the years following World War II became involved in the Campaign for Nuclear Disarmament (CND) and, just two years before assuming the lead role in this organization, joined with Albert Einstein (1879–1955) in issuing *The Russell-Einstein Manifesto*, the tract anthologized in this part. What this manifesto makes clear is the danger foreseen by its proponents: nuclear war will be catastrophic for the human race. The underlying fear of Russell and Einstein is simply that global wars once started will drift unavoidably into nuclear wars. And so *The Manifesto* is nothing short of a call for the renunciation of war. It is worth noting that Russell followed up on his joint initiative with Einstein by sending letters in the late 1950s to Soviet Premier Nikita Khruschev and US President Dwight D. Eisenhower, urging them to reconsider the dangers of nuclear war between their two nations. Clearly the danger outlined by Russell and Einstein is a danger to which we must return in speaking of Environmentalism and Fundamentalism.

While Huxley and Russell articulate a pacifism that stands apart from religion, Ursula Franklin, a Canadian feminist, pacifist, and environmentalist, embraces a pacifism grounded in Quakerism, a seventeenth-century protestant religious movement founded by George Fox. It is clear from what she says that her anti-militarism flows from her understanding of the teachings and spirit of Jesus, and in this sense represents, in part, a return to the pacifism of Gandhi. Central to her understanding of the pacifism of Quakerism is the attempt to live an internally consistent value system that brings the whole of one's daily life under the ordering of the spirit of Christ, encourages living adventurously, advocates exercising imagination and sympathy with others, and maintains attesting to the inconsistency of war with the spirit and teachings of Jesus. But Franklin does not stop her analysis of pacifism here. She goes on to argue for a link between militarism, which she clearly opposes, and the hierarchical structures that oppress women, again something that she resists. Since militarism is, in her opinion, the ultimate expression of the threat system, and since women, she believes, understand threat systems, feminism and pacifism can join hands. Finally, Franklin is emphatic in saying with Gandhi, that pacifism seeks not just peace but also justice. For this reason she is eager to explore in a lucid way unjust involuntary inclusion and exclusion from social activities caused by technology. Her illustrations of unjust involuntary inclusion include the absence of any line between soldiers and civilians in modern warfare as well as the effect of pollution on polluters and non-polluters alike. Finally, her illustrations of unjust involuntary exclusion include the displacement of workers by machines. While some of these examples are ones with long historical roots, Franklin's treatment of them in the context of pacifism, feminism, and justice is remarkably original.

As indicated above, pacifism stands as a foil for Fascism and its veneration of war and conflict. And while Fascism venerates courage in the context of war, it is difficult to avoid the conclusion that pacifists in their own right comprise a group of deeply committed and courageous individuals. This conclusion is incontrovertible in the case of Gandhi, but in its own way it is also illustrated in Tolstoy, Huxley, Russell, and Franklin. There is no doubt but that each of these individuals could have found much less dangerous ground to till by endorsing conventional and popular beliefs of the masses. That they did not do this is a testament to their intellectual and moral courage.

CHAPTER 34

Nobel's Bequest:
A Letter Addressed to a Swedish Editor

Leo Tolstoy

There has lately appeared in the papers information that in connection with Nobel's will the question has been discussed as to who should be chosen to receive the £10,000 bequeathed to the person who has best served the cause of peace. This has called forth certain considerations in me, and you will greatly oblige me by publishing them in your paper.

I think this point in Nobel's will concerning those who have best served the cause of peace is very difficult. Those who do indeed serve this cause do so because they serve God, and are therefore not in need of pecuniary recompense, and will not accept it. But I think the condition expressed in the will would be quite correctly fulfilled if the money were transmitted to the destitute and suffering families of those who have served the cause of peace.

I am alluding to the Caucasian Dukhobors or Spirit-Wrestlers. No one in our time has served, and is continuing to serve, the cause of peace more effectively and powerfully than these people.

Their service of the cause of peace consists in this. A whole population, more than ten thousand persons, having come to the conviction that a Christian cannot be a murderer, decided not to participate in the military service. Thirty-four men who were summoned to enter the service refused to take the oath and serve, for which they have been confined to a penal battalion—one of the most dreadful of punishments. About three hundred men of the reserve returned their certificates to the authorities,

declaring that they could not and would not serve. These three hundred men were incarcerated in the Caucasian prisons, their families being transported from their homes and settled in Tartar and Georgian villages, where they have neither land nor work to live by.

Notwithstanding the admonitions of the authorities, and threats that they and their families will continue to suffer until they consent to fulfill military duties, those who have refused to do so do not change their decision. And their relatives—their fathers, mothers, wives, sisters—not only do not seek to dissuade them from, but encourage them in, this decision. These men say:—

"We are Christians, and therefore cannot consent to be murderers. You may torture and kill us, we cannot hinder that, but we cannot obey you, because we profess that same Christian teaching which you yourself also accept."

These words are very simple, and, so far from being new, it seems strange to repeat them. Nevertheless, these words, spoken in our time and under the conditions in which the Dukhobors find themselves, have a great importance. In our time everybody speaks of peace, and of the means of instituting it. Peace is spoken of by professors, writers, members of Parliament and of peace societies, and these same professors, writers, members of Parliament and of peace societies, when the occasion offers, express patriotic feelings; and when their time comes they quietly enter the ranks of the army, believing that war will cease, not through their efforts, but through somebody else's, and not in their time, but in some time to come.

Priests and pastors preach about peace in their churches, and zealously pray God for it, but they are careful not to tell their flocks that war is incompatible with Christianity. All the emperors, kings, and presidents, travelling from capital to capital, lose no opportunity to speak of peace. They speak of peace when embracing each other at the railway stations; they speak of peace when receiving deputations and presents; they speak of peace with a glass of wine in their hands, at dinners and suppers; above all they lose no opportunity to speak of peace in front of those same troops which are collected for murder, and of which they boast one before another.

And, therefore, in the midst of this universal falsehood, the conduct of the Dukhobors, who say nothing about peace, but only say that they themselves do not wish to be murderers, has a special significance, because it exhibits to the world that ancient, simple, unerring, and only means of establishing peace long ago revealed to man by Christ, but from which the people of former times were so far off that it seemed impracticable; while in our time it has become so natural that one can only be astonished how it is that all men of the Christian world have not yet adopted it.

This means is simple, because for its application it is not necessary to undertake anything new, but only for each man of our time himself to refrain from doing that which he regards as bad and shameful for himself as well as for others; and not to consent to be the slave of those who prepare men for murder. This means is certain, because, if Christians were only to admit—what they must admit—that a Christian cannot be a murderer, there would then be no soldiers; because all are Christians, and there would be lasting and inviolable peace between them. And this means is the only one, because, as long as Christians will not regard participation in the military service as impossible for themselves, so long will ambitious men involve others in this service, and there will be armies; and if there be armies, there will also be wars.

I know this means has already for long been practised. I know how the ancient Christians who refused the military service were executed by the Romans for doing so (these refusals are described in the lives of the saints). I know how the Paulicians were, every one of them, destroyed for the same conduct. I know how the Bogomili were persecuted, and how the Quakers and Mennonites suffered for this same cause. I know also how, at the present time, in Austria, the Nazarenes are languishing in prisons; and how people have been martyred in Russia.

But the fact that all these martyrdoms have not abolished war in no way proves that they have been useless. To say that this means is not efficacious because it has already been applied for a long time and yet war still exists, is the same as to say that in spring the sun's warmth is not efficacious because the ground has not yet become bare of snow, and flowers have not yet sprung up.

The meaning of these refusals in former times and now is quite different; then they were the first rays of the sun falling on the frozen winter earth, now they are the last touch of warmth necessary to destroy the remains of the seeming winter which has lost its power. And in fact there never was before that which now is; never before was the absurdity so evident that all men, without exception, strong and weak, disposed for war and abhorring it, should be equally obliged to take part in military service; or that the greater part of the national wealth should be spent on continually increasing military preparations; never before was it so clear as in our time that the continual excuse for the gathering and maintenance of armies—the supposed necessity of defence from an imaginary attack of enemies—has no basis in reason, and that all these threats of attack are only the invention of those to whom armies are necessary for their own purpose of maintaining power over the nations.

It has never occurred before, that war threatened man with such dreadful devastations and calamities, and such massacres of whole populations, as it does at the present time. And, lastly, never before have those feelings of unity and good will among nations owing to which war appears to be something dreadful, immoral, senseless, and fratricidal, been so widely spread. But, above all never, as it is now, was the deceit so evident by which some people compel others to prepare for war, burdensome, unnecessary, and abhorrent to all.

It is said that, to destroy war by this means, too much time would have to elapse; that a long process of the union of all men in the one and the same desire to avoid participation in war would have to be gone through. But love of peace and abhorrence of war, like love of health and abhorrence of disease, have long since been the continual and general desire of all men not corrupted, intoxicated, and deluded.

So that, if peace has not yet been established, it is not because there does not exist among men the universal desire for it; it is not because there is no love for peace and abhorrence of war; but only because there exists the cunning deceit by which men have been, and are, persuaded that peace is impossible and war indispensable. And therefore, to establish peace amongst men, first of all amongst Christians, and to abolish war, it is not necessary to inculcate in men anything new; it is only necessary to liberate them from the deceit which has been instilled into them, causing them to act contrary to their general desire. This deceit is being

more and more revealed by life itself, and in our time it is so far revealed that only a small effort is necessary in order that men should completely free themselves from it. Precisely this effort the Dukhobors are making in our time by their refusal of the military service.

The conduct of the Dukhobors is tearing off the last covering which hides the truth from man. And the Russian government knows this and is endeavouring with all its strength to keep up, if only for a time, that deceit upon which its power is founded; and that government is, for this purpose, using the cruel and secret measures usual, in such cases, to those who know their guilt.

The Dukhobors who have refused the military services are confined to penal battalions and exiled to the worst parts of Siberia and the Caucasus; while their families—old men, children, wives—are driven out of their dwellings and settled in localities where, homeless and without means of earning their food, they are gradually dying out from want and disease. And all this is being done in the greatest secrecy. Those incarcerated in prisons, and those who are being exiled, are kept separate from everyone else; the exiled are not allowed to communicate with Russians, they are kept exclusively among non-Russian tribes, true information concerning the Dukhobors is forbidden in the press, letters from them are not forwarded, letters to them do not reach them, special police guard against any communication between the Dukhobors and Russians, forbidding it; and those who have endeavoured to help the Dukhobors, and spread information about them among the public, have been banished to distant places or else altogether exiled from Russia. And, as is always the case, these measures only produce the reverse result to that which the government desires.

CHAPTER 35

The Theory and Practice of Satyagraha

M.K. Gandhi

[The following is taken from an article by Gandhiji contributed to the Golden Number of *Indian Opinion* which was Issued in 1914 as a souvenir of the eight years' Satyagraha in South Africa:]

Carried out to its utmost limit, Satyagraha is independent of pecuniary or other material assistance; certainly, even in its elementary form, of physical force or violence. Indeed, violence is the negation of this great spiritual force, which can only be cultivated or wielded by those who will entirely eschew violence. It is a force that may be used by individuals as well as by communities. It may be used as well in political as in domestic affairs. Its universal applicability is a demonstration of its permanence and invincibility. It can be used alike by men, women, and children. It is totally untrue to say that it is a force to be used only by the weak so long as they are not capable of meeting violence by violence. This superstition arises from the incompleteness of the English expression, *passive resistance*. It is impossible for those who consider themselves to be weak to apply this force. Only those who realize that there is something in man which is superior to the brute nature in him and that the latter always yields to it, can effectively be Satyagrahis. This force is to violence, and, therefore, to all tyranny, all injustice, what light is to darkness. In politics, its use is based upon the immutable maxim, that government of the people is possible only so long as they consent either consciously or unconsciously to be governed. We did not want to be governed by the Asiatic Act of 1907 of the

Transvaal, and it had to go before this mighty force. Two courses were open to us: to use violence when we were called upon to submit to the Act, or to suffer the penalties prescribed under the Act, and thus to draw out and exhibit the force of the soul within us for a period long enough to appeal to the sympathetic chord in the governors or the law-makers. We have taken long to achieve what we set about striving for. That was because our Satyagraha was not of the most complete type. All Satyagrahis do not understand the full value of the force, nor have we men who always from conviction refrain from violence. The use of this force requires the adoption of poverty, in the sense that we must be indifferent whether we have the wherewithal to feed or clothe ourselves. During the past struggle, all Satyagrahis, if any at all, were not prepared to go that length. Some again were only Satyagrahis so called. They came without any conviction, often with mixed motives, less often with impure motives. Some even, whilst engaged in the struggle, would gladly have resorted to violence but for most vigilant supervision. Thus it was that the struggle became prolonged; for the exercise of the purest soul-force, in its perfect form, brings about instantaneous relief. For this exercise, prolonged training of the individual soul is an absolute necessity, so that a perfect Satyagrahi has to be almost, if not entirely, a perfect man. We cannot all suddenly become such men, but if my proposition is correct—as I know it to be correct—the greater the spirit of Satyagraha in us, the better men will we become. Its use, therefore, is, I think, indisputable, and it is a force, which, if it became universal, would revolutionize social ideals and do away with despotisms and the ever-growing militarism under which the nations of the West are groaning and are being almost crushed to death, and which fairly promises to overwhelm even the nations of the East. If the past struggle has produced even a few Indians who would dedicate themselves to the task of becoming Satyagrahis as nearly perfect as possible, they would not only have served themselves in the truest sense of the term, they would also have served humanity at large. Thus viewed, Satyagraha is the noblest and best education. It should come, not after the ordinary education in letters, of children, but it should precede it. It will not be denied, that a child, before it begins to write its alphabet and to gain worldly knowledge, should know what the soul is, what truth is, what love is, what powers are latent in the soul. It should be an essential of real education that a child should learn, that in the struggle of life, it can easily conquer hate by love, untruth by truth, violence by self-suffering.

CHAPTER 36

Morality of Pacifism

Aldous Huxley

It is often objected that pacifism is morally unjustifiable. "Your position in society," the critic of pacifism argues, "is that of a parasite. You are profiting by what the armed forces of your country are doing to preserve you and your family from danger but you refuse to undertake defence work yourself and you try to persuade others to follow your example. You have no right to take from the society in which you live without giving anything in return."

Several answers to these criticisms present themselves:

(1) In the contemporary world, the armed forces of a country do not provide its inhabitants with protection. On the contrary, their existence is one of the principal sources of national danger. There is no more effective way of provoking people to attack than to threaten them. At the present time Great Britain combines extreme vulnerability with formidable aggressive armament. Our policy of rearmament with weapons of aggression is one which positively invites attack. The pacifist is criticized as a shirker who seeks security behind a line of soldiers, sailors, and airmen, whom he refuses to help. In reality, his dearest wish is to get rid of the soldiers, sailors, and airmen, and all their machinery of destruction; for he knows that so long as they are there, security will be unattainable. Tanks, bombers, and battleships do not give security; on the contrary, they are a constant source of danger.

(2) Those who accuse pacifists of being parasites upon the society in which they live should pause for a moment to consider a few facts and figures. Since the last war this country has spent sixteen hundred millions of pounds upon its armaments, and the rate of expenditure is now to be increased. The world as a whole spends nearly two thousand millions a year on its "defence forces." These "defence forces" live at the expense of the working community,

performing no constructive work, absorbing an increasing amount of the world's energy and not only failing to provide the individual citizens of the various nations with adequate protection, but actually inviting attack from abroad. To the inhabitant of a bombarded London it will be no satisfaction to learn that the planes for which he has been paying so heavily in taxation are bombarding some foreign capital.

(3) Refusal to obey the government of the society of which one is a member is a very serious matter. Still, most moralists and political philosophers have been of opinion that individuals are fully justified in disobeying the State if the State commands them to do something which they are convinced to be wrong. Social solidarity is not always desirable. There is such a thing as solidarity with evil as well as solidarity with good. A man who finds himself on a pirate ship is morally justified in refusing to co-operate with his shipmates in their nefarious activities. All reformers have been men who refused to co-operate, on some important issue, with the societies of which they were members. That is why so many of them have been persecuted by their contemporaries. The Christian religion takes its name from a persecuted reformer.

Criticisms and answers:

(1) The State provides free schools, libraries, pensions, etc. In return the individual should do what the State demands of him.

Answer: (*a*) The individual pays for State services in taxation.

(*b*) The State is not God and its demands are not categorical imperatives. The State was made for man, not man for the State. The State is a convenience, like drains or the telephone; its demand that it should be treated as an all-wise divinity is inadmissible and leads, as the history of tyrannies and dictatorships shows, to every kind of crime and disaster.

(*c*) If the State may justifiably demand of an individual that he should commit murder for the sake of his country, then it is equally justified in demanding that he should commit lesser crimes. But we can imagine the outcry that would be raised by pious militarists if for example, in an effort to raise the birth-rate and improve the quality of the race, the State were to conscribe all women and compel them to have sexual intercourse with eugenically selected men.

(2) "The pacifist method of dealing with war is too slow and there will be another war before there are enough pacifists to stop it."

The pacifist method is certainly slow; but the militarist's method is far slower. Indeed, the militarist's method is foredoomed to make no advance whatever toward the goal of peace. War produces more war. Only non-violence can produce non-violence. Pacifism is admittedly slow and hard to practise; but the fact remains that it is the only method of getting universal peace which promises to be in the least effective.

(3) "There is something worse than war, and that is injustice." But war inevitably commits injustices far greater and more widespread than those it was called upon to redress.

(4) "Pacifism tends to increase the arrogance and power of dictators."

(*a*) None of the modern dictators has been faced with large-scale pacifism. Where non-violence has been used on a large scale [. . .] even violent and ruthless rulers have been nonplussed.

(*b*) What increases the arrogance of dictators is not so much pacifism as the half-hearted use of their own violent methods. The violence of dictators must be opposed either by violence greater than theirs (with the certainty of prolonging the war habit and the possibility of doing irreparable damage to civilization) or else by complete pacifism (which, however slow and difficult, will ultimately lead to the establishment of peace).

CHAPTER 37

The Russell-Einstein Manifesto

Bertrand Russell and Albert Einstein

Issued in London, 9 July 1955

In the tragic situation which confronts humanity, we feel that scientists should assemble in conference to appraise the perils that have arisen as a result of the development of weapons of mass destruction, and to discuss a resolution in the spirit of the appended draft.

We are speaking on this occasion, not as members of this or that nation, continent, or creed, but as human beings, members of the species Man, whose continued existence is in doubt. The world is full of conflicts; and, overshadowing all minor conflicts, the titanic struggle between Communism and anti-Communism.

Almost everybody who is politically conscious has strong feelings about one or more of these issues; but we want you, if you can, to set aside such feelings and consider yourselves only as members of a biological species which has had a remarkable history, and whose disappearance none of us can desire.

We shall try to say no single word which should appeal to one group rather than to another. All, equally, are in peril, and, if the peril is understood, there is hope that they may collectively avert it.

We have to learn to think in a new way. We have to learn to ask ourselves, not what steps can be taken to give military victory to whatever group we prefer, for there no longer are such steps; the question we have to ask ourselves is: what steps can be taken to prevent a military contest of which the issue must be disastrous to all parties?

The general public, and even many men in positions of authority, have not realized what would be involved in a war with nuclear bombs. The general public still thinks in terms of the obliteration of cities. It is understood that the new bombs are more powerful than the old, and that, while one A-bomb could obliterate Hiroshima, one H-bomb could obliterate the largest cities, such as London, New York, and Moscow.

No doubt in an H-bomb war great cities would be obliterated. But this is one of the minor disasters that would have to be faced. If everybody in London, New York, and Moscow were exterminated, the world might, in the course of a few centuries, recover from the blow. But we now know, especially since the Bikini test, that nuclear bombs can gradually spread destruction over a very much wider area than had been supposed.

It is stated on very good authority that a bomb can now be manufactured which will be 2,500 times as powerful as that which destroyed Hiroshima. Such a bomb, if exploded near the ground or under water, sends radio-active particles into the upper air. They sink gradually and reach the surface of the earth in the form of a deadly dust or rain. It was this dust which infected the Japanese fishermen and their catch of fish. No one knows how widely such lethal radio-active particles might be diffused, but the best authorities are unanimous in saying that a war with H-bombs might possibly put an end to the human race. It is feared that if many H-bombs are used there will be universal death, sudden only for a minority, but for the majority a slow torture of disease and disintegration.

Many warnings have been uttered by eminent men of science and by authorities in military strategy. None of them will say that the worst results are certain. What they do say is that these results are possible, and no one can be sure that they will not be realized. We have not yet found that the views of experts on this question depend in any degree upon their politics or prejudices. They depend only, so far as our researches have revealed, upon the extent of the particular expert's knowledge. We have found that the men who know most are the most gloomy.

Here, then, is the problem which we present to you, stark and dreadful and inescapable: Shall we put an end to the human race; or shall mankind renounce war? People will not face this alternative because it is so difficult to abolish war.

The abolition of war will demand distasteful limitations of national sovereignty. But what perhaps impedes understanding of the situation more than anything else is that the term "mankind" feels vague and abstract. People scarcely realize in imagination that the danger is to themselves and their children and their grandchildren, and not only to a dimly apprehended humanity. They can scarcely bring themselves to grasp that they, individually, and those whom they love are in imminent danger of perishing agonizingly. And so they hope that perhaps war may be allowed to continue provided modern weapons are prohibited.

This hope is illusory. Whatever agreements not to use H-bombs had been reached in time of peace, they would no longer be considered binding in time of war, and both sides would set to work to manufacture H-bombs as soon as war broke out, for, if one side manufactured the bombs and the other did not, the side that manufactured them would inevitably be victorious.

Although an agreement to renounce nuclear weapons as part of a general reduction of armaments would not afford an ultimate solution, it would serve certain important purposes. First, any agreement between East and West is to the good in so far as it tends to diminish tension. Second, the abolition of thermonuclear weapons, if each side believed that the other had carried it out sincerely, would lessen the fear of a sudden attack in the style of Pearl Harbour, which at present keeps both sides in a state of nervous apprehension. We should, therefore, welcome such an agreement though only as a first step.

Most of us are not neutral in feeling, but, as human beings, we have to remember that, if the issues between East and West are to be decided in any manner that can give any possible satisfaction to anybody, whether Communist or anti-Communist, whether Asian or European or American, whether white or black, then these issues must not be decided by war. We should wish this to be understood, both in the East and in the West.

There lies before us, if we choose, continual progress in happiness, knowledge, and wisdom. Shall we, instead, choose death, because we cannot forget our quarrels? We appeal as human beings to human beings: Remember your humanity, and forget the rest. If you can do so, the way lies open to a new Paradise; if you cannot, there lies before you the risk of universal death.

Resolution:

We invite this Congress, and through it the scientists of the world and the general public, to subscribe to the following resolution:

> In view of the fact that in any future world war nuclear weapons will certainly be employed, and that such weapons threaten the continued existence of mankind, we urge the governments of the world to realize, and to acknowledge publicly, that their purpose

cannot be furthered by a world war, and we urge them, consequently, to find peaceful means for the settlement of all matters of dispute between them.

Max Born
Percy W. Bridgman
Albert Einstein

Leopold Infeld
Frederic Joliot-Curie
Herman J. Muller
Linus Pauling
Cecil F. Powell
Joseph Rotblat
Bertrand Russell
Hideki Yukawa

CHAPTER 38

The Nature of War in a Technological Society

Ursula Franklin

The principles of the testimony against war and violence remain unchanged to this day, but the world in which conscientious objection is exercised has altered dramatically. What follows is a brief outline of these changes, particularly as they affect the nature of modern war and war preparations, and the resultant changes in the practices of conscientious objection to war and conscription in a modern technological society. As countries become increasingly dominated by technology, as they in fact become "technological societies," we see a dramatic shift in the nature of war, both as an activity and as a social institution. This shift was perceived by keen observers even before 1914 and led to the formation of the first world peace societies. By the end of the Second World War the changes were painfully apparent to all, and today it is clear that the historical notion of war as a separate and distinct activity, set apart in terms of time, territory, and participants, no longer exists.

For the modern practice of conscientious objection, two aspects of the changing nature of warfare are particularly important. The first is the disappearance of a clear boundary or demarcation between military and civil activities or aspects of national life. The second is the intrusion of war planning and preparation into "peacetime" activities of national governments, an intrusion that, in fact, blurs the temporal, emotional, and economic boundaries between war and peace. I do not wish to dwell on the fact that in modern war civilians (that is, women and children) are considered targets; the bombings of Coventry, Dresden, Rotterdam, Berlin, and Hiroshima and the attacks on refugee camps in the Middle East and Latin America are sufficient evidence. Nor do I wish to stress that nuclear fallout, be it from tests or bombs, does not respect national boundaries. For those who believe that war is wrong, these horrors do not make war any "more wrong," but they do make work and witness against war and violence more urgent. The important point is that such horrors are the consequences of the pivotal role of technology and science in modern warfare. The Second World War marked the end of a period in which science and technology provided special tools—such as gas, tanks, aircraft, and submarines—for use in more or less conventional warfare. Since then, technology has laid down the complete pattern of war and preparations for war. The arms race is driven by "technological imperative," and the intrinsic structural demands of highly advanced armament technologies have essentially eliminated "peace" as a political reality. A state of peace—in which nations do not maintain standing armies in constant readiness poised at a publicly identified enemy—has not existed for the last three decades at least, except as political fiction.

Critical Thinking Questions

1. What does Tolstoy accomplish when he expresses disbelief about private individuals who commit gruesome acts on behalf of public institutions? Why does Tolstoy praise the Doukhobors? Tolstoy rejects the use of violence in confronting human enslavement and oppression. How does he justify this renunciation? What (if any) circumstances exist that might force us to violate Tolstoy's maxim?

2. What is the definition of *Satyagraha* as Gandhi describes it in the opening passages of the selection? How does *Satyagraha* manifest itself in politics? Why might it be difficult for a person to practise *Satyagraha*? Gandhi argues that the adoption of perfect chastity, poverty, truthfulness, and fearlessness will be sufficient to overcome militarism. Why might this remedy succeed? Why might it fail?

3. Identify the implicit economic argument in favour of pacifism, as Huxley articulates it. Which institutional elements would promote pacifism? Does Huxley offer a false choice between pacifism and traditional notions of security?

4. How does *The Russell-Einstein Manifesto* attempt to alert the public to the dangers of nuclear war? How would you describe the ideological orientation of *The Russell-Einstein Manifesto*? How realistic does the agenda of *The Russell-Einstein Manifesto* strike you?

5. According to Franklin, how has the "technological imperative" changed the notion of warfare (and its various political aspects such as disarmament negotiations)? Discuss (where available) with references to historical and contemporary examples. What are the specific similarities (as Franklin identifies them) between militarism and hierarchical structures that oppress women? How would you synthesize her views about the role of technology in warfare with her views on feminism?

Biographies

Leo Tolstoy (1828–1910)

Born into a powerful branch of Russia's ruling nobility, this scion of feudalistic privilege chose to live out his final years like one of the humble peasants who frequently appear in his novels. This renunciation of material wealth and social status in exchange for a stark but simple life full of spirituality and intellectual pursuits unfolded against the revolutionary tapestry of the nineteenth century. Its real-life personalities and ever-changing political, social, and literary threads provided Tolstoy with the very raw material that he eventually weaved into some of the greatest novels ever written. Better yet, the realistic, occasionally horrific grandeur of works such as *War and Peace* effectively restates Tolstoy's wish for humanity to transcend its own cruelty. While Tolstoy did not always live up to his own message, it would eventually echo in the works of his spiritual co-equals such as American civil rights leader Martin Luther King Jr and Mohandas Gandhi.

Mohandas Gandhi (1869–1948)

Gandhi could have easily lived a life of relative comfort, had he accommodated himself with the British rulers of India during the *Raj* period. Gandhi's privileged caste membership certainly opened doors during his youth, when he experimented with the social customs of the colonizers while studying law in London. It is more than ironic, then, to learn that Gandhi would frequently rely on his knowledge of Western ideas and thoughts to undermine the hollow foundations of British imperialism, first in South Africa, then in his homeland. Yes, Gandhi paid the ultimate price for his vision of a multi-ethnic, multi-religious India, free from its social and gender traditions. But his successful use of non-violent means in the face of superior power might have found a worthy legacy in the American civil rights movements of the 1960s and remains an inspiration to this very day.

Aldous Huxley (1894–1963)

Member of a prominent English family, whose accomplishments and ambitions stretched across multiple fields, Huxley gained literary acclaim with writings that challenged scientific progress. *A Brave New World* ranks as the most famous manifestation of the cultural pessimism that pervaded the philosophy of Huxley. Some see Huxley, who promoted Indian mysticism and English romanticism, as an intellectual godfather of the LSD-fuelled counterculture movement of the 1960s, an ironic twist by any measure.

Bertrand Russell (1872–1970)

How does one re-trace the life of a man whose long and extremely productive life lasted nearly a century? One can only offer fleeting signposts. They include the *Principia Mathematica* (1910–1913), an account of Russell's attempt to ground mathematics in logic; the wide-ranging *History of Western Philosophy* (1945) that showed Russell's breadth; and the Nobel Prize in Literature (1950) for his revealing, even shocking autobiography. This accounting of Russell's accomplishments severely neglects his contributions to epistemology and metaphysics. But Russell's intellectual world was from far abstract. As a young man, he witnessed the dawn of the nuclear age. As an elderly man, he joined youth decades his junior to protest the nuclear armament policies of the world's major powers. Russell might have been old in age toward the end, but not in spirit.

Albert Einstein (1879–1955)

His very name has become a synonym for genius and deservingly so. Einstein's insights into the relative, interrelated nature of matter, energy, and time transformed the universe of human knowledge and consciousness. Yet Einstein, born in Ulm, Germany, to German-Jewish parents, was more than just the destroyer of the scientific world that had existed prior to 1905 when he published (with little fanfare) his groundbreaking theories. He also sought to close the gap between humanity's unrelenting march toward technological progress and its limping moral maturity. Yes, Einstein himself acted more than once without morals in his personal life. But he also possessed the clarity of thought to fight mortal threats to humanity, whether they appeared in the form of the Nazis, whom he eventually escaped for the United States, or the threat of a global nuclear war.

Ursula Franklin (1921–)

Franklin (née Martius) experienced at a young age the wide range of human cruelties that defined the twentieth century. The Jewish heritage of her mother condemned Franklin to a Nazi internment camp during World War II. She left her native Germany shortly after war's end for Canada, where she continued her academic career in physics at the University of Toronto. Franklin's research into radioactive material eventually ended nuclear tests above ground. Broader research interests such as the political and social role of technology exposed Franklin to a wider audience as she emerged as one of the most prominent Canadian peace activists during the Cold War era. Franklin's resistance against various forms of oppression—whether technological or political—has also found expression in her role as a spokesperson for feminist causes such as pay equity.

Part VIII

Neo-liberalism and Globalization

Neo-liberalism and Globalization

Neo-liberalism and globalization share much in common with classical liberalism; in particular, they share with Adam Smith's ideology an affirmation of natural liberty. Moreover, they share with classical liberalism an endorsement of internationalism through trade and a repudiation of the principles of mercantilism. Where the two ideologies separate is over the ideal of justice. Classical liberals such as Smith repudiated the injustice associated with slavery and the seizing of indigenous land in the Americas. Neo-liberalism prevails today in a much rougher form, with little mention of the principle of justice. Inspired by the work of Hayek in 1944 as well as the political effectiveness of former Prime Minister Margaret Thatcher in the United Kingdom and former President Regan in the United States (in the 1970s and 1980s respectively), neo-liberalism has gained traction in North America and in the World Trade Organization. Despite its current success, advocates of neo-liberalism and globalization have yet to resolve the ideological tension they have with the state capitalism of the People's Republic of China. How this tension will resolve itself over the next ten to fifteen years is unclear.

Major Figures

Frédéric Bastiat (1801–1850), Friedrich Hayek (1899–1992), James Buchanan (1919–), Alan Greenspan (1926–), and Jagdish Bhagwati (1934–)

Period of Influence

1944 to the present

Introduction

The classical liberalism of Adam Smith has in more recent times come back with a vengeance. Whereas Smith advocated laissez-faire principles with respect to trade, he tended to temper these with considerations of the principle of justice and decency. This is perhaps nowhere so clearly expressed as it is in his comments on slavery in the New World and in his comments on the brutality to which Europeans subjected indigenous peoples all in the name of religion and gold. Neo-liberalism, on the other hand, picks up where Smith's views on laissez-faireism left off, and then extends them to apply not only to the free flow of market goods but also to the free flow of capital and labour, all the while narrowing the notion of justice to contractual principles. The connection between neo-liberalism and globalization is simply expressed in the following terms: the former diminishes a robust notion of justice in its analysis of the free flow of market goods, while the latter diminishes this notion in its analysis of the free flow of market goods and capital. Both the former and the latter are therefore distinct from the classical liberalism found in Smith.

A very good starting point for the seeds of neo-liberalism is Frédéric Bastiat (1801–1850), a French political economist who was influenced by Richard Cobden (1804–1865) and the Anti-Corn Law League. Bastiat thinks that in many ways his contemporaries are the dupes of "one of the strangest illusions," namely the belief that government can supply "milk for infancy" and "wine for old age," yet not tax the people. The result of this illusion is the creation of government which Bastiat defines, in highly original terms, as the great fiction through which everyone endeavours to live at the expense of everyone else. An advocate of minimal government and free trade, Bastiat defends what others call a "theory" as simply practice expounded: the actions of men are impelled by the instinct of preservation and progress.

The cultivation of the ideas of the Austrian-born economist Friedrich Hayek (1899–1992) has been undertaken by James Buchanan (1919–), a political economist influenced by Frank Knight (1885–1972) of the University of Chicago. Buchanan is a strong advocate of the public choice theory, a theory that focuses on the indivisibility and non-excludability of public goods. Buchanan affirms the following two central elements in this theory: (i) the conceptualization of politics as exchange, and (ii) the model of *Homo Economicus*. It is the first of these elements that distinguishes public choice theory from social choice theory commonly associated with Kenneth Arrow (1921–), an American Nobel Prize–winning economist. In a nutshell, for Buchanan, the market coordinates the activities of self-seeking persons without the requirement of any detailed political direction. This is the position that he takes in *Economics from the Outside In* (2007), and that he affirms earlier in the present extract of 2005 when he says, "economics reconciles the separated pursuits of individual interests . . . without the necessary services of a choice maker." Fundamental to Buchanan's view of economics is the notion of exchange or "catallaxy" rather than allocation—moreover, the exchange of which he speaks occurs between natural equals. Here, Buchanan unashamedly affirms natural equality as a normative value, but it is a normative value that, he believes, rests upon individual liberty. In the end, Buchanan affirms a normative notion of equal liberty. In all of this, one is well aware of the ghosts of Thomas Hobbes and his affirmation of equality as a law of nature and Adam Smith and his endorsement of the invisible hand. There is more than a trace of the thoughts of these two men in the trenchant writings of James Buchanan.

The transition from neo-liberalism to globalization is seamless. It is a transition from the integration of national economies through trade to the integration of national economies through trade, direct foreign investment, short-term capital flows, international flows of workers and humanity, and flows of technology. Globalization is simply neo-liberalism amplified. In the excerpt below, Jagdish Bhagwati (1934–) of Columbia University writes in defence of globalization. He singles out for analysis two very different kinds of criticisms arrayed against it: (i) altruistic criticisms that proceed from empathy and allege that globalization is malign in its impact on social issues, and (ii) self-interested criticisms that proceed from fear and allege that wages and standards will collapse owing to globalization. In response to the first of these criticisms, Bhagwati argues that the expanded form of neo-liberalism does not occlude citizens' issues such as the environment and indigenous culture. By making use of David Hume's concentric circles of empathy, this Columbia economist argues that Hume's circles have been inverted and death has occurred to distance because of globalization. As the result, Bhagwati argues, "virtually every social concern" has had its interests advanced via globalization. In response to the second of the foregoing arguments, he attempts to show the benefits of trade for prosperity, as found not only in increased annual growth rate but also in increased wages in rich and poor countries alike. Bhagwati argues that sluggish earnings of workers are not attributable to international trade and illegal unskilled immigration. Whether one is persuaded by the response of Bhagwati to the two foregoing criticisms will depend on the details of his argument. Suffice it to say at the very least this advocate of globalization provides the beginning of a metric to help separate rhetoric from sound empirical evidence in weighing up the pros and cons of this new form of integrated national economies. Autarky be forewarned!

With enthusiasm equal to Bhagwati's, Alan Greenspan (1926–), former Chair of the Federal Reserve in the United States from 1987–2006, endorses globalization. Known as a devotee of the uncompromising advocate of capitalism Ayn Rand, Greenspan in the present article tries to mitigate the downside of globalization. He does this by focusing upon the problem in advanced industrial and technological societies of growing inequality—especially in income—which tends to undermine support for competitive markets. He believes that functioning capitalistic economic institutions "must be perceived as fair" in order for these same institutions to receive broad support. So how does he address the problem of income inequality and the perceived lack of fairness? First he affirms that, under the rubric of globalization, innovation and competition have increased the concentration of income "virtually everywhere." Greenspan argues that the income concentration of the early part of the twentieth century is attributable to interest, dividend, and capital gains from wealth, in contrast to the income concentration that presently exists, which is attributable to the "imbalance between the demand for skilled workers and their supply." Having laid out the source of the problem, Greenspan then goes on to argue that the key to solving the problem of income inequality, as found in income concentration, lies in education and immigration. In the result, Greenspan recommends opening up elementary and secondary schools to market forces, even possibly making use of vouchers. But he believes education reform will take too long to address the inequality problem and therefore endorses, in addition, the idea of opening the doors to the immigration of skilled workers into the United States. It is in this way that the former Chairman of the Federal Reserve addresses the income inequality problem and its perceived lack of fairness.

In striking contrast to the foregoing writers and their optimism and support for neo-liberal principles and globalization, stands Naomi Klein (1970–), Canadian author and activist. In her recent writings she has taken aim at corporate globalization. She does this on the grounds that, far from being born of freedom, deregulated capitalism has been "midwifed" by the most "brutal forms of coercion" and therefore does not go hand in hand with democracy. Klein indicts unbridled capitalism and its associated globalization on the grounds that it subscribes to the shock doctrine, a doctrine that asserts that only a crisis can bring about real change. She also describes this capitalism of Milton Freedman and Alan Greenspan as "disaster capitalism," a form of capitalism that feeds upon the carcases of those who experience catastrophe. It is in countries such as Russia, China, and Chile, as well as the United States at the time of disaster associated with hurricane Katrina, that Klein believes one sees illustrations of disaster capitalism. The underlying message of Klein is that those subscribing to this form of capitalism and globalization all subscribe to a new policy trinity: the elimination of public sphere, the liberation of corporations, and "bare bones" in social spending. Through the use of this new policy trinity, neo-liberals and defenders of globalization make use of disasters, shocks, and lies to disorient those who would oppose them in the rewriting of public policy. Greenspan himself acknowledges that public policy is about choices. Klein acknowledges Greenspan's point but attempts to provide her readers with weapons that allow them to disarm disaster capitalists who would foist on them a new ideology that does not serve their interests.

All of the foregoing individuals, with the exception of Klein, embrace a view of politics that privileges economic matters in the determination of public policy. Some—including Buchanan and Bhagwati—do this more skillfully than others, and their approaches are more nuanced. Nonetheless, they all share an abiding faith in what Klein perceptively calls "a fundamentalist form of capitalism." It is still too early in the game to say how such a view of capitalism will play out in spite of the successes it may have had. Before the game is over, serious consideration has to be had of trenchant criticisms that have been independently made by others, including those in the environmentalism camp, such as David Suzuki and Rachel Carson, as well as those in the democratic socialism camp, such as Peter Self.

CHAPTER 39

Government

M. Frédéric Bastiat

I wish some one would offer a prize—not of a hundred francs, but of a million, with crowns, medals, and ribbons—for a good, simple, and intelligible definition of the word "Government."

What all immense service it would confer on society!

The Government! What is it? Where is it? What does it do? What ought it to do? All we know is, that it is a mysterious personage; and, assuredly, it is the most solicited, the most tormented, the most overwhelmed, the most admired, the most accused, the most invoked, and the most provoked, of any personage in the world.

I have not the pleasure of knowing my reader, but I would stake ten to one, that for six months he has been making Utopias, and if so, that he is looking to Government for the realization of them.

And should the reader happen to be a lady, I have no doubt that she is sincerely desirous of seeing all the evils of suffering humanity remedied, and that she thinks this might easily be done, if Government would only undertake it.

But, alas! that poor unfortunate personage, like Figaro, knows not to whom to listen, nor where to turn. The hundred thousand mouths of the press and of the platform cry out all at once:—

"Organize labour and workmen.

"Do away with egotism.

"Repress insolence and the tyranny of capital. [. . .]"

"Do have a little patience, gentlemen," says Government, in a beseeching tone. "I will do what I can to satisfy you, but for this I must have resources. I have been preparing plans for five or six taxes, which are quite new, and not at all oppressive. You will see how willingly people will pay them."

Then comes a great exclamation:—"No, indeed! where is the merit of doing a thing with resources? Why, it does not deserve the name of a Government! So far from loading us with fresh taxes, we would have you withdraw the old ones.

"You ought to suppress

"The salt tax,

"The tax on liquors,

"The tax on letters,

"Custom-house duties,

"Patents."

In the midst of this tumult, and now that the country has two or three times changed its Government, for not having satisfied all its demands, I wanted to show that they were contradictory. But what could I have been thinking about? Could I not keep this unfortunate observation to myself?

I have lost my character for ever! I am looked upon as a man without *heart* and without *feeling*—a dry philosopher, an individualist, a plebeian—in a word, an economist of the English or American school. But, pardon me, sublime writers, who stop at nothing, not even at contradictions. I am wrong, without a doubt, and I would willingly retract. I should be glad enough, you may be sure, if you had really discovered a beneficent and inexhaustible being, calling itself the Government, which has bread for all mouths, work for all hands, capital for all enterprises, credit for all projects, oil for all wounds, balm for all sufferings, advice for all perplexities, solutions for all doubts, truths for all intellects, diversions for all who want them, milk for infancy, and wine for old age—which can provide for all our wants, satisfy all our curiosity, correct all our errors, repair all our faults, and exempt us henceforth from the necessity for foresight, prudence, judgment, sagacity, experience, order, economy, temperance, and activity.

[. . .]

I will venture to say that I fear we are, in this respect, the dupes of one of the strangest illusions which have ever taken possession of the human mind.

Man recoils from trouble—from suffering; and yet he is condemned by nature to the suffering of privation, if he does not take the trouble to work. He has to choose, then, between these two evils. What means can he adopt to avoid both? There remains now, and there will remain, only one way, which is, *to enjoy the labour of others*; such a course of conduct prevents the trouble and the satisfaction from preserving their natural proportion, and causes all the trouble to become the lot of one set of persons, and all the satisfaction that of another. This is the origin of slavery and of plunder, whatever its form may be—whether that of wars, impositions, violence, restrictions, frauds, &c.,—monstrous abuses, but consistent with the thought which has given them birth. Oppression should be detested and resisted,—it can hardly be called absurd.

Slavery is subsiding, thank heaven! and on the other hand, our disposition to defend our property, prevents direct and open plunder from being easy.

One thing, however, remains—it is the original inclination which exists in all men to divide the lot of life into two parts, throwing the trouble upon others, and keeping the satisfaction for themselves. It remains to be shown under what new form this sad tendency is manifesting itself.

The oppressor no longer acts directly and with his own powers upon his victim. No, our conscience has become too sensitive for that. The tyrant and his victim are still present, but there is an intermediate person between them, which is, the Government—that is, the Law itself. What can be better calculated to silence our scruples, and, which is perhaps better appreciated, to overcome all resistance? We all, therefore, put in our claim, under some pretext or other, and apply to Government. We say to it, "I am dissatisfied at the proportion between my labour and my enjoyments. I should like, for the sake of restoring the desired equilibrium, to take a part of the possessions of others. But this would be dangerous. Could not you facilitate the thing for me? Could you not find me a good place? or check the industry of my competitors? or, perhaps, lend me gratuitously some capital, which you may take from its possessor? Could you not bring up my children at the public expense? or grant me some prizes? or secure me a competence when I have attained my fiftieth year? By this means I shall gain my end with an easy conscience, for the law will have acted for me, and I shall have all the advantages of plunder, without its risk or its disgrace!"

As it is certain, on the one hand, that we are all making some similar request to the Government; and as, on the other, it is proved that Government cannot satisfy one party without adding to the labour of the others, until I can obtain another definition of the word Government, I feel authorized to give my own. Who knows but it may obtain the prize? Here it is:

Government is the great fiction, through which everybody endeavours to live at the expense of everybody else.

CHAPTER 40

Classical Liberalism as an Organizing Ideal

James M. Buchanan

Markets and Social Choice

The fundamental principle of economics reconciles the separated pursuits of individual interests and the emergence of mutually satisfactory outcomes without the necessary services of a choice maker, as such. Market outcomes emerge from the interactions of separated but interdependent choosers within a structure of rules that define the parameters of the game. The specific outcomes are not within the choice set of participants or anyone else. There is no social choice, and it becomes highly misleading to model markets as if the institutions perform specific functions.

Economists were distracted from what should have been their classical philosophical understandings of their discipline by the seminal methodological essay by Lionel Robbins in the 1930s (Robbins, 1932). While properly puncturing utilitarian absurdities, Robbins offered the widely accepted definition of "the economic problem," as the allocation of scarce means among alternative ends. With this definition, the way was set for the disciplinary domination of the maximizing paradigm at the expense of the almost total neglect of "catallaxy," which offers the only mind-set from which the implications of the science of economics for socio-political order can emerge.

When viewed in this catallactic perspective, the implications for political philosophy are evident. Market organization, to the extent that it is operative, replaces hierarchical organization. Markets make evaluative social orderings, by whomever done, unnecessary if the purpose is that of providing some basis for choosing among the feasible options. There is no need for some all-powerful authority, some sovereign, to orchestrate the productive, allocative, distributive, and evaluative processes summarized as "the economy." Writing a full century before the great discoveries of classical political economy, Thomas Hobbes failed to see that resolution of the problem raised by the presumed anarchistic chaos does not require the all-powerful sovereign, and that such resolution requires, instead, only the limited sovereign which enforces property and contract, or provides in Adam Smith's terminology, the appropriate "laws and institutions," without which markets can scarcely work at all.

Unfortunately, ideas in political theory did not fully incorporate the understandings developed by the classical economists. And the political role of markets in reducing or even eliminating the need for hands-on politicized intrusions in market processes was understood by neither political theorists nor economists themselves. We find, even into the middle twentieth century, economists spending much time and energy discussing the derivation of "social welfare functions."

How Do Markets Work?

Markets operate to generate order out of apparent chaos, and without the necessity of hands-on political intrusion. But just how do they accomplish this apparent miracle? The great discovery of the eighteenth-century moral philosophers was the recognition that the uniformities in human nature that prompted all persons to seek their own interests, a simple behavioural norm, created the complex order that is observed. Indeed, we, as economists, should claim precedence from Stephen Wolfram (2002) whose recent emphasis on cellular automata generalizes to all of science the relationship between simple rules and the complex order they produce.

The presuppositions that we, both as economists and classical liberals, carry around with us when we interpret this market-processed transformation, from simple rules of behaviour to the order of the economy, warrant further consideration. The units of analysis are individuals or persons who engage, one with another, in exchanges or trades, and in the act of so doing secure mutual benefits. We presuppose, often without recognition, that all persons in the economic nexus are willing participants in the sense that they are both autonomous and responsible for themselves, that individuals do not willingly sacrifice their innate power to make exchanges; in other words, that persons "choose to be free." And, almost as a corollary to this presupposition of autonomy and responsibility, we also presume that participants in markets acknowledge the necessary reciprocity that any workable exchange relationship embodies.

Trade among Natural Equals

These presuppositions of autonomy and reciprocity imply a more fundamental normative proposition to the effect that all persons in the trading nexus are to be considered as natural equals, each one of whom is assumed to be equally capable of making exchanges and living with the consequences. This postulate of natural equality places the classical liberal directly and specifically at odds with all those who, explicitly or implicitly, accept the Platonic postulate of natural hierarchy. To Plato there are natural slaves and natural masters, with the consequences that follow for social organization, be it economic or political. To Adam Smith, by contrast, who is in this as in other aspects the archetype classical liberal, the philosopher and the porter are natural equals with observed differences readily explainable by culture and choice. It is not surprising that the nineteenth-century followers of Adam Smith, the economists, were as one in their opposition to human slavery, the institution that was so strongly defended by the dominant intelligentsia, and Carlyle in particular, all of whom were followers of Plato in their putative claim for natural hierarchy. We owe a debt of gratitude to my colleague David Levy (2001) for his exposure of this dark side of the early "humanist" criticism of markets.

David Ricardo was not at all helpful in carrying forward the teachings of Adam Smith in this respect. His doctrine of comparative advantage locates the origins of trade in differences between prospective traders. The Smithean logic, by contrast, locates the origins of trade in the advantages of specialization, as such, and does not require differences among prospective traders at all.[1]

Empirical Realism and Normative Relevance

Empirically, of course, persons differ, one from another, along almost any one of the multiplicity of dimensions that might be used for comparative evaluation. This statement would have provoked no response from Thomas Jefferson, whose phraseology about created equality in the American Declaration of Independence has been so seriously misinterpreted. Jefferson was not advancing scientific hypotheses concerning the equality of persons along any one or any set of the dimensions that might be descriptively introduced for classification purposes. He was, instead, saying that as an identified member of the human species, a person possesses natural qualities that cannot, in any way, be aggregated so as to allow for some location in an hierarchical ordering. Persons must, therefore, be considered as equals in any sense that involves the sorting and screening processes out of which social ordering relationships finally emerge.

As a straightforward value stance, this may be sufficient unto itself to explain the attraction of classical liberalism. The empirical reality of individual differences may be simply ignored as being normatively irrelevant for purposes of discussing the organization of society, and the "as if" presumption of equality that the liberal order must embody may become central in some final evaluation.

Equality and Individual Liberty

There is more to be said, however, in the effort to explain and understand why and how the principles of classical liberalism provide the motivating force for our zealotry, if you will, for our willingness to stand up and be counted in opposition to sometimes popular causes. The "as if" presumption of socio-political equality, as such, rests, in turn, on a more basic value than equality, that of individual liberty itself. And this is the distinguishing value that does, indeed, set members of our clan apart from so many of our peers.

But how does the value placed on liberty relate to the necessary presumption of socio-political equality? The connection is straightforward once it is recognized that, for the classical liberal, discriminatory liberty involves a contradiction. The only meaningful liberty is equal, as emphasized by J.S. Mill and John Rawls. The putative libertarian who claims maximal liberty for himself but places others lower in some hierarchical ordering, simply does not qualify for membership in the clan.

Equal liberty is a two-way street. A person may be quite firm in a commitment involving attempts by others to impose their values; freedom from coercion is a quasi-universal desire. But a willingness to refrain from imposing one's own values on others is a less recognized and surely less widely accepted commitment that is also essential. "Don't tell me what to do" and "Do what I say"—these are not compatible admonitions. Classical liberalism allows for no naturally privileged class or group, along any dimension. Acceptance of this elemental principle is difficult for many.[2] It is as difficult in this new century as it was a full century and a half ago to hold fast to the postulate of natural equality and to accept its implications, in a practicable sense, even if, perhaps especially, in the face of empirical evidence from evolutionists and others, we acknowledge its necessary normative place in our imagined utopia.

Notes

1. For a discussion of the implications of these differences in the origins of trade, see Buchanan and Yoon (2002). For a general treatise that builds from the presupposition of ex ante equality, see Yang (2001).

2. In over four and a half decades of participation in Mont Pelerin society meetings, I recall only two occasions where I experienced extremely negative reactions to intervention by speakers from the audience. In both instances, arguments were made in support of special treatment for a privileged elite.

References

Buchanan, James M., and Yong J. Yoon (2002), "Globalization as framed by the two logics of trade," *Independent Review*, 6 (3), 399–405.

Levy, David M. (2001), *How the Dismal Science Got Its Name: Classical Economics and the Ur-Text of Racial Politics*, Ann Arbor, MI: University of Michigan Press.

Robbins, Lionel (1932), *The Nature and the Significance of Economic Science*, London: Macmillan.

Wolfram, Stephen (2002), *A New Kind of Science*, Champaign, IL: Wolfram Media.

Yang, Xioakai (2001), *Economics: New Classical versus Neoclassical Frameworks*, Malden, MA: Blackwell.

CHAPTER 41

Two Critiques of Globalization

Jagdish Bhagwati

At the outset, I can do no better than to recall what Rabbi Hillel, who lived in the time of Herod, said: "If I am not for myself, then who will be for me? And when I am only for myself, what am I?" What the Rabbi was saying was that we have, or must have, both altruism and self-interest to define our lives. But, in truth, on this spectrum, few lie in the centre but tend to gravitate toward one end or the other. And this is just what we find among the critics of globalization. Several are *altruistic*; they proceed from *empathy*, thinking that globalization is malign in its impact on humanity, on what might be called "social issues." But a large number are also proceeding instead from *self-interest*, actuated by *fear*. These include mainly the labour unions that fear their wages and standards will collapse with globalization, and others who fear that the overall prosperity of their nation is also at risk.

I find, far too often, that many who proceed from self-interest and fear also mask their concerns by claiming to be altruistic as well. Thus, one will often come across arguments from union leaders or some NGOs that protectionism of the rich countries is also beneficial to the poor countries, as when some opponents of NAFTA claim that freer trade between the United States and Mexico has hurt both countries and also the poor in each of them.[1] This makes them more comfortable, to be sure. But beyond exposing these arguments as specious so that our public policy discourse gets more informed as is necessary for a well-functioning democracy, the only thing one can suggest to those who advance them is to admit, with Rabbi Hillel, that the pursuit of self-interest is part of our nature, but that pretense at altruism, as distinct from actual altruism, should not be.

As it happens, both sets of critics are mistaken; and so let me treat each separately, starting briefly with the criticisms based on altruism and empathy, which I have addressed fully in this book, *In Defense of Globalization*, and then proceed to a more substantial discussion of the current arguments that are based instead on self-interest and fear.

Altruism and Empathy

In Defense of Globalization met with a huge response precisely because it uniquely addressed the "social impact" questions which the young students and the civil society groups were raising.[2] The book itself was prompted by the 1999 WTO Ministerial Meeting, which sank under the onslaught of massive disruptive demonstrations that were only matched by the Clinton Administration's lack of preparation to confront and contain the mayhem. As I debated civil society leaders, including Ralph Nader in the town hall, and appeared on the opening panel for NGOs (which had to be postponed to the afternoon because of a bomb threat) with Pascal Lamy, Clare Short, Charlene Barshefsky, Alec Erwin, and other trade ministers, and then talked with the demonstrators on the streets, I felt that these were not people who were worried about whether free trade was good for aggregate GNP and prosperity or whether protection was more appropriate. Rather, they were concerned with what might be called the social implications of economic globalization. They were concerned, indeed were convinced, that globalization put us behind on several "citizens' issues" such as the environment, indigenous culture (à la President Eva Morales) and mainstream culture (à la Monsieur Bove), democracy, poverty in the poor countries, and child labour there as well. To use the phraseology that Bill Clinton, Gerhard Schroeder, and Tony Blair made fashionable, they claimed that *globalization lacks a human face*. But was this true?

In Defense of Globalization was precisely addressed to this overriding issue. Before analyzing this issue, however, I tried to understand what had brought about the remarkable growth of altruistic concerns, much of it from the idealistic young. I found the explanation largely in what I called the "inversion of Hume's concentric circles." David Hume and Adam Smith were both members of the Scottish Enlightenment. Both had written how distance diminished empathy. In a classic passage, quoted and discussed in *In Defense of Globalization*, Adam Smith had written in *The Theory of Moral Sentiments* in 1760 that a European man of sensibility would continue to snore through the loss of a hundred million Chinese in an earthquake "provided he never saw them," but "if he was to lose his little finger to-morrow, he would not sleep to-night." David Hume had written of concentric circles of empathy, which declined as one went further from the centre. Today, however, we have the death of distance; and television brings ever closer to us the hitherto-hidden pestilence, famine, and tragic afflictions of the countless in misery. At the same time, as the political scientist Robert Putnam has argued, there is increasing tendency for civic life to decline in communities that Americans in particular no longer "bowl together." So, the outermost circle has become the innermost circle, whereas the innermost circle is now beginning to be the outermost circle. The idealist young therefore are agitated and animated by the distant afflictions that they witness close at hand today; and they cry out for solutions, which they often find in anti-globalization rhetoric and advocacy.

By looking at virtually every social concern I could lay my hands on, I argued that globalization, by and large, advanced these social agendas instead of handicapping them. In short, globalization *has* a human face. I can only illustrate with one compelling example the kind of argumentation and evidence that I marshalled to arrive at this startling conclusion: the reader has the entire book to judge for herself the case I build patiently and without an ideological straitjacket, against the entire range of current anti-globalization critiques.

Thus, take the wage differential against women. Take the phenomenon that, for the same type of work and the same qualifications, a firm pays men more than women. Using Gary Becker's theory of price and prejudice, we may hypothesize that the willingness of firms to pay more for equally qualified men will begin to shrink once they face stiff international competition. So, in traded industries, you would see the wage differential closing faster than in non-traded industries. Lo and behold that is just what two splendid women economists found to be the case in the United States over a long period. Globalization, in the shape of trade, was a force for good, not harm.

But take the differential in pay that comes, not at the level of the firm, but because women traditionally have been confined to jobs that pay less: like teaching and nursing. But even here, take the example of Japanese multinationals. In Japan the glass ceiling beyond which women cannot go used to be so low that women could barely stand up! One went to Japan and found that, in a land that produced the world's first great female novelist (Lady Murasaki in the eleventh century), today the women typically were either housewives or in jobs such as serving tea to male executives who did all of the talking and negotiating. When Japanese multinationals started going abroad in massive numbers in the late 1980s, the men, of course, remained executives. Their wives who lived in New York, Paris, Rome, and London, suddenly saw how Western men treated their wives differently and how the women were up-wardly mobile in business and other occupations. That turned them into powerful agents of change when they returned. And so now we have had Madame Ogata as the UN High Commissioner for Refugees, Madame Tanaka as the Foreign Minister and many women getting into the Diet and also rising in executive ranks. Japanese investment abroad was among the phenomena that fostered the change in attitudes that led to the promotion of equality for Japanese women.[3]

Self-interest and Fear

If the concerns about globalization that proceed from altruism and empathy can be laid to rest, those arising from self-interest and fear are not so easily dismissed, though they are even less grounded in objective reality. As the Russian proverb goes: fear has big eyes. But it also has deaf ears.

The fear of trade and multinationals today particularly afflicts the rich countries, where many are afraid that economic prosperity is imperilled by trade with the poor countries. Additionally, the working classes and the unions typically fear that their wages and standards are in peril from trade with poor countries. But it was only a few decades ago that the fear was rampant among the poor countries that were in such peril from trade with the rich countries: how ironic this seems. A few economists and some cash-rich NGOs have worked hard to renew the fear among the poor countries as well. Let me, therefore, urge the reader to work through the extended analysis and empirical evidence that I have produced, on the benefits of trade for prosperity in the poor countries (Chapter 5 of my book), and on the need to discount the alleged adverse effect of trade on wages and labour standards in the rich countries (in the earlier cited Chapter 10). But let me add a few salient points here, on the question of the relationship between trade and prosperity, while dealing with the question of wages and labour standards more robustly later. I will also start with conventional worries; and then I will address worries (such as the fear of India and China) that have emerged in recent years, reinforcing the old concerns, in regard to both overall prosperity and wages.

1. *Prosperity from Trade.* First, my colleague Professor Arvind Panagariya has noted that, if one examines the growth and trade record (where available) of rich and poor countries for nearly 40 years in the post-war period, you

see a remarkable phenomenon. The "economic miracle" countries which averaged a high annual growth rate of per capita income at about 3 per cent, also showed similar growth in their trade; and the "economic debacle" countries that experienced negligible or even negative growth rates were also characterized by similarly dismal trade performance.[4] Now, this does not necessarily imply that trade led to growth instead of the other way around. Anyone who has studied the experience of developing countries in depth knows—and I know because I have participated in two major projects (one where I was a country co-author and one which I co-directed) in the 1960s and 1970s on the trade and development policies of several countries—the argument that growth happened independently of trade, which simply followed as a "trickle-down" effect of growth, is little short of crazy.[5] But this area does invite entry by crazy people, or people who are not crazy but act as if they were because the market incentives, as I argue below, are such today that they reward craziness.

Second, note that it is possible to observe periods, which may last over almost two decades in rare cases, where autarky and high growth rates may be observed together. But it is impossible to find cases where this has been a "sustainable" relationship over very long periods. The Soviet Union collapsed after making many economists, including me at one stage, believe that its autarky was no barrier. Well, just look at a chart on Soviet Russia's steadily declining growth rate in the face of huge investment rates.[6] You see a decline in productivity that must be at least partly attributed to a virtually closed economy and rigid central planning laced with massive restrictions on production and investment. After a huge spurt in the 1920s and 1930s, these ill-advised policies finally caught up with them.

Let me also recall a funny, and true, story about my Cambridge teacher Joan Robinson.

In the mid-1960s, she and Gus Ranis of Yale, one a radical and the other a mainstream economist, were overheard agreeing that Korea was an economic miracle. How could this harmony have arisen? It turned out that she was thinking of North Korea whereas Ranis was talking about South Korea! Now, after over a quarter of a century, we know who was right: North Korea simply failed to sustain its high growth rate. Autarky, and total lack of political and economic freedoms, turned the short-run miracle into a debacle.[7]

Third, much is made these days of the cliché that "one (shoe) size does not fit all," implying that general advice that trade is good is unsound and that we must vary the prescription with each country, presumably advocating protection here and there, on an ad hoc basis, and without an overarching philosophy that progress towards freeing trade is desirable. This sounds so right; but it is downright shallow and silly. Science, and good policy, require that certain general propositions be taken as guiding principles, as distinct from reliance on ad hoc prescriptions. One has to decide whether one wants to go barefoot or wear shoes. And once one decides to wear shoes, the shoe size will inevitably tend to vary, as the policy gets grounded in reality. Thus, one has to decide whether the central policy has to be openness or autarky. After the post-war experience, it is clearly possible to argue that good policymaking requires a policy of freer trade. But this does not mean that the actual freeing of trade must not take into account the political and economic difficulties that may attend the transition from one system to another: the transition to freer trade, and working with an open economy, require policy and institutional support that have in fact been the subject of rich analysis by trade economists for decades.[8]

2. Globalization: Trade, Immigration, and Wages. The longstanding stagnation, or at best very sluggish rise, in workers' earnings in the

United States has given rise to the fear that globalization, involving trade with the poor countries and also illegal unskilled immigration from them, is at the heart of the problem. Yet, this causation should not be taken at face value, no matter how plausible it seems to many in the rich countries.

First, all empirical studies, including those done by some of today's top trade economists (such as Paul Krugman and Robert Feenstra), show that the adverse effect of trade on wages is not substantial. My own empirical investigation, reported also in Chapter 10 in this book, in fact argues that the effect of trade with poor countries may even have been to moderate the downward pressure on wages that rapid unskilled-labour-saving technical change would have caused.[9]

Second, the same goes for the econometric studies by the best labour economists today, regarding the effects of the influx of unskilled illegal immigrants into the United States. The latest study by George Borjas (no friend of illegal immigrants) and Larry Katz, both of Harvard, once necessary adjustments are made, also shows a virtually negligible impact on US workers' wages.

So, despite the popular fears, globalization does not appear to be the cause of the problem. What then explains the disturbing situation regarding wages? Can it be that globalization has significantly reduced the bargaining ability of workers and thus puts a downward pressure on wages? I strongly doubt this. First, the argument is not relevant when employers and workers are in a competitive market and workers must be paid the going wage. As it happens, less than 10 per cent of the workers in the private sector in the United States are now unionized. Second, if it is claimed that acceleration in globalization has decimated unionization, that is dubious. The decline in unionization has been going on for longer than the last two decades of globalization, shows no

dramatic acceleration in the last two decades, and is to be attributed to the union-unfriendly provisions of the half-century-old Taft-Hartley provisions that crippled the ability to strike. Third, it seems plausible that unionization has also suffered because fewer workers now expect that unions can deliver higher wages. In the public sector, the wages are squeezed because of budget constraints: as the recent New York Transit strike showed, the public utilities are increasingly unable to raise the price of services or to get more subsidies to finance losses and therefore the ability of unions in such a situation to get more for their workers is crippled. Again, increasing numbers work at home, in no small measure due to technical change such as online transactions, that facilitates such decentralized work, in a return to the pre-factory-work era, and are therefore less amenable to unionization.

Again, can we turn to yet another element of globalization for an explanation? Has the outflow of Direct Foreign Investment (DFI) to the poor countries with cheap labour caused a decline in the capital which works at home with unskilled labour and hence to a decline in wages? As I look at the data, the United States has received more or less as much equity investment as it has lost over the last two decades. One cannot just look at one side of the ledger; I might add that I was once in a BBC radio debate with the Mayor of the French town, which had lost its Hoover factory to England. He was lamenting the loss and holding up multinationals as somewhat wicked in their pursuit of profits. So, I told him: Mr. Mayor, Hoover is an American firm. When it came to your town, you applauded. Now that they have travelled on, you are agitated. You cannot have it both ways. Again, as I argue below, the econometric evidence on location by multinationals does not show that cheap labour is a big draw; and many other factors producing competitiveness are at play, making the rich countries also major attractions for the inflow of equity investments by multinationals.

So, in lieu of globalization as the culprit, one has to fall back on the argument that substantial unskilled-labour-saving technical change is putting pressure on the wages of the unskilled. Technical change (except for the Green Revolution, where the new seeds led to increases in both the demand for landless labour and real wages because the application of irrigation and fertilizers to the new seeds led to more intensive land use with multiple shifts) happens to be continually economizing on the use of unskilled labour. Much empirical argumentation and evidence exists on this, coming from world-class economists such as Alan Krueger of Princeton. But, as always, anecdotes (which obviously cannot substitute for systematic evidence) can make this point come alive.[10] The effect of technical change in increasing the demand for skilled and reducing that for unskilled labour today can be illustrated by two examples.

First, to take an example from my own professorial life, secretaries are increasingly hard to get from the university administration on campuses. Instead, universities now offer you computers. Whereas secretaries are generally semi-skilled—though in the past highly educated and gifted females often became secretaries because they had few other options—the computers have to be looked after, and fixed frequently due to failure (especially when one has a deadline), by "electronic plumbers" who are skilled and get paid much more. So the rapid spread of computers is steadily reducing demand for secretaries and increasing the demand for the electronic plumbers.

A more striking example comes from Charlie Chaplin's famous film, *Modern Times*. You will recall how he goes berserk on the assembly line, the mechanical motion of turning the spanner finally getting to him (illustrating Adam Smith's famous observation that

the division of labour, and concentration on repetitive, narrow tasks could turn workers into morons and that education for them had to provide the antidote). Suppose that you take your child to see the film and she asks you: Daddy, take me to see an assembly line so I can actually see the people working at it. Well, it is going to be increasingly difficult to find such an assembly line for your child to see. Yes, there are assembly lines today; but they are without workers; they are managed by computers in a glass cage above, with highly skilled engineers in charge. The disoriented Charlie Chaplins have increasingly disappeared, at least from the assembly lines. Amusingly, this was brought home to Americans when, having decided to investigate the production of potato and semiconductor chips because of the widespread perception that potato chips were produced by primitive techniques and semiconductors were made with advanced technology, a reporter found that the facts were the other way around. He visited a factory that produced semiconductors and found that it involved moronic fitting of little wires onto small boards, whereas the Pringles factory he visited for potato chips was fully automated on its assembly line, with Pringles fitting beautifully on one another, each a total replica of the other, in the red and green boxes one finds in hotel mini-bars.

The facts are that this is rapidly occurring in the United States, and in other rich countries, as technical change is quickly spreading through the system. This naturally creates, in the short-run, pressure on the jobs and wages of the workers being displaced. But we know from past experience with technical change that we usually get a J-curve where, as productivity increase takes hold, it will (except in cases where macroeconomic difficulties may occur and are not addressed by macroeconomic remedies) result in wage increases. A Luddite response, therefore, is hardly called for. So, why has there been no such effect—or at least a significant effect—in the statistics on wages for almost two decades?

I suspect that the answer lies in the intensity of displacement of unskilled labour by IT-based technical change—its potency is dramatic, as is evident from nearly everyone's daily experience—and in the fact that it is continuous now, unlike such discrete changes as the invention of the steam engine. Before the workers get on to the rising part of the J-curve, they run into yet more such technical change, so that the working class gets to go from one declining segment of the J-curve to another, to yet another. The pressure on wages gets to be relentless, lasting over longer periods than in earlier experience with unskilled-labour-saving technical change. But this technical change, which proceeds like a tsunami, has nothing to do with globalization.

Notes

1. See, for instance, Chapters 4 and 7 in a polemical book by a US Democrat, Congressman Sherrod Brown, *Myths of Free Trade*, (New York: The New Press, 2004). Unfortunately, at the time of this essay going to press, Mr Brown was elected to the new US Congress and can be expected to bring his misguided views assiduously to the floor in that legislative body.

2. The earlier work of my Columbia University colleague Joe Stiglitz promised much but delivered little: it was focused largely, and then again with little nuance, on the policies and conditionalities of the Bretton Woods institutions, the IMF and the World Bank, with little bearing on the issues that ailed most of the agitated. See Joseph Stiglitz, *Globalization and Its Discontents* (New York: W.W. Norton, 2002). Strangely enough, Nancy Birdsall has argued that the Stiglitz book deals with "social justice," whereas mine does not, because the indexes of the two books show minimal references to the phrase in my book unlike his. The absurdity of this conclusion, and the fact that my book deals with virtually all social-justice issues whereas his uses the phrase without

addressing any of these issues meaningfully, if at all, is demonstrated in my note, "In Defense of *In Defense of Globalization*," posted on my website www.columbia.edu/~jb38.

3. This trend has also been helped by the increasing flow of Japanese students to the West, where they learn our way of life and our values. Thus, the early Japanese students used to be deferential and called me "sensei," the revered teacher: I sometimes joke that I used to love it as no American students would ever do that! But now, they put their feet on the table like the American students and even blow those horrid bubbles from their chewing gums. This "acculturation" of Japan is a gathering force that shows itself up in several ways. I have described the phenomenon by titling a 1994 *Foreign Affairs* article of mine, on the US–Japan trade negotiations where the Japanese refused to accept demands for import targets, "Samurai No More": our negotiators thought they were dealing with the samurai when, in fact, they were dealing with GIs. Another apt metaphor is: "Crossing Against the Light": whereas the traditional Japanese dutifully waited for the green traffic light to flash before they crossed a road, now they are like New Yorkers dashing across despite red and yellow lights.

4. See Arvind Panagariya, "Miracles and Debacles: In Defense of Trade Openness," *The World Economy*, Vol. 27 (8), August 2004, pp. 1149–71.

5. I use the word "crazy," which is not very polite, in the tradition of Keynes who wrote famously that it would be crazy to prefer bilateral trade agreements to multilateralism in trade.

6. See, for instance, the chart on the Soviet growth rates in Padma Desai's introductory chapter in her *Soviet Economy: Problems and Prospects* (Oxford: Basil Blackwell, 1987), Chart 1.1.

7. There is consensus now that the cocktail made with three liqueurs—greater reliance on markets, political democracy, and openness to the world economy—is enormously productive of prosperity and hence of attack on poverty. Both Soviet Union and North Korea rejected the cocktail, foregoing markets, denying democracy, and embracing autarky. In this regard, see also the discussion in my 1993 Rajiv Gandhi Memorial Lecture, *Democracy and Development*, reprinted

in my essays, *A Stream of Windows* (Cambridge, MA: MIT Press, 2000).

8. In fact, I and other trade economists began writing about the rationale for, and design of, adjustment assistance in import-competing industries in the 1970s. I have often lectured also about the need to remedy the absence of such a safety net in the poor countries. They have now seen the benefits of trade liberalization and would like to profit from it, but are fearful to move on to the high wire when there is no safety net.

9. This is also the conclusion of Robert Feenstra and Gordon Hanson, reviewed in this book, in their study of outsourcing of components to Mexico from the United States and its effects on US wages. While the wage differential between skilled and unskilled workers rises, the real wage of the unskilled rises as well.

10. The use of anecdotes and *bon mots* is a device for making abstruse economic arguments accessible and plausible to the public at large. Wit, irony, and even sarcasm are excellent aides in putting one's points across to the general public. I might also add that there is now a fetish, among even serious economists like Dani Rodrik, Jeffrey Sachs, and Robert Barro (all associated with Harvard University, strangely enough), for mindless cross-country regressions, which serve as a substitute for analysis. The use of these regressions as "evidence," and the pretense that they are superior to, and a desirable substitute for conceptual and analytical arguments—Dani Rodrik once described conceptual analysis as "rhetoric" and his regressions as "evidence," committing two errors in one breath—are increasingly coming under fire.

CHAPTER 42

Education and Income Inequality

Alan Greenspan

Overshadowing the current anxiety is a problem of longer standing: many people's day-by-day experiences in the job market seem to contradict the well-documented evidence that competitive markets over the decades have elevated standards of living for the vast majority of Americans and much of the rest of the world. Too many perceive the increasingly competitive markets that are the hallmark of today's high-tech globalized economy as continually destroying jobs, and those losses are all too visible. Large layoffs are publicized in the media. Reductions in job slots in America's factories and offices appear unending.

It is thus not surprising that competition is often seen as a threat to job security. It is not perceived as a creator of higher wages either, although in the end it always has been and inevitably will be now as well. [. . .]

It does no good to argue that unrestrained competition leaves a society *on average* better off, when, in recent years, workers see their bosses gaining large bonuses as they themselves get tepid wage increases. People have to experience competition's advantages firsthand. If they do not, some will turn to populist leaders who promise, for example, to erect tariff walls. Such protectionism is perceived, erroneously, as securing high-paying jobs in steel, autos, textiles, and chemicals—the icons of America's *past* economic might. But twenty-first-century consumers are less disposed to the products of those industries than were their parents; the US domestic economy, by implication, will no longer support the relative wages and job levels contracted in those industries during negotiations of an earlier period. Accordingly, steel and textile industry employment is off sharply from the peaks of the 1950s and 1960s. The declines will likely continue.

The loss of traditional manufacturing jobs is often considered a worrisome hollowing out of the economy. It is not. On the contrary, the shift of manufacturing jobs in steel, autos, and textiles, for example, to their more modern equivalents in computers, telecommunications, and information technology is a plus, not a minus, to the standard of living. Traditional manufacturing companies are no longer the symbol of cutting-edge technologies; their roots lie deep in the nineteenth century or earlier. The world's consumers have increasingly been drawn to products embodying new ideas—cell phones over bicycles, for example. Global trade gives us access to a full range of products without requiring us to manufacture all of them domestically.

Were we to bow to the wishes of the economically uninformed and erect barriers to foreign trade, the pace of competition would surely slow, and tensions, I suppose, might at first appear to ease. After all, Richard Nixon's wage and price controls were highly popular when they were imposed in August 1971. The euphoria dissipated quickly as shortages began to appear. It is likely that such a scenario of growing discontent would be repeated were tariff walls raised. The American standard of living would soon begin to stagnate, and even decline, as a consequence of rising prices, deteriorating product choice, and, perhaps most visibly, our trading partners retaliating by shutting out our job-creating exports.

Manufacturing jobs can no longer be highly paid, since it is consumers who at the end of the day pay the wages of factory workers. And

they have balked. They prefer Wal-Mart prices. Those prices, reflecting Chinese low wages, are inconsistent with a funding of high-wage traditional US factories. Forcing US consumers to pay above-market prices to support factory salaries eventually would run into severe resistance. But by then, the American standard of living would have fallen. The Peterson Institute of International Economics estimates that the cumulative effect of globalization since the end of World War II has added 10 per cent to the level of the GDP of the United States. Shutting our doors to trade would bring the American standard of living down by that percentage. By comparison, the hugely painful retrenchment in real GDP from the third quarter of 1981 to the third quarter of 1982 was only 1.4 per cent. Those who say it is better that fewer people experience the stress of globalization even if it means that some people are less wealthy are creating a false choice. Once walled off, a country loses its competitive verve and begins to stagnate, and stagnation leads to even more intense pain for more people.

If these dire outcomes are unacceptable, as I trust they are, what can be done to counter the distorted perception of how jobs are gained and lost and how incomes are generated? And how can we redress the reality of the continuing advance of income inequality? Both are, among other considerations, undermining support for competitive markets. As I have noted many times, competitive markets and, by extension, globalization and capitalism cannot be sustained without the support of a large proportion of society. The rule of law under which capitalist economic institutions function must be perceived as "fair" if these institutions are to continue to receive broad support. The only way to temper the bias against an economy that entails the timely repositioning of labour is to continue to support market incentives that create jobs and to find productive ways to ease the pain of job losers. That problem is not new.

The growing inequality of income, however, is new, and it requires analysis as to its roots, and policy action where appropriate.

[. . .]

Until quite recently, judging from the numerous rounds of successful trade negotiations, globalization has been generally accepted. There is little doubt, however, that, driven by rapidly expanding innovation and competition, globalization has been a major contributor to the increasing concentration of income virtually everywhere. In the past couple of decades, innovation, especially Internet-related, has been moving faster than we can educate ourselves to apply advancing technologies. Thus, the shortfall of the supply of advanced skills relative to the demand for them is pressing the wages of skilled workers higher relative to the wages of the less skilled. There is no compelling reason why the pace of innovative ideas, which often come in bunches, should be immediately matched by a supply of skilled workers to implement them. The insights that advance cutting-edge technologies emerge from a very small part of that workforce.

As globalization increased the skilled wage premium, technological innovation was also taking a toll on lesser-skilled workers. The demand for moderately skilled workers declined as repetitive jobs were gradually displaced by computer programs. I recall architectural and engineering firms with acres of people drawing detailed designs for the newest building complex or jet aircraft. Those jobs are all gone—programmed out of existence. Lower-income workers, mainly in services not subject to global competition, have fared somewhat better. Fears of Americans that immigration is undercutting their wage levels have yet to be confirmed by hard evidence. In general, lower-income US workers did poorly in the 1980s but have fared somewhat better in recent years.

During the past quarter century, as incomes at the middle and lower levels of the US income

distribution lagged, those of the most affluent rose rapidly. Americans have seen this before. The last time income in the United States was concentrated in the hands of such a relatively few people was a brief period in the late 1920s and, I suspect more durably, in the years preceding World War I. Owing to the rapid development of the United States as a national market in the latter part of the nineteenth century, income had become highly concentrated by the early years of the twentieth century, as the Rockefellers, Fords, Morgans, and Carnegies were able to reach beyond their local fiefdoms to leverage their incomes by many multiples. The newly rich were a much larger group than the prominent few families that so engaged the society pages at the turn of the century. The striking income disparities of the early twentieth century, however, were driven by a substantially larger concentration of wealth than exists today. Much of the income concentration of those days reflected interest, dividends, and capital gains from that wealth, rather than wage and salary differentials.[1]

[. . .]

The key policy levers to address the problem of increasing inequality, as I see it, are thus primarily education and immigration. Markets are already working in that direction. We need to quicken the process. Specifically, we need to harness better the forces of competition that have shaped the development of education in the United States, and we need to make immigration easier for highly skilled individuals. I'll return to these points below.

[. . .]

Enhancing elementary and secondary school sensitivity to market forces should help restore the balance between the demand for and supply of skilled workers in the United States. I do not know whether vouchers, which bring an element of competition to public schools, are the final answer. But I suspect that Rose and Milton Friedman, devoting the end of their distinguished careers to advancing the policy, were on the right track. (I do not recall either ever being off track.)

[. . .]

Unless our resident population, with the assistance of our schools, can supply the level of skills we need, which to date they have not, as our skilled baby boomers retire we will require a significant increase in the number of skilled workers migrating to the United States. As Bill Gates, the chairman of Microsoft, succinctly testified before Congress in March 2007, "America will find it infinitely more difficult to maintain its technological leadership if it shuts out the very people who are most able to help us compete." He added that we are "driving away the world's best and brightest precisely when we need them most."

Much of our skill shortage can be resolved with education reform. But at best, that will take years. The world is moving too fast for political and bureaucratic dawdling. We need to address quickly a double US disability: the increasing income concentration and the increasing cost of staffing our highly complex capital stock. Both could be "cured" by opening up the United States to the world's very large and growing pool of skilled workers. Our skilled jobs are the highest paid in the world. Accordingly, were we to allow open migration of skilled workers to this country, there would soon be a lower wage premium of skilled over lesser skilled and an end to our shortages of skilled workers.[2] The shortages occur because we are inhibiting world competitive labour markets from functioning. Administrative exclusionary rules have been substituted for the pricing mechanism. In the process, we have created in this country a privileged, native-born elite of skilled workers whose incomes are being supported at non-competitively high levels by immigration quotas on skilled professionals. Eliminating such restrictions would, at the stroke of a pen, reduce much income inequality

and address the problem of a potentially non-competitive capital stock.

The politics of immigration policy, of course, is influenced by far more than economics. Immigration policy confronts the considerably more difficult issue of the desire of the population to maintain the cultural roots that tie the society together and foster voluntary exchange to mutual advantage. The United States has always been able eventually to absorb waves of immigration and maintain the individual rights and freedoms bestowed by our Founding Fathers. But the transitions were always more difficult than hindsight makes them appear. If we are to continue to engage the world and improve our standard of living, we will have to either markedly improve our elementary and secondary education or lower our barriers to skilled immigrants. In fact, implementing both measures would confer important economic benefits.

Public policy is a series of choices. We can build exclusionary walls around the United States to keep out the goods, services, and people that compete with domestic producers and workers. The result would be a loss of competitive spark, leading to a stagnant and weakened economy. Our standard of living would fall and societal discontent would fester and rise, as the once-vaunted superpower fell from its position of world leadership.

Alternatively, we can engage the increasingly competitive high-tech world, address our domestic school system's failure to supply a level of newly skilled workers sufficient to quell our disturbing increase in income inequality, and further open our borders to the world's growing skilled-worker pool.

No alternative offers a rising American standard of living without the challenge and stress of borders open to goods and people. Choice is what public policy is all about. And with choice come both benefits and costs. To achieve the benefits, we need to accept the costs.

Notes

1. Data on wealth distribution in the late nineteenth century are sparse, but the large prevalence of property income confirms the vast anecdotal evidence of those years. The decline in the concentration of income in the 1930s and through World War II owed to weakened asset values and capital losses, the hypertight labour markets of World War II, and the wage and price controls that inhibited supply and demand from functioning. Parenthetically, one consequence of those controls was the emergence of company-supplied medical insurance as a means to attract workers whose wages were frozen. The consequences of that system are all too evident to today's US manufacturers.

2. The rise in the income spread between skilled and less-skilled workers worldwide suggests that the shortage of skills is a global problem. Because international migration is so inhibited, the "price" for skills does not converge globally. It is clearly more of a problem in the United States than elsewhere. Hence, opening skilled immigration into the United States would put upward pressure on wages of non-US skilled workers and increase income concentration by a modest amount; it would also lower the US skilled wage level.

CHAPTER 43

Blank Is Beautiful: Three Decades of Erasing and Remaking the World

Naomi Klein

One of those who saw opportunity in the floodwaters of New Orleans was Milton Friedman, grand guru of the movement for unfettered capitalism and the man credited with writing the rulebook for the contemporary, hypermobile global economy. Ninety-three years old and in failing health, "Uncle Miltie," as he was known to his followers, nonetheless found the strength to write an op-ed for the *Wall Street Journal* three months after the levees broke. "Most New Orleans schools are in ruins," Friedman observed, "as are the homes of the children who have attended them. The children are now scattered all over the country. This is a tragedy. It is also an opportunity to radically reform the educational system."[1]

Friedman's radical idea was that instead of spending a portion of the billions of dollars in reconstruction money on rebuilding and improving New Orleans' existing public school system, the government should provide families with vouchers, which they could spend at private institutions, many run at a profit that would be subsidized by the state. It was crucial, Friedman wrote, that this fundamental change not be a stopgap but rather "a permanent reform."[2]

A network of right-wing think tanks seized on Friedman's proposal and descended on the city after the storm. The administration of George W. Bush backed up their plans with tens of millions of dollars to convert New Orleans schools into "charter schools," publicly funded institutions run by private entities according to their own rules. Charter schools are deeply polarizing in the United States, and nowhere more than in New Orleans, where they are seen by many African-American parents as a way of reversing the gains of the civil rights movement, which guaranteed all children the same standard of education. For Milton Friedman, however, the entire concept of a state-run school system reeked of socialism. In his view, the state's sole functions were "to protect our freedom both from the enemies outside our gates and from our fellow-citizens: to preserve law and order, to enforce private contracts, to foster competitive markets."[3] In other words, to supply the police and the soldiers—anything else, including providing free education, was an unfair interference in the market.

In sharp contrast to the glacial pace with which the levees were repaired and the electricity grid was brought back online, the auctioning-off of New Orleans' school system took place with military speed and precision. Within 19 months, with most of the city's poor residents still in exile, New Orleans' public school system had been almost completely replaced by privately run charter schools. Before Hurricane Katrina, the school board had run 123 public schools; now it ran just 4. Before the storm, there had been 7 charter schools in the city; now there were 31.[4] New Orleans teachers used to be represented by a strong union; now the union's contract had been shredded, and its 4700 members had all been fired.[5] Some of the younger teachers were rehired by the charter, at reduced salaries; most were not.

New Orleans was now, according to the *New York Times*, "the nation's pre-eminent laboratory for the widespread use of charter schools," while the American Enterprise Institute, a Friedmanite think tank, enthused that "Katrina accomplished in a day . . . what Louisiana school reformers couldn't do after years of trying."[6] Public school teachers, meanwhile, watching money allocated for the victims of the flood being diverted to erase a public system and replace it with a private one, were calling Friedman's plan "an educational land grab."[7]

I call these orchestrated raids on the public sphere in the wake of catastrophic events, combined with the treatment of disasters as exciting market opportunities, "disaster capitalism."

[. . .]

Most people who survive a devastating disaster want the opposite of a clean slate: they want to salvage whatever they can and begin repairing what was not destroyed; they want to reaffirm their relatedness to the places that formed them. "When I rebuild the city I feel like I'm rebuilding myself," said Cassandra Andrews, a resident of New Orleans' heavily damaged Lower Ninth Ward, as she cleared away debris after the storm."[8] But disaster capitalists have no interest in repairing what once was. In Iraq, Sri Lanka, and New Orleans, the process deceptively called "reconstruction" began with finishing the job of the original disaster by erasing what was left of the public sphere and rooted communities, then quickly moving to replace them with a kind of corporate New Jerusalem—all before the victims of war or natural disaster were able to regroup and stake their claims to what was theirs.

[. . .]

When I began this research into the intersection between super-profits and mega-disasters, I thought I was witnessing a fundamental change in the way the drive to "liberate" markets was advancing around the world. Having been part of the movement against ballooning corporate power that made its global debut in Seattle in 1999, I was accustomed to seeing similar business-friendly policies imposed through arm-twisting at World Trade Organization summits, or as the conditions attached to loans from the International Monetary Fund. The three trademark demands—privatization, government deregulation, and deep cuts to social spending—tended to be extremely unpopular with citizens, but when the agreements were signed there was still at least the pretext of mutual consent between the governments doing the negotiating, as well as a consensus among the supposed experts. Now the same ideological program was being imposed via the most baldly coercive means possible: under foreign military occupation after an invasion, or immediately following a cataclysmic natural disaster. September 11 appeared to have provided Washington with the green light to stop asking countries if they wanted the US version of "free trade and democracy" and to start imposing it with Shock and Awe military force.

As I dug deeper into the history of how this market model had swept the globe, however, I discovered that the idea of exploiting crisis and disaster has been the modus operandi of Milton Friedman's movement from the very beginning—this fundamentalist form of capitalism has always needed disasters to advance. It was certainly the case that the facilitating disasters were getting bigger and more shocking, but what was happening in Iraq and New Orleans was not a new, post–September 11 invention. Rather, these bold experiments in crisis exploitation were the culmination of three decades of strict adherence to the shock doctrine.

Seen through the lens of this doctrine, the past 35 years look very different. Some of the most infamous human rights violations of this era, which have tended to be viewed as sadistic acts carried out by anti-democratic regimes, were in fact either committed with the deliberate intent of terrorizing the public or actively harnessed to prepare the ground for the introduction of radical free-market "reforms." In Argentina in the seventies, the junta's "disappearance" of 30,000 people, most of them leftist activists, was integral to the imposition of the country's Chicago School policies, just as terror had been a partner for the same kind of economic metamorphosis in Chile. In China in 1989, it was the shock of the Tiananmen Square massacre and the

subsequent arrests of tens of thousands that freed the hand of the Communist Party to convert much of the country into a sprawling export zone, staffed with workers too terrified to demand their rights. In Russia in 1993, it was Boris Yeltsin's decision to send in tanks to set fire to the parliament building and lock up the opposition leaders that cleared the way for the fire-sale privatization that created the country's notorious oligarchs.

[. . .]

There have, of course, been cases in which the adoption of free-market policies has taken place democratically—politicians have run on hard-line platforms and won elections, the US under Ronald Reagan being the best example, France's election of Nicolas Sarkozy a more recent one. In these cases, however, free-market crusaders came up against public pressure and were invariably forced to temper and modify their radical plans, accepting piecemeal changes rather than a total conversion. The bottom line is that while Friedman's economic model is capable of being partially imposed under democracy, authoritarian conditions are required for the implementation of its true vision. For economic shock therapy to be applied without restraint—as it was in Chile in the seventies, China in the late eighties, Russia in the nineties, and the US after September 11, 2001—some sort of additional major collective trauma has always been required, one that either temporarily suspended democratic practices or blocked them entirely. This ideological crusade was born in the authoritarian regimes of South America, and in its largest new conquered territories—Russia and China—it co-exists most comfortably, and most profitably, with an iron-fisted leadership to this day.

[. . .]

Friedman's Chicago School movement has been conquering territory around the world since the seventies, but until recently its vision had never been fully applied in its country of origin. Certainly Reagan had made headway, but the US retained a welfare system, social security, and public schools, where parents clung, in Friedman's words, to their "irrational attachment to a socialist system."[9]

When the Republicans gained control of Congress in 1995, David Frum, a transplanted Canadian and future speechwriter for George W. Bush, was among the so-called neo-conservatives calling for a shock therapy–style economic revolution in the US. "Here's how I think we should do it. Instead of cutting incrementally—a little here, a little there—I would say that on a single day this summer we eliminate 300 programs, each one costing a billion dollars or less. Maybe these cuts won't make a big deal of difference, but, boy, do they make a point. And you can do them right away."[10]

Frum didn't get his home-grown shock therapy at the time, largely because there was no domestic crisis to prepare the ground. But in 2001 that changed. When the September 11 attacks hit, the White House was packed with Friedman's disciples, including his close friend Donald Rumsfeld. The Bush team seized the moment of collective vertigo with chilling speed—not, as some have claimed, because the administration deviously plotted the crisis but because the key figures of the administration, veterans of earlier disaster capitalism experiments in Latin America and Eastern Europe, were part of a movement that prays for crisis the way drought-struck farmers pray for rain, and the way Christian-Zionist end-timers pray for the Rapture. When the long-awaited disaster strikes, they know instantly that their moment has come at last.

For three decades, Friedman and his followers had methodically exploited moments of shock in other countries—foreign equivalents of 9/11, starting with Pinochet's coup on September 11, 1973. What happened on September 11, 2001, is that an ideology hatched in American universities and fortified in

Washington institutions finally had its chance to come home.

The Bush administration immediately seized upon the fear generated by the attacks not only to launch the "War on Terror" but to ensure that it is an almost completely for-profit venture, a booming new industry that has breathed new life into the faltering US economy. Best understood as a "disaster capitalism complex," it has much farther-reaching tentacles than the military-industrial complex that Dwight Eisenhower warned against at the end of his presidency: this is global war fought on every level by private companies whose involvement is paid for with public money, with the unending mandate of protecting the United States homeland in perpetuity while eliminating all "evil" abroad. In only a few short years, the complex has already expanded its market reach from fighting terrorism to international peacekeeping, to municipal policing, to responding to increasingly frequent natural disasters. The ultimate goal for the corporations at the centre of the complex is to bring the model of for-profit government, which advances so rapidly in extraordinary circumstances, into the ordinary and day-to-day functioning of the state—in effect, to privatize the government.

[. . .]

Amid the weapons trade, the private soldiers, for-profit reconstruction, and the homeland security industry, what has emerged as a result of the Bush administration's particular brand of post–September 11 shock therapy is a fully articulated new economy. It was built in the Bush era, but it now exists quite apart from any one administration and will remain entrenched until the corporate supremacist ideology that underpins it is identified, isolated, and challenged. The complex is dominated by US firms, but it is global, with British companies bringing their experience in ubiquitous security cameras, Israeli firms their expertise in building high-tech fences and walls, the

Canadian lumber industry selling prefab houses that are several times more expensive than those produced locally, and so on. "I don't think anybody has looked at disaster reconstruction as an actual housing market before," said Ken Baker, CEO of a Canadian forestry trade group. "It's a strategy to diversify in the long run."[11]

[...]

In the attempt to relate the history of the ideological crusade that has culminated in the radical privatization of war and disaster, one problem recurs: the ideology is a shape-shifter, forever changing its name and switching identities. Friedman called himself a "liberal," but his US followers, who associated liberals with high taxes and hippies, tended to identify as "conservatives," "classical economists," "free marketers," and, later, as believers in "Reaganomics" or "laissez-faire." In most of the world, their orthodoxy is known as "neo-liberalism," but it is often called "free trade" or simply "globalization." Only since the mid-nineties has the intellectual movement, led by the right-wing think tanks with which Friedman had long associations—Heritage Foundation, Cato Institute, and the American Enterprise Institute—called itself "neo-conservative," a worldview that has harnessed the full force of the US military machine in the service of a corporate agenda.

All these incarnations share a commitment to the policy trinity—the elimination of the public sphere, total liberation for corporations, and skeletal social spending—but none of the various names for the ideology seem quite adequate. Friedman framed his movement as an attempt to free the market from the state, but the real-world track record of what happens when his purist vision is realized is rather different. In every country where Chicago School policies have been applied over the past three decades, what has emerged is a powerful ruling alliance between a few very large corporations and a class of mostly wealthy politicians—with hazy and ever-shifting lines between the two groups.

In Russia the billionaire private players in the alliance are called "the oligarchs"; in China, "the princelings"; in Chile, "the piranhas"; in the US, the Bush–Cheney campaign "Pioneers." Far from freeing the market from the state, these political and corporate elites have simply merged, trading favours to secure the right to appropriate precious resources previously held in the public domain—from Russia's oil fields, to China's collective lands, to the no-bid reconstruction contracts for work in Iraq.

A more accurate term for a system that erases the boundaries between Big Government and Big Business is not liberal, conservative, or capitalist but corporatist. Its main characteristics are huge transfers of public wealth to private hands, often accompanied by exploding debt, an ever-widening chasm between the dazzling rich and the disposable poor, and an aggressive nationalism that justifies bottomless spending on security. For those inside the bubble of extreme wealth created by such an arrangement, there can be no more profitable way to organize a society. But because of the obvious drawbacks for the vast majority of the population left outside the bubble, other features of the corporatist state tend to include aggressive surveillance (once again, with government and large corporations trading favours and contracts), mass incarceration, shrinking civil liberties, and often, though not always, torture.

[...]

From Chile to China to Iraq, torture has been a silent partner in the global free-market crusade. But torture is more than a tool used to enforce unwanted policies on rebellious peoples; it is also a metaphor of the shock doctrine's underlying logic.

Torture, or in CIA language "coercive interrogation," is a set of techniques designed to put prisoners into a state of deep disorientation and shock in order to force them to make concessions against their will. The guiding logic is elaborated in two CIA manuals that were declassified in the late nineties. They explain that the way to break "resistant sources" is to create violent ruptures between prisoners and their ability to make sense of the world around them.[12] First, the senses are starved of any input (with hoods, earplugs, shackles, total isolation), then the body is bombarded with overwhelming stimulation (strobe lights, blaring music, beatings, electroshock).

The goal of this "softening-up" stage is to provoke a kind of hurricane in the mind: prisoners are so regressed and afraid that they can no longer think rationally or protect their own interests. It is in that state of shock that most prisoners give their interrogators whatever they want—information, confessions, a renunciation of former beliefs.

[...]

The shock doctrine mimics this process precisely, attempting to achieve on a mass scale what torture does one on one in the interrogation cell. The clearest example was the shock of September 11, which, for millions of people, exploded "the world that is familiar" and opened up a period of deep disorientation and regression that the Bush administration expertly exploited. Suddenly we found ourselves living in a kind of Year Zero, in which everything we knew of the world before could now be dismissed as "pre-9/11 thinking." Never strong in our knowledge of history, North Americans had become a blank slate—"a clean sheet of paper" on which "the newest and most beautiful words can be written," as Mao said of his people.[13] A new army of experts instantly materialized to write new and beautiful words on the receptive canvas of our post-trauma consciousness: "clash of civilizations," they inscribed. "Axis of evil," "Islamo-fascism," "homeland security." With everyone preoccupied by the deadly new culture wars, the Bush administration was able to pull off what it could only have dreamed of doing before 9/11: wage privatized wars abroad and build a corporate security complex at home.

[...]

This book is a challenge to the central and most cherished claim in the official story—that the triumph of deregulated capitalism has been born of freedom, that unfettered free markets go hand in hand with democracy. Instead, I will show that this fundamentalist form of capitalism has consistently been midwifed by the most brutal forms of coercion, inflicted on the collective body politic as well as on countless individual bodies. The history of the contemporary free market—better understood as the rise of corporatism—was written in shocks.

[...]

I am not arguing that all forms of market systems are inherently violent. It is eminently possible to have a market-based economy that requires no such brutality and demands no such ideological purity. A free market in consumer products can co-exist with free public health care, with public schools, with a large segment of the economy—like a national oil company—held in state hands. It's equally possible to require corporations to pay decent wages, to respect the right of workers to form unions, and for governments to tax and redistribute wealth so that the sharp inequalities that mark the corporatist state are reduced. Markets need not be fundamentalist.

Keynes proposed exactly that kind of mixed, regulated economy after the Great Depression, a revolution in public policy that created the New Deal and transformations like it around the world. It was exactly that system of compromises, checks, and balances that Friedman's counter-revolution was launched to methodically dismantle in country after country. Seen in that light, the Chicago School strain of capitalism does indeed have something in common with other dangerous ideologies; the signature desire for unattainable purity, for a clean slate on which to build a re-engineered model society.

This desire for godlike powers of total creation is precisely why free-market ideologues are so drawn to crises and disasters. Non-apocalyptic reality is simply not hospitable to their ambitions. For 35 years, what has animated Friedman's counter-revolution is an attraction to a kind of freedom and possibility available only in times of cataclysmic change—when people, with their stubborn habits and insistent demands, are blasted out of the way—moments when democracy seems a practical impossibility.

Believers in the shock doctrine are convinced that only a great rupture—a flood, a war, a terrorist attack—can generate the kind of vast, clean canvases they crave. It is in these malleable moments, when we are psychologically unmoored and physically uprooted, that these artists of the real plunge in their hands and begin their work of remaking the world.

Notes

1. "The Promise of Vouchers," *Wall Street Journal*, 5 December 2005.
2. Ibid.
3. Milton Friedman, *Capitalism and Freedom* (1962, repr. Chicago: University of Chicago Press, 1982), 2.
4. Interview with Joe DeRose, United Teachers of New Orleans, 18 September 2006; Michael Kunzelman, "Post-Katrina, Educators, Students Embrace Charter Schools," Associated Press, 17 April 2007.
5. Steve Ritea, "N.O. Teachers Union Loses Its Force in Storm's Wake," *Times-Picayune* (New Orleans), 6 March 2006.
6. Susan Saulny, "U.S. Gives Charter Schools a Big Push in New Orleans," *New York Times*, 13 June 2006; Veronique de Rugy and Kathryn G. Newmark, "Hope after Katrina?" *Education Next*, 1 October 2006, www.aei.org.
7. "Educational Land Grab," *Rethinking Schools*, Fall 2006.
8. Nicholas Powers, "The Ground below Zero," *Indypendent*, 31 August 2006, www.indypendent.org.
9. Bob Sipchen, "Are Public Schools Worth the Effort?" *Los Angeles Times*, 3 July 2006.
10. Paul Tough, David Frum, William Kristal et al., "A Revolution or Business as Usual?: A Harper's Forum," *Harper's*, March 1995.
11. Wency Leung, "Success Through Disaster: B.C.-Made Wood Houses Hold Great Potential for Disaster Relief," *Vancouver Sun*, 15 May 2006.
12. Central Intelligence Agency, *Kubark Counterintelligence Interrogation*, July 1963, 1, 101. Declassified manual is available in full, www.gwu.edu/~nsarchiv.
13. Mao Tse-Tung, "Introducing a Cooperative," *Peking Review* 1, no. 15 (10 June 1958), 6.

Critical Thinking Questions

1. It was the nineteenth century when Bastiat argued that government is the "great fiction through which everybody endeavours to live at the expense of everybody else." How does this historical context support or undermine his case? If Bastiat were to have witnessed the financial collapse of 2008 and the economic crisis that followed it, how might he have responded to the various government policies designed to shore up various industries?

2. Bhagwati accuses globalization critics of being disingenuous by framing fearful self-interest as emphatic altruism. How does Bhagwati explain this apparent

phenomenon? How valid are the assumptions upon which Bhagwati bases his argument? Bhagwati argues that critics of globalization unfairly blame it for developments unrelated to globalizations. Discuss one of the examples that Bhagwati cites. Might the critics of globalization have a point after all?

3. Buchanan rejects the "need for some all-powerful authority, some sovereign" to steer the economy specifically and society generally in offering the free market as an alternative mechanism. Identify its basic features. Can this mechanism cover all aspects of society? Which nineteenth-century political philosopher does Buchanan attack when he (i) denies the existence of hierarchies within society, and (ii) identifies the individual as the primary unit of economic and political analysis? What is your assessment of Buchanan's claim that "the empirical reality of individual differences" does not matter in the organization of society?

4. While Greenspan acknowledges the massive discrepancy in incomes between the richest and poorest segments of society, he argues that this inequity is less serious than it appears. Assess the veracity of this claim. Greenspan identifies immigration (read: the voluntary transfers of individuals from one region to another) as a remedy to the effects of globalization. Assess the efficacy and the feasibility of this proposal by listing potential advantages and disadvantages. While Greenspan identifies education as a response to the harmful effects of globalization, he implicitly rejects a greater role for the state in this process. How consistent or inconsistent is this argument?

5. How credible does Klein's argument appear? What are her strongest arguments? Where does her argument fall flat? What (if any) other factors other than the mechanisms that Klein identifies might have contributed to the conditions she describes?

Biographies

Frédéric Bastiat (1801–1850)

Joseph Schumpeter (1883–1950) once called Bastiat "the most brilliant economic journalist who ever lived." Other prominent economists including Friedrich A. Hayek (1899–1992) and James Buchanan (1919–) offered comparable assessments in praising Bastiat's sarcastic but insightful writing in favour of the free market. But Bastiat, who once sardonically urged the French state to protect the candle industry against the sun, has so far failed to match the intellectual reach of his contemporary rivals Karl Marx (1818–1883) and Joseph Proudhon (1809–1865). Former British Prime Minister Margaret Thatcher (1925–)—who calls Bastiat her favourite economic thinker—discovered his relative anonymity firsthand during a state visit to his native France. Few, if any, of Thatcher's hosts had ever heard of Bastiat, whose popularity has recently risen, with the emergence of the populist Tea Party movement in the United States.

James Buchanan (1919–)

Buchanan dabbled in libertarian socialism before taking graduate classes at the University of Chicago, where he fell under the immediate spell of free-market advocate Frank Knight (1885–1972). During this period, Buchanan also discovered the Swedish economist Knut Wicksell (1851–1926), who in 1896 had published an obscure essay that previewed several key positions of the Austrian School in its hostile critique of the state and taxation. Inspired by this research, Buchanan applied the techniques and tools of neo-classical economics toward the study of politics, an approach that now appears in the literature as public choice theory. This adaptation eventually earned Buchanan the 1986 Nobel Prize in Economics. But Buchanan's legacy as a co-founder of public choice theory goes far beyond his many awards and his role as the founder of several academic institutions. His work has not only changed the study of politics, but also its practice.

Jagdish Bhagwati (1934–)

Born in what is now Mumbai during the dying final years of the British Raj, Bhagwati's biography shares many similarities with another important Indian economist, Amartya Sen (1933–). Both hail from prominent families and both enjoyed the privilege of studying in England as well as the United States. But whereas Sen criticizes globalization, Bhagwati has emerged as one of its most powerful defenders during his prolific career as an academic and past advisor to the Director General of the General Agreement on Tariffs and Trade (GATT), the forerunner of the modern-day World Trade Organization (WTO), and the United Nations. But Bhagwati is more than just a partisan defender of globalization who blissfully ignores its shadows. His support for human rights and migrants says otherwise.

Alan Greenspan (1926–)

Alan Greenspan, to use his own words, rarely displayed signs of "irrational exuberance" during his cool, calculating, and often cryptic tenure as head of US Federal Reserve Board from 1987 through 2006. Greenspan's calmness though belied the radical vision that defined the ideology of one of his early and important mentors—author and journalist Ayn Rand (1905–1982), whose fictional and non-fictional writings promoted the virtues of selfishness. While no would accuse Greenspan of being an avatar for Rand, few would deny her influence on one of the most powerful individuals through the late twentieth century into the early twenty-first century. This said, some might claim that Greenspan bears plenty of personal responsibility for his role in promoting policies that contributed to the American housing bubble whose burst nearly brought down the global economy in 2008.

Naomi Klein (1970–)

When journalist and author Naomi Klein grew up in her native Montreal, she showed no interest in politics. In fact, Klein appeared to rebel against the activism of her mother, a documentary filmmaker, by indulging in the teen-oriented consumerism, which she later condemned in *No Logo*. Klein has since long abandoned such ways. Writing for a series of renowned magazines and newspapers on both sides of the 49th parallel as well as the *Atlantic*, Klein has emerged as one the best known and prolific critics of globalization. She also put a unique spin on Carol Hanish's thesis that the personal is political by marrying Canadian filmmaker Avi Lewis—the son of Canadian diplomat Stephen Lewis and the grandson of David Lewis, who co-founded the Co-operative Commonwealth Federation, the forerunner of the contemporary New Democratic Party.

Part IX

Feminism

Feminism

Feminism is a political philosophy that advocates civil, political, social, and economic equality for the sexes. There is a tendency among advocates of this political ideology to draw a distinction between sex and gender, with the former biologically and the latter culturally understood. Further, among such feminists, sex differences are minimized. Mary Wollstonecraft of England and her *A Vindication of the Rights of Woman* (1792) are compelling to cite as the beginning of the first wave of feminism. Simone de Beauvoir of France and Betty Friedan of the United States are equally compelling persons to note as the initiators of the second wave of this political philosophy. Their writings, *The Second Sex* (1953) and *The Feminine Mystique* (1963), respectively, began the struggle for economic and social equality. In this struggle, feminists ingeniously explored motifs such as domination, patriarchy, the private domain, the public domain, the political role of the family, an ethic of care, and sexism in political theory. The role that women played during World War II, coupled with the civil rights movement in the United States, emboldened women of Europe and the United States and Canada to assert what they saw as their natural rights.

Major Figures

Christine de Pisan (1364–c. 1430), Lady Damaris Masham (1658–1708), Mary Astell (1666–1731), Mary Wollstonecraft (1759–1797), John Stuart Mill (1806–1873), Harriet Taylor Mill (1807–1858), Elizabeth Cady Stanton (1815–1902), Richard Pankhurst (1834–1898), Emmeline Pankhurst (1858–1928), Nellie McClung (1873–1951), Simone de Beauvoir (1908–1986), Betty Friedan (1921–2006), Kate Millett (1934–), Carol Gilligan (1936–), Lorraine Code (1937–), Germaine Greer (1939–), Alice Schwarzer (1942–), Catharine McKinnon (1946–), Susan Okin (1946–2004), Martha Nussbaum (1947–), and Ayaan Hirsi Ali (1969–)

Period of Greatest Influence

First Wave from 1792 to the 1930s; the Second Wave from 1960 to the present

Introduction

Feminism has a much longer history than many assume. Its first wave occurred in the years following the publication of Mary Wollstonecraft's (1759–1797) *A Vindication of the Rights of Woman*, written as a feminist answer to Thomas Paine's (1737–1809) *The Rights of Man*. Soon after the publication of these works, other feminist publications appeared, including Harriet Taylor's (1807–1858) *The Enfranchisement of Women* and John Stuart Mill's (1806–1873) *The Subjection of Women*. But it was not just publications that shaped this first wave of feminism; there were political events—such as the Seneca Falls Convention in 1848, which adopted the Declaration of Sentiments demanding female suffrage—that served as defining moments in the rising tide of interest in and organization around women's issues by women. Other events, such as the suffrage movement in the early twentieth century, took place in connection with women's rights in the years that followed, but it was not until the publication of two works, Simone de Beauvoir's (1908–1986) *The Second Sex* in 1949 and Betty Friedan's (1921–2006) *The Feminine Mystique* in 1963, that the second wave of feminism began to have an impact on Western culture and the hegemonic power that men held in Western societies. It is from this second wave of feminism that the following excerpts are drawn, beginning with Lorenne Clark's (1936–) analysis of John Locke's view of women.

As a lawyer, criminologist, and philosopher, Lorenne Clark has provided keen observations on feminism in two fields: sexism of political theory and sexual assault law. In the following excerpt, she concerns herself with the former and singles out for analysis and criticism the views of John Locke on patriarchy and the dominion of a husband over his wife. She argues with great effectiveness that Locke denounces patriarchy but endorses the husband's dominion over his wife, thereby creating a logical problem for himself. Clark tantalizingly traces the distinctions that Locke draws between "paternal power" and "parental power" and draws attention to Locke's views on monogamy. She thus sets the stage for a closer examination of the connection these distinctions and ideas have to contractual relationships and the institution of property.

The next feminist to be read is Susan Okin (1946–2004). An admirer of John Rawls, Okin nonetheless takes issue with his omission of a serious analysis of the role of the family in his magisterial work *A Theory of Justice*. Of particular concern to Okin is Rawls' failure to apply his principles of justice—the principles of liberty and difference—to the structure of the family. Rather, according to Okin, Rawls simply assumes that family institutions are just, something that Okin finds questionable when considering gendered families, which can give rise to dependence and domination rather than equality and reciprocity. Okin concludes her assessment of Rawls' notion of justice by developing, in rudimentary form, a feminist reading of Rawls that in the end, she believes, can strengthen Rawls' theory against some of its criticisms.

The impact of Rawls' thinking on feminist philosophy is further revealed in the writings of the well-known Martha Nussbaum (1947–). In her *Frontiers of Justice*, written in memory of John Rawls, Nussbaum affirms the convergence between her own theory of justice, called the capabilities approach, and Rawls' theory of justice, called the informed-desire approach. This convergence is analyzed by Nussbaum in her earlier work *Women and Human Development*, though in the present extract only the capabilities approach is treated by her. Under both approaches, the state's concern for its citizens would embrace laws against marital rape, laws protecting marital consent, laws mandating compulsory education, and laws banning child labour, to name only a few areas of agreement. However, Nussbaum is specifically attracted to the capabilities approach because, as she makes clear in *Women and Human Development*, it provides the "philosophical underpinning" for those entitlements required for human dignity. With this background in mind, Nussbaum lays out her "minimum core social entitlements" in terms of central human capabilities essential for a minimum account of social (political) justice. Those familiar with classical Greek philosophy will recognize the influence of Aristotle's (384–322 BCE) thought on Nussbaum, at least with respect to their shared concept of the person as one who is both capable and needy.

A more radical and theoretical feminism than that of Nussbaum is the feminism of Lorraine Code (1937–). Writing in 1991 in *What She Can Know?*, Code explores epistemological questions, in other words, questions concerning the foundations of knowledge, along a mitigated relativist path. She does this by arguing, with some success, in favour of the claims that the sex of the knower is epistemologically significant and that knowledge is a construct that "bears the marks of its constructors." Notwithstanding this, Code does not want to encourage a feminist epistemology based upon gynocentric (female) concerns that replace androcentric (male) concerns. Rather, she wishes to argue for a well-mapped middle position that allows room for subjectivity and a measure of relativism that challenges the ideals of objectivity, impartiality, universality, and univocity without collapsing into antirealism—the position that denies external reality. Code is well aware, as the extract makes clear, of the difficulty faced by feminists who opt for an absolute relativism—a relativism that denies the existence of "facts of the matter." Absolute relativism cannot be countenanced by feminists, Code believes, owing to the indisputable reality of sexism, wage gaps between men and women, violence against women, inadequate day care, and racial injustices. The mitigated relativism Code offers is challenging, thought-provoking, and at odds with postpositivist empiricism, beginning with David Hume (1711–1776) and working through to Rudolf Carnap (1891–1970). Code's ideas aim at something new, namely non-reductive explanations and a general ecological or holistic treatment of knowledge and human activity.

While Susan Okin and Lorraine Code represent perspectives of American and Canadian feminists respectively, Alice Schwarzer (1942–) represents a perspective of European feminists. In *The Little Difference and Its Huge Consequences*, Schwarzer advances the proposition—very much in keeping with the ideas of Simone de Beauvoir—that masculinity and femininity are products of culture not nature. According to Schwarzer, culture produces an ideology of domination and subjection, of power and powerlessness, resulting in a gap between the two genders that is "seemingly impossible to overcome." It is this same ideology that has embedded at its core the belief in the vaginal orgasm, which leads some men to practise sexual control over women. This in turn functions, thinks Schwarzer, as the foundation of "the public monopoly of male society over women." From Schwarzer's perspective, compulsory heterosexuality is political and cultural, lacking any biological basis. From this same perspective, she argues in favour

of treating people "first and foremost" as people and only secondarily as gendered creatures. There is much in Schwarzer's position that is reminiscent of that of the Canadian
Shulamith Firestone (1945–), as found in *The Dialectic of Sex*.

The contribution of Ayaan Hirsi Ali (1969–), a Somali-born strident feminist, can
only be described as an uncompromising critique of the role of women in Muslim societies. In very blunt language, Hirsi Ali, herself a Dutch citizen, marks what are in her
opinion the three possible categories of Muslim women in present-day Dutch society:
Muslim women who choose to assimilate in Western society, all the while running the
risk of losing their lives in an effort to achieve their dreams; Muslim women who lead a
"double life," living as a Muslim women in the company of their larger family but living
as Western women outside it; and, finally, Muslim women who succumb to the pressures of Islamic customs and end up as modern slaves inside Muslim homes—either of
their parents or of their Muslim husband. Hirsi Ali pleads for European Union governments to provide education to such women—arguing that education is the best tool for
empowering women—in order to combat directly the major obstacle, namely violence,
to Muslim women "leading dignified and free lives." The violence that she refers to here
assumes three different forms: physical, mental, and sexual as committed by close families. In the present extract, Hirsi Ali proceeds to give more detailed illustrations of these
different forms of violence. Despite the seriousness of the problems that Hirsi Ali identifies here, she ends her lecture on a cautiously optimistic note, saying that awareness of
the scope of the problems that Muslim women face in European societies is growing.
By implication, she affirms that the education of both the subjects of this violent abuse
as well as the wider social community is a necessary step in the alleviating the plight of
Muslim women in European countries.

The second wave of feminism has undoubtedly reinvigorated political and philosophical issues concerned with the present position of women in the global community.
It is obvious that political philosophies cannot go back to "business as usual" nor to a
time prior to the second wave. Issues of equality, justice, domination, subjection, exploitation, and patriarchy have now infiltrated political philosophy in such a way that gender
issues must be considered as salient and deserving of serious analysis in the same spirit
as class and race issues. There is no turning back the clock. What Clark, Okin, and others
provide us with in the excerpts that follow are very robust and carefully crafted ideas that
need to be integrated into our way of seeing the world. The challenge that each of the
above individuals offers is, at the end of the day, rather liberating, not only for individuals but also for societies, and not only for women but also for men. It is time for societies
and people to begin to see things this way.

CHAPTER 44

Women and Locke: Who Owns the Apples in the Garden of Eden?

Lorenne M.G. Clark

The idea of creating a society guaranteeing equality between the sexes has never been considered by most political theorists. They have either endorsed, or simply accepted, the assumption of a natural inequality of the sexes which ought to be preserved in civil society.[1] This same presupposition has excluded the family from the theorists' framework of what are thought to be distinctively *political* institutions. Despite the central role of the family in human life, it has been consigned to the domain of purely natural phenomena. The related belief that women and children must be relegated for theoretical purposes to the family, to be safely ignored in a realm of brute nature, suffices to allow such theorists to exclude women from the ontology of politics (except insofar as they do productive work).

In looking at major theorists from this perspective, the task is not simply to show that they display sexist attitudes. The main purpose is to demonstrate that their theories rest on these assumptions and that they would be vastly different theories if these assumptions were not made. The point of such a demonstration is to establish that the theories which have been advanced on these foundations are not workable as blueprints for political institutions guaranteeing sexual equality. It remains to show how major political theorists demonstrate these assumptions, what use they make, either explicitly or implicitly, of these premises, and what problems this causes in their theories.

I wish to examine Locke from this point of view. To what extent does Locke illustrate the basic sexist assumptions which I have argued lie at the foundation of Western political theory? The specific premises I take to be central to Western political theory are, first, that there is a "natural" inequality of the sexes and a "natural" superiority of the male; second, that reproduction is not a central fact of political life and is of no value in creating a significant life for man; and, third, that the family is not a political, but a "natural" institution which remains outside the political framework in an ahistorical state of nature.

In addition to these major assumptions, there are further minor or derivative hypotheses which require examination. Among these, and of particular relevance to Locke, are questions relating to inheritance and the ownership of property. How do Locke's major premises function to justify ownership and inheritance of private property in order to preserve dominant sex and class position? Is ownership of the means and products of reproduction, as well as those of production, really needed to generate the kind of political society which Locke thinks is needed to secure "the peace, safety, and public good of the people" which is, he argues, the end of government?[2]

The first assumption, that there is an inequality of the sexes and that the male is superior, is both implicit and explicit in Locke. In the *First Treatise,* in attempting to refute Filmer's claim that Adam rules over Eve by dint of the law of God, Locke is at great pains to show that the source of the condition in which women are subjugated to men does not lie in law, but in nature: "Farther it is to be noted, that these words here of 3 *Gen.* 16 which our A. calls the Original Grant of Government were not spoken to Adam, neither indeed was there any Grant in them made to Adam, but a Punishment laid upon Eve; and if we will take them as they were directed in particular to her, or in her, as their representative to all other Women, they will at most concern the Female Sex only, and import no more but that Subjection they should ordinarily be in to their Husbands: But there is here no more Law to oblige a Woman to such a Subjection, if the Circumstances either of her Condition or Contract with her Husband should exempt her from it, then there is, that she should bring forth her Children in Sorrow and Pain, if there could be found a Remedy for it, which is also a part of the same Curse upon her."[3]

Thus the subjection in which most women are ordinarily found with respect to men is explicitly not the result of law, or any sort of arbitrary convention, not even that most Divine convention established by the will and authority of God. Rather it lies in the punishment laid on her, and on her alone, which consists in her being, as he says later in the same passage, "the weaker Sex," and forced to bring forth children in pain and sorrow.

Women are, then, by nature weaker than men, and this weakness is itself a direct result of the unique capacities women have with respect to reproduction. The Curse of God laid on women consists in her being by nature disadvantaged, and the disadvantage is clearly considered to be her reproductive capacities. The fact that women and women alone can bear children is a natural disadvantage which leads to a natural inequality between the sexes. Despite the fact that Locke believes that the inequality of the sexes is contingent,

grounded in natural differences between the sexes with respect to reproduction, this nonetheless establishes the superiority of the male: For though as a helper in the Temptation, as well as a Partner in the Transgression, Eve was laid below him, and so he had accidentally a Superiority over her.[4]

But given that there is this natural inequality, the common condition of women is to be under the subjection of men. However, precisely because this is a natural inequality, it is one which can, on rare occasions, be overcome. Should she be of noble birth, or ample means, these qualities compensate for her natural disadvantages, and she can, by means of these qualities, escape the condition of subjugation to which she would otherwise be liable: "And will anyone say, that Eve, or any other Woman sinn'd, if she were brought to Bed without those multiplied Pains God threatens her here with? Or that either of our Queens Mary or Elizabeth, had they Married any of their Subjects, had been by this Text put into a Political Subjection to him? or that he thereby should have had Monarchical Rule over her? God, in this Text gives not, that I see, any Authority to Adam over Eve, or to Men over their Wives, but only foretells what should be Woman's Lot, how by his Providence he would order it so, that she should be subject to her husband, as we see that generally the Laws of Mankind and customs of Nations have ordered it so; and there is, I grant, a Foundation in Nature for it."[5] Locke explicitly here acknowledges that the subjection of women to men is codified in law and custom. But he finds its source in nature and is, by this means, able to argue that in some few instances it is a natural liability which can be overcome.

Locke's objective in chapter V of the *First Treatise,* "Of Adam's Title to Sovereignty by the Subjection of Eve," is to show that God's creation of a natural basis for inequality between the sexes does not establish any basis, natural or otherwise, for Absolute Sovereignty and the absolute duty of obedience Filmer alleges to exist between subjects and monarch. The most Genesis establishes, says Locke, are "the Subjection of the Inferior Ranks of Creatures to Mankind," (1:28) and "the Subjection that is due from a Wife to her Husband" (3:16).[6] Thus he neither questions nor criticizes the alleged basis of the inequality and endorses the assumption that the natural difference between the sexes leads to the creation of an obligation on the part of a wife to be subjected to the will and authority of her husband: it is what is *due* from her to him.

In the *Second Treatise,* in "Of Paternal Power," he states that "though I have said above that all men by nature are equal, I cannot be supposed to understand all sorts of equality." He cites age, virtue, excellence of parts and merit, birth, alliance, and benefits as differences in respect of which some men gain a precedence over others. He goes on to say that none of these differences in respect of which men are not in some sense equal, conflicts with the way in which they are equal, namely, "in respect of jurisdiction or dominion one over another . . . that equal right that every man has to his natural freedom, without being subjected to the will or authority of any other men."[7]

Thus Locke does not deny that there are differences among men.[8] He argues instead that men are equal with respect to the right to autonomy *despite* these differences. However, as we have already seen, the allegedly "natural" differences between the sexes do justify the natural domination of women by men. His explicit statement on this issue in the *Second Treatise* is as follows: "it therefore being necessary that the last determination—i.e., the rule—should be somewhere, it naturally falls to the man's share, as the abler and the stronger."[9] The rule *naturally* falls to the man's share. Here he stresses that it is man's natural superiority (by virtue of his being "abler and the stronger"), rather than woman's natural disadvantage, which gives rise

to men's rightful rule over women. I agree here with Elrington, who says that this implies that the right of the husband arises solely from superior power. There are more similarities between Locke and Hobbes than are sometimes assumed.[10]

Two things are immediately obvious from this. In the First *Treatise* Locke appeared to argue that it is simply as a consequence of women's natural disadvantage that men do, as a matter of fact, ordinarily rule over women, but in the end he concludes that wives have a duty to obey. Thus there is a curious asymmetry between the sexes with respect to the consequences which follow from the fact that there are differences, natural and otherwise, between one person and another. The presupposition of a fundamental right to autonomy overrides any differences which may exist between individual men.

The natural differences between the sexes, however, override any presupposition of an equal right to autonomy for men and women. Here and only here a natural difference creates a justified domination of one person by another. However, the existence of clearly non-natural differences between one woman and another may sometimes override the presumption of female inferiority which explains and justifies the general subjugation of women by men. Thus, exceptional women may, because of the presence of social differences, overcome their natural disadvantage and so escape subjection. But in general the natural differences between men and women overrule any presupposition of equality between the sexes. Differences between individual men do not negate the presumption of equality among men, and differences between individual women may overcome the presumption of inferiority and so create a right to autonomy in some cases.

It seems abundantly clear, however, that Locke believed that there was a natural inequality between the sexes, that men were superior, and that this superiority ordinarily gave them a right to the obedience of their wives. It also seems clear that he believed that the source of women's inferiority lay in their reproductive capacities, and that he regarded this as a natural rather than a conventional disadvantage. It must be pointed out, however, that it is difficult to say that Locke saw this as the sole source and nature of women's inferior status. It is far from clear what her reproductive disadvantage has to do with the "greater strength" and being "abler" he attributes to males and which he uses to justify the authority of husband over wife in the *Second Treatise*.

How these assumptions affected the development of his theory can best be seen by considering how they shaped his assumptions about the family and its relation to other, political, institutions. Throughout both treatises Locke assumes that the natural condition of women is to be in the family. The subjection of women by men is the subjection of wife by husband. He nowhere discusses the status of the single woman. Women are, for Locke, married women, and, hence, most women are under the subjection of men. And most women are married women, because it is woman's nature to reproduce children which she is incapable of providing for on her own.[11] When he discusses the role of women, he explicitly states that they were created as companions for men and that they are incapable of bearing and rearing children without the assistance of men at least until all of the children are, as he says, "out of a dependency for support." Thus it is the natural fate of women to be married as a consequence of their reproductive capacities, and to be under the subjection of their husbands because they are dependent on them for the support of their offspring. Locke thus assumes that the family and its structure of authority are a natural association created in the state of nature.

The problem for Locke was then to distinguish political authority from natural authority.

Political authority must rest on consent and, hence, must be distinguished and distinguishable from natural familial authority which rests on a natural superiority of the male over the female which is itself grounded in a natural difference between them with respect to their reproductive roles.

In discussing the beginning of political societies, Locke admits that most civil societies began under the government and administration of one man: "the government commonly began in the father, for the father, having by the law of nature the same power with every man else to punish as he thought fit any offences against that law, might thereby punish his transgressing children even when they were men."[12] This is an *admission* for Locke because, for other reasons which we know very well, he was out to attack the concept of patriarchal government but nonetheless had to acknowledge the historical fact that most governments began as forms of paternal power and were, therefore, patriarchal governments. He did not want legitimate government to hang on the natural dominion man has in the family.

The interesting and important point to be seen is that since he himself assumes that male dominion in the family is natural, he must show that paternal power is to be distinguished from political power in order to argue that the basis for legitimate government is consent. Since he assumed that in the state of nature men exercised a natural dominion over women, he could hardly argue that even patriarchal dominion in the family is artificial and so cannot be used to justify patriarchal concepts of government. This would have been the most believable argument to advance to effect that conclusion. But he did not use it, and that is just the point. So far as he was concerned, that position was of no use. He simply assumes that the family and the division of power within it are a natural and not a political creation. As will become apparent, what is even more important is that he *must* assume this in order to arrive at a theory of society which conforms to the principles he thinks it must.

In the state of nature, women are naturally disadvantaged, men are naturally superior, and the family arises as a natural institution based on these natural differences between the sexes.[13] Thus, everything he says about equality in the state of nature pertains only to men. Men, and men only, are naturally free from the dominion of one over another, though this is consistent with his belief that some women do manage to maintain some measure of control over their lives and their property.[14] The vast majority of women are already under the domination of individual men because they are "naturally" weaker and less able. They share the common natural disadvantage to which all women are subject, and have none of the compensating virtues to offset their natural liability and so place them in a position where they do not have to accept the will and authority of men in order to survive. Thus, Locke's hypothetical state of nature is as full of presumptions about the different reproductive natures and relations of the sexes as it is about the different productive natures and relations of men, which have been so often and so thoroughly dealt with by others.[15] Locke's state of nature is simply seventeenth-century England devoid of legitimate Lockean law and authority.

However, in his attempts to undermine the concept of patriarchal government Locke was forced to take a somewhat less conservative view of the relations between the sexes in the family than might otherwise have been the case. He also cites anthropological evidence which in fact challenges his unrecognized assumptions about sexual inequality in the state of nature. But of course he did not draw from these any conclusions as to the conventional nature of existing familial relationships.

His basic argument in chapter IV, "Of Paternal Power," in the *Second Treatise*, is that no support for patriarchal government can be derived from the existence of paternal power in the family because the power in the family, which consists in the exercise of parental authority over children, is equally shared between father and mother. He argues that "paternal" power is really a misnomer, and should be replaced with "parental" power, because "paternal" "seems so to place the power of parents over their children wholly in the father, as if the mother had no share in it; whereas, if we consult reason or revelation, we shall find she has an equal title."[16] He hardly mentions the dominion of husband over wife. He did not see this as relevant to his attack on patriarchal government. He wanted to establish that no one man, by right and without consent, could rule over another, not that no one man by right could rule over a woman. He assumed that men would continue to exercise dominion over women in the political as well as the familial sphere, and so there was no need to question the authority of husband over wife.

But it was important to him to show that the father did not have absolute authority over his children. As he puts the case himself: "it will but very ill serve the turn of those men who contend so much for the absolute power and authority of the fatherhood, as they call it, that the mother should have any share in it; and it would have but ill supported the monarchy they contend for, when by the very name it appeared that that fundamental authority from whence they would derive their government of a single person only was not placed in one but two persons jointly." Thus, the family provides no justification for one-man rule in government because the authority over children devolves on two persons.

The joint authority of parents is, however, a theme he relentlessly repeats, and in fact, he goes as far as he can in denigrating the authority over children which paternity legitimizes, in order to undermine as far as possible patriarchal concepts of what constitutes legitimate government: "But what reason can hence advance this care of the parents due to their offspring into an absolute arbitrary dominion of the father, whose power reaches no farther than . . . to give such strength and health to their bodies . . . as may best fit his children to be most useful to themselves and others . . . But in this power the mother, too, has her share with the father. Nay, this power so little belongs to the father by any peculiar right of nature, but only as he is guardian of his children, that when he quits his care of them he loses his power over them . . . so little power does the bare act of begetting give a man over his issue." Mere fatherhood establishes nothing, says Locke. Authority, in this case, proceeds not from simple paternity but from the acceptance of responsibility—and so, of course he wants to say, in government. Notice, too, that he here wishes to construe the parental role as one of *guardianship*, which is certainly more applicable to civil than to natural relationships. In his enthusiasm to denaturalize politics, he verges on politicizing the family.

One could, in fact, push this somewhat further. While he has said elsewhere that the power of a husband over his wife is one form of power a man can have,[17] he wants to distinguish it both from the power a father has over his children, and the power a magistrate has over his subjects. Only the latter is *political* power. But more importantly for our point here, only a father's power over his children presents us with a relationship in any way relevant to a consideration of the nature and limits of political power. The relationship between husband and wife, in which the husband is in the superior position, does not even have to be justified as does the power of a father over his children. That form of power simply comes about as a result of a natural inequality which, unlike that between parents and children, does not disappear through time and tutelage. This is a natural dominion of one sex over the other.

Thus the relationship between parents and children is more like the relationship between a legitimate sovereign and his subjects. It is a limited power in which the period of dominion is grounded on natural inequalities which disappear over time. Of course, it is unlike legitimate sovereignty in that the latter never licenses an absolute authority since there are no natural inequalities of even a temporary sort between the persons so organized: "But these two powers, political and paternal, are so perfectly distinct and separate, are built upon so different foundations, and given to so much different ends, that every subject that is a father has as much a paternal power over his children as the prince has over his, and every prince that has parents owes them as much filial duty and obedience as the meanest of his subjects do theirs, and cannot therefore contain any part or degree of that kind of dominion which a prince or magistrate has over his subjects."

Thus, while Locke rejects "paternal" in favour of "parental," he is deliberately distinguishing "paternal" power from the power of husband over wife. While we may now have a better name for the relationship existing between father and children, we now have no name to refer to the relationship between husband and wife! It almost ceases to be a power relationship, since it is not seen as a species of power deserving a unique name. In any case, both a father's power over his children and political power are to be contrasted with the power of husband over wife, which, clearly, does not change over time. This is not, of course, an argument which Locke makes, but it obviously lies behind his thinking. If it did not, he would not have advanced his attack on patriarchal government by an analysis of the parental role of a father vis-à-vis his children. Further, he would not have construed patriarchal power as exclusively parental power; he would have invoked as well the relation of husband and wife.

In his zeal to find arguments against

patriarchal government his rudimentary anthropology almost gets him too far, however: "And what will become of this paternal power in that part of the world where one woman has more than one husband at a time, or in those parts of America where, when the husband and wife part, which happens frequently, the children are all left to the mother, follow her, and are wholly under her care and provision?" He does not go the whole way here and begin to question the assumed naturalness of monogamy and male dominance, but the implications are clear that he believes that there are some real "states of nature" in which even the dominion of male over female does not exist.

However, it must be said that he does at times seem to be aware that the dominion of husband over wife poses something of a problem for his arguments against patriarchal government. He does, for example, argue that marriage is a contractual relationship: "Conjugal society is made by a voluntary compact between man and woman." Thus, he is trying to make marriage as analogous as possible to his view of legitimate government. Just as legitimate authority rests on the consent of the governed, so the authority of husband over wife is legitimized by her consent. And he allows that the power of a husband over a wife is not unlimited: "the power of the husband being so far from that of an absolute monarch that the wife has in many cases a liberty to separate from him where natural right or their contract allows it, whether that contract be made by themselves in the state of nature, or by the customs or laws of the country they live in; and the children upon such separation fall to the father's or mother's lot, as such contract does determine." He also stresses that it is the obligation of both parents to care for their offspring: "God having made the parents instruments in his great design of continuing the race of mankind and the occasion of life to their children, as he has laid on them an obligation to nourish, preserve, and bring up

their offspring." He explains monogamy on the basis of the fact that infant human beings require more nurture than the offspring of other animals: "the father, who is bound to take care for those he has begot, is under an obligation to continue in conjugal society with the same woman longer than other creatures whose young being able to subsist of themselves before the time of procreation returns again, the conjugal bond dissolves of itself and they are at liberty."

Thus, it is apparently a natural duty that a father should provide for those he has helped to create, and, hence, it could reasonably be maintained that it is a natural right of women to be assisted in the raising of the young they bear. But since he also believes that women, like the females of other animals who give birth to their young alive, are incapable of providing on their own for their offspring, it is clear that they do not have much option but to get married if they desire to have children or if they find they are going to have a child (whether they desire the child or not).

Notes

1. See Lorenne Clark, "Rights of Women," in J. King-Farlow and W. Shea, eds, *Contemporary Issues in Political Philosophy* (New York 1976), 49–65.
2. Locke, *Two Treatises of Government,* ed. Peter Laslett (New York 1963), 131.
3. Ibid. 47.
4. Ibid. 44.
5. Ibid. 47.
6. Ibid. 49, and see also 49: " . . . this Text gave not Adam that Absolute *Monarchical Power* our A[uthor, Filmer] Supposes . . . but the Subjection of Eve to Adam, a Wife to her Husband."
7. Ibid. 54.
8. He is singularly silent, however, on the issue of whether these are "natural" differences. Given the things he cites, it hardly seems possible to construe all of them as in any way "natural." Thus, the differences between individual women, which

can compensate for their "natural" disadvantage, are likewise social and not natural.

9. *Treatises* 82.

10. See Hobbes, *Leviathan,* chapter 20, and *Treatises* 364n.

11. *Treatises* 79–80.

12. Ibid. 105.

13. At the heart of traditional political theory's inability to devise a theory which guarantees sexual equality is the assumption that women's unique capacities with respect to reproduction are natural, rather than social or conventional, disadvantages. Reproduction is consistently regarded as a natural *liability.* The point of the present paper is to show the centrality and necessity of this assumption within Locke's theoretical perspective.

14. I am much indebted to Professor John King-Farlow for many helpful comments he made on an earlier draft of this paper, particularly with respect to the conditions under which women's "natural" inferiority may be overcome.

15. The most notable treatment is in C.B. Macpherson, *The Political Theory of Possessive Individualism* (Oxford 1962). My own work has been greatly influenced by his views. Macpherson sees Locke as beginning from certain assumptions, which he designates "natural," which he then uses to justify gross inequality, when the reality of the case is that he must arrange social affairs to create the allegedly "natural" state of affairs which is in fact necessary to bring about the state of inequality which he considers desirable.

16. *Treatises* 52. The quotations which follow in this section are from *Second Treatise,* chapter 4, unless otherwise stated.

17. *Treatises* 2.

CHAPTER 45

The Barely Visible Family

Susan Moller Okin

In part 1 of *A Theory of Justice,* Rawls derives and defends the two principles of justice—the principle of equal basic liberty, and the "difference principle" combined with the requirement of fair equality of opportunity. These principles are intended to apply to the basic structure of society. They are "to govern the assignment of rights and duties and to regulate the distribution of social and economic advantages."[1] Whenever the basic institutions have within them differences in authority, in responsibility, or in the distribution of resources such as wealth or leisure, the second principle requires that these differences must be to the greatest benefit of the least advantaged and must be attached to positions accessible to all under conditions of fair equality of opportunity.

In part 2, Rawls discusses at some length the application of his principles of justice to almost all the institutions of the basic social structure that are set out at the beginning of the book. The legal protection of liberty of thought and conscience is defended, as are democratic constitutional institutions and procedures; competitive markets feature prominently in the discussion of the just distribution of income; the issue of the private or public ownership of the means of production is explicitly left open, since Rawls argues that his principles of justice might be compatible with certain versions of either.[2] But throughout all these discussions, the issue of whether the monogamous family, in either its traditional or any other form, is a just social institution, is never raised. When

Rawls announces that "the sketch of the system of institutions that satisfy the two principles of justice is now complete,"[3] he has paid no attention at all to the internal justice of the family. In fact, apart from passing references, the family appears in *A Theory of Justice* in only three contexts: as the link between generations necessary for the just savings principle; as an obstacle to fair equality of opportunity (on account of the inequalities among families); and as the first school of moral development. It is in the third of these contexts that Rawls first specifically mentions the family as a just institution—not, however, to *consider* whether the family "in some form" is a just institution but to *assume* it.[4]

Clearly, however, by Rawls's own reasoning about the social justice of major social institutions, this assumption is unwarranted. The serious significance of this for the theory as a whole will be addressed shortly. The central tenet of the theory, after all, is that justice as fairness characterizes institutions whose members could hypothetically have agreed to their structure and rules from a position in which they did not know which place in the structure they were to occupy. The argument of the book is designed to show that the two principles of justice are those that individuals in such a hypothetical situation would agree upon. But since those in the original position are the heads or representatives of families, they are not in a position to determine questions of justice within families. As Jane English has pointed out, "By making the parties in the original position heads of families rather than individuals, Rawls makes the family opaque to claims of justice."[5] As far as children are concerned, Rawls makes an argument from paternalism for their temporary inequality and restricted liberty.[6] (This, while it may suffice in basically sound, benevolent families, is of no use or comfort in abusive or neglectful situations, where Rawls's principles would seem to require that children be protected through the intervention of outside authorities.) But wives (or whichever adult member[s] of a family are *not* its "head") go completely unrepresented in the original position. If families are just, as Rawls later assumes, then they must become just in some different way (unspecified by him) from other institutions, for it is impossible to see how the viewpoint of their less advantaged members ever gets to be heard.

There are two occasions when Rawls seems either to depart from his assumption that those in the original position are "family heads" or to assume that a "head of a family" is equally likely to be a woman as a man. In the assignment of the basic rights of citizenship, he argues, favouring men over women is "justified by the difference principle . . . only if it is to the advantage of women and acceptable from their standpoint." Later he seems to imply that the injustice and irrationality of racist doctrines are also characteristic of sexist ones.[7] But in spite of these passages, which appear to challenge formal sex discrimination, the discussions of institutions in part 2 implicitly rely, in a number of respects, on the assumption that the parties formulating just institutions are (male) heads of (fairly traditional) families, and are therefore not concerned with issues of just distribution within the family or between the sexes. Thus the "heads of families" assumption, far from being neutral or innocent, has the effect of banishing a large sphere of human life—and a particularly large sphere of most women's lives—from the scope of the theory.

During the discussion of the distribution of wealth, for example, it seems to be assumed that all the parties in the original position expect, once the veil of ignorance is removed, to be participants in the paid labour market. Distributive shares are discussed in terms of household income, but reference to "individuals" is interspersed into this discussion as if there were no difference between the advantage or welfare of a household and that of an individual.[8] This confusion obscures the fact that wages are paid to employed members of the labour force, but that in societies characterized by gender (all current societies) a much larger proportion of women's than men's labour is unpaid and is often not even acknowledged as labour. It also obscures the fact that the resulting disparities in the earnings of men and women, and the economic dependence of women on men, are likely to affect power relations within the household, as well as access to leisure, prestige, political power, and so on, among its adult members. Any discussion of justice *within* the family would have to address these issues. [...]

Later, in Rawls's discussion of the obligations of citizens, his assumption that justice is agreed on by heads of families in the original position seems to prevent him from considering another issue of crucial importance: women's exemption from the draft. He concludes that military conscription is justifiable in the case of defence against an unjust attack on liberty, so long as institutions "try to make sure that the risks of suffering from these imposed misfortunes are more or less evenly shared by all members of society over the course of their life, and that there is no avoidable *class* bias in selecting those who are called for duty" (emphasis added).[9] The complete exemption of women from this major interference with the basic liberties of equal citizenship is not even mentioned.

In spite of two explicit rejections of the justice of formal sex discrimination in part 1, then, Rawls seems in part 2 to be heavily influenced by his "family heads" assumption. He does not consider as part of the basic structure of society the greater economic dependence of women and the sexual division of labour within the typical family, or any of the broader social ramifications of this basic gender structure. Moreover, in part 3, where he takes as a given the justice of the family "in some form," he does not discuss any alternative forms. Rather, he sounds very much as though he is thinking in terms of traditional, gendered family structure and roles. The family, he says, is "a small association, normally characterized by a definite hierarchy, in which each member has certain rights and duties." The family's role as moral teacher is achieved partly through parental expectations of the "virtues of a good son or a good daughter." In the family and in other associations such as schools, neighbourhoods, and peer groups, Rawls continues, one learns various moral virtues and ideals, leading to those adopted in the various statuses, occupations, and family positions of later life. "The content of these ideals is given by the various conceptions of a good wife and husband, a good friend and citizen, and so on."[10] Given these unusual departures from the supposedly generic male terms of reference used throughout the book, it seems likely that Rawls means to imply that the goodness of daughters is distinct from the goodness of sons, and that of wives from that of husbands. A fairly traditional gender system seems to be assumed.

Rawls not only assumes that "the basic structure of a well-ordered society includes the family *in some form*" (emphasis added); he adds that "in a broader inquiry the institution of the family might be questioned, and other arrangements might indeed prove to be preferable."[11] But why should it require a broader inquiry than the colossal task in which *A Theory of Justice* is engaged, to raise questions about the institution and the form of the family? Surely Rawls is right in initially naming it as one of those basic social institutions that most affect the life chances of individuals and should therefore be part of the primary subject of justice. The family is not a private association like a church or a university, which vary considerably in the type and degree of commitment each expects from its members, and which one can join and leave voluntarily. For although one has some choice (albeit a highly constrained one) about marrying into a gender-structured family, one has no choice at all about being born into one. Rawls's failure to subject the structure of the family to his principles of justice is particularly serious in the light of his belief that a theory of justice must take account of "how [individuals] get to be what they are" and "cannot take their final aims and interests, their attitudes to themselves and their life, as given."[12] For the gendered family, and female parenting in particular, are clearly critical determinants in the different ways the two sexes are socialized—how men and women "get to be what they are."

If Rawls were to assume throughout the construction of his theory that all human adults are participants in what goes on behind the veil of ignorance, he would have no option but to require that the family, as a major social institution affecting the life chances of individuals, be constructed in accordance with the two principles of justice. [...] I turn to a major problem for the theory that results from its neglect of the issue of justice within the family: its placing in jeopardy Rawls's account of how one develops a sense of justice.

Gender, the Family, and the Development of a Sense of Justice

Apart from being briefly mentioned as the link between generations necessary for Rawls's just savings principle, and as an obstacle to fair equality of opportunity, the family appears in Rawls's theory in only one context—albeit one of considerable importance: as the earliest school of moral development. Rawls argues, in a much-neglected section of part 3 of *A Theory of Justice,* that a just, well-ordered society will be stable only if its members continue to develop a sense of justice, "a strong and normally effective desire to act as the principles of justice require."[13] He turns his attention specifically to childhood moral development, aiming to indicate the major steps by which a sense of justice is acquired.

It is in this context that Rawls *assumes* that families are just. Moreover, these supposedly just families play a fundamental role in his account of moral development. First, the love of parents for their children, which comes to be reciprocated, is important in his account of the development of a sense of self-worth. By loving the child and being "worthy objects of his admiration . . . they arouse in him a sense of his own value and the desire to become the sort of person that they are." Rawls argues that healthy moral development in early life depends upon love, trust, affection, example, and guidance.[14]

At a later stage in moral development, which he calls "the morality of association," Rawls perceives the family, though he describes it in gendered and hierarchical terms, as the first of many associations in which, by moving through a sequence of roles and positions, our moral understanding increases. The crucial aspect of the sense of fairness that is learned during this stage is the capacity—which, as I shall argue, is essential for being able to think *as if* in the original position—to take up the different points of view of others and to learn "from their speech, conduct, and countenance" to see things from their perspectives. We learn to perceive, from what they say and do, what other people's ends, plans, and motives are. Without this experience, Rawls says, "we cannot put ourselves into another's place and find out what we would do in his position," which we need to be able to do in order "to regulate our own conduct in the appropriate way by reference to it." Building on attachments formed in the family, participation in different roles in the various associations of society leads to the development of a person's "capacity for fellow feeling" and to "ties of friendship and mutual trust." Just as in the first stage "certain natural attitudes develop toward the parents, so here ties of friendship and confidence grow up among associates. In each case certain natural attitudes underlie the corresponding moral feelings: a lack of these feelings would manifest the absence of these attitudes."[15]

This whole account of moral development is strikingly unlike the arid, rationalist account given by Kant, whose ideas are so influential in many respects on Rawls's thinking about justice. For Kant, who claimed that justice must be grounded in reason alone, any feelings that do not follow from independently established moral principles are morally suspect—"mere inclinations."[16] By contrast, Rawls clearly recognizes the importance of feelings, first nurtured within supposedly just families, in the development of the capacity for moral thinking. In accounting for his third and final stage of moral development, where persons are supposed to become attached to the principles of justice themselves, Rawls says that "the sense of justice is continuous with the love of mankind." At the same time, he acknowledges our particularly strong feelings about those to whom we are closely attached, and says that this is rightly reflected in our moral judgments: even though "our moral sentiments display an independence from the accidental circumstances of our world, . . . our natural attachments to particular persons and groups still have an appropriate place." He indicates clearly that empathy, or imagining oneself in the circumstances of others, plays a major role in moral development. It is not surprising that he turns away from Kant, and toward moral philosophers such as Adam Smith, Elizabeth Anscombe, Philippa Foot, and Bernard Williams in developing his ideas about the moral emotions or sentiments.[17]

Rawls's summary of his three psychological laws of moral development emphasizes the fundamental importance of loving parenting for the development of a sense of justice. The three laws, Rawls says, are

not merely principles of association or of reinforcement. . . . [but] assert that the active sentiments of love and friendship, and even the sense of justice, arise from the manifest intention of other persons to act for our good. Because we recognize that they wish us well, we care for their well-being in return.[18]

Each of the laws of moral development, as set out by Rawls, depends upon the one before it, and the first assumption of the first law is: "given that family institutions are just, ..." Thus Rawls frankly and for good reason acknowledges that the whole of moral development rests at base upon the loving ministrations of those who raise small children from the earliest stages, and on the moral character—in particular, the *justice*—of the environment in which this takes place. At the foundation of the development of the sense of justice, then, are an activity and a sphere of life that, though by no means necessarily so, have throughout history been predominantly the activity and the sphere of women.

Rawls does not explain the basis of his assumption that family institutions are just. If gendered families are *not* just, but are, rather, a relic of caste or feudal societies in which roles, responsibilities, and resources are distributed not in accordance with the two principles of justice but in accordance with innate differences that are imbued with enormous social significance, then Rawls's whole structure of moral development would seem to be built on shaky ground. Unless the households in which children are first nurtured, and see their first examples of human interaction, are based on equality and reciprocity rather than on dependence and domination—and the latter is too often the case—how can whatever love they receive from their parents make up for the injustice they see before them in the relationship between these same parents? How, in hierarchical families in which sex roles are rigidly assigned, are we to learn, as

Rawls's theory of moral development requires us, to "put ourselves into another's place and find out what we would do in his position"? Unless they are parented equally by adults of both sexes, how will children of both sexes come to develop a sufficiently similar and well-rounded moral psychology to enable them to engage in the kind of deliberation about justice that is exemplified in the original position? If both parents do not *share* in nurturing activities, are they both likely to maintain in adult life the capacity for empathy that underlies a sense of justice?[19] And finally, unless the household is connected by a continuum of just associations to the larger communities within which people are supposed to develop fellow feelings for each other, how will they grow up with the capacity for enlarged sympathies such as are clearly required for the practice of justice? Rawls's neglect of justice within the family is clearly in tension with the requirements of his own theory of moral development. Family justice must be of central importance for social justice.

I have begun to suggest a feminist reading of Rawls, drawing on his theory of moral development and its emphasis on the moral feelings that originate in the family. This reading can, I think, contribute to the strengthening of Rawls's theory against some of the criticisms that have been made of it.[20] For, in contrast with his account of moral development, much of his argument about how persons in the original position arrive at the principles of justice is expressed in terms of mutual disinterest and rationality—the language of rational choice. This, I contend, leaves what he says unnecessarily open to three criticisms: it involves unacceptably egoistic and individualistic assumptions about human nature; taking an "outside" perspective, it is of little or no relevance to actual people thinking about justice; and its aim to create universalistic and impartial principles leads to the neglect of "otherness" or difference.[21] I think all three criticisms are mistaken,

but they result at least in part from Rawls's tendency to use the language of rational choice.

In my view, the original position and what happens there are described far better in other terms. As Rawls himself says, the combination of conditions he imposes on them "forces each person in the original position to take the good of others into account."[22] The parties can be presented as the "rational, mutually disinterested" agents characteristic of rational choice theory only because they do not know *which* self they will turn out to be. The veil of ignorance is such a demanding stipulation that it converts what would, without it, be self-interest into equal concern for others, including others who are very different from ourselves. Those in the original position cannot think from the position of *nobody*, as is suggested by those critics who then conclude that Rawls's theory depends upon a "disembodied" concept of the self. They must, rather, think from the perspective of *everybody*, in the sense of *each in turn*. To do this requires, at the very least, both strong empathy and a preparedness to listen carefully to the very different points of view of others. As I have suggested, these capacities seem more likely to be widely distributed in a society of just families, with no expectations about or reinforcements of gender.

Notes

1. John Rawls, *A Theory of Justice* (Cambridge: Harvard University Press, 1971), p. 61.

2. For a good recent discussion of Rawls's view of just property institutions, see Richard Krouse and Michael McPherson, "Capitalism, 'Property-Owning Democracy,' and the Welfare State," in *Democracy and the Welfare State*, ed. Amy Gutmann (Princeton: Princeton University Press, 1988).

3. Rawls, *Theory*, p. 303.

4. Ibid., pp. 463, 490. See Deborah Kearns, "A Theory of Justice—and Love; Rawls on the Family," *Politics (Australasian Political Studies*

Association Journal) 18, no. 2 (1983): 39–40, for an interesting discussion of the significance for Rawls's theory of moral development of his failure to address the justice of the family.

5. English, "Justice Between Generations," *Philosophical Studies* 31, no. 2 (1977): 95.
6. Rawls, *Theory*, pp. 208–9.
7. Ibid., pp. 99,149.
8. Ibid., pp. 270–74, 304–9.
9. Ibid., pp. 380–81.
10. Ibid., pp. 467, 468.
11. Ibid., pp. 462–63.
12. Rawls, "The Basic Structure as Subject," *American Philosophical Quarterly* 14, No. 2 (1977): 160.
13. Rawls, *Theory*, p. 454.
14. Ibid., pp. 465, 466.
15. Ibid., pp. 469–71.
16. See Okin, "Reason and Feeling in Thinking About Justice," *Ethics* 99, no. 2 (1989): 231–35.
17. Rawls, *Theory*, pp. 476, 475, 479ff.
18. Ibid., p. 494; see also pp. 490–91.
19. On the connections among nurturing, empathy, and gender, see, for example, Judith Kegan Gardiner, "Self Psychology as Feminist Theory," *Signs* 12, no. 4 (1987), esp. 771 and 778–80; Sara Ruddick, "Maternal Thinking," *Feminist Studies* 6, no. 2 (1980).
20. See Okin, "Reason and Feeling," for the more detailed argument from which this and the following paragraph are summarized.

21. Thomas Nagel, "Rawls on Justice," in *Reading Rawls,* ed. Norman Daniels (New York: Basic Books, 1974), (reprinted from *Philosophical Review* 72 [1973]), makes the first argument Michael J. Sandel, *Liberalism and the Limits of Justice* (Cambridge: Cambridge University Press, 1982), makes the first two arguments. The second argument is made by both Alasdair MacIntyre, in *After Virtue* (Notre Dame: University of Notre Dame Press, 1981), for example, pp. 119 and 233, and Michael Walzer, in *Spheres of Justice* (New York: Basic Books, 1983), pp. xiv and 5, and *Interpretation and Social Criticism* (Cambridge: Harvard University Press, 1987), pp. 11–16. The third argument, though related to some of the objections raised by Sandel and Walzer, is primarily made by feminist critics, notably Seyla Benhabib, in "The Generalized and the Concrete Other," in *Feminism as Critique,* ed. Benhabib and Drucilla Cornell (Minneapolis: University of Minnesota Press, 1987); and Iris Marion Young, in "Toward a Critical Theory of Justice," *Social Theory and Practice* 7 (1981), and "Impartiality and the Civic Public," in *Feminism as Critique.* The second and third objections are combined in Carole Pateman's claim that "Rawls's original position is a logical abstraction of such rigour that nothing happens there" (*The Sexual Contract* [Stanford: Stanford University Press, 1988], p. 43).
22. Rawls, *Theory*, p. 148.

CHAPTER 46

The Capabilities Approach

Martha C. Nussbaum

The basic intuitive idea of my version of the capabilities approach is that we begin with a conception of the dignity of the human being, and of a life that is worthy of that dignity—a life that has available in it "truly human functioning," in the sense described by Marx in his 1844 *Economic and Philosophical Manuscripts.* (I use the Marxian idea for political purposes only, not as the source of a comprehensive doctrine of human life; Marx makes no such distinction.)

Marx speaks of the human being as a being "in need of a totality of human life-activities," and the approach also takes its bearing from this idea, insisting that the capabilities to which all citizens ate entitled are many and not one, and are opportunities for activity, not simply quantities of resources.[1] Resources are inadequate as an index of well-being, because human beings have varying needs for resources, and also varying abilities to convert resources into functioning. Thus two people with similar quantities of resources may actually differ greatly in the ways that matter most for social justice. This issue will become especially salient when we confront the theory with issues of impairment and disability.

With this basic idea as a starting point, I then attempt to justify a list of ten capabilities as central requirements of a life with dignity. As with Rawls's principles, so here: the political principles give shape and content to the abstract idea of dignity (cf. Rawls [1971], 586). These ten capabilities are supposed to be general goals that can be further specified by the society in question as it works on the account of fundamental entitlements it wishes to endorse. But in some form all are held to be part of a minimum account of social justice: a society that does not guarantee these to all its citizens, at some appropriate threshold level, falls short of being a fully just society, whatever its level of opulence. And although in practical terms priorities may have to be set temporarily, the capabilities are understood as both mutually supportive and all of central relevance to social justice. Thus a society that neglects one of them to promote the others has short-changed its citizens, and there is a failure of justice in the short-changing.

The capabilities approach is not intended to provide a complete account of social justice. It says nothing, for example, about how justice would treat inequalities above the threshold. (In that sense it does not answer all the questions answered by Rawls's theory.) It is an account of minimum core social entitlements, and it is compatible with different views about how to handle issues of justice and distribution that would arise once all citizens are above the threshold level. Nor does it insist that this list of entitlements is an exhaustive account of political justice; there may be other important political values, closely connected with justice, that it does not include.[2]

The list itself is open-ended and has undergone modification over time; no doubt it will undergo further modification in the light of criticism. But here is the current version.

The Central Human Capabilities

1. *Life*. Being able to live to the end of a human life of normal length; not dying prematurely, or before one's life is so reduced as to be not worth living.

2. *Bodily Health*. Being able to have good health, including reproductive health; to be adequately nourished; to have adequate shelter.

3. *Bodily Integrity*. Being able to move freely from place to place; to be secure against violent assault, including sexual assault and domestic violence; having opportunities for sexual satisfaction and for choice in matters of reproduction.

4. *Senses, Imagination, and Thought*. Being able to use the senses, to imagine, think, and reason—and to do these things in a "truly human" way, a way informed and cultivated by an adequate education, including, but by no means limited to, literacy and basic mathematical and scientific training. Being able to use imagination and thought in connection with experiencing and producing works and events of one's own choice, religious, literary, musical, and so forth. Being able to use one's mind in ways protected by guarantees of freedom of expression

with respect to both political and artistic speech, and freedom of religious exercise. Being able to have pleasurable experiences and to avoid non-beneficial pain.

5. *Emotions*. Being able to have attachments to things and people outside ourselves; to love those who love and care for us, to grieve at their absence; in general, to love, to grieve, to experience longing, gratitude, and justified anger. Not having one's emotional development blighted by fear and anxiety. (Supporting this capability means supporting forms of human association that can be shown to be crucial in their development.)

6. *Practical Reason*. Being able to form a conception of the good and to engage in critical reflection about the planning of one's life. (This entails protection for the liberty of conscience and religious observance.)

7. *Affiliation.*
   A. Being able to live with and toward others, to recognize and show concern for other human beings, to engage in various forms of social interaction; to be able to imagine the situation of another. (Protecting this capability means protecting institutions that constitute and nourish such forms of affiliation, and also protecting the freedom of assembly and political speech.)
   B. Having the social bases of self-respect and non-humiliation; being able to be treated as a dignified being whose worth is equal to that of others. This entails provisions of non-discrimination on the basis of race, sex, sexual orientation, ethnicity, caste, religion, national origin.

8. *Other Species*. Being able to live with concern for and in relation to animals, plants, and the world of nature.

9. *Play*. Being able to laugh, to play, to enjoy recreational activities.

10. *Control over One's Environment.*
    A. *Political*. Being able to participate effectively in political choices that govern one's life; having the right of political participation, protections of free speech and association.
    B. *Material*. Being able to hold property (both land and movable goods), and having property rights on an equal basis with others; having the right to seek employment on an equal basis with others; having the freedom from unwarranted search and seizure. In work, being able to work as a human being, exercising practical reason and entering into meaningful relationships of mutual recognition with other workers.

The basic idea is that with regard to each of these, we can argue, by imagining a life without the capability in question, that such a life is not a life worthy of human dignity.[3] The argument in each case is based on imagining a form of life; it is intuitive and discursive. Nonetheless, I believe that the process, and the list, can gather broad cross-cultural agreement, similar to the international agreements that have been reached concerning basic human rights. Indeed, the capabilities approach is, in my view, one species of a human rights approach, and human rights have often been linked in a similar way to the idea of human dignity.

The capabilities approach is fully universal: the capabilities in question are held to be important for each and every citizen, in each and every nation, and each person is to be treated as an end. The approach is in this way similar to the international human rights approach; indeed I view the capabilities approach as one species of a human rights approach.[4] Arguing in favour of a set of cross-cultural norms and against the positions of cultural relativists has been an important dimension of the approach.[5]

Notes

1. Marx (1844/1978), 88, 91; translation modified.
2. Stability is clearly one such value, but stability is already incorporated in the justification of the capabilities list itself, since I argue that we can justify any account of core political commitments only by showing that it can remain stable: see Nussbaum (2000), chap. 2.
3. In Nussbaum (1995) I make this argument in detail for affiliation and practical reason.
4. See Chapter 3 and Nussbaum (2003).
5. See, for example, Nussbaum (2000), chap. 1.

References

Marx, Karl. 1844/1978. *Economic and Philosophical Manuscripts of 1844.* In *The Marx-Engels Reader*, Ed. Robert C. Tucker. New York: Norton. Pp. 66–125.

Nussbaum, Martha C. 1995. "Aristotle on Human Nature and the Foundations of Ethics." In *World, Mind, and Ethics: Essays on the Philosophy of Bernard Williams.* Ed. J.E.G. Altham and Ross Harrison. Cambridge: Cambridge University Press.

———. 2000. *Women and Human Development.* Cambridge: Cambridge University Press.

———. 2003. "Capabilities as Fundamental Entitlements: Sen and Social Justice." *Feminist Economics* 9 (July/November): 33–59.

Rawls, John. 1971. *A Theory of Justice.* Cambridge, MA: Harvard University Press.

CHAPTER 47

A Feminist Epistemology

Lorraine Code

As long as "epistemology" bears the stamp of the postpositivist, empiricist project of determining necessary and sufficient conditions for knowledge and devising strategies to refute skepticism, there can be no feminist epistemology. I have shown that the conceptions of knowledge and subjective agency that inform this project are inimical to feminist concerns on many levels: ontological, epistemological, moral, political. Ideals central to the project—ideals of objectivity, impartiality, and universality—are androcentrically derived. Their articulation maps onto typical middle-class white male experiences to suppress the very possibility that the sex of the knower could be epistemologically significant. But my project has been to take that possibility very seriously and to argue that once its implications are examined, "the epistemological project" will demand reconstruction. It would not be possible to develop a feminist epistemology that retained allegiance to the pivotal ideas around which epistemology—for all its variations—has defined itself. Hence there can be no feminist epistemology in any of the traditional senses of the term.

Feminists can be epistemologists, however, and epistemologists can be feminists. Feminists have to understand "the epistemological project" to be in a position to see its androcentrism and to comprehend the political consequences of its hegemony. They need to engage in dialogues with the tradition to analyze its strengths and limitations; they need to develop politically informed critiques and to create space for productive relocations of knowledge in human lives. My contention that feminists have to engage in epistemological analysis without articulating their project as the creation of "a feminist epistemology" is not merely a semantic quibble. Epistemological analyses that are compatible with feminist political commitments—however varied—sit uneasily with amalgamating the labels while attempting to decentre androcentricity so that it can include women. Feminists cannot participate in the construction of a monolithic, comprehensive epistemological *theory* removed from the practical-political issues a theory of knowledge has to address. My discussions of women and madness, of the nurses in the Grange Inquiry, and of the creation of the Poverty Game have shown why theories that transcend the specificities of gendered and otherwise situated subjectivities are impotent to come to terms with the politics of knowledge. So there can be no feminist epistemology in the received sense—yet epistemological questions are fundamental to feminist inquiry.

Even if androcentricity could be decentred to make space for gynocentric concerns, it is not obvious that "a feminist epistemology" would be the most desirable result. A feminist epistemology would seem to require a basis in assumptions about the essence of women and of knowledge. Hence it would risk replicating the exclusionary, hegemonic structures of the masculinist epistemology, in its various manifestations, that has claimed absolute sovereignty over the epistemic terrain. A politically adequate "successor epistemology" would have to give pride of place to questions such as, Whose knowledge are we talking about? Is

it the knowledge that interchangeable observers have of cups, pens, and books on tables, or is it knowledge that committed Marxists have about capitalism? that committed supporters of apartheid have about blacks? Is it the knowledge of privileged intellectuals with the leisure to analyze the nature of freedom and oppression, or is it the knowledge that women who desperately need work must have so that they can weigh the dangers of radiation in a factory job against the humiliation of unemployment and welfare? The diversity of situations and circumstances in which people need to be in a position to know makes it difficult to see how *a* theory of knowledge, *an* epistemology, could respond to their questions.

Some of these reservations bear on the difficulty of seeing in feminist empiricism the best alternative to androcentric epistemology.[1] Feminist empiricism advocates a new empiricist project informed by the privileged vision of feminist consciousness and hence peculiarly equipped to eradicate sexism and androcentrism, represented as social biases. In its feminist dimension, it disrupts the smooth impartiality of the standard empiricist credo by introducing a specificity—a declaration of specific interests—to contest the very possibility of a disinterested epistemology. Hence it can claim subversive potential. But its scope is constricted by the fact that it makes these claims from within a structure that is itself indelibly tainted.

In arguing that social biases permeate "the context of discovery" in any inquiry so thoroughly that it would be naive to hope for their eradication in the "context of justification," feminist empiricism demonstrates its radical potential. In requiring—especially in the social sciences—that researchers locate themselves on the same critical plane as their "objects of study," feminist empiricism takes issue with the very idea that there could be valid, detached observation. And in urging more rigour in scientific and other inquiry, to detect the influence of gender bias in shaping research, feminist empiricism refuses to accept any claims for value-free inquiry.[2] Paradoxically, by acknowledging its engaged, interested position and taking the socio-political identity of inquirers into account *epistemologically*, feminist empiricism promises enhanced objectivity and diminished bias.

Yet that very emphasis on screening for bias restricts the promise of feminist empiricism. The idea that a "truer" account of reality, a more rigorously empirical and hence objective account, can be achieved through self-conscious stripping away of bias threatens to reproduce the old liberal split between "the individual" and the discourses and power structures constitutive of her or his place on the epistemic terrain. It evinces a belief in a detached position from which biases will indeed be visible and can be washed away. The thought that the—possibly unconscious—androcentrism of mainstream epistemology is imposed and maintained from outside on an otherwise neutral subject matter fails to take into account the constitutive role of ideologies, stereotypes, and structures of epistemic privilege in creating the only institutionally legitimate possibilities for the construction and growth of knowledge. It does not grant sufficient credence to the claim that facts are often made, not found. Feminist empiricism—like the master discourse from which it takes its name—opts for a position outside the material and historical conditions that most urgently require analysis. Hence, despite its subversive potential, it cannot, alone, provide the theoretical position that feminist epistemologists require.[3]

How, then, can the terrain be remapped so that the space required for feminist epistemological analyses can be created? A productive imagery is that of creating a clearing, an open middle ground where an inquirer can take up a position, a standpoint, within a forest of absolutes: the exigencies of objectivism, the fervour of ideology, the quietism of extreme relativism,

and the hegemony of universal Truth—to mention only a few. This idea of "taking up a position" resumes the positionality analyses of previous chapters. Positionality, I think, is a sophisticated elaboration of earlier feminist standpoint theories that argued for the possibility of developing a unified, authoritative construction of reality anchored in the experiences and socio-economic positions of women, deriving their inspiration from Marxist analyses of the standpoint of the proletariat.[4] Recent feminist concentration on differences and specificities makes the possibility of *a* feminist standpoint both remote and suspect, for it would presuppose an artificial unity in diversity. Intricated as it is with a complex configuration of specificities, *positionality* responds more adequately to the historical/political exigencies of the 1990s.

On this middle ground, responsible critical inquiry could take place, and effective forms of cognitive agency could thrive. Yet middle grounds have a bad name in professional philosophy. Too often, occupying such a position is condemned as a refusal to take a stand, a plea for undecidability and indifferent tolerance, a desire to have things both—or all—ways, hence a feeble form of fence sitting. Moreover, [...] the dichotomous thinking of most mainstream philosophy obliterates the very possibility of "middle grounds." My claim, however, is that a well-mapped middle ground offers a place to take up positions of strength and maximum productivity from which exclusionary theories can be tapped critically and creatively for criticism and reconstruction. Occupancy of these positions is compatible with a strong commitment to engagement in practices designed to eradicate women's oppression and to the creation of environments ecologically committed to the promotion of social/political well-being. It draws on the theoretical and practical resources that surround it to incorporate what is best in them and to reject what is damaging and oppressive. From these positions it is clear that analyses of damage, constraint, well-being, and empowerment are all themselves situated and revisable, based on the best understanding available at the time, open to renegotiation. The provisionality—the revisability—of the resources no more leaves them "undecided," unstable sites for theory building and activism than a "fallibilist" standpoint in scientific inquiry would make it impossible to proceed with research. Like scientific research, politically informed activism and theory building have to go on, from where they are, for the gaps in their knowledge will not become visible except in practice, in further research that shows where revision is demanded. "Second wave" feminists made remarkable progress working from the hypothesis that women could be analyzed as a class; that same progress destabilized the hypothesis, yet while it was in place it made quantities of high-quality, emancipatory research and action possible.

Feminists committed to breaking with the monolithic, hegemonic tradition, to working as philosophers and feminists at once, have revealed gaps in the malestream totalizing discourse which leave them no choice but to refuse obedience to it. These refusals are *anarchic* in breaking away from the rules of established methodologies, challenging the most taken-for-granted philosophical assumptions, theories, and goals.[5] Challenges and refusals are marks not of truculence and aimless rebellion, but of strategies for uncovering the structures of an order that is imposed to check an imagined threat of "chaos," the exaggeration of whose dangers conceals its emancipatory potential. This is a "chaos" of plurality, ambiguity, and differences: plurality of methods and methodologies; ambiguity in theoretical conclusions; differences that refuse the reductivism of universality and univocity. Only by thinkers wedded to a rigid conception of order and orthodoxy could this multiplicity be interpreted as chaotic in a derogatory sense. Yet such thinkers prevail, and

such interpretations are the stuff of which their theories are made. For Stenstad, an anarchist persists in "questioning, working and playing with ambiguities, being alert for the presence of the strange within the familiar, and allowing for concealment or unclarity in the midst of disclosure."[6] The questioning takes place *from somewhere* and is committed to finding answers that make action possible.

One of the traditionally problematic features of a middle ground is that a refusal to occupy a position of pure objectivism is equated with an assertion of value in relativism. I have made such a claim at many places in this book. I have done so cognizant of the fact that there are cogent and persuasive arguments against relativism available in the philosophical tradition: that relativism can take an "anything goes" form that would make criticism and responsible epistemic choice into meaningless ephemera—hence that absolute relativism forces perfect tolerance, which would have to include tolerance of sexism, racism, homophobia, and other oppressive practices. But the middle ground has no place for absolutes, relativist or otherwise. Participants in standard objectivist/relativist debates work with a false dichotomy according to which any move toward relativism amounts to a flat rejection of realism. My claim is that epistemological relativism does not entail antirealism.

Politically, feminists could not opt for an absolute relativism that recognized no facts of the matter—no objective, external reality—but only my, your, or our negotiated reality. Consider feminist concern with what "science has proved" about women's natural inferiority to men, about the safety of drugs to safeguard or prevent pregnancy, about the harmlessness of pesticides and nuclear power. That concern will not be put to rest by an assurance that there are many ways of looking at these things, all equally valid. No politically informed woman will be convinced by an argument that it is all relative—that for some people these things are wrong or harmful and for others they are valid and harmless. Nor could feminists agree that "the realities" of sexism, the wage gap, violence against women, inadequate day care, class and racial injustices are all in their minds. It would fly in the face of the well-documented experiences of countless women to deny that these are realities, if perhaps not in the idealized physical science sense. If there are no objective social realities—in a sense that allows for perspectival differences—there are no tools for the realization of feminist political projects.

However various their political allegiances, feminists are united in their commitments to ending women's oppression in patriarchal societies. Their ideological differences may produce different causal analyses of oppression and prompt diverse solutions. Yet differences in knowledge about oppression do not preclude possibilities of transformative dialogue. Were the oppression not demonstrably there *at all*, no debate would be possible; were it known identically by everyone, no debate would be necessary. Hence the impact of feminism on epistemology recommends a mitigated relativism. Mitigated relativism takes different perspectives into account. The claim that it must be mitigated affirms that there is something there, in the world, to know and act on—hence to constrain possibilities of knowledge and analysis. Were this not so, the findings of feminist research could simply be dismissed as one set of opinions, no better than any others. Indeed, they could be read as manifestations of ideological paranoia, and a relativist would have no way of countering the charge. Feminists need to demonstrate the reality of social injustices and practices and to work as hard for change in larger social structures and institutions as for change in the "personal" areas of women's lives. Because of the dominance of received "objectivist" knowledge in producing the social institutions in which they live, women cannot opt

for a *radical* relativism that is unable to name those institutions and productions. They can, and I think must, opt for the mitigated, critical relativism implicit in asking, *Whose* knowledge are we talking about? Such a relativism would recognize the perspectival, locatedness of knowledge *and* its associations with subjective purposes. Yet it would develop strategies for evaluating perspectives and purposes.

This claim for evaluative possibilities might appear to recommend a mitigated *objectivism* instead of a mitigated relativism, and the suggestion would be plausible.[7] On a continuum between extreme objectivism and radical relativism, the mitigated versions of each would approach one another quite closely. I prefer to characterize the position I advocate as a mitigated relativism, however, for the freedom it offers from the homogenizing effects of traditional objectivism, in which differences, discrepancies, and deviations are smoothed out for the sake of achieving a unified theory. With its commitment to difference, critical relativism is able to resist reductivism and to accommodate divergent perspectives. Mitigated in its constraints by "the facts" of material objects and social/political artifacts, yet ready to account for the mechanisms of power (in a Foucauldian sense) and prejudice (in a Gadamerian sense) that produce knowledge of these facts, and committed to the self-critical stance that its mitigation requires, such relativism is a resourceful epistemological position.

Notes

1. In examining feminist empiricism and a version of feminist standpoint theory as possible "successor epistemologies," I am drawing on Harding's classifications in *The Science Question in Feminism*. In her "Conclusion: Epistemological Questions" in *Feminism and Methodology*, Harding characterizes them aptly as *transitional epistemologies* (p. 186). It will be apparent that the

"standpoint" I sketch here is somewhat different from Harding's.

2. In her book *Toward a Feminist Epistemology* (Totowa, NJ: Rowman & Littlefield, 1990), which I read after this book had gone to press, Jane Duran develops a version of empiricism that draws on "naturalized epistemologies." Her analysis aims to make it possible for empiricists to take human specificities more plausibly into account while retaining their central empiricist commitments.

3. Wylie notes that "feminist empiricists are caught in the awkward position of exploiting the epistemic advantages of their standpoint as women while endorsing the ideal of scientific inquiry is objective in that an inquirer's social, political standpoint is irrelevant." Wylie, "The Philosophy of Ambivalence: Sandra Harding on *The Science Question in Feminism*," in Hanen and Nielsen, eds, *Science, Morality, and Feminist Theory*, p. 64.

4. A landmark feminist standpoint position is elaborated in Nancy Hartsock, "The Feminist Standpoint: Developing the Ground for a Specifically Feminist Historical Materialism," in Harding and Hintikka, eds, *Discovering Reality*.

5. I borrow the "anarchic" characterization from Stenstad, "Anarchic Thinking."

6. Ibid., p.89.

7. Marilyn Friedman made this suggestion to me.

Bibliography

Duran, Jane. *Toward a Feminist Epistemology*. Totowa, NJ: Rowman & Littlefield, 1990.

Hanen, Marsha, and Kai Nielson, eds. *Science, Morality, and Feminist Theory.* Calgary, Alberta: University of Calgary Press, 1987.

Harding, Sandra. *The Science Question in Feminism*. Ithaca: Cornell University Press, 1986.

———, ed. *Feminism and Methodology*. Bloomington: Indiana University Press, 1987.

Harding, Sandra, and Merrill Hintikka, eds. *Discovering Reality: Feminist Perspectives on Epistemology, Methodology, and the Philosophy of Science*. Dordrecht: Reidel, 1983.

Hartsock, Nancy. "The Feminist Standpoint: Developing the Ground for a Specifically Feminist Historical Materialism." In Harding and Hintikka, eds, *Discovering Reality*.

Stenstad, Gail. "Anarchic Thinking." *Hypatia: A Journal of Feminist Philosophy* 3 (Summer 1988): 87–100.

Wylie, Alison. "The Philosophy of Ambivalence: Sandra Harding on *The Science Question in Feminism*." In Hanen and Nielsen, eds, *Science, Morality, and Feminist Theory*.

CHAPTER 48

The Function of Sexuality in the Oppression of Women

Alice Schwarzer

Almost always (in these past years) when I have tried to speak with men about emancipation—quite apart from whether they were friends or colleagues, on the left or the right—these talks would end up with that one "slight difference." Emancipation was all well and good, but that slight difference—we didn't want to get rid of that, too, did we?

Oh no! We would never dare. Most definitely not! There would always be the eternal *petite différence*, of course. Right? And the more progressive the circles in which it was debated, the smaller the difference was—except the consequences remained equally great.

It is time, therefore, to ask ourselves finally what this oft-quoted slight difference consists of and whether it justifies making "people" into "men" and "women" instead of just letting them be "people." You don't have to look far in this potency-crazed society for said difference.

Actually, it's not very big. In a state of rest, the experts assure us, it's three to three and one-half inches; aroused, another two to three inches.

And in this nubbin resides manhood, the magical power to make women lustful and to rule the world? The nubbin-wearers, at least, seem to be convinced of it. I think it's nothing more than a pretext. Not this *biological* difference, but its *ideological* consequences must be categorically eliminated. Biology is not destiny. Masculinity and femininity are not nature but culture. In every generation they represent a renewed, forced identification with dominance and subjection. Penises and vaginas don't make us men and women, but power and powerlessness do.

The ideology of the two halves that supposedly complement each other so well has crippled us and created a rift which is seemingly impossible to overcome. Men and women feel differently, think differently, move differently, live differently. Everyone knows only too well how the stigma of masculinity or of femininity branded on our foreheads confines and defines us. Nothing, neither race nor class, determines human life to the extent that gender does. Here women and men are both victims of their roles—but women are still victims of victims.

The fear, dependence, distrust, and powerlessness experienced by women are enormous. [. . .] The closer we look, the deeper the rift between the sexes. Only those who dare to bridge this gap will—one distant day—be able to overcome it. Only those who admit existing conditions will be able to make changes. In the long run, both sexes stand to gain; in the short run, women stand to lose their chains and men their privileges.

All who speak of equality—in the face of the inequality between the sexes—are compounding their guilt daily. They are not interested in humanizing men and women but rather in maintaining prevailing conditions, from which they themselves profit. The exploitation of women has not diminished in recent decades but has rather become more acute. Women work more than ever before.

Only the forms of this exploitation have sometimes become more subtle, more difficult to detect. What is officially understood by the word *emancipation* often means nothing more than that women who were slaves have now become free slaves. [. . .]

Vaginal Orgasm and Sex Monopoly

What can we say in favour of penetration? Nothing for women, a lot for men. Coitus, which damns women to passivity, is for men the most uncomplicated and comfortable way of practising sex: They don't have to communicate with women, don't have to stimulate them mentally or physically—passive compliance is enough.

You really can't underestimate the psychological implications for men of this violent act of invasion. *Screwing,* as it is so aptly called in everyday language, is the highest demonstration of male potency! Besides, for many men power is pleasure and that's why penetration is perhaps the most erotic stimulation for them today. (That women, on the other hand, have become largely unable to experience sex as satisfying because of their oppression and the perversion of relations between the sexes, seems to me to be an indication of their physical integrity. They are evidently not prepared for the perverse separation of physical and mental communication which male society openly practises.)

But that alone does not entirely explain the absolute compulsion for sexual norms which are contrary to the needs of one half of humanity (the female half) and which bring with them the enormous burden of contraception. Imagine: The horror of unwanted pregnancies and abortions, the attendant side effects of the pill, and inflammations caused by the diaphragm—all of this—would become superfluous with one blow if women were allowed to experience their sexuality in accordance with their natural needs. Heterosexual penetration would no longer be a form of making love but would be reserved for procreation. Unwanted pregnancies would no longer be possible.

But neither the misery of abortion nor female frigidity was able to shake the dogma of the vaginal orgasm. The reasons for this have to be momentous. My theory: Only the myth of the vaginal orgasm (and of the importance of penetration) insures sexual monopoly of men over women, which, in turn, is the foundation of the public monopoly of male society over women.

In other words: in this society, people are lonely without a love relationship in which they must buy affection and tenderness with sex; thus, women, like men, must resort to sexual relationships. If this sexuality is only possible under the guise of that certain "difference," if heterosexuality is given absolute priority, then women and men must turn to each other. The monopoly is therefore reversible, it would seem. But only apparently. A man without a woman in our society is still a man, but a woman without a man is not a woman.

[. . .]

A woman has no existence as an autonomous being—only in relation to a man. Her definition is that of a sexual being. Every attempt at emancipation must come to a dead end sooner or later, as long as every woman is individually subject to a man on a private level. And as long as she has no alternative, she cannot choose her relationships freely.

That's the important point: the sexual monopoly of men over women ensures their emotional monopoly (women fall in love only with men, of course), their social monopoly (for social recognition women must depend on marriage or a relationship with a man), and their economic monopoly (women accept gratis work in the home and "additional income" jobs out of love for men).

Thus only the destruction of the male sexual

monopoly from the foundation up will cause gender roles to collapse.

Why Compulsory Heterosexuality Is So Political

Categories like heterosexuality and homosexuality are cultural in nature and cannot be justified on a biological basis. The prevailing heterosexuality is a culturally induced, forced heterosexuality. Just how insupportable the concept of a "natural" heterosexuality is was illustrated by [Alfred] Kinsey in his report on *Sexual Behavior of Women*.

[…]

In a culture in which procreation is not the primary impulse for human sexuality, homosexuality as well as heterosexuality and a sexuality with one's self would have to be taken for granted as part of the free development of the individual.

There are political reasons for why things are not that way. The only way the male sexual monopoly can be ensured is through a heterosexuality that is elevated to the status of dogma. Its pretext is that "little difference."

[…]

In her militant book, *The Dialectic of Sex*, Shulamith Firestone places the question of sexuality in relation to the question of class:

Just as the end goal of socialist revolution was not only the elimination of the economic class *privilege* but of the economic class *distinction* itself, so the end goal of feminist revolution must be . . . not just the elimination of male *privilege* but of the sex *distinction* itself. (11)

Because this way of thinking regularly elicits fears of castration and hysterical reactions in males and because it is not a common perspective, I want to explain it in my own words once again:

What this means is that people are first and foremost people and only secondarily female and male. Gender would no longer be destiny. Women and men would not be forced into role behaviour, and the masculine mystique would be as superfluous as the femininity complex. Sex-specific divisions of labour and exploitation would be suspended. Only biological motherhood would be woman's affair; social motherhood [the rearing of children] would be men's affair just as much as women's. […] People would communicate with one another in unlimited ways, sexually and otherwise, according to their individual needs at any given time and regardless of age, race, and gender. (There would be no class system in this liberated society.) A utopia for tomorrow, but also goals and perspectives which we cannot lose sight of today. From now on, these things must determine what we do.

CHAPTER 49

Portrait of a Heroine as a Young Woman

Ayaan Hirsi Ali

One of my current heroines is Samira Ahmed, a 24-year-old girlishly pretty woman with large, brown, doelike eyes, dark, curly hair, and a smile that seduces even the gloomiest of faces to lighten up and smile back. Besides her good nature, she is also inquisitive and has a strong will to be her own person. Born to a family who left Morocco in the early 1980s and settled in The Netherlands, she is one of ten children.

In the summer of 2005, I attended her graduation ceremony at a training college in Amsterdam. Samira received a diploma for pedagogy and a record 10 score (the highest score possible) for her thesis.

This is the celebratory side of Samira's story, for there is also a tragic side. When I arrived for Samira's graduation I was received like all the other guests in a reception area just outside of the auditorium where the ceremony was to take place. I noticed the happy class, a total of 35 students, gathered in clusters around coffee stands. Family and friends accompanied them, chatting, carrying gifts and flowers wrapped in cellophane. Proud fathers and mothers, flushed siblings teasing their red-faced brothers and sisters, boyfriends and girlfriends happy just to be there to witness an achiever in the family.

On Samira's stand none of her family showed up: no brother, no sister, no cousin, no nephew, no niece. Two years earlier, Samira had to sneak away from home because she wanted to live in a student house like her Dutch friends Sara and Marloes. At home she had shared a bedroom with some of her siblings and had no privacy at all. Every move she made in the house was monitored by her mother and sisters; outside the house her brothers kept watch. They all wanted to make sure that under no circumstances would she become Westernized.

Samira had endured terrible physical and psychological violence at home. Her family always had a pretext to question her, go through her stuff and forbid her from setting foot outside the house. She was beaten frequently. There were rumours in her community that she had a Dutch boyfriend. The beatings at home became harsher. Samira could bear it no longer and left. Soon afterwards, in the summer of 2003, she got in touch with me. I went with her to the police to file a complaint against her brothers, who had threatened to murder her. According to them, Samira's death was the only way to avenge the shame she brought upon the family for leaving their parents' house.

The police said they could do nothing to help her except file the complaint. They said there were thousands of other women like her and it was not the police's duty to intervene in family matters. Ever since she left, Samira has been in hiding, moving from house to house and depending on the kindness of strangers. Mostly she is brave and faces life with a powerful optimism. Samira reads her textbooks, does her homework, and turns her papers in on time. She accepts invitations to student parties from Sara and Marloes and makes an effort to enjoy herself.

Sometimes, however, she has a sad, drawn look on her face that betrays her worries. Once in a while she just weeps and confides that she wishes her life were different, perhaps more like the lives of her Dutch friends. Today, however, on her graduation day, she is glowing, clutching her diploma and returning the kisses of her friends. Her worries are far from over, though. She has no money; she has to find a job, and with her Moroccan name that will be far from easy in The Netherlands; she has to find another new place to live; she lives in an unending fear of being discovered by her brothers and slaughtered by them. This is no joke, for in just two police regions in Holland (The Hague area and the southern section of the province of South Holland), 11 Muslim girls were killed by their own families between October 2004 and May 2005 for "offences" similar to those committed by Samira.

In my mind, there are three categories of Muslim women in Dutch society. I suspect that this distinction applies to other European Union countries with large Muslim populations as well. First, there are girls such as Samira—strong-willed, intelligent, and willing to take a chance on shaping their individual futures along a path they choose for themselves. They face many obstacles as they try to assimilate in Western society and some may lose their lives trying to attain their dreams.

Second, there are girls and women who are very dependent and attached to their families but who cleverly forge a way to lead a double life. Instead of confronting their families and arguing about their adherence to custom and religion, these girls use a more tactful approach. When with family (in the broadest sense of the word, which also includes their community), they put on their headscarves and at home obey every whim of their parents and menfolk.

Outside the home, however, they lead the life of an average Western woman: they have a job, dress fashionably, have a boyfriend, drink alcohol, attend cocktail parties, and manage to travel away from home for a while.

The third group are the utterly vulnerable. Some of these girls are imported as brides or domestic workers from the country of origin of the immigrants with whom they come to live. Some are daughters of the more conservative families. These girls are removed from school once they attain puberty and locked up at home. Their families get away with this form of modem slavery because the authorities rarely take notice of these young women. The girls have often been brought up to be absolutely obedient; they perform household chores without question. Their individual wills have been bent to the servitude taught at their parents' house and put into practice in their husbands' homes or the homes of the people who import and enslave them. They can hardly read or write.

When they marry, they generally bear as many children as their individual fertility allows. When they miscarry, most of them view this as God's will, not as a lack of proper health care, which they are usually prevented from seeking because of their families' religious reasons.

When a woman in this subjugated state is violently abused by husband, brother, or father, she considers it a result of her own wrongdoing. In response, she promises to behave better in the future, Some abused women may be tempted to rebel by running away or informing the authorities when their life becomes too painful. Those who act on such a temptation are likely to be killed by their own family or husband, or end up in prostitution or in the women's shelters. Some who have shown signs of rebellion are lured back to their country of origin by parents or husbands and simply dumped there, abandoned, disowned, with or without children, and with no financial resources or people to help them.

For a while now I have been asserting that the most effective way for European Union governments to deal with their Muslim minorities is to empower the Muslim women living within their borders. No one has offered a convincing argument against this position, but no one outside my own part seems to want to make the first step to help these women. The best tool for empowering these women is education. Yet the education systems of some European Union countries are going through a crisis of neglect, particularly with regard to immigrant children. We are paying the price of mixing education with ideology. However, let me stick to the important subject of freeing women from the shackles of superstitious belief and tribal custom.

The biggest obstacle that hinders Muslim women from leading dignified, free lives is violence—physical, mental, and sexual—committed by their close families. Here is only a sample of some of the violence perpetrated on girls and women from Islamic cultures:

- Four-year-old girls have their genitals mutilated: some of them so badly that they die of infections; others are traumatized for life from the experience and will later suffer recurrent infections of their reproductive and urinary systems.
- Teenage girls are removed from school by force and kept inside the house to stop their schooling, stifle their thinking and suffocate their will.
- Victims of incest and sexual abuse are beaten, deported, or killed to prevent them from filing complaints.
- Some pregnant victims of incest or abuse are forced by their fathers, older brothers, or uncles to have abortions in order to keep the family honour from being stained. In this era of DNA testing, the girls could demonstrate that they have been abused. Yet instead of punishing the abusers, the family treats the daughter as if she had dishonoured the family.
- Girls and women who protest their maltreatment are beaten by their parents in order to kill their spirits and reduce them

to a lifelong servitude that amounts to slavery.
- Many girls and women who can't bear to suffer any more take their own lives or develop numerous kinds of psychological ailments, including nervous breakdown and psychosis. They are literally driven mad.
- A Muslim girl in Europe runs more risk than girls of other faiths of being forced into marriage by her parents with a stranger. In such a marriage—which, since it is forced, by definition starts with rape—she conceives child after child. She is an enslaved womb. Many of her children will grow up in a household with parents who are neither bound by love nor interested in the well-being of their children. The daughters will go through life as subjugated as their mothers and the sons become—in Europe—dropouts from school, attracted to pastimes that can vary from loitering in the streets to drug abuse to radical Islamic fundamentalism.

European policy-makers have not yet understood the huge potential of liberating Muslim women. They are squandering the single best opportunity they have to make Muslim integration a success within one generation. Morally, governments need to eradicate violence against women in Europe. This would make clear to fundamentalists that Europeans take their constitutions seriously. Now, most abusers simply think that Western rhetoric about the equality of men and women is cowardly and hypocritical, since Western governments tolerate the abuse of millions of Muslim women when they're told it's in the name of freedom of religion.

Muslim women like Samira would make sure to prepare their own children for a life in modern society. These women would plan their family with a chosen partner. This planning reduces the chances for dropouts among their children. They value education and would emphasize its importance for their children. They value work and aspire to make a contribution to the economy. They would provide the greying European economy with the human resources it needs instead of adding to its social welfare rolls.

The children of successful Muslim women are more likely to have a positive attitude towards the societies in which they live. They will learn at an early age to appreciate the freedom and prosperity they live in and perhaps even understand how vulnerable these freedoms are and defend them.

Why are European leaders so slow to appreciate the great role Muslim women can play in a successful integration of immigrants in the European Union? Some blame can be attributed to the passivity of universities and non-governmental organizations in addressing immigrant women's rights. The academic community unanimously condemns violence against women, whether it is committed by family or the state, but it has been negligent in investigating and providing the necessary legal framework and data to help policy-makers make women's rights a priority.

The classic argument of professors that universities are not political arenas seems disingenuous, since many faculties and colleges across Europe indulge in all sorts of ideological and political practices. For instance, Oxford University has just given a chair to Tariq Ramadan, the Swiss Muslim ideologist seen by some as a moderate voice propounding the assimilation of Muslims into European society by "psychological integration" and by some Americans and Europeans as a radical. He was hired in the summer of 2005 by the University of Notre Dame in the United States to teach Islamic philosophy and ethics at its Joan B. Kroc Institute for Peace and Justice, but he was denied entry into the country, his visa revoked just days before he was to begin working there. Ultimately, he resigned from the post, since he could not get there to teach. His hiring by Oxford appears to be not solely because of his outstanding academic record but because he is seen as buffer against radical Islam.

Yet, in spite of having Arab and Islam faculties, most universities in Europe serve as activist centres to further the Palestinian cause, instead of research and teaching centres for Muslim students. There is as yet no chair, no study, no course on the subjugation of Muslim women and how that affects Europe and the future of this major population of European Muslims. There are no researchers gathering facts and figures on the intensity of violence faced by Muslim women, how that violence hinders them in their daily lives, and how that prevents Muslims from integrating successfully into European society.

Non-governmental organizations are embarrassingly silent on this fight for human rights. Oh, yes, there is one in Norway that pays attention, Human Rights Watch, run by a brave, determined woman, Hege Storhaus. But in the bigger countries, no NGO yet monitors the number of times an honour killing is committed in a member state, or the number of times a girl is circumcised, or the number of times a girl is removed from school and forced into a life of virtual slavery.

However, there is room for some optimism. Awareness is growing in Europe about the breadth and persistence of violence against Muslim women and girls, justified by culture and religion, committed by family. Some governments have acknowledged that they should take action to fight against this and all types of violence against women. Yet we are a long way from conditions where girls like Samira can lead a life without fear. What a waste that Europe is blind to this golden opportunity that lies at her feet.

Critical Thinking Questions

1. What are the specific premises of Western political theory, as Clark identifies them? How does Locke's attempt to undermine patriarchal government end up reinforcing these very positions?

2. Why does Okin's critique of Rawls' theory of justice attach so much importance to the family as a societal institution? What are the possible implications of Okin's critique? Does it, for example, open the door for a greater role of the state in private affairs? And if not the state, which institution might ensure that the family becomes more just?

3. Consider Nussbaum's list of Central Human Capabilities. Which feature a feminist angle without necessarily saying so? Why would Nussbaum prefer to present her list in a rather neutral language? How advantageous or disadvantageous might such a move be?

4. Why does Code shy away from advocating absolute relativism from a feminist perspective? Why does she embrace a mitigated relativism? Code talks about a "middle position" in outlining how it is that knowledge "bears the marks of its constructors." What does she mean by a "middle position"?

5. According to Schwarzer, which factor ultimately determines the cultural assignment of gender? How does she think the "sexual monopoly of men" impacts gender relations? What is the political significance of homosexuality for Schwarzer?

6. Why does Hirsi Ali attach so much importance to the treatment of Muslim women in European societies? Which link does she see between their rights and the broader assimilation of Muslims into Western societies? Hirsi Ali accuses Western governments of tolerating the abuse of millions of Muslim women. How credible do you find this claim as well as her broader assumptions?

Biographies

Lorenne Clark (1936–)

The resume of Canadian Lorenne Clark leaves little doubt about her status as one of the leading authorities on feminist legal theory. A graduate of the University of British Columbia, the University of Oxford, and Toronto's Osgoode Hall Law School, Clark has helped shape public and legal opinions on matters such as rape, pornography, and prostitution during the course of her long and multifaceted career. She has achieved this influence through several avenues: as an activist who helped prostitutes and rape victims when few did so during the 1970s, as an academic (University of Toronto, Dalhousie Law School) who authored several leading pieces on legal and political theory, as a prominent Nova Scotian lawyer, and as a government official (Deputy Minister of Justice, Yukon).

Susan Okin (1946–2004)

Like Martha Nussbaum (1947–) today, Susan Okin considered herself to be a liberal philosopher in the broader tradition of John Rawls (1921–2002). Yet it was she who revealed significant gaps in Rawls' philosophy through her political analysis of the family, an institution that *A Theory of Justice* ignores. This critique—which links sexism in the private sphere of the family with sexism in the public realm—revolutionized political theory and established Okin as one of the most important thinkers of her era. Born in New Zealand, Okin studied and taught at some of the most renowned schools in the world. But this stature never stopped her practical advocacy on behalf of women everywhere but especially in the developing world, which had emerged as a major research interest toward the end of Okin's all-too-brief career and life.

Martha Nussbaum (1947–)

Born into an aristocratic WASP family with lines to the original Mayflower settlers, Nussbaum's liberalism emerged during an early age. One day she "integrated" her affluent suburban surroundings by bringing home a black girl on a play date, much to the stated chagrin of her conservative, southern father. This defiance of established, perhaps encrusted, authority is a central theme in Nussbaum's academic career, which rests on the premise that philosophers should be "lawyers of humanity." This utilitarian approach has nourished the fierce and occasionally ferocious advocacy Nussbaum has exhibited on behalf of women and sexual minorities. Some of these clashes, including her famous exchange with theory-obsessed feminist Judith Butler, have revealed the jesting sharpness of Nussbaum's intellect. Yet she has seemingly maintained a regal air, without succumbing to snobbery herself.

Lorraine Code (1937–)

How does gender affect knowledge creation? Calgary-born Lorraine Code raised this simple but "outrageous" question in her famous essay (1981) "Is the Sex of the Knower Epistemologically Significant?" While it would be a mistake to reduce her research interests to issues at the intersection of feminism and knowledge production, Code has consistently shown that established ways of creating and acquiring knowledge have failed to consider women in advancing feminist epistemology. This contribution has earned Code, who speaks fluent French and German, an international reputation that has exposed her work to top-flight academic audiences in the United

States, the United Kingdom, continental Europe, Australia, and South Africa. More recently, she has drawn a bridge that connects epistemology with environmental ethics, as she continues to research at York University in Toronto.

Alice Schwarzer (1942–)

Growing up in post-war West Germany, Schwarzer appeared to be headed toward a career in commercial trading before entering the world of journalism and academia. While working in France as a freelance reporter, Schwarzer befriended Simone de Beauvoir (1908–1986) and studied under Michel Foucault (1926–1984). Never shy about breaking taboos, Schwarzer publicly confessed in 1971 that she had an abortion as West Germam feminists challenged the restrictive anti-abortion law of their country. *The Little Difference and Its Huge Consequences* (1975) established Schwarzer as a feminist with global reach. Schwarzer continues to cause controversy to this very day. On the one hand, she oversees *Emma*, a feminist magazine that she founded in 1977. On the other, she has written for the country's leading tabloid, *Bild*, which regularly features pin-ups on its pages.

Ayaan Hirsi Ali (1969–)

Adjectives such as "controversial" and "polarizing" only get close to describing the political views of Ayaan Hirsi Ali. Born in Somalia, Hirsi Ali received an Islamic education and sympathized with the Muslim Brotherhood during her youth. But her views changed with age and she eventually sought asylum in the Netherlands while on her way to Canada, where she was to be the bride in an arranged marriage. She continued to distance herself from Islam as she established herself in Dutch political life to emerge as a fierce critic of the religion in a country with a history of religious tolerance. Her collaboration with the late, assassinated filmmaker Theo van Gogh eventually turned Hirsi Ali into a target of Muslim extremists, which has forced her to live in relative seclusion. While this critique of Islam as a misogynistic religion has earned Hirsi Ali support inside and outside of feminist circles, others have accused her of stifling dialogue.

Part X

Environmentalism

Environmentalism

Environmentalism is a political philosophy that gives priority to the environment over such things as class, nations, gender, or race. Its first wave, beginning in Europe, the United States, and Mexico, comprised three phases: a moral and cultural one, a scientific conservation one, and a wilderness one. Environmentalism's second wave, beginning with Rachel Carson, comprised an empirically based biological and economic approach to the world around us, viewed in a holistic way. Recognition by Carson of the "elixirs of death"—namely, 2,4-D and DDT—in the early 1960s contributed greatly to the development of this second wave. Carson captures the essence of this new political philosophy by echoing the words of Albert Schweitzer: we have lost the capacity to foresee and forestall. It is instructive to learn that it is Schweitzer to whom Carson dedicates her famous *Silent Spring* (1962).

Major Figures

Alexander von Humboldt (1769–1859), William Wordsworth (1770–1850), George Perkins Marsh (1801–1882), John Ruskin (1819–1900), William Morris (1834–1896), John Muir (1838–1914), Edward Carpenter (1844–1929), Miguel Angel de Quevedo (1862–1946), Gifford Pinchot (1865–1946), Aldo Leopold (1887–1948), Rachel Carson (1907–1964), Arne Naess (1912–2009), Rudolf Bahro (1935–1997), and Murray Bookchin (1921–2006)

Period of Greatest Influence

First wave from 1800–1949; the second wave from 1960 to the present

Introduction

The Bhopal environmental disaster of 2–3 December 1984—in which highly toxic methyl isocynate gas leaked from a Union Carbide factory, killing thousands of people and maiming up to 200,000 others in Bhopal, India—together with the Chernobyl nuclear disaster in 1986—which resulted in an estimated 30,000 to 60,000 cancer deaths in the surrounding area—and the Fukushima nuclear accident of 2011—in which three nuclear reactors experienced a meltdown, releasing radioactive caesium 137 and plutonium in sufficient quantities to cause concern—are but reminders of the truth of the words of the Nobel Prize winner Albert Schweitzer (1875–1965): that humankind has lost the capacity to foresee and forestall, at least with respect to what humankind does to the environment.

Writing in 1962 in her famous *Silent Spring*, a book dedicated to Schweitzer, Rachel Carson (1907–1964) draws to our attention the "needless havoc" that humans have created in the natural world through the senseless use of insecticides. Carson affirms unequivocally the thoughtless destructive urge of humans in their "conquest of nature." In taking this stand as a professional biologist for the US Fish and Wildlife Service, Carson launches what turned out to be the second wave of environmentalism, a wave that had been preceded by the first wave, itself originating in 1860 with the effects of the Industrial Revolution of the eighteenth and nineteenth centuries. In the readings that follow attention will be given solely to writers who help shape the second wave of environmentalism after Carson, but this should not obscure the indebtedness these writers have to the individuals comprising the first wave, including William Wordsworth (1770–1850), George Perkins Marsh (1801–1882), John Ruskin (1819–1900), William Morris (1834–1896), John Muir (1838–1914), Edward Carpenter (1844–1929), Miguel Angel de Quevedo (1862–1946), Gifford Pinchot (1865–1946), Mohandas Gandhi (1869–1948), and Aldo Leopold (1887–1948).

Undoubtedly one of the more passionate and articulate defenders of environmentalism, especially in its version of deep ecologism, is the Norwegian Arne Naess (1912–2009). In some ways the credo that he affirms under the heading of "deep ecology" resonates with some of the themes of Schweitzer and his notion of "reverence for life." It also resonates with some of the sentiments of Aldo Leopold in his claim that—with respect to humans and their interaction with the environment—they are modelling the gardens of Alhambra of the Moorish monarchs of Granada with a steam shovel. Naess' credo is no expression of a sentimentalist but rather of a sophisticated professional philosopher who expresses in blunt and clear terms some of the ideas that are later argued for by Anne Ehrlich (1933–) and Paul Ehrlich (1932–). Naess affirms, among others the following points: human and non-human life has intrinsic value, diversity of life forms has value in itself, and ideological change is rooted in the appreciation of life quality.

Of course, once one enters the den of a deep ecologist such as Naess, serious moral questions begin to arise. Andrew Dobson (1957–) raises some of these questions when he says that deep ecologists want to advance "deeper" reasons for the care of the environment than do shallow ecologists, such as those who advocate, in the spirit of the Brundtland Report, sustainable development. Among the questions Dobson raises are the following: to whom or what does the ethical theory of the deep ecologist apply? And, according to deep ecologists, what attributes does a person need to be a member of the ethical community? After canvassing some answers to these questions as proposed by philosophers and ecologists, Dobson rejects biospherical egalitarianism, a theory that affirms equality among all living things, and maintains that environmental ethicists generally endorse a hierarchy of valued entities and collection of entities. Dobson shows clearly the difficulty of giving meaning to the term "intrinsic value" as applied to all living things and endorsing a hierarchy of valued entities. In brief, he teases out serious issues that must be resolved by anyone wishing to advance deep ecology.

In 1992, famous world scientists issued *World Scientists' Warning to Humanity*, a report that gave empirical teeth to some of the things discussed in the Brundtland Report and by Dobson. The warning, secular in nature, issued by such distinguished scientists as Murray Gell-Mann, Stephen Hawking, Dorothy Crowfoot Hodgkin, and Stephen Jay Gould, affirms five imperatives if "vast misery" to our species is to be averted. These imperatives include the following: environmentally damaging activities must be brought under control, resources must be managed more effectively, human population must be stabilized, poverty must be eliminated, and sexual equality must be ensured. These imperatives speak for themselves, but it is more than just a little interesting that the final exhortation affirms the importance of an ideal that feminists such as Susan Okin and Martha Nussbaum endorse, namely the importance of sexual equality. These show a vital interconnection between some themes in feminism and environmentalism that is often overlooked.

When one turns to Murray Bookchin (1921–2006), one sees a resurfacing of some of the skepticism of Andrew Dobson. In rejecting "biocentrism," Bookchin effectively endorses Dobson's rejection of biospherical egalitarianism. From Bookchin's perspective, biocentrism "denies humanity its real place in natural evolution" and denies "the most distinctive of human natural attributes: the ability to foresee, to will, and to act insightfully." He advocates in place of a philosophy of denial of the human spirit a philosophy of social ecology, which recovers the continuity of human nature with the creative process of natural evolution and which explores the roots of the cultural in the natural phenomena. Quite intriguingly, Bookchin comes close to rejecting Schweitzer's notion of reverence for life when he argues that a revered nature is a dominating nature and thus the very antithesis of the liberal and Marxian image of nature dominated by humans. What Bookchin advocates in place of Schweitzer's view is one which sees societal and cultural matters as ecologically derivative and cumulative—in short, according to Bookchin, there is a causal connection here between the organic and societal.

In the final excerpt, John Barry (1966–) presents a rather compelling picture of the origins of green theory. Along the way, he highlights the importance to green theory of overcoming the separation of "human" from "nature," of stressing the importance of the "embodiedness" of humans, of recognizing for human society the constitutive dimension of social-environmental relations, and of underlining the need to extend the "moral community" beyond the species barrier. It is worth noting that Barry rightly acknowledges the strong basis that green social theory has in the natural sciences of ecology, evolutionary and environmental psychology, the biological sciences, and thermodynamics.

Barry then turns his attention to historical progression of green social theory from development to sustainable development; in the process, he makes an unavoidable reference to the Brundtland Report, *Our Common Future* (1987). However, Barry does not stop with this report but consolidates some of the key elements found in the discourses that have evolved on the subject of sustainable development, among which he includes human dependence on the natural environment as well as the fragility of local and global environments to human collective action. While it would be misleading to say that Barry offers us something radically new in talking about green social theory, it would be quite accurate to say he provides a fine consolidation of ideas that have arisen in connection with this theory, especially as related to its origins and connection with sustainable development.

The moving credo of Arne Naess provides a well articulated basis for deep ecology. A more secular approach to deep ecology and ecology generally is provided in the thoughts of the *World Scientists' Warning*, Dobson, Bookchin, and Barry. Collectively—from Naess to Barry—their works provide a two-fold challenge for anyone advocating deep ecology, a challenge that asks what metaphysics—secular or religious—is needed to sustain this form of ecology and how far the moral net can be cast before the boat to which it is attached sinks under the weight of its catch. The views of all of the foregoing individuals allow for ample room of personal reflection on one's own journey through and in the environment.

CHAPTER 50

A Platform of the Deep Ecology Movement

Arne Naess

(1) The flourishing of human and non-human life on earth has intrinsic value. The value of non-human life forms is independent of the usefulness these may have for narrow human purposes.

(2) Richness and diversity of life forms are values in themselves and contribute to the flourishing of human and non-human life on earth.

(3) Humans have no right to reduce this richness and diversity except to satisfy vital needs.

(4) Present human interference with the non-human world is excessive, and the situation is rapidly worsening.

(5) The flourishing of human life and cultures is compatible with a substantial decrease of the human population. The flourishing of non-human life requires such a decrease.

(6) Significant change of life conditions for the better requires change in policies. These affect basic economic, technological, and ideological structures.

(7) The ideological change is mainly that of appreciating *life quality* (dwelling in situations of intrinsic value) rather than adhering to a high standard of living. There will be a profound awareness of the difference between big and great.

(8) Those who subscribe to the foregoing points have an obligation directly or indirectly to participate in the attempt to implement the necessary changes.

The eight formulations are of course in need of clarification and elaboration. A few remarks:

Re (1) Instead of "biosphere" we might use the term "ecosphere" in order to stress that we of course do not limit our concern for the life forms in a biologically narrow sense. The term "life" is used here in a comprehensive non-technical way to refer also to things biologists may classify as non-living: rivers (watersheds), landscapes, cultures, ecosystems, "the living earth." Slogans such as "let the river live" illustrate this broader usage so common in many cultures.

Re (2) So-called simple, lower, or primitive species of plants and animals contribute essentially to the richness and diversity of life. They have value in themselves and are not merely steps toward the so-called higher or rational life forms. The second principle presupposes that life itself, as a process over evolutionary time, implies an increase of diversity and richness.

Why talk about diversity *and* richness? Suppose humans interfere with an ecosystem to such a degree that 1000 vertebrate species are each reduced to a survival minimum. Point (2) is not satisfied. *Richness*, here used for what some others call "abundance," has been excessively reduced. The maintenance of richness has to do with the maintenance of habitats and the number of individuals (size of populations). No exact count is implied. The main point is that life on earth may be excessively interfered with even if complete diversity is upheld.

What is said about species holds also for habitats and ecosystems which show great similarity so that it makes sense to count them.

Re (3) This formulation is perhaps too strong. But, considering the mass of ecologically irresponsible proclamation of human rights, it may be sobering to announce a norm about what they have no right to do.

The term "vital need" is vague to allow for considerable latitude in judgment. Differences in climate and related factors, together with differences in the structures of societies as they now exist, need to be considered. Also the difference between a means to the satisfaction of the need and the need must be considered. If a whaler in an industrial country quits whaling he may risk unemployment under the present economic conditions. Whaling is for him an important means. But in a rich country with a high standard of living whaling is not a vital need.

Re (4) Status of interference. For a realistic assessment of the global situation, see the unabbreviated version of the IUCN's *World Conservation Strategy* (1980). There are other works to be highly recommended such as Gerald Barney's *Global 2000 Report to the President* of the United States (1980).

People in the materially richest countries cannot be expected to reduce their excessive interference with the non-human world to a moderate level overnight. Less interference does not imply that humans should not modify some ecosystems as do other species. Humans have modified the earth and will continue to do so. At issue is the nature and extent of such interference.

The fight to preserve and extend areas of wilderness or near-wilderness should continue and should focus on the general ecological functions of these areas (one such function: large wilderness areas are required by the biosphere to allow for continued evolutionary speciation of animals and plants). Present designated wilderness areas and game preserves are not large enough to allow for speciation of large birds and mammals.

Re (5) Limitation of population. The stabilization and reduction of the human population will take time. Interim strategies need to be developed. But this in no way excuses the present complacency. The extreme seriousness of our current situation must first be more widely recognized. But the longer we wait the more drastic will be the measures needed. Until deep changes are made, substantial decreases in richness and diversity are liable to occur; the rate of extinction of species will be greater than in any other period of earth history.

A legitimate objection may be that if the present billions of humans deeply change their behaviour in the direction of ecological responsibility, non-human life could flourish. Formulation (5) presupposes that the probability of a deep enough change in economics and technology is too small to take into account.

Re (6) Policy changes required. Economic growth as conceived and implemented today by the industrial states is incompatible with points (1) to (5).

Present ideology tends to value things because they are scarce and because they have a commodity to market value. There is prestige in vast consumption and waste, to mention only two of many relevant factors. Economic growth registers mainly growth in marketable values, not in values generally, including ecological values. Whereas "self-determination," "local community," and "think globally, act locally" will remain key slogans, the implementation of deep changes nevertheless requires increasingly global action in the sense of action across every border, perhaps contrary to the short-range interests of local communities.

Support for global action through non-governmental organizations becomes increasingly important. Many of these organizations are able to act locally from grass roots to grass roots, thus avoiding negative governmental interference.

Cultural diversity today requires advanced

technology, that is, techniques that advance the basic goals of each culture. So-called soft, intermediate, and appropriate technologies are steps in this direction.

Re (7) Some economists criticize the term "quality of life" because it is supposed to be too vague. But, on closer inspection, what they consider to be vague is actually the non-quantifiable nature of the term. One cannot quantify adequately what is important for the quality of life as discussed here, and there is no need to do so.

Re (8) There is ample room for different opinions about priorities. What should be done first, what next? What is most urgent? What is necessary as opposed to what is highly desirable? Different opinions in these matters should not exclude vigorous co-operation.

What is gained from tentatively formulating basic views shared today by most or all supporters of the deep ecology movement? Hopefully it makes it a little easier to localize the movement among the many "alternative" movements. Hopefully this does not lead to isolation but rather to even better co-operation with many other alternative movements. It might also make some of us more clear about where we stand, and more clear about which disagreements might profitably be reduced and which ones might profitably be sharpened. After all, as we shall see, "diversity" is a high-level norm!

Bibliography

Barney, Gerald, ed. (1980) *Global 2000 Report to the President* (Oxford: Pergamon Press).

World Conservation Strategy (1980) Gland, Switzerland: International Union for the Conservation of Nature (IUCN).

CHAPTER 51

Deep Ecology:
Ethics as a Code of Conduct

Andrew Dobson

Some years ago, "deep ecology" was regarded as a keystone of radical political-ecological thinking (Curry, 2006, pp. 71–81). It was believed that a fundamental ethical shift was required that would dethrone human interests as the centrepiece of political life and extend ethical concern deep into the natural world. In recent years, this ethical move has itself been decentred in favour of a more political response which calls for an extension of political voice that would include nature. What these two moves have in common is a questioning of the overriding centrality—the "trumping" effect—of human interests over those of other parts of the natural world. I shall say more about the democratizing move later [. . .] but the ethical arguments that paved the way for it are critical and I shall deal with them now.

The first influential use of the term "deep ecology" is generally credited to the Norwegian Arne Naess. In September 1972 Naess gave a lecture in Bucharest in which he drew a distinction between what he called the "shallow" and the "deep" ecology movements. The distinction had to do with the difference between a shallow concern at "pollution and resource depletion," for the damaging effects this might have on human life, and the deep concern—for its own sake—for ecological principles such as complexity, diversity, and symbiosis (Naess, 1973, p. 95). I suggest that deep ecology informs a certain type of radical green politics in a way that will not be obvious to those who make such politics synonymous with environmentalism. Indeed, ecologism's being informed by deep ecology is precisely what (partly) helps distinguish it from environmentalism: environmentalists will be happy with so-called "shallow" ecological reasons for care for the environment, while deep ecologists will want to advance "deeper" reasons which take the natural world as an entity worthy of moral concern in its own right.

The first question to which any ethical theory must have an answer is: To whom or to what should it apply? This is tied to a second question: In respect of the possession of what attributes do we admit a subject to membership of the ethical community? One ethical theory might hold, for example, that it should cover human beings (and only human beings), and that this is in virtue of their possession of the capacity to reason. In this way, the attribute (possession of a rational faculty) defines the boundaries of the ethical community. Environmental philosophy in general, and deep ecology in particular, may be regarded as a series of answers to these two questions. In this context the influence of the animal rights movement and its intellectual backers has been

profound. It is largely true to say that the extension by the animal rights movement and its theorists of the ethical domain from human to (some) animals has until recently been seen by ecophilosophers and deep ecology theorists as the right course to pursue in their aim to produce an ethic for non-sentient nature.

An ethic for animals is by no means the same as an ethic for the environment, but, to the extent that it constitutes a foray across the species divide, it is a start. As long ago as the third century BCE, Epicurus argued that just as humans can experience pleasure and pain so can animals, and more recently Peter Singer has famously turned this argument into reasons for moral constraint in our behaviour towards animals (Singer, 1975). Tom Regan builds a different bridge across the divide by arguing that human beings and some animals may similarly be regarded as "subjects-of-a-life," and that if this is the reason why we regard humans as morally considerable, it would be inconsistent to deny (some) animals similar moral considerability too (Regan, 1988).

Neither Singer nor Regan get anywhere near an environmental ethic, however. Singer restricts moral considerability to sentient beings, while Regan's extension of the moral community is even more circumscribed: besides humans it includes no more than "normal mammalian animals aged one or more" (Regan, 1988, p. 81). However, both theories do raise the spectre of "speciesism"—discrimination on the grounds of species alone—and ask us whether such discrimination can be rationally justified. Rationalist approaches to a properly *environmental* ethic proceed along similar lines, with ethicists seeking less restrictive attributes for non-human entities than either sentience or a degree of mental complexity.

Lawrence Johnson, for example, argues that organisms and collections of organisms (including species and ecosystems) have well-being needs, and therefore an interest in having them met. This "well-being interest" is the attribute, according to Johnson, which accords moral significance to those entities said to possess it (Johnson, 1991). This is an environmental ethic in two senses: first, it may be argued to apply to the whole environment; and second, it grants moral considerability to "wholes" (species, ecosystems) as well as to individuals. It therefore covers the ground outlined by Aldo Leopold in his classic statement of the reach of an environmental ethic in *A Sand County Almanac*:

> All ethics so far evolved rest upon a single premise: that the individual is a member of a community of interdependent parts. His instincts prompt him to compete for his place in that community; but his ethics prompt him also to co-operate (perhaps in order that there be a place to compete for).
>
> The land ethic simply enlarges the boundaries of the community to include soils, waters, plants, and animals, or collectively: the land. (Leopold, 1949, p. 204)

Leopold also provided us with a general rule of thumb for sound environmental action by writing that "[A] thing is right when it tends to preserve the integrity, stability, and beauty of the biotic community. It is wrong when it tends otherwise" (Leopold, 1949, pp. 224–5). This has worried subsequent commentators for its apparent implication that *individual* entities can justifiably be sacrificed for the *general* good, thereby bearing out Tom Regan's worries regarding "environmental fascism" (Regan, 1988, p. 362).

Rationalist seekers after an environmental ethic have responded to this common criticism by advancing the cause of attributes which grant moral considerability to both individuals *and* wholes. Lawrence Johnson's "well-being interests" are a case in point, as is the attribute of "autopoiesis" which Robyn Eckersley describes

as the "characteristic of self-reproduction or self-renewal" (Eckersley, 1992, p. 60), building on Fox's observation that "[L]iving systems . . . are not merely *self-organizing* systems, they are *self-regenerating* or *self-renewing* systems" (Fox, 1990, p. 170). Eckersley continues:

> [A]n autopoietic approach to intrinsic value is not vulnerable to the objections that are associated with either extreme atomism or extreme holism. Whereas atomistic approaches attribute intrinsic value only to individual organisms, and whereas an unqualified holistic approach attributes intrinsic value only to whole ecosystems (or perhaps only the biosphere or ecosphere itself), an autopoietic approach recognizes . . . the value not only of individual organisms but also of species, ecosystems, and the ecosphere ("Gaia"). (Eckersley, 1992, p. 61)

Of course, this attribution of moral considerability to wholes as well as parts does not preclude the possibility of clashes between them—in fact, such clashes are inevitable. Attfield has pointed out, while considering the "Gaian" argument that the biosphere as a whole has moral standing, that "there can be a conflict between maximizing its excellences and maximizing the intrinsic value of its components" (Attfield, 1983, p. 159). The difficulties involved in resolving conflicts between the claims of different "ecological subjects" have proved very awkward, and these problems emerged early on in the history of deep ecology with Naess' "Principle Two" of deep ecology, described in his seminal 1973 paper. The idea is: "Biospherical egalitarianism in principle" (Naess, 1973, p. 95). The difficulty with this becomes clear if one focuses on the small-print clause "in principle" and Naess' own comment upon it: "The 'in principle' clause is inserted because any realistic praxis necessitates some killing, exploitation, and suppression" (Naess,

1973, p. 95). This has become a famous phrase in environmental-ethical literature—how much killing, and who or what is to be exploited and suppressed?

The notion of biospherical egalitarianism is evidently problematic. Mary Midgley caustically rejects the principle of an "equal right to live and blossom" when she says that biospherical egalitarians:

> have . . . made things extremely hard for themselves lately by talking in a very wholesale, *a priori* French-revolutionary sort of way about all animals being equal, and denouncing "speciesism" as being an irrational form of discrimination, comparable to racism. This way of thinking is hard to apply convincingly to locusts, hookworms, and spirochaetes, and was invented without much attention to them. (Midgley, 1983, p. 26)

So how are problems of conflict to be resolved? How is the "in principle" clause to be filled out?

In general terms, environmental ethicists cope with this in the same way as the rest of us: by constructing a *hierarchy* of valued entities and collections of entities. These hierarchies are usually arrived at on the basis of taking the valued attribute in question and arguing that some entities or collections of entities have more of this attribute than others and therefore weigh more heavily in the moral balance. So Lawrence Johnson bases moral considerability on the possession of well-being interest. But it becomes clear that not all entities have the same (kind of) well-being interest: "certainly it seems that humans are capable of a much higher level of well-being than is the smallpox organism" (Johnson, 1991, p. 261).

Indeed, it is striking how often these intrepid philosophical adventurers return, in a fairly traditional way, to home base. Complexity is a favourite datum around which to construct the requisite hierarchies. Warwick Fox has related value to complexity in the following way:

> To the extent that value inheres in complexity of relations, and to the extent that complexity of relations is evidenced in the degree of an organism's central organization (and therefore for capacity of richness of experience), then organisms are entitled to moral consideration commensurate with their degree of central organization (or capacity for richness of experience) for the duration of their existence. (Fox, 1984, p. 199)

He goes on: "Recognizing this, we should be clear that the central intuition of deep ecology does not entail the view that intrinsic value is spread evenly across the membership of the biotic community" (Fox, 1984, p. 199), and that therefore "these hierarchical conceptions of intrinsic value . . . provide a guide to action in situations where values come into genuine conflict" (Fox, 1990, p. 182).

In this way, attempts to solve the difficulties with Naess' principle have often ended by undermining the principle itself. This is clear evidence of the intractability of the problem—and it is an absolutely practical problem for the politics of the green movement. Anyone who has drowned slugs in a cup of beer to stop them eating the lettuces may be congratulated on a certain ecological sensibility (by not using a chemical pesticide), but was the action environmentally ethical? As Richard Sylvan has commented: "The guidelines as regards day-to-day living and action for a follower of deep ecology remain unduly and unfortunately obscure" (Sylvan, 1984, p. 13).

At the root of all of this is the search for a way of investing value in beings other than in human beings such that we cannot legitimately treat them only as means to our ends: "We need an ethic that recognizes the intrinsic value of all aspects of the nonhuman world" (Bunyard and Morgan-Grenville, 1987, p, 284). Thus, it is hoped, an ethical non-anthropocentrism will underpin responsible behaviour towards the non-human natural world.

But what would intrinsic value look like? In a detailed survey, John O'Neill outlines three possibilities. First, "[A]n object has intrinsic value if it is an end in itself [as opposed to] a means to some other end"; second, "[I]ntrinsic value is used to refer to the value an object has solely in virtue of its 'intrinsic properties'"; and third, "[I]ntrinsic value is used as a synonym for 'objective value,' i.e., the value that an object possesses independently of the valuation of valuers" (O'Neill, 1993, p. 9). O'Neill concludes that holding an environmental ethic involves holding that "non-human beings have intrinsic value in the first sense," but that holding a *defensible* environmental ethic might involve commitment to intrinsic value in the second or third senses (ibid., pp. 9–10).

As far as the issue of objective value is concerned, several attempts have been made to counter the subjectivist's objection that value is a quality invested in objects by human beings—in other words, objects do not possess value in their own right, rather we confer it upon them. Often, these attempts amount to an appeal to our intuition. For example, Holmes Rolston writes that "We can be thrilled by a hawk in a windswept sky, by the rings of Saturn, the falls of Yosemite." He admits that "All these experiences are mediated by our cultural education," but asserts that they "have high elements of giveness, of finding something thrown at us, of successful observation" (Rolston, 1983, p. 144). Similarly, he says that "we have sometimes found values so intensely delivered that we have saved them wild, as in the Yellowstones, the Sierras, and the Smokies" (ibid., p. 156). It is not the demand on our intuition that offends here, but while Rolston might persuade us to agree about the value of nature's "spectaculars," it might not stretch

as far as other offerings such as the anopheles mosquito and the tsetse fly.

Another favourite gambit of the intrinsic valuers is to ask us to conduct a thought experiment so as to test our susceptibility to their suggestions. The experiment can take many forms but the general idea is always the same. Consider, for example, Robin Attfield's version. Attfield asks us to think of the last surviving human being of a nuclear holocaust confronted by the last surviving elm tree. Attfield's question is: Would this human being be doing anything wrong in cutting down the elm tree, knowing that she or he would die before the tree? He reports that "most people who consider this question conclude that his (*sic*) act would be wrong" (Attfield, 1983, p, 155), and that this is evidence of a visceral feeling for intrinsic value. His rationalization of this effect is that trees have a "good of their own" and "are thus at least serious candidates for moral standing" (ibid., p. 145).

It will be clear that cashing out all the complexities of intrinsic value involves detailed argumentation—any more of which would be misplaced here. The point at present is to contrast instrumental with non-instrumental value—and to say that although O'Neill (above) talks only of non-human "beings," environmental ethicists also talk of the "states, activities, and/or experiences" of objects as potential sites of intrinsic value (e.g. Attfield, 1990, p. 63), and *collections* of entities, likewise.

Some ecophilosophers regard the difficulties of extending the work of animal rights theorists and sustaining an "intrinsic value" position for nature as insurmountable, and have preferred to concentrate on the cultivation of a "state of being" rather than a "code of conduct" (Fox, 1986b, p. 4). This approach involves the belief that the development of an ecologically sound ethics is not possible within the current mode of ethical discourse (rights, duties, rational actors, the capacity for pain and suffering, and so on), and that such an ethics can only, and must, emerge front a new worldview. Those who argue from this perspective point out that the current mode of discourse demands that ecologists present reasons why the natural world should *not* be interfered with. What is required, they suggest, is the cultivation of an alternative worldview within which justifications would have to be produced as to why it *should* be interfered with (Fox, 1986a, p. 84).

Bibliography

Attfield, R. (1983) *The Ethics of Environmental Concern* (Oxford: Blackwell).

——. (1990) "Deep ecology and intrinsic value," *Cognito* 4(1).

Bunyard, P., and Morgan-Grenville, F. (eds) (1987) *The Green Alternative* (London: Methuen).

Curry, P. (2006) *Ecological Ethics: An Introduction* (Cambridge: Polity Press).

Eckersley, R. (1992) *Environmentalism and Political Theory: Toward an Ecocentric Approach* (London: UCL Press).

Fox, W. (1984) "Deep ecology: a new philosophy of our time?" *The Ecologist*, 14 (5/6).

——. (1986a) *Approaching Deep Ecology: A Response to Richard Sylvan's Critique of Deep Ecology* (Tasmania: University of Tasmania).

——. (1986b) "Ways of thinking environmentally," talk given to Fourth National Environmental Education Conference, Australia, September.

——. (1990) *Towards a Transpersonal Ecology: Developing New Foundations for Evironmentalism* (Boston, MA: Shambhala Press).

Johnson, L. (1991) *A Morally Deep World: An Essay on Moral Significance and Environmental Ethics* (Cambridge: Cambridge University Press).

Leopold, A. (1949) *A Sand County Almanac* (Oxford: Oxford University Press).

Midgley, M. (l983) *Animals and Why They Matter* (Harmondsworth: Penguin).

Naess, A. (1973) "The shallow and the deep, long-range ecology movement. A summary," *Inquiry*, 16.

O'Neill, J. (1993) *Ecology, Policy and Politics: Human Well-being and the Natural World* (London: Routledge).

Regan, T. (1988) *The Case Jar Animal Rights* (London: Routledge).

Rolston, H. (1983) "Are values in nature subjective or objective?" in R. Elliot and A. Gare (eds) *Environmental Philosophy* (Milton Keynes: Open University Press).

Singer, P. (1975) *Animal Liberation* (New York: Review Books).

Sylvan, R. (1984) "A critique of deep ecology" (part two), *Radical Philosophy*, 41.

CHAPTER 52

World Scientists' Warning to Humanity[1]

Introduction

Human beings and the natural world are on a collision course. Human activities inflict harsh and often irreversible damage on the environment and on critical resources. If not checked, many of our current practices put at serious risk the future that we wish for human society and the plant and animal kingdoms, and may so alter the living world that it will be unable to sustain life in the manner that we know. Fundamental changes are urgent if we are to avoid the collision our present course will bring about.

The Environment

The environment is suffering critical stress:

The Atmosphere
Stratospheric ozone depletion threatens us with enhanced ultraviolet radiation at the earth's surface, which can be damaging or lethal to many life forms. Air pollution near ground level, and acid precipitation, are already causing widespread injury to humans, forests, and crops.

Water Resources
Heedless exploitation of depletable groundwater supplies endangers food production and other essential human systems. Heavy demands on the world's surface waters have resulted in serious shortages in some 80 countries, containing 40 per cent of the world's population. Pollution of rivers, lakes, and groundwater further limits the supply.

Oceans
Destructive pressure on the oceans is severe, particularly in the coastal regions, which produce most of the world's food fish. The total marine catch is now at or above the estimated maximum sustainable yield. Some fisheries have already shown signs of collapse. Rivers carrying heavy burdens of eroded soil into the seas also carry industrial, municipal, agricultural, and livestock waste—some of it toxic.

Soil
Loss of soil productivity, which is causing extensive land abandonment, is a widespread by-product of current practices in agriculture and animal husbandry. Since 1945, 11 per cent of the earth's vegetated surface has been de-graded—an area larger than India and China combined—and per capita food production in many parts of the world is decreasing.

Forests
Tropical rain forests, as well as tropical and temperate dry forests, are being destroyed rapidly. At present rates, some critical forest types will be gone in a few years, and most of the tropical rain forest will be gone before the end of the next century. With them will go large numbers of plant and animal species.

Living Species
The irreversible loss of species, which by 2100 may reach one-third of all species now living, is especially serious. We are losing the potential they hold for providing medicinal and other benefits, and the contribution that genetic diversity of life forms gives to the robustness of the world's biological systems and to the astonishing beauty of the earth itself.

Much of this damage is irreversible on a scale of centuries or permanent. Other processes appear to pose additional threats. Increasing levels of gases in the atmosphere from human activities, including carbon dioxide released from fossil fuel burning and from deforestation, may alter climate on a global scale. Predictions of global warming are still uncertain—with projected effects ranging from tolerable to very severe—but the potential risks are very great.

Our massive tampering with the world's interdependent web of life—coupled with the environmental damage inflicted by deforestation, species loss, and climate change—could trigger widespread adverse effects, including unpredictable collapses of critical biological systems whose interactions and dynamics we only imperfectly understand.

Uncertainty over the extent of these effects cannot excuse complacency or delay in facing the threats.

Population

The earth is finite. Its ability to absorb wastes and destructive effluent is finite. Its ability to provide food and energy is finite. Its ability to provide for growing numbers of people is finite. And we are fast approaching many of the earth's limits. Current economic practices that damage the environment, in both developed and underdeveloped nations, cannot be continued without the risk that vital global systems will be damaged beyond repair.

Pressures resulting from unrestrained population growth put demands on the natural world that can overwhelm any efforts to achieve a sustainable future. If we are to halt the destruction of our environment, we must accept limits to that growth. A World Bank estimate indicates that world population will not stabilize at less than 12.4 billion, while the United Nations concludes that the eventual total could reach 14 billion, a near tripling of today's 5.4 billion. But, even at this moment, one person in five lives in absolute poverty without enough to eat, and one in ten suffers serious malnutrition.

No more than one or a few decades remain before the chance to avert the threats we now confront will be lost and the prospects for humanity immeasurably diminished.

Warning

We the undersigned, senior members of the world's scientific community, hereby warn all humanity of what lies ahead. A great change in our stewardship of the earth and the life on it is required if vast human misery is to be avoided and our global home on this planet is not to be irretrievably mutilated.

What We Must Do

Five inextricably linked areas must be addressed simultaneously:

1. We must bring environmentally damaging activities under control to restore and protect the integrity of the earth's systems we depend on. We must, for example, move away from fossil fuels to more benign, inexhaustible energy sources to cut greenhouse gas emissions and the pollution of our air and water. Priority must be given to the development of energy sources matched to Third World needs—small-scale and relatively easy to implement.

   We must halt deforestation, injury to and loss of agricultural land, and the loss of terrestrial and marine plant and animal species.

2. We must manage resources crucial to human welfare more effectively. We must give high priority to efficient use of energy, water, and other materials, including expansion of conservation and recycling.

3. We must stabilize population. This will be possible only if all nations recognize that it requires improved social and economic conditions, and the adoption of effective, voluntary family planning.

4. We must reduce and eventually eliminate poverty.

5. We must ensure sexual equality, and guarantee women control over their own reproductive decisions.

The developed nations are the largest polluters in the world today. They must greatly reduce their overconsumption if we are to reduce pressures on resources and the global environment. The developed nations have the obligation to provide aid and support to developing nations, because only the developed nations have the financial resources and the technical skills for these tasks.

Action on this recognition is not altruism, but enlightened self-interest: whether industrialized or not, we all have but one lifeboat. No nation can escape from injury when global biological systems are damaged. No nation can escape from conflicts over increasingly scarce resources. In addition, environmental and economic instabilities will cause mass migrations with incalculable consequences for developed and undeveloped nations alike.

Developing nations must realize that environmental damage is one of the gravest threats they face and that attempts to blunt it will be overwhelmed if their populations go unchecked. The greatest peril is to become trapped in spirals of environmental decline, poverty, and unrest, leading to social, economic, and environmental collapse.

Success in this global endeavour will require a great reduction in violence and war. Resources now devoted to the preparation and conduct of war—amounting to over $1 trillion annually—will be badly needed in the new tasks and should be diverted to the new challenges.

A new ethic is required—a new attitude toward discharging our responsibility for caring for ourselves and for the earth. We must recognize the earth's limited capacity to provide for us. We must recognize its fragility. We must no longer allow it to be ravaged. This ethic must motivate a great movement, convincing reluctant leaders and reluctant governments and reluctant peoples themselves to effect the needed changes. The scientists issuing this warning hope that our message will reach and affect people everywhere. We need the help of many.

We require the help of the world community of scientists—natural, social, economic, political;

We require the help of the world's business and industrial leaders;

We require the help of the world's religious leaders; and

We require the help of the world's peoples.

We call on all to join us in this task.

The following is an abridged list of signatories of the Warning. Over 1670 scientists, including 104 Nobel laureates—a majority of the living recipients of the Prize in the sciences— have signed it so far. These men and women represent 71 countries, including all of the 19 largest economic powers, all of the 12 most populous nations, 12 countries in Africa, 14 in Asia, 19 in Europe, and 12 in Latin America.

Walter Alvarez, Geologist, National Academy of Sciences, USA

Philip Anderson, Nobel laureate, Physics; USA

Christian Anfinsen, Nobel laureate, Chemistry; USA

Werner Arber, Nobel laureate, Medicine; Switzerland

Michael Atiyah, Mathematician; President, Royal Society; Great Britain

Mary Ellen Avery, Pediatrician, National Medal of Science, USA

Julius Axelrod, Nobel laureate, Medicine; USA

Howard Bachrach, Biochemist, National Medal of Science, USA

John Backus, Computer Scientist, National Medal of Science, USA

David Baltimore, Nobel laureate, Medicine; USA

David Bates, Physicist, Royal Irish Academy, Ireland

Georg Bednorz, Nobel laureate, Physics; Switzerland

Baruj Benacerraf, Nobel laureate, Medicine; USA

Sune Bergström, Nobel laureate, Medicine; Sweden

Hans Bethe, Nobel laureate, Physics; USA

Konrad Bloch, Nobel laureate, Medicine; USA

Nicholaas Bloembergen, Nobel laureate, Physics; USA

Bert Bolin, Meteorologist, Tyler Prize, Sweden

Norman Borlaug, Agricultural Scientist; Nobel laureate, Peace; USA & Mexico

E. Margaret Burbidge, Astronomer, National Medal of Science, USA

Adolph Butenandt, Nobel laureate, Chemistry; Former President, Max Planck Institute; Germany

Ennio Candotti, Physicist; President, Brazilian Society for the Advancement of Science; Brazil

Georges Charpak, Nobel laureate, Physics; France

Paul Crutzen, Chemist, Tyler Prize, Germany

Jean Dausset, Nobel laureate, Medicine; France

Margaret Davis, Ecologist, National Academy of Sciences, USA

Gerard Debreu, Nobel laureate, Economics; USA

Paul-Yves Denis, Geographer, Academy of Sciences, Canada

Thomas Eisner, Biologist, Tyler Prize, USA

Mohammed T. El-Ashry, Environmental scientist, Third World Academy, Egypt & USA

Mahdi Elmandjra, Economist; Vice President, African Academy of Sciences; Morocco

Richard Ernst, Nobel laureate, Chemistry; Switzerland

Dagfinn Follesdal, President, Norwegian Academy of Science, Norway

Otto Frankel, Geneticist, Australian Academy of Sciences, Australia

Konstantin V. Frolov, Engineer; Vice President, Russian Academy of Sciences; Russia

Kenichi Fukui, Nobel laureate, Chemistry; Japan

Robert Gallo, Research scientist, Lasker Award, USA

Murray Gell-Mann, Nobel laureate, Physics; USA

Donald Glaser, Nobel laureate, Physics; USA

Sheldon Glashow, Nobel laureate, Physics; USA

Marvin Goldberger, Physicist; Former President, California Institute of Technology, USA

Stephen Jay Gould, Paleontologist, Author, Harvard University, USA

Stephen Hawking, Mathematician, Wolf Prize in Physics, Great Britain

Dudley Herschbach, Nobel Prize, Chemistry; USA

Dorothy Crowfoot Hodgkin, Nobel laureate, Chemistry; Great Britain

Ronald Hoffmann, Nobel laureate, Chemistry; USA

Nick Hoionyak, Electrical Engineer, National Medal of Science, USA

Sarah Hrdy, Anthropologist, National Academy of Sciences, USA

Kun Huang, Physicist, Chinese Academy of Sciences, China

Hiroshi Inose, Electrical Engineer; Vice President, Engineering Academy; Japan

Francois Jacob, Nobel laureate, Medicine; France

Carl-Olof Jacobson, Zoologist; Secretary-General, Royal Academy of Sciences; Sweden

Daniel Janzen, Biologist, Crafoord Prize, USA

Harold Johnston, Chemist, Tyler Prize, USA

Robert Kates, Geographer, National Medal of Science, USA

Frederick I.B. Kayanja, Vice-Chancellor, Mbarara University, Third World Academy, Uganda

Henry Kendall, Nobel laureate, Physics;

Chairman, Union of Concerned Scientists; USA

Gurdev Khush, Agronomist, International Rice Institute, Indian National Science Academy, India & Philippines

Klaus von Klitzing, Nobel laureate, Physics; Germany

Aaron Klug, Nobel laureate, Chemistry; Great Britain

E.F. Knipling, Agricultural Researcher, National Medal of Science, USA

Walter Kohn, Physicist, National Medal of Science, USA

Torvard Laurent, Physiological chemist; President, Royal Academy of Sciences; Sweden

Leon Lederman, Nobel laureate, Physics; Chairman, American Association for the Advancement of Science; USA

Wassily Leomief, Nobel laureate, Economics; USA

Luna Leopold, Geologist, National Medal of Science, USA

Rita Levi-Montalcini, Nobel laureate, Medicine; USA & Italy

William Lipscomb, Nobel laureate, Physics; USA

Jane Lubchenco, Zoologist; President-Elect, Ecological Society of America; USA

Lynn Margulis, Biologist, National Academy of Sciences, USA

George Martine, Institute for Study of Society, Population & Nature; Brazil

Ernst Mayr, Zoologist, National Medal of Science, USA

Digby McLaren, Past President, Royal Society of Canada; Canada

James Meade, Nobel laureate, Economics; Great Britain

Jerrold Meinwald, Chemistry, Tyler Prize, USA

M.G.K. Menon, Physicist; President, International Council of Scientific Unions; India

Gennady Mesiatz, Physicist; Vice President, Russian Academy of Sciences; Russia

César Milstein, Nobel laureate, Medicine; Argentina & Great Britain

Franco Modigliani, Nobel laureate, Economics; USA

Walter Munk, Geophysicist, National Medal of Science, USA

Lawrence Mysak, Meteorologist; Vice President, Academy of Science, Royal Society of Canada; Canada

James Neel, Geneticist, National Medal of Science, USA

Louis Néel, Nobel laureate, Physics; France

Howard Odum, Ecologist, Crafoord Prize, USA

Yuri Ossipyan, Physicist; Vice President, Russian Academy of Sciences; Russia

Autar Singh Paintal, Physiologist; Former President, Indian National Science Academy; India

Mary Lou Pardue, Biologist, National Academy of Sciences, USA

Linus Pauling, Nobel laureate, Chemistry & Peace; USA

Roger Penrose, Mathematician, Wolf Prize in Physics, Great Britain

John Polanyi, Nobel laureate, Chemistry; Canada

George Porter, Nobel laureate, Chemistry; Great Britain

Ilya Prigogine, Nobel laureate, Chemistry; Belgium

Edward Purcell, Nobel laureate, Physics; USA

G.N. Ramachandran, Mathematician, Institute of Science, India

Peter Raven, Director, Missouri Botanical Garden; National Academy of Sciences, USA

Tadeus Reichstein, Nobel laureate, Medicine; Switzerland

Gustavo Rivas Mijares, Engineer; Former President, Academy of Sciences, Venezuela

Wendell Roelofs, Entomologist, National Medal of Science, USA

Miriam Rothschild, Biologist, Royal Society, Great Britain

Sherwood Rowland, Chemist; Past

President, American Association for the Advancement of Science; USA

Carlo Rubbia, Nobel laureate, Physics; Italy & Switzerland

Albert Sabin, Virologist, National Medal of Science, USA

Carl Sagan, Astrophysicist & Author, USA

Roald Sagdeev, Physicist, Russian & Pontifical Academies, Russia & USA

Abdus Salam, Nobel laureate, Physics; President, Third World Academy of Sciences; Pakistan & Italy

José Sarukhan, Biologist, Third World Academy, México

Richard Schultes, Botanist, Tyler Prize, USA

Glenn Seaborg, Nobel laureate, Physics; USA

Roger Sperry, Nobel laureate, Medicine; USA

Ledyard Stebbins, Geneticist, National Medal of Science, USA

Janos Szentgothai, Former President, Hungarian Academy of Sciences; Hungary

Jan Tinbergen, Nobel laureate, Economics; Netherlands

James Tobin, Nobel laureate, Economics; USA

Susumu Tonegawa, Nobel laureate, Medicine; Japan & USA

James Van Allen, Physicist, Crafoord Prize, USA

Harold Varmus, Nobel laureate, Medicine; USA

George Wald, Nobel laureate, Medicine; USA

Gerald Wasserburg, Geophysicist, Crafoord Prize, USA

James Watson, Nobel laureate, Medicine; USA

Victor Weisskopf, Wolf Prize in Physics, USA

Fred Whipple, Astronomer, National Academy of Sciences, USA

Torsten Wiesel, Nobel laureate, Medicine; USA

Geoffrey Wilkinson, Nobel laureate, Chemistry; Great Britain

Edward O. Wilson, Biologist, Crafood Prize, USA

Solly Zuckerman, Zoologist, Royal Society, Great Britain

Note

1. Sponsored by the Union of Concerned Scientists, 26 Church Street, Cambridge, MA 02238.

CHAPTER 53

Freedom and Necessity in Nature: A Problem in Ecological Ethics

Murray Bookchin

One of the most entrenched ideas in Western thought is the notion that nature is a harsh realm of necessity, a domain of unrelenting lawfulness and compulsion. From this underlying idea, two extreme attitudes have emerged. Either humanity must yield with religious or "ecological" humility to the dicta of "natural law" and take its abject place side by side with the lowly ants on which it "arrogantly" treads, *or* it must "conquer" nature by means of its technological and rational astuteness, in a shared project ultimately to "liberate" all of humanity from the compulsion of natural "necessity"—an enterprise that may well entail the subjugation of human by human.

The first attitude, a quasi-religious quietism, is typified by "deep ecology," antihumanism, and sociobiology, while the second, an activist approach, is typified by the liberal and Marxian image of an omniscient humanity cast in a commandeering posture toward the natural world. Modern science—despite its claims to value-free objectivity—unwittingly takes on an ethical mantle when it commits itself to a concept of nature as comprehensible, as orderly in the sense that nature's "laws" are rationally explicable and basically necessitarian.

The ancient Greeks viewed this orderly structure of the natural world as evidence of a cosmic *nous* or *logos* that produced a subjective presence in natural phenomena as a whole. Yet with only a minimal shift in emphasis, this same notion of an orderly nature can yield the dismal conclusion that "freedom is the recognition of

necessity" (to use Friedrich Engels's rephrasing of Hegel's definition). In this latter case, freedom is subtly turned into its opposite: the mere *consciousness* of what we can or cannot do.

Such an internalized view of freedom as subject to higher dicta, of "Spirit" (Hegel) or "History" (Marx), not only served Luther in his break with the Church's hierarchy; it provided an ideological justification for Stalin's worst excesses in the name of dialectical materialism and his brutal industrialization of Russia under the aegis of society's "natural laws of development." It may also yield an outright Skinnerian notion of an overly determined world in which human behaviour is reduced to mere responses to external or internal stimuli.

These extremes aside, the conventional wisdom of our time still sees nature as a harsh "realm of necessity"—morally, as well as materially—that constitutes a challenge to humanity's survival and well-being, not to speak of its freedom. With the considerable intellectual heritage of dystopian thinkers like Hobbes and utopian ones like Marx, the self-definition of major academic disciplines embodies this tension, indeed, this conflict. Economics was forged in the crucible of a necessitarian, even "stingy" nature whose "scarce resources" were thought to be insufficient to meet humanity's "unlimited needs." Psychology, certainly in its psychoanalytic forms, stresses the importance of controlling human internal nature, with the bonus that the individual's sublimated energy will find its expression in the subjugation of external nature. Theories of work, society, behaviour, and even sexuality turn on an image of a necessitarian nature that must in some sense be "dominated" to serve human ends—presumably on the old belief that what is natural disallows *all* elements of choice and freedom. Nor is nature philosophy itself untainted by this harshly necessitarian image. Indeed, more often than not, it has served as an ideological justification for a hierarchical society, modeled on a hierarchically structured "natural order."

This image and its social implications, generally associated with Aristotle, still live in our midst as a cosmic justification for domination in general—in its more noxious cases, for racial and sexual discrimination, and in its most nightmarish form, for the outright extermination of entire peoples. Raised to a moral calling, "man" emerges from this massive ideological apparatus as a creature to whom "Spirit" or "God has imparted a supranatural quality of a transcendental kind and a mission to govern an ordered universe that "He" or "It" created.

[...]

If liberal and Marxist theorists prepared the ideological bases for plundering the natural world, "biocentrically" oriented antihumanists and "natural law" devotees may be preparing the ideological bases for plundering the human spirit. In the course of "revering nature," they have created an insidious image of a humanity whose "intrinsic worth" is no more or less than that of other species. "Biocentrism" denies humanity its real place in natural evolution by completely subordinating humanity to the natural world. Paradoxically, "biocentrism" and antihumanism also contribute to the alienation and reification of nature such that a "reverence" for nature can easily be used to negate any existential respect for the diversity of life. Against the background of a cosmic "Nature," human life and individuality are completely trivialized, as witness James Lovelock's description of people as merely "intelligent fleas" feeding on

the body of Gaia. Nor can we ignore a growing number of "natural law" acolytes who advocate authoritarian measures to control population growth and forcibly expel urban dwellers from large congested cities, as though a society that is structured around the domination of human by human could be expected to leave the natural world intact.

It is grossly misleading to invoke "biocentrism," "natural law," and antihumanism for ends that deny the most distinctive of human natural attributes: the ability to reason, to foresee, to will, and to act insightfully to enhance nature's own development. In a sense, it deprecates nature to separate these subjective attributes from it, as though they did not emerge out of evolutionary development and were not implicitly part of animal development. A humanity that has been rendered oblivious to its own responsibility to evolution—a responsibility to bring reason and the human spirit to evolutionary development, to foster diversity, and to provide ecological guidance such that the harmful and the fortuitous in the natural world are diminished—is a humanity that *betrays its own evolutionary heritage* and that ignores its species-distinctiveness and uniqueness.

Ironically, then, a nature that is reverentially hypostatized is a nature set apart from humanity—and in the very process of being hypostatized over humanity, it is defamed. A nature reconstructed into forms apart from itself, however "reverentially," easily becomes a mere object of utility. Indeed, a revered nature is the converse of the old liberal and Marxian image of nature "dominated" by man. Both attitudes reinstate the theme of domination in ecological discussion.

Here the limited form of reasoning based on *deduction*, so commonplace in conventional logic, supplants an organismic form of reasoning based on *eduction*—that is, on derivation, so deeply rooted in the dialectical outlook. *Potentially*, human reason is an expression of nature rendered self-conscious, a nature that finds its voice in being of its own creation. It is not only we who must have our own place in nature but nature that must have its place in us—in an ecological society and in an ecological ethics based on humanity's catalytic role in natural evolution.

[. . .]

Along with the antihumanistic ideologies that foster misanthropic attitudes and actions, the reduction of human beings to commodities is steadily denaturing and degrading humanity. The commodification of humanity takes its most pernicious form in the manipulation of the individual as a means of production and consumption. Here, human beings are employed (in the literal sense of the term) as techniques either in production or in consumption, as mere devices whose creative powers and authentic needs are equally perverted into objectified phenomena. As a result, we are witnessing today not only the "fetishization of commodities" (to use Marx's famous formulation) but the fetishization of needs.[1] Human beings are becoming separated from their own nature as well as from the natural world in an existential split that threatens to give dramatic reality to Descartes's theoretical split between the soul and the body. In this sense, the claim that capitalism is a totally "unnatural order" is only too accurate.

The terrible tragedy of the present social era is not only that it is polluting the environment; it is also simplifying natural ecocommunities, social relationships, *and even the human psyche.* The pulverization of the natural world is being accompanied by the pulverization of the social and psychological worlds. In this sense, the conversion of soil into sand in agriculture can be said, in a metaphorical sense, to apply to society and the human spirit. The greatest danger we face—apart from nuclear immolation—is the homogenization of the world by a market society and its objectification of all human relationships and experiences into commodities.

To recover human nature is not only to recover its continuity with the creative process of natural evolution but to recognize its distinctiveness. To conceive of the participation of life forms in evolution is to understand that nature is a realm of incipient freedom. It is freedom and participation—not simply necessity—that we must emphasize, an emphasis that involves a radical break with the conventional image of nature.

Social ecology, in effect, stands at odds with the notion that culture has no roots whatever in natural evolution. Indeed, it explores the roots of the cultural in the natural and seeks to ascertain the gradations of biological development that phase the natural into the social. By the same token, it also tries to explore the important differences that distinguish the societal from the natural and to ascertain the gradations of social development that, hopefully, will yield a new, humanistic ecological society. The two lines of exploration go together in producing a larger whole, indeed, one that must transcend even the present capitalist society based on perpetual growth and profit. To identify society as such with the *present* society, to see in capitalism an "emancipatory" movement precisely because it frees us from nature, is not only to ignore the roots of society in nature but to identify a perverted society with humanism and thereby to give credence to the antihumanist trends in ecological thinking.

This much is clear: the way we view our position in the natural world is deeply entangled with the way we organize the social world. In large part, the former derives from the latter and serves, in turn, to reinforce social ideology. Every society projects its own perception of itself onto nature, whether as a tribal cosmos that is rooted in kinship communities, a feudal cosmos that originates in and underpins a strict hierarchy of rights and duties, a bourgeois cosmos structured around a market society that fosters human rivalry and competition, or a corporate cosmos diagrammed in flow charts, feedback systems, and hierarchies that mirror the operational systems of modern corporate society. That some of these images reveal a truthful aspect of nature, whether as a community or a cybernetic flow of energy, does not justify the universal, almost imperialistic claims that their proponents stake out for them over the world as a whole. Ultimately, only a society that has come into its "truth," to use Hegelian language—a rational and ecological society—can free us from the limits that oppressive and hierarchical societies impose on our understanding of nature.

The power of social ecology lies in the association it establishes between society and ecology, in understanding that the social is, potentially at least, a fulfillment of the *latent* dimension of freedom in nature, and that the ecological is a major organizing principle of social development. In short, social ecology advances the guidelines for an ecological society. The great divorce between nature and society—or between the "biological" and the "cultural"— is overcome by shared developmental concepts such as greater diversity in evolution; the wider and more complete participation of all components in a whole; and the ever more fecund potentialities that expand the horizon of freedom and self-reflexivity. Society, like mind, ceases to be sui generis. Like mind, with its natural history, social life emerges from the loosely banded animal community to form the highly institutionalized human community.[2]

Social ecology challenges the image of an unmediated natural evolution, in which the human mind, society, and even culture are sui generis, in which non-human nature is irretrievably separated from human nature, and in which an ethically defamed nature finds no expression whatever in society, mind, and human will. It seeks to throw a critical and meaningful light on the phased, graded, and cumulative development of nature into society, richly mediated by the prolonged dependence of the human young on parental care, by the blood tie as the earliest social and cultural bond beyond immediate parental care, by the so-called "sexual division of labour," and by age-based status groups and their role in the origin of hierarchy.

Ultimately, it is the institutionalization of the human community that distinguishes society from the non-human community—whether for the worse, as in the case of pre-1789 France or tsarist Russia, where weak, unfeeling tyrants like Louis XVI and Nicholas II were raised to commanding positions by bureaucracies, armies, and social classes; or for the better, as in forms of self-governance and management that empower the people as a whole, like the Parisian sections during the French Revolution and the anarchosyndicalist collectives during the Spanish Civil War. We see no such contrived institutional infrastructures in non-human communities, although the rudiments of a social bond do exist in the mother– offspring relationship and in common forms of mutual aid.

With a growing knowledge that sharing, cooperation, and concern foster healthy human consociation, with the technical disciplines that open the way for a creative "metabolism" between humanity and nature, and with a host of new insights into the presence of nature in so much of our own civilization, it can no longer be denied that nature is still with us. Indeed, it has returned to us ideologically as a challenge to the devouring of "natural resources" for profit and the mindless simplification of the biosphere. We can no longer speak meaningfully of a "new" or "rational" society without also tailoring our social relationships and institutions to the ecocommunities in which our social communities are located. In short, any rational future society must be an ecological society, conjoining humanity's capacity for innovation, technological development, and intellectuality with the non-human natural world on which civilization itself rests and human well-being depends.

The ecological principles that enter into biotic evolution do not disappear from social evolution, any more than the natural history of mind can be dissolved into Kant's ahistorical epistemology. Quite the contrary: the societal and cultural are ecologically derivative, as the men's and women's houses in tribal communities so clearly illustrate. The relationship between nature and society is a cumulative one, while each remains distinctive and creative in its own right. Perhaps most significant, the nature of which the societal and cultural are derivative—and cumulative—is a nature that is a potential realm of freedom and subjectivity, and humanity is potentially the most self-conscious and self-reflexive expression of that natural development.

[. . .]

Social ecology, by definition, takes on the responsibility of evoking, elaborating, and giving an ethical content to the natural core of society and humanity.[3] Granting the limitations that society imposes on our thinking, the development of mind out of "first nature" produces an objective ground for an ethics, indeed, for formulating a vision of a rational society that is neither hierarchical nor relativistic: an ethics that is based neither on atavistic appeals to "blood and soil" and inexorable "social laws" ("dialectical" or "scientific") on the one hand, nor on the wayward consensus of public opinion polls, which will support capital punishment one year and life imprisonment the next. Freedom becomes a desideratum as self-reflexivity, as self-management, and most excitingly, as a creative and active process that, *with its ever-expanding horizon*, resists the moral imperatives of a rigid definition and the jargon of temporally conditioned biases.[4]

An ecological ethics of freedom would provide an objective directiveness to the human enterprise. We have no need to degrade nature or society into a crude biologism at one extreme or a crude dualism at the other. A diversity that nurtures freedom, an interactivity that enhances complementarity, a wholeness that fosters creativity, a community that strengthens individuality, a growing subjectivity that yields greater rationality—all are desiderata that provide the ground for an objective ethics. They are also the real principles of any graded evolution, one that renders not only the past explicable but the future meaningful.

Notes

1. See Murray Bookchin, *The Ecology of Freedom* (Palo Alto: Cheshire Books, 1982; Montreal: Black Rose Books, 1991), pp. 68–69.

2. An ecological approach can spare us some of the worst absurdities of sociobiology and biological reductionism. The popular notion that our deep-seated "reptilian" brain is responsible for our aggressive, "brutish," and cruel behavioural traits may make for good television dramas like *Cosmos*, but it is ridiculous science. Like all the great animal groups, most Mesozoic reptiles were almost certainly gentle herbivores, not carnivores—and those that were carnivores were probably neither more nor less aggressive, "brutish," or "cruel" than mammals. Our images of Tyrannosaurus rex (a creature whose generic name is sociological nonsense) may be inordinately frightening, but they grossly distort the reptilian life forms on which the carnivore preyed. If anything, the majority of Mesozoic reptiles were probably very pacific and easily frightened, all the more because they were not particularly intelligent vertebrates. What remains unacknowledged in this imagery of fierce, fire-breathing, and "unfeelingly cruel" reptiles is the implicit assumption of different psychic sensibilities in reptiles and mammals, the latter presumably being more "sensitive" and "understanding" than the former. A psychic evolution

in non-human beings thus goes together with the evolution of intelligence. Yet confronted with the unstated premises of such evolutionary trends, few scientists would find them comfortable.

3. This project is elaborated in considerable detail in my book *The Ecology of Freedom.*

4. Hence freedom is no longer resolvable into a strident nihilistic negativity or a trite instrumental positivity. Rather, in its open-endedness, it contains both and transcends them as a continuing process. Freedom thus resists precise definition just as it resists terminal finality. It is always becoming, hopefully surpassing what it was in the past and developing into what it can be in the future.

CHAPTER 54

Greening Social Theory

John Barry

Origins of Green Theory

Often a "green" or "environmental" perspective is caricatured as something that is "countercultural," hippy, and out of touch with the "realities" of modern, late twentieth-century life. In modern Britain "green" is most vividly associated with groups such as "New Age Travellers" and the animal rights and anti-roads protest movement, in North America with the 1960s "counterculture" and "hippies." However, the focus here is not public perceptions of "greenies" or a sociological analysis of green groups and movements, but rather origins and principles of green social, moral, and political theory.

For reasons of space, some origins of green social theory are listed below:

1. the "romantic" and negative reaction to the Industrial Revolution;

2. the positive reaction to the French (democratic) Revolution;

3. a negative reaction to "colonialism" and "imperialism" in the nineteenth and twentieth centuries;

4. the emergence of the science of ecology;

5. growing public perception of an "ecological crisis" in the 1960s, claims of "limits to growth" in the 1970s, and the emergence of "global environmental problems" in the 1980s and 1990s;

6. transcending the politics of "industrialism" (organized on a left–right continuum) by a politics of "post-industrialism" (beyond left and right);

7. increasing awareness of and moral sensitivity to our relations with the non-human world (from the promotion of "animal rights" to ideas that the earth is "sacred");

8. the integration of progressive social, political, and economic policies with the politics of transition to a sustainable society, principally the universal promotion of human rights, socio-economic equality, democratization of the state and the economy.

Of particular importance is the central concern of green theory and practice to overcome both the separation of "human" from "nature" and also the misperception of humans as above or "superior" to nature. Green social theory may be seen as an attempt to bring humanity and the study of human society "back down to earth." The science of ecology played an important part in arguing that humans as a species of animal (that is, we are not just *like* animals, we are animals) are ecologically embedded in nature, and exist in a web-like relation to other species, rather than being at the top of some "great chain of being." It is crucial to note the significance of green social theory having a strong basis in the natural sciences (mainly ecology, evolutionary and environmental psychology, the biological life sciences and thermodynamics), because, as will be suggested below, this gives us a strong indication of what the "greening" of social theory may involve.

A second and related point is that green social theory, in transcending the culture/nature split, begins its analysis based on a view of humans as a species of natural being, which like other species has its particular species-specific characteristics, needs and modes of flourishing. Central to green social theory, unlike other forms of social theory, is a stress on the "embodiedness" of humans.

A third issue which green social theory raises is the ways in which social–environmental relations are not only important in human society, but also *constitutive* of human society. What is meant by this is that one cannot offer a theory of society without making social–environmental interaction, and the natural contexts and dimensions of human society a central aspect of one's theory. In its attention to the naturalistic bases of human society, the green perspective is "materialistic" in a much more fundamental way than materialism within Marxist theory. Unlike the latter, green social theory concerns itself with the external and internal natural conditions of human individual and social life, whereas the "material base" for Marx is economic not natural. At the same time,

this materialist reading of green social theory questions the "post-materialist" character often ascribed to green politics and issues, as given by Inglehart's popular explanation for green politics as "post-materialist" (Inglehart, 1977) and mainly a middle-class phenomenon. This middle-class characterization of green politics is one that Marxists have drawn attention to and used to demonstrate the "anti-working-class" interests of green theory [. . .]. However, both this Marxist critique and Inglehart's thesis fail to explain the "environmentalism of the poor" (Martinez-Alier, 2001), the class, ethnic, and race dynamics of the environmental justice movement (Schlosberg, 1999), or "resistance eco-feminism" [. . .]. The Eurocentric perspective of Inglehart's analysis is of course limiting, as is the empirically weak connection he makes between wealth/income levels and post-materialist values (Cudworth, 2003: 71) and his limiting of "environmental concern" to aesthetic/amenity rather than material or productive interests which people have with their environments.

A fourth issue to note about green social theory is its moral claim about our relationship to the natural environment. What makes green moral theory distinctive is that it wishes to extend the "moral community" beyond the species barrier to include our interaction with the non-human world as morally significant. In part, this moral concern with the non-human world is what gives green politics its self-professed character as "beyond left and right." As Lester Brown puts it, "Both capitalists and socialists believe that humans should dominate nature. They perceive nature as a resource base to be exploited for the welfare and comfort of humans" (1989: 136).

Some of the basic principles of green social theory are listed below:

- Overcoming the separation between "society" and "environment" (which includes extending environment to include the human, built environment).

- Appreciation of the *biological embodiedness* and *ecological embeddedness* of human beings and human society.
- Views humans as a species of natural being, with particular species-specific needs and characteristics.
- Accepts both internal and external natural limits, those relating to the particular needs and vulnerable and dependent character of "human nature," and external, ecological scarcity in terms of finite natural resources and fixed limits of the environment to absorb human-produced wastes.
- As a critical mode of social theory, green social theory criticizes not just "economic growth" but the dominant industrial model of "development," "modernization," and progress.
- Claims that how we treat the environment is a moral issue, and not just a "technical" or "economic" one. This ranges from claims that the non-human world has intrinsic value, to the idea of animal rights.
- Prescriptive aspects: restructuring social, economic, and political institutions to produce a more ecologically sustainable world.
- "Act local, think global": ecological interconnectedness and interdependence which transcends national boundaries.
- Futurity: timeframe of green social theory is expanded to include concern for future generations.
- Scientific: based on ecological science (but also other natural sciences such as biology and physics).

Green Social Theory: From "Development" to "Sustainable Development" and Beyond

[. . .] [M]odern social theory as a body of knowledge begins as the systematic study of modern or industrial society, explaining its emergence from a pre-industrial stage, and analyzing its internal dynamics and processes. In this way social theory is intimately connected with the theory and practice of the "development" or "modernization" of modern societies. That is, modern social theory takes the processes of development as its object of study and aims to provide a critical analysis of *what* development consists of, *how* it occurs, *who* or what are the main features or actors of development, and *where* and *when* it occurs or has occurred. As such, the increasing concern with "sustainable development" within political and economic theory and practice (particularly since the 1992 Rio "Earth Summit" conference organized by the United Nations Conference on Environment and Development) presents social theory (and the social and natural sciences more generally) with an opportunity (some might say obligation) to expand its parameters to include key aspects of this "sustainable development" agenda (which is based upon, but not co-extensive with, the "green" political agenda).

The essence of sustainable development is that it integrates a concern for the environment and environmental protection with obligations to current and future human generations. In terms of its most famous definition, contained in the Brundtland Report *Our Common Future*:

> Sustainable development is development that meets the needs of the present without compromising the ability of future generations to meet their own needs. It contains within it two key concepts: the concept of "needs," in particular the essential needs of the world's poor, to which overriding priority should be given; and the idea of limitations imposed by the state of technology and social organization in the environment's ability to meet present and future needs. (WCED, 1987: 43)

Sustainable development is thus development that is ecologically sustainable; that is, development that is consistent with external, natural ecological constraints and limits. Another way of looking at it has been advanced by Jacobs (1996):

> The concept of "sustainability" is at root a simple one. It rests on the acknowledgment, long familiar in economic life, that maintaining income over time requires that the capital stock is not run down. The natural environment performs the function of capital stock for the human economy, providing essential resources and services. Economic activity is presently running down this stock. While in the short term this can generate economic wealth, in the longer term (like selling off the family silver) it reduces the capacity of the environment to provide these resources and services at all. *Sustainability is thus the goal of "living within our environmental means." Put another way, it implies that we should not pass the costs of present activities on to future generations.* (1996: 17: emphasis added)

The discourse (or rather discourses) of sustainability and sustainable development acknowledge:

1. human dependence upon the natural environment, i.e., that the human economy is a subset of ecological systems;
2. the existence of external natural limits on human economic activity;
3. the detrimental effect of certain industrial activities on local and global environments;
4. the fragility of local and global environments to human collective action;
5. that one cannot talk about "development" without also linking it to the environmental preconditions for development;
6. following on from 4, development decisions now may have environmental (and thus development) consequences for future generations and those living in other parts of the world.

In this way, green social theory, together with the emerging centrality of the theoretical and practical dimensions of sustainable development, are suggestive of why and how social theory can be "greened."

Bibliography

Brown, L. (1989) *Envisioning a Sustainable Society: Learning Our Way Out,* New York: State University of New York Press.

Cudworth, E. (2003) *Environment and Society,* London: Routledge.

Inglehart, R. (1977) *The Silent Revolution: Changing Values and Political Styles among Western Publics,* Princeton, NJ: Princeton University Press.

Jacobs, M. (1996) *The Politics of the Real World,* London: Earthscan.

Martinez-Alier, J. (2001) *Environmentalism of the Poor,* Cheltenham: Edward Elgar.

Schlosberg, D. (1999) *Environmental Justice and the New Pluralism,* Oxford: Oxford University Press.

World Commission on Environment and Development (WCED) (1987) *Our Common Future,* Oxford: Oxford University Press.

Critical Thinking Questions

1. What are the strengths and weaknesses of Naess' argument that the "flourishing of human life" in the future depends on a "substantial decrease" of the human population? What are the potential impacts of measures designed to stabilize and reduce the human population? Would you support or reject such measures? Why?

2. Which conceptual differences distinguish ecologism from environmentalism, according to Dobson? Which questions does deep ecology attempt to answer, according to Dobson? Identify some of the answers concerning the status of animals. With which do you agree? Why?

3. Why do the World Scientists ask the developed nations (like Canada) to shoulder the burden of action? How do the scientists justify this demand on developed nations? How have they in turn acted since 1992, when the World Scientists made their demands? How has the larger global context changed since then?

4. What is the nature of the "existentialist split" that Bookchin identifies? Whom (or what) does Bookchin blame for this condition? Why must any "rational future society" be an "ecological society," according to Bookchin?

5. What is the primary agenda of green theory, according to Barry? Why is green social theory more and simultaneously less "materialistic" than Marxist theory, according to Barry? Review the Brundtland Report's definition of sustainable development as described by Barry. What (if any) contradictions does it contain?

Biographies

Arne Naess (1912–2009)

Arne Naess pursued a number of intellectual interests during his professional philosophical career, which began 1939 in his native Norway where he taught for more than 30 years. As one of his editors said, Naess was "the philosophical equivalent of a hunter-gatherer," whose passions, not to mention positions, roamed across the philosophical landscape. Topics other than environmental philosophy that have benefited from his insights include semantics and the philosophy of science as Naess fought for both sides in the enduring epistemological dispute over the validity of scientific reasoning—first as a militant defender of it, then as an ardent critic in expressing considerable skepticism about the short-term prospects of humanity. Naess, who nonetheless remained hopeful about the long-term prospects of humanity, also displayed considerable skills in other fields such as mountaineering and political activism. In fact, he once combined both in an effective fashion when he successfully prevented the construction of a dam by chaining himself to the mountain wall of a fjord.

Andrew Dobson (1957–)

Academics, fairly or unfairly, often suffer from the perception that they stand apart from society, removed from its daily realities. Andrew Dobson, however, has immunized himself against such charges by testing his theoretical positions in the political marketplace of the United Kingdom. Dobson has run for the British Green Party twice (2005, 2006), losing both times. He has, however, remained active in political life as the main author of his party's 2010 electoral platform. He has also contributed to the opinion pages of leading British newspapers as a frequent letter-to-the-editor writer. He has balanced this practical approach to the political arts with his ongoing academic contributions, particularly through his involvement on the editorial boards of various leading journals, including *Environmental Politics*, which he co-founded. Green candidates are still trying to make a significant breakthrough in Commonwealth countries that have a first-past-the-post electoral system. Dobson, however, speaks to the quality of Green candidates.

Murray Bookchin (1921–2006)

Biographical accounts of Bookchin, who grew up in New York as the only child of Russian immigrants, often paint him as a radical and confrontational figure whose taste for direct activism only matches his sharp polemic. While this image is far from baseless if we consider he once denounced capitalism as a "social cancer," it ignores his forward-thinking, subtle side. Writing under the pseudonym Lewis Herber, Bookchin warned about the perils of environmental decline well before Rachel Carson published *Silent Spring*. His future writings also anticipated contemporary environmental and social issues such as global warming, the effects of globalization, and obesity. Far from being divisive, Bookchin has served as a rallying point for a variety of historic and contemporary social movements such as the student movement during the 1960s and the current anti-globalization movement. One might not agree with everything Bookchin has written or said as an author, academic, and activist, but it would be a mistake to ignore him and his insights, particularly his observation that "the domination of nature by man stems from the very real domination of human by human."

John Barry (1966–)

The schism between Catholics and Protestants that has defined the distant and recent history of the Irish Isle in countless measures has begun to fade into history with the Good Friday Agreement of 1998. But sectarian tensions have a habit of dying slowly, if ever, and it takes a great deal of personal courage to offer a political vision that aims to close the deep trenches that have divided Republicans and Unionists in Northern Ireland, and Northern Ireland from the Republic of Ireland. Barry has successfully managed this difficult feat through his role in the creation of an all-island Green Party in 2006. While this party continues to secure its place in the aftermath of the Troubles, its very presence sends a powerful signal about the need to transcend past divisions in the face of anticipated ecological disturbances. At this stage, one should also note the extensive body of academic scholarship Barry has produced over the years as a well-travelled expert on environmental politics. Yet the many honours and publications that bear his name, as impressive as they might be, somehow appear to lose their lustre when held up against Barry's shining vision of an inclusive future in a place that has become almost synonymous for metaphysical strife.

Part XI

Religious Fundamentalism

Religious Fundamentalism

Religious fundamentalism in all its varieties (Christian, Jewish, and Muslim) endorses unequivocally a strict adherence to the social and moral codes and metaphysical beliefs of revealed religion as found in sacred and infallible texts. The rejection of the values of the Enlightenment, secularism, and impiety stands at the core of all three versions of religious fundamentalism. For Islamic fundamentalism, this rejection occurred most prominently in the late 1700s in Saudi Arabia; for Jewish fundamentalism, it occurred around 1775; and for Christian fundamentalism, it occurred in 1909 and 1915 with the publication of booklets called *The Fundamentals*. The rise of modern science beginning in 1660 and the discovery of Darwin's theory of natural selection in 1859, along with the forces of secularism, have contributed greatly to the growth of these movements. All three versions of fundamentalism have made a comeback in the late twentieth and early twenty-first centuries. Curiously, though different religious perspectives, they all have similar values with respect to the family, marriage, the role of women, divorce, abortion, contraception, drugs, and alcohol.

Major Figures

Ibn Abd al-Wahhab (1703–1792), Rabbi Abraham Isaac Kook (1865–1935), Rabbi Zvi Yehuda Kook (1891–1982), Ayatollah Khomeini (1902–1989), Sayyid Abul-Ala Maududi (1903–1979), Hasan al-Banna (1906–1949), Sayyid Qutb (1906–1966), Pat Robertson (1930–), Rabbi Meir Kahane (1932–1990), Jerry Falwell (1933–2007), and Bob Jones III (1939–)

Period of Greatest Influence

Islamic fundamentalism: 1800s, and then from 1928 to the present; Jewish fundamentalism: from Yom Kippur War of 1973 to the present; Christian fundamentalism: from 1909 to the 1930s, and then from 1979 to the present

Introduction

The intellectual movement of the eighteenth century called the Enlightenment was expected to put an end to self-incurred subordination and to replace it with an understanding of the universe, society, and the individual based on reason and empirical research. This was certainly the hope of its most famous advocate Immanuel Kant (1724–1804). The writings of Karl Marx (1818–1883) and Sigmund Freud (1856–1939), among others, as well as the events associated with the Industrial Revolution in the nineteenth century and the Great War (1914–1918) in the twentieth century began to cast a dark shadow over the efficacy of this intellectual movement. It was in this context that religious fundamentalism began to emerge, at least in North America, between 1909 and 1915. Very briefly, what religious fundamentalism represents is a strict adherence to the social and moral code of revealed religion—as distinct from natural religion which is based on rational proofs—and a belief in the rewards for a life lived in faith as grounded in sacred and infallible texts such as the Koran, the New Testament, and the Torah.

It is in response to a growing religious fundamentalism in the United States of America that the well-known and fondly remembered preacher Harry Emerson Fosdick (1878–1969) delivers his famous sermon "Shall the Fundamentalists Win?" on 21 May 1922 at the First Presbyterian Church, New York City. Fosdick takes issue with the importance for the Christian church of such beliefs as the virgin birth, the inerrancy of scripture, and the Second Coming. Indeed, he rejects a literal reading of the scriptures and sees in them a source of spiritual inspiration that rests, at times, on something more akin to an allegorical interpretation of the revealed word of God.

In epic fashion, Fosdick marks the difference between fundamentalist and liberal Christians and affirms his support for the latter, and, in doing so, makes the case for tolerance and Christian liberty as well as for a re-orientation of Christian thinking toward the main issues of modern Christianity such as law, justice, mercy, and faith.

In a more contemporary setting than that addressed by Fosdick, Kevin Phillips (1940–) excoriates Christian fundamentalism and its influence on politics in the United States. Phillips, writer of *American Dynasty* (2004) and *Bad Money* (2008), speaks of American disenlightenment and attributes it to the influence of the religious right in that country, especially after the events of 9/11 in which the World Trade Center of New York and the Pentagon were attacked by Al Qaeda. Given his Republican roots, Phillips adopts a surprising position that runs counter to the prevailing Christian fundamentalism typically found under the presidency of George W. Bush (2001–2009). Rather than venerate theological correctness (which he abbreviates TC), Phillips, in sobering language, traces a causal connection between religious fundamentalism and the decline of empires in the past. Among those empires he lists Rome, Hapsburg Spain, the Dutch Republic, and Britain. He expresses his concern that the United States risks decline in a similar fashion if it marches on the same road as these empires, a road that includes widespread concern over cultural and economic decay, growing religious fervour, the eclipse of reason by faith, millennial expectations, and military overreach. Small wonder that Phillips denounces the "emergence of the Republican party as a powerful vehicle for religiosity"! It is difficult not to find in his words more than a little food for thought.

While Hasan al-Banna (1906–1949) is the founder of the Muslim Brotherhood, a fundamentalist Islamic group, Sayyid Qutb (1906–1966) is the Islamic leader who advances al-Banna's ideas in more recent times. It is Qutb who, with resolution, draws a sharp distinction between Islamic and permissive Western societies, such as those that exist in the United States and Europe. According to Qutb, the whole world is in a state of "convulsion" and in search of new foundations that will enable it to address the hunger, destitution, and misery of the whole globe. Islam, for Qutb, is this foundation, but it will only be able to provide the Islamic order to life if Muslims redouble their efforts to confront the hostility of the Western world to Islam. This hostility is found, he believes, in two facts: first, the evil created by contemporary crusaders in both a military and cultural direction; and second, the imperialism the West exerts over the Islamic spirit. Qutb makes it clear that religion is a "spiritual" and "organizational" force and one that can be renewed in Islam against crusader imperialists whether they be capitalists, communists, or Zionists—those who favour a secular Israel in the Middle East. Qutb's antipathy to these three groups is further refined by other comments he makes, especially when generalizing about Jews and not just Zionist Jews. There he says, uncompromisingly, that Jews have confronted Islam with enmity, more so than the polytheists, and attributes atheistic materialism to a Jew (Marx), animalistic sexuality to a Jew (Freud), and the destruction of the family to a Jew (Durkheim). For Qutb, the Muslim community will meet hard times, but with a return to the foundational principles it will prevail and "survive intact until the End of Days."

In a scholarly publication, the anthropologist and sociologist Michael Feige (1957–) attempts in modern dress to delineate the "meaning of the presence of others on the Holy Land" as seen through the eyes of those adhering to Zionism and those adhering to Gush Emunim—that is, as seen through the eyes of those adhering to a belief in a secular Israel and those adhering to a belief in a fundamentalist religious Israel. "Secular" in this context means those who base their belief on reason, while "fundamentalist religious" means those who base their belief on faith alone. Furthermore, the "other" in this context means "Palestinians," and Feige carefully examines similarities and differences in the beliefs that Zionists and Gush Emunim have of Palestinians. Both share the worldview that they, as Jews, came to Israel as an "empty land," or more exactly "a land whose residents had no political rights," but they disagree on other points, including the relevance of the religious-messianic world of Gush Emunim. Feige also considers the Gush Emunim view of Palestinian Arabs, not simply as "other" but as "primitive" and "partners in the redemption process"—but only so long as they do not demand national rights and do not object to the "Judaization of the entire land." Finally, Feige describes the Gush Emunim view of Palestinian Arabs as "temporary sojourners" and accordingly "an integral part of the Arab people and not a nation in their own right." In forthright fashion, he makes clear that the settlers of Gush Emunim "stress that the conflict [between settlers and Palestinian Arabs] is a perennial one based on absolute religious values that preclude any possibility of compromise." What emerges from Feige's discussion in the minds of his readers is the intractable nature of the Middle East conflict between Gush Emunim—as a Jewish fundamentalist movement—and Palestinian Arabs in search of a state they can call their own.

In his work *Jewish Fundamentalism and the Temple Mount*, Motti Inbari (1970–), among other things, does a commendable job of tracing the rise of the Gush Emunim to Rabbi Avraham Yitzhak Hacohen Kook (1865–1935) and his son Rabbi Zvi Yehuda Hacohen Kook (1891–1982). Inbari makes clear that the latter Kook and his followers were inspired by the "new reality" created by the Six Day War (1967), a war won by Israel against the forces of Egypt, Syria, Jordan, and Iraq which helped "propagate the perception" that the victory of Israel was a sign of God's will to redeem his people. In addition, Inbari explains that Yehuda Kook stood at odds with the Chief Rabbi of the Israel Defense Forces, Shlomo Goren, by opposing the latter's endorsement of the idea of Jews entering the Temple Mount in order to pray.

The religious fundamentalism of the twenty-first century severely challenges the spirit of the Enlightenment articulated by Immanuel Kant in the eighteenth century. Indeed, when religious fundamentalism is combined with the ideology of postmodernism—a school of thought that rejects the values of truth, objectivity, values, facts, and meaning and replaces them with subjectivism and consensus—the Kantian spirit of shaking off self-incurred tutelage is under great threat. Whether reason can prevail not only against unmitigated relativism as found in postmodernism but also against religious fundamentalism is something this century awaits. At this stage, one can only say that Fosdick's query "Shall the Fundamentalists win?" is not rhetorical.

CHAPTER 55

Shall the Fundamentalists Win?

Harry Emerson Fosdick

This morning we are to think of the Fundamentalist controversy which threatens to divide the American churches, as though already they were not sufficiently split and riven.

[...]

There is nothing new about the situation. It has happened again and again in history, as, for example, when the stationary earth suddenly began to move and the universe that had been centred in this planet was centred in the sun around which the planets whirled. Whenever such a situation has arisen, there has been only one way out: the new knowledge and the old faith had to be blended in a new combination. Now, the people in this generation who are trying to do this are the liberals, and the Fundamentalists are out on a campaign to shut against them the doors of the Christian fellowship. Shall they be allowed to succeed?

It is interesting to note where the Fundamentalists are driving in their stakes to mark out the deadline of doctrine around the church, across which no one is to pass except on terms of agreement. They insist that we must all believe in the historicity of certain special miracles, pre-eminently the virgin birth of our Lord; that we must believe in a special theory of inspiration—that the original documents of the Scripture, which of course we no longer possess, were inerrantly dictated to men a good deal as a man might dictate to a stenographer; that we must believe in a special theory of the atonement—that the blood of our Lord, shed in a substitutionary death, placates an alienated Deity and makes possible welcome for the returning sinner; and that we must believe in the

second coming of our Lord upon the clouds of heaven to set up a millennium here, as the only way in which God can bring history to a worthy dénouement. Such are some of the stakes which are being driven, to mark a deadline of doctrine around the church.

If a man is a genuine liberal, his primary protest is not against holding these opinions, although he may well protest against their being considered the fundamentals of Christianity. This is a free country and anybody has a right to hold these opinions or any others, if he is sincerely convinced of them. The question is: has anybody a right to deny the Christian name to those who differ with him on such points and to shut against them the doors of the Christian fellowship? The Fundamentalists say that this must be done. In this country and on the foreign field they are trying to do it. They have actually endeavoured to put on the statute books of a whole state binding laws against teaching modern biology. If they had their way, within the church, they would set up in Protestantism a doctrinal tribunal more rigid than the Pope's. In such an hour, delicate and dangerous, when feelings are bound to run high, I plead this morning the cause of magnanimity and liberality and tolerance of spirit. I would, if I could reach their ears, say to the Fundamentalists about the liberals what Gamaliel said to the Jews, "Refrain from these men, and let them alone: for if this counsel or this work be of men, it will be overthrown: but if it is of God ye will not be able to overthrow them; lest haply ye be found even to be fighting against God."

That we may be entirely candid and concrete and may not lose ourselves in any fog of generalities, let us this morning take two or three of these Fundamentalist items and see with reference to them what the situation is in the Christian churches. Too often we preachers have failed to talk frankly enough about the differences of opinion which exist among evangelical Christians, although everybody knows that they are there. Let us face this morning some of the differences of opinion with which somehow we must deal.

We may well begin with the vexed and mooted question of the virgin birth of our Lord. I know people in the Christian churches, ministers, missionaries, laymen, devoted lovers of the Lord and servants of the Gospel, who, alike as they are in their personal devotion to the Master, hold quite different points of view about a matter like the virgin birth. Here, for example, is one point of view: that the virgin birth is to be accepted as historical fact; it actually happened; there was no other way for a personality like the Master to come into this world except by a special biological miracle. That is one point of view, and many are the gracious and beautiful souls who hold it. But, side by side with them in the evangelical churches is a group of equally loyal and reverent people who would say that the virgin birth is not to be accepted as an historic fact. To believe in virgin birth as an explanation of great personality is one of the familiar ways in which the ancient world was accustomed to account for unusual superiority. Many people suppose that only once in history do we run across a record of supernatural birth. Upon the contrary, stories of miraculous generation are among the commonest traditions of antiquity. Especially is this true about the founders of great religions. According to the records of their faiths, Buddha and Zoroaster and Lao-Tsze and Mahavira were all supernaturally born. Moses, Confucius, and Mohammed are the only great founders of religions in history to whom miraculous birth is not attributed. That is to say, when a personality arose so high that men adored him, the ancient world attributed his superiority to some special divine influence in his generation, and they commonly phrased their faith in terms of miraculous birth. So Pythagoras was called virgin born, and Plato, and Augustus Caesar, and many more. Knowing this, there are within the evangelical churches large groups of people whose opinion about our Lord's coming would run as follows: those first disciples adored Jesus—as we do; when they thought about his coming they were sure that he came specially from God—as we are; this adoration and conviction they associated with God's special influence and intention in his birth—as we do; but they phrased it in terms of a biological miracle that our modern minds cannot use. So far from thinking that they have given up anything vital in the New Testament's attitude toward Jesus, these Christians remember that the two men who contributed most to the church's thought of the divine meaning of the Christ were Paul and John, who never even distantly allude to the virgin birth.

Here in the Christian churches are these two groups of people and the question which the Fundamentalists raise is this: shall one of them throw the other out? Has intolerance any contribution to make to this situation? Will it persuade anybody of anything? Is not the Christian church large enough to hold within her hospitable fellowship people who differ on points like this and agree to differ until the fuller truth be manifested? The Fundamentalists say not. They say that the liberals must go. Well, if the Fundamentalists should succeed, then out of the Christian church would go some of the best Christian life and consecration of this generation—multitudes of men and women, devout and reverent Christians, who need the church and whom the church needs.

Consider another matter on which there is a sincere difference of opinion between evangelical Christians: the inspiration of the Bible. One point of view is that the original documents of the Scripture were inerrantly dictated by God to men. Whether we deal with the story of creation or the list of the dukes of Edom or the narratives of Solomon's reign or the Sermon on the Mount or the thirteenth chapter of First Corinthians, they all came in the same way and they all came as no other book ever came. They were inerrantly dictated; everything there—scientific opinions, medical theories, historical judgments, as well as spiritual insight—is infallible. That is one idea of the Bible's inspiration. But side by side with those who hold it, lovers of the Book as much as they, are multitudes of people who never think about the Bible so. Indeed, that static and mechanical theory of inspiration seems to them a positive peril to the spiritual life. The Koran similarly has been regarded by Mohammedans as having been infallibly written in heaven before it came to earth. But the Koran enshrines the theological and ethical ideas of Arabia at the time when it was written. God an Oriental monarch, fatalistic submission to his will as man's chief duty, the use of force on unbelievers, polygamy, slavery—they are all in the Koran. The Koran was ahead of the day when it was written, but, petrified by an artificial idea of inspiration, it has become a millstone about the neck of Mohammedanism. When one turns from the Koran to the Bible, he finds this interesting situation. All of these ideas, which we dislike in the Koran, are somewhere in the Bible. Conceptions from which we now send missionaries to convert Mohammedans are to be found in the Book. There one can find God thought of as an Oriental monarch; there, too, are patriarchal polygamy, and slave systems, and the use of force on unbelievers. Only in the Bible these elements are not final; they are always being superseded; revelation is progressive.

The thought of God moves out from Oriental kingship to compassionate fatherhood; treatment of unbelievers moves out from the use of force to the appeals of love; polygamy gives way to monogamy; slavery, never explicitly condemned before the New Testament closes, is nevertheless being undermined by ideas that in the end, like dynamite, will blast its foundations to pieces. Repeatedly one runs on verses like this: "It was said to them of old time . . . but I say unto you"; "God, having of old time spoken unto the fathers in the prophets by divers portions and in divers manners, hath at the end of these days spoken unto us in his Son"; "The times of ignorance therefore God overlooked; but now he commandeth men that they should all everywhere repent"; and over the doorway of the New Testament into the Christian world stand the words of Jesus: "When he, the Spirit of truth is come, he shall guide you into all the truth." That is to say, finality in the Koran is behind; finality in the Bible is ahead. We have not reached it. We cannot yet compass all of it. God is leading us out toward it. There are multitudes of Christians, then, who think, and rejoice as they think, of the Bible as the record of the progressive unfolding of the character of God to his people from early primitive days until the great unveiling in Christ; to them the Book is more inspired and more inspiring than ever it was before; and to go back to it mechanical and static theory of inspiration would mean to them the loss of some of the most vital elements in their spiritual experience and in their appreciation of the Book.

Here in the Christian church today are these two groups, and the question which the Fundamentalists have raised is this: shall one of them drive the other out? Do we think the cause of Jesus Christ will be furthered by that? If he should walk through the ranks of this congregation this morning, can we imagine him claiming as his own those who hold one idea of inspiration and sending from him into outer darkness those who hold another? You cannot fit the Lord Christ into that Fundamentalist mould. The church would better judge his judgment. For in the Middle West the Fundamentalists have had their way in some communities and a Christian minister tells us the consequence. He says that the educated people are looking for their religion outside the churches.

Consider another matter upon which there is a serious and sincere difference of opinion between evangelical Christians: the second coming of our Lord. The second coming was the early Christian phrasing of hope. No one in the ancient world had ever thought, as we do, of development, progress, gradual change, as God's way of working out his will in human life and institutions. They thought of human history as a series of ages succeeding one another with abrupt suddenness. The Graeco-Roman world gave the names of metals to the ages—gold, silver, bronze, iron. The Hebrews had their ages too—the original Paradise in which man began, the cursed world in which man now lives, the blessed Messianic Kingdom some day suddenly to appear on the clouds of heaven. It was the Hebrew way of expressing hope for the victory of God and righteousness. When the Christians came they took over that phrasing of expectancy and the New Testament is aglow with it. The preaching of the apostles thrills with the glad announcement, "Christ is coming!"

In the evangelical churches today there are differing views of this matter. One view is that Christ is literally coming, externally on the clouds of heaven, to set up his kingdom here. I never heard that teaching in my youth at all. It has always had a new resurrection when desperate circumstances came and man's only hope seemed to lie in divine intervention. It is not strange, then, that during these chaotic, catastrophic years there has been a fresh rebirth of this old phrasing of expectancy. "Christ is coming!" seems to many Christians the central

message of the Gospel. In the strength of it some of them are doing great service for the world. But unhappily, many so overemphasize it that they outdo anything the ancient Hebrews or the ancient Christians ever did. They sit still and do nothing and expect the world to grow worse and worse until he comes.

Side by side with these to whom the second coming is a literal expectation, another group exists in the evangelical churches. They, too, say, "Christ is coming!" They say it with all their hearts; but they are not thinking of an external arrival on the clouds. They have assimilated as part of the divine revelation the exhilarating insight which these recent generations have given to us, that development is God's way of working out his will. They see that the most desirable elements in human life have come through the method of development. Man's music has developed from the rhythmic noise of beaten sticks until we have in melody and harmony possibilities once undreamed. Man's painting has developed from the crude outlines of the cavemen until in line and colour we have achieved unforeseen results and possess latent beauties yet unfolded. Man's architecture has developed from the crude huts of primitive men until our cathedrals and business buildings reveal alike an incalculable advance and an unimaginable future. Development does seem to be the way in which God works. And these Christians, when they say that Christ is coming, mean that, slowly it may be, but surely, his will and principles will be worked out by God's grace in human life and institutions, until "he shall see of the travail of his soul and shall be satisfied."

These two groups exist in the Christian churches and the question raised by the Fundamentalists is: shall one of them drive the other out? Will that get us anywhere? Multitudes of young men and women at this season of the year are graduating from our schools of learning, thousands of them Christians who may make us older ones ashamed by the sincerity of their devotion to God's will on earth. They are not thinking in ancient terms that leave ideas of progress out. They cannot think in those terms. There could be no greater tragedy than that the Fundamentalists should shut the door of the Christian fellowship against such.

I do not believe for one moment that the Fundamentalists are going to succeed. Nobody's intolerance can contribute anything to the solution of the situation which we have described. If, then, the Fundamentalists have no solution of the problem, where may we expect to find it? In two concluding comments let us consider our reply to that inquiry.

The first element that is necessary is a spirit of tolerance and Christian liberty. When will the world learn that intolerance solves no problems? This is not a lesson which the Fundamentalists alone need to learn; the liberals also need to learn it. Speaking, as I do, from the viewpoint of liberal opinions, let me say that if some young, fresh mind here this morning is holding new ideas, has fought his way through, it may be by intellectual and spiritual struggle, to novel positions, and is tempted to be intolerant about old opinions, offensively to condescend to those who hold them and to be harsh in judgment on them, he may well remember that people who held those old opinions have given the world some of the noblest character and the most rememberable service that it ever has been blessed with, and that we of the younger generation will prove our case best, not by controversial intolerance, but by producing, with our new opinions, something of the depth and strength, nobility and beauty of character that in other times were associated with other thoughts. It was a wise liberal, the most adventurous man of his day—Paul the Apostle—who said, "Knowledge puffeth up, but love buildeth up."

Nevertheless, it is true that just now the Fundamentalists are giving us one of the worst exhibitions of bitter intolerance that the churches of this country have ever seen. As one watches them and listens to them, he remembers the remark of General Armstrong of Hampton Institute: "Cantankerousness is worse than heterodoxy." There are many opinions in the field of modern controversy concerning which I am not sure whether they are right or wrong, but there is one thing I am sure of: courtesy and kindliness and tolerance and humility and fairness are right. Opinions may be mistaken; love never is.

As I plead thus for an intellectually hospitable, tolerant, liberty-loving church, I am of course thinking primarily about this new generation. We have boys and girls growing up in our homes and schools, and because we love them we may well wonder about the church which will be waiting to receive them. Now, the worst kind of church that can possibly be offered to the allegiance of the new generation is an intolerant church. Ministers often bewail the fact that young people turn from religion to science for the regulative ideas of their lives. But this is easily explicable. Science treats a young man's mind as though it were really important. A scientist says to a young man: "Here is the universe challenging our investigation. Here are the truths which we have seen, so far. Come, study with us! See what we already have seen and then look further to see more, for science is an intellectual adventure for the truth." Can you imagine any man who is worthwhile turning from that call to the church, if the church seems to him to say, "Come, and we will feed you opinions from a spoon. No thinking is allowed here except such as brings you to certain specified, predetermined conclusions. These prescribed opinions we will give you in advance of your thinking; now think, but only so as to reach these results." My friends, nothing in all the world is so much worth thinking of as God, Christ, the Bible, sin and salvation, the divine purposes for humankind, life everlasting. But you cannot challenge the dedicated thinking of this generation to these sublime themes upon any such terms as are laid down by an intolerant church.

The second element which is needed if we are to reach a happy solution of this problem is a clear insight into the main issues of modern Christianity and a sense of penitent shame that the Christian church should be quarreling over little matters when the world is dying of great needs. If, during the war, when the nations were wrestling upon the very brink of hell and at times all seemed lost, you chanced to hear two men in an altercation about some minor matter of sectarian denominationalism, could you restrain your indignation? You said, "What can you do with folks like this who, in the face of colossal issues, play with the tiddledywinks and peccadillos of religion?" So, now, when from the terrific questions of this generation one is called away by the noise of this Fundamentalist controversy, he thinks it almost unforgivable that men should tithe mint and anise and cumin, and quarrel over them, when the world is perishing for the lack of the weightier matters of the law, justice, and mercy, and faith. These last weeks, in the minister's confessional, I have heard stories from the depths of human lives where men and women were wrestling with the elemental problems of misery and sin—stories that put upon a man's heart a burden of vicarious sorrow, even though he does but listen to them. Here was real human need crying out after the living God revealed in Christ. Consider all the multitudes of men who so need God, and then think of Christian churches making of themselves a cockpit of controversy when there is not a single thing at stake in the controversy on which depends the salvation of human souls. That is the trouble with this whole

business. So much of it does not matter! And there is one thing that does matter—more than anything else in all the world—that men in their personal lives and in their social relationships should know Jesus Christ.

Just a week ago I received a letter from a friend in Asia Minor. He says that they are killing the Armenians yet; that the Turkish deportations still are going on; that lately they crowded Christian men, women, and children into a conventicle of worship and burned them together in the house where they had prayed to their Father and to ours. During the war, when it was good propaganda to stir up our bitter hatred against the enemy we heard of such atrocities, but not now! Two weeks ago, Great Britain, shocked and stirred by what is going on in Armenia, did ask the Government of the United States to join her in investigating the atrocities and trying to help. Our Government said that it was not any of our business at all. The present world situation smells to heaven! And now, in the presence of colossal problems, which must be solved in Christ's name and for Christ's sake, the Fundamentalists propose to drive out from the Christian churches all the consecrated souls who do not agree with their theory of inspiration. What immeasurable folly!

Well, they are not going to do it; certainly not in this vicinity. I do not even know in this congregation whether anybody has been tempted to be a Fundamentalist. Never in this church have I caught one accent of intolerance. God keep us always so and ever increasing areas of the Christian fellowship: intellectually hospitable, open-minded, liberty-loving, fair, tolerant, not with the tolerance of indifference as though we did not care about the faith, but because always our major emphasis is upon the weightier matters of the law.

CHAPTER 56

Church, State, and National Decline

Kevin Phillips

Religious, secular, or somewhere in between, most Americans of early 2000s shared some concern about a broad range of threats to the nation's future: immorality, decadence, crime, terrorism, private and public corruption, mon-eyed politics, greed and luxury, and the strati-fication of wealth and power. But how they defined them or what they chose to emphasize varied greatly.

Conservatives saw a threat that was predom-inantly religious and moral, and the gloomy, neo-Calvinist preoccupation of important el-ements of the religious right emerged all too clearly in their leaders' immediate, unthinking interpretation of the meaning of September 11. Jerry Falwell and Pat Robertson agreed that the United States had been attacked because of God's displeasure with secular immorality. Their comments, although quickly retracted, painted a picture of the stern Old Testament God hurling thunderbolts and death at his way-ward chosen people.

Secular Americans and those who only oc-casionally attended religious services had a somewhat different point of view. Their fears had more to do with economics, society, and the successes or failures of US foreign policy. Not a few worried about the excesses of organized re-ligion and the influence of the Christian right. Between 2001 and 2005, after the Terri Schiavo episode, national polls showed such concern doubling. Among secular voters a startling two-thirds expressed antipathy to evangelicals.[1] To many of the born-again, "secular"—as in secular humanist—was an expletive to be cul-turally deleted.

Controversy also began to collect around the fundamentalist pulpiteers' prophecies of rapture, end times, and Armageddon. By 2005 a counterattack was apparent in mainline reli-gious responses, Catholic and Protestant alike. This was exemplified by publications such as *The Rapture Exposed*, Lutheran theologian Barbara Rossing's contention that rapture theology was little better than a racket, and comparable works on the Catholic side, replete with charges that what was really left behind in Tim LaHaye's series was biblical truth.[2] Polls are few, but those taken showed that majorities of Catholics, Lutherans, Episcopalians, Congregationalists, Presbyterians, and Methodists disbelieved in the event so central to the *Left Behind* books and fundamentalist jeremiads.[3]

The historical dilemma is that while reli-gion has generally served humankind well, cer-tainly in framing successful societies around the world, there have been conspicuous ex-ceptions—bloody religious wars, malevolent crusades, and false prophecies. Indeed, the precedents of past leading world economic powers show that blind faith and religious ex-cesses—the rapture seems to be both—have of-ten contributed to national decline, sometimes even being in its forefront.

As with Charles Kimball's five criteria for the mutation of religion, I believe that a yard-stick can be set up for Rome, Hapsburg Spain, the Dutch Republic, Britain, and the United States that isolates and profiles five critical symptoms of decline in the past leading world economic powers. Just as Kimball's five criteria are broadly framed and need not all be present simultaneously—one or two, he says, can be enough to suggest trouble—likewise for these five symptoms of a power already at its peak and starting to decline. These broad categories are mine, in no firm order and based on research for several of my books over two decades. However, the relevant history has many sources and confirmations.

One symptom is widespread public concern over cultural and economic decay, with its many corollaries. The second is a growing religious fervour, church–state relationship, or crusading insistence. Next comes a rising commitment to faith as opposed to reason and a corollary downplaying of science. Fourth, we often find a considerable popular anticipation of a millennial timeframe: an epochal battle, emergence of the antichrist, or belief in an imminent second coming or Armageddon. Last, empires are prone to a hubris-driven national strategic and military overreach, often pursuing abstract international missions that the nation can no longer afford, economically or politically.

I have not included high debt levels in this set of symptoms, partly because it seems a familiar facet of great-power economic aging [. . .]. In its most deadly form, debt accompanies corrupt politics, hubris, and international overreach and then—as we shall see—becomes crippling in its own right.

[. . .]

A Twenty-First-Century American Disenlightenment?

[. . .]

The essential political preconditions fell into place in the late 1980s and 1990s with the emergence of the Republican party as a powerful vehicle for religiosity and church influence, while state Republican parties, most conspicuously in the South and Southwest, endorsed so-called Christian-nation party platforms.[4]

These unusual platforms, as yet nationally uncatalogued, set out in varying degrees the radical political theology of the Christian Reconstruction movement, the tenets of which range from using the Bible as a basis for domestic law to emphasizing religious schools and women's subordination to men. The 2004 platform of the Texas Republican party is a case in point. It reaffirms the status of the United States as "a Christian nation," regrets "the myth of the separation of church and state," calls for abstinence instead of sex education, and broadly mirrors the reconstructionist demand for the abolition of a large group of federal agencies and departments, including the Energy Department and the Environmental Protection Agency.[5]

George W. Bush's election to the presidency and his unusual choice of former Missouri senator John Ashcroft to head the Justice Department were true milestones. We have already seen Bush's involvement in intensifying the religiosity of the Republican party and in linking White House policy statements to Scripture and prophecy. When Ashcroft, a long-time favourite of the religious right, had explored seeking the presidency in 1997 and 1998, most of his financial support came from Christian evangelicals such as Pat Robertson.[6] Conservatives subsequently mobilized in favour of his selection as attorney general. Son and grandson of Pentecostal preachers, Ashcroft, more than any previous attorney general, viewed law and politics through a religious lens. He made no effort to shade this connection. In Ashcroft's memoirs, explained one critic, "he describes each of his many electoral defeats as a crucifixion and every important political victory as a resurrection, and recounts scenes in which he had friends and family anoint him with oil in the manner 'of the ancient kings of Israel' with each new public office."[7] While in the Senate, Ashcroft enjoyed a 100 per cent approval rating from both the Christian Coalition and the National Right to Life Committee, pleasing the latter by sponsoring a constitutional amendment that extended protection to the "unborn" at "every stage of their biological development, including fertilization," a breadth that might have criminalized birth control.[8] As attorney general, the Missourian was accused of dragging his heels on the prosecution of abortion-clinic bombers.[9]

Earlier in his political career, Ashcroft had decried the barrier between church and state as "a wall of religious oppression." Midway through the first Bush administration Americans United for Separation of Church and State, a liberal group, condemned his actions as attorney general: "Whenever cases deal with government funding or promotion of religion," said its spokesperson, "the Justice Department under Ashcroft is always on the side of bringing church and state together."[10] Perhaps, but it is also fair to say that Bush's religious constituencies thrill to criticisms of such hostile groups.

During Ashcroft's time in the Senate, he had also authored successful legislation to let states turn over welfare and other social services to religious providers, a program that George W. Bush embraced as governor of Texas and which helped to inspire his 2001 proposal for federal faith-based initiatives.[11] Where possible, religious agencies would take over the provision of federal social services. When Bush's legislation stalled in the Senate, he used a federal executive order to establish faith-based-initiative units in six departments (Justice, Education, Health and Human Services, Housing and Urban Development, Labor, and Agriculture), as well as in the Agency for International Development. At the General Services Administration, the office-maintenance arm of the federal government, Bush appointees held lunch-hour revival meetings in the front hall, making it seem, in the words of *The Washington Post*, "more like the foyer of a Pentecostal storefront church."[12]

The House and Senate lobbies had some of that same look. House Majority Leader Tom DeLay and Oklahoma senator James Inhofe, chairman of the Senate Committee on Environment and Public Works, were two who insisted that all the answers were in the Bible, and two-thirds of Republican House and Senate members enjoyed 80 per cent or better voting ratings from groups such as the Christian Coalition, the Traditional Values Coalition, the National Right to Life Committee, and the Family Research Council.[13] Dozens of legislators anxious to be theologically correct competed to maintain perfect ratings.

As for the interaction of church and state in the White House, characterizations peculiar to George W. Bush—his salute from religious-right leaders in 2001 as the national head of their movement and his seeming self-image as someone who spoke for God—added to the perception of a unique presidency. That a chief executive could be described in these ways without sparking a heated national debate bespoke the public's willingness to accept religion and authority in the aftermath of September 11.

The way in which Bush White House policies were the application of hard-line, preformed doctrine rather than the results of evidence seeking explained by two departing and disillusioned officials. Former treasury secretary Paul O'Neill recalled his dismay that ideology dwarfed real-world analysis: "Ideology is a lot easier, because you don't have to anything or search for anything. You already know the answer to everything. It's not penetrable by facts."[14] John DiIulio, the first head of the White House Office of Faith-Based and Community Initiatives, ruefully described "the complete lack of a policy apparatus" or "meaningful, substantive policy discussions" because everything was political, with much of the policy coming from right-wing think tanks and the Christian right.[15]

The president was most comfortable with black-and-white, good-versus-evil portraiture, acknowledging that nuance was not in his playbook.[16] Anti-intellectualism, which profited George Wallace so much in his 1968 presidential campaign, became a Bush prop, too, as in his mockery of high grades during a visit to Yale, his alma mater, to receive an honorary degree in 2002.[17] An unidentified senior administration official dismissed the intellectual elites, "what we call the reality-based community . . . [people] who believe that solutions emerge from your judicious study of discernible reality."[18] In the Oval Office, instinct, prayer, and faith took precedence.

Several cartoonists went so far as to draw Bush in robes like those worn by the Iranian ayatollahs, and [. . .] portraits of fundamentalist movements around the world displayed considerable resemblance to those of the George W. Bush administration. Nor was that behaviour governed simply by deep commitment to religion and religiosity. Esther Kaplan, in her book *With God on Their Side*, identified a much narrower worldview:

> He really isn't interested in faith in general. The president didn't flick an eyelash when the National Council of Churches and the US Council of Catholic Bishops opposed his war on Iraq. He didn't listen when the Council on American-Islamic Relations filed a suit challenging the constitutionality of the Patriot Act. When the Union for Reformed Judaism announced that an antigay marriage amendment would "defile the constitution," the president took no notice. Nor did Bush respond to a joint call, signed by 50 prominent Christian leaders, including Richard Cizik of the National Association of Evangelicals and Jim Wallis of Call to Renewal, for policies that promote "quality health care, decent housing and a living income for the poor." His is not

an embrace of spirituality or ethics broadly speaking, or of faith as an important voice among many in the national debate. It is, instead, an embrace of right-wing Christian fundamentalism.[19]

Even more to the point, many of Bush's views exuded a theological correctness that was almost a mirror image of the political correctness displayed by secular liberals in discussing minority groups, women's rights, and environmental sanctity. By 2005 words such as "theocrat" and "theocon" were gaining traction in political journalism, and with cause. As religious conservatives became the dominant Republican constituency in the 1990s, their tune became the essential party dance music. Swings to the right and then bows to various church-related partners took over conservative choreography.

In Republican politics theological correctness—call it TC—became a policy-shaping force in determining Middle Eastern geopolitics, combating global AIDS, defining the legal rights of fetuses, pretending that oil was not a cause for the invasion of Iraq, and explaining geological controversies in language compatible with the Book of Genesis. As church congregations became GOP auxiliaries and a host of religious-right organizations provided essential scorecards of senators and congressmen up for re-election, the nature of constituency pressure changed from share our values to support our doctrine—or else.

A few Republican centrists became openly critical of this juggernaut. Arizona senator John McCain had criticized the Jerry Falwells, Pat Robertsons, and Bob Joneses during his confrontation with Bush in the 2000 Republican presidential primaries. In 2004 Rhode Island senator Lincoln Chafee suggested that Bush's "I carry the word of God" posture warranted voter attention. In 2005 Connecticut GOP congressman Christopher Shays, as we have seen, sparked attention simply by describing the Republican party as a "theocracy."[20]

As public skepticism grew, even one-third of self-identified Republicans found themselves critical when poll takers queried whether the religious right had too much or too little influence in Washington.[21] But they were too late. Theology had moved from church pulpits into the decision-making circles of the nation's capital.

Notes

1. Louise Bolce and Gerald De Maio, "Our Secularist Democratic Party," *The Public Interest*, No. 149, Fall 2002, pp. 3–20, see p. 4.

2. Barbara Rossing, *The Rapture Exposed: The Message of Hope in the Book of Revelations* (Boulder, CO: Westview Press, 2004).

3. James L. Guth and John C. Green, eds., *The Bible and the Ballot Box: Religion and Politics in the 1988 Election* (Boulder, CO: Westview Press, 1991).

4. Between the "Christian nation" platform adopted by the Texas Republican party in 2004 and the kindred action by the Arizona GOP in 1988, dozens of other related pronouncements have been made by state parties, mostly in the South and West. The Oklahoma GOP, for one, came out against the separation of church and state. Amazingly, no full compilation exists.

5. The details of the 2004 Texas GOP platform can be perused at www.theocracywatch.com.

6. Esther Kaplan, *With God on Their Side: How Christian Fundamentalists Trampled Science, Policy, and Democracy in George W. Bush's Whitehouse* (New York, NY: The New Press, 2004), p.134.

7. Ibid., p. 34.

8. Ibid., p. 134.

9. Ibid., pp. 135–36.

10. Ibid., pp. 34–35.

11. Ibid., p. 39.

12. Hamil R. Harris, "Putting Worship into Their Workdays," *The Washington Post*, 19 November 2001.

13. Indeed, many of the GOP's House and Senate leaders earned 100 per cent ratings.

14. Ron Suskind, *The Price of Loyalty* (New York: Simon & Schuster, 2004), p. 292.

15. www.raticol.org/ratville/CAH/DiIulio.html.

16. "Joe, I don't do nuance." George W. Bush to Senator Joseph Biden as quoted in *Time*, 15 February 2004.

17. "Bush Mixes Humor with Humility in Commencement Talk," *Yale Daily News*, 22 May 2001.

18. Ron Suskind, "Without a Doubt," *The New York Times Magazine*, 17 October 2004.

19. Kaplan, *With God on Their Side*, p. 4.

20. Shays was quoted in *The New York Times* of March 23. 2005; Chafee in Ron Suskind, "Without a Doubt."

21. Such results came in various flavours, but one of the most revealing followed the Schiavo controversy, when an NBC/*Wall Street Journal* poll reported one-third of Republicans saying that Congress should prevent Bush and party leaders from "going too far in pushing their agenda." John Harwood, "Republicans Splinter on Bush Agenda," *The Wall Street Journal*, 7 April 2005.

CHAPTER 57

The Present and Future of Islam

Sayyid Qutb

64. Some may be surprised that the spirit of fanaticism against Islam remains so strong in the feelings of Europe after it rejected Christianity and the shouts of the pilgrims and the priests no longer fill its ears as they did during the days of the Crusades, but this surprise vanishes when we consider two actual facts:

65. *The first fact:* "The evil stirred up by the crusaders was not limited to the clash of arms but was first and foremost a cultural evil. The poisoning of the European mind against Islam arose from the distorted version of the teachings and ideals of Islam that the European leaders gave to the ignorant masses in the West. It was at that time that the ridiculous idea became established in European minds that Islam was a religion of sensualism and bestial violence, and that it held to formalistic rules but did not seek to cleanse or purify the heart. Having been established, this idea remained. It was also at this time that they insulted the Apostle Muhammad by calling him "my dog."[1]

66. "The seeds of hatred were sown . . . The enthusiasm of the ignorant crusaders had its sequels in many parts of Europe and encouraged the Christians of Spain to go to war to save their country from "the yoke of the heathens"! As for the destruction of Muslim Spain (al-Andalus) it took many centuries to be accomplished. But precisely because this fighting lasted so long, the anti-Islamic feeling in Europe begin to put down its roots and then became permanent. It completely eradicated the traces of the Islamic age in Spain after the most savage and brutal persecution the world had ever seen. Echoes of rejoicing reverberated

through Europe in the wake of this, though they knew that the result was the destruction of learning and culture and their replacement by medieval ignorance and crudeness.

67. "But before the echoes of these events had the chance to die away in Spain, there occurred a third event of great importance that further marred the relations between the Western world and Islam. That was the fall of Constantinople into the hands of the Turks. Europe saw the remnant of the old Greek and Roman splendor in Byzantium (Constantinople) and looked upon it as Europe's bulwark against the barbarians of Asia, and with the fall of Constantinople the gateway of Europe was thrown open to the Islamic flood. In the following war-torn centuries, hostility of Europe to Islam became a matter not only of cultural importance, but of political importance too, and this increased its intensity.

68. "In spite of all this, Europe profited considerably from this conflict. The 'Renaissance' or revival of the arts and sciences in Europe based on considerable borrowing from Islamic and particularly Arab sources was due mostly to the material contact between East and West. Europe profited from this more than the Islamic world did, but it did not recognize the favour by diminishing its hatred of Islam. On the contrary, that hatred grew with the progress of time and hardened into custom. It overshadowed the popular feeling whenever the word 'Muslim' was mentioned. It entered the realm of popular proverbs and until it took up its abode in the heart of every European, man or woman. Stranger than all this, it survived through all the

stages of cultural change. Then came the age of the Reformation when Europe split into sects and every sect was armed to the teeth against every other sect, but hostility to Islam was common to them all. After that there came a time when religious feeling in Europe began to vanish, but hostility to Islam continued. One of the most outstanding examples of this is the fact that the French philosopher and poet, Voltaire, who was one of the most vigorous enemies of Christianity and its church in the eighteenth century, was at the same time extreme in his hatred of Islam and the Apostle of Islam. After some decades there came a time when learned men in the West began to study foreign cultures and approach them with same degree of sympathy, but so far as Islam was concerned, the traditional scorn crept as an irrational partisanship into their scholarly investigations, and the gulf that history had dug between Europe and the Islamic world remained unbridged. Then contempt for Islam became a basic part of European thinking. The fact is that the first orientalists in modern times were Christian missionaries working in Islamic countries. The distorted picture which they drew from Islamic teachings and history was calculated to influence the Europeans' attitude toward the 'heathen.' But this mental twist has continued even though the orientalist sciences have freed themselves from missionary influence and no longer have the excuse that ignorant religious fanaticism misguides them. Thus the orientalist prejudice against Islam is an inherited instinct and a natural characteristic, based upon the effects created by the crusades with all their sequels on the minds of the early Europeans.

69. "Perhaps someone will ask: how does it happen that such an ancient revulsion as this—which was fundamentally religious and possible in its time because of the spiritual predominance of the Christian church—continues in Europe at a time when religious feeling is only a matter of the past?

70. "Entanglements such as these are by no means astonishing, for it is well known in psychology that a person can lose all the religious beliefs imparted to him in his childhood and yet particular superstitions—that were at formerly connected with those discarded beliefs—may remain in force, defying all rational analysis throughout the whole life of that person. Such is the case of the European attitude toward Islam. Although the religious feeling that was the cause of the revulsion toward Islam has in the meantime given way to a more materialistic outlook on life, the old revulsion itself has remained as a factor in the inward consciousness of European minds. Its degree of strength undoubtedly varies from one person to another, but there is no doubt of its existence. The spirit of the crusades—albeit in diminished form—still hangs over Europe and the attitude of its civilization toward Islam bears distinct traces of that die-hard ghost."[2]

71. *The Second Fact*: European and American Crusaderist[3] imperialism cannot leave out of its account the fact that the Islamic spirit is a bulwark resisting the spread of imperialism and it must destroy this bulwark or at least shake it. Thus, we must pay no attention to those who are gullible or mercenary and say that Europe does not care about religion and does not see it as a source of strength and fears from the Islamic world only its material strength. In reality, religion has a spiritual strength which must be taken into account in order to renew material strength. Furthermore, Islam in its essence is not like Christianity, for it commands the preparation of material forces and urges resistance and struggle, and warns the surrenderers and the weak-hearted of an evil outcome in this world and the next. "Make ready for them whatever force and strings of horses you can, to terrify thereby the enemy of God and your enemy"[4] "O believers, take not the unbelievers as friends instead of the believers."[5] "So let them fight in the way of God who sell the present life

for the world to come."[6] "Faint not, neither sorrow; you shall be the upper ones if you are believers. If a wound touches you, a like wound has touched the heathen."[7]

72. Religion is a spiritual and an organizational[8] force, and call for material strength. Religion is a resisting bulwark and a call for strong resistance. European and American[9] imperialism cannot avoid being hostile to this religion. The only thing is that the forms[10] of hostility change according to each nation's *(ummah)* style of imperialism and according to conditions and circumstances. France, for example, announces open and undisguised war in the whole Arab Maghrib against Islam under the name of the "Berber Decree"[11] or some other name, and its representatives in Damascus announce in the broad light of day that they are the descendants of the crusaders.[12] England acts more deviously and stealthily influences the teaching institutes in Egypt to create a general mentality that scorns the Islamic elements in life, indeed all the Eastern ones, and when it has created a generation of teachers with this mentality it sends them into the schools and the offices of the Ministry of Education to influence the mentalities of the following generations and to produce the programs and the plans that lead to the formation of this mentality, with great caution to keep the elements that represent Islamic culture from the centres of control in the Ministry. In this way they do not need to confront religious feeling with undisguised hostility. This task they leave to a large party who have far reaching influence in the formation of the general Egyptian mentality. In the Sudan, on the other hand, they find no need for such indirection, but take the position we have described in relation to the Christian missionaries and Muslim traders. America establishes practices and systems that crush all aspects of Islam, doctrinal, ethical, and practical, in all parts of the Islamic world.[13]

73. Thus every imperialist state has followed one or another way of opposing and stifling this religion for centuries.[14] And they continue to co-operate in essentially the same policy as appears from the positions they take on every issue in which Islam is directly or indirectly involved.[15]

74. Those who reckon that Jewish financial influence in the United States and elsewhere is what leads Westerners in this direction, those who reckon that English ambitions or Anglo-Saxon cunning is what directs their positions, and those who reckon that the struggle between the Eastern and Western blocs is the effective factor—all of these neglect a real element in the matter which must be added to all these others. This is the Crusader spirit that all Westerners carry in their blood and that lies hidden deep in their minds, to which is added imperialism's fear of the Islamic spirit and the effort to destroy the strength of Islam,[16] whereby the Westerners are all linked by a single feeling and a single interest in destroying it. This unites communist Russia and capitalist America. And let us not forget the role of worldwide Zionism in the plot against Islam and in uniting the forces against it both in the Crusaderist imperialist world and in the materialist communist world. It is the continuing role that the Jews have always played since the Hijrah of the Apostle to Medina and the founding of the Islamic state.[17]

75. There is something amazing about the spirit of Islam in spite of all the shocks it has faced since the earliest period of its life until today, in spite of the effect of the premature shocks it suffered in its infancy, then in spite of the victory of Western civilization with its material and cultural strength, which has turned some who bear the names of Muslims[18] into willing[19] instruments of the demolition and destruction of Islam at the hands of the imperialists.

76. In spite of all of this the spirit of Islam has remained essentially sound and its hidden power has influenced the general course of

the life of humanity. It also has influenced the shape and orientation of international politics for the last 14 centuries and right until today. There has been no political or military movement in which Islam has not been taken into account, even in the ages of weakness, division, and spiritual, social, and economic convulsion in the Islamic world.

77. The period of weakness and obscurity has ended, and the tide of Islam has begun to rise everywhere in spite of the crushing blows directed at the vanguards of the Islamic renaissance everywhere. These are[20] manifestations that cannot be ignored, indicating the latent vitality of Islam, and the fact that it has sufficient spiritual capital for the restoration of a new Islamic life, not based on mere desire or optimism but also on actual practical foundations visible to the eyes. Today these are at the stage of assembling and preparation in spite of the factors of resistance and relapse that sometimes appear, for these are but bubbles that will soon burst or summer clouds that will soon be dispersed.[21]

78. But in spite of my absolute faith in the inevitability[22] of the restoration of Islamic life in the Islamic world and of the readiness[23] of Islam to be a worldwide—not just local—order in the future, I would not want to be so impetuous as to claim that this will be easy or simple.

79. Indeed not. There are many and enormous obstacles, and there are great works that must be accomplished before the restoration of a sound Islamic life can be rendered easy even in Islamic society. An appreciation of these great obstacles and an awareness of these necessary works is something that must follow from a true feeling for the greatness of the goal at which we aim and the momentous results to be expected by the one who undertakes to accomplish this end.[24]

80. It is not enough for one to send forth a resounding cry of fervent zeal for the hope to become an actual reality, if he does not appreciate all of the obstacles and all of the responsibilities

and if he does not make those whom his cry reaches aware of the prodigious effort that he is asking them to expend.

81. It is natural that the opening of a yawning gap between the conduct of government and the spirit of Islam over a long period of time makes the return to a conduct derived from this spirit more difficult because the machinery of the state and of society, the foundations of life in all its components and the psychological and intellectual orientation, all of these stand on specific bases that are hard to change without expending prodigious and lengthy efforts. The more time goes on, the greater these difficulties become, requiring even more prodigious and lengthy efforts.

82. Then added to the factor of a long time is another present-day factor, that we do not live alone in this world and we do not live in isolation from the rest of the world. Our interests and concerns are interwoven with this world which is dominated by a particular civilization, whose mentality is completely contradictory to the Islamic mentality—as we shall explain below—and this makes our steps along the path to a restoration of a sound Islamic life slow on one hand and burdensome on the other.

83. The importance of this last factor is increased by the fact that this Western world with which our interests are interwoven is stronger than we are at present. We have no control over it and no strength equal to its strength, as we did in the early days of Islam. Furthermore, it is at the same time hostile to us and hostile to our religion in particular. Therefore, it will not let us create an Islamic order anew or restore a sound Islamic life unless we expend redoubled efforts which we could otherwise save if we had control over the Western world or strength equal to its strength or if it were friendly to us and to the religion to which we wish to return.

84. However, all of this does not mean that a return to the Islamic order is impossible. It means only that it is a difficult and massive task

requiring uncommon effort. Also, and more than anything else, it requires a zealous faith, a boldness to leap over the obstacles placed in its path, fortitude for the extremely difficult effort needed, confidence that it is necessary for the Islamic world and for the whole human world, and a creative and inventive mentality whose task is not to patch up the reality that exists but to create a whole new unpatched reality.

[. . .]

86. Among the facts[25] worth noting in this connection is that contemporary Western civilization has led the world to two comprehensive wars and since the second war has led it to a division[26] between Eastern and Western blocs and to the ever-present threat of a third war, to disturbances everywhere and to hunger, destitution and misery in three-quarters of the globe. The whole world order today is in a state of convulsion and disturbance, seeking for new foundations and searching for spiritual sustenance that will give back to the human race its trust in humane principles.

Notes

1.   Author's [Sayyid Qutb] note: "Based on the similarity of the forms 'Mahomed' and 'Mahound,' Ma is the first person possessive pronoun and 'Hound,' from the German 'Hund,' meaning dog. Thus those insulters played with the external forms of words, Mahomed and Mahound." From the book, *Islam at the Cross Roads,* by Leopold Weiss (Muhammad Asad) and translated by Doctor 'Umar Farrukh. Translator's [William Shepherd] note: paragraphs 65 to 70 correspond to pp. 70–76 of the sixth edition of the English version. I have consulted the English version and sometimes followed it but usually try to reproduce the Arabic version where its wording or meaning diverges from the English. Such evidence as is available to me suggests that this book was written in English, although Weiss was originally Austrian, or at least that the Arabic translation was done from English.

2.   Author's note: From the book, *Islam at the Cross Roads,* by Leopold Weiss. (Muhammad Asad) and translated by Doctor 'Umar Farrukh. Translator's note: The information on the book is repeated at this point by the author.

3.   Eds. 1–5 omit "and American Crusaderist."

4.   Author's note: Surat al-Anfal (8), 60.

5.   Author's note: Surat al-Nisa' (4), 144.

6.   Author's note: Surat al-Nisa' (4), 74.

7.   Author's note: Surat Al 'Imran (3), 139–140.

8.   Eds. 1–5 omit "organizational."

9.   Eds. 1–5 omit "and American."

10.   Ed. 1 reads "policy" instead of "forms (*mazāhir*)".

11.   Translator's note: A Moroccan decree of 1930 removing Berbers from the jurisdiction of Islamic law. Generally seen as a French "divide and rule" policy to split Berbers from Arabs as well as an attack on Islam.

12.   Ed. 1 omits "and its representatives in Damascus announce to the broad light of day that they are the descendants of the crusaders." Ed. 3 omits only "in Damascus." Cf. Ch. 7§128.

13.   Eds. 1–5 omit the last sentence, "America establishes . . . Islamic world."

14.   Eds. 1–5 read: "since the last century and before" instead of "for centuries."

15.   Eds. 1–5 read: "from the positions the United Nations takes on the cases of Indonesia and Holland, Kashmir between India and Pakistan, Hyderabad between India and the Nizam and then tops it off with its position on Palestine" instead of "from the positions . . . indirectly involved."

16.   Ed. 1 reads "the Arabs" instead of "Islam."

17.   Eds. 1–3 omit "And let us not forget the role of worldwide Zionism . . . the founding of the Islamic state."

18.   Eds. 1–5 omit "who bear the names of."

19.   Eds. 1–2 omit "willing."

20.   Eds. 1–5 read "The formation of the Arab world, east and west, into one bloc, and the appearance of two great Islamic blocs in Pakistan and Indonesia, these are . . . " instead of "everywhere in spite of . . . these are . . . "

21.   Ed. 1 lacks the last sentence: "Today these are at the stage . . . soon be dispersed." Eds. 2–3 lack only, "in spite of the factors . . . soon be dispersed."

22. Eds. 1–5 read "possibility" instead of "inevitability."
23. Eds. 1–5 read "suitability" instead of "readiness."
24. Eds. 1–5 add: "as it must from an awareness of the consequences of essaying an opinion in such great matters."
25. Eds. 1–5 read "happenstances (muṣādafāt)" instead of "facts (haqā'iq)."
26. Eds. 1–5 read "complete division" instead of "division."

Bibliography

Asad, Muhammad (Leopold Weiss), *Islam at the Cross Roads,* sixth edition. Lahore: Arafat Publications, 1947 (1975 reprint; first ed., 1934).

CHAPTER 58

Hostile Visitors: The Palestinians in the Settlers' Worldview

Michael Feige

The Palestinians as the "Other" for Zionism and Gush Emunim

Gush Emunim's treatment of the Palestinians has to be understood against the backdrop of the Zionist relation to the Arabs over the years, which is itself based on Western images of the Orient. As stated before, the settlers have appropriated many of the symbols and values of secular Zionism as part of their religious ethos. The place of the Arab as the ultimate "other" was also adapted from secular Zionism, including some of the methods of either confronting or ignoring the intricate issues involved.[1] Basically, their situations were similar: communities of immigrants who moved to reside on a land inhabited by natives who violently resisted their arrival. Both the early Zionists and the Gush Emunim settlers may have had economic considerations

that supported their move, but their settlements were primarily legitimated by an ideology of homecoming. Both came, according to their worldview, to what they considered an empty land or, rather, a land whose residents had no political rights and therefore little moral ground for objection to the act of homecoming. Both saw themselves as representing the values of the West in the East, of modernity in a traditional setting, while simultaneously criticizing the West for its decay and shallowness. And both had a commitment (albeit not the same one) to the Bible, which framed the meaning of return and the status of the local Arabs. It's little wonder that we find great similarities between the views of the Palestinian Arabs of Gush Emunim and the early Zionists.

However, there are also important differences. The context of the early twentieth century can hardly be compared with that of the late twentieth century. Early Zionists acted within the confines of Ottoman rule or the British Mandate, against an Arab community that enjoyed the same rights that they did, whereas Gush Emunim operates under the auspice of a Jewish state that rules contested territories. The settlement of Westerners among native people isn't accepted any longer by the international community as it was in the time of the early Zionists. The religious-messianic world of Gush Emunim was never part of the Zionist ethos, and biblical precepts, such as the obligation to settle everywhere on the land or to treat the Arabs as *gerim*—the halakhic term for "resident aliens"—was never seriously debated by Zionist leaders. Dov Schwartz (1997), a researcher with a National Religious ideology, wrote, "The intellectuals of religious Zionism seemingly had easy ideological work with respect to rights to the land. They did not need to employ apologetic tones, historical or political utilitarian, in presenting the crucial place of the land of Israel in Zionist action. The presence of the Arab people did not lead adherents of religious Zionism to doubt the sovereignty of the people on its land" (13). Perhaps most importantly, the secular Zionist movement and the liberal Israeli state could reach agreement and compromise with the Arabs nations and the Palestinians, including territorial concessions, whereas Gush Emunim, because of its political extremism and religious zealotry, could accept no compromise.

Over the years, a gradual process took place within the Israeli public in which the Arab gradually ceased to be the menacing other and became a partner in negotiation. This process was by no means unilinear, and the Second Intifada revived primeval fears. From a wide historical perspective, however, the menacing connotations of Arabs for Gush Emunim settlers grew just as the Arabs' threatening position was declining in the rest of Israeli society. Gush

Emunim initiated its demonstrations against the Israeli government over the interim peace negotiations with Egypt and Syria, and continued to protest the attempts at reconciliation with the Palestinians. As the Arabs increasingly became possible negotiation partners for most Israelis, the Gush Emunim settlers did their utmost to perpetuate the Arabs' status as ultimate others. The settlers see their role as constantly reminding the Israeli public of the long history of the conflict by showing how menacing and hateful the Arabs actually are.

The Palestinian as an Authentic Primitive

Like the Zionist settlers that preceded them, the Gush Emunim settlers see no inherent conflict between themselves and the individual Arab, as long as he or she is not attached to a movement seeking national rights. They display examples of personal friendship and compassion. One of the first *Nekuda* issues displayed a picture of a settler helping an old blind Arab across a road. Elyakim Haetzni, one of the settlers' leaders from Kiryat Arba and a lawyer, helped individual Arabs deal with Israeli authorities. A resident of the Neve Tzuf settlement explains, "You can say that their [the Arabs'] lives have changed completely since we arrived, because their standard of living has risen substantially. They have never earned as much . . . Their mentality has changed, too: they dress differently, behave differently—our effect on them has been considerable" (Ben-Pazi 1988, 69).

In general, the settlers reproduced the old Zionist stand that has strong orientalist undertones—that the arrival of Jewish settlement benefits the Arab natives, so the natives should be thankful. According to the settlers, accepting and approving the Gush Emunim project are in the interest of the local Palestinians, primarily for economic reasons. Rabbi Zalman Melamed (1988) suggests a different concept: since the settlement is part of a divine process, objection is sacrilegious, and the Muslims, who share the same God, should be the first to realize that. He says, "We must explain this to them. They must be partners in the redemption process of the people of Israel, not fight it. Quite the opposite, they bring disaster upon themselves through their current behaviour; not physically, but mentally and morally" (11).

Accepting the Arabs is possible as long as they remain isolated individuals who do not demand national rights. For the Palestinians to remain so, it is preferable that they stay "simple" *fellahin* ("farmers"), as they presumably were for generations and as befits their nature. Their Palestinization—namely, their demand for political rights—counters the interests of the Jewish settlers, but also, as the settlers see it, counters their self-interest. From the settlers' perspective, it is not "natural"—let alone beneficial—for Arab villagers to align themselves with the national movement and rise up against the Jewish neighbours that bring prosperity to their villages. Often, when villagers become hostile, the settlers attribute the behaviour to a small group of manipulative agitators who abuse the kind nature of the Arab *fellah* for political purposes. As a Jewish resident in the Muslim quarter of the Old City of Jerusalem explains, "When the agitation started, there was a change in their behaviour. We feel they are possessed by hatred and depression. All at once they stopped meeting our eyes. They are easily agitated by the threatening force of a minority that overpowers them, they are frightened and hateful" (Ben-Pazi 1988, 109). Here, the orientalist concept of the childlike native with no will of its own is unmistakable.

Accordingly, Gush Emunim solutions for the conflict and their understanding of the status of local Arabs depoliticize and denationalize the Arabs. The Arabs may remain on the land for as long as they stay in their pristine "authentic" situation without objecting to the Judaization of the entire land. Gush Emunim has never openly resorted to the radical solutions of the extreme Right—the transfer of the Palestinians from the land—though doubtless many activists would not object to the implementation of a solution by ethnic cleansing. The typical Gush Emunim solution hints at the possibility of population transfer, not as a mass solution, but reserved only for those who refuse to accept Israeli presence and sovereignty; namely, the presumably relatively small and identifiable group of agitators. Rabbi Dan Be'ri (1985) suggests what he regards as autonomy, which includes the Palestinian citizens of the state: "We must clarify to them that while we have the power they will not receive any sovereignty in our land. Citizenship is for the sons of the Jewish nation alone: we should render them the status of *gerim*, autonomous as much as possible. If they display hostility—[we should] evict them from the land or fight them honourably." The halakhic term *gerim* suggests placing the Palestinians in a status conceived by religious rather than state law.

A children's book by Emuna Elon (1988) displays the relationship between a settler boy from "Ramat El" (a thin disguise for the author's settlement Beit El) and a Palestinian boy, Fatchi, from the refugee camp of "Jisafon" (Jilabun). The Jewish boy learns of the lifestyle of his friend and the history of his people, including the deportation from his former village, and they become friends in the shadow of the national conflict. The story ends with an ironic twist: the Arab child Fatchi, with the assistance of his Jewish friend, finds a treasure, which belonged to Fatchi's family, near the mosque in the former village where there is now a kibbutz. Unsurprisingly, the kibbutz members oppose the actions of the settlers and hold leftist views that morally contradict their residing in homes built on the ruins of an Arab village.

The Arab boy intends to use the money to build a better future for himself and his family outside of the land of Israel. Meanwhile, he lectures the kibbutz members: "Now I know that the Arabs have many lands and the Jews have only one land. Allah has created it for you. If we take this land—where will you go?" (82). The book is empathic toward the Arab boy (who has conveniently converted to Zionism) and proposes that the settlers learn their neighbours' culture and lifestyle. It concludes with a solution to the private problem of Fatchi and his family (emigration) while offering the Palestinians no collective solution.

The Arab boy's lecture exemplifies another important point: according to the settlers, deep in their heart the Arabs know that justice is with the Jews returning home. A boy from a refugee camp can tell the story to the guilt-stricken kibbutz members better than any representative of Gush Emunim. The reason why the Arabs know that which the Israelis are unsure of is that the Arabs have not been tainted and contaminated by modernity and secularization, and "simple" traditional people easily recognize the eternal truths of life and time. Whereas in Elon's story a boy holds this knowledge, usually the settlers attribute such understanding to old Arabs. A resident of Alon Shvut tells of a young Arab shepherd who resents a settler's demand that the boy move his herd from a fenced area. His old father tells him, "The Jews settled on a land that never was ours" (Ben-Pazi 1988, 51). Possibly (assuming the settler's account is credible), the father was trying to avoid a violent confrontation that he could not hope to win, but his words touched a favourable chord in the settler's heart because he cites them as a true expression of Arab understanding.

The religious settlers often confront their rabbis with questions regarding relations with Arabs. This is another difference from secular Zionists, who allowed no intermediaries, certainly not religious authorities, to explain the presence of the Palestinians. When Rabbi Shlomo Aviner (1990) was asked whether meetings with Arabs should be commended and initiated, he replied,

> It is a good idea, in order to increase peace, to meet the Arabs who live in the land of Israel, but only on the condition that it will be based on the truth; namely, that they recognize the fact that this land is ours, this state is ours, and that we have taken no state from them, nor do we owe them any state. If they recognize this, it is good to meet them and, if they don't, then they are liars, and we have no dealings with liars. (67)

According to Aviner, an Arab who claims national rights to the land is neither a Palestinian nationalist nor a proud patriot; he is not even deluded. He is simply a liar because he, along with all his compatriots, know that the Arabs hold no rights to the land. The early Zionists never made such claims regarding the Palestinians, although they, too, hoped that the Arab national movement would not take hold.

Being a natural native, the Arab "senses" the truth of the Jewish claim. He can comprehend the deep devotion of a people to their land—something that is lost on the modern and postmodern man of hyperspace and rapid mobility. Ironically, the settlers see the Palestinians as sharing their worldview: while they stand against the Arabs on one—shallow and superficial—level, they believe them to be partners in a deeper struggle against fellow Israelis—a struggle common to all who share devotion to tradition. Therefore, it is not surprising that, in Elon's book, the Palestinian refugee boy knows what the kibbutz members have long forgotten: that he must be loyal to the land given to his people by God. He should therefore also recognize that he and his people do not belong to the land.

An interesting, yet atypical, story relates to Rabbi Menachem Fruman (1993) of the Tekoah settlement and his attempts to create links with

Muslim religious leaders. In his reasoning, the religious leaders of both sides should meet because they have a better chance of reaching an agreement than political leaders. To the queries of his friends and the skepticism from all sides of the political spectrum, he answered,

> It is important to stress that, in a Jewish-Muslim religious dialogue, the fact that the Jewish side is linked to the idea of a Greater Israel is not a problem. Quite the opposite. In a religious dialogue, I, as a man of Greater Israel or, more specifically, a settler, have much to discuss with the Palestinians. The attachment to the land that characterizes the men of Greater Israel and most of the Arabs is a potential basis for co-existence. He who conceives of himself as living within the context of his traditional culture will be able to respect the attachment to the land and the culture of the other. (43)

The possibility of conceiving of a religious peace stems from a basic principle shared by both religions: It is God who owns the land and He can give it to the believers. Fruman suggests a depolitization of the land—a declaration that, because of its sacredness, both religions should share control.

Fruman found no support among his fellow settlers, including the rabbis of his own camp: he was criticized harshly in his home settlement to the point of being evicted, and the Muslim fundamentalists he met were also not enthusiastic about his plan. Fruman himself maintained his rightist views and supported harsh measures against Hamas leaders, including the killing of his interlocutors from Hamas, Sheikhs Ahmad Yasin and Abdul Aziz Rantisi, by the Israeli Defense Forces. His marginal views are nevertheless important because they show an inventive development of the logic of Gush Emunim. For Fruman, the Palestinians are first and foremost Muslims, just as, for him,

the nature of the Jews is basically religious. His solution bypasses political Palestinian representation because militant political representation fails to grasp the true nature of the people: basically, the "authentic" Jews and Arabs can reach an agreement based on their mutual understanding, common to true believers, of the nature of the attachment to the land and their standing before God. Unlike Fruman, most settlers found no point in discussing the rights of the Palestinians, neither as a nation nor as part of a religion, and the Palestinians never accredited the settlers with any rights worth discussing.

The Palestinians as Temporary Sojourners

According to the settlers' view, the land belongs to the Jewish people, and the Arabs have no true claim to be discussed, negotiated, or compromised. The Arabs, like the Romans or Crusaders before them, are only temporary sojourners in the home of others. Rabbi Yitzhak Shilat (1988) writes,

> We did not invite the Palestinians to come and reside in our land: they penetrated and invaded it, as foreign nomads, when we were not home. Only because of the compassion that lies deep in the soul of our people did we not evict them from here and allowed them to live peacefully and quietly in homes they built on our historical land. To this generosity they reply on each recurring occasion with cries of "itbach el-Yahud" ["butcher the Jew"] . . . For those who do not wish to live with us in peace, our verdict is this—that they be sent away to their people and their ancient lands. Had they any self-respect, they would have gone there by own free will. (48)

Since they are visitors—and it is unconceivable for the rabbi to think that they do not realize what they are—they have other places that they can call their own ancient homes. The settlers were very late in using the term that the rabbi uses—"Palestinians"—to designate the local Arabs, because it implies a certain acceptance of their rights to the land.

Gush Emunim settlers see the Arab world as threatening the return of the Jewish people to their homeland mainly for reasons of religion, anti-Semitism, and greed. While they realize the differences between various groups within the Arab world and among the Palestinian people, they tend to see them as a unitary whole, without relevant subgroups. The Palestinians are, according to the settlers and the Israeli Right in general, an integral part of the Arab people and not a nation in their own right. The Israeli Arab citizens are basically similar to their brothers who are not Israeli citizens. If the whole land of Israel includes both sides of the Green Line, it stands to reason that the fate of the entire Palestinian population under the rule of Israel should be the same.

The view of the Arabs is a mirror image of the basic ideology of Gush Emunim: they are "whole" just like the land of Israel is "whole" and the people of Israel are "whole." Differentiation, especially regarding the Palestinians who are Israeli citizens, divides the land, as well as its people. Differences among factions of Palestinians, such as those between secular nationalists and extreme Muslim fundamentalists, also receive scant attention. If any subdivision is analytically useful for the settlers, it is the one between the common man or woman, who are pastoral and non-political and willing to live in peace with the Jews, and the militant agitators, who are usually a minority and act against the true interests of their people and the divine course of history. Israeli political and territorial concessions are dangerous because they encourage extremists and enable them to lure more common Arabs into a circle of pointless hate.

The interests behind the inclusive view of the Arabs are apparent: if the Palestinians are no different than other Arabs, then the Palestinians belong to a powerful nation and not to a relatively small group of mostly refugees, and their claim to the land is petty and greedy. The Arabs, as the settlers never tire of mentioning, already have 22 states that may be considered homelands. Apart from rejecting Palestinian national claims to the land, and pitting the small Jewish nation against hundreds of millions of Arabs or Muslims, this view also absolves Israel of moral responsibility toward the Palestinians. Their larger national family, the Arabs, can and should take care of them, and their claim to someone else's home is morally flawed. According to Gush Emunim, there is no "Palestinian problem," and if that non-problem were to be "solved" through a Palestinian state and Israeli concessions, it would endanger the future of Israel and compromise the eternal rights of the Jewish people. The settlers stress that the conflict is a perennial one based on absolute religious values that preclude any possibility of compromise.

The discourse about the Israeli Arabs, though the settlers rarely encounter them, is important.[2] Gush Emunim supporters claim that the Arabs have little right to participate in Israeli political life and practically no right to participate in the discussion over basic issues determining the future of Israel, such as arguments regarding peace, territory, and the future of the settlements. They are seen as a fifth column, potential traitors, loyal to Israel only when convenient, and never to be trusted. According to Gush Emunim, Israel is and should be an ethnocracy: a state dedicated to the public good of one ethnic group and actively participating in social conflicts in favour of the sacred ethnos rather than the demos (namely, the entire body of citizens).[3] One of their main arguments against the Oslo Accords was that, since they were passed by the Israeli parliament only with the support of the Arab parties, they were illegitimate.[4]

Author Mira Kedar (2002) of Ofra tried to understand why, at the outset of the Second Intifada, the land that had waited faithfully for the Jews to return and had not accepted any other nation's permanent presence, had produced a second nation once the Jews had decided to return. The eternal rights of the Jews are, for Kedar, undeniable, as is the newly conceived nature of the Palestinian people. Just as she believes that the Jewish return has divine meaning independent of the will of individuals, so, too, has the Palestinian emergence and their violent uprising. What, she wonders, is the divine role that God has allotted the unwelcomed intruders? Here are her conclusions:

> The Palestinians are the clouded mirror that the God Almighty has set before us—with the murderous inclinations and their moral decay and so on—[God says,] "Here, have a look: this is what a people that cleaves to the land of Israel as ordinary people look like; look, if you insist on building here a state like all other countries."

After years of living side by side with the Palestinians, Kedar cannot merely dismiss them as passing overnight visitors and seeks to account for their function in the divine order of things. They still are visitors, but not accidental ones. Again, her explanation takes no account of Palestinian demands and regards the Palestinian people as manipulated objects of God's will. She does not suggest a dialogue with her neighbours: rather, she understands their existence as part of the most important of dialogues, which is that between the people of Israel and God, as another test that the people have to pass. Like other groups of gentiles, their meaning stems from their role as a mirror for the Jewish people in the divine plan.

Notes

1. On the Arabs in Zionist ideology; see Yadgar (2003).
2. The Israeli Arabs number currently about one million. They received citizenship right after the establishment of the state. On their history, situation, and identity issues, see Rabinowitz (1997) and Yiftachel (2006).
3. On the theory of Israeli ethnocracy, see Yiftachel (2006).
4. It is interesting to note that the support of a "Jewish majority" was first presented by Yitzhak Rabin himself, and later strengthened in the election campaign of Ehud Barak, both leaders of the Labor Party.

References

Works in Hebrew

Aviner, Shlomo. 1990. *Shu't* [Questions and answers] *intifada*. Beit El.

Ben-Pazi, Rina, ed. 1988. Like in the beginning. Beit El.

Be'ri, Rabbi Dan. 1985. Autonomy to the land of Israel Arabs. *Nekuda* 87:10–11.

Elon, Emuna. 1988. *Fatchi's treasure*. Beit El.

Fruman, Menachem. 1993. Only men of truth, men of religion, can settle the conflict. *Nekuda* 165:40–43.

Kedar, Mira. 2002. Clouded mirror. *Nekuda* 252:48–49.

Melamed, Z. 1988. A new stage in the redemption process. *Nekuda* 119: 10–11.

Schwartz, Dov. 1997. *The land of reality and imagination*. Tel Aviv: Am Oved.

Shilat, Rabbi Yitzhak. 1988. The fear to use force comes from moral weakness. *Nekuda* 119: 48–49.

Works in English

Rabinowitz, Dani. 1997. *Overlooking Nazareth: The ethnography of exclusion in Galilee.* Cambridge: Cambridge University Press.

Yadgar, Yaacov. 2003. Between "the Arab" and "the Religious Rightist": "Significant others" in the construction of Jewish-Israeli national identity. *Nationalism and Ethnic Politics* 9: 52–74.

Yiftachel, Oren. 2006. *Ethnocracy: Land and identity politics in Israel/Palestine.* Philadelphia: University of Pennsylvania Press.

CHAPTER 59

Rabbi Avraham Yitzhak Hacohen Kook and Merkaz Harav Yeshiva

Motti Inbari

The activist messianic approach of Religious Zionism, which was fuelled by the vision of Rabbi Avraham Yitzhak Hacohen Kook (1865–1935), mandated the goal of the reestablishment of the Temple as a key Zionist objective. Secular reality was perceived as temporary and transient—an external shell that would later be replaced by a messianic future, whose overt purpose was the reinstatement of the religious ritual on Mount Moriah.[1] This dialectic was also manifested in the positions of Rabbi Kook on entering the Temple Mount in the present period and on the construction of the Third Temple.

According to Rabbi Kook, the process of national revival of the Jewish people was perceived as a Revealed End, and was ultimately due to lead to the full redemption of Israel, namely, the establishment of the religious kingdom and the renewal of the rites on the Temple Mount. To this end, he established the Torat Cohanim yeshiva in 1921. This institute of religious higher learning was intended, as its declared intentions stated, to study the "Talmudic order of Kodashim, the regulation of worship in the Temple, the commandments that relate to the Land of Israel and the religious laws relating to the state."[2] The yeshiva was founded on the basis of the expectation that the movement of national revival led by Zionism, which was characterized by a disconnection from religion, would rapidly return to the fold of sanctity, the completion of ultimate redemption, and the building of the Temple. As is clear from his pamphlet *Sefatei Cohen* (Lips of a Priest) in which he described the goals of the new yeshiva, Kook believed that the revival of the Hebrew nation, despite the fact that it constituted primarily a secular initiative by Jews who rejected religious authority, was nevertheless intended to secure a sublime spiritual purpose. It would ultimately emerge that the final purpose of this revival was to bring religious redemption to the Jewish people, the zenith of which is the building of the Temple:

The anticipation of seeing the priests at their worship and the Levites on their stand and Israel in their presence—this is the foundation that bears this entire revival.[3]

According to Rabbi Kook, this day was steadily emerging, and preparations must therefore be made. Torat Cohanim yeshiva was thus intended to attend to the practical preparation of priests and Levites for their worship in the Temple, based on the acute messianic expectation that the Temple would indeed be built "speedily and in our days." Rabbi Kook may well have found a precedent for this approach—which demanded that priests and Levites be prepared for the Temple worship on the basis of the expectation that redemption was near—in the spiritual heritage of an important Orthodox leader, Israel Meir Hacohen (1838–1933), the author of the *Chafetz Chaim*, who was considered one of the architects of the Orthodox position.[4]

Hacohen's position on the issue was articulated in "The Anticipation of Redemption," which was composed in Radin, Russia, where he lived. The Chafetz Chaim attempted to address the question of the secularization of the Jewish people, and to withstand the powerful attraction of the Hovevei Zion and Zionist movements among the Jewish masses. In his article, which was dominated by a pessimistic sense that Jewish religious values and tradition were being abandoned, the rabbi offered a dialectic interpretation of the phenomenon of secularization, seeing the very weakness of religion as a positive sign. He believed that the period in which he found himself was consonant with the "birth pangs of Messiah"—the period that preceded the ultimate redemption, which is characterized by a serious decline in both spiritual and material terms.[5]

In the face of the Orthodox vulnerability when challenged by the changes of the period and by the pseudomessianic fervour aroused by Theodor Herzl and his Zionist message,[6] the Chafetz Chaim proposed a different messianic program: In previous generations, when affairs were running smoothly, there was no great need to accelerate the process of redemption, since the Torah passed from father to son in an orderly and uninterrupted manner. In the present generation, however, there was a real danger that no one would remain to whom the Torah could be transferred, and traditional Judaism would be obliterated from memory. Accordingly, God must open the eyes of the people through the miracles of redemption. This call seems to have been formulated, in part, as a response to the sense among observant circles that the Jewish masses had abandoned religion and embraced sin to the point that it was no longer worthy of redemption.[7]

The Chafetz Chaim did not confine himself to messianic rhetoric, and sought to show his audience that Torah study also leads to action. To this end, he established a special yeshiva for priests, teaching the Talmudic tractate of Kodashim, which includes sections discussing the Temple worship that had been largely neglected over the long period of exile. The Chafetz Chaim also demanded that every Jew (and not only every priest) familiarize himself with the Temple worship and the sacrifices. He explained that this was necessary because if the Messiah were to appear suddenly and the people did not know how to worship the Lord, "this would be a disgrace to him [the Messiah]."[8]

Rabbi Kook taught the tractate of Kodashim in the context of this hope that the sacrifices would be reinstated, and this seems to have formed the background for the establishment of Torat Cohanim yeshiva.

A correspondent with the London newspaper *The Christian* visited the yeshiva, which was situated in the Muslim Quarter of the Old City of Jerusalem. He informed his readers that Rabbi Kook had established the yeshiva because of his sense of extreme urgency regarding the establishment of the Temple. The Zionist executive in London demanded an explanation following this report, and Rabbi Kook replied that the requirement to study the

Temple worship was now more pressing than ever:

> Our faith is firm that days are coming when all the nations shall recognize that this place, which the Lord has chosen for all eternity as the site of our Temple, must return to its true owners, and the great and holy House must be built thereon . . . An official British committee some time ago asked for my opinion regarding the location of the Temple according to our estimation. I told them that just as you see that we have the right to the entire Land [following the Balfour Declaration of 1917], even though the entire world was distant from this . . . so days shall come when all the nations shall recognize our rights to the site of the Temple.[9]

This position reflects the characteristic dynamics of Rabbi Kook's work. His messianic activism, which led him to prepare priests and Levites for their worship, stopped at the gates of the Temple Mount. He argued that the building of the Temple was conditioned on the recognition by the gentiles of the Jewish people's right to the Temple Mount. The preparation of the priests was intended to take place outside the area of the Temple Mount, and the establishment of the yeshiva did not imply that he actually intended to enter the site with his students, let alone commence the sacrificial rituals.

In support of my argument, I would note an additional source from the period, found in a rabbinical responsum published by Rabbi Avraham Yitzhak Hacohen Kook in his book *Mishpat Cohen*, published in 5681 (1921). In the responsum, Rabbi Kook issues a strong warning against entering the Temple Mount area.[10] It seems that this responsum was issued in reaction to the proposal by Rabbi Chaim Hirschenson, mentioned in the book *Malki Ba-Kodesh*, to construct a house of prayer on the Temple Mount.[11] In his responsum, Rabbi

Kook gives the explanation of *mora hamikdash* (Awe of the Temple), according to which, given the sanctity with which this holy place is to be treated (and since its holiness has not been lost[12]), the public must stay away from the Temple Mount and refrain from entering the area. The dialectical explanation he offered for this was that distancing oneself from the site of the Temple would lead to a deeper spirituality, and hence to a profound sense of attachment: "The power of the memory of honour and the awe of sanctity is all the greater when it comes through denying proximity and through distancing." The rabbi ended his responsum with the following comments:

> And when, through God's infinite mercy, a fragment of the light of the emergence of salvation has begun to shine, the Rock of Israel will, with God's help, add the light of his mercy and truth, and will reveal to us the light of his full redemption, and bring us speedily our true redeemer, the redeemer of justice, our just Messiah, and will speedily fulfill all the words of his servants the prophets, and will build the Temple, speedily in our days. . . . And, until then, all Israel shall as friends associate in a single union to steer their hearts toward their Father in heaven, without bursting out and without departure, *without any demolition of the fence and without any hint of transgressing against the prohibition of profanity and impurity of the Temple and its holinesses.* (emphasis added)[13]

The Six-Day War created a new reality in the Middle East. In the course of the war, Israel occupied the West Bank, the Gaza Strip, the Golan Heights, and the Sinai Peninsula. The Israeli victory created fervent hope among the younger generation of Religious Zionists. The dominant school within this population, the graduates of Mercaz Harav yeshiva in Jerusalem, headed by Rabbi Zvi Yehuda Hacohen Kook, propagated the perception that the Israeli victory in this war reflected God's will to redeem His people. The post-war era therefore represented a higher stage in the process of redemption. The Gush Emunim mass settlement movement, established in 1974 and led by the graduates of the yeshiva, aimed to settle the territories occupied by the IDF to establish facts on the ground, and to settle the biblical Land of Israel with Jews. They saw settlement as a manifestation of God's will to redeem His people.

On the issue of the Temple Mount, however, Rabbi Zvi Yehuda Hacohen Kook did not diverge from his father. Although Zvi Yehuda is considered the spiritual guide of the Gush Emunim movement, which acted out of a strong sense of messianic urgency, he continued to view the Temple Mount as out of bounds. Zvi Yehuda signed the declaration issued by the Chief Rabbinate immediately after the occupation of the site, prohibiting Jews from entering the Temple Mount.

Indeed, Zvi Yehuda sharply criticized Shlomo Goren, the Chief Rabbi of the Israel Defense Forces, and later a Chief Rabbi of the State of Israel, who advocated Jewish prayer on the Mount [. . .]. Zvi Yehuda felt compelled to oppose in the fiercest possible terms the idea of Jews entering the Temple Mount area in order to pray.[14] Indeed, both of the Kooks ruled that the sanctity of the Temple Mount was so great that it was prohibited even to place one's fingers inside the cracks in the Western Wall. Zvi Yehuda fiercely opposed the demand to undertake archaeological excavations on the Temple Mount, since it "is surrounded by a wall. We do not pass this wall and we have no need for [the site] to be studied."[15]

It should be emphasized that the principled position of Zvi Yehuda against Jews entering the Temple Mount was not intended to weaken the demand for Israel to demonstrate its sovereignty on the site. He argued that the Jewish people enjoyed "property ownership" of the area of the Temple Mount. However, he explained that the State of Israel had not yet attained a spiritual level permitting Jews to enter the area of Mt Moriah. Only after the state had been built in the spirit of the Torah, in both the practical and spiritual realms, would it be possible to enter the holy site.

Notes

1. See Dov Schwartz, *Faith at a Crossroads: A Theological Profile of Religious Zionism* (Leiden: Brill, 2002), 156–192.

2. The pamphlet *Sefati Cohen* (Lips of a Priest), dated 12 Heshvan 5681 (24 October 1920), appears in Shlomo Zalman Shragai, "Rabbi Avraham Hacohen Kook, Zatsa"l, on the Restitution of the Place of Our Temple to the People of Israel," *Sinai* 85 (5739/1978): 193–198 (in Hebrew).

3. Ibid., 194.

4. Despite the importance of this thinker in consolidating the Orthodox approach, he has received limited research attention. Further biographical details on the Chafetz Chaim may be found in Eliezer Schweid, *Between Orthodoxy and Religious Humanism* (Jerusalem: Van Leer Institute, 1977), 12–14 (in Hebrew).

5. For example: Babylonian Talmud, Tractate Soteh, 49b.

6. See Robert Wistrich, "In the Footsteps of the Messiah," in Gideon Shimoni and Robert S. Wistrich (eds), *Theodor Herzl, Visionary of the Jewish State* (Jerusalem: Hebrew University and Magnes Press, 1999), 231–238.

7. Israel Meir Hacohen, *Anticipation of Redemption* (Bnei Brak: Netzach, 5749/1989), 11 (in Hebrew).

8. Ibid., 17–24.

9. Shragi, "Rabbi Avraham Hacohen Kook," 197.

10. Avraham Iitzhak Kook, *Mishpat Cohen* (Jerusalem: Rav Kook Institute, 5745/1984), 183 (in Hebrew).

11. Hayyim Hirschenshon, *Malki Ba-Kodesh A* (St. Louise: Moinster Printing, 1919), 10–13, 41–89 (in Hebrew). Cf. Zalman Koren, "Memorandum concerning the Position of the Chief Rabbinate through the Generations on the Question of the

Temple Mount," *Iturei Kohanim* 201 (5761/2000), 27–32 (in Hebrew).

12. Rabbi Kook's position differs from the position of Rabbi Avraham Ben David, who argued that since the destruction of the Temple the physical site where the Temple stood had lost its sanctity. According to Ben David's approach, the site can only regain its sanctity when the Temple is reconstructed; accordingly, the prohibition of *Karet* does not apply to those entering the Temple Mount area in this era. Rabbi Kook rejected this approach, preferring that of Maimonides, who argued that the sanctity of the Temple Mount sire is eternal because of the primeval sanctification of the site by God as the dwelling place of the Divine Presence. See Kook, *Mishpat Cohen*, 182–227.

13. Ibid., 203.

14. Koren, "Memorandum," 29–30.

15. Shlomo Aviner, *Lemikdashcha Tov* (Jerusalem: Hava Library, 5760/1999), 12–13 (in Hebrew).

Critical Thinking Questions

1. By which method does Fosdick reach the conclusion that holy books such as the Koran or the Bible are millstones around the necks of major monotheistic religions? What does Fosdick predict will happen if fundamentalist interpretations of Christianity prevail? While Fosdick never states it explicitly, he argues that scientific and religious thinking are reconcilable. Which evidence does he cite in support of his claim?

2. Phillips suggests that the United States has drifted toward a theocratic form of government since 9/11, citing a number of developments during the presidency of Republican George W. Bush. How credible does the claim appear in light of contemporary circumstances? How does it buttress or undermine his broader claim that fierce religious intolerance fuels national decline in the long run? Phillips suggests that secular and religious Americans share mutual concerns "over cultural and economic decay, with its many corollaries." If that is the case, what other feelings might they have in common?

3. Which historic event continues to be the central source of European prejudices against Islam, according to Qutb, who argues that this bias is an "inherent instinct" and a "natural characteristic"? How credible is this claim? Qutb suggests that foreign imperialists of various ideological stripes and "worldwide Zionism" are conspiring to destroy Islam because they fear its spirit and strength. What (if any) evidence does he cite in support? Whom does Qutb address when he attacks the historic and contemporary ills of Western civilization? What is his purpose?

4. Which recent historical event echoes in the background when Qutb speaks of treating Jews as if they were a "disease"? While Qutb blames a worldwide Jewish conspiracy for a number of historic and contemporary ills in Islamic societies, he suggests elsewhere that Islam has been resilient, even dominant, in world affairs. If Qutb is correct, why would he continue to frame Muslims as victims? When

Qutb attacks secular Muslims in the mould of Ataturk, the founder of modern-day Turkey, what does he implicitly concede about the state of the Islamic community?

5. How do Jewish groups like Gush Emunim use language to deny the political demands of Palestinians living in the Occupied Territories? Who is doing whom a favour for which purpose, according to this discourse? What role do Palestinians play in the unverifiable claim that God divined Israel to the Jews? What is the fate of voices among Jewish settlers who advocate a perhaps more nuanced approach in dealing with Palestinians?

6. Why does the Temple Mount occupy such an important place in the minds of Jewish fundamentalists? What (if any) tensions has the status of the Temple Mount caused among various fundamentalist factions? As the readings note, Jewish fundamentalists believe that current events have led them to anticipate the end of times. How reliable are the methods by which they arrive at their conclusion?

Biographies

Harry Emerson Fosdick (1878–1969)

Two figures personified the schism that split American Protestantism during the 1920s. One was the three-time Democratic presidential candidate William Jennings Bryan (1860–1925), the extraordinary spokesperson for the working class who used his inexhaustible oratory skills to indict Darwinism during the famous Scopes Monkey Trial (1925). The other was Fosdick, an ordained Baptist priest whose attempt to reconcile Christianity with liberal modernity earned him the financial support of none other than oil tycoon John D. Rockefeller (1839–1937), whose name once served as the standard of greed. So ran the front lines of a conflict fought increasingly across the airwaves through radio, a carrier which exposed millions of listeners to the still-popular sermons of Fosdick, who was born in Buffalo, NY. While it is uncertain whether his views will prevail, Fosdick has left behind a permanent mark on Christendom through the founding of the Riverside Church in New York City. Its interdenominational, multi-racial congregation worships in a neo-gothic cathedral where it has heard speeches and sermons from the likes of Nelson Mandela (1918–) and Martin Luther King Jr (1929–1968).

Kevin Phillips (1940–)

Members of the Republican Party in the United States have more than sufficient reason to call Kevin Phillips a turncoat, for he was once a senior strategist for the party before becoming one of its harsh critics as a columnist and author. His personal biography identifies Phillips as a "Yankee" with the academic resume (Colgate, Harvard) to prove it. Yet Phillips correctly anticipated that the future electoral fortunes of his party would lie beyond the northern Frost Belt in the southern and southwestern regions of the United States. This view—which he later recorded in the groundbreaking *The Emerging Republican Majority* (1969)—laid the foundation for the 1968 election of Richard Nixon, whom he had served as an advisor. Phillips though soon distanced himself from the Conservative chic of the Nixon era to condemn the creation that he helped to conceive.

Sayyid Qutb (1906–1966)

The biography of Sayyid Qutb acquires an ironic angle seen through the prism of 9/11. Born in Egypt, Qutb was living in the United States during the late 1940s and early 1950s when he became what one might call a born-again Muslim. Qutb had come to the United States to escape political persecution as an opponent of the ruling monarchy. But the experience of living in a society that he deemed to be materialistic, racist, and promiscuous inspired Qutb to explore Islam, which until then had played a limited role in his life. Qutb lived out his newly discovered religious fervour by joining the Muslim Brotherhood, where he quickly advanced to become its leading theoretician. This status earned Qutb the hostility of the despotic but secular regime of nationalist Gamal Abdel Nasser (1918–1970), who used the occasion of a failed assassination attempt in 1954 to crush the organization by arresting several leading members, including Qutb. Like Adolf Hitler (1889–1945), Qutb used his time in prison to record his anti-Jewish, anti-Western views, which continue to influence contemporary Arab actors in the Middle East such as Hamas. Nasser's regime eventually executed Qutb by hanging him. Qutb might be an historic figure, but his life reveals several threads that continue to run through the fabric of the contemporary Middle East.

Michael Feige (1957–)

The Six Day War of 1967 between Israel and its Arab neighbours looms large in the research of Michael Feige, for it led to the formation of Gush Emunim, a political movement committed to the territorial expansion of Israel beyond its borders of 1948 as defined by the Torah. While Gush Emunim has formally ceased to exist as a political institution, its influence on contemporary politics as the chief ideology for a Greater Israel has been undeniable. By encouraging the permanent settlement of Jews in the territories occupied in 1967, Gush Emunim sought to produce facts on the ground. Feige's accomplishment lies in tracing the various aspects of this practice over the course of his academic career as a sociologist and anthropologist at universities in Israel and the United States. The Middle East is a massive arsenal of ancient myths and collective memories that have fused into a complex minefield of grievances. While it might be impossible to clear this minefield of all its explosive devices, Feige has made it more passable.

Motti Inbari (1970–)

A self-described secular Jew, Inbari has emerged as one of the leading scholars of fundamentalist groups in Israel that pursue messianic ambitions and harbour millennial expectations. Growing up in what he called a "leftist, almost anti-religious" family, Inbari developed this academic interest by accident when he and his wife accepted a journalistic assignment to investigate a police incident near Tel-Aviv that involved a messianic rabbi and his followers. The incident eventually inspired a master's thesis at the Hebrew University of Jerusalem, where he also completed his Ph.D. dissertation. A revised version of his thesis has since appeared under the title *Jewish Fundamentalism and the Temple Mount. Who Will Build the Third Temple?* Inbari has recently moved to the United States, where he currently teaches at the University of North Carolina-Pembroke.

Additional Readings and Web Links

Part I: Classical Liberalism

Additional Readings

Buchanan, James M. *Why I, Too, Am Not a Conservative: The Normative Vision of Classical Liberalism.* Cheltenham, England; Northampton, MA: Edward Elgar, 2005.

Davies, Howard, and David Green. *Banking on the Future.* Princeton: Princeton University Press, 2010.

Friedman, Milton. *Capitalism and Freedom.* Chicago: Chicago University Press, 1962.

Gordon, Joy. "The Concept of Human Rights: The History and Meaning of Its Politicization." *Brooklyn Journal of International Law 23* (1998): 689–791.

Griffith-Jones, Stephany, Jose Antonio Ocampo, and Joseph E. Stiglitz, eds. *Time for a Visible Hand.* New York: Oxford University Press, 2010.

Hayek, Friedrich A. *Economic Freedom and Representative Government.* London: Institute of Economic Affairs, 1973.

Seaford, Ricard. "World Without Limits." *Times Literary Supplement,* 19 June 2009, 14–15.

Tett, Gillian. *Fool's Gold: How Unrestrained Greed Corrupted a Dream, Shattered Global Markets and Unleashed a Catastrophe.* London: Little Brown, 2009.

Tuck, Richard. *Natural Rights Theories: Their Origin and Development.* Cambridge: Cambridge University Press, 1979.

Web Links

Adam Smith Institute
www.adamsmith.org/

LockeSmith Institute—Belmont University
www.belmont.edu/lockesmith/index.html

The Locke Institute
www.thelockeinstitute.org/index.html

Library of Economics and Liberty
www.econlib.org/index.html

The Digital Locke Project
www.digitallockeproject.nl/

Immanuel Kant—Stanford Encyclopedia of Philosophy
http://plato.stanford.edu/entries/kant/

Baron de Montesquieu, Charles-Louis de Secondat—Stanford Encyclopedia of Philosophy
http://plato.stanford.edu/entries/montesquieu/

Part II: Conservatism

Additional Readings
Buckley Jr, William F. *God and Man at Yale: The Superstitions of Academic Freedom*. Chicago: Regnery Publishing, 1951.

Farber, David. *The Rise and Fall of Modern American Conservatism: A Short History*. Princeton: Princeton University Press, 2010.

Honderich, Ted. *Conservatism: Burke, Nozick, Bush, Blair?* London: Pluto, 2005.

Kirk, Russell. *The Conservative Mind from Burke to Eliot,* seventh revised edition. Washington, DC: Regnery Publishing, 2001.

Oakeshott, Michael. *Rationalism in Politics and Other Essays*. London: Methuen, 1962.

Oretega y Gasset, José. *The Revolt of the Masses*. New York: Norton, 1932.

Web Links
William F. Buckley Jr Collection
https://cumulus.hillsdale.edu/Buckley/

Roger Scruton
http://www.roger-scruton.com/articles.html

The Russell Kirk Center for Cultural Renewal
www.kirkcenter.org/

The Federalist Society for Law and Public Policy Studies
www.fed-soc.org/

The Heritage Foundation
www.heritage.org/

Part III: Reform Liberalism

Additional Readings
English, John. *Just Watch Me: The Life of Pierre Elliott Trudeau: 1968–2000*. Toronto: Random House, 2009.

Gray, John N. *Liberalisms: Essays in Political Philosophy*. New York: Routledge, 2010.

Hodge, Rodger D. *The Mendacity of Hope: Barack Obama and the Betrayal of American Liberalism*. New York: HarperCollins, 2010.

Lippmann, Walter. *The Good Society*. Princeton: Princeton University Press, 2008.

Nussbaum, Martha. *Not for Profit: Why Democracy Needs the Humanities*. Princeton: Princeton University Press, 2010.

Rawls, John. *A Theory of Justice*. Cambridge, MA: Harvard University Press, 1971.

——. *Political Liberalism*. New York: Columbia University Press, 1993.

Sen, Amartya K. *Collective Choice and Social Welfare*. San Francisco: Holden-Day, 1970.

——. *The Idea of Justice*. Cambridge, MA: Harvard University Press, 2009.

Web Links
Center for American Progress
www.americanprogress.org

European Liberal Forum
www.liberalforum.eu

John Maynard Keynes
www.maynardkeynes.org

Liberal International
www.liberal-international.org

The John Dewey Society
http://doe.concordia.ca/jds/

The New Republic
www.tnr.com

The Nation
www.thenation.com

Part IV: Marxism

Additional Readings

Althusser, Louis. *For Marx*. London: Verso, 1990.
Berlin, Isaiah. *Karl Marx: His Life and Environment*. New York: Oxford University Press, 1996.
Bremmer, Ian. *The End of the Free Market: Who Wins the War Between States and Corporations?* New York: Portfolio (Penguin USA), 2010.
Held, David. *Introduction to Critical Theory. Horkheimer to Habermas*. Berkeley: University of California Press, 1980.
Kolakowski, Leszek. *Main Currents of Marxism: The Founders, the Golden Age, the Breakdown* (translated from the Polish by P.S. Falla). New York: W.W. Norton, 2005.
McLellan, David. *Karl Marx: His Life and Thought*. London: Papermac, 1973, 1987.
Schoenhals, Michael, ed. *China's Cultural Revolution, 1966–1969: Not a Dinner Party*. Armonk, NY: M.E. Sharpe, 1996.
Tucker, Robert C., ed. *The Lenin Anthology*. New York: Norton, 1975.

Web Links
Marxists Internet Archive
http://www.marxists.org/

World Socialist Web Site
http://wsws.org/

Critique of the Gotha Programme (Marx & Engels Internet Archive)
www.marxists.org/archive/marx/works/1875/gotha/index.htm

Trotsky Internet Archive
www.marxists.org/archive/trotsky/index.htm

Part V: Democratic Socialism

Additional Readings

Barman, Sheri. *The Primacy of Politics: Social Democracy and the Making of Europe's Twentieth Century*. Cambridge: Cambridge University Press, 2006.

Beveridge, William H. *The Pillars of Security*. New York: MacMillian, 1943.

Callinicos, Alex. *Against the Third Way: An Anti-Capitalist Critique*. Cambridge, UK: Polity Press, 2001.

Laxer, James. *In Search of a New Left: Canadian Politics after the Neo-Conservative Assault*. Toronto: Viking, Penguin, 1996.

Macpherson, C.B. *Democratic Theory. Essays in Retrieval*. Oxford: Oxford University Press, 1973.

Merkel, Wolfgang, et al. *Social Democracy in Power: The Capacity to Reform*. New York, NY: Routledge, 2008.

Nove, Alec. *The Economics of Feasible Socialism Revisited*. New York: HarperCollins Academia, 1991.

Offe, Claus. *Contradictions of the Welfare State*. Cambridge, MA: MIT Press, 1984.

Self, Peter. *Rolling Back the Market: Economic Dogma and Political Choice*. New York: St. Martin's Press, 2000.

Sombart, Werner. *Why Is There No Socialism in the United States?* (translated by Patricia M. Hocking and C.T. Husbands; edited and with an introductory essay by C.T. Husbands; and with a foreword by Michael Harrington) London: Macmillan, 1976.

Web Links

Chancellor Willy Brandt Foundation
www.willy-brandt.de/en/the-foundation.html

Douglas-Coldwell Foundation
www.dcf.ca/

Eugene V. Debs Foundation
http://debsfoundation.org/

Labour: Politics—The Guardian
www.guardian.co.uk/politics/labour

Monthly Review
http://.monthlyreview.org

New Politics Initiative
http://web.archive.org/web/20040421031913/http://www.newpolitics.ca/

New Democratic Party of Canada (Official Site)
www.ndp.ca/

Québec solidaire
www.quebecsolidaire.net/

People's History Museum
www.phm.org.uk/

The Party of European Socialists (PES)
www.pes.eu/

Part VI: Fascism and Neo-nationalism

Additional Readings

Berezin, Mabel. *Illiberal politics in Neoliberal Times: Culture, Security and Populism in the New Europe.* Cambridge, UK: Cambridge University Press, 2009.

Danchev, Alex, ed. *100 Artists' Manifestos: From the Futurists to the Stuckists.* London: Penguin Classic, 2011.

Evans, Richard J. *The Coming of the Third Reich.* London: Allen Lane, 2003.

Griffin, Roger. *The Nature of Fascism.* New York: St. Martin's Press, 1991.

———. *A Fascist Century: Essays by Roger Griffin* (edited by Matthew Feldman; with a preface by Stanley G. Payne). New York: Palgrave Macmillan, 2008.

Kershaw, Ian. *Hitler, the Germans, and the Final Solution.* New Haven: Yale University Press, 2008.

Paxton, Robert O. *The Anatomy of Fascism.* New York: Knopf, 2004.

Shirer, William L. *The Rise and Fall of the Third Reich: A History of Nazi Germany.* New York: Simon and Schuster, 1960, 1990.

Smith, Anthony D. *Nations and Nationalism in a Global Era.* Cambridge: Polity Press, 1995.

Weber, Thomas. *Hitler's First War: Adolf Hitler, The Men of the List Regiment, and the First World War.* Oxford: Oxford University Press, 2010.

Web Links

Hannah Arendt—Stanford Encyclopedia of Philosophy
http://plato.stanford.edu/entries/arendt/

Holocaust Memorial
www.stiftung-denkmal.de/en/home/html

Geert Wilders Weblog
www.geertwilders.nl/

Simon Wiesenthal Centre
www.wiesenthal.com/site/pp.asp?c=lsKWLbPJLnF&b=6212365

South Poverty Law Center
www.splcenter.org/

United States Holocaust Memorial Museum
www.ushmm.org/

Part VII: Pacifism

Additional Readings

Dombrowski, Daniel. *Christian Pacifism*. Philadelphia: Temple University Press, 1991.

Fiala, Andrew. *The Just War Myth. The Moral Illusions of War*. Lanham, MD: Rowman and Littlefield, 2008.

Gandhi, Mohandas K. *Non-Violence in Peace and War, 1942–1949*. New York: Garland Press, 1972.

Hauerwas, Stanley. *Performing the Faith: Bonhoeffer and the Practice of Nonviolence*. Grand Rapids: Brazos, 2004.

Kant, Immanuel. "Perpetual Peace," in *Kant's Political Writings*. Cambridge: Cambridge University Press, 1991.

Narveson, Jan. "Pacifism: A Philosophical Analysis." *Ethics 74*, 4 (1965): 259–71.

Schweitzer, Albert. *Civilization and Ethics*. London: A. & C. Black, 1949.

Thoreau, Henry David. "Civil Disobedience," in *Walden and Other Writings*. New York: The Modern Library, 2000.

Web Links

A Force More Powerful
www.aforcemorepowerful.org/

Center for Peace and Justice—Villanova University
www1.villanova.edu/villanova/artsci/peaceandjustice.html

Concerned Philosophers for Peace
http://peacephilosophy.org/

The Complete Site on Mahatma Gandhi
www.mkgandhi.org/

Global Peace Index—Vision of Humanity
www.visionofhumanity.org/

International Peace Research Association Foundation
www.iprafoundation.org/

International Centre on Nonviolent Conflict
www.nonviolent-conflict.org/

Just War Theory
www.justwartheory.com/

Centre for Peace Studies— McMaster University
www.humanities.mcmaster.ca/~peace/

Mennonite Church Canada's Peace and Justice Ministries
www.mennonitechurch.ca/programs/peace/

MIR Centre for Peace—Selkirk College
http://selkirk.ca/research/mir-centre-for-peace/

Peace & Justice Studies Association
www.peacejusticestudies.org/

Peace Voice
www.peacevoice.info/

Peace and Conflict Studies—University of Waterloo
http://uwaterloo.ca/peace-conflict-studies

Part VIII: Neo-liberalism and Globalization

Additional Readings

Della Porta, Donatella, ed. *The Global Justice Movement: Cross-national and Transnational Perspectives*. New York: Paradigm, 2006.

Harvey, David. *A Brief History of Neoliberalism*. Oxford: Oxford University Press, 2005.

Hacker, Jacob, and Paul Pierson. *Winner-Take-All-Politics: How Washington Made the Rich Richer and Turned Its Back on the Middle Class*. New York: Simon Schuster, 2010.

Saad-Filho, Alfredo, and Deborah Johnston, eds. *Neoliberalism: A Critical Reader*. Ann Arbor, MI: Pluto Press, 2005.

Shaxson, Nicholas. *Treasure Islands: Tax Havens and the Men Who Stole the World*. London: Bodley Head, 2011.

Stiglitz, Joseph E. *Making Globalization Work*. New York: W.W. Norton, 2006.

Wolf, Martin. *Why Globalization Works*. New Haven, CT: Yale Nota Bene, 2005.

Web Links

Ludwig von Mises Institute
http://mises.org/

Mont Pelerin Society
www.montpelerin.org/montpelerin/index.html

International Policy Network
www.policynetwork.net/about-ipn

American Enterprise Institute
www.aei.org/

Fraser Institute
www.fraserinstitute.org/

World Trade Organization
www.wto.org/

Mapping Globalization
www.princeton.edu/~mapglobe/HTML/home.html

Attac International
www.attac.org/en

Part IX: Feminism

Additional Readings
Basu, Amrita, ed. *Women's Movement in the Global Era: The Power of Local Feminisms*. Boulder, CO: Westview Press, 2010.
Beauvoir, Simone de. *The Second Sex*, translated and edited by H.M. Parshley. New York: Vintage Books, 1974 (1952).
Code, Lorraine. *Encyclopedia of Feminist Theories*. London: Routledge, 2004.
Gilbert, Sandra, and Susan Gubar. *The Madwoman in the Attic: The Women Writer in the Nineteenth-Century Literary Imagination*. New Haven: Yale University Press, 1979.
Gubar, Susan. *Critical Condition: Feminism at the Turn of the Century*. New York: Columbia University, 2000.
Hanisch, Carol. "The Personal is Political" in *Notes from the Second Year: Women's Liberation: Major Writings of the Radical Feminists*, edited by Shulamith Firestone and Anne Koedt. New York: Radical Feminism, 1970.
Hansen, Karen V., and Ilene J. Philipson. *Women, Class and the Feminist Imagination: A Socialist Feminist Reader*. Philadelphia: Temple University Press, 1990.
Maxwell, Sarah. *Success and Solitude: Feminist Organizations Fifty Years after the Feminist Mystique*. Lanham, MD: University Press of America, 2009.
Nicholson, Linda, ed. *The Second Wave: A Reader in Feminist Theory*. New York: Routledge, 1997.
Sunstein, Cass R., ed. *Feminism and Political Theory*. Chicago: University of Chicago Press, 1990.

Web Links
National Council of Women in Canada
www.ncwc.ca/ip_ncwcdo.html

Canadian Council of Muslim Women
www.ccmw.com/

Canadian Federation of Business and Professional Women
www.bpwcanada.com/

Canadian Federation for Sexual Health
www.cfsh.ca/

Feminist.com
www.feminist.com/

International Council of Women
www.icw-cif.org/

Ms. Magazine
www.msmagazine.com/index.asp

Part X: Environmentalism

Additional Readings

Brundtland, Gro Harlem. *Our Common Future*. New York: Oxford University Press, 1987.
Carson, Rachel. *Silent Spring*. Cambridge, MA: The Riverside Press, 1962.
Carter, Neil. *The Politics of the Environment: Ideas, Activism, Policy*. New York: Cambridge University Press, 2007.
Dobson, Andrew. *Justice and the Environment: Conceptions of Environmental Sustainability and Dimensions of Social Justice*. Oxford: Oxford University Press, 1998.
Hardin, Garrett, "The Tragedy of the Commons," *Science 162*, 3859 (1968): 1243–48.
IPCC. *Climate Change 2007: Synthesis Report. Contribution of Working Groups I, II and III to the Fourth Assessment Report of the Intergovernmental Panel on Climate Change*. Geneva: International Panel on Climate Change, 2007.
Lomborg, Bjørn. *The Skeptical Environmentalist*. Cambridge: Cambridge University Press, 2001.
Lovelock, James. *Gaia: A New Look at Life on Earth*, third edition. Oxford: Oxford University Press, 2000, 1979.
Schweitzer, Albert. *Civilization and Ethics*. London: Adam & Charles Black, 1994.
Wall, Derek. *The No-Nonsense Guide to Green Politics*. Ottawa, ON: The New Internationalist, 2010.

Web Links

Association for Environmental Studies and Sciences
www.aess.info/

Ecoportal Canada
www.planetfriendly.net/ecoportal.html

Greenpeace Canada
www.greenpeace.org/canada/

Grist: Environmental News, Commentary, Advice
www.grist.org/

Friends of the Clayoquot Sound
www.focs.ca/

International Institute for Sustainable Development
www.iisd.org/

Sierra Club
www.sierraclub.org/

Wilderness Committee
wildernesscommittee.org/

Part XI: Religious Fundamentalism

Additional Readings

Armstrong, Karen. *The Battle for God: Fundamentalism in Judaism, Christianity and Islam.* New York: Ballantine Books, 2000.

Dawkins, Richard. *The God Delusion.* London: Bantam Press, 2006.

Hamer, Dean H. *The God Gene: How Faith is Hardwired into Our Genes.* New York: Doubleday, 2004.

Inbari, Motti. *Jewish Fundamentalism and the Temple Mount: Who Will Build the Third Temple.* Albany, NY: SUNY Press, 2009.

Lewis, Bernard. *Islam and the West.* New York: Oxford University Press, 1993.

Marsden, George M. *Fundamentalism and American Culture.* New York: Oxford University Press, 2006.

Marty, Martin E., and Scott R. Appleby. *The Fundamentalism Project* (Vol. 1–5). Chicago: University of Chicago Press, various dates.

Nussbaum, Martha C. *The Clash Within: Democracy, Religious Violence and the India's Future.* Cambridge, MA: Harvard University Press, 2007.

Onfray, Michael. *Atheist Manifesto: The Case Against Christianity, Judaism, and Islam.* New York: Arcade Publishing, 2007.

Tibi, Bassam. *Islam's Predicament with Modernity: Religious Reform and Cultural Change.* New York: Routledge, 2009.

Web Links

Bharatiya Janata Party
www.bjp.org/

Christian Coalition of America
www.cc.org/

Evangelical Christian Church in Canada
www.cecconline.com/

Friends of Mercaz HaRav
www.mercazharav.org/

Jihad Watch
www.jihadwatch.org/

Revolutionary Association of the Women of Afghanistan
www.rawa.org/index.php

Religious Tolerance (Ontario Consultants on Religious Tolerance)
www.religioustolerance.org/

Southern Baptist Convention
www.sbc.net/

Southern Poverty Law Center
www.splcenter.org/

Ikhwanweb: The Muslim Brotherhood
www.ikhwanweb.com/

The Religious Zionists of America
www.rza.org/

Women Against Fundamentalism
www.womenagainstfundamentalism.org.uk/

Glossary

Absolutism: A form of government in which all political power is concentrated in the hands of either one or a few individuals.

Abstract rights: Rights divorced from history and tradition, singled out for praise by French Revolutionaries, and for criticism by the conservative Edmund Burke.

Activism: The struggle for social change. Examples include participation in the anti–Vietnam War movement, the struggle for the decriminalization of abortion, the civil disobedience advocated by Mohandas Gandhi, and the civil rights movement in the United States in the 1960s.

Affirmative action: Programs that ameliorate the conditions of disadvantaged individuals or groups, including those that suffer owing to race, national or ethnic origin, colour, religion, sex, age, or mental or physical disability.

Agenda: Term used by Jeremy Bentham in contrast to "Non-Agenda." Keynes asserts that the chief task of economists is to distinguish afresh those things comprising the Agenda, namely those things that are of priority to the government of the day. Again, according to Keynes, the companion task for politics and politicians is structuring a form of government that shall be capable of fulfilling the Agenda.

Ahimsa: School of thought derived from Buddhism and Jainism that practises harmlessness, from which are derived—according to Aldous Huxley—both humanitarianism and pacifism. Cf. **Satyagraha**.

Alienation: Being estranged from one's essential nature, work, or fellow human beings. This idea played a role in the writings of Georg Hegel and Karl Marx.

Al Qaeda: A decentralized, global network of Sunni Islamic terror cells founded by Osama Bin Laden (1957–2011), the son of a wealthy Saudi Arabian entrepreneur. Al Qaeda, which translates as "the Base," emerged in the late 1980s during the waning days of the Cold War and gained global prominence in the 1990s and 2000 through a series of attacks, most notably on New York and Washington, DC, on 11 September 2001. The death of Bin Laden at the hands of US special forces in 2011 has by all accounts weakened Al Qaeda and its global Jihad (Holy War) agenda.

Altruism: Contrasts with egoism and manifests a concern for the interests and welfare of others. Like egoism, it can be interpreted normatively or psychologically; according to the former, people should be concerned for the interests and welfare of others, while according to the latter, people are by nature so concerned.

Anarchism: Political movement that advocates the abolition of authority on the grounds that coercion is evil. Without government, it aims to achieve social harmony. By the end of the nineteenth century, many anarchists became interested in the revolutionary potential of anarcho-syndicalism or revolutionary trade unionism.

Androcentrism: Literally, "male-centred." Feminists, whether liberal, socialist, or radical, oppose male-centredness in society for the adverse effect it has on women economically, politically, and socially.

Androgyny: The condition of possessing both male and female characteristics. It implies that humans are sexless persons and that therefore sex is irrelevant to social and political roles. Some feminists claim that one goal for the future should be the cultivation of individuals who are androgynous.

Anti-Semitism: Discrimination against Jews. This discrimination became institutionalized in the Third Reich in Germany during the years 1933–1945.

Antithetical ideals: Ideals that are opposed. Liberty and equality are examples of antithetical ideas.

Apartheid: Racial segregation of blacks, whites, and "coloureds," especially as practised by the National Party in South Africa from 1948 to 1994.

Arab Spring: A period of political turmoil across the Arab Middle East, which witnessed the demise of several totalitarian regimes that had clung to power for decades, often with the help of Western nations who had coddled them for economic and strategic reasons. This phase began with a peaceful revolution in Tunisia, which then spread to Egypt, where protestors aided by the Internet forced the resignation of long-time potentate Hosni Mubarak. But this pattern did not repeat elsewhere, particularly in Libya, where a civil war had preceded the death of long-time ruler Muammar al-Gaddafi.

Aristocracy: Rule by the best, usually comprising the elite or prominent citizens. One of six constitutional regimes as identified by Aristotle, the others being monarchy, polity, tyranny, oligarchy, and democracy.

Aryans: In Nordic mythology, a pure and noble-blooded race of northern Europe, especially those of German stock. Belief in this mythology served as the background for belief in Aryan supremacy as found in the Nazi Party.

Atheistic materialism: Position that affirms the centrality of material or natural forces in explanation of social phenomena while rejecting the belief in god or gods.

Autarky: An economic policy that emphasizes self-sufficiency through the reduction of imported goods. In pre-Nazi Germany this idea was used by Johann Gottlieb Fichte and Friedrich List to explain the failures of economic policies based on free trade and to attack the positions of Adam Smith, Richard Cobden, and David Ricardo.

Authority: Political power that is legitimate.

Autonomy and reciprocity: Presupposition of classical and neo-liberal economists. This presupposition, at least as developed by James Buchanan, implies the normative claim to the effect that all persons in the trading context are natural equals, each one assumed to be equally capable of both making exchanges and living with the consequences.

Banlieue Revolt (2005): A series of violent clashes between French police and youth that occurred in the poorer suburbs of Paris and other French cities in 2005. The riots—which lasted some 20 nights from late October through the middle of November that year—caused extensive property damage and two deaths. It also exposed the deep cracks between the mainstream of French society and its growing underclass of disaffected, unemployed youth of Muslim-Arab heritage.

Barely visibly family: The minimal recognition given the family in John Rawls' *A Theory of Justice*. Rawls gives this minimal recognition in spite of his assumption that families are not only just but also where moral development takes place in the first instance. Susan Okin finds this minimalism on the part of Rawls counterintuitive and in need to serious modification.

Biocentrism: Theory that places all life forms on the same ethical level. It condemns anthropocentrism for placing humans at the centre of ethical considerations in the cosmos.

Biodiversity: A term that allows the scientific community to describe the variability of life forms and ecosystems. The concept serves as a measure of ecological health and sustainability. Consider the following examples. Whereas the Amazon qualifies as a region of high biological diversity, a mono-cultural tree plantation would rank low in terms of diversity.

Bolshevism: Derived from the Russian word *bolshinstvo* meaning "majority." In 1903, the Russian Social Democratic Labour Party split into two groups. The Bolsheviks, headed by Vladimir Ilyich Lenin, were radical and endorsed the use of violence, while the Mensheviks, or "minority," were moderate in outlook.

Bourgeoisie: Term used by Marx to refer to the owners of the means of production (land, banks, natural resources) in a capitalist society. It was this class that emerged to challenge the old feudal class. Used loosely, it refers to the middle class. Cf. **Proletariat**.

Brundtland Report: The name of a groundbreaking environmental report, where the concept of sustainable development first gained a global audience. Named after the former Norwegian Prime Minister Gro Harlem Brundtland, the report describes the findings of an eponymous UN commission into the state of the global environment and development. Published in 1987, the report pushed global environmental problems up the political agenda and prepared the path for a series of high-level meetings such as the Rio Conference in 1992.

Bureaucracy: One of five parts of the state, the others being the cabinet, legislature, judiciary, and military/police. Normally, it comprises the non-elected administrative arm of the state.

Capabilities approach: As advanced by Martha Nussbaum, an incomplete account of social justice that draws special attention to "minimum core social entitlements." These entitlements include those pertaining to bodily health, bodily integrity, thought, and emotions. Nussbaum supports this position and maintains that it is but one species of the human rights approach.

Capitalism: An economic system in which the means of production and the mechanics of distribution are controlled by a narrow class of property owners. It is predicated on competition, free trade, and the absence of monopoly control. In Adam Smith's writings it is clearly distinguished from two other economic systems: mercantilism and physiocracy.

Caste: A rigid hereditary class system—often associated with Hinduism in India—where sharp social divisions, as determined by occupations, are strictly enforced.

Catallactic perspective: Economic perspective, spoken of by James Buchanan, that claims that market organization replaces hierarchical organization. "Market outcomes" and "market ends," as they are called, simply emerge from the interactions of "interdependent choosers" within a structure of rules that "define the parameters of the game." On this view, the anarchism feared by Thomas Hobbes can be avoided, not by requiring an all-powerful and hierarchical sovereign power but a market backed by a limited sovereign who enforces the laws of property and contract.

Christian fundamentalism: Early twentieth-century American religious movement that subscribed to the following beliefs: the virgin birth of Jesus, the inerrancy of scripture, a special theory of atonement, and the second coming of Jesus as a denouement of history.

Civil disobedience: Non-violent resistance of the law. This was advocated by Henry David Thoreau and William Lloyd Garrison in the United States, Leo Tolstoy in Russia, and most famously Mohandas Gandhi in India during the independence movement against the British in the 1940s. It was also used by Martin Luther King Jr in the civil rights movement in the United States during the 1960s.

Civil rights: Usually coupled with political rights to embrace those rights found in liberal constitutions: the right to freedom of speech, association, the press, conscience, and religion, and the right to vote (suffrage). These rights are contrasted with economic and social rights as applied to property, health, education, and employment.

Civil society: The domain of autonomous groups or associations that stand at arm's length from government. Such groups would include families, churches, unions, and clubs.

Classical liberalism: The version of liberalism advocated by John Locke and Adam Smith and resuscitated by neo-liberals such as Milton Friedman and Robert Nozick. Under this version of liberalism, the rights of individuals to life, liberty, and property are emphasized.

Class struggle: The contradiction identified by Marx as the fundamental mechanism explaining change in history. During the phase of capitalism, the capitalists, or bourgeoisie, dominated the proletariat, according to Marx. The former represented the owners of the means of production and the latter represented those who were exploited, namely, the workers.

Cold War: The term describes a period that roughly lasted from 1946 to 1991 during which the former Soviet Union and the United States competed for global influence as the respective leaders of the eastern (socialist) and the western (capitalistic) bloc. This competition unfolded through a series of direct political confrontations between the two superpowers, as well as a series of proxy wars between some of their respective allies in the developing, post-colonial world in places such as Vietnam, the Korean Peninsula, the African Continent, and the Middle East. This Cold War threatened to turn "hot" on at least one major occasion—the so-called Cuban Missile Crisis (1962)—when the prospect of Soviet nuclear missiles stationed off the American mainland pushed both nations to the edge of a nuclear conflict. It would have likely destroyed planetary life as both nations maintained massive arsenals under the deterrence doctrine of Mutually Assured Destruction (MAD). The Cold War ended with the dissolution of the Soviet Union, whose state-run economy had failed to keep up with its more productive American competitor.

Collective rights: The view that the community is a self-originating source of moral, social, and historical claims. As argued by Kymlicka, such alleged rights or claims are the source of some of the opposition among aboriginal peoples to Trudeau's White Paper of 1969. In a nutshell, this opposition expressed clearly the conflict between individualism and collectivism.

Collectivism: Following Friedrich Hayek, the organizing of the whole of society and its resources for a unitary end and the rejection of autonomous spheres that affirm the supremacy of individuals' ends.

Colour-blind constitution: Following Kymlicka, the removal of all legislation differentiating among people in terms of race and ethnicity.

Common purpose: Common good, general welfare, or general interest.

Communism: Political ideology, distinct from democratic socialism, advocating the use of violence by the vanguard of the proletariat, or intelligentsia, to overturn the dominance of the bourgeoisie. Marx was the most famous proponent of this ideology, though others almost as famous were Lenin, Leon Trotsky, Mao Tse-Tung, and Fidel Castro.

Communist Manifesto, The: One of the central sources of Marxism, the ideology bearing the name of German philosopher Karl Marx (1818–1883). Published in 1848 during a revolutionary period in European history, this text written by Marx and his collaborator Friedrich Engels (1820–1895) argues that the "history of all hitherto existing society is the history of class struggles" in describing one of the central tenets of Marxism. The text also introduced terms such as **proletariat** and **bourgeoisie** to a wider audience in detailing the nature, evolution, and (predicted) decline of capitalism. The title remains one of the most influential and referenced sources of political commentary and analysis.

Communitarianism: A political philosophy that emphasizes the role of community and tradition in defining the interests and rights of persons. This position has classical roots in Plato and Aristotle, but more recently it has been advanced by Alasdair MacIntyre.

Comparative advantage: Theory of Adam Smith, developed by David Ricardo, that nations should play upon their strengths by trading that which they produce efficiently and importing that which they do not.

Consequentialism: A moral school of thought that assesses the morality of actions by the extent to which they contribute to the realization of the good, conceived as including happiness or pleasure and, importantly, values other than these, e.g., self-realization and the appreciation of beauty.

Conservatism: Political philosophy wedded to the idea of preserving traditions, practices, and institutions. Edmund Burke is the most famous proponent of this view, though it is also advanced by David Hume.

Constitutionalism: Belief in government working within the framework of a constitution that defines general principles of government institutions such as the legislature, executive, and judiciary. Sometimes, though not always, these general principles will specify political rights.

Convention: Unwritten law that lacks legal enforcement but include penalties of various political, social, and economic kind. Conventions play a particularly important role in the life of states, whose political institutions draw inspiration from the parliamentary traditions of the United Kingdom, where conventions are treated as if they were codified laws.

Conventionalism: School of moral thought maintaining that morality is grounded in practices that have evolved without the need of some contract. Nonmoral examples of evolving practices include the use of money and the use of language.

Corporativism (corporatism): Type of socio-political system used in Italy under Benito Mussolini with his vision of the corporate state. Under this theory, business interests and labour interests should be incorporated into the processes of government. In this way, the interests of labourers, managers, state, and nation are brought together.

Crimes against humanity: A concept introduced by the Greek jurist Nicolas Politis for the purpose of international prosecution of Turkish authorities in connection with atrocities they committed against the Armenian people at the end of the nineteenth and beginning of the twentieth century. Other countries—from Germany and other Nazi-occupied nations during World War II to, more recently, Cambodia, Rwanda, and the former Yugoslavia—have witnessed such crimes. Cf. **War crimes**.

Critical anti-realism: Metaphysical position that claims reality is something constructed by humans rather than something existing independently of them. Pluralism and relativism are products of this position.

Critical symptoms of decline: As suggested by Kevin Phillips, concern over cultural and economic decay, growing religious fervour, rising commitment to faith over reason, popular anticipation of a millennial time frame, and strategic and military over-reach.

Crusades: Christian military expeditions or holy wars initiated in Europe to take control of the Holy Land from Muslims. Eight such expeditions occurred from 1095 to 1212. In 1095, Pope Urban II encouraged Christian men of Europe to support the plight of their eastern Christian brothers as well as the movement of pilgrims to Jerusalem by recovering the sacred land of their lord.

Cultural Revolution: Movement in China launched by Mao Tse-Tung in 1966 to purge the country of his opponents. The Red Guard comprised the leaders of this movement. Cf. **Maoism**.

Das Kapital: A text that contains many of the central positions held by German philosopher Karl Marx (1818–1883), the main founder of the political ideology bearing his name. *Das Kapital* explores and eviscerates various aspects of capitalism in laying out an extensive critique that continues to enjoy support and court controversy since 1867, when the first of what would eventually become four volumes appeared. The opening volume arguably qualifies as the most important one, since it includes central elements of Marxist theory about the role of economics as the driving force of history. It is also the only one that appeared during Marx's lifetime. Collaborator and benefactor Friedrich Engels (1820–1895) published the remaining volumes posthumously.

Deep ecologism: Radical environmentalism whose advocates, such as Arne Naess, focus on what they consider to be the roots of environmental despoliation. These roots extend to the anti-social aspects of industrialization, whether under capitalism or Marxism.

Democracy: Derived from the Greek word *demokratia*, meaning "rule by the people." In contemporary discussions this takes two forms: participatory democracy and representative democracy, the former found in some city-states of ancient Greece, and the latter found in present-day industrialized Western nations. According to Thomas Paine, democracy should strive to bring out the genius in everyone.

Democratic centralism: Lenin's theory that the central leadership of the Communist Party of the Soviet Union is to permit open discussions prior to, but not after, policy decisions. It affirmed the need for subordination to properly constituted authority.

Democratic revolution: As advocated by Peter Self, a revolution that extends democratic practices to institutions other than the state, aspires to more economic equality, and encourages the responsible exercise of rights by citizens.

Democratic socialism: A political ideology originating in the nineteenth century in response to the social problems created by the Industrial Revolution and the inability of classical liberalism to address these same problems. It emphasizes equality, especially economic equality, as an ideal.

Demography: Strictly, writing about the *demos,* or people. It is a field of study that examines human populations in terms of their structure (e.g., age, sex, marital status) and dynamics (e.g., births, deaths, and migratory habits).

Dialectic: The art of critical examination into the truth of an opinion. Plato's dialectical thinking made use of the method of questions and answers. Hegel's dialectical idealism postulated a struggle between the thesis and the anti-thesis of an idea. Marx turned Hegel's dialectic on its head and established a position called "dialectical materialism," in which material things (such as classes of persons) formed the entities that engaged in the struggle as thesis and anti-thesis. In the thinking of both Hegel and Marx, the dialectical struggle resulted in a new synthesis being reached, which in turn formed the thesis of a new struggle.

Dialectical materialism: Marx's conception of social systems driven by modes of production and property relations. These causal forces influence law, religion, art, and philosophy, among other things, in a dialectical or Hegelian fashion.

Dialectical naturalism—A term that American philosopher Murray Bookchin coined to highlight the interplay between social and ecological problems. As such, dialectical naturalism stands in philosophical opposition to the dialectical materialism informing Marxism, since it ignores ecological concerns in framing history as the outcome of economic forces. Dialectical naturalism challenges this perspective in linking human existence to ecological limits.

Dictatorship of the proletariat: According to Marx and Lenin, the transitory period of rule by the proletariat which follows the overthrow of the bourgeoisie. During this time, the proletariat would have to be vigilant in suppressing attempts by the bourgeoisie to re-establish its dominance. Cf. **Immiseration of the proletariat**.

Difference principle: A principle advocated by the liberal philosopher John Rawls according to which the lowest individual endowment is maximized. Hence, *caeteris paribus,* social goods should be distributed equally unless unequal distributions have the effect of normally providing an advantage to the poor and unless all members of society have equal chances of acquiring greater-than-average shares of social goods.

Direct foreign investment (DFI): The outflowing of capital, sometimes, though not always, to poor countries with cheap labour.

Disaster capitalism: Following Naomi Klein, raids on the public sphere in the aftermath of catastrophic events such as Hurricane Katrina. Disaster capitalism views disasters as presenting market opportunities.

Dispensationalism: Christian fundamentalist view of history according to which history is divided up into seven dispensations or parts, whose character is fixed by God.

Division of labour: The practice of specialization in labour, noted and advocated by Adam Smith and David Ricardo in the eighteenth and nineteenth centuries but also recognized by Plato in *The Republic,* written in the early part of the fourth century BCE.

Doctrine of Surplus Value: A concept critical to the understanding of Marxism, the political ideology founded by German philosopher Karl Marx (1813–1889). Marx argues that the success of capitalism lies in its ability to accumulate the value, which workers create in excess of their labour costs. Entrepreneurs collect this "surplus" as profit, then re-invest portions of it into additional production capacities, thereby improving their potential to accumulate additional investment capital, not to mention profits.

Dominant protective association: In the absence of government, the dominant association that exists to protect the interests of certain persons. Churches, unions, and gangs are examples of such associations that exist even in the presence of government. Cf. **Protective association**.

Ecology: The study of the interactions of organisms with their physical environment and with each other.

Economic determinism: The theory that economic matters such as modes and relations of production determine social and political matters such as legal and religious institutions.

Egalitarianism: School of thought that affirms a principle of procedural and substantive equality.

Elitism: Belief in rule by a minority justified either on the grounds of merit or on the grounds of inevitability, other forms of leadership being inefficient, impractical, or unattainable.

Enabling Act: Legislation passed in March 1933 in Germany that transferred all legislative powers to Hitler's cabinet, including the power to amend the constitution. The third clause of the bill provided that laws enacted by the government (cabinet) should be drafted by the Chancellor (Hitler) and should come into effect the day after publication.

Enlightenment: An intellectual movement of the eighteenth century in Europe that aimed to rid persons of their self-incurred subordination. It promoted the understanding of the universe, society, and humans based on reason and empirical research. Immanuel Kant is perhaps its most famous proponent.

Environmentalism: Political philosophy that advocates heightened sensitivity for the environment, popularly referred to by the use of the adjective "green." Its advocates range from proponents of moderate change to those such as the organization Greenpeace and deep ecologists, who are more aggressive in their approach.

Equality: One of three ideals of the French Revolution—the other two being liberty and fraternity

(i.e., brotherhood)—that has found its way into constitutions of liberal societies as a protected ideal. It applies most frequently to the idea of procedural rather than substantive equality. Cf. **Legal and political equality**.

Equal liberty principle: A principle advanced by John Rawls guaranteeing all members of liberal society equal political liberties, liberties of conscience, property rights, and legal rights.

Essentialism: Philosophical position that asserts that the essence of any natural kind found in the sciences comprises a set of characteristics required of members of that kind. Applied to inanimate things, such as chemical elements, this position works better than it does when applied to biological species, such as humans, especially in light of Darwin's theory of evolution. Specifically applied to the human species, essentialism maintains that humans have an essence that exists independent of free choice. Cf. **Existentialism.**

Ethic of care: Position of some feminists that women differ from men, with the former having an ethic of responsibility and relations in contrast to an ethic of justice and rights.

European Union: Union of 27 counties in Europe. It evolved from the European Coal and Steel Community, the Common Market, and Euratom in the 1950s. Today, in many parts, it allows for free movement of goods, services, and labour and most recently, again in many parts, makes use of a common currency, the Euro.

Events of 9/11—A shorthand reference for the attacks on New York and Washington, DC, which Al Qaeda staged almost simultaneously on 11 September 2011. The attacks began when 19 suicide terrorists of Arab-Muslim background seized four commercial passengers jets. The hijackers eventually crashed three of the planes into their intended targets—one plane hitting each of the twin towers part of World Trade Center complex in New York and the Pentagon in Washington, DC. A fourth plane intended for Washington, DC, crashed in rural Pennsylvania after passengers rose against the hijackers. The Republican administration of US President George W. Bush responded to this particular event—which claimed some 3,000 victims that day—with the Global War on Terror.

Exchange: Following Bastiat, the calculation made by all to discontinue direct production when obtaining it indirectly saves time and money.

Existentialism: Philosophical school of twentieth century that laid emphasis on freedom, individuality, and the human condition generally. Captured nicely in Jean-Paul Sartre's phrase that "we are what we choose to be."

Externalities: The effects on third parties resulting from transactions between two other parties under the conditions of a free market. Such externalities might include diseconomies (e.g., pollution, congestion, and ugliness) or economies (e.g., reliable postal services and efficient urban transportation).

Factionalism: Adverse division among the citizenry. This division results in the promotion of the interests of some citizens against the interests of the wider community.

Fascism: A political ideology and movement, established by Benito Mussolini in 1919, calling for the abandonment of liberal and communist ideals, and the adoption of totalitarian ideals of leadership, ethno-national unity, irrationality, the leadership principle, and the corporate state.

Federalism: A constitutional system in which legislative powers are divided between a central government and regional governments at the state or provincial level. Accordingly, the citizens are subject to the legislative authority of two levels of government.

Feminism: A political ideology and movement that aims to advance the interests of women. Several philosophical positions have emerged from this movement, including liberal, socialist, and radical ones. These positions vary in how they deal with the dichotomy between public man and private woman, patriarchy, and sex and gender.

Feminist empiricism: A form of empiricism that attempts to combat inimical and androcentrically

centred epistemology. Some feminists, such as Lorraine Code, reject feminist empiricism in favour of a "middle ground" empiricism that affirms "mitigated relativism" and "realism."

Feudalism: The peculiar association of vassalage with fief-holding that was established in the Carolingian Empire (ninth century CE) and that spread subsequently from the Frankish kingdom to Italy, Spain, Germany, England, Scotland, and Ireland. It was a social system of rights of lords and duties of vassals based on land tenure and personal relationships.

Fidesz: A political party in Hungary. The emergence of Fidesz dates back to the concluding days of the Cold War, when Hungary became one of the first Soviet satellites to stage free, democratic elections. Political, economic, and social developments inside and outside of Hungary have subsequently pushed the party to the conservative side of the political spectrum, where it employs nationalistic rhetoric with great success to secure votes. During the most recent parliamentary election, it secured about two-thirds of the electorate.

Final Solution: A Nazi euphemism for the organized extermination of European Jews during World War II. While German special forces (*Kampfeinsatzgruppen*) might have killed up to one million Jews during the early years of the war as the German army was advancing across Europe, efforts took an organized and deadlier turn in early 1942 at the Wannsee Conference, where high-level Nazi officials signed off on an action plan to accelerate the killings by organizing them along industrial scales through the use of mass extermination camps such as the infamous Auschwitz.

Fiscal policy: The spending and revenue-producing (e.g., taxation) policy of a government. As an example, Keynesian economics (economics based on the ideas of John Maynard Keynes) promoted increased spending and lower taxes when unemployment was high, and reduced spending and increased taxes when inflation was high.

Forces of production: Equivalent to modes of production in Marxist thinking. Accordingly, the forces of production worked on property relations to produce, jointly, the superstructure comprising law, religion, philosophy, family, entertainment, etc.

Freedom: Made up of negative and positive freedom. The former refers to the absence of constraints imposed by the state, and the latter refers to the existence of opportunities to develop one's self.

Free Market, The: A system of economic exchanges that features the near-absence of state regulation and interference. Proponents of this concept, which has never existed and may never exist in its ideal form, are skeptical if not hostile toward measures such as taxes, regulations of various sorts, and state participation in industry. They instead favour a laissez-faire attitude in economic matters based on the writings of Scottish philosopher Adam Smith (1723–1790).

Free rider problem: A problem that arises when the use of goods by someone who has not contributed to their production cannot be excluded. In such a situation, it is no longer rational for such a person to contribute to the production of such goods.

French Revolution: A revolution in France, beginning in 1789, that aimed to limit the powers of the monarchy and the privileges of the aristocracy and clergy. Though based on the ideals of liberty, equality, and fraternity, it quickly gave way to a reign of terror during which time many were sent to the guillotine. Edmund Burke's *Reflections on the Revolution in France* was a treatise aimed at showing the strengths of conservatism against the principles of revolution.

Füehrer: Literally, "leader." In National Socialism of the Third Reich, it referred to the chief or supreme leader—i.e., Adolf Hitler. The equivalent of this position in Fascism was Il Duce—i.e., Mussolini.

Füehrerprinzip: Leadership principle adhered to in Nazi Germany and Fascist Italy that required absolute obedience to the leader and correspondingly to his subordinates as in a military chain of command.

Fundamentalism: Ideology that emphasizes the basic ideas of a creed and the literal interpretation of sacred texts. Examples can be found in at least three major world faiths: Judaism, Christianity, and Islam.

Futurists: A group of artists whose various works informed not only modern art during the first half of the twentieth century but also fascism. While their contributions varied, they took their name from the Futurist Manifesto penned by Italian writer Filippo Tommaso Emilio Marinetti (1876–1944) in 1909. The movement that would eventually bear the name of Marinetti's manifesto embraced modern technology and war in attacking the perceived decadence and liberalism of European society, then teetering on the edge of World War I. Marinetti himself would later serve Benito Mussolini (1883–1945) as a cabinet minister and front-line soldier in Russia.

Gaia hypothesis: It postulates that the totality of all organic beings and their inorganic surroundings form a self-regulating system of immense complexity that functions as if it were alive itself. First developed by British scientist and physician James Lovelock (1919–), the hypothesis draws inspiration from Gaia, the bearer of all things in Greek mythology. While the scientific community had initially challenged this argument, its level of acceptance has increased since its initial appearance in the 1960s.

Gender: Roles women and men play in society. Cf. **Sex**.

General Agreement on Tariffs and Trace (GATT): It was established in 1948 to reduce trade barriers through the operation of the most-favoured-nation principle. This agreement now is administered under the World Trade Organization (WTO).

Genocide Convention: A resolution that the General Assembly of the United Nations adopted in 1948 to prevent and punish genocide. The convention legally defines genocide, incorporates it into international law, and spells out a punishment mechanism. The convention responded to the Holocaust of World War II but also earlier genocides such as Armenian Genocide during and after World War I.

Globalization: The drive of corporations and capitalists to maximize profit through deregulation and international trade law.

Global War on Terror: A series of measures with which the United States responded to the events of

9/11, when the Islamic terror network of Al Qaeda successfully attacked the World Trade Center in New York and the Pentagon in Washington, DC—symbols of America's commercial and military supremacy respectively. Notable elements of this response included the following: the 2001 invasion of Afghanistan, whose Islamic fundamentalist government had offered Al Qaeda moral and material support in staging the initial attacks; the 2003 invasion and occupation of Iraq, which the United States had falsely accused of maintaining so-called weapons of mass destruction (WMD); and the legally sanctioned limitation if not outright suspension of various civil rights for the purpose of apprehending and preventing of future (Islamic) terrorists (or if you wish, acts of terrorists) through measures such as the Patriot Act, extraordinary rendition, and "enhanced interrogation techniques" such as water-boarding. Critics of this Global War on Terror have argued that it has undermined the moral and economic standing of the United States.

Gnosticism: A syncretic religious and philosophical movement in the second century CE that emphasized esoteric knowledge. This knowledge (*gnosis*) was of the mysteries of the universe, and through gnosis came the power to overcome the demons of the universe and to answer such questions as "Whence evil?" and "Whither man?"

Government: In a broad sense, the central mechanisms of the state: the executive, the legislature, the bureaucracy, and the judiciary. A strikingly different definition is given by Frédéric Bastiat: government is the great fiction, through which everybody endeavours to live at the expense of everyone else.

Great Society: An ambitious but unrealized agenda, which Democratic President Lyndon B. Johnson proposed in the 1960s to drain the remaining pools of poverty in the United States. Developed during a period of unprecedented American political influence abroad and economic prosperity at home, this blueprint for reform followed in the ideological footsteps of the New Deal. But its success was questionable from the very start as it clashed with the challenges of the coinciding Vietnam War and the emerging conservatism of Republican Barry Goldwater, whose extremist defence of personal virtues such as individual

responsibility left no room for the perceived vices of the welfare state.

Great Western Transmutation: Term coined by Marshall Hodgson to refer to the irreversible occurrence of cultural change, including industrialization, that occurred at the end of the eighteenth century. Not to be confused with the **Industrial Revolution**.

Growing inequality of income: Considered by neo-liberals to erode the support for the competitive market. Neo-liberals see job losses as an old problem in new dress, but believe growing inequality of income to be a new problem that must be addressed by policy action where appropriate. The policy action that neo-liberals endorse turns on better education and the easing of immigration.

Gujarat, India: Site of gruesome attacks on Muslims by Hindus in 2002, resulting in more than 2,000 deaths.

Gush Emunim: Hebrew for "Bloc of the Faithful." Political movement in Israel inspired by Rabbi Avraham Kook and his son Rabbi Yehuda Kook. As a group, it is responsible for many of the settlements in territory occupied by Israel after the Six Day War of 1967.

Halakha: Hebrew expression for "proper way." It refers to the accumulated laws and ordinances as they evolved from Old Testament times.

Hamas: Islamic political organization active in Gaza. Ideologically influenced by the Muslim Brotherhood.

Harm: The effect of causing deterioration in the functioning of something. A notion heavily relied on by utilitarians, harm is too often confused with pain caused to a sentient being. Plato gives a better account of this notion than do utilitarians by advancing a functional definition.

Hasidism: Sect of Orthodox Judaism that originated in eighteenth-century Poland under the tutelage of Rabbi Israel ben Eliezer (c. 1700–1760). His teachings emphasized prayer, piety, and joyful observance of God's commandments. The ideas of Hasidism are in some cases rooted in Jewish mysticism (the Kabbalah).

Hezbollah: Party of God, backed by Iran, and active in Lebanon. Its present leader is Sayyed Hassan Nasrallah. It aims to eliminate Western colonialism, establish an Islamic state in Lebanon, and bring people to justice for crimes committed in Lebanon's civil war.

Holism: A term introduced by Jan Smuts of South Africa to refer to our understanding of the interconnectedness of the ecosystem. This is sometimes contrasted by environmentalists with an atomistic or linear approach to the ecosystem.

Holocaust: Literally, "wholesale sacrifice" or "destruction." The first wholesale slaughter of a people in the twentieth century occurred in 1915 when more than a million—perhaps a million and a half—Armenians were killed by Turkish authorities. The second such slaughter occurred under the Nazis and the Third Reich of Adolf Hitler when six million Jews were exterminated under a program called the **Final Solution**.

Homo Economicus: Simply, "economic man." Those who subscribe to the view that man is economic by nature go on to assert that humans are ineluctably driven by the desire of endless accumulation. The thematic connection between this view of human nature and human tendencies toward greed or pleonexia, as discussed by Plato, is obvious.

Hubris: A term that signals the absence of humility and the abundance of arrogance. The term often appears in Classical Greek literature to describe humans who dared to challenge the gods, only to experience some form of deserving retribution (Nemesis). Modern uses of the term often refer to individuals whose ambitions far exceed their actual abilities.

Humanism: A secular philosophy that emphasizes the basic needs and interests of human beings. This idea was extant during classical times but was rediscovered during the Renaissance.

Ideologue: Intransigent supporter of an ideology.

Imagination: The faculty of humans on which Adam Smith places emphasis in developing his theory of moral sentiments. Pity or compassion is, for Smith, dependent on our own ability to imagine ourselves in the situation in which others find themselves. As he says, imagination is the source of our fellow-feeling for the misery of others.

Immiseration of the proletariat: Marx thought that capitalism would, by virtue of economic competition, cause systemic downward mobility, eventually leading to its overthrow by the proletariat. Democratic socialists such as Eduard Bernstein and R.H. Tawney do not subscribe to this, thereby drawing a distinction between Marxists and democratic socialists. Cf. **Dictatorship of the proletariat**.

Imperialism: The practice of a country acquiring and administering colonies and dependencies. Lenin thought imperialism to be the highest stage of capitalism. At its zenith, imperialist nations included Great Britain, Belgium, France, the Netherlands, and Portugal.

Individualism: Liberal view that asserts that individuals are the ultimate units of moral worth. Keynes' view explains the rise of individualism as attributable to ideas of natural liberty, social compact, toleration, utility, and rational self-love. Friedrich Hayek adds to the above, claiming that the whole of the philosophy of individualism is based on the impossibility of any person surveying more than a limited number of human needs. Thus, he concludes, the ends about which any person can have concerns will always be but a small fraction of all the needs of humans.

Indivisibility: Under public choice theory, the idea that benefits produced for one person are available to a wider group as well.

Industrial absolutism: According to Justice Brandeis of the United States Supreme Court, a form of authority that is quasi-governmental. This form of authority, possessed by industrialists, is thought by some to give rise to a private jurisdiction and relations between owners and workers that resembles that between rulers and subjects.

Industrial Revolution: Dramatic industrial change in the eighteenth and nineteenth centuries that profoundly influenced the politics of modern man. This period witnessed the transformation of the modes of production from handcrafted work to mechanization, and still later to automation. The Industrial Revolution was the product of the rise of modern science, beginning with the foundation of professional scientific bodies, such as the Royal Society of London in 1660. Cf. **Great Western Transmutation**.

Inerrancy: A belief in religious fundamentalism that all sacred scriptures, being divinely inspired, are without error.

Institutions: Rule-governed structures in society. These include public institutions, such as courts, schools, and governmental and administrative units, as well as private institutions, such as the Red Cross, Exxon, and the Royal Bank of Canada.

International Monetary Fund (IMF): Established together with the World Bank under Bretton Woods in 1944. This organization was originally created to help ensure stability of foreign exchange. In contemporary times, the organization assists debtor and developing states. Often the assistance to debtor states is tied to the introduction by the debtor state of particular policies. A good example of this occurred under Anwar Sadat of Egypt in the early 1980s who accepted loans from the IMF in exchange for removing subsidies for bread in Egypt—an action that eventually led to his assassination. Another example is presently underway as the IMF, together with the European Central Bank and the European Commission, aim to salvage the euro by demanding a "trimming" of the sovereign debt of Greece in exchange for economic bailouts. Initially the agreement establishing the IMF worked on a gold exchange standard but this was discarded in 1978 in favour of allowing member states the freedom to choose their own system of exchange rate.

Invisible Committee: The (so-far) anonymous authors of *The Coming Insurrection,* an anarchist text first published in France but popular throughout several Western countries. Several media accounts have linked this group with the Tarnac Nine, a group of middle-class French graduate students accused of plotting to commit various acts of terrorism.

Invisible hand: Notion advanced by Adam Smith to describe the convergence of individual and public interest in a free market society. It is sometimes thought to be the tendency of supply and demand toward self-correction. Economist John Maynard Keynes criticized this doctrine as unproved and almost certainly false.

Iron law of oligarchy: Theory of Robert Michel that organizations are controlled by the few active people in them because of the requirements of efficiency and organization.

Iron law of wages: Theory of David Ricardo to the effect that owners of the means of production, the capitalists, would pay the workers no more than was needed to survive.

Islamization: A term that populists in Europe and North American use to warn their respective societies against the perceived spread of radical Islamist ideology by recent immigrants from Arab-Muslim nations. More broadly, it assumes that Muslim practices, beliefs, and values are incompatible with what populists such as Geert Wilders have called Judeo-Christian traditions. This fear has encouraged the emergence of populist parties in several European countries and contributed to the 2011 massacre of 69 mostly young Norwegians at the hands of Andres Behring Breivik.

Jim Crow: A short-hand term for the body of laws that denied black Americans various political, social, and economic rights during the period that lasted from the mid-1870s to mid-1960s. Jim Crow laws segregated black Americans from white Americans by creating supposedly "separate but equal" public institutions and facilities. Attempts to break this institutionalized racism advanced in the 1950s thanks to legal rulings (*Brown v. Board of Education*) and the personal courage of figures such as Rosa Parks and Dr. Martin Luther King Jr. This movement reached a temporary apex in the mid-1960s when the Democratic administration of Lyndon B. Johnson passed several ground-breaking pieces of legislation such as the Civil Rights Act (1964).

Justice: Along with courage and wisdom, considered by the Greeks to be one of the fundamental virtues. As a principle of right conduct it is usually thought of along procedural and substantive lines, the former applying to the way in which one is treated (e.g., the recipient of due process) and the latter applying to the distribution of scarce goods.

Koran: The holy manuscript of Muslims.

Kristallnacht: An episode of anti-Semitic violence, which the Nazi government of Germany orchestrated on 9 November 1938. The effects of this particular pogrom extended through several days and marked a sharp escalation in the state-sanctioned terror against Germans with Jewish ancestry. Whereas previous measures had added up to legalized discrimination, the Night of the Broken Glasses foreshadowed the regime's use of violence to solve what it euphemistically called the Jewish Problem.

Labour theory of value: An idea put forward by David Ricardo, stating that prices of goods are proportional to the value of labour embodied in them.

Laissez-faire: Literally, "let things be." This is a principle of capitalism espoused by Adam Smith according to which economic activity should be free of government interference. Smith was, accordingly, against protectionism.

Law of nations: Laws relating to the association between nations. In contemporary terms, the law of nations is known as international law with Hugo Grotius its most famous founder.

Laws of nature: In the study of human nature, laws that are discoverable by the use of reason alone. Thomas Hobbes is one of the more famous advocates of such laws, but others noteworthy in this regard include Plato, Aristotle, and Locke.

League of Nations: International organization established in 1920 under a covenant of the Treaty of Versailles, which ended World War I. Precursor of the United Nations. The idea of the League was found in US President Woodrow Wilson's Fourteen Points, although the US Senate refused to ratify the Treaty or join the League.

Lebensraum: German word meaning "living space." The term was used by the Nazis between 1933 and 1945 as a slogan to justify German acquisition of territory, particularly in eastern Europe.

Legal and political equality: The possession of the same legal and political rights in a political community. For legal equality, these would normally include the right to procedural justice, the right to be secure against unreasonable search and seizure, and the right not to be subject to cruel and unusual treatment or punishment. For political equality, these would usually include freedom of conscience, of thought, of association, and of religion.

Legitimacy: Rule or governance that is justified by some principle of right or justice. According to Max Weber, the main principles were charisma, tradition, and rationality/legality.

Liberalism: A political philosophy emphasizing the rights of individuals within society. The first version of this philosophy—classical liberalism—was articulated by John Locke, who stood in favour of the rights of individuals to life, liberty, and property, and by Adam Smith, who stood in favour of economic freedoms. The second, later version—reform liberalism—was spelled out by T.H. Green, John Dewey, and John Maynard Keynes, who believed that political institutions should facilitate the goal of personal self-realization.

Libertarianism: A late twentieth-century anti-statist political philosophy. Economic and social freedoms, coupled with an unregulated free market, rank high among its ideals. As a political philosophy it shares much with public choice theory. This position has been advanced by Robert Nozick and Jan Narveson, both of whom advocate the widest possible domain of freedom for the individual. It differs from anarchism in that it subscribes to the notion of the minimal state.

Lockean proviso: Argues that a permanent property right in a previously unowned thing is unacceptable if the position of those who are no longer at liberty to use that thing is thereby worsened. This proviso originates with Locke, who argues that in the appropriation process there must be "enough and as good left in common for others."

Maoism: Political philosophy of Mao Tse-Tung, who adapted Marxist ideas to serve China's needs. The term is sometimes used to refer to the cult surrounding Chairman Mao, a cult which reached its climax in the Cultural Revolution, launched by Mao in 1966.

March on Rome: An insurrection that allowed Benito Mussolini to come to power in October 1922.

Market failures: Economic problems that arise from an unregulated free market system. Such problems include pollution, ugliness, and congestion.

Marxism: School of political thought advocated by Karl Marx and Friedrich Engels and developed by Lenin and others. According to this ideology, the modes of production and property relations constitute the economic foundation upon which are built the political and legal superstructures. In the capitalist phase of history, which follows the aristocratic phase, Marxists believe the bourgeoisie controls the means of production—control that will not be released into the hands of the proletariat except by revolution.

Materialism: In political theory, the belief that natural resources and modes of production are the primary explanation of social and political structures and activity. In philosophical theory, the belief that the mind can be reduced to, without residue, the brain.

Mein Kampf: The title of the book, which Nazi leader Adolf Hitler (1889–1945) published in mid-1920s. Part autobiography, part political blueprint, part anti-Semitic tirade, Hitler wrote portions of *Mein Kampf* ("My Struggle") while serving a relatively light prison sentence for his treasonous role in the Beer Hall Putsch (1923), a failed attempt by a group of German politicians and former military leaders to seize power during the early years of the Weimar Republic, the period of parliamentary democracy that defined Germany from the end of World War I in 1918 to 1933, when Hitler seized power through a combination of electoral politics and political violence and intimidation.

Mensheviks: Literally, "the minority." These individuals, followers of Georgi Plekhanov (1857–1918), were more consistent followers of Marx than were the Bolsheviks. They believed socialism would be established in Russia only after the establishment of capitalism. For Lenin and the Bolsheviks, this was too slow. Cf. **Bolshevism**.

Mercantilism: Economic theory common in the fifteenth and sixteenth centuries, and advocated by some as late as the eighteenth century. According to this theory, the power of a given country is determined by its wealth as measured by its gold and silver reserves. State power could thus be enhanced by monopolizing these precious metals. Adam Smith argued forcefully against this theory in *The Wealth of Nations*.

Meritocracy: System in which social position and advancement are measured by ability and industry. In Western democratic countries, typically the public or civil service is predicated on merit, thereby impeding nepotism or patronage.

Metaphysics: A term used to describe the branch of philosophy that studies the fundamental nature of existence and reality. The term itself originated with an editor of Aristotle, who used it to describe a collection of works that had appeared after Aristotle's *Physics*. But these observations hardly describe the complexities and controversies that characterize this field, which some scholars say does not even represent a legitimate line of inquiry.

Militarism: The glorification of military force by the state. Practical consequences of this sentiment may include substantial economic and political privileges for members of the military at the expense of other groups, and a heightened willingness to use military force in the pursuit of political goals. Militarism counts as one of the defining characteristics of Fascist regimes, but may also wax and wane in less totalitarian societies according to their circumstances.

Modes of production: Techniques of production, including those that are agricultural and those that are industrial.

Monetarism: School of economic thought that claims that the control of money supply is the most important mechanism in the control of the national economy and inflation.

Moral Majority: A political organization founded in 1979, largely through the initiative of Jerry Falwell, for the purpose of having an effective body that could lobby government from an evangelical Christian point of view. It ceased to exist in 1989.

Multiculturalism: A movement and idea that is a response to nationalism and that emphasizes cultural pluralism and group-differentiated rights. According to Will Kymlicka, multiculturalism as an idea is sometimes made use of by liberals against a conformist view of culture, and sometimes made use of by conservatives to support a conformist view of minority culture.

Multilateralism: In international affairs, multilateralism means a commitment to many nation-states in the joint pursuit of specific goals. As contrasted with unilateralism, bilateralism, and trilateralism.

Munich Agreement: The agreement made among France, Germany, Italy, and the United Kingdom in 1938 that provided for the cession of parts of Czechoslovakia to Germany.

Muslim Brotherhood: A Muslim movement established in 1928 in Egypt by Hasan al-Banna for the purpose of offsetting the negative effects of Westernization and secularism in Egyptian society.

Myth of the vaginal orgasm: According to Alice Schwarzer, the dogma of the "sexual monopoly of men over women," which in turn provides "the foundation of the public monopoly of male society over women."

Nation: A group of people sharing a common language, ethnic background, history, and culture.

National Action Committee of the Status of Women (NAC): This Canadian women's advocacy group became a target for neo-liberals in 2004.

Nationalism: The veneration of the idea of the nation by a group of people who share ethnic, linguistic, historical, and religious backgrounds. Nationalism played an important role in the Balkans in the nineteenth century and in Africa in the twentieth century. In more recent years nationalism has reared its head in

the former Yugoslavia, Chechnya, and East Timor, and less violently in Spain and Quebec. Sometimes this term is confused with patriotism—the love of one's homeland. The earliest mention of the term "nationalism" is in the work of Johann Gottfried Herder in 1774.

National Religious Party: The political face of the Gush Emunim.

Natural law: Principles discoverable by reason that pertain to human conduct. It precedes all enacted law. Its advocates include Thomas Hobbes and his younger contemporary Samuel Pufendorf (1632–1694).

Natural rights: Rights that people have simply as human individuals. The theory of natural rights emerged to provide political safeguards for the individual.

Negative liberty: The freedom one has when one is unconstrained by government. Cf. **Positive liberty**.

Neo-liberalism: Political philosophy that reverts back to the economic and political ideals of classical liberalism, and couples these with the practices of deregulation, privatization, and monetarism. Equivalent to neo-conservatism.

New capitalism: The twenty-first century attempt by the financial elite to roll back egalitarian gains. As described by Linda McQuaig, the effort to reverse egalitarian gains is but a return to laissez-faireism, or old capitalism, with the addition of international treaties that help to establish an "unfettered capitalism" as legally binding.

New Deal: The totality of political and economic reforms that Democratic President Franklin Delano Roosevelt initiated and implemented in the United States during the 1930s to relieve and reverse the effects of the Great Depression, a period of economic turmoil caused by excessive financial speculation and lax regulations. While some measures proved to be successful in creating employment for millions of American who lost everything in the wake of the 1929 stock-market crash that had triggered the Great Depression, other policies proved to be less effective in the face of resistance from FDR's political opponents, including the US Supreme Court. Subsequent US administrations have since ameliorated, even reversed, significant aspects of the New Deal agenda.

New Economic Policy (NEP): Introduced in the Soviet Union by Lenin in 1921 to rebuild the economy. It resulted in a temporary withdrawal from centralization and doctrinaire thinking. Freedom of trading and overtime for workers were permitted, as was the privatization of agriculture and small factories.

Night watchman: Metaphorical image used to capture the role classical liberals, neo-liberals, and libertarians assign to the state. Accordingly, the state plays the role of ensuring the protection of the rights of life, liberty, and possessions.

Nihilism: The radical rejection of values as found in morality, order, and authority. This idea was advanced by Friedrich Nietzsche (1844–1900), philologist and critic of culture.

Non-excludability: Under Public Choice Theory, the idea that goods, if supplied to one group, cannot be restricted to the people who organized its provision.

Normative discourse: Discourse that evaluates the moral element in persons' actions by means of criteria for what is right, wrong, good, or bad.

NSDAP—Acronym for *Nationalsozialistische Deutsche Arbeiterpartei,* the German National Socialist German Workers' Party. The "Nazi" party emerged in 1920 out of the short-lived German Workers' Party, one of the countless nationalistic groups that had sprung up on far-right fringes of Germany's political spectrum following the end of World War I and the emergence of the Weimar Republic. Adolf Hitler (1889–1945) eventually became its undisputed leader after he had become aware of it through his work as a government informant.

Nulla poena sine lege: Latin for "no penalty without a law."

Nuremberg Laws—A body of laws that the ruling Nazi government of Germany passed in 1935 to legalize social Darwinistic ideas about Eugenics (racial hygiene). The laws turned primarily but not exclusively Germans of Jewish ancestry into second-class citizens subject to humiliating treatment. While this particular community had been facing various repressions and restrictions since the Nazis had risen to power in 1933, the Nuremberg Laws institutionalized this pattern of state-sanctioned force and lowered the societal threshold for actions that eventually culminated in the Holocaust, the extermination of some six million European Jews.

Nuremberg Tribunals: A series of trials that prosecuted and punished the surviving leaders of Germany's Nazi regime following the end of World War II. Convened in the spiritual capital of the Nazi movement, the tribunals broke new ground in international law by holding leading politicians and generals personally accountable for their actions, particularly Germany's war of aggression. It also introduced new ideas such as the concept of crimes against humanity in the aftermath of the Holocaust. While the tribunals—particularly the main trial against leading figures such as Herman Göring—have faded into historical memory, their methodology and outcomes have significantly shaped the evolution of international law and its application in events since World War II.

Original position: A hypothetical position advanced by John Rawls for determining principles of fairness. The position assumes a veil of ignorance, as free and equal citizens engage in co-operation in attempting to determine the principles by which they will live together.

Ottoman Empire: Major Muslim power that controlled southeastern Europe, the Middle East, and North Africa from the thirteenth century until the early part of the twentieth century. The empire established itself in a significant way with the seizure of much of what was Byzantium in 1453.

Pacifism: A school of thought that believes in the nonviolent opposition to the use of violence and injustice in any form. It has religious and anarchistic roots dating back to early Christianity and such figures as Tertullian and Origen.

Palestinian cause: The aspiration among Palestinians to return to their homeland following their displacement in 1948 at the hands of Israeli Jews. This aspiration has given rise to the call of a "right of return" among Palestinian groups, both in the West Bank and in Gaza.

Palingenetic: From Greek, meaning having the attribute of being reborn or regenerated. In politics, it represents the desire to create a new political order following a period considered corrupt or decadent.

Pareto principle: A principle claiming that any change in welfare must be acceptable to all those affected by it. Named after the Italian economist and sociologist Vilfredo Pareto.

Parliamentary system: Sometimes called the Westminster system of government. This system embraces a parliamentary executive and opposition with a significant role ascribed to the latter. The Westminster model contrasts with the Congressional model insofar as the latter lacks a Congressional executive.

Paris Commune: The name of the revolutionary body that ruled Paris from March through May of 1871. This council, whose leading members represented a wide range of Marxist, socialist, and anarchist factions, rose to power during the power vacuum that had appeared following the defeat of France during her war (1870–1871) with Prussia, leading to the formation of the German Reich. Regular government forces eventually ended this interregnum by storming the defensive barricades that had appeared throughout the city.

Participatory democracy: A form of democracy in which those affected by decisions participate directly in making them. This form is usually contrasted with **representative democracy**.

Party for Freedom: A Dutch populist party, whose agenda reflects many of the political positions held by comparable organizations across western and northern Europe. Defining policy positions include a marked hostility toward Islam, immigrants generally but especially from Muslim-Arab countries, and supranational organizations such as the European Union.

Patriarchal government: Form of government attacked by John Locke as illegitimate. Government by the patriarchs is government by the head of the family, the father. Locke's attack was directed at Robert Filmer who attempted to legitimize the growth of government through God's licence to Adam to govern Eve.

Patriarchy: Literally, "rule by the father." As a social system it represents the domination of women by men, and as such is strongly opposed by feminists.

Perennial inflationary pressure: Ongoing and inevitable inflationary pressures for higher wages. According to Joseph Schumpeter, this pressure results from high-level unemployment in capitalist society, which in turn leads to the weakening of the social framework and, curiously, to the breakdown of the capitalist society. Hence Schumpeter's turn of phrase "creative destruction."

Permanent revolution: A theory of Leon Trotsky (1879–1940) that promoted the idea that revolution should be continuous and international in scope. The effect of this was to institutionalize revolution.

Petite difference: The biological difference possessed by men but lacked by women that is made to have ideological consequences. These ideological consequences are rooted, however, not in biology but in culture and represent "in every generation" an identification with "dominance and subjection."

Physiocracy: An economic theory advocated by a French physician, François Quesnay, in the eighteenth century. According to this theory, the wealth of a nation consists in the consumable goods produced by the labour of that society, where the only productive labour is that which is employed upon the land. Agriculture is thus considered the key industry in the economy.

Pluralism: A theory that maintains that political power is distributed among interest groups in a civil society. Such groups include unions, churches, professional organizations, and ethnic groups. Accordingly, government policy is the result of the resolution of conflict among these groups.

Plutocracy: Literally, "rule by the wealthy." Aristotle claimed that oligarchy (rule by the few) is nothing but plutocracy.

Polygamy: Marital practice that endorses the marriage of a single male to many women. John Stuart Mill examines this practice in connection with the Mormons of the nineteenth century in his discussion of liberty.

Positive liberty: The liberty one has when impediments to self-realization, such as poverty and disease, are removed through government action. Cf. **Negative liberty**.

Positivism: A philosophical perspective about the nature of scientific knowledge and research methodology. Subscribers of this perspective argue that knowledge of every kind should emerge exclusively through the use of value-neutral, quantitative observations, and verifications. This view holds the scientific method in high esteem and rejects more subjective conceptions of reality.

Postmodernism: A school of thinking that rejects the values of the Enlightenment (truth, objectivity, value, facts, and meaning) and replaces them with consensus and subjectivism.

Pragmatism: A theory of knowledge distinct from rationalism and empiricism. It was advocated by William James, Charles Sanders Peirce, and John Dewey. In political theory, it refers to the practice of determining political action on the basis of practical and expedient factors rather than on the basis of rigid principles.

Prisoners' dilemma: A rational choice dilemma that arises when individually rational behaviour turns out to be jointly inefficient because it leads to an outcome or result that each agent prefers less than another.

Procedural justice: Justice that prescribes the manner in which duties, rights, and responsibilities are exercised and enforced in a court of law. Cf. **Substantive justice**.

Progressive taxation: A system of taxation in which the percentage of income tax paid increases with one's earned income.

Proletariat: The class of wage earners with no property who subsist through the sale of their labour. In Marx's dialectical materialism, the proletariat would ultimately be victorious over the bourgeoisie, but only after a violent revolution. Cf. **Bourgeoisie**.

Property: The institution of ownership. It is divided, typically, into private and public, with the former owned by individual persons and the latter owned by the state. The right to private property has been a cornerstone of liberal thinking since Locke. The institution of property is thoroughly examined by Plato in *The Republic* and by Aristotle in *Politics*.

Property relations: Relations of production that during stable times influence the ideology as found in law, politics, religion, art, and philosophy, and that during unstable times come into conflict with the techniques or modes of production. Property relations form part of the substructure of the social system.

Protective association: A term used by Robert Nozick to refer to protective organizations that naturally spring into existence in a state of nature such as that described by Thomas Hobbes and John Locke. Contemporary illustrations of such associations would include gangs in urban areas, where the state, through its law enforcement agency, has lost control—i.e., where there is a no man's land.

Public choice theory: A theory that represents the invasion of economists in the neoclassical tradition into the domain of political science. Supporters of this position, such as Mancur Olson, argue that all organizational life can be dissolved into the competing interests of individuals.

Public goods: Goods whose benefit is indivisible. Illustrations of this are national defence and public health.

Public sector: Sector of the economy embracing services rendered by the state, including education, transportation, health, and postal services. These and other services are subject to attack by libertarians and public choice theorists.

Quakers: Mid-seventeenth-century group in England and the American colonies, also known as the

Friends. They advocated silent waiting for the "inward light" in the search for God. In addition, they were known for being non-violent advocates of social reform under the leadership of George Fox. In this respect, they represented a rediscovery of pacifism rather than its continuation.

Radicalism: A political philosophy looking for far-reaching and sometimes immediate change. Marxists, and the Jacobins of the French Revolution, are illustrative of this school of thinking.

Reactionary: The intransigent resistance to change, or, occasionally, the desire to return to the past.

Realism: A metaphysical position affirming the existence of an independent and objective world.

Realism and romance in sexual politics: Contrast identified by Kate Millett between the approaches to sexual politics as found in the writings of J.S. Mill and John Ruskin from the nineteenth century.

Reform liberalism: A version of liberalism that developed during the nineteenth and twentieth centuries. T.H. Green of England was the first spokesperson of this movement, with John Dewey of the United States and J.M. Keynes of England soon following. What these three thinkers shared was a recognition of the importance of individual liberties and of the need for forceful state action to create conditions favourable to the enhancement of these liberties.

Regina Manifesto: Manifest of the Co-operative Commonwealth Federation as adopted in Regina, Saskatchewan, in 1933. It promoted principles regulating production, distribution, and exchange that aimed at satisfying human needs rather than making a profit.

Relativism: Epistemological position that denies the existence of an objective and independent world. Mitigated relativism endorses a modified form of this position by affirming a form of objectivity that is conditioned by historic and natural matters rooted in time and place. In the result, in keeping with Lorraine Code's view on mitigated relativism, things are not unequivocally objective.

Renaissance: The rebirth of arts and sciences following the Medieval period in Europe. It is usually associated with the humanistic works of Erasmus and the rediscovery, mediated by the Arabs, of the works of Plato and Aristotle. The forces of secularism and individualism began to dominate in a way in which they had not since the classical period. Noteworthy among the emerging class of humanists of this period were the likes of Leonardo da Vinci, Giotto, Michelangelo, Botticelli, and Titian.

Representative democracy: A form of democracy in which elected candidates represent people in constituencies. It contrasts with **participatory democracy**, in which each citizen is free to participate in the decision making of public policy.

Republicanism: Constitutional form of government. Republics stand in contrast to monarchies in lacking a monarch as head of state but possessing a political or quasi-political figure as commander in chief.

Revolution: Radical or dramatic social change in a country. Illustrations of such events include the French, American, Russian (Bolshevik), and Chinese Communist Revolutions.

Rights: Justifiable legal or moral claim to something or to some practice. Positively enacted rights are those created by legislation, while natural rights are those which one has by virtue of being a human being or sentient creature. Both Hobbes and Locke made use of the notion of natural rights, and in time this notion became incorporated into the American Declaration of Independence. Still later, it became a clarion call of many constitutions, and indeed in the United Nations' Universal Declaration of Human Rights (1948) itself. The notion is slow to emerge in political thinking, with hardly a trace of it to be found in the writings of Plato or Aristotle.

Sapere aude: Literally, "dare to know." This was Immanuel Kant's motto of the Enlightenment.

Satyagraha: A philosophy of Mohandas Gandhi that excludes the use of violence and embraces civil disobedience and non-co-operation. Cf. **Ahimsa.**

Scientific image of the world: Wilfrid Sellars' term that he applies to a view of the world derived from the postulation of imperceptible entities and principles pertaining to them that help to explain the behaviour of these entities. The scientific image is constructed making use of different procedures to connect theoretical entities, via different instruments, to intersubjectively accessible features of the manifest world. Sellars contrasts the scientific image with the manifest image of the world.

Secularism: Position denouncing religious values while affirming rational ones. Religious fundamentalism opposes it as atheistic, materialistic, and focused on a "transient and temporary reality."

Seneca Falls Convention: A conference held in 1848 in Seneca Falls, New York, that marked the birth of the American women's rights movement. The Convention adopted Elizabeth Cady Stanton's Declaration of Sentiments and called for female suffrage.

Sephardim: Jews who have gone to Israel from Arab lands. The ancestors of these people originally lived in Spain, but were expelled by Ferdinand and Isabella in 1492.

Sermon on the Mount: The discourse of Jesus, as found in Matthew 5–7, which sets forth the principles of Christian ethics. It includes the beatitudes, Jesus' naming of those who are blessed—including the meek, the merciful, and the peacemakers.

Sex: Biological differences that separate men and women. Cf. **Gender**.

Sharia: The religious law of Islam. Drawn from various sources including the Koran itself, this code covers a wide range of public and private matters among Muslims. Several Muslim nations recognize Sharia as the solitary source of civil and criminal law, often doling out penalties deemed to be harsh and barbarous by Western observers. Other Muslim nations have combined Sharia with elements of Western-style jurisprudence.

Shi'ism: A sect of Islam found in Iran and Iraq that believes that it is possible to remove the stains of sin through living a simple and devout life, as well as through suffering. It is especially attractive to the poor and dispossessed. Cf. **Sunnism**.

Social contract: The hypothetical agreement found at the base of civil society, according to Hobbes, Locke, and Rousseau, but disputed by Hume. It is this agreement that moves persons from a state of nature—with a life that is "nasty, brutish, and short"—to a civil or political society.

Social Darwinism: A school of thought that attempts to transfer Charles Darwin's ideas regarding natural selection in biology to the cultural, social, and economic domains. Herbert Spencer, in the nineteenth century, and William Graham Sumner, in the twentieth century, promoted this school of thought.

Social ecology: Theory advanced by Murray Bookchin claiming that the natural world represents first nature, while the cultural, social, and political represent second nature. The second emerges out of the first by a process of evolution, and gives rise to the present ecological crisis. Evolution has conferred a responsibility on human beings as part of second nature.

Socialism: Political philosophy that approves of public ownership of the means of production. Frequently the result of this is the nationalization of key industries or modes of transportation.

Social responsibility: Obligation to contribute to the common good. In a democracy, there exists a balance, if not a tension, between social responsibility and individual liberty.

Soviet Union (Union of Soviet Socialist Republics): A former Marxist-socialist territorial state in Eurasia that existed from 1922 to 1991. The state emerged after the Bolsheviks under the leadership of Vladimir Lenin had consolidated their political and territorial control following the events of the Russian Revolution (1917) and Russian Civil War (1917–1922). The state, which succeeded the Imperial Russian Empire of the Romanov Dynasty, played a crucial role during the twentieth century, first as a member of the military alliance that defeated Nazi Germany during World War I (1939–1945), then as the central antagonist to the United States during the Cold War (1946–1991).

State: Comprises the executive and legislative branches of government, together with the bureaucracy, judiciary, and military/police.

State of nature: Hobbesian and Lockean term that refers to the pre-political condition of humanity. Out of this condition emerges a social contract between a sovereign and his or her people (Hobbes) and among equally free individuals (Locke).

Substantive justice: Called "distributive justice" by Aristotle, it applies to the distribution of goods according to principles of fairness. Cf. **Procedural justice**.

Substructure: Applies to the techniques or modes of production and the property relations in a Marxist analysis of society. Cf. **Superstructure**.

Suffrage: The right to vote in electing public officials. The Seneca Falls Convention in 1848 represented the first major initiative in the United States to advance women's right to vote, and similar initiatives occurred in other countries such as Canada and the United Kingdom. But the issue of suffrage extended not only to women but also to other identifiable groups, including blacks in South Africa and the United States, and First Nations people in Canada. With the demise of apartheid in South Africa in the early 1990s, the advance of the civil rights movement in the United States in the early 1960s, and amendments to the Indian Act in Canada in 1960, the franchise was extended in these countries to different recognizable groups.

Sunnism: The dominant sect of Islam that embraces the traditional social and legal practices of the Muslim community. Cf. **Shi'ism**.

Superstructure: The dimension of social life that is explained in terms of the means of production and property relations. According to Marxists, it includes religion, law, philosophy, culture, and the family. Cf. **Substructure**.

Survival of the fittest: A term that English philosopher Herbert Spencer (1820–1903) coined in attempting

to extend Charles Darwin's theory of evolution into social realms. This extension earned Spencer posthumous membership in the school of social Darwinism. Its various European and North American members argued that human societies must abide by the same laws as other non-human life forms. This view—which echoes but abuses Darwin's concept of natural selection—informed nineteenth century imperialism, the Eugenics (racial hygiene) movement of the early twentieth century, and German aggressions and atrocities (the Holocaust of European Jews) during the 1930s and 1940s in the quest for *Lebensraum* (living space).

Sustainable development: A pattern of economic development that considers ecological limits. While definitions for this concept vary, the Brundtland Report of 1987 defines it as "development that meets the needs of the present without comprising the ability of future generations to meet their own needs." The usage of this concept, which challenges previous assumptions about the possibility of limitless growth, has since expanded beyond its initial environmental context into other public policy fields.

Syndicalism: Trade-unionism. It specifically refers to the version of trade unionism before 1914 in Spain and Italy.

TC: Abbreviation for theological correctness. The term is inspired by its secular counterpart, PC, or political correctness.

Temple Mount: Mount Moria; the most sacred site of Judaism and the third most sacred site of Islam. It is located in Jerusalem. In 1966 a group of Orthodox Rabbis affirmed that Jews were allowed to enter the Temple Mount. The First Temple in Judaism was destroyed in 586 BCE, while the Second Temple was built in 516 BCE and destroyed in 70 CE. The hope of the members of the Temple Mount Faithful is to build the next temple on Mount Moria.

Theocracy: Rule by the priestly class, or rule by those who emphasize religious beliefs in political decision making.

Theory of Evolution: A scientific explanation of the diversity and changes in biological life. It rests on the writings of English naturalist Charles Darwin (1809–1882), who argued in his groundbreaking publication *On the Origin of Species* (1859) that all past and present forms of life share a common ancestry, from which they evolved in separate direction through natural selection, a process that favours populations capable of adapting to their circumstances. Lacking any knowledge of genetics, Darwin developed his theory by careful observation of natural life, most famously through his journey to the Galapagos Island in Pacific. While the scientific community of Darwin's era initially treated his views with hostility, they have since become widely accepted, despite rearguard challenges from theories that favour a religious element such as Creationism or Intelligent Design.

Third Reich: The Nazi regime in Germany from 1933 to 1945. The passing of the Enabling Act in March 1933 ended the Weimar Republic and established a new political order in Germany. The First Reich was the Holy Roman Empire (962–1806), and the Second Reich was the German Empire (1871–1918). Hitler expected the Third Reich to last a thousand years.

Third Way, The: Efforts by social democratic parties to re-address their policies in the post-1989 period in Europe. According to Anthony Giddens, the third way can be viewed as progressivism.

Third World: The developing countries of Africa, Asia, and Latin America. The first and second worlds comprise the industrialized democratic countries and the orthodox communist countries.

Toleration: A moral dimension that reached a critical phase in European civilization during the Protestant Reformation. In contemporary times, following the works of J.S. Mill and John Rawls, discussions pertaining to it have focused on specifying how far liberal peoples are to tolerate non-liberal people's practices. The urgency of addressing this issue has arisen at the centre of the talk of the clash of civilizations and fear of the Islamization of Europe.

Totalitarianism: A political system in which all aspects of the community are controlled by the state. This control would extend to include control over fundamental institutions such as schools, churches, courts, families, the workplace, and even recreational organizations. Such a system typically emerges at the far right of the political spectrum.

Traditional principles of justice: A notion addressed by John Rawls in his later writings. Rawls presents eight traditional principles that he takes to be standard principles of justice found among free and democratic societies. Many of these principles are drawn from writings of publicists in international law.

Treaty of Versailles: The agreement, which formally ended World War I between the victorious Allies (led by United States, the United Kingdom, and France) and defeated Germany. The treaty, which served as the centre plank of the post-war settlement, imposed a range of penalties on Germany. They included the loss of her overseas colonies, the loss of territory along her eastern and western frontiers, restrictions on the size and composition of her military, and extensive reparation payments. The treaty also included the so-called War Guilt Clause (Article 231), which assigned Germany responsibility for the damages caused during the war. German nationalistic forces used the perceived harshness of these provisions to undermine the Weimar Republic.

Twenty-Five Program: A political action agenda proposed by Adolf Hitler in 1920 in which he foreshadowed many of the militaristic, racist, and later genocidal policies that would define the Nazi regime that ruled Germany from 1933 to 1945. The program appeared when the National Socialist German Workers' Party (NSDAP) still existed under the label of the German Workers' Party (DAP).

United Nations Charter: The treaty that founded the United Nations on 26 June 1945. Signed in San Francisco by the original member countries, the treaty describes the structure of the UN and its various bodies in spelling out organizational principles, purposes, and procedures. As of this writing in June 2012, the United Nations has 193 members.

Utilitarianism: A school of ethics claiming that the value of actions is to be assessed in terms of their ability to produce pleasure or pain. Early members of this school included Jeremy Bentham, James Mill, and

John Stuart Mill. According to the first of these, the proper course of action was always that which produced the greatest happiness for the greatest number.

Utopia: An ideal state or condition, which English humanist, philosopher, and political advisor Thomas More first coined in the early sixteenth century to describe an imaginary, far-off island with a perfect political system. This definition has since expanded to encompass creative and critical imaginations of future social, political, and technological worlds. Scholars, for example, describe Marxism as utopian, because it foresees unlimited material prosperity, in lamenting current conditions. In this sense, utopian thought qualifies as contemporary social criticism.

US Naval Base Guantanamo Bay: A military base located on the Island of Cuba, where the United States maintains a separate detention and interrogation complex for individuals suspected of being (Islamic) terrorists. Opened after the events of 9/11 in 2001, the site with its peculiar legal status has become synonymous for American excesses in its execution of the Global War on Terror, especially during its early stages when US officials denied inmates—so-called Unlawful Combatants—various privileges afforded to them under American and international law. While the treatment of prisoners has improved in the aftermath of various court rulings and political pressure, the site remains a controversial part of the American response to so-called Islamic terrorism as of this writing in 2012.

Volk: Literally, "the people." National socialists attached mythological significance to this term and its referent, grafting on to the German people deeds and accomplishments of epic proportion.

Vouchers: In neo-liberal thought, state-endorsed coupons that are redeemable at either public or private institutions for purposes such as health and education. Both Milton Friedman and Alan Greenspan support the use of vouchers, at least in the field of education.

Wahhabism: Sunni Islamic movement that emerged in 1747 under Ibn Abd al-Wahhab. It advocates the excoriating of anything extraneous to Islam, including Shi'ism.

War crimes: Acts of soldiers or civilians that may be considered breaches of the laws or customs of war. At the conclusion of World War II, an International Military Tribunal was established—one in Germany and one in Japan—to investigate crimes against peace, war crimes, and crimes against humanity as committed by Germany and Japan and their allies. Cf. **Crimes against humanity**.

Welfare state: A political state that has a social safety net in the form of social programs such as employment insurance, old age security, medical coverage, and assistance to those who are individually challenged.

World Trade Organization (WTO): Successor organization to the General Agreement on Tariffs and Trade (1995). This body aims to support the principles of neo-liberalism. Among the WTO's basic provisions are the following: concessions offered to one member must be available to other members, tariff-binding provisions can be reduced but not increased, products that enter from abroad must be treated the same as domestically produced goods, and countervailing and anti-dumping duties can be imposed to counter subsidies and dumping.

World War II: The (so far) most devastating and destructive conflict in human history, whose political, social, economic, and demographic consequences can still be felt today. Spanning the globe, historians estimate that the conflict could have caused up to 80 million casualties. Key causes include the geopolitical instability that characterized the decade that followed World War I (1914–1918) and the Great Depression of 1929. This combination of events paved the path for the emergence of expansionist totalitarian regimes in Europe (Nazi Germany, Fascist Italy) and Asia (Imperial Japan). This Berlin-Rome-Tokyo "Axis" eventually launched a series of aggressive wars in their respective spheres of influence. German aggression in Europe also featured a genocidal dimension (cf. **Holocaust**). An alliance, which at its height included the British Commonwealth, the Soviet Union, and the United States, eventually succeeded in defeating this agenda due to superior military leadership and resources, including the inaugural use of nuclear weapons against Japanese targets during the waning days of the war, which also set the stage for the Cold War.

Yeshiva: School that instructs in Judaic learning. Its origins date back to 500–300 BCE to the time of the Men of the Great Assembly.

Zionism: A Jewish nationalist movement and ideology whose goal is the creation of a Jewish state in Palestine. This movement originated in eastern Europe during the nineteenth century, and the first Zionist Congress was convened in 1897 by Theodor Herzl.

References

Arendt, H. (2006 [1963]). *Eichmann in Jerusalem: A Report on the Banality of Evil*. New York: Penguin, pp. 37–46.

Barry, J. (2007). *Environment and Social Theory*, 2nd edn. London and New York: Routledge, pp. 295–300.

Bastiat, M.F. (1850). *Essays on Political Economy*. London: A.W. Bennett, pp. 3–8.

Bhagwati, J. (2007 [2004]). *In Defense of Globalization*. Oxford: Oxford University Press, pp. 268–276.

Bookchin, M. (1995). *The Philosophy of Social Ecology: Essays on Dialectical Naturalism*, second revised edition. Montreal, New York, and London: Black Rose Books, pp. 71–90.

Buchanan, J.M. (2005). *Why I, Too, Am Not a Conservative: The Normative Vision of Classical Liberalism*. Cheltenham, UK/Northampton, MA: Edward Elgar, pp. 65–69.

Buckley Jr, W.F. (2002, December 12). To preserve what we have. *The Wall Street Journal*.

Burke, E. (1993). *Reflections on the Revolution in France*. Edited by L.G. Mitchell. Oxford: Oxford University Press, pp. 58–62.

Clark, L.M. (1979). Women and Locke: Who owns the apples in the Garden of Eden? In L.M. Clark & L. Lange (Eds.), *The Sexism of Social and Political Theory: Women and Reproduction from Plato to Nietzsche* (pp. 16–25). Toronto: University of Toronto Press.

Chimni, B.S. (1999). Marxism and international law: A contemporary analysis. *Economic and Political Weekly* 34: 337–349.

Code, L. (1991). *What Can She Know? Feminist Theory and the Construction of Knowledge*. Ithaca: Cornell University Press, pp. 314–321.

de Secondat, Baron de Montesquieu, C. (1952). *The Spirit of Laws*. Chicago: William Benton/ Encyclopaedia Britannica, pp. 9–12.

Dewey, J. (1963). *Liberalism and Social Action*. New York: Capricorn Books/G. Putnam and Sons, pp. 61–67.

Dobson, A. (2007). *Green Political Thought*, 4th edn. London and New York: Routledge, pp. 31–37.

Feige, M. (2009). *Settling in the Hearts: Jewish Fundamentalism in the Occupied Territories*. Detroit: Wayne State University, pp. 115–124.

Fosdick, H.E. (1999). *Shall the Fundamentalists Win?* New York: The Riverside Church Archives Committee, pp. 3, 5–14.

Franklin, U. (2006). *The Ursula Franklin Reader: Pacifism as a Map*. Toronto: Between the Lines, pp. 53–54.

Freud, S. (1961). *Civilization and Its Discontents*. Edited and translated by J. Strachey. New York: W.W. Norton and Company, Ltd., pp. 59–61.

Gandhi, M.K. (1961 [1951]). *Non-Violent Resistance*. New York: Schoken Books, pp. 34–36.

Giddens, A. (2003). *The Progressive Manifesto:New Ideas for the Centre-Left*. Cambridge, UK: Polity Press, pp. 1–7.

Greenspan, A. (2007). *The Age of Turbulence: Adventures in a New World*. New York: The Penguin Press, pp. 392–408.

Hirsi Ali, A. (2006). *The Caged Virgin: An Emancipation Proclamation for Women and Islam*. New York: Free Press.

Huxley, A. (1962 [1944]). *The Perennial Philosophy*. Cleveland and New York: Meridian Books/The World Publishing Company, pp. 77–80.

———. (1972). *An Encyclopaedia of Pacifism*. New York and London: Garland Publishing, Inc., pp. 72–75.

Hitler, A. (1958). The Twenty-Five Points of the German Workers' Party. In L.L. Snyder, (Ed.), *Documents of German History* (pp. 393–396). New Brunswick, NJ: Rutgers University Press.

Inbari, M. (2009). *Jewish Fundamentalism and the Temple Mount: Who Will Build the Third Temple?* Translated by S. Vardi. Albany, NY: Suny Press, pp. 18–22.

Kant, I. (1963). *On History*. Edited by L.W. Beck and translated by L.W. Beck, R.E. Anchor, and E.L. Fackenheim. New York: The Bobbs-Merrill Company, Inc., pp. 3–10.

Keynes, J.M. (1972 [1931]). *The Collected Writings of John Maynard Keynes. Essays in Persuasion*, Volume IX. London: The Macmillan Press Ltd./ Cambridge University Press, pp. 272, 284–292.

Kirk, R. (1993). *The Politics of Prudence*. Wilmington, DE: ISI Books, pp. 15–26.

Klein, N. (2007). *The Shock Doctrine: The Rise of Disaster Capitalism.* Toronto: Alfred A. Knopf, pp. 5–24.

Kymlicka, W. (1989). *Liberalism, Community and Culture.* Oxford: Oxford University Press, pp. 140–144.

Lenin, V.I. (1973). *Imperialism, The Highest Stage of Capitalism: A Popular Outline.* Peking: Foreign Languages Press, pp. 104–111.

Lewis, D., & Scott, F. (2001). *Make This Your Canada: A Review of* CCF *History and Policy*, 2nd edn. Winnipeg, MA: Wallingford Press, pp. 163–175.

Locke, J. (2003). *Two Treatises of Government and a Letter Concerning Toleration.* Edited by I. Shapiro. New Haven: Yale University Press, 111–121.

Luxemburg, R. (1981 [1961]). *The Russian Revolution and Leninism or Marxism?* Westport, CT: Greenwood Press, Publishers, pp. 47–56.

McQuaig, L. (2001). *All You Can Eat: Greed, Lust, and the New Capitalism.* Toronto: Viking, pp. 6–22.

Madison, J. (1961). No. 10. In A. Hamilton, J. Madison & J. Jay (Eds.), *The Federalist Papers* (pp. 77–84). New York and Scarborough, ON: The New American Library of World Literature.

Marinetti, F.T. (2006). *Critical Writings.* Edited by Gunter Berghaus. New York: Farrar, Straus, Giroux, pp. 13–15.

Marx, K., & Engels, F. (1998). *The Communist Manifesto.* New York: Monthly Review Press, pp. 1–24.

Mill, J.S. (1999). *On Liberty.* Edited by E. Alexander. Peterborough, ON: Broadview Literary Texts, pp. 51–55.

Mussolini, B. (1933). *The Political and Social Doctrine of Fascism.* Translated by J. Soames. London: Leonard and Virginia Woolf at the Hogarth Press, pp. 11–26.

Naess, A. (1989). A platform of the deep ecology movement. In D. Rothenberg (Ed. and Trans.), *Ecology, Community and Lifestyle: Outline of an Ecosophy* (pp. 29–33). Cambridge: Cambridge University Press.

Nussbaum, M.C. (2006). *Frontiers of Justice: Disability, Nationality, Species Membership.* Cambridge, MA: The Belknap Press of Harvard University, pp. 74–78.

Okin, S.M. (1989). *Justice, Gender, and the Family.* New York: Basic Books Inc., pp. 93–101.

Phillips, K. (2006). *American Theocracy: The Peril and Politics of Radical Religion, Oil, and Borrowed Money in the 21st Century.* New York: Viking, pp. 218–220, 232–236.

Qutb, S. (1996). The present and the future of Islam. In W.E. Shepard (Ed.), *Sayyid Qutb and Islamic Activism: A Translation and Critical Analysis of Social Justice in Islam* (pp. 283–290). Leiden, New York, and Koln: E.J. Brill.

Rawls, J. (1999). *The Law of the Peoples.* Cambridge, MA: Harvard University Press, pp. 36–37.

Russell B. & Einstein, A. The Russell-Einstein Manifesto [issued at a press conference in London on July 9, 1955]. www.pugwash.org/about/manifesto.htm

Schwarzer, A. (2001). The function of sexuality in the oppression of women. In P.A. Herminghouse & M. Mueller (Eds.), *German Feminist Writings* (pp. 223–226). New York and London: The Continuum International Publishing Group Inc.

Scrunton, R. (2007). *Culture Counts: Faith and Feeling in a World Besieged.* New York: Brief Encounters/Encounter Books, pp. 16–26.

Self, P. (2000). *Rolling Back the Market: Economic Dogma and Political Choice.* New York: St. Martin's Press, 222–228, 247–251.

Smith, A. (1995 [1805]). *An Inquiry into the Nature and Causes of the Wealth of Nations.* Edited by W. Playfair. London: William Pickering, pp. 184–195.

Tawney, R.H. (1971). *Equality*, 2nd edn. London: Unwin Books, pp. 164–173.

Tolstoy, L. (1967). *Tolstoy's Writings on Civil Disobedience and Non-Violence.* New York: Bergman Publishers, pp. 175–179.

Trudeau, P.E. (1968). *Federalism and the French Canadians.* Toronto: The Macmillan Company of Canada Limited, pp. xx–xxvi.

Tse-Tung, M. (1973). *Selected Works of Mao Tse-Tung, Volume I.* Peking: Foreign Languages Press, pp. 311–315, 343–345.

Vagts, D.F. (1990). International law in the Third Reich. *The American Journal of International Law* 84: 699–702.

Wilders, G. (n.d.). Speech Geert Wilders berlijn (Engels). www.pvv.nl/index.php/component/content/article/36-geert-wilders/3586-speech-geert-wilders-berlijn.html

World Scientists' Warning to Humanity. (1996). In. P.R. Ehrlich & A.H. Ehrlich (Eds.), *Betrayal of Science and Reason: How Anti-Environmental Rhetoric Threatens Our Future* (pp. 242–250). Washington, DC, and Covelo, CA: Shearwater Books.

Credits

Readings

Adam Smith, *An Inquiry into the Nature and Causes of the Wealth of Nations* (London: William Pickering, 1995).

Alan Greenspan, "Education and Income Inequality" adapted from *The Age of Turbulence: Adventures in a New World*, copyright © 2007, 2008 by Alan Greenspan. Used by permission of The Penguin Press, a division of Penguin Group (USA) Inc.

Aldous Huxley, *An Encyclopaedia of Pacifism*. Copyright © 1937 by Aldous Huxley. Reprinted by permission of Georges Borchardt, Inc., for the Estate of Aldous Huxley.

Aldous Huxley, *The Perennial Philosophy*, excerpt from pp. 77-80 (996 words). Copyright 1944, 1945 by Aldous Huxley. Copyright renewed 1973, 1974 by Laura A. Huxley. Reprinted by permission of HarperCollins Publisher.

Alexander Hamilton, James Madison, John Jay, *The Federalist Papers* (New York and Scarborough, Ontario: The New American Library of World Literature, 1961).

Andrew Dobson, *Green Political Thought*, fourth edition (London and New York: Routledge, 2007).

Anthony Giddens, *The Progressive Manifesto* (Cambridge, England: Polity Press, 2003), pages 1-7.

Ayaan Hirsi Ali, *The Caged Virgin: An Emancipation Proclamation for Women and Islam,* reprinted with the permission of Free Press, a Division of Simon & Schuster, Inc. Copyright © De Zoontjesfabriekm de Maagdenkool, Submission, Vreemde Situaties Copyrihht © 2002, 2004 by Ayaan Hirsi Ali and Augustus Publishers; Ik Wil dty Hier en Nu Gefeurt © 2002 by Colet Van der Ven; Politiek Schalelyk voor myn Ideaal © 2002 by Aryan Visser, English translation © 2006 by Jane Brown. All rights reserved.

Benito Mussolini, *The Political and Social Doctrine of Fascism*, translated by Jane Soames (London: Leonard and Virginia Woolf at the Hogarth Press, 1933).

Bertrand Russell and Albert Einstein, *The Russell-Einstein Manifesto.*

B.S. Chimni, 'Marxism and International Law', Economic and Political Weekly 34 (1999); pp. 337-349 .

Charles de Secondat, Baron de Montesquieu, *The Spirit of Laws* (Chicago: William Benton/Encyclopaedia Britannica, 1952).

David Lewis and Frank Scott, *Regina Manifesto*, second edition (Winnipeg, Manitoba: Wallingford Press, 2001).

David Rothenberg, ed., *Ecology, Community and Lifestyle: Outline of an Ecosophy* (Cambridge: Cambridge University Press, 1989). Reprinted with the permission of Cambridge University Press.

Detlev F. Vagts, 'International Law in the Third Reich', The American Journal of International Law 84 (1990) 661-702.

Edmund Burke, *Reflections on the Revolution in France* (1790; reprint, Oxford: The World's Classics/Oxford University Press, 1993).

F.T. Marinetti, "The Futurist Manifesto" from *Critical Writings,* edited by Gunter Berghaus, translated by Doug Thompson. Copyright © 2006 by Luce Marninetti, Vittoria Marinetti Piazzoni, and Ala Marinetti Clerici. Translation, compilation, editorial work, foreword, preface, and introduction copyright © 2006 by Farrar, Straus and Giroux, LLC. Reprinted by permission of Farrar, Straus and Giroux, LLC.

Geert Wilders, Speech, Berlign (Engels).

Hannah Aredndt, "An Expert on the Jewish Question" from *Eichmann in Jerusalem*, copyright © 1991, 1992 by Lotte Kohler. Used by permission of Viking Penguin, a division of Penguin Group (USA) Inc.

Harry Emerson Fosdick, *Will the Fundamentalists Win?* (New York: The Riverside Church Archives Committee, 1999).

Immanual Kant, *On History* (New York: The Bobbs-Merrill Company, Inc., 1963).

Jagdish Bhagwati, *In Defense of Globalization* (Oxford: OUP, 2007), pages 268-276.

James M. Buchanan, *Why I, Too, Am Not a Conservative: The Normative Vision of Classical Liberalism* (Cheltenham, UK/Northampton, MA: Edward Elgar, 2005), pages 65-69.

John Barry, *Environment and Social Theory*, second edition (London and New York: Routledge, 2007).

John Dewey, *Liberalism and Social Action* (New York: Capricorn Books/G. Putnam and Sons, 1963).

John Maynard Keynes, *Essays in Persuasion*, Volume IX (London: The Macmillan Press Ltd./Cambridge University Press, 1972).

John Locke, *The Second Treatise on Government and a Letter Concerning Toleration* (New Haven: Yale University Press, 2003).

John Stuart Mill, *On Liberty* (1859; reprint, Peterborough, Ontario: Broadview Literary Texts, 1999).

John Rawls, *The Law of Peoples*: With "The Idea of Public Reason Revisited", pp. 36-37, 59-62, Cambridge, Mass.: Harvard University Press, Copyright © 1999 by the President and Fellows of Harvard College. Reprinted by permission of the publisher.

Karl Marx and Friedrich Engels, *The Communist Manifesto* (New York: Monthly Review Press, 1998.

Kevin Phillips, "Church, State, and National Decline", from *American Theocracy*. Copyright © 2006 by Kevin Phillips. Used by permission of Viking Penguin, a division of Penguin Group (USA) Inc.

Leon Tolstoy, *Tolstoy's Writings on Civil Disobedience* (New York: Bergman Publishers, 1967).

Linda McQuaig, *All You Can Eat: Greed, Lust, and the New Capitalism* (Toronto: Viking, 2001).

Lorenne M.G. Clark and Lynda Lange, eds., *The Sexism of Social and Political Theory: Women and Reproduction from Plato to Nietzsche* (Toronto: University of Toronto Press, 1979).

Lorraine Code, *What Can She Know? Feminist Theory and the Construction of Knowledge*,1991. Used by permission of the publisher, Cornell University Press.

Louis L. Snyder, ed., *Documents of German History* (New Brunswick, New Jersey: Rutgers University Press, 1958).

Mao Tse-tung, *Selected Works of Mao Tse-tung*, Volume I (Peking: Foreign Languages Press, 1973).

Martha C. Nussbaum, "The Capabilities Approach" from *Frontiers of Justice: Disability, Nationality, Species Membership*, pp. 74-78, Cambridge, Mass.: The Belknap Press of Harvard University Press, Copyright © 2006 by the President and Fellows of Harvard College. Reprinted by permission of the publisher.

M. Frederic Bastiat, *Essays on Political Economy* (London: A.W. Bennett, mid-nineteenth century).

Michael Feige, *Hostile Visitors: The Palestinians in the Settlers' Worldview*.

M.K. Gandhi, *Non-Violent Resistance* (New York: Schoken Books, 1961; copyright Navajivan Trust, 1951).

Motti Inbari, *Jewish Fundamentalism and the Temple Mount: Who Will Build the Third Temple?* (Albany, New York: Suny Press, 2009).

Murray Bookchin, *The Philosophy of Social Ecology: Essays on Dialectical Naturalism*, second revised edition (Montreal, New York, and London: Black Rose Books, 1995).

Naomi Klein, excerpt from *The Shock Doctrine: The Rise of Disaster Capitalism*. Copyright © 2007 Naomi Klein. Reprinted by permission of Knopf Canada.

Patricia A. Herminghouse and Magda Mueller, eds., *German Feminist Writings* (New York/London: The Continuum International Publishing Group Inc., 2001).

Paul R. Ehrlich and Anne H. Ehrlich, *Betrayal of Science and Reason*. Copyright © 1996 by Paul R. Ehrlich and Anne H. Ehrlich. Reproduced by permission of Island Press, Washington, DC.

Peter Self, *Rolling Back the Market: Economic Dogma and Political Choice* (New York: St. Martin's Press, 2000).

Pierre Elliott Trudeau, *Federalism and the French Canadian* (Toronto: The Macmillan Company of Canada Limited, 1968).

R.H. Tawney, *Equality*, second edition (London: Unwin Books, 1971).

Roger Scruton, *Culture Counts: Faith and Feeling in a World Besieged* (New York: Brief Encounters/ Encounter Books, 2007).

Rosa Luxemburg, *The Russian Revolution and Leninism or Marxism?* University of Michigan Press.

Russell Kirk, *The Politics of Prudence* (Wilmington, Delaware: ISI Books, 1993).

Sigmund Freud, *Civilization and Its Discontents* (1930; reprint, New York: W.W. Norton and Company, Ltd., 1961).

Susan Moller Okin, *Justice, Gender, and the Family* (New York: Basic Books Inc. 1989).

Ursula Franklin, *The Ursula Franklin Reader: Pacifism as a Map* (Toronto: Canada Council for the Arts, 2006).

Vladimir I. Lenin, *Imperialism, The Highest Stage of Capitalism: A Popular Outline* (Peking: Foreign Languages Press, 1973).

William F. Buckley Jr., 'To Preserve What We Have', Wall Street Journal, Dec. 12, 2002.

Will Kymlicka, *Liberalism, Community and Culture* (Oxford: Oxford University Press, 1989).

William E. Shepard, ed., *Sayyid Qutb and Islamic Activism: A translation and Critical Analysis of Social Justice in Islam* (Leiden/New York/Koln: E.J. Brill, 1996).